Reading Literature and Writing Argument

Missy James
Tallahassee Community College

Alan Merickel
Tallahassee Community College

Prentice Hall

Upper Saddle River, New Jersey 07458

Library of Congress Cataloging-in-Publication Data
James, Missy.
    Reading literature and writing argument/Missy James and Alan Merickel.
    p.cm.
    Includes bibliographical references and index.
    ISBN 0-13-088011-6
    1. English language–Rhetoric. 2. Persuasion (Rhetoric) 3. College readers. 4. Report
writing. I. Merickel, Alan. II. Title.
    PE1408 .J36 2001
    808'.0427–dc21   2001018515

Editor in Chief: Leah Jewell
Senior Acquisitions Editor: Carrie Brandon
Editorial Assistant: Tom DeMarco
Senior Managing Editor: Mary Rottino
Production Liaison: Fran Russello
Editorial/Production Supervision: Jessica Balch (Pine Tree Composition)
Prepress and Manufacturing Buyer: Sherry Lewis
Senior Marketing Manager: Brandy Dawson
Cover Designer: Robert Farrar-Wagner
Cover Image: Marjory Dressler

This book was set in 10/12 Caslon by Pine Tree Composition, Inc.,
and was printed and bound by Courier Companies, Inc.
The cover was printed by Phoenix Color Corp.

© 2002 by Pearson Education, Inc.
Upper Saddle River, New Jersey 07458

Printed in the United States of America

10   9   8   7   6   5   4   3

ISBN 0-13-088011-6

Pearson Education LTD., *London*
Pearson Education Australia PTY, Limited, *Sydney*
Pearson Education Singapore, Pte. Ltd
Pearson Education North Asia Ltd, *Hong Kong*
Pearson Education Canada, Ltd., *Toronto*
Pearson Educaión de Mexico, S. A. de C. V.
Pearson Education–Japan, *Tokyo*
Pearson Education Malaysia, Pte. Ltd
Pearson Education, *Upper Saddle River, New Jersey*

Contents

2 Writing to Evaluate and Articulate   24

3 Individuality and Community   58

6 Power and Responsibility   503

Preface

Reading Literature and Writing Argument springs directly from our classroom experiences as teachers of two college composition courses: "Writing Argument and Persuasion" and "Writing about Literature." In teaching the argument-based composition course, we delight in witnessing our students' development of the critical processes and rhetorical tools needed for constructing an argument. In the literature-based composition course, we delight in witnessing our students' discovery, or rediscovery, of the magic of imaginative literature and their deepening awareness of their humanity. In both courses, students are enriched, as readers and as writers, through their active engagement with ideas in written language. Also, in both courses, students are challenged to examine their thinking and to contrast their ideas with the ideas of others. We want our students to experience the best of these two worlds. Thus, to merge the distinct values of each course, we have written *Reading Literature and Writing Argument*.

    Reading Literature and Writing Argument is based on the premise that writing is valued when it makes readers think. This premise implies, of course, that a person must have ideas—something to say—in order to put pen to paper or fingers to keyboard. However, the notion that these ideas must have value can be daunting to the individual who is staring at the blank page or screen. This is where literature—stories, poems, plays, essays—can play a vital role, one too often overlooked in students' overly busy, information-laden lives. Literature can unlock the gate to students' imaginations and open the window for creative envisioning. Likewise, the study of argument is vital to compelling students to think clearly and objectively.

    Students can practice the skills of analysis and evaluation and, in doing so, develop critical standards and criteria for judging ideas. For example, Henry David Thoreau's essay, "Civil Disobedience," is an argument, and students learn when they examine his assertion that the individual's first responsibility is to maintain his or her own integrity. Similarly, students learn from examining the arguments made in a play by Sophocles, in a poem by Gwendolyn Brooks, or in a story by Ed Vega.

Literature liberates thinking, and argument disciplines it. The combined and complementary forces are inspiring and empowering. With our students' experiences in the two composition courses as our guide, we have attempted to harness the courses' complementary strengths in *Reading Literature and Writing Argument.*

ORGANIZATION

Chapters 1 and 2 introduce and explain the terms and tools of argument. Chapters 3 through 6 present literature pieces centered on four enduring themes: "Individuality and Community," "Nature and Place," "Family and Identity," and "Power and Responsibility." Following each reading selection are questions that invite students to apply the argument terms and tools from Chapters 1 and 2. In this way, the literature pieces offer a practice field for the tools of critical thinking. Also, a number of writing topics are provided to generate longer written responses and, thus, to prompt students' ideas for writing their own arguments. Following Chapter 6, the appendices, "Notes on the Writing Process" and "Notes on Using Sources and Creating a Draft," address specific challenges of writing an argument and include references to student sample papers in Chapter 2. Also, a student sample Rogerian argument paper is presented at the end of Appendix A.

Chapter 1, "Reading to Explore and Examine," opens with a brief discussion of academic argument and presents a core concept: Reading literature is a prompt for rooting out and exploring the underlying values that inform our responses to the world around us. We then introduce basic argument structure and several rhetorical concepts that relate argument to audience appeal and tone. In selecting terms and concepts to feature in *Reading Literature and Writing Argument,* we chose the tools our classroom teaching experiences have identified as particularly useful to students, both as readers and as writers. Chapter activities reinforce the argument terms and concepts and give students a chance to practice applying them to their reading of some literature pieces.

Chapter 2, "Writing to Evaluate and Articulate," features the reasoning process—how we form opinions and arrive at conclusions. To begin, we challenge students to develop a habit of questioning the foundation of their opinions by evaluating their thinking process. Again, taking a lead from our experiences in the first-year college composition classroom, we decided to highlight the common fallacy of hasty generalization. Also, a brief overview of deduction and induction helps students see how the reasoning process works in argumentation and gives them an additional tool for evaluating their own thinking, ideas, and opinions, as well as those of others—from a speaker in a poem to a character in a play.

From thinking about how we think, we move in Chapter 2 to the process of *writing* argument, which we present as five basic tasks. We offer illustrations of writers, both professional and student, applying these tasks. The last section of the chapter presents a four-part written exploration and articulation activity, a process that draws on the concepts from Chapters 1 and 2 and culminates in the students' writing their own arguments. The four-part activity directs students to explore their own thinking about a designated subject; to explore the subject in the context of several literature pieces; to explore the subject by doing some research; and, finally, to articulate an issue and claim, gather support, and compose their own arguments. We present four sample student essays, including two longer research projects: one illustrates the process of the four-part exploration and articulation activity and one features the final product, the research-based argument paper. Lastly, chapter activities are provided to give students some hands-on engagement with the core concepts introduced in the chapter.

For the anthology chapters (Chapters 3–6), we chose theme headings that are broad and that directly affect students' individual lives. We believe that students appreciate the opportunity to explore their own thinking processes within these contexts. Also, the themes invite students to draw connections, not only among the readings within a single chapter, but also among readings in any of the four chapters. For example, some family issues that students may identify in Chapter 5 readings can be related to responsibility issues in Chapter 6 readings. Students may draw on their reading experiences from several chapters as they explore an issue and move toward the writing of their own arguments. Again, we include chapter activities to stimulate students' thinking about their reading experiences and about potential issues for writing an argument.

To borrow from Robert Frost's statement on poetry, *Reading Literature and Writing Argument* is designed to bring both "delight" and "wisdom" to first-year college students' composition experiences. We believe that students will enjoy reading the literature pieces, practicing critical thinking skills, and exploring different perspectives on issues close to their own lives. And finally, students will discover they have a wealth of ideas as well as the critical acumen to compose a written argument that will compel their readers to think. The blank page or computer screen will present a welcome invitation to students to speak out and to be heard, to make choices, and to make a difference in their own lives and in the lives of others.

ACKNOWLEGMENTS

In writing this book, our colleagues of the Tallahassee Community College English Department and in the Writing Center, as well as our Academic Dean, have provided a steady source of encouragement, and we gratefully thank each of them for their queries, empathetic comments, and pats on the back. For their keen editors' eyes and creative suggestions, we offer special thanks to freelance developmental editor, Heather Hoyt of Arizona State University, and to friend and companion, Victoria Merickel. At Prentice Hall, we are grateful to editor-in-chief, Leah Jewell, for her early-on interest in our concept for this book and to senior acquisitions editor, Carrie Brandon, for her persistent support and guidance. We also appreciate Lisa M. Black's indefatigable efforts to secure copyright permissions, and we offer a hearty thank you to project coordinator, Jessica Balch, for her cheerful efficiency in producing the book.

Finally, we owe thanks to the following reviewers whose comments and suggestions helped to shape the book: Lynee Lewis Gaillet, Georgia State University; Michael Hennessy, Southwest Texas State University; Shawn Schumaker, DeVry Institute of Technology, Dupage Campus; Matt Smith, Heartland Community College.

Chapter One

Reading to Explore and Examine

The term argument evokes images of confrontation. As two people challenge one another over conflicting views, their voices rise, their moods darken, and their minds become fixed upon winning.

> "How can you say sexual harassment in the workplace is an overstated problem? Being a male, you've never experienced it. You don't know what you're talking about!"
> "Oh, so just because I'm a male, I can't understand this issue? What an unbelievably sexist thing to say!"

Of course, this confrontational form of argument can be heard throughout our society, from dorm rooms to courtrooms, from public hearings to legislative debates. The popular television program "Crossfire" is built around exactly such a form of argument as nationally known political analysts spend a half hour attacking one another during prime time. And the 1990s vintage talk shows—from Ricki Lake to the Jerry Springer show—thrive on divisiveness and confrontation. When people join a confrontational argument, they often close their minds. Their emotions displace their reason as their desire for victory overcomes any inclination to listen to their opposition's point of view.

In an academic setting, however, argument means more than confrontation. **Academic argument** implies a reasoned approach to issues. In an academic community, people also hold opposing viewpoints, but they debate in order to modify and strengthen their positions. Through the deliberative and respectful exchange of viewpoints, each side "wins" by attaining a deeper understanding of the issue. Two history professors, for example, may well view the World War II bombings of Hiroshima and Nagasaki quite differently. Two paleontology professors may debate the cause of the extinction of the dinosaurs. Two students may hold differing views regarding the use of capital punishment. However, in academic argument, despite the intensity of the debate, emotion should never replace reason.

Reason dictates that we not only make our own position clear, but that we also do our best to understand opposing positions. After all, the purpose of the college experience is learning, whether that learning comes through classroom discussion, through research, or through the general interaction of members in the academic community. Academic argument is an integral part of that learning process.

EXPLORE

". . . you go to a great school not so much for the knowledge as for arts and habits: for the habit of attention, for the art of expression, for the art of assuming at a moment's notice a new intellectual position, for the art of entering quickly into another person's thoughts, for the habit of submitting to censure and refutation, for the art of indicating assent or dissent in graduated terms, for the habit of regarding minute points of accuracy, for the art of working out what is possible in a given time, for taste, for discrimination, for mental courage and mental soberness."

—WILLIAM JOHNSON CORY (1823–1892)[1]
ETON COLLEGE

Written over one hundred years ago, William Johnson Cory's description of the learning process endures. Each semester, many contemporary social issues wash across a college campus, touching the academic disciplines both directly and indirectly: euthanasia, affirmative action, freedom of speech, genetic engineering, gender equity, global warming, immigration. Although in society at large, sharply focused debates emerge as people establish positions around these issues, in a college setting, students and faculty have the opportunity to step back from the moment and create some emotional distance. The college experience enables us to probe the values and belief systems which underlie issues and ideas. Looking inward and outward, we practice the *habit of attention* which enables us to make choices, deliberately and thoughtfully, and to participate in shaping a free society.

Imaginative literature allows us to explore *"the art of expression, . . . the art of assuming at a moment's notice a new intellectual position, . . . the art of entering into another person's thoughts."* Anchoring one of humanity's fundamental questions—how should I live my life?—in the concrete language of time and place, literature both personalizes and focuses this question for us. Reading literature, we are transported from the particular details of our individual lives to the lives of other persons, their places, and their times. We emerge from the pages of the literary work with fresh perspectives. As the poet Wallace Stevens noted, "Imagination is one of the forces of nature." Through literature we may examine with a clear vision both the personal issues that sometimes cloud our daily lives and the social issues that often divide our communities. The literature provided in this textbook is grouped around four

---

[1]William Johnson Cory was a British educator and lyric poet who taught at Eton College from 1845 to 1871. In 1882, he published *Guide to Modern History from 1815 to 1835.*

themes: Individuality and Community, Nature and Place, Family and Identity, and Power and Responsibility.

"Once upon a time . . ."

Listening to stories as young children, we were not only entertained but also informally instructed in values: honesty, competition, pride, loyalty, compassion, empathy. As readers in a first-year college composition course, we continue to learn from stories about our beliefs and ideas, the **value assumptions,** which underlie our behavior and attitudes and inform our opinions and conclusions. Through our reading and our writing about literature, we can step back and explore these value assumptions; we can ferret out underlying beliefs and ideas and scrutinize their logic and reasonableness. To illustrate, we will briefly explore three stories, whose full texts are included in later chapters.

In reading Raymond Carver's "Cathedral" (Chapter 6), we witness the narrator's personal growth through his reluctant interaction with his "wife's blind friend," Robert. As active readers, we can trace our evolving response to the narrator. For example, here are some excerpts from early in the story:

> My idea of blindness came from the movies. In the movies, the blind moved slowly and never laughed. Sometimes they were led by seeing-eye dogs.
>
> At first glance, his [Robert's] eyes looked like anyone else's eyes. But if you looked close, there was something different about them. Too much white in the iris, for one thing, and the pupils seemed to move around in the sockets without his knowing it or being able to stop it. Creepy.

While the narrator shows himself to be observant, his comments are likely to strike us as simple-minded, crass, and insensitive. By the end of the story, however, the narrator reveals a softer, more serious, and thoughtful side of his character. But careful readers will ask questions: Is the narrator's transformation authentic? Has this one night's encounter changed his outlook? By writing to record our reaction to the narrator at various points in the story, we can draw our individual conclusions about the character of the narrator. Also, we can explore our personal reactions to each of the story's three characters—the narrator/husband, the wife, and the wife's friend Robert—which may reveal something about how we form judgments.

In writing an informal, reflective response to the story, we may recall our own experiences with individuals who were different from us—in physical or mental abilities, in ethnicity, in economic class, in religious faith—and around whom we felt uncomfortable. In the act of recalling and writing, we can become readers of our own "stories" and explore the underlying themes: *What assumptions, beliefs, or ideas accounted for our feelings about and actual reaction in that particular situation?* Also, using Carver's story as a model, we can "role play"; we can imagine ourselves in a situation similar to the narrator's and write our own script. How would we respond to a visitor who is uncomfortably different from us? Again, from this outward perspective, viewing ourselves as a character in a story, we can explore and examine our range of feelings and reactions: What ideas or beliefs about how a person *should* act or look shape our reaction to and interaction with this "different" individual? Finally, as we move beyond ourselves, these underlying questions—how we view "the other," those who are not "like us"—may lead us to a deeper level of scrutiny of contemporary issues: for example, the scope of the American Disabilities Act, the purpose of affirmative action programs, or the reform of immigration policies.

Tim O'Brien's short story, "The Things They Carried" (Chapter 6) introduces us, firsthand, to the Vietnam foot soldier, and Louise Erdrich's story, "The Red Convertible" (Chapter 3), to a recent Vietnam veteran. Reading O'Brien's story and empathizing with Lieutenant Jimmy Cross and his men, we may see today's middle-aged veterans as yesterday's young men with names and girlfriends and families back home, as individuals who are struggling to survive in a hostile environment: ". . . afraid of dying . . . they were even more afraid to show it. . . . They used a hard vocabulary to contain the terrible softness. . . . *zapped while zipping*. . . ." Likewise, reading Erdrich's story, we see Lyman Lamartine's brother, Henry, who has recently returned home after serving as a Marine in Vietnam. Here is how Lyman describes his brother, who spends much of his time watching TV: "He sat in front of it, watching it, and that was the only time he was completely still. But it was the kind of a stillness you see in a rabbit when it freezes and before it will bolt. . . . his smile had changed, or maybe it was gone."

Living with these characters in the pages of O'Brien's and Erdrich's stories, we see the actual human faces behind the cliche, "war is hell." As a result, we may look a bit differently upon the middle-aged man at the street corner with the weathered face, scraggly hair, and "Veteran, will work for food" sign. Perhaps, too, this deliberative reflection will lead us to investigate homeless issues or programs and benefits for veterans in our own communities.

EXAMINE

If academic argument implies both understanding opposing positions as well as articulating our own positions, then we must begin with analysis. Thoughtfully and objectively analyzing the views of others, including their underlying assumptions, is a necessary first step in understanding our own beliefs. However, this task is not simple. First, we must understand some of the basic elements of argument.

The Greek philosopher Aristotle in his *Rhetoric* identifies several elements of argument which will be important for us. His three appeals, *logos, pathos,* and *ethos* (**rhetorical triangle**), mark three human characteristics: reason, emotion, and perception of character. Understanding these three elements will give us insights into the positions of others as well as our own. In addition, Aristotle describes a three-part **syllogism,** consisting of a major premise, a minor premise, and a conclusion:

Major Premise:	College graduates are critical thinkers.
Minor Premise:	Michael and Meredith are college graduates.
Conclusion:	Michael and Meredith are critical thinkers.

Such a syllogism creates an outline, revealing the logical structure of an argument. Although not all arguments can be so neatly dissected and outlined, our attempts to reduce an argument to its bare elements can help us examine its underlying logic.

To allow more flexibility and openness in examining argument structure, a twentieth-century British philosopher, Stephen Toulmin, created new terminology to rework the elements of Aristotle's syllogism. According to the Toulmin model for argument, the warrant replaces the syllogism's major premise; the grounds or evidence replaces its minor premise; and the claim replaces its conclusion:

> Since dogs are bred for human companionship [the *warrant*], and schnauzers are dogs [the *grounds*], schnauzers would make companionable pets [the *claim*].

Because this textbook emphasizes reading, writing, and critical thinking rather than advanced logic and rhetoric, we will focus on those elements of argument which will help us examine and articulate positions efficiently: claims, evidence, warrants, and rhetorical appeals.

ARGUMENT STRUCTURE

Claims

The **claim** is the assertion made in an argument, the main point or thesis. We can also think of the claim as the conclusion the writer has drawn. Some claims are easily seen. For example, in the essay, "Truer to the Game," Randy Horick makes this statement: "The women play a superior brand of basketball." For readers, there can be no misunderstanding—in fact, every word in Horick's essay leads readers to accept his claim.

Truer to the Game

RANDY HORICK

Out in our driveway, where my 12-year-old daughter dreams of becoming the next Chamique Holdsclaw, we have been working together on a few of the finer points of competitive basketball. Like how to use your elbow semi-legally to establish position (an old Don Meyer bit of wisdom). Or how to inbound the ball to yourself by thunking it off the buttocks of an unsuspecting opponent. Or the deep personal satisfaction, to say nothing of the psychological advantage, gained from setting a teeth-rattling screen.

As part of this regimen, I have tried to use games on TV as teaching tools. I point out, for example, a good blockout on a rebound, a properly executed pick and roll, or the way to run a two-on-one fast break (or, more often, the way *not* to run a break).

Being a quick study, my daughter has observed one of the game's truths just from viewing two telecasts: the women's Final Four games on Friday and the corresponding men's contests on Saturday evening. "Dad," she observed, "the guys can't shoot."

This is either basketball's deep, dark secret or a cause for excitement, depending on your point of view. The truth is that the women take better shots than their male counterparts. As their respective NCAA tournaments made it ever clearer this March, when it comes to putting the pill in the hoop, girls' basketball rocks. Boys' basketball, well, doesn't.

But not only that: The women play a superior brand of basketball. These are not the tilted rantings of some addle-brained pot-stirrer, as accustomed as you may profess to be to seeing such things on these pages. You can find a whole pantheon of old NBA stars—including no less of a luminary than Bill Russell his own bad shot-blocking self—who proclaim that women's basketball is much truer to the game they played than the men's version today.

Claims of superiority, of course, all depend upon your definitions. If you measure quality by physical measures—speed, play above the rim, dazzling one-on-one moves—it's still a man's world. (Don't imagine, however, that the women in the Final Four aren't superbly conditioned athletes.)

If you're looking for solid fundamentals and all-around team play, well, um, fellas, y'all got next. Ironically, the relative physical inferiority of today's women players provides the basis for a superior game.

The ability of men to complete acrobatic, soaring drives and dunks increasingly has led them to become infatuated with "taking it to the tin"—regardless of which defenders are in the way or which teammates may be open elsewhere. It's as if the guys have all graduated from some funky basketball camp that teaches that style points count for even more than real ones.

If you had $250 for every time during the men's NCAAs that a player passed up a jump shot, faked with the ball, then put his head down and headed toward the hole, they'd make you an honorary member of the bar association. The predictable results of such reckless driving, all too often, are offensive fouls, ugly collisions, and loads of bricks. For every dunk, we are forced to witness several thunks. For every electrifying play, there are several short-circuits. The literal rise of countless would-be Jordans has corresponded with a steady fall in field goal and free throw percentages in the men's game.

Contrast that with the women's game, where the play is decidedly below the rim and dunks are rarer than incorruptible state legislators.

Because the girls aren't yet throwing it down, they're forced to concentrate on the aspects of the game that many of the boys seem to regard as beneath them. Like practicing free throws. Running patterned offenses. Looking for back-door cutters. Making routine shots. Executing the fundamentals.

For all of these reasons, if you want to teach someone to play the game, women's basketball today is far more instructive. In part, that's because their game runs at a slightly slower speed, allowing you more clearly to see plays develop. Much more, however, it has to do with better shot selection, better ball movement, and more faithful adherence to the concept of team play.

Off the court, of course, women's college basketball looks even better in comparison. At the Division I Level, men's hoops today less and less exemplifies the old ideals of amateur competition and more and more resembles a corporate leviathan.

In the way that drug cartels have corrupted the institutions in countries like Columbia and Mexico, those who control the money and labor supply have leeched into men's basketball. AAU coaches serve as talent brokers who wield inordinate influence. Shoe companies sponsor posh summer camps for top high school players and sign college coaches to cushy contracts, hoping to win future endorsements from those who become stars.

Meanwhile, the pressures to win are so enormous upon coaches, and the financial allure of an NBA career so powerful to players, that almost any action can be rationalized in the name of winning. Top high school players with marginal grades may be shipped off to basketball trade schools that pass themselves off as institutions of academic learning.

Collegiate coaches recruit the nation's elite players knowing all too well that they will be gone within a year or two, and that their only real interest in the college experience lies in gaining experience that will prepare them for the pros.

Things are so whomperdejawed that the NCAA, which blithely presided over the creation of this mess, is now declaring that the entire culture of men's basketball is diseased and needs a radical cure. (Good luck, guys.)

Against this backdrop, the women's game looks like a fount of purity. Star players don't bug out early for the professional league; they stay and earn their degrees.

Coaches don't have to hire bodyguards to protect their athletes from contact by predatory agents. The recruiting process does not begin in the eighth or ninth grades. There are no televised McDonald's all-American games or dunk contests that teach the best players that they belong to some sort of celebrity elite.

Those days may be coming. As the popularity of women's basketball continues to increase (Sunday's championship between Tennessee and Connecticut was the most watched women's game ever), so too will the pressures.

The retirement last week of Louisiana Tech coach Leon Barmore is a reminder of where the game is going. Tech and Old Dominion are perhaps the last of the "little" schools that remain powers in women's basketball today. It's easy to forget that, barely two decades ago, the game was dominated by colleges you never heard of: Delta State, Immaculata, Stephen F. Austin, Wayland Baptist.

Women's basketball belongs to the big schools now. With the WNBA successfully established, it is conceivable that collegians might turn pro early if salaries become attractive enough. Coaches might cut corners and grease palms to lure the best high schoolers to their programs. A whole industry might rise up and enshroud the game, as it has with men's basketball.

Until then, though, I'll keep offering up as role models the kind of unspoiled, we-first players who were evident in the women's tournament.

Meanwhile, we won't forget at our house that the men's pro league still offers enormous entertainment value. Just last Sunday, during the Knicks-Lakers game, my daughter came rushing in breathlessly. "Dad, dad, come check it out. Kobe Bryant and Chris Childs are having a fight!"

On the other hand, a claim can be implied or indirect rather than explicit or directly stated, particularly in imaginative literature. Do you recall reading *The Scarlet Letter* by Nathaniel Hawthorne? Like many high school students, you probably encountered this novel sometime during your four years, but can you state the claim Hawthorne makes? Something about deception perhaps? Maybe something about values? Readers are not likely to find a single sentence in Hawthorne's novel equivalent to Horick's assertion regarding women's basketball. However, in a classroom discussion, through the interplay of varying interpretations, readers can articulate a central claim or assertion for this novel.

Of course, some imaginative literature offers no claim whatsoever. Look, for example, at a short poem by Kenneth Rexroth:

Cold before Dawn

Cold before dawn,
Off in the misty night,
Under the gibbous moon,
The peacocks cry to each other,
As if in pain.

Do you see an implicit claim in this poem? If you do, you are probably reading too much into this five-line, imagist poem. As a further example, look at this Ezra Pound poem:

In a Station at the Metro

The apparition of these faces in the crowd,
Petals on a wet, black bough.

You will discover no claim here, no matter how proficiently you analyze this poem. But look at the following poem by the eighteenth-century British poet William Blake:

London

I wander thro' each charter'd street,
Near where the charter'd Thames does flow,
And mark in every face I meet
Marks of weakness, marks of woe.

In every cry of every Man,
In every Infant's cry of fear,
In every voice, in every ban,
The mind-forg'd manacles I hear.

How the Chimney-sweeper's cry
Every black'ning Church appalls;
And the hapless Soldier's sigh
Runs in blood down Palace walls.

But most thro' midnight streets I hear
How the youthful Harlot's curse
Blasts the new born Infant's tear,
And blights with plagues the Marriage hearse.

What do you see as the claim in this poem? Is the claim about the young children used as chimney sweeps and doomed to early deaths? Is it about venereal disease? Yes, the poem says something about both of these subjects; indeed, a number of subclaims usually can be identified in any example of writing. In this poem, however, Blake indirectly accuses the religious, military, and legal institutions of being responsible for the human suffering endured by so many people in the late 1700s. No single line makes such a claim, but when you re-read the poem, you will see that the indictment is certainly the poem's central focus, the conclusion the writer wishes the reader to draw from this evidence.

Argument theorists identify several types of claims, including a claim of fact, a claim of policy, and a claim of value. If you state that the world loses ten acres of rainforest every minute, then you are making a **claim of fact,** which may be useful as evidence in an argument calling for new environmental laws to protect the rainforest. The call for new laws would be a **claim of policy** because it asks for a specific action to take place. If the argument makes a judgment labeling something good or bad, then you have a **claim of value:** Rainforests are an invaluable and irreplaceable natural resource.

Evidence

Evidence is the body of information used to support claims. This information may be based on subjective personal experience, on objective facts, on the authority of an expert. Toulmin calls this information the grounds for the claims. There are various types of evidence, but for our purposes, let's concentrate on three: personal experience, reports, and authority.

In an essay, a student claims euthanasia should be legalized and cites his experience of watching his grandmother suffer a prolonged and painful death as the result of cancer. The student's choice of descriptive details coupled with his sincere tone creates a strong, emotional response in his readers. His use of **personal experience** provides strong evidence for the validity of his argument, particularly among readers who have had similar experiences.

On the other hand, some readers may not have any experience with cancer and may never have experienced the death of a family member or loved one. For these people, despite the obvious emotional pull of the evidence, further proof will be required. In this case, the writer might want to provide some statistics of the numbers of patients on life-support in this country, as well as the costs to families and health care providers. Taking this approach, the writer is using **reports,** objective facts gathered from outside sources, to support his argument.

The student writer might take one further step towards validating his argument for legalizing euthanasia by citing an **authority.** In this case, a quote from a health care professional would be a good choice. In fact, any field has authorities, people recognized as experts. Citing Dr. Spock as an authority on babies, Bill Gates when discussing the computer industry, or Michael Jordan in relation to professional basketball, a writer could be certain readers would recognize these people as authorities. They have credibility.

Applying the concept of evidence to imaginative literature complicates and enriches our reading experience. To begin with, we must address the **dramatic context** of the writing itself, including the actions, words, and thoughts of the characters within that work. Examining the characters' arguments, their positions, framed within the dramatic context, we look beyond ourselves and ultimately gain a better perception of our own positions.

For example, perhaps if you saw the film *Rain Man,* you recall watching Tom Cruise's character transform his attitude toward his mentally challenged, older brother (played by Dustin Hoffman) as the two travel together. That transformation is based on the evidence of personal experience within the context of the film. In fact, that particular film had a great impact on audiences, for many people left the theater examining their own perceptions of mentally challenged people. Similarly, readers of Harper Lee's novel, *To Kill A Mockingbird,* not only see the transformation of attitudes within the characters as they confront the issue of racial discrimination, but they may also come away from that reading experience examining their own attitudes about prejudice. Thus, analyzing the evidence in the dramatic context of a particular work leads you to understand the position of the character within the work and to explore your own beliefs and values.

Moving beyond the dramatic context, we also can examine the **social context** of a story, poem, or play as evidence of the writer's claim. However, an understanding of that evidence often requires us to gather additional information.

Look back at the poem "London," cited earlier. If William Blake wants the reader to believe the social institutions of eighteenth-century England were to blame for much of the suffering endured by its citizens, he must offer us some evidence. At that time, poor families often sold one of their children to the chimney sweeps who used them to slide down London's many tight chimneys. As they brushed the soot from those chimneys, the children's lungs filled with black dust, and they regularly died while still in their early teens. The fact that such an abuse of children was legal in London is clear evidence in support of Blake's claim. By acquainting yourself with this historical background, you enrich your understanding of Blake's implied argument.

Warrants

Warrants are the assumptions, general principles, or commonly accepted beliefs which underlie an argument. According to Toulmin's argument model, warrants link the evidence to the claim; they are the bonding element that justifies or warrants the audience's movement from evidence to claim. Although a warrant may be stated in an argument, it frequently is a hidden or an unstated assumption. Furthermore, warrants are often value-based, that is, based on principles or beliefs that guide our behavior and inform our attitudes about people, events, and issues.

For example, in arguing for strict environmental regulation of rainforests (claim of policy), a writer may offer statistical data and scientific facts to show how rainforests are being destroyed (evidence). The warrant—rainforests are valuable resources—may be readily accepted by American readers and require no backing. However, for the Brazilian landowner, his property may seem more valuable as a clear-cut and plowed field than as a rainforest. Perhaps the writer should not assume all of her readers will accept her warrant. Depending on whom the writer envisions as her audience, she may need to back her warrant with evidence to show how rainforests are valuable. Of course, within our own boundaries, from the Pacific Northwest to the Everglades, similar disputes rage over how to use our wilderness areas. First, how do we define *wilderness?* And how is our view of wilderness impacted by the economic or cultural factors in our lives? Responses will vary among individuals. Yet these responses are crucial to any discussion of wilderness issues. Our personal definition informs the value we assign to wilderness areas; this value assignment (the warrant) then shapes our viewpoint about specific land use issues. Similarly, in the case of euthanasia or physician-assisted suicide, the sanctity and dignity of human life are values that influence our positions. In articulating a claim for physician-assisted suicide, the warrant would be based on our degree of allegiance to each of these values.

Because warrants are often value-based, they can be difficult for us to recognize. How often do we stop to examine the values that affect our judgment of a person or groups of people? When do we have the time for this deliberative introspection? Voice mail, cell phones, and e-mail are efficient means of communicating, for example, but they also make us even busier, as we rush to respond. In contrast, reading literature can relax us. It can take us out of the hectic rush of our daily lives and provide a window for us to look more deeply into ourselves and beyond ourselves—inside the lives and emotions of other persons. Literature, therefore, provides an ideal playing field for examining warrants.

For example, in Blake's poem, "London," we identified a claim (the social institutions of eighteenth-century England were to blame for much of the suffering of its citizens) and pointed out evidence (the practice of selling children to chimney sweeps). What warrant underlies the argument, binding the evidence to the claim? Interestingly, the warrant, a value assumption, is so readily accepted by contemporary readers that we don't think to question it: The use of child labor is an affront to the principles of compassionate people everywhere. In eighteenth-century England, however, children, especially children of poor families, were viewed as property; the selling and buying of children were not widely condemned. Fortunately, enlightened thinkers, such as Blake, stood apart and questioned social institutions that supported the exploitation and abuse of children.

But the child labor issue is still complicated for contemporary readers. What about those expensive athletic shoes or the designer silk shirt we may have recently purchased? Where were they manufactured? And by whom? Recently, the employment practices of several well-known U.S. manufacturers of name-brand shoes and clothing have come under critical scrutiny. Many U.S. manufacturers have opened factories in foreign countries where operating costs are far lower: Land is cheaper, and environmental and labor laws are often either nonexistent or far less stringent than in the United States. In some cases, boys and girls younger than sixteen work long hours in brutal working conditions for meager wages. Is this practice not abusive and exploitative, an affront to our principles of compassion? Even though we are not directly responsible for hiring the twelve-year-old girl who works in the factory where our silk shirts were manufactured, do we share some portion of responsibility? Reading Blake's poem as an argument and examining its warrant from this perspective, we bridge the centuries that seemed to divide us from eighteenth-century London.

AUDIENCE APPEAL AND TONE

Over two thousand years ago, Aristotle's *Rhetoric* introduced the three appeals, *pathos, logos, ethos,* which focus on the specific effects of an argument—its language and tone—on its audience. Drawing on these three appeals, the writer of argument addresses the basic human characteristics of his or her audience: emotion and empathy (***pathos***), logic and reasoning (***logos***), credibility and trust (***ethos***). Today, any lawyer who expects to win over a jury understands the necessity for making these appeals. Martin Luther King Jr.'s essay, "Letter from Birmingham Jail," written in 1963 (Chapter 3), stands as a modern classic of argumentation, in part because of King's use of rhetorical appeals. Reading this essay, you will see how King builds trust with his audience (*ethos*): "I hope this letter finds you strong in the faith. I also hope that circumstances will soon make it possible for me to meet each of you, not as an integrationist or a civil rights leader, but as a fellow clergyman and a Christian brother"; reasons deliberately and analytically (*logos*): "How does one determine whether a law is just or unjust? A just law is a manmade code.... An unjust law is a code that is out of harmony with the moral law...."; and evokes his audience's empathy and compassion (*pathos*): "...when you suddenly find your tongue twisted and your speech stammering as you seek to explain to your six-year-old daughter why she can't go to the amusement park that has just been advertised on television, and see tears welling up in her eyes...." Although addressed to a specific audience, eight "fellow" Alabama clergymen, more than thirty-five years ago, King's "Letter" speaks compellingly to a universal audience.

If we are not accustomed to examining essays as arguments, certainly we are familiar with the Western tradition of courtroom confrontation. Using Aristotle's rhetorical appeals to examine several poems, we can appreciate the poems as argumentation, as well as deepen our understanding of the appeals as ways that writers connect with their readers.

Pathos

"Federico's Ghost" by Martín Espada provides a striking illustration of *pathos* appeal. The poem tells the story of a boy's defiant gesture of protest against the abusive treatment of workers by those in positions of power:

Federico's Ghost

The story is
that whole families of fruitpickers
still crept between the furrows
of the field at dusk,

when for reasons of whiskey or whatever
the cropduster plane sprayed anyway,
floating a pesticide drizzle
over the pickers
who thrashed like dark birds
in a glistening white net,
except for Federico,
a skinny boy who stood apart
in his own green row,
and, knowing the pilot
would not understand in Spanish
that he was the son of a whore,
instead jerked his arm
and thrust an obscene finger.

The pilot understood
He circled the plane and sprayed again,
watching a fine gauze of poison
drift over the brown bodies
that cowered and scurried on the ground,
and aiming for Federico,
leaving the skin beneath his shirt
wet and blistered,
but still pumping his finger at the sky.

After Federico died,
rumors at the labor camp,
told of tomatoes picked and smashed at night,
growers muttering of vandal children
or communists in camp,
first threatening to call Immigration,
then promising every Sunday off
if only the smashing of tomatoes would stop.
Still tomatoes were picked and squashed
in the dark,
and the old women in camp
said it was Federico,
laboring after sundown
to cool the burns on his arms,
flinging tomatoes
at the cropduster
that hummed like a mosquito
lost in his ear,
and kept his soul awake.

Using sensory language and specific details, Espada pulls us inside—behind the words—to where we cannot avoid seeing the human faces of the tomato pickers, who are not unlike ourselves: "whole families," "a skinny boy," "old women." By acknowledging our common humanity, we must acknowledge the injustice and the oppression of the field laborers' lives. Poetic structure also heightens *pathos* appeal. Because we are accustomed to reading margin-to-margin prose, the poem's line breaks slow down our reading. We cannot rush, or skip over words, as we may do in reading an essay. Espada isolates images in short lines, which surprise and shock us as readers:

> over the pickers
> who thrashed like dark birds
> in a glistening white net,
> . . . .
> leaving the skin beneath his shirt
> wet and blistered,

With these images fixed in our imaginations, we are compelled to confront the reality of "man's inhumanity to man" and also to examine our own attitudes toward day laborers, migrant workers, and illegal aliens. Appealing to our emotions and moral values, Espada's poem makes a powerful statement about prejudice and power and about human dignity and heroism. "Federico's Ghost" may, indeed, keep our own "soul[s] awake."

Logos

Shakespeare's sonnets can provide excellent illustrations for the *logos* point of Aristotle's triangle. Compare the form of the English or Shakespearean sonnet itself, a logical, fixed structure (fourteen lines—three quatrains and a couplet) to Espada's free-verse (open-form poetry), for example. The sonnet's structure reinforces the poem's argumentative emphasis. As noted earlier, Espada's free-form line breaks counter logical structure and dramatize emotion. In the case of a Shakespearean sonnet, however, its ordered structure and regular rhythm underscore its pattern of reasoning and logic, as illustrated in "Sonnet 18":

Sonnet 18

> Shall I compare thee to a summer's day?
> Thou art more lovely and more temperate:
> Rough winds do shake the darling buds of May,
> And summer's lease hath all too short a date:
> Sometime too hot the eye of heaven shines,
> And often is his gold complexion dimmed;
> And every fair from fair sometimes declines
> By chance or nature's changing course untrimmed;
> But thy eternal summer shall not fade,
> Nor lose possession of that fair thou ow'st,
> Nor shall death brag thou wander'st in his shade,
> When in eternal lines to time thou grow'st:
> > So long as men can breathe or eyes can see,
> > So long lives this, and this gives life to thee.

In the sonnet, the poet's claim is explicitly stated in the final quatrain: For as long as men live, this poem shall live and so, too, shall his beloved. In the preceding twelve lines, the poet provides evidence for his claim. Beginning with "a summer's day," he lists comparisons, each of which he finds deficient: "Sometime too hot the eye of heaven shines,/ And often is his gold complexion dimmed." As readers, we are invited to think and reason with the poet as he makes his case for his beloved's immortality.

Ethos

Questioning the speaker's reliability leads us to the last point of Aristotle's rhetorical triangle: *ethos* appeal—how a speaker or writer establishes credibility and builds trust with his readers. One way to examine *ethos* is to examine *tone*—the attitude the speaker or writer conveys through specific word choices. For example, read the following, "Sonnet 130" by Shakespeare:

Sonnet 130

My mistress' eyes are nothing like the sun;
Coral is far more red than her lips' red;
If snow be white, why then her breasts are dun;
If hairs be wires, black wires grow on her head.
I have seen roses damasked, red and white,
But no such roses see I in her cheeks;
And in some perfumes there is more delight
Than in the breath that from my mistress reeks.
I love to hear her speak, yet well I know
That music has a far more pleasing sound;
I grant I never saw a goddess go;
My mistress, when she walks, treads on the ground.
  And yet, by heaven, I think my love as rare
  As any she belied with false compare.

As in "Sonnet 18," the poet states his claim in the final quatrain: "And yet, by heaven, I think my love as rare/ As any she belied with false compare." And again, the poet laces the first twelve lines with comparisons as evidence for his claim.

However, studying the specific images, readers are led to scrutinize the poet's tone and to question the sincerity of his declaration of "love as rare." Would one whose love is "rare" describe his mistress' breasts as "dun," her hair as "black wires," her breath as "reek[ing]"? Does the poet intend to compliment her or to poke fun at her? And what does he mean by "rare"—rare as in precious or rare as in unusual? Finally, how do we as individual readers respond to our perception of his character? Do we admire him for his down-to-earth honesty and witty outlook, or do we fault him for a mean-spirited, sexist attitude? Debates over the *ethos* of the poet/speaker can spark lively classroom discussions and prompt us to examine our own attitudes and assumptions about men and women and relationships.

For a different perspective on *ethos* appeal, read the following short fiction piece, "Girl," by Jamaica Kincaid:

Girl

JAMAICA KINCAID

Wash the white clothes on Monday and put them on the stone heap; wash the color clothes on Tuesday and put them on the clothesline to dry; don't walk barehead in the hot sun; cook pumpkin fritters in very hot sweet oil; soak your little clothes right after you take them off; when buying cotton to make yourself a nice blouse, be sure that it doesn't have gum on it, because that way it won't hold up well after a wash; soak salt fish overnight before you cook it; is it true that you sing benna in Sunday school?; always eat your food in such a way that it won't turn someone else's stomach; on Sundays try to walk like a lady and not like the slut you are so bent on becoming; don't sing benna in Sunday school; you mustn't speak to wharf-rat boys, not even to give directions; don't eat fruits on the street—flies will follow you; *but I don't sing benna on Sundays at all and never in Sunday school;* this is how to sew on a button; this is how to make a buttonhole for the button you have just sewed on; this is how to hem a dress when you see the hem coming down and so to prevent yourself from looking like the slut I know you are so bent on becoming; this is how you iron your father's khaki shirt so that it doesn't have a crease; this is how you iron your father's khaki pants so that they don't have a crease; this is how you grow okra—far from the house, because okra tree harbors red ants; when you are growing dasheen, make sure it gets plenty of water or else it makes your throat itch when you are eating it; this is how you sweep a corner; this is how you sweep a whole house; this is how you sweep a yard; this is how you smile to someone you don't like too much; this is how you smile to someone you don't like at all; this is how you smile to someone you like completely; this is how you set a table for tea; this is how you set a table for dinner; this is how you set a table for dinner with an important guest; this is how you set a table for lunch; this is how you set a table for breakfast; this is how to behave in the presence of men who don't know you very well, and this way they won't recognize immediately the slut I have warned you against becoming; be sure to wash every day, even if it is with your own spit; don't squat down to play marbles—you are not a boy, you know; don't pick people's flowers—you might catch something; don't throw stones at blackbirds, because it might not be a blackbird at all; this is how to make a bread pudding; this is how to make doukona; this is how to make pepper pot; this is how to make a good medicine for a cold; this is how to make a good medicine to throw away a child before it even becomes a child; this is how to catch a fish; this is how to throw back a fish you don't like, and that way something bad won't fall on you; this is how to bully a man; this is how a man bullies you; this is how to love a man, and if this doesn't work there are other ways, and if they don't work don't feel too bad about giving up; this is how to spit up in the air if you feel like it, and this is how to move quickly so that it doesn't fall on you; this is how to make ends meet; always squeeze bread to make sure it's fresh; *but what if the baker won't let me feel the bread?;* you mean to say that after all you are really going to be the kind of woman who the baker won't let near the bread?

Kincaid's narrator would seem to be a mother lecturing her daughter, "girl." The mother's advice and admonitions are salt-of-the-earth, basic survival skills for a girl or woman: from how to cook, how to clean, and how to spit or smile to how to take care of a man or to administer her own birth control. Clearly, the mother is intent on her daughter's listening; the daughter manages only two brief rebuttals: *"but I don't sing benna on Sundays . . . but what if the baker won't let me feel the bread?"* Furthermore, the mother's tone is authoritative and domineering; her lecture is spiked with imperative clauses: do this, do that, don't do that, never do this, etc. Yet it also is a catalogue of practical information: "this is how...; this is how...." The mother is passing on to her daughter all of her own hard-earned knowledge. As readers, what is our attitude toward this mother? Is she a "good" mother? Do we respect her? Trust her? Why or why not? In response, we find ourselves scrutinizing the tone of the voice we hear as we read this short piece and examine the narrator's motives. Would we describe the tone as simple yet elegant, a message of "tough love," or crude and haranguing, a belittling message of misguided love? Like "Sonnet 130," Kincaid's short fiction piece can provoke energetic discussion and prompt us to explore our underlying assumptions about the role of a parent or an authority figure.

ROGERIAN ARGUMENT STRATEGY

Common sense dictates that successful argument depends on our success in engaging audiences—in particular, those audiences with opposing or conflicting viewpoints. Yet how often have we witnessed or participated in an argument, such as the following:

MICHAEL: I think the use of animals for medical science research and laboratory testing should be banned. It's unethical, immoral, and inefficient to use animals for these experimentations.

MEREDITH: That's easy for you to say. But what if your own child or your mother or your brother had a life-threatening illness and needed a certain drug or maybe an organ transplant? Wouldn't you want the best medical science could do for your loved one? And wouldn't you want that treatment to have been laboratory-tested on animals?

MICHAEL: No. Animals have as much right to life as we do. We're no better. In fact, when I look around the world today, I think we may be less deserving than animals.

MEREDITH: You're a fanatic. I love animals, too, but a human life is more valuable than an animal's.

...End of the argument. But what was accomplished? Each party has had his or her moment at the podium to justify his or her position. Each party walks away from the argument, unchanged, unmoved by the opposing viewpoint, indeed, perhaps even more entrenched in his or her position. How can we avoid these dead-end arguments? If we and our audience have strong viewpoints on a divisive issue, how can we build that essential bridge between our views and our audience's?

Earlier we noted that Stephen Toulmin adapted Aristotle's classical model of argument to suit the needs of modern and contemporary audiences. Similarly, in studying audience appeal and tone, the work of Carl R. Rogers, an American psychotherapist and communication theorist, complements Aristotle's rhetorical triangle. According to Rogers, we engage our audience by demonstrating empathy with their viewpoints; we present an objective summation of the opposing viewpoints. In this way, we acknowledge their validity and, therefore, open the doors for communication—a first and crucial step for argumentation. At the same time, we present ourselves as individuals of good will and character, thus, building trust with our audience (*ethos* appeal*).

Rogers's theory of argumentation and audience empathy, **Rogerian strategy,** appears frequently in argument textbooks. In fact, Rogerian strategy follows the commonsense wisdom of the "golden rule": "Do unto others as you would have them do unto you." In other words, I will listen openly to your views; in exchange, you will agree to listen openly to mine. Furthermore, the conclusion or claim of Rogerian argument is a well-qualified, compromise position. For example, in the dialogue above, a Rogerian conclusion might read: "Recognizing that the use of animals for tests and laboratory experiments is inherently unfair to the animals, we must strictly regulate research laboratories to ensure that conditions are humane and to limit the use of animal testing." All in all, negotiation and compromise are the ruling principles of Rogerian argument strategy (see Appendix A).

In theory, the Rogerian strategy seems wholly sensible, based, as it is, on a practical understanding of people and an awareness of human nature. But in our competitive society ("Winning's not everything—it's the only thing") and amidst a media culture that seems to thrive on an "in-your-face" hollering match, the Rogerian style takes a backseat. Indeed, in presenting Rogerian argument in the composition classroom, as teachers we find that students often protest its non-aggressive tone ("where's the fun?") and question its tactics ("manipulative, deceptive?"). We respond that Rogerian argument does not mean giving up one's beliefs, nor does it mean accepting whatever anyone says or writes; rather we ask our students to agree to listen to opposing viewpoints with the purpose of understanding them.

For example, let's consider one current and enduring environmental issue: the preservation of wilderness or "green spaces." Clearly, these areas are shrinking, squeezed out by the needs of a growing population and technological culture. And in the case of some of the more popular national parks, Yellowstone, for example, the visitors themselves are literally the vehicles of much ecological degradation. Given these premises, the conclusion seems simple: Take action before it's too late, before there are no remaining wilderness areas to preserve. But action requires money—taxpayers' dollars. Meanwhile, other environments, not likely featured on a glossy Sierra Club calendar, are also threatened and endangered; these are our cities, our large urban areas where thousands of citizens live. We worry about the drug culture and violent crimes, yet send young children off to schools with overcrowded classrooms, overworked teachers, and too few textbooks. Again, given these premises, the conclusion seems simple: Take action now to improve urban schools and provide these children with a quality education. Again, action requires money—taxpayers' dollars.

The wilderness and urban environments would seem to be competing factions, and indeed, public discussion fosters this division. Meanwhile, the media, hungry for drama, fan the flames of divisiveness by couching the different groups in extreme terms. Serious thinking evaporates. The fight is on: "us against them." In the headlong rush to win, each side must beat its drums more loudly and attempt to drown out others. Of course, serious thinking does not have to be overcome by contentious rhetoric. If we practice the habit of listening—of understanding and empathizing with other persons' perspectives—we are less likely to be waylaid by simplistic thinking.

Reading stories, poems, plays, and essays fosters empathetic understanding and provides practice in receptive listening. For example, we may never have lived in a large urban environment, but reading Lucille Clifton's poem, "For de Lawd," gives us, at least for a moment, an insider's viewpoint:

For de Lawd

people say they have a hard time
understanding how I
go on about my business
playing my Ray Charles
hollering at my kids—
seem like my Afro
cut off in some old image
would show I got a long memory
and I come from a line
of black and going on women
who got used to making it through murdered sons
and who kept on pushing
who fried chicken
ironed
swept off the back steps
who grief kept
for their still alive sons
for their sons coming
for their sons gone
just pushing
in the inner city
or
like we call it
home
we think a lot about uptown
and the silent nights
and the houses straight as
dead men
and the pastel lights
and we hang on to our no place
happy to be alive
and in the inner city
or
like we call it
home

This black woman and mother of sons, who lives in the "inner city," speaks to us directly and plainly about "home": we see people who are going about the daily doings of living; who love, who grieve, and who are proud, "happy to be alive." Thus, rather than an abstract slogan or label, the "inner city" becomes a real place for us.

Similarly, N. Scott Momaday's poem, "New World," invites us to go out in nature and witness the unfolding of a day:

New World

1.
First Man,
behold:
the earth
glitters
with leaves;
the sky
glistens
with rain.
Pollen   2.
is borne   At dawn
on winds   eagles
that low   hie and
and lean   hover
upon   above   3.
mountains.   the plain   At noon
Cedars   where light   turtles
blacken   gathers   enter
the slopes—   in pools.   slowly
and pines.   Grasses   into   4.
                        shimmer   the warm   At dusk
                        and shine.   dark loam.   the gray
                        Shadows   Bees hold   foxes
                        withdraw   the swarm.   stiffen
                        and lie   Meadows   in cold;
                        away   recede   blackbirds
                        like smoke.   through planes are fixed
                                       of heat   in the
                                       and pure   branches.
                                       distance.   Rivers
                                                     follow
                                                     the moon,
                                                     the long
                                                     white track
                                                     of the
                                                     full moon.

The poem's short, one- or two-word lines demand our close attention as readers. We must practice patience and slow ourselves down to follow the text of the poem accurately. Then, like the "First Man," we can "behold" the treasures which the day reveals: "the earth/ glitters. . . grasses shimmer. . . ."

The study of literature and the study of argument are complementary and mutually empowering; both contribute to creative envisioning and critical thinking. Even as we hold fast to opposing viewpoints, we share the common ground of our humanity. Literature can lead us to this common ground. By tapping into our imaginations, literature can help us see from a broader and more in-depth perspective, our personal, day-to-day issues as well as enduring, public issues. In this way, we are better prepared to articulate a thoughtful position and to argue it with heartfelt emotion, clear logic, and valid reasoning. Through the interplay of arguments, we participate in shaping our lives and the affairs of our communities.

CHAPTER ACTIVITIES

1. In a group of three or more, select an issue that prompts local or national debate. Pick one side in the debate and write its claim in one sentence. List several examples of evidence this side uses to support its claim. What assumptions (warrants) do the followers of this side hold? List them. And finally, which rhetorical appeals does this side use? List them and include examples.

2. a. What assumption about suburban neighborhoods does the editorial cartoon below challenge?

   b. Bring to class an editorial cartoon which challenges a widely held assumption.

Mike Smith reprinted by permission of United Feature Syndicate, Inc.

3. After reading "Those Winter Sundays" by Robert Hayden, write out the poet's claim in one sentence. Now list the poem's evidence which supports that claim. Is the claim valid only within the dramatic context of the poem? Or is the claim valid universally? Can you find evidence within your own personal experience which would support the claim? What warrant underlies the claim?

Those Winter Sundays

Sundays too my father got up early
and put his clothes on in the blueblack cold,
then with cracked hands that ached
from labor in the weekday weather made
banked fires blaze. No one ever thanked him.

I'd wake and hear the cold splintering, breaking,
When the rooms were warm, he'd call,
and slowly I would rise and dress,
fearing the chronic angers of that house,

Speaking indifferently to him,
who had driven out the cold
and polished my good shoes as well.
What did I know, what did I know
of love's austere and lonely offices?

4. Read Wilfred Owen's poem *"Dulce et Decorum Est."* How does the poet use Aristotle's three rhetorical appeals to convince us of his claim that the phrase, *"Dulce et decorum est/ Pro patria mori,"*[2] lacks merit? Is there a logical presentation of evidence? Is there an emotional presentation of evidence? Does the speaker seem to have credibility?

Dulce Et Decorum Est

Bent double, like old beggars under sacks,
Knock-kneed, coughing like hags, we cursed through sludge,
Till on the haunting flares we turned our backs
And towards our distant rest began to trudge.
Men marched asleep. Many had lost their boots
But limped on, blood-shod. All went lame; all blind;
Drunk with fatigue; deaf even to the hoots
Of tired, outstripped Five-Nines that dropped behind.

Gas! Gas! Quick boys!—An ecstasy of fumbling,
Fitting the clumsy helmets just in time;
But someone still was yelling out and stumbling
And floundr'ing like a man in fire or lime . . .

---

[2]Quotation from Horace, meaning, "It is sweet and dutiful to die for one's country."

Dim, through the misty panes and thick green light,
As under a green sea, I saw him drowning.

In all my dreams, before my helpless sight,
He plunges at me, guttering, choking, drowning.

If in some smothering dreams you too could pace
Behind the wagon that we flung him in,
And watch the white eyes writhing in his face,
His hanging face, like a devil's sick of sin;
If you could hear, at every jolt, the blood
Come gargling from the froth-corrupted lungs,
Obscene as cancer, bitter as the cud
Of vile, incurable sores on innocent tongues,—
My friend, you would not tell with such high zest
To children ardent for some desperate glory,
The old Lie: *Dulce et decorum est
Pro patria mori.*

Chapter Two

Writing to Evaluate and Articulate

Mark Twain, well-known for his skepticism about the human race, was particularly scathing in his comments about man's ability to think independently. "We are creatures of outside influences; as a rule we do not think, we only imitate," Twain writes in his essay, "Corn-Pone Opinions." Indeed, everyone has an opinion... "you have your opinion; I have mine."[1] How often have we heard this comment? We arrive at these opinions through our reasoning. This reasoning process secures our status as a higher order of animal than, say, a mole, which reacts to stimuli (although when ranking reasoning abilities, Twain probably would have placed the mole above humans). Throughout our waking moments, we are forming opinions, many of these, quickly and subconsciously, seemingly without thinking or at least without examining our reasoning process.

The enormous influence of mass media in our culture undermines any impulse toward independent thought. In an increasingly complex world, any one person cannot hope to have more than a rudimentary understanding of such issues as welfare reform in the United States, inflation and interest rates, global warming, or ethnic conflicts in the Balkan region. In their efforts to fill our information gap, news magazines serve us up predigested facts leading to undeniably *correct* conclusions, and televised news programs often seem to make little distinction between fact and opinion. Movies also present us with distinct perspectives of current affairs. Whether another's opinion or our own, we must constantly question the foundation of that opinion: what assumptions do we make about the world; what inferences do we unwittingly want to accept; and to what extent is our thinking based on flawed logic?

---

[1]Mark Twain, *The Family Mark Twain* (New York and London: Harper & Brothers Publishers, 1935), p.1402.

Copyright © 1998 by Don Wright. Used by permission of Don Wright/The Palm Beach Post.

EVALUATE

If we pay attention to the media, we are likely to believe crime is a major problem in the United States. Our newspapers and television programs are filled with graphic reports of criminal activities, from fraudulent corporate schemes to random mass shootings. Popular films regularly depict criminal situations culminating in extreme violence. Let's put ourselves in the place of an elderly man living alone in a suburban neighborhood. Through the influence of the media, such a person might fear for his life. And such fears may well restrict this person's daily activities—he may no longer feel safe taking the bus to his doctor's appointments; he may avoid the local mall where he encounters, in his view, many oddly dressed adolescents; and he may feel too insecure to take an evening walk in his neighborhood. On the other hand, living where he does, the probability of this man's becoming a victim of crime is minimal. Nevertheless, acting on his **assumption**—crime is epidemic—he has narrowed his life. From his perspective of the world, shaped by the media's daily news reports, his argument is clear: Because I do not want to become a victim of crime, I must stay at home where I feel somewhat secure.

This elderly man's thinking is based on flawed reasoning. Although it is true that crime can occur anywhere, he has used inadequate evidence to generalize about the crime risk in his own suburban community. His error in reasoning, moving from inadequate evidence to a broad generalization, illustrates a common logical fallacy: **hasty generalization.** We also know this fallacy as the clichéd expression, *jumping to conclusions*.

When we move from particular evidence to make a broad assertion, we are thinking inductively. Although hasty generalization is a fallacy, **inductive reasoning** also sparks creative thinking which can lead us to personal insights or profound discoveries. Based on a careful examination of *what is,* we envision what *could be.* For example, when a college instructor notices her students are experiencing difficulty understanding the assigned readings and notes that her students' scores on the verbal portion of the SAT have fallen, she could reasonably conclude that students at her particular institution are reflecting a national trend toward weaker reading skills. This conclusion would provide the motivation for the professor to seek a creative solution to the problem. A conclusion reached through inductive reasoning is also called an **inference,** which the linguist S. I. Hayakawa defined as "a statement about the unknown based on the known."[2] Although we cannot know for certain that an inference is 100 percent true, based on what we do know, we can feel convinced it is probably true.

Not uncommonly, however, people make their inductive leaps too soon; they jump to a conclusion when their evidence is inadequate. For example, a toddler may burn his fingers on a stove, and after that incident he may say, "Hot! Hot!" whenever entering a kitchen and seeing a stove. The toddler's parents, although amused by his simplistic conclusion (of course, not all stoves are hot at all times), are also glad that he views the stove as a dangerous beast. However, in some cases, a person's hasty generalization can have tragic consequences. For example, you may have read Shakespeare's *Romeo and Juliet* in high school or have seen a movie adaptation. In the end, although Juliet is merely pretending to have taken her own life, Romeo immediately jumps to the conclusion she is dead and takes his own life. In Act V, Romeo meets his servant on the streets of Mantua:

ROMEO: News from Verona! How now Balthasar?
              Dost thou not bring me letters from the friar?
              How doth my lady? Is my father well?
              How fares my Juliet? That I ask again,
              For nothing can be ill if she be well.

BALTHASAR: Then she is well, and nothing can be ill.
              Her body sleeps in Capel's monument,
              And her immortal part with angels lives,
              I saw her laid low in her kindred's vault
              And presently took post to tell it you.
              O, pardon me for bringing thee ill news,
              Since you did leave it for my office, sir.

---

[2]S. I. Hayakawa, *Language in Thought and Action* (New York: Harcourt, Brace, Jovanovich, 1978), p. 35.

ROMEO:	Is it e'en so? Then I defy you, stars!
	Thou knowest my lodging. Get me ink and paper
	And hire post horses. I will hence tonight.
BALTHASAR:	I do beseech you, sir, have patience.
	Your looks are pale and wild and do import
	Some misadventure.

[Although the servant has delivered terrible news to Romeo, he can also see that Romeo is in no state of mind to think the situation through clearly. The key word in Balthasar's speech is "patience," something Romeo does not possess at the moment. Nor has he gained any patience when, later arriving at the tomb, he kills Paris and lays him in the tomb near Juliet. And as he turns his attention to Juliet herself, Romeo still is not thinking clearly.]

ROMEO:	. . .O my love, my wife!
	Death, that hath sucked the honey of thy breath,
	Hath had no power yet upon thy beauty.
	Thou art not conquered. Beauty's ensign yet
	Is crimson in thy lips and in thy cheeks.
	And death's pale flag is not advanced there.
	…Ah, dear Juliet,
	Why art thou yet so fair? Shall I believe
	That unsubstantial Death is amorous,
	And that the lean abhorrèd monster keeps
	Thee here in dark to be his paramour?
	For fear of that I will stay with thee
	And never from this pallet of dim night
	Depart again

* * *

[*Drinks*] O true apothecary!
Thy drugs are quick. Thus with a kiss I die.

[Of course, as we know, Juliet is not dead but merely drugged. Romeo's confusion is understandable; after all, his servant has told him Juliet is dead, and he himself has seen her lying in a tomb. However, Romeo also has seen quite clearly that she does not look dead ("crimson in thy lips and in thy cheeks"). Even so, his emotional state overpowers his reason, and he ignores this important piece of evidence. Romeo jumps to a fatal conclusion: he drinks the poison he has brought with him and dies beside his, yet living, beloved Juliet.]

Arthur Miller's twentieth-century play, *The Crucible*, based on the Salem witch trials of 1692, also illustrates how our emotions, in this case, fear, can derail reasoning and clear thinking. In the play, as in historical Salem, Massachusetts, the townspeople jump to the conclusion that the women are witches, although their evidence, the testimony of young girls, is inadequate. At the close of Act One, the girls, Abigail and Betty, begin their accusations:

HALE: Take courage, you must give us all their names. How can you bear to see this child suffering? Look at her, Tituba. *He is indicating Betty on the bed.* Look at her God-given innocence; her soul so tender; we must protect her Tituba; the Devil is out and preying on her like a beast upon the flesh of the pure lamb. God will bless you for your help.

Abigail rises, staring as though inspired, and cries out.

ABIGAIL: I want to open myself! *They turn to her, startled. She is enraptured, as though in a pearly light.* I want the light of God, I want the sweet love of Jesus! I danced for the Devil; I saw him; I wrote in his book; I go back to Jesus; I kiss His hand. I saw Sarah Good with the Devil! I saw Goody Osburn with the Devil! I saw Bridget Bishop with the Devil!

As she is speaking, Betty is rising from the bed, a fever in her eyes, and picks up the chant.

BETTY, *staring too:* I saw George Jacobs with the Devil! I saw Goody Howe with the Devil!
PARRIS: She speaks! *He rushes to embrace Betty.* She speaks!
HALE: Glory to God! It is broken, they are free!
BETTY, *calling out hysterically and with great relief:* I saw Martha Bellows with the Devil!
ABIGAIL: I saw Goody Sibber with the Devil! *It is rising to a great glee.*
PUTNAM: The marshal, I'll call the marshal!

Parris is shouting a prayer of thanksgiving.

BETTY: I saw Alice Barrow with the Devil!

The curtain begins to fall.

HALE, *as Putnam goes out*: Let the marshal bring irons!

[The dialogue and stage directions depict the strong emotions that surround this situation. The men, who very much *want* to believe the girls' accusations, readily make the inductive leap to condemn the accused women. And once made, they secure exactly what they want: the accused women's guilty verdict. In contrast, at the start of Act Two, Miller shows us two people for whom the evidence is inadequate:]

ELIZABETH: ...There be fourteen people in jail now. *Proctor simply looks at her, unable to grasp it.* And they'll be tried, and the courts have power to hang them too.
PROCTOR, *scoffing, but without conviction*: Ah, they'd never hang—

ELIZABETH: The Deputy Governor promises hangin' if they'll not confess, John. The town's gone wild, I think. She speaks of Abigail, and I thought she were a saint, to hear her. Abigail brings the other girls into the court, and where she walks the crowd will part like the sea for Israel. And folks are brought before them, and if they scream and howl and fall to the floor—the person's clapped in the jail for bewitchin' them.

PROCTOR, *wide-eyed:* Oh, it is a black mischief.

ELIZABETH: I think you must go to Salem, John. *He turns to her.* I think so. You must tell them it is a fraud.

[John Proctor does, indeed, go to Salem, but to no avail. The town has "gone wild," allowing emotion to overcome all reason. Based on inadequate evidence, the people of Salem have made a hasty generalization. As a result, fourteen people are hanged.]

Perhaps we are inclined to tell ourselves that these events in Salem took place over three hundred years ago and, therefore, do not apply to our contemporary world. However, we need only to look back to the mid-twentieth century to see a series of events dominated by emotion rather than reason—the McCarthy hearings in which the House UnAmerican Activities Commission investigated persons accused of being communists. In fact, this occurrence inspired Miller to write *The Crucible*. Appealing to fear—the post–World War II threat of Communism, the "Red Scare"—this group in Congress thwarted or ruined the careers of many journalists and actors in this country. Again, as in colonial Salem, reason was overcome by emotion. Indeed, the term, "witch hunt," has as much viability today as it did in the late 1600s. We must remain vigilant to avoid becoming victims of our own flawed reasoning, slaves to purely emotional appeals. Examining literature, like *Romeo and Juliet* and *The Crucible*, helps us to practice this vigilance.

Hasty generalization, when it fosters **stereotyping,** can have considerable negative impact on individuals and far-reaching implications on our policies and institutions. When we form quick judgments about other persons, based on their outward appearance—their dress, their hairstyle, their accent, or their gender, race, or age—we may be making a hasty generalization. As we suggested in Chapter 1, for example, the narrator in the short story "Cathedral" (Chapter 6) has formed simplistic generalizations about "blindness" from images in movies. Standing apart as readers, we clearly see the narrator's own blindness, his narrow-mindedness and prejudicial thinking. In contrast, we may not so readily detect our own narrow thinking when it is reinforced by popular culture and media images.

Of course, we should take individual responsibility for our opinions about others and about issues and events. Taking this responsibility, however, demands hard thinking—the continuous questioning of the underlying evidence that affects our generalizations and inferences. But hard thinking sounds like hard work. Perhaps, "ignorance is bliss"? Of course not. Most of us would not knowingly choose to be prejudicial thinkers. In reading literature, our imaginations allow us to practice using our mental energy: we journey with characters to Vietnam; we hear about the inner city; or we see the boy in the tomato field thrust his finger toward the sky in protest. In writing about literature, we develop the habit of inquiry and scrutiny. We explore the roots of our thinking, examine the underlying logic of our assumptions, evaluate the validity of our generalizations, and articulate our conclusions. And once committed to living the examined life—to scrutinizing assumptions, to questioning evidence, and to analyzing arguments—we cannot turn away from the task of taking responsibility for our choices and opinions.

DEDUCTION AND INDUCTION: AN OVERVIEW

Logicians use the terms, **inductive** (specific to general) and **deductive** (general to specific), to describe our reasoning process. Inductive reasoning is an open-ended process in that the conclusion reached is *always* based on probability. Deductive reasoning, on the other hand, aims to *prove* its conclusion by confining or limiting its scope. To practice the habit of self-inquiry and evaluation, inductive and deductive thinking are useful tools of analysis. For example, let's consider Percy Bysshe Shelley's poem, "Ozymandias":

Ozymandias

I met a traveler from an antique land
Who said: Two vast and trunkless legs of stone
Stand in the desert...Near them, on the sand,
Half sunk, a shattered visage lies, whose frown,
And wrinkled lip, and sneer of cold command,
Tell that its sculptor well those passions read
Which yet survive, stamped on these lifeless things,
The hand that mocked them, and the heart that fed:
And on the pedestal these words appear:
"My name is Ozymandias, king of kings:
Look on my works, ye Mighty and despair!"
Nothing beside remains. Round the decay
Of that colossal wreck, boundless and bare
The lone and level sands stretch far away.

Using the model of Aristotle's syllogism (Toulmin terms in parentheses), we can outline Ozymandias's reasoning:

Major premise (warrant):	The monuments of great and powerful leaders will last forever.
Minor premise (support):	I am a great and powerful leader who has built monuments.
Conclusion (claim):	Therefore, my monuments will last forever.

Ozymandias bases his argument on an underlying, unstated assumption that seems true to him—the monuments of kings are eternal. However, on what evidence is his assumption based? Propelled by self-pride and arrogance, the "king of kings" has made an inductive leap to arrive at his major premise. From this premise, he reasons deductively that his "works" will last forever. In the last lines of the poem, however, the poet proclaims the error of Ozymandias's reasoning:

> Nothing beside remains. Round the decay
> Of that colossal wreck, boundless and bare
> The lone and level sands stretch far away.

Inductive reasoning, often occurring beneath the surface, that is, subconsciously, is risky, prone to error, as in the case of Ozymandias. However, as noted earlier, inductive reasoning also can lead to profound discoveries. For example, the research scientist first must risk an inductive leap in her search for a cure for a disease. After observing patterns of reactions of certain viruses to a particular agent in laboratory experiments, she may predict (hypothesize) that this virus would react similarly to this agent within a human subject. She then would use deductive reasoning to test her hypothesis: she would set up specific laboratory conditions to prove or disprove her theory. We see, therefore, how inductive and deductive reasoning are intertwined in argumentation. The two processes are not contradictory; rather, they are complementary, as inextricably linked as wings are to a bird: one does not "fly" without the other.

ARTICULATE

When we sit down to write our own arguments, we face several tasks:

1. We must be certain we have clearly identified the *issue*.
2. We must gather and analyze the information logically.
3. We must create a *claim* which uses well-defined terminology and is limited in scope.
4. We must provide adequate support by selecting specific, accurate, and relevant *evidence*.
5. We must organize our evidence in a way that effectively presents our argument to the audience.

To see how these five elements come together in writing an argument, let's look at two excerpts from Martin Luther King, Jr.'s "Letter from Birmingham Jail" (Chapter 3).

In the following example of **deductive** organization, King makes a general statement as a major premise (warrant), then states his claim, and, finally in the succeeding five paragraphs, supports his claim with evidence:

> In any nonviolent campaign there are four basic steps: collection of the facts to determine whether injustices exist; negotiation; self-purification; and direct action

[*major premise*]. We have gone through all of these steps in Birmingham [*claim*].
…Birmingham is probably the most thoroughly segregated city in the United
States.…[*evidence* for collection of facts].

Then, last September, came the opportunity to talk to leaders of Birmingham's economic community.…[*evidence* for negotiation] Mindful of the difficulties involved, we decided to undertake a process of self-purification. We began a
series of workshops on non-violence,.…[*evidence* for self-purification]

Then it occurred to us that Birmingham's mayoral election was coming up in
March, and we speedily decided to postpone direct action until after election day.…
Having aided in this community need, we felt our direct-action program could be de-
layed no longer. [*evidence* for direct action]

King later uses a pattern of **inductive** organization to refute his audience's position that his direct-action program was "untimely" and that he should have waited
for the new civic administration to remedy segregation. First, King piles on specific
examples and personal testimonies as his evidence, and then he presents his claim:

We have waited for more than 340 years for our constitutional and God-
given rights. The nations of Asia and Africa are moving with jetlike speed toward gaining political independence, but we still creep at horse-and-buggy pace toward gaining a cup of coffee at a lunch counter. Perhaps it is easy for those who have never
felt the stinging darts of segregation to say, "Wait." But when you have seen vicious
mobs lynch your mothers and fathers at will and drown your sisters and brothers at
whim; when you have seen hate-filled policemen curse, kick and even kill your
black brothers and sisters; when you see the vast majority of your twenty million
Negro brothers smothering in an airtight cage of poverty in the midst of an affluent
society; when you suddenly find your tongue twisted and your speech stammering
as you seek to explain to your six-year-old child why she can't go to the amusement
park that has just been advertised on television, and see tears welling up in her eyes
when she is told that Fun-town is closed to colored children, and see ominous
clouds of inferiority beginning to form in her little mental sky, and see her beginning to distort her personality by developing an unconscious bitterness toward
white people; when you have to concoct an answer for a five-year-old son who is
asking: "Daddy, why do white people treat colored people so mean?"; when you
take a cross-country drive and find it necessary to sleep night after night in your automobile because no motel will accept you; when you are humiliated day in and day
out by nagging signs reading "white" and "colored"; when your first name becomes
"nigger," your middle name becomes "boy" (however old you are) and your last
name becomes "John," and your wife and mother are never given the respected title
"Mrs."; when you are harried by day and haunted by night by the fact that you are a
Negro, living constantly at tiptoe stance, never quite knowing what to do next, and
are plagued with inner fears and outer resentments; when you are forever fighting a
degenerating sense of "nobodiness" [*evidence*]—then you will understand why we
find it difficult to wait. There comes a time when the cup of endurance runs over,
and men are no longer willing to be plunged into the abyss of despair [*claim*].

Despite his strong emotional involvement, King obviously has analyzed the situation logically. Within his letter, he has composed claims that are narrowly fo-

cused and thus provable. His examples in support of these claims are concrete rather than general. And, finally, King has used both deductive and inductive patterns of organization to structure his argument effectively for his audience.

While not everyone will be able to write as skillfully as Martin Luther King, Jr., creating clear, effective position statements is certainly within the grasp of any college student. In his Birmingham jail cell, King had many long hours to compose his letter, and the result shows this hard work. Although time is a scarce commodity for most college students, several sessions of concentrated effort should produce a presentable argument. For example, let's examine a topic which is relevant and familiar to college students, *working while attending college:*

1. What do you know about working and attending college (your job, friends' jobs, classmates' jobs and academic experiences, student expenses, etc.)?
2. Do you hold any principles (warrants) that direct your thinking on this subject? Or have specific experiences led you to draw conclusions about working and attending college?
3. Can you make a claim of value (good/bad) or a claim of policy (should do/should not do) regarding this subject? Or does your experience lead you to make a claim of fact (true/false)? Is your claim focused and therefore supportable?
4. Do you have sufficient concrete examples, gleaned from your experience and observations, to prove your claim?
5. How can you most effectively organize your argument? Should you follow a deductive pattern, first, stating the claim and then supporting it with examples; or should you follow an inductive pattern, first, offering examples and then concluding with the claim? Or does the length of your argument allow you to use both organizational patterns effectively?

In reading the following student essay, notice how Shawn Mullin has addressed the five writing tasks listed above:

Yes, the Future Looks Bright, but the Moment Is Hell

My share of the rent, all $220 of it, is due next Friday. Today my business management professor asked the class to buy another textbook and read chapter one before we meet again; that's $46.50 I'll need by Wednesday. The utility bill is probably already in the mail, and my girlfriend is expecting me to take her out to dinner Saturday to celebrate our "six-month anniversary." I have $36.87 in my checking account and a big problem.

According to my calculations, I need to come up with about $300. by the end of the week. Perhaps I could make one of those desperation calls to Mom and Dad although I can already hear their answer: "Shawn, we are paying your tuition and sending some spending money. We expect you to contribute as well. After all, both your brothers will be attending college in the coming years. You wouldn't want us to spend their money on you, would you!" At this point, I wouldn't object, but I know I'll never make that call. No, I already have a job; what I need are more hours— more hours in the day so I can find the time to work, study, attend class, sleep, and, when all else is done, even have a social life.

Since my boss typically pays me in cash on Fridays, all I need to do is work more hours. But at $6.50 an hour, I'll need to add quite a few hours by Friday afternoon. When school began last fall, I promised myself I would not work more than 25 hours a week, and my position at the print shop has worked out well when compared to my friends' working conditions. Their bosses also promised to hold down their hours and be considerate of exams and research papers; however, those promises were hardly made before the managers began demanding more and more time at work. My friends' protests about chemistry exams or English papers were completely ignored. They regularly work 35 to 40 hours a week; their grades reflect the lack of study time. And now I am about to join them.

Dr. Robert Jones, my history professor, recently told me that due to working while attending school, most students now take five years to complete a four-year degree. And further corroborating that news is my academic counselor, Dr. Elizabeth French, who told me that she found that the grades of students working more than 20 hours per week fell with each increase of five hours. She also explained that she found a significant decrease in participation in campus life as working hours increased because these students have no extra time for student government, clubs, or other campus organizations. That information is not good news for me since I have no choice in this situation. It's work more hours or live on the streets.

Working more than twenty hours a week has negative effects on college students. That much is clear. Nevertheless, this time I'll ask for the extra hours and accept the consequences. However, I intend to find a cheaper place to live, so I will not be in this position again next term. And who knows? Maybe my girlfriend will be just as happy celebrating our one-year anniversary over coffee at Starbucks.

For this short, first-person point of view argument, the writer chose to follow an inductive pattern of organization. The first four paragraphs present the *evidence*—personal experience and testimony—which leads to an explicit *claim* (position statement) in the conclusion paragraph: *Working more than twenty hours a week has negative effects on college students.* Using the same set of considerations that guided this writer, students can create an argumentative essay in response to assigned readings in literature. Look, for example, at Daphine Beckham's essay below, prompted by two poems, Walt Whitman's "I Saw in Louisiana a Live-Oak Growing" (page 53) and T. S. Eliot's "The Love Song of J. Alfred Prufrock" (Chapter 3):

Perspective on Men

When I was a little girl, I thought my father was a rock, hard and unmoving. I come from a family of strong men. These male relatives were bread-winners, stoic, and without a doubt the leaders of their respective prides. Later, I realized these rocks had cracks which defined their characters and souls. These men cried, they made mistakes, and they could feel.

My earlier attitudes towards men can be summed up in the poem by Walt Whitman entitled, "I Saw in Louisiana a Live-Oak Growing." In the poem, the speaker compares himself to a live-oak tree:

> I saw in Louisiana a live-oak growing,
> All alone stood it and the moss hung down from the
>   branches,
> Without any companion it grew there uttering joyous
>   leaves of dark green,
> And its look, rude, unbending, lusty, made me think of
>   myself.

Like the tree, the speaker believes himself to be deeply rooted. He has a vision of himself as a dominating figure who is in control of his environment.

As I got older, I began to realize that men are not the stereotypical figures I once believed. In T. S. Eliot's poem, "The Love Song of J. Alfred Prufrock," a different kind of man is introduced. This man feels insecure, fragmented, and confused. Prufrock states, "I am not Prince Hamlet, nor was meant to be." Unlike Whitman's speaker who thinks of himself as a master of his environment, Prufrock is unsure of his ability to command respect, admiration, or to choose the direction of his own life. He calls himself, "an attendant lord," who is not worthy of leadership privileges, and, "Almost, at times, the fool." When I was young, the men around me seemed strong, secure, and certain, like Whitman's live-oak tree. Later, however, I noticed a trace of Prufrock's insecurities.

In Whitman's poem, the speaker is confident of his physical and sexual appeal. The poem makes allusions to this confidence through the use of such phrases as, "lusty," and, "manly love." In contrast, Prufrock suffers doubts about his physical attractiveness:

> And indeed there will be time,
> To wonder, "Do I dare?" and, "Do I dare?"
> Time to turn back and descend the stair,
> With a bald spot in the middle of my hair—
> [They will say: "How his hair is growing thin!"]

When I was young, the last thing I would expect to see was my father, fretting in front of the mirror, worrying about a few extra pounds, or some new wrinkle around his eyes. But now I know better—he dyes his hair!

Prufrock, moreover, is deeply concerned about growing old; he places an inordinate value on youth. In contrast, Whitman's speaker celebrates the older man. He envisions his aging self like the unyielding oak tree and identifies with the noble characteristics of the tree, growing strong and more appealing with age. Prufrock's self-comparisons are cynical and demeaning. In one instance, he makes an analogy between himself and an insect, a mere bug put on display: "And when I am formulated, sprawling on a pin,/ When I am pinned and wriggling on the wall," he says. In another line, Prufrock compares himself to an insignificant crustacean laboring in obscurity on the bottom of the sea: "I should have been a pair of ragged claws,/ Scuttling across the floors of silent seas." Clearly, Prufrock holds a low opinion of himself.

Reflecting on these two poems, I am reminded of an incident with my father when I was around eleven years old. I sat on the rough, splintered, wood of the community dock of the small Gulf coast village of Cedar Key, Florida. I was waiting for my father. He paid the bills and fed the family by working on the water. It was sticky and summer, and I was swatting mosquitoes while I watched a stray mutt rummage through an overturned garbage can. "Can we take him home?" I pleaded, when my father showed up. "He looks so hungry and kinda pitiful."

"What do we need with a mutt like that?" he snapped. "The damn thing looks like more trouble than it's worth. Leave it be."

I knew better than to argue, but later that evening, the dog showed up at our house, and my father was feeding him table scraps. "Must have followed us home," he grumbled as the dog gobbled up the food, "But tomorrow he's gotta go." The dog stayed, and, despite the constant complaining from my father, they were friends for many years.

Many years later, I learned that the dog did not follow us home; my father went back to get him. I guess a man can be Prufrock and a live-oak at the same time.

In writing this essay, Daphne Beckham chose to follow a deductive pattern of organization. The *claim* is presented in the introduction paragraph—*These men cried, they made mistakes, and they could feel*—and is followed by the *evidence*, examples from her personal experience and selected quotations from each of the poems.

As Daphne's essay illustrates, when we examine a theme dramatized in literature, we have the opportunity to gain insight into our own thinking. We move forward, attempting to clarify our own position on an aspect of the theme and, finally, to present our position to an audience. Moving beyond the personal perspective argument to construct an academic argument, we then face the challenging task of identifying an issue within that theme, researching that issue, and articulating a defensible position for an audience. The following response activities provide a process for moving from self-reflection and exploration to the articulation of a defensible position.

Four-Part Written Exploration and Articulation

I. **Exploration**. Examine your own thinking on a subject. As an example, let's use *materialism*.

You can try one of the following prewriting techniques:

a. Write the word *materialism* at the top of a page, and write nonstop about it for five to ten minutes just to see what ideas emerge.

b. Write the word *materialism* and list all the ideas, concepts, and terms that are associated with the word. List but do not edit; allow your creative mind to work.

c. Similar to listing, you can cluster. Write *materialism* in the center of a page, circle the word, and cluster around it any ideas and concepts that come to mind. Once you have become familiar with your own thinking on the subject, examine your reasoning process. To do so, respond to the following questions:

1) What assumptions or broad generalizations about materialism are revealed in your prewriting?

2) Can you identify specific, personal experiences that may have led you to make an inductive leap in reaching those generalizations?

II. **Exploration.** Read four or five pieces of literature focusing on your chosen subject [*materialism*, in our example] and examine each one separately by looking at the argument made within its dramatic context.

    a. What is a significant claim in the piece?

    b. What evidence is offered in support of that claim?

    c. What rhetorical appeals (*ethos, logos, pathos*) does the writer use in order to move the reader toward acceptance of the claim?

    d. Upon reflection, how might you defend, refute, and or qualify each writer's claim?

III. **Exploration.** Research your subject [we will continue to use *materialism*] in its social context.

    a. Can you find additional examples of literature, art, and film that address this subject of materialism?

    b. Can you find any statistics related to materialism? Perhaps you can locate the number of pounds of raw resources consumed by an American as compared to the pounds consumed by a Brazilian. Or perhaps you can discover the amount of money spent annually on clothes and music by American teenagers.

    c. Gather commentaries from sources with different perspectives on materialism. For example, if you look in the magazine *The Utne Reader*, where you will find a social critic's perspective, also look in *Forbes* magazine, where you will find a business perspective.

    d. Interview an authority on the subject and/or create your own survey instrument and implement it locally.

    e. Compile your research under specific, descriptive headings.

IV. **Articulation.** Create your own argument on the subject you have explored.

    a. Narrow the general subject to a particular issue.

    b. Identify a specific issue question and formulate a tentative claim for the issue.

    c. Gather support for your claim.

    d. Write your argument.

Student Sample

Continuing with our example of *materialism,* here is Lisa Coletti's response to the four-part assignment:

I. **Exploration.** Examine your own thinking on the subject you have selected. [Lisa chose option a: Write the word *materialism* at the top of a page, and write nonstop about it for five or ten minutes just to see what ideas emerge.]

Materialism

It's about buying things. About things being important to you.

About things being more important to you than people. The 1980s, the "me" generation, consuming. Consumers. Americans and their wealth, so much wealth they forget what is important and so buy things . . . They try to buy love instead of earning it. Shopping malls. Rows of people going up and down on the escalators, people clus-Rows of people going up and down on the escalators, people clustered around the fountains tossing pennies in. People looking at their watches. Crying children, angry wives. People, gluttons of consumer-ism. Capitalism? The evil one that Marx was trying to arm the worker against. PROFIT, the guiding principle. Cal, Adam's son in *East of Eden,* a pile of thousand-dollar bills (or hundred-dollar bills?) setting fire to them one by one. Think of the way children crowd around a pinata that has just been broken. GREED. The difference between wanting and needing things. When we invest meaning in things instead of people . . ."You can't take it with you."

II. **Exploration.** Read four or five pieces of literature focusing on your chosen subject and examine each one separately by looking at the argument within its dramatic context.
   a. What is a significant claim in the piece?
   b. What is the evidence offered in support of the claim?
   c. What rhetorical appeals does the writer use in order to move the reader toward acceptance of the claim?
   d. How might you defend, refute, and/or qualify each writer's claim?

[Lisa read a dramatic monologue, "Rodeo" by Jane Martin, and poems by William Wordsworth, Marge Piercy, and Gary Snyder. (The four works follow this chapter.) Here are her responses to each of these readings.]

"Rodeo" by Jane Martin

<u>Claim</u>: This piece seems to claim that there is a certain integrity to traditional things which is lost when they are commercialized.

<u>Evidence</u>: The evidence which is presented is the fact that the elements of commercialism which have been brought into the rodeo have lowered its quality and authenticity.

<u>Rhetorical Appeal</u>: In the first part of the monologue, the first three paragraphs, Big Eight focuses on the rodeo she was raised with. From her description of how she started riding to stories of rodeo tradition and the original procedure, she communicates a feeling of belonging, which she expresses with the word "us." By showing her firsthand commitment and connection to the rodeo,

the narrator creates *ethos*. Because of her involvement, I respect her viewpoints, even though her language is a bit rough.

In the second part of the monologue, Big Eight moves on to describe "them," the big-time hot shots who have taken over rodeo. To convey her feelings about these newcomers, Big Eight begins by rattling off a list of famous names with contempt: "Them. Coca-Cola, Pepsi Cola, Marlboro damn cigarettes. You know the ones I mean. Them." With her tone and repetition of the word "them," Martin establishes Big Eight's negative feelings toward the forces of commercialism, therefore, appealing to *pathos*. Further developing these feelings in Big Eight's character, Martin continues to splice the word "damn" into otherwise recognizable famous names: "Marlboro damn cigarettes," "Ice damn Capades," and "Minnie damn Mouse." This selective use of an expressive word, especially in the case of "Ice Capades" and "Minnie Mouse"—generally not seen as malevolent influences—leaves no doubt as to the speaker's distaste for the popular commercial influence in rodeo. Big Eight's disapproval of commercial values, her disdain for "them," also appeals to *pathos*.

<u>Defend</u>: From my experience, money interests often corrupt. College football is one example. Also, it's not unusual to see a nice stand of trees bulldozed to build a shopping center directly across from another one.

"The World Is Too Much with Us" by William Wordsworth

<u>Claim</u>: Wordsworth is claiming that modern life has lost its magic because we are preoccupied with material things.

<u>Evidence</u>: The evidence put forth for this claim is the fact that despite the knowledge which modern people have, they are not as happy as ancient peoples who had to rely much more on imagination and mythology for explanation.

<u>Rhetorical Appeal</u>: The main appeal is *logos*. Wordsworth uses logic in drawing a contrast between his nineteenth-century world, the world which is "too much with us" (line 1), and the ancient pagan world in which connections between humans and nature were considered fundamental to an understanding of life. Also, the poem's Elizabethan Sonnet form appeals to *logos*. The poet presents his evidence in a coherent and logical structure. After stating his main premise in the first line, he follows with his evidence, rhythmically ordered, line by line. The language of this poem is vivid,

but it doesn't really grab my emotions, although it may have worked on an emotional level for nineteenth-century readers. I can appreciate Wordsworth's metaphors, such as in line 5, "The sea that bares her bosom to the moon," but it doesn't really strike an emotional chord for me.

<u>Qualify</u>: Wordsworth leaves me thinking about his claim. The sentiment of yearning for a simpler time and a purer form of joy which the poet communicates is common still today, nearly two hundred years later. This suggests that materialism and short-sightedness are not just characteristic of humans in the twentieth century. Contrary to what we might think, materialism is not unique to modern society; however, just because a person drives a BMW doesn't necessarily mean that he or she is insensitive. For example, I enjoy possessing material things, but I also enjoy nature, taking a walk in the park at sunset.

"To Be of Use" by Marge Piercy

<u>Claim</u>: This poem claims that well-done, necessary work has a substance to it which is lacking in more frivolous pursuits.

<u>Evidence</u>: The evidence which is offered to support this claim is that men and women of action are more likable than those who sit still and live in fear.

<u>Rhetorical Appeal</u>: Overall, this poem appeals to my emotions (*pathos*) because of its language—choice of images and sounds of words and phrases. In the first stanza, Piercy talks about the people who go at their work with confidence and assertiveness. She uses words like "sure" (line 4), "sleek" (line 6), and "bouncing" (line 7) to convey these qualities. Also, for me, the image of the seals and and bouncing ball (lines 6 to 7) is happy. She makes work sound like fun! In the second stanza, Piercy pays tribute to people who persist in slow, laborious work. Using words like "harness" (line 8), "massive" (line 9), "strain", and "muck" (line 10), Piercy relates the lack of glamour in such work, and yet dignifies it at the same time. In the third stanza, the speaker admires the rhythm of those who work communally and for a common purpose. In the last line of this stanza, Piercy applies this idea of "common rhythm" to the poem itself: "when the food must come in or the fire be put out," (line 17).

Additionally, with the last two lines, "The pitcher cries for water to carry/ and a person for work that is real" (line 25), Piercy sets up an analogy which states that water is to a pitcher as real work is to a human; the former fulfills the latter. This analogy appeals to reasoning (*logos*). Finally, Piercy does not try to say that only one way of working or one type of work is useful. This open-mindedness, looking at her subject from several perspectives, creates *ethos*.

Defend: I never thought about work in quite this way. Piercy takes the drudgery out of the word. Also, I like how she celebrates the common worker, the laborer—that would include students who wait tables to pay their tuition.

"After Work" by Gary Snyder

Claim: Happiness comes from simple things.

Evidence: The couple in the poem do not have many material goods, and yet they are happy.

Rhetorical Appeals: Like Piercy, Snyder appeals to my emotions (*pathos*) through his choice of words and images. To communicate feelings of "home" which his audience can identify with, Snyder uses words that appeal to the senses. The phrases, "peeling garlic" (line 7), "hot iron stove" (line 8), and "stew simmering" (line 13), all evoke sensory responses. Also, in the second stanza, in the repetitive phrasing of "the axe, the rake/ the wood" (line 9), Snyder uses heavy words to describe heavy objects. All the things mentioned in the poem are simple, and many words are monosyllabic. Yet Snyder communicates to me a very deep feeling of happiness and pleasure. This is definitely a feel-good poem, one to read when I need to change my mood!

Also, I find myself really liking Snyder's speaker. This is a guy with downhome (nonmaterialistic) values that I respect (*ethos*).

Defend: Snyder's speaker supports what I said earlier in qualifying Wordworth's claim. In our material world, people can still appreciate the simpler things in life.

Summary: These four pieces of literature all relate to materialism. In their own way, they each make a claim which is based on the same underlying value assumptions: material things are impermanent; happiness can be found in simple things, like a pot of stew, a hard day's work, a daydream, and a good old-fashioned rodeo. Also, commercial values should not rule our lives and undercut our respect for traditions and for other beings.

IV. Articulation. Create your own argument on the subject you have explored.
  a. Narrow the general subject to a particular issue.
  b. Identify a specific issue question and formulate a tentative claim for the issue.
  c. Gather support for your claim.
  d. Write your argument.

[For this section of the assignment, Lisa narrowed her subject from the broad topic of *materialism* to focus on consumerism and fast food. She created a claim, found support for that claim, and wrote her paper.]

Super-Size It!

Modern Americans are, by definition, consumers. Whether it be satellite dishes or diamonds, SUVs, or gold jewelry, Americans spend a great deal of resources on the acquisition of goods. People's reasons for consumption of specific goods vary widely, but un-doubtedly, our culture's emphasis on material possessions has in some way affected each of us. Just a glance at our waistlines offers jiggling proof of our misplaced values.

The British poet, William Wordsworth, saw our consumer society coming two hundred years ago when he wrote the famous lines, "The world is too much with us; late and soon,/ Getting and spending, we lay waste our powers..." He continues, "We have given our hearts away..." (Wordsworth 433). And perhaps we have given our hearts away, traded our appreciation for nature and the simple pleasures in life for a stereo with wrap-around sound and a big-screen television. In a consumer society like ours, that's called marketing. That we prefer a Little Debbie to a carrot or six-teen ounces of rare steak to a serving of beans and rice may have more to do with marketing than any conscious decision on our part to ruin our health.

The Western, and more specifically, American focus on con-sumption has been held responsible for the nation's tendency to-ward obesity. The seriousness of this ailment is specific to the United States in that fully 20 percent of Americans are obese (30 percent or more over one's ideal weight), up from about 12.5 per-cent in 1991 (Reaves 1). That is a shocking statistic—20 percent of us are not merely fat, we are obese. In light of the position of the United States as a leading consumer society and the fact of rising American obesity rates, it seems Americans' problem with weight control is directly related to the country's economic prosperity and tendency toward materialism.

Materialism is not a purely American invention, however. Some historians begin the study of consumer society in relatively recent times, but others place its birth much earlier. For example, in John Storey's *Cultural Consumption and Everyday Life*, Julia Bermingham is said to have argued that the beginnings of consumer society can be traced to "the sixteenth, and certainly no later than the eighteenth century" (1). Once scarce and, hence, expensive commodities, fat and sugar slowly became more available to the general population, and what was once coveted—for example a couple of pieces of hard candy at holiday time—now is so common we hardly take notice. Feeling a little hungry? Just buy a candy bar from a nearby machine. For that matter, buy two. Or perhaps opt for the super-sized bar offering a full half pound of instant satisfaction.

The consumer society came to the United States on a large scale with the development of the assembly line by Henry Ford in the manufacture of his Model T's (Robbins 13). With the money he saved in the manufacturing process of these cars, Ford raised wages and lowered the cost of the automobile. This rise in wages led to more money being made available to workers to spend on consumer goods (13). But in addition to rising wages, a more widespread change in the economy which greatly increased spending power was instigated by the introduction of credit. Credit allowed consumers to buy with only the promise to pay. This new spending power, in effect, "created" money and led to, among other things, a housing boom throughout the 1940s, 50s, and 60s (Robbins 20). The post–World War II housing boom is critical in an examination of the components of contemporary American consumer culture, for this increase in homes led to an increase in demand for such products as appliances, furnishings, and automobiles (20). While the products which entered the market directly after World War II, for instance, were much less technologically advanced than the devices which line store shelves today, there is little doubt that these symbols of convenience and middle-class prosperity were the precursors of today's Cuisinarts, bagel slicers, and pasta makers.

Along with this flood of new consumer products came the increase in social emulation, which is seen as a "key factor in the dramatic birth of consumerism" (Storey 4). The modern consumer society began to take root, and as the economy grew, so did Americans' desire for material possessions. In the rush for spending power, Americans grew busier and busier, adjusting their working patterns to accommodate their desires. Americans' busy lifestyles are blamed for the tendency of Americans to be overweight, literally driving Americans to fast-food restaurants.

Beef and sugar, primary ingredients in most fast-food meals, are both inefficient to produce and detrimental to our diet. For example, the production of 28 metric tons of animal protein from beef requires 150 million tons of vegetable and cereal protein, not particularly efficient use of the land (Robbins 220). At the same time, beef, which is high in fat and cholesterol, has been linked to cardiovascular disease, colon cancer, breast cancer, and osteoporosis. Yet, in spite of these drawbacks, beef remains the most popular meat in America, having replaced pork as the top choice in the 1960s (Robbins 220). Every year, 6.7 billion hamburgers are sold in the United States in fast-food restaurants alone (220). A popular sandwich choice, McDonald's Big Mac, has a "whopping" 530 total calories (Twitchell 211).

But what is the effect of the Big Mac on the growth of American obesity? Perhaps the answer lies not in the Big Mac itself but rather in the technology which makes the Big Mac both necessary and possible. Technology has allowed Americans to produce more while expending less energy. As is stated in "The Long-Run Growth in Obesity as a Function of Technological Change" by Tomas J. Philipson and Richard A. Posner,

> Technological change caused the price of calories to fall because food prices have declined while at the same time the amount of physical exertion required when supplying labor has also fallen. In an agricultural or industrial society, work is strenuous; in effect, the worker is paid to exercise... In a postindustrial and redistributive society, such as that of the United States today, most work entails little exercise... As a result, people must pay for undertaking... physical activity... leisure weight control must be substituted for job weight control. (4)

In effect, an attempt to control this weight problem, brought on by too much consumption, is made by (what else?) more consumption. Americans spent $8.4 billion on diet products and services in 1991, with total sales, including things like artificial sweeteners and health club memberships, reaching $33 billion. This figure is, incidentally, roughly equal to the gross national product of Pakistan, Egypt, or Hungary (Averett and Korenman 6). As with everything else to do with consumption, whether it is a Jenny Craig Weight Reduction Program or a Weight Watchers Frozen Dinner, Americans lead the world on weight-loss expenditures.

So why, if Americans are weight-conscious enough to spend so much on diet aids, do they continue to become obese and at increasingly higher rates? One argument that has been put forth is that the $33 billion has not been spent to lose weight, but rather to feel better about not losing weight. As *Time* writer Joel Stein says in an article by Jessica Reaves, ". . . spending $33 billion on weird fad diets is actually quite easy when you look at the options. . . . It's a lot easier to fumble around with complicated diets and then blame the diet for a failure than it is to take responsibility for gaining weight" (1). Meanwhile, the diet industry's growth helps keep the economy plump.

Given that obesity is a complicated problem which cannot be completely attributed to any one cause, one can conclude that while American prosperity and materialism are not solely responsible for the rise in obesity, these factors are not entirely without responsibility. But perhaps our desire for comfort and convenience is also to blame. After all, when the fast-food patron pulls up to the drive-through window and says, "Super-size it!", he knows what he is buying—a large serving of fat and sugar packaged for immediate consumption as he sits behind the wheel of his new SUV talking on his cell phone . . . "Let me put you on hold just a minute. I gotta mop a little mayo off my tie."

American society is not going to change soon. It will continue to fuel its economy with elevated consumer spending. And, of course, there is an undeniable pleasure in owning nice things. However, individually we can choose how we spend our time and resources. We can make rational decisions. We can protect our health and need not have heart attacks at age 48 . . . nor awaken some day to realize we have "given our hearts away."

Works Cited

Averett, Susan and Sandern Korenman. "The Economic Reality of *The Beauty Myth.*" *Working Paper Series # 4521*. The National Bureau of Economic Research, Inc. Cambridge, MA: Nov. 1993.

Karon, Tony. "Supersize Nation." *Time.com*. 20 Oct. 1998. 22 March 2000. <http://www.time/com/time/daily/0,2960,15347,00 html>.

Philipson, Tomas J., and Richard A. Posner. "The Long-Run Growth in Obesity as a Function of Technical Change." Working Paper Series #7423. Nov. 1999.

Reaves, Jessica. "The Unbearable Heaviness of Being American." *Time.com*. 7 Oct. 1999. 22 March 2000. <http://www.time.com/time/daily/ 0,2960,33259,00.html>.

Robbins, Richard H. *Global Problems and the Culture of Capitalism*. Needham Heights, Massachusetts: Allyn and Bacon, 1999.

Stein, Joel. "I Wouldn't Eat That If I Were You." *Time.com*. 31 May 1999. 22 March 2000. <http://www.time.com/time/magazine/ article/0,3266,25700,00.html>.

Storey, John. *Cultural Consumption and Everyday Life*. New York: Oxford University Press, 1999.

Twitchell, James B. *Lead Us Into Temptation: The Triumph of American Materialism*. New York: Columbia University Press, 1999.

Wordsworth, William. "The World Is Too Much With Us." *Literature: Reading and Writing the Human Experience*. 7th ed. Richard Abcarian and Marvin Klotz, eds. New York: St. Martin's Press, 1998. 433.

Any part of the assignment sequence is valuable; however, it is the end product, an articulated expression of your own particular position, that promises the most rewards. Here is another example of that final product, in this case, student Meredith Newmon Blanco's paper dealing with alcoholism and the family. (For some discussion of Meredith's writing process, see Appendix A.)

Who Are the Real Victims of Alcoholism?

The knocking at the door was so loud that I thought my heart was going to explode. We had been asleep for hours. Neither one of us was prepared to be awakened so abruptly. Once the sleepy fog began to lift from my head, I realized that it was my father-in law who was making so much noise outside of my door. Like so many other times, he was drunk and yelling in a high-pitched babble about needing to borrow ten dollars. Ten dollars, I thought to myself. It's two o'clock in the morning; he's got to be out of his mind! My husband jumped to his feet, and as always, dismissed his father with money in hand and tried to salvage some of his own dignity.

As he came back to the room, he had an unusual look on his face. Enrique said to me, "My mother was driving him, this time." He turned the light off and went to sleep. I realized at that moment, there was a substance abuse problem that involved everyone and would eventually explain some of my husband's peculiar habits and behaviors. Molly Peacock's poem, "Say You Love Me," brilliantly illustrates the emotional and sometimes physical damage done to children of alcoholics.

Children of alcoholic parents suffer from a variety of problems directly linked to their parents' alcohol abuse. The abuse is widespread and not particular. It doesn't seek out the poor and disadvantaged; it seeks out any soul who will give it a home, no matter what or who is lost in the process. Researchers Charles D. Weddle and Phillip Wishon state, "There are estimates of some twenty-eight million children of alcoholics in this country" (8). Children of alcoholics are challenged by their own development as well as their experiences of living in a dysfunctional home environment. Moreover, children of alcoholics are a unique group of people, in that, if they can survive, their survival skills are unparalleled.

Children in homes with alcoholics grow up with inconsistency and disciplinary fluctuations that may cause them to take on certain types of identity roles as a defense mechanism. These roles are the "hero," who is often the elder child and who takes on responsibility and shoulders adult responsibilities. The "scapegoat" is another role. This child typically shoulders all the blame for the family problems and disturbances. The middle child is typically the ignored child, or the "lost-one." The last child, the youngest, is often shielded from the family problems and nasty secrets (Weddle and Wilson 9). All of these children have a variety of characteristics, each unique to its own circumstances. Regardless of how differently these children may be labeled, they each long for their parent's approval, whether or not the parent is sober. This longing is illustrated in "Say You Love Me": "Do you love me? Say You Do. / I love you Dad, I whispered leveled by defeat" (Peacock 1036). This child displays the same type of behavior that children of alcoholics do. The pattern of succumbing to the dependent parent's needs is a typical behavior in children who grow up in these environments.

Alcoholic parents may not realize the devastation they impose on those they love. Peacock writes, "He'll get mean, my sister hissed, just tell him. / I brought my knee up to kick him, but I was too scared" (1035). Children of alcoholics live in an environment laced with fear and darkness ("Alcoholism and Alcohol"). As a consequence, these children have more psychological, health, and social problems. These problems range from migraines to frequent illnesses, poor schoolwork, and, the most devastating one, suicide attempts ("Answers to Frequently"). These children cannot cope with their problems alone, nor should they have to.

If one is going to help a child of an alcoholic, one must know what alcoholism is. Alcoholism is defined as,

> primary chronic disease with genetic, psychosocial and environmental factors influencing its development and manifestations. The disease is often progressive and fatal. It is characterized by continuous or periodic: impaired control over drinking, preoccupation with the drug alcohol, use of alcohol despite adverse consequences, and distortions in thinking most notably denial. ("Definition")

This is a very clinical and detailed definition of the disease and its effects; however, aside from the effects on the consumer of alcohol, it fails to mention the other victims affected by this disease. The victims in an alcoholic family are primarily the other family members. The victims in "Say You Love Me" are clearly the two young girls: "He gazed through hysteria as a wet baby thing repeating 'do you love me?' 'Say you do,' in baby chokes, only loud because he was man./ There wouldn't be any rescue from my mother" (Peacock 1036). The children in this poem, like so many other children of alcoholics, are the true victims of this illness.

Alcoholism is extremely prevalent in the United States. It is a vicious cycle that, left untreated, will replicate itself: "Sons of alcoholic father are 4 or 5 times more likely to become alcoholics than sons of non-alcoholics. Daughters of alcoholic parents are also more likely to marry alcoholic men and have children with high risk for addictive behavior" ("Answers"). This cycle of dysfunctional behavior will not be broken if the abuse is not treated and intervention is not accomplished. The world can seem like a horrible, dangerous place for children whose parents drink, as Peacock's poem depicts, "There was no world out there, so there we remained, completely alone" (1036). Children in these dysfunctional environments often have a grim and dark outlook on life and themselves. These views will carry over into their adult lives and adult relationships. The views and feelings of these children are supported by a multitude of statistics on alcoholism.

The statistics on alcoholism are staggering: "76 million people have been exposed to alcoholism in the family. . . . Alcohol attributes to 100,000 deaths annually making it the third leading cause of preventable mortality in the US" ("Alcoholism"). Children of alcoholics experience higher levels of conflict within the family. Their development is delayed, and they are four times more likely than other children to develop alcoholism. There is a higher risk that a child of an alcoholic will marry into families where alcoholism is prevalent ("Children"). Also, their communication skills and problem-solving skills are often delayed and ineffective. These children have a lower self-esteem than children who grow up in homes where alcohol is not abused. As the research conclusively demonstrates, children of alcoholics face a multitude of challenges, both in the family they are born into and in the family they create.

As we know, art imitates life, and Molly Peacock's poem, "Say You Love Me," paints a starkly realistic and dark portrait of a chronic social problem. The poem dramatizes the extremely volatile relationship between an alcoholic father and his two young daughters. In the family home, if an alcoholic adult's illness is left untreated, the chances of its resurfacing or being passed on to the next generation are extremely high. Children of alcoholics face a variety of complex challenges in their homes, and once they "leave the nest," they will confront a whole new set of challenges. If these children are not taught conflict resolution tools and effective communication skills, they will be sorely disadvantaged throughout their childhoods and adult lives. These children need to be provided with community resources to teach them skills to help them cope and manage their lives. Adults in our community must realize the severity of this problem and work towards this common goal. The children in our society are the real victims of alcoholism, and we, the adults, are the responsible party.

Works Cited

"Alcoholism and Alcohol-Related Problems: A Sobering Look." *Infinet Internet Service. National Council on Alcohol and Drug Dependency.* 13 Nov. 1999. <http://www.ncadd.org>.

"Answers to Frequently Asked Questions about Being a Child of an Alcoholic." *Infinet Internet Service. National Council of Alcohol*

and Drug Dependency. 11 Nov. 1999. <http://www.alcoholism
help.com>.

"Chemical Dependency: Myths and Facts about Alcoholism." *Infinet
Internet Service. Baptist Hospital East*. 13 Nov. 1999. <http://
www.baptisteast.com>.

"Children of Alcoholics: Important Facts." *Infinet Internet Service*.
August, 1998. *National Association of Children of Alcoholics*.
13 Nov. 1999. <http://www.healthorg/nacoa/impfacts.htm>.

"Definition of Alcoholism." *Infinet Internet Service*. 25 Feb. 1990.
National Council on Alcoholism and Drug Dependency. 11 Nov.
1999. <http://www.ncadd.org>.

"FYI: Drinking in America." *Infinet Internet Service. National
Council of Alcohol and Drug Dependency*. 12 Nov. 1999.
<http://www.ncadd.org/fyidina.html>.

Peacock, Molly. "Say You Love Me." *Literature: Reading and Writing the Human Experience*. 7th ed. Richard Abcarian and Marvin Klotz, eds. New York: St. Martin's Press, 1998. 1056–1057.

Weddle, Charles D. and Phillip Wishon. "Children of Alcoholics."
Children Today Jan–Feb. 1986: 8–12.

CHAPTER ACTIVITIES

1. In a group of three or more, select several categories of people with whom you are familiar, such as college athletes, rappers, motorcyclists, or sorority women. Make a list of five or so commonly held characteristics associated with each group. Under each list, write out the underlying evidence which has fostered these perceptions.

2. Read through the cartoon on p. 52:
   a. List the gender stereotypes that are presented in the cartoon.
   b. Using one of the groups from activity #1, create your own comic strip to poke fun at that group's stereotypes.

3. a. What conclusions did you make about college before you came to campus? What evidence led you to make these conclusions? Which proved to be inaccurate? Which accurate?
   b. What conclusions do you think people might make about you? Why? What are these conclusions based on?

4. Can you recall a specific situation in which you jumped to a conclusion? Spend several minutes writing about it. Try to step back and analyze the situation. What caused you to "jump" too quickly? Would you characterize it as an "innocent mistake," or did you have a strong emotional interest in coming to that conclusion?

5. Using a newspaper's letters to the editor, find examples of both inductive and deductive thinking. Is the writer reasoning from specific evidence to reach a broader conclusion (induction)? Or does the writer's conclusion follow from the specific application of a general principle (deduction)?

Walt Whitman

I Saw in Louisiana a Live-Oak Growing

I saw in Louisiana a live-oak growing,
All alone stood it and the moss hung down from the branches,
Without any companion it grew there uttering joyous leaves of dark
    green,
And its look, rude, unbending, lusty, made me think of myself,
But I wonder'd how it could utter joyous leaves standing alone there without
    its friend near, for I knew I could not,
And I broke off a twig with a certain number of leaves upon it, and
    twined around it a little moss,
And brought it away, and I have placed it in sight in my room,
It is not needed to remind me as of my own dear friends,
(For I believe lately I think of little else than of them,)
Yet it remains to me a curious token, it makes me think of manly
    love;
For all that, and though the live-oak glistens there in Louisiana
    solitary in a wide flat space,
Uttering joyous leaves all its life without a friend a lover near,
I know very well I could not.

Jane Martin

Rodeo

A young woman in her late twenties sits working on a piece of tack. Beside her is a Lone Star beer in the can. As the lights come up we hear the last verse of a Tanya Tucker song or some other female country-western vocalist. She is wearing old worn jeans and boots plus a long-sleeved workshirt with the sleeves rolled up. She works until the song is over and then speaks.

Big Eight: Shoot—Rodeo's just goin' to hell in a handbasket. Rodeo used to be somethin'. I loved it. I did. Once Daddy an' a bunch of 'em was foolin' around with some old bronc over to our place and this ol' red nose named Cinch got bucked off and my Daddy hooted and said he had him a nine-year-old girl, namely me, wouldn't have no damn trouble cowboyin' that horse. Well, he put me on up there, stuck that ridin' rein in my hand, gimme a kiss, and said, "Now there's only on thing t' remember Honey Love, if ya fall off you jest don't come home." Well I stayed up. You gotta stay on a bronc eight seconds. Otherwise the ride don't count. So from that day on my daddy called me Big Eight. Heck! That's all the name I got anymore . . . Big Eight.

Used to be fer cowboys, the rodeo did. Do it in some open field, folks would pull their cars and pick-ups round it, sit on the hoods, some ranch hand'd bulldog him some rank steer and everybody'd waver their hats and call him by name. Ride us some buckin' stock, rope a few calves, git throwed off a bull, and then we'd jest git us to a bar and tell each other lies about how good we were.

Used to be a family thing. Wooly Billy Tilson and Tammy Lee had them five kids on the circuit. Three boys, two girls and Wooly and Tammy. Wasn't no two-beer rodeo in Oklahoma didn't have a Tilson entered. Used to call the oldest girl Tits. Tits Tilson. Never seen a girl that top-heavy could ride so well. Said she only fell off when the gravity got her. Cowboys used to say if she landed face down you could plant two young trees in the holes she'd leave. Ha! Tits Tilson.

Used to be people came to a rodeo had a horse of their own back home. Farm people, ranch people—lord, they *knew* what they were lookin' at. Knew a good ride from a bad ride, knew hard from easy. You broke some bones er spent the day eatin' dirt, at least ya got appreciated.

Now they bought the rodeo. Them. Coca-Cola, Pepsi Cola, Marlboro damn cigarettes. You know the ones I mean. Them. Hire some New York faggot t' sit on some ol' stuffed horse in front of a sagebrush photo n' smoke that junk. Hell, tobacco wasn't made to smoke, honey, it was made to chew. Lord wanted ya filled up with smoke he would've set ya on fire. Damn it gets me!

There's some guy in a banker's suit runs the rodeo now. Got him a pinky ring and a digital watch, honey. Told us we oughta have a watchamacallit, choriographus or somethin', some ol' ballbuster used to be with the Ice damn Capades. Wants us to ride around dressed up like Mickey Mouse, Pluto, crap like that. Told me I had to haul my butt through the barrel race done up like Minnie damn Mouse in a tu-tu. Huh uh, honey! Them people is so screwed-up they probably eat what they run over in the road.

Listen, they got the clowns wearin' Astronaut suits! I ain't lyin'. You know what a rodeo clown does! You go down, fall off whatever—the clown runs in front of the bull so's ya don't git stomped. Pin-stripes, he got 'em in space suits tellin' jokes on a microphone. First horse see 'em, done up like the Star Wars went crazy. Best buckin' horse on the circuit, name of Piss 'N' Vinegar, took one look at them clowns, had him a heart attack and died. Cowboy was ridin' him got hisself squashed. Twelve hundred pounds of coronary arrest jes fell right through 'em. Blam! Vio con dios. Crowd thought that was funnier than the astronauts. I swear it won't be long before they're strappin' ice-skates on the ponies. Big crowds now. Ain't hardly no ranch people, no farm people, nobody I know. Buncha disco babies and dee-vorce lawyers—designer jeans and day-glo Stetsons. Hell, the whole bunch of 'em wears French perfume. Oh it smells like money now! Got it on the cable T and V—hey, you know what, when ya rodeo yer just bound to kick yerself up some dust—well now, seems like that fogs up the ol' TV camera, so they told us a while back that from now on we was gonna ride on some new stuff called Astro-dirt. Dust free. Artificial damn dirt, honey. Lord have mercy.

Banker Suit called me in the other day said "Lurlene . . ." "Hold it," I said, "Who's this Lurlene? Round here they call me Big Eight." "Well, Big Eight," he said, "My name's Wallace." "Well that's a real surprise t' me," I said, "Cause aroun' here everybody jes calls you Dumb-ass." My, he laughed real big, clapped his big ol' desk, an' then he said I wasn't suitable for the rodeo no more. Said they was lookin' fer another type, somethin' a little more in the showgirl line, like the Dallas Cowgirls maybe. Said the ridin' and ropin' wasn't the thing no more. Talked on about floats, costumes, dancin' choreog-aphy. If I was a man I woulda pissed on his shoe. Said he'd give me a lifetime pass though. Said I could come to his rodeo any time I wanted.

Rodeo used to be people ridin' horses for the pleasure of people who rode horses—made you feel good about what you could do. Rodeo wasn't worth no money to nobody. Money didn't have nothing to do with it! Used to be seven Tilsons riding in the rodeo. Wouldn't none of 'em dress up like that Donald damn Duck so they quit. That there's the law of gravity!

There's a bunch of assholes in this country sneak around until they see ya havin' fun and then they buy the fun and start in sellin' it. See, they figure if ya love it, they can sell it. Well you look out, honey! They want to make them a dol-lar out of what you love. Dress *you* up like Minnie Mouse. Sell your rodeo. Turn *yer* pleasure into Ice damn Capades. You hear what I'm sayin'? You're jus' mer-chandise to them, sweetie. You're jus' merchandise to them.

Blackout.

William Wordsworth

The World Is Too Much With Us

> The world is too much with us; late and soon,
> Getting and spending, we lay waste our powers;
> Little we see in nature that is ours;
> We have given our hearts away, a sordid boon.
> This sea that bares her bosom to the moon,
> The winds that will be howling at all hours,
> And are up-gathered now like sleeping flowers,
> For this, for everything, we are out of tune;
> It moves us not.—Great God! I'd rather be

A pagan suckled in a creed outworn;
So might I, standing on this pleasant lea,
Have glimpses that would make me less forlorn;
Have sight of Proteus rising from the sea;
Or hear old Triton blow his wreathèd horn.

Marge Piercy

To Be of Use

The people I love the best
jump into work head first
without dallying in the shallows
and swim off with sure strokes almost out of sight.
They seem to become natives of that element,
the black sleek heads of seals
bouncing like half-submerged balls.

I love people who harness themselves, an ox to a heavy cart,
who pull like water buffalo, with massive patience,
who strain in the mud and the muck to move things forward,
who do what has to be done, again and again.

I want to be with people who submerge
in the task, who go into the fields to harvest
and work in a row and pass the bags along,
who are not parlor generals and field deserters
but move in a common rhythm
when the food must come in or the fire be put out.

The work of the world is common as mud.
Botched, it smears the hands, crumbles to dust.
But the thing worth doing well done
has a shape that satisfies, clean and evident.
Greek amphoras for wine or oil,
Hopi vases that held corn, are put in museums
but you know they were made to be used.

The pitcher cries for water to carry
And a person for work that is real.

Gary Snyder

After Work

The shack and a few trees
float in the blowing fog

I pull out your blouse,
warm my cold hands
　　　　on your breasts.
you laugh and shudder
peeling garlic by the
　　　　hot iron stove.
bring in the axe, the rake,
the wood

we'll lean on the wall
against each other
stew simmering on the fire
as it grows dark
　　　　drinking wine.

Chapter Three

Individuality and Community

The goals of an individual sometimes conflict with the goals of the society in which he or she lives. People naturally want to live in an orderly environment and, as a result, generally choose to obey the rules of their society. For example, a person cannot choose to grow cabbages in a public park just because the park makes a convenient spot for a garden: usurping public land for private enterprise is against the law. Similarly, although the temperature soars to 100 degrees on an August afternoon, a person cannot elect to walk the streets naked: Public nudity is usually prohibited by local law. And, of course, even beyond the authority of the law, society may enforce codes of behavior simply through the power of its approval or its disapproval. Yet what teenager has not enjoyed the thrill of non-conformity accompanying socially unacceptable behavior, whether it comes in the form of purple hair, a pierced navel, or simply lighting a cigarette? Nevertheless, in most areas of life, adults generally are forced to conform to community standards of conduct, and while some people may find such conformity comforting, others find it irritating, even demeaning.

History is filled with examples of conflicts created when individuals have felt their own paths blocked by the constraints of the societies in which they lived. Galileo was certain the earth revolved around the sun and ultimately paid a high price for his iconoclastic belief. Other than seeing his innovative art ridiculed by contemporary critics, Vincent van Gogh received almost no recognition during his lifetime; however, today we view him as one of the most talented Impressionists, and his paintings are valued in the millions of dollars. James Joyce's *Ulysses* was banned in the United States when it was first published in Paris in 1922, yet by the end of the century, it was acclaimed as one of the world's most important novels. Whether, in the end, such conflicts affect the flow of history or merely create friction for people as they go about their daily lives, they create powerful emotions which inform our literature.

Many of us have read *Huckleberry Finn* by Mark Twain. Huck, certainly the prototype rebellious American child, at first simply finds ways to get around both his father's and his aunt's demands, but later defies the values and laws of the larger society as he befriends the freed slave Jim in their trip down the Mississippi River. We tend to approve of Huck's rebelliousness and applaud the trouble it causes for those around him. Similarly, readers often find the language and behavior of the main character, Holden Caulfield, in J. D. Salinger's *Catcher in the Rye* acceptable, even insightful, as he displays the characteristic teenage behavior that questions rather than accepts the standards of adults. In these two instances, as well as innumerable other examples in literature, the emotions surrounding conflicts between individuals and their communities create powerfully moving experiences for readers.

In order to evaluate our own behavior, we can analyze the motives and reasoning behind the actions of individuals who accept the constraints of society and bend to its wishes as well as those individuals who choose to resist. Clearly, history and literature provide many examples. Plato's *Crito*, included in this chapter, is an account of the ancient Greek philosopher Socrates' suicide. A renowned teacher and respected thinker, Socrates finds himself accused by the Athenian government of corrupting the youth of the city. For this crime, Socrates is sentenced to death. His friends urge him to flee, for another city-state is sure to offer him refuge; however, Socrates believes so strongly in the need for order and in his duty to uphold civil law that he yields to his sentence and drinks poisonous hemlock. In accepting his death, was Socrates holding on to the generalization that civic duty is more important than personal happiness? Is he to be honored for this ultimate personal sacrifice? Or is he to be judged a fool for not taking the advice of his friends and students?

Thomas Jefferson argued that all citizens must respect the law or face the threat of anarchy, yet he also helped author the Declaration of Independence, which itself justifies instances of civil disobedience. Later in American history, Henry David Thoreau and Martin Luther King, Jr. willingly risked anarchy in the hopes of evoking social change. Included in this chapter are essays by Thoreau and King, both of whom, in contrast to Socrates, chose to resist the demands of their governments. During the Vietnam War, thousands of young men were drafted to serve in the military to fight a war which many Americans considered to be immoral. Upon receiving their draft notices, some young men chose to resist their orders and, in protest, fled to Canada; others, however, accepted their military orders as their patriotic and civic duty. Reading Tim O'Brien's story, "On the Rainy River," we witness the narrator's wrestling with this moral decision.

In each selection in this chapter, we encounter the question of the individual's place in his or her society. In some cases, such as "A&P" and "The Bride Comes to Yellow Sky," the situation evokes humor; however, in others, such as *Antigone*, the conflict is one of life and death. Kurt Vonnegut's short story, "Harrison Bergeron," offers both humor and a life or death struggle. Both our personal experiences and our reading of works by such writers as Claude McKay, Richard Rodriguez, Frank Chin, and John Hope Franklin, demonstrate that finding our place as individuals in a complex society such as ours is always a struggle. And in a democratic society such as ours, we are granted the privilege and obliged with the responsibility to articulate and to defend our positions, our choices, to others. Thus, in creating an argument based on morals and values, we must define and clarify, explain and elaborate those principles which have guided our decision.

When we argue that this particular action is the right action because it is the morally right thing to do, we create arguments that are not quite like the standard argument. For example, we might well argue that having multiple sex partners is dangerous to one's health. To support our claim we could easily find reliable statistics showing a higher incidence of sexually transmitted diseases among people who do have multiple sex partners when compared to people who do not have multiple sex partners. That would be strong evidence for our claim, and those statistics alone might be adequate to convince readers to avoid sexual promiscuity. We would be making an appeal to fear, and that fear would be well founded. On the other hand, if we argue that people should avoid sexual promiscuity because having sex before marriage is immoral, then we have created an argument whose support will be quite different.

When we make a claim of policy based on a moral judgment, we cannot so easily find statistics or objective facts to use as evidence. Rather we will have to look for support in the form of authoritative opinions and testimonies and personal experience. Perhaps promiscuity is unhealthy, but that is not our point; this time we want to prove to our readers that promiscuity violates a moral code. And to make our case, we will have to cite moral authorities our audience will recognize and respect. Perhaps Reverend Billy Graham would impress our Christian readers. In that case, we might also want to quote some Biblical text as well. Most religions have recognizable leaders who have commented on the immorality of multiple sexual partners, but what if we are unsure about our readers' adherence to an organized religion? Where do we turn for evidence then? Certainly a person does not have to be religious to have strong moral convictions. In families, grandparents are often enforcers of moral code: "Don't do that. You know your grandfather would not approve." Most cultures respect the wisdom gained through years of living, so we might look for an older person with some positive name-recognition. We might also turn to philosophers whose writings address ethical principles and matters of right and wrong. Or perhaps we might cite respected public figures who have a generally credible quality to their actions and words; former President Jimmy Carter and Mother Teresa, for example, both seem to have achieved that kind of credibility with a wide range of people today. As a result, many readers would take seriously their comments on promiscuity even though their expertise and experience have nothing directly to do with the subject.

Personal experience also sometimes supports a moral claim. Reading Martin Luther King, Jr.'s "Letter from Birmingham Jail," we will notice that King cites religious authorities St. Augustine and St. Thomas Aquinas, as well as modern philosopher Martin Buber. But he also offers his readers evidence in the form of personal experience as he recounts incidents of segregation that affected his children. In our argument about promiscuity, we could offer readers our own experience watching promiscuous friends suffer due to their choice of having multiple sexual partners. As with most personal experience, the emotional impact of such anecdotes is often strong, making this type of evidence effective in persuading an audience.

Sexual promiscuity is a personal choice that certainly affects an individual, yet there are also many moral choices whose ripples of influence more overtly extend far out into society. For example, in the 1980s, some citizens of the United States chose to harbor illegal aliens from Central American countries because deportation by the Immigration Service might mean torture or death at the hands of conflicting groups vying for power. These people knowingly violated U.S. law, making that choice on moral grounds. Earlier in our history, abolitionists hid run-away slaves traveling the underground railroad; they too made the choice to violate U.S. law since it conflicted with their own sense of what was right. Although we may respect those who made that decision in the 1800s and those who did so in the 1980s and admire them for the risk they took in making that moral decision, we must also recognize that no country can afford to have its citizens deciding which laws they will obey and which they will ignore.

Any time a person chooses to break the law, that decision has an impact on the rest of society. How many people illegally use marijuana to relieve the effects of chemotherapy or the pain of glaucoma? And at what point will their numbers be so large that the nation will begin to re-examine its drug laws? Perhaps the impact of our moral decisions is minor, or perhaps, as in President Nixon's case, the impact can be felt by the entire nation.

How do we know right from wrong? In a given situation, why is one action preferable to another? Is our action based on a religious conviction? Do we choose a path based on social code? Is there some innate instinct within all humans guiding us toward right-action? Literature often portrays our struggles in making moral choices. Acknowledging these struggles provides further incentive for us to exercise patience and discipline, both in responding to and in creating an argument based on values and moral principles.

PREWRITING AND DISCUSSION

1. What do we mean when we use the word *community?* Is a community merely a group of people joined by the fac that they live in the same small geographic area? Or are there other ways in which a group can be held together to form a community?

2. Consider both the positive as well as the negative effects of belonging to a community. What pressures are exerted by communities? Think about a community you have experienced or seen friends experience; how do they describe themselves, and are those descriptions consistent with the way outsiders would describe them?

3. Write for a few minutes about what it means to be an individual in our contemporary society. Is it outward appearance that signals one's individuality? List some people you consider to be strong, independent individuals. In small groups of four or five, discuss your ideas of individuality.

Kate Chopin

Désirée's Baby

As the day was pleasant, Madame Valmondé drove over to L'Abri to see Désirée and the baby.

It made her laugh to think of Désirée with a baby. Why, it seemed but yesterday that Désirée was little more than a baby herself; when Monsieur in riding through the gateway of Valmondé had found her lying asleep in the shadow of the big stone pillar.

The little one awoke in his arms and began to cry for "Dada." That was as much as she could do or say. Some people thought she might have strayed there of her own accord, for she was of the toddling age. The prevailing belief was that she had been purposely left by a party of Texans, whose canvas-covered wagon, late in the day, had crossed the ferry that Coton Maïs kept, just below the plantation. In time Madame Valmondé abandoned every speculation but the one that Désirée had been sent to her by a beneficent Providence to be the child of her affection, seeing that she was without child of the flesh. For the girl grew to be beautiful and gentle, affectionate and sincere,—the idol of Valmondé.

It was no wonder, when she stood one day against the stone pillar in whose shadow she had lain asleep, eighteen years before, that Armand Aubigny riding by and seeing her there, had fallen in love with her. That was the way all the Aubignys fell in love, as if struck by a pistol shot. The wonder was that he had not loved her before; for he had known her since his father brought him home from Paris, a boy of eight, after his mother died there. The passion that awoke in him that day, when he saw her at the gate, swept along like an avalanche, or like a prairie fire, or like anything that drives headlong over all obstacles.

Monsieur Valmondé grew practical and wanted things well considered: that is, the girl's obscure origin. Armand looked into her eyes and did not care. He was reminded that she was nameless. What did it matter about a name when he could give her one of the oldest and proudest in Louisiana? He ordered the *corbeille* from Paris, and contained himself with what patience he could until it arrived; then they were married.

Madame Valmondé had not seen Désirée and the baby for four weeks. When she reached L'Abri she shuddered at the first sight of it, as she always did. It was a sad looking place, which for many years had not known the gentle presence of a mistress, old Monsieur Aubigny having married and buried his wife in France, and she having loved her own land too well ever to leave it. The roof came down steep and black like a cowl, reaching out beyond the wide galleries that encircled the yellow stuccoed house. Big, solemn oaks grew close to it, and their thick-leaved, far-reaching branches shadowed it like a pall. Young Aubigny's rule was a strict one, too, and under it his negroes had forgotten how to be gay, as they had been during the old master's easy-going and indulgent lifetime.

The young mother was recovering slowly, and lay full length, in her soft white muslins and laces, upon a couch. The baby was beside her, upon her arm, where he had fallen asleep, at her breast. The yellow nurse woman sat beside a window fanning herself.

Madame Valmondé bent her portly figure over Désirée and kissed her, holding her an instant tenderly in her arms. Then she turned to the child.

"This is not the baby!" she exclaimed, in startled tones. French was the language spoken at Valmondé in those days.

"I knew you would be astonished," laughed Désirée, "at the way he has grown. The little *cochon de lait!* Look at his legs, mamma, and his hands and fingernails— real fingernails. Zandrine had to cut them this morning. Isn't it true, Zandrine?"

The woman bowed her turbaned head majestically, "Mais si, Madame."

"And the way he cries," went on Désirée, "is deafening. Armand heard him the other day as far away as La Blanche's cabin."

Madame Valmondé had never removed her eyes from the child. She lifted it and walked with it over to the window that was lightest. She scanned the baby narrowly, then looked as searchingly at Zandrine, whose face was turned to gaze across the fields.

"Yes, the child has grown, has changed," said Madame Valmondé, slowly, as she replaced it beside its mother. "What does Armand say?"

Désirée's face became suffused with a glow that was happiness itself.

"Oh, Armand is the proudest father in the parish, I believe, chiefly because it is a boy, to bear his name; though he says not,—that he would have loved a girl as well. But I know it isn't true. I know he says that to please me. And mamma," she added, drawing Madame Valmondé's head down to her, and speaking in a whisper, "he hasn't punished one of them—not one of them—since baby is born. Even Négrillon who pretended to have burnt his leg that he might rest from work—he only laughed, and said Négrillon was a great scamp. Oh, mamma, I'm so happy; it frightens me."

What Désirée said was true. Marriage, and later the birth of his son had softened Armand Aubigny's imperious and exacting nature greatly. This was what made the gentle Désirée so happy, for she loved him desperately. When he frowned she trembled, but loved him. When he smiled, she asked no greater blessing of God. But Armand's dark, handsome face had not often been disfigured by frowns since the day he fell in love with her.

When the baby was about three months old, Désirée awoke one day to the conviction that there was something in the air menacing her peace. It was at first too subtle to grasp. It had only been a disquieting suggestion; an air of mystery among the blacks; unexpected visits from far-off neighbors who could hardly account for their coming. Then a strange, an awful change in her husband's manner, which she dared not ask him to explain. When he spoke to her, it was with averted eyes, from which the old love-light seemed to have gone out. He absented himself from home; and when there, avoided her presence and that of her child, without excuse. And the very spirit of Satan seemed suddenly to take hold of him in his dealings with the slaves. Désirée was miserable enough to die.

She sat in her room, one hot afternoon, in her *peignoir,* listlessly drawing through her fingers the strands of her long, silky brown hair that hung about her shoulders. The baby, half-naked, lay asleep upon her own great mahogany bed, that was like a sumptuous throne, with its satin-lined half canopy. One of La Blanche's little quadroon boys—half naked too—stood fanning the child slowly with a fan of peacock feathers. Désirée's eyes had been fixed absently and sadly upon the baby, while she was striving to penetrate the threatening mist that she felt closing about her. She looked from her child to the boy who stood beside him, and back again; over and over. "Ah!" It was a cry that she could not help; which she was not conscious of having uttered. The blood turned like ice in her veins, and a clammy moisture gathered upon her face.

She tried to speak to the little quadroon boy; but no sound would come, at first. When he heard his name uttered, he looked up, and his mistress was pointing to the door. He laid aside the great, soft fan, and obediently stole away, over the polished floor, on his bare tiptoes.

She stayed motionless, with gaze riveted upon her child, and her face the picture of fright.

Presently her husband entered the room, and without noticing her, went to a table and began to search among some papers which covered it.

"Armand," she called to him, in a voice which must have stabbed him, if he was human. But he did not notice. "Armand," she said again. Then she rose and tottered towards him. "Armand," she panted once more, clutching his arm, "look at our child. What does it mean? tell me."

He coldly but gently loosened her fingers from about his arm and thrust the hand away from him. "Tell me what it means!" she cried despairingly.

"It means," he answered lightly, "that the child is not white; it means that you are not white."

A quick conception of all that this accusation meant for her nerved her with unwonted courage to deny it. "It is a lie; it is not true, I am white! Look at my hair, it is brown; and my eyes are gray, Armand, you know they are gray. And my skin is fair," seizing his wrist. "Look at my hand; whiter than yours, Armand," she laughed hysterically.

"As white as La Blanche's," he returned cruelly; and went away leaving her alone with their child.

When she could hold a pen in her hand, she sent a despairing letter to Madame Valmondé.

"My mother, they tell me I am not white. Armand has told me I am not white. For God's sake tell them it is not true. You must know it is not true. I shall die. I must die. I cannot be so unhappy, and live."

The answer that came was as brief:

"My own Désirée: Come home to Valmondé; back to your mother who loves you. Come with your child."

When the letter reached Désirée she went with it to her husband's study, and laid it open upon the desk before which he sat. She was like a stone image: silent, white, motionless after she placed it there.

In silence he ran his cold eyes over the written words. He said nothing.

"Shall I go, Armand?" she asked in tones sharp with agonized suspense.

"Yes, go."

"Do you want me to go?"

"Yes, I want you to go."

He thought Almighty God had dealt cruelly and unjustly with him; and felt, somehow, that he was paying Him back in kind when he stabbed thus into his wife's soul. Moreover he no longer loved her, because of the unconscious injury she had brought upon his home and his name.

She turned away like one stunned by a blow, and walked slowly towards the door, hoping he would call her back.

"Good-by, Armand," she moaned.

He did not answer her. That was his last blow at fate.

Désirée went in search of her child. Zandrine was pacing the sombre gallery with it. She took the little one from the nurse's arms with no word of explanation, and descending the steps, walked away, under the live-oak branches.

It was an October afternoon; the sun was just sinking. Out in the still fields the negroes were picking cotton.

Désirée had not changed the thin white garment nor the slippers which she wore. Her hair was uncovered and the sun's rays brought a golden gleam from its brown meshes. She did not take the broad, beaten road which led to the far-off plantation of Valmondé. She walked across a deserted field, where the stubble bruised her tender feet, so delicately shod, and tore her thin gown to shreds.

She disappeared among the reeds and willows that grew thick along the banks of the deep, sluggish bayou; and she did not come back again.

Some weeks later there was a curious scene enacted at L'Abri. In the centre of the smoothly swept back yard was a great bonfire. Armand Aubigny sat in the wide hallway that commanded a view of the spectacle; and it was he who dealt out to a half dozen negroes the material which kept this fire ablaze.

A graceful cradle of willow, with all its dainty furbishings, was laid upon the pyre, which had already been fed with the richness of a priceless *layette*. Then there were silk gowns, and velvet and satin ones added to these; laces, too, and embroideries; bonnets and gloves; for the *corbeille* had been of rare quality.

The last thing to go was a tiny bundle of letters; innocent little scribblings that Désirée had sent to him during the days of their espousal. There was the remnant of one back in the drawer from which he took them. But it was not Désirée's; it was part of an old letter from his mother to his father. He read it. She was thanking God for the blessing of her husband's love:—

"But, above all," she wrote, "night and day, I thank the good God for having so arranged our lives that our dear Armand will never know that his mother, who adores him, belongs to the race that is cursed with the brand of slavery."

CRITICAL THINKING QUESTIONS

1. Community standards are sometimes applied by those in control for the purpose of maintaining their control. This situation can be positive; for example, most societies find ways to curb the impulses of their adolescent males. On the other hand, Chopin describes a situation in which those in control unfairly manipulate others in the name of community standards. Can you think of situations in which such control occurs today?

2. To what degree do you feel community control is an outdated concept today?

Stephen Crane

The Bride Comes to Yellow Sky

The great Pullman was whirling onward with such dignity of motion that a glance from the window seemed simply to prove that the plains of Texas were pouring eastward. Vast flats of green grass, dull-hued spaces of mesquit and cactus, little groups of frame houses, woods of light and tender trees, all were sweeping into the east, sweeping over the horizon, a precipice.

A newly married pair had boarded this coach at San Antonio. The man's face was reddened from many days in the wind and sun, and a direct result of his new black clothes was that his brick-colored hands were constantly performing in a most conscious fashion. From time to time he looked down respectfully at his attire. He sat with a hand on each knee, like a man waiting in a barber's shop. The glances he devoted to other passengers were furtive and shy.

The bride was not pretty, nor was she very young. She wore a dress of blue cashmere, with small reservations of velvet here and there, and with steel buttons abounding. She continually twisted her head to regard her puff sleeves, very stiff, straight, and high. They embarrassed her. It was quite apparent that she had cooked, and that she expected to cook, dutifully. The blushes caused by the careless scrutiny of some passengers as she had entered the car were strange to see upon this plain, under-class countenance, which was drawn in placid, almost emotionless lines.

They were evidently very happy. "Ever been in a parlor-car before?" he asked, smiling with delight.

"No," she answered; "I never was. It's fine, ain't it?"

"Great! And then after a while we'll go forward to the diner, and get a big lay-out. Finest meal in the world. Charge a dollar."

"Oh, do they?" cried the bride. "Charge a dollar? Why, that's too much—for us—ain't it, Jack?"

"Not this trip, anyhow," he answered bravely. "We're going to go the whole thing."

Later he explained to her about the trains. "You see, it's a thousand miles from one end of Texas to the other; and this train runs right across it, and never stops but four times." He had the pride of an owner. He pointed out to her the dazzling fittings of the coach; and in truth her eyes opened wider as she contemplated the sea-green figured velvet, the shining brass, silver, and glass, the wood that gleamed as darkly brilliant as the surface of a pool of oil. At one end a bronze figure sturdily held a support for a separated chamber, and at convenient places on the ceiling were frescos in olive and silver.

To the minds of the pair, their surroundings reflected the glory of their marriage that morning in San Antonio; this was the environment of their new estate; and the man's face in particular beamed with an elation that made him appear ridiculous to the negro porter. This individual at times surveyed them from afar with an amused and superior grin. On other occasions he bullied them with skill in ways that did not make it exactly plain to them that they were being bullied. He subtly used all the manners of the most unconquerable kind of snobbery. He oppressed them; but of this oppression they had small knowledge, and they speedily forgot that infrequently a number of travellers covered them with stares of derisive enjoyment. Historically there was supposed to be something infinitely humorous in their situation.

"We are due in Yellow Sky at 3:42," he said, looking tenderly into her eyes.

"Oh, are we?" she said, as if she had not been aware of it. To evince surprise at her husband's statement was part of her wifely amiability. She took from a pocket a little silver watch; and as she held it before her, and stared at it with a frown of attention, the new husband's face shone.

"I bought it in San Anton' from a friend of mine," he told her gleefully.

"It's seventeen minutes past twelve," she said, looking up at him with a kind of shy and clumsy coquetry. A passenger, noting this play, grew excessively sardonic, and winked at himself in one of the numerous mirrors.

At last they went to the dining-car. Two rows of negro waiters, in glowing white suits, surveyed their entrance with the interest, and also the equanimity, of men who had been forewarned. The pair fell to the lot of a waiter who happened to feel pleasure in steering them through their meal. He viewed them with the manner of a fatherly pilot, his countenance radiant with benevolence. The patronage, entwined with the ordinary deference, was not plain to them. And yet, as they returned to their coach, they showed in their faces a sense of escape.

To the left, miles down a long purple slope, was a little ribbon of mist where moved the keening Rio Grande. The train was approaching it at an angle, and the apex was Yellow Sky. Presently it was apparent that, as the distance from Yellow Sky grew shorter, the husband became commensurately restless. His brick-red hands were more insistent in their prominence. Occasionally he was even rather absent-minded and far-away when the bride leaned forward and addressed him.

As a matter of truth, Jack Potter was beginning to find the shadow of a deed weigh upon him like a leaden slab. He, the town marshal of Yellow Sky, a man known, liked, and feared in his corner, a prominent person, had gone to San Antonio to meet a girl he believed he loved, and there, after the usual prayers, had actually induced her to marry him, without consulting Yellow Sky for any part of the transaction. He was now bringing his bride before an innocent and unsuspecting community.

Of course people in Yellow Sky married as it pleased them, in accordance with a general custom; but such was Potter's thought of his duty to his friends, or of their idea of his duty, or of an unspoken form which does not control men in these matters, that he felt he was heinous. He had committed an extraordinary crime.

Face to face with this girl in San Antonio, and spurred by his sharp impulse, he had gone headlong over all the social hedges. At San Antonio he was like a man hidden in the dark. A knife to sever any friendly duty, any form, was easy to his hand in that remote city. But the hour of Yellow Sky—the hour of daylight—was approaching.

He knew full well that his marriage was an important thing to his town. It could only be exceeded by the burning of the new hotel. His friends could not forgive him. Frequently he had reflected on the advisability of telling them by telegraph, but a new cowardice had been upon him. He feared to do it. And now the train was hurrying him toward a scene of amazement, glee, and reproach. He glanced out of the window at the line of haze swinging slowly in toward the train.

Yellow Sky had a kind of brass band, which played painfully, to the delight of the populace. He laughed without heart as he thought of it. If the citizens could dream of his prospective arrival with his bride, they would parade the band at the station and escort them, amid cheers and laughing congratulations, to his adobe home.

He resolved that he would use all the devices of speed and plains-craft in making the journey from the station to his house. Once within that safe citadel, he could issue some sort of vocal bulletin, and then not go among the citizens until they had time to wear off a little of their enthusiasm.

The bride looked anxiously at him. "What's worrying you, Jack?"

He laughed again. "I'm not worrying, girl; I'm only thinking of Yellow Sky."

She flushed in comprehension.

A sense of mutual guilt invaded their minds and developed a finer tenderness. They looked at each other with eyes softly aglow. But Potter often laughed the same nervous laugh; the flush upon the bride's face seemed quite permanent.

The traitor to the feelings of Yellow Sky narrowly watched the speeding landscape. "We're nearly there," he said.

Presently the porter came and announced the proximity of Potter's home. He held a brush in his hand, and, with all his airy superiority gone, he brushed Potter's new clothes as the latter slowly turned this way and that way. Potter fumbled out a coin and gave it to the porter, as he had seen others do. It was a heavy and muscle-bound business, as that of a man shoeing his first horse.

The porter took their bag, and as the train began to slow they moved forward to the hooded platform of the car. Presently the two engines and their long string of coaches rushed into the station of Yellow Sky.

"They have to take water here," said Potter, from a constricted throat and in mournful cadence, as one announcing death. Before the train stopped his eye had swept the length of the platform, and he was glad and astonished to see there was none upon it but the station-agent, who, with a slightly hurried and anxious air, was walking toward the watertanks. When the train had halted, the porter alighted first, and placed in position a little temporary step.

"Come on, girl," said Potter, hoarsely. As he helped her down they each laughed on a false note. He took the bag from the negro, and bade his wife cling to his arm. As they slunk rapidly away, his hang-dog glance perceived that they were unloading the two trunks, and also that the station-agent, far ahead near the baggage-car, had turned and was running toward him, making gestures. He laughed, and groaned as he laughed, when he noted the first effect of his marital bliss upon Yellow Sky. He gripped his wife's arm firmly to his side, and they fled. Behind them the porter stood, chuckling fatuously.

2

The California express on the Southern Railway was due at Yellow Sky in twenty-one minutes. There were six men at the bar of the Weary Gentleman saloon. One was a drummer who talked a great deal and rapidly; three were Texans who did not care to talk at that time; and two were Mexican sheep-herders, who did not talk as a general practice in the Weary Gentleman saloon. The barkeeper's dog lay on the board walk that crossed in front of the door. His head was on his paws, and he glanced drowsily here and there with the constant vigilance of a dog that is kicked on occasion. Across the sandy street were some vivid green grassplots, so wonderful in appearance, amid the sands that burned near them in a blazing sun, that they caused a doubt in the mind. They exactly resembled the grass mats used to represent lawns on the stage. At the cooler end of the railway station, a man without a coat sat in a tilted chair and smoked his pipe. The fresh-cut of the Rio Grande circled near the town, and there could be seen beyond it a great plum-colored plain of mesquit.

Save for the busy drummer and his companions in the saloon, Yellow Sky was dozing. The new-comer leaned gracefully upon the bar, and recited many tales with the confidence of a bard who has come upon a new field.

"—and at the moment that the old man fell downstairs with the bureau in his arms, the old woman was coming up with two scuttles of coal, and of course—"

The drummer's tale was interrupted by a young man who suddenly appeared in the open door. He cried: "Scratchy Wilson's drunk, and has turned loose with both hands." The two Mexicans at once set down their glasses and faded out of the rear entrance of the saloon.

The drummer, innocent and jocular, answered: "All right, old man. S'pose he has? Come in and have a drink, anyhow."

But the information had made such an obvious cleft in every skull in the room that the drummer was obliged to see its importance. All had become instantly solemn. "Say," said he, mystified, "what is this?" His three companions made the introductory gesture of eloquent speech; but the young man at the door forestalled them.

"It means, my friend," he answered, as he came into the saloon, "that for the next two hours this town won't be a health resort."

The barkeeper went to the door, and locked and barred it; reaching out of the window, he pulled in heavy wooden shutters, and barred them. Immediately a solemn, chapel-like gloom was upon the place. The drummer was looking from one to another.

"But say," he cried, "what is this, anyhow? You don't mean there is going to be a gun-fight?"

"Don't know whether there'll be a fight or not," answered one man, grimly; "but there'll be some shootin'—some good shootin'."

The young man who had warned them waved his hand. "Oh, there'll be a fight fast enough, if any one wants it. Anybody can get a fight out there in the street. There's a fight just waiting."

The drummer seemed to be swayed between the interest of a foreigner and a perception of personal danger.

"What did you say his name was?" he asked.

"Scratchy Wilson," they answered in chorus.

"And will he kill anybody? What are you going to do? Does this happen often? Does he rampage around like this once a week or so? Can he break in that door?"

"No; he can't break down that door," replied the barkeeper. "He's tried it three times. But when he comes you'd better lay down on the floor, stranger. He's dead sure to shoot at it, and a bullet may come through."

Thereafter the drummer kept a strict eye upon the door. The time had not yet been called for him to hug the floor, but, as a minor precaution, he sidled near to the wall. "Will he kill anybody?" he said again.

The men laughed low and scornfully at the question.

"He's out to shoot, and he's out for trouble. Don't see any good in experimentin' with him."

"But what do you do in a case like this? What do you do?"

A man responded: "Why, he and Jack Potter—"

"But," in chorus the other men interrupted, "Jack Potter's in San Anton'."

"Well, who is he? What's he got to do with it?"

"Oh, he's the town marshal. He goes out and fights Scratchy when he gets on one of these tears."

"Wow!" said the drummer, mopping his brow. "Nice job he's got."

The voices had toned away to mere whisperings. The drummer wished to ask further questions, which were born of an increasing anxiety and bewilderment; but when he attempted them, the men merely looked at him in irritation and motioned him to remain silent. A tense waiting hush was upon them. In the deep shadows of the room their eyes shone as they listened for sounds from the street. One man made three gestures at the barkeeper; and the latter, moving like a ghost, handed him a glass and a bottle. The man poured a full glass of whisky, and set down the bottle noiselessly. He gulped the whisky in a swallow, and turned again toward the door in immovable silence. The drummer saw that the barkeeper, without a sound, had taken a Winchester from beneath the bar. Later he saw this individual beckoning to him, so he tiptoed across the room.

"You better come with me back of the bar."

"No, thanks," said the drummer, perspiring; "I'd rather be where I can make a break for the back door."

Whereupon the man of bottles made a kindly but peremptory gesture. The drummer obeyed it, and, finding himself seated on a box with his head below the level of the bar, balm was laid upon his soul at sight of various zinc and copper fittings that bore a resemblance to armor-plate. The barkeeper took a seat comfortably upon an adjacent box.

"You see," he whispered, "this here Scratchy Wilson is a wonder with a gun—a perfect wonder; and when he goes on the war-trail, we hunt our holes—naturally. He's about the last one of the old gang that used to hang out along the river here. He's a terror when he's drunk. When he's sober he's all right—kind of simple— wouldn't hurt a fly—nicest fellow in town. But when he's drunk—whoo!"

There were periods of stillness. "I wish Jack Potter was back from San Anton'," said the barkeeper. "He shot Wilson up once—in the leg—and he would sail in and pull out the kinks in this thing."

Presently they heard from a distance the sound of a shot, followed by three wild yowls. It instantly removed a bond from the men in the darkened saloon. There was a shuffling of feet. They looked at each other. "Here he comes," they said.

3

A man in a maroon-colored flannel shirt, which had been purchased for purposes of decoration, and made principally by some Jewish women on the East Side of New York, rounded a corner and walked into the middle of the main street of Yellow Sky. In either hand the man held a long, heavy, blue-black revolver. Often he yelled, and these cries rang through a semblance of a deserted village, shrilly flying over the roofs in a volume that seemed to have no relation to the ordinary vocal strength of a man. It was as if the surrounding stillness formed the arch of a tomb over him. These cries of ferocious challenge rang against walls of silence. And his boots had red tops with gilded imprints, of the kind beloved in winter by little sledding boys on the hillsides of New England.

The man's face flamed in a rage begot of whisky. His eyes, rolling, and yet keen for ambush, hunted the still doorways and windows. He walked with the creeping movement of the midnight cat. As it occurred to him, he roared menacing information. The long revolvers in his hands were as easy as straws; they were moved with an electric swiftness. The little fingers of each hand played sometimes in a musician's way. Plain from the low collar of the shirt, the cords of his neck straightened and sank, straightened and sank, as passion moved him. The only sounds were his terrible invitations. The calm adobes preserved their demeanor at the passing of this small thing in the middle of the street.

There was no offer of fight—no offer of fight. The man called to the sky. There were no attractions. He bellowed and fumed and swayed his revolvers here and everywhere.

The dog of the barkeeper of the Weary Gentleman saloon had not appreciated the advance of events. He lay yet dozing in front of his master's door. At sight of the dog, the man paused and raised his revolver humorously. At sight of the man, the dog sprang up and walked diagonally away, with a sullen head, and growling. The man yelled, and the dog broke into a gallop. As it was about to enter an alley, there was a loud noise, a whistling, and something spat the ground directly before it. The dog screamed, and, wheeling in terror, galloped headlong in a new direction. Again there was a noise, a whistling, and sand was kicked viciously before it. Fear-stricken, the dog turned and flurried like an animal in a pen. The man stood laughing, his weapons at his hips.

Ultimately the man was attracted by the closed door of the Weary Gentleman saloon. He went to it and, hammering with a revolver, demanded drink.

The door remaining imperturbable, he picked a bit of paper from the walk, and nailed it to the framework with a knife. He then turned his back contemptuously upon this popular resort and, walking to the opposite side of the street and spinning there on his heel quickly and lithely, fired at the bit of paper. He missed it by a half-inch. He swore at himself, and went away. Later he comfortably fusilladed the windows of his most intimate friend. The man was playing with this town; it was a toy for him.

But still there was no offer to fight. The name of Jack Potter, his ancient antagonist, entered his mind, and he concluded that it would be a glad thing if he should go to Potter's house, and by bombardment induce him to come out and fight. He moved in the direction of his desire, chanting Apache scalp-music.

When he arrived at it, Potter's house presented the same still front as had the other adobes. Taking up a strategic position, the man howled a challenge. But this house regarded him as might a great stone god. It gave no sigh. After a decent wait, the man howled further challenges, mingling with them wonderful epithets.

Presently there came the spectacle of a man churning himself into deepest rage over the immobility of a house. He fumed at it as the winter wind attacks a prairie cabin in the North. To the distance there should have gone the sound of a tumult like the fighting of two hundred Mexicans. As necessity bade him, he paused for breath or to reload his revolvers.

4

Potter and his bride walked sheepishly and with speed. Sometimes they laughed together shamefacedly and low.

"Next corner, dear," he said finally.

They put forth the efforts of a pair walking bowed against a strong wind. Potter was about to raise a finger to point the first appearance of the new home when, as they circled the corner, they came face to face with a man in a maroon-colored shirt, who was feverishly pushing cartridges into a large revolver. Upon the instant the man dropped his revolver to the ground and, like lightning, whipped another from its holster. The second weapon was aimed at the bridegroom's chest.

There was a silence. Potter's mouth seemed to be merely a grave for his tongue. He exhibited an instinct to at once loosen his arm from the woman's grip, and he dropped the bag to the sand. As for the bride, her face had gone as yellow as old cloth. She was a slave to hideous rites, gazing at the apparitional snake.

The two men faced each other at a distance of three paces. He of the revolver smiled with a new and quiet ferocity.

"Tried to sneak up on me," he said. "Tried to sneak up on me!" His eyes grew more baleful. As Potter made a slight movement, the man thrust his revolver venomously forward. "No; don't you do it, Jack Potter. Don't you move a finger toward a gun just yet. Don't you move an eyelash. The time has come for me to settle with you, and I'm goin' to do it my own way, and loaf along with no interferin'. So if you don't want a gun bent on you, just mind what I tell you."

Potter looked at his enemy. "I ain't got a gun on me, Scratchy," he said. "Honest, I ain't." He was stiffening and steadying, but yet somewhere at the back of his mind a vision of the Pullman floated: the sea-green figured velvet, the shining brass, silver, and glass, the wood that gleamed as darkly brilliant as the surface of a pool of oil—all the glory of the marriage, the environment of the new estate. "You know I fight when it comes to fighting, Scratchy Wilson; but I ain't got a gun on me. You'll have to do all the shootin' yourself."

His enemy's face went livid. He stepped forward, and lashed his weapon to and fro before Potter's chest. "Don't you tell me you ain't got no gun on you, you whelp. Don't tell me no lie like that. There ain't a man in Texas ever seen you without no gun. Don't take me for no kid." His eyes blazed with light, and his throat worked like a pump.

"I ain't takin' you for no kid," answered Potter. His heels had not moved an inch backward. "I'm takin' you for a damn fool. I tell you I ain't got a gun, and I ain't. If you're goin' to shoot me up, you better begin now; you'll never get a chance like this again."

So much enforced reasoning had told on Wilson's rage; he was calmer. "If you ain't got a gun, why ain't you got a gun?" he sneered. "Been to Sunday-school?"

"I ain't got a gun because I've just come from San Anton' with my wife. I'm married," said Potter. "And if I'd thought there was going to be any galoots like you prowling around when I brought my wife home, I'd had a gun, and don't you forget it."

"Married!" said Scratchy, not at all comprehending.

"Yes, married. I'm married," said Potter, distinctly.

"Married?" said Scratchy. Seemingly for the first time, he saw the drooping, drowning woman at the other man's side. "No!" he said. He was like a creature allowed a glimpse of another world. He moved a pace backward, and his arm, with the revolver, dropped to his side. "Is this the lady?" he asked.

"Yes; this is the lady," answered Potter.

There was another period of silence.

"Well," said Wilson at last, slowly, "I s'pose it's all off now."

"It's all off if you say so, Scratchy. You know I didn't make the trouble." Potter lifted his valise.

"Well, I 'low it's off, Jack" said Wilson. He was looking at the ground. "Married!" He was not a student of chivalry; it was merely that in the presence of this foreign condition he was a simple child of the earlier plains. He picked up his starboard revolver, and, placing both weapons in their holsters, he want away. His feet made funnel-shaped tracks in the heavy sand.

CRITICAL THINKING QUESTIONS

1. Scratchy's behavior is based on several *assumptions*, and in the end he is disappointed to learn that they no longer hold true. What assumptions does he hold?

2. If we generalize from this story, we might say that Crane is arguing that women are a force which serves to diminish men's natural tendency to fight and brawl. Do you think this is a fair statement to make about the old West? Does it hold true today?

WRITING TOPIC

People naturally shape their behavior and attitudes to the social conditions they encounter. When those conditions change, people are thrown off balance. Have you witnessed social changes that have forced you to confront your behavior and attitudes?

Louise Erdrich

The Red Convertible

Lyman Lamartine

I was the first one to drive a convertible on my reservation. And of course it was red, a red Olds. I owned that car along with my brother Henry Junior. We owned it together until his boots filled with water on a windy night and he bought out my share. Now Henry owns the whole car, and his youngest brother Lyman (that's myself), Lyman walks everywhere he goes.

How did I earn enough money to buy my share in the first place? My own talent was I could always make money. I had a touch for it, unusual in a Chippewa. From the first I was different that way, and everyone recognized it. I was the only kid they let in the American Legion Hall to shine shoes, for example, and one Christmas I sold spiritual bouquets for the mission door to door. The nuns let me keep a percentage. Once I started, it seemed the more money I made the easier the money came. Everyone encouraged it. When I was fifteen I got a job washing dishes at the Joliet Cafe, and that was where my first big break happened.

It wasn't long before I was promoted to busing tables, and then the short-order cook quit and I was hired to take her place. No sooner than you know it I was managing the Joliet. The rest is history. I went on managing. I soon became part owner, and of course there was no stopping me then. It wasn't long before the whole thing was mine.

After I'd owned the Joliet for one year, it blew over in the worst tornado ever seen around here. The whole operation was smashed to bits. A total loss. The fryalator was up in a tree, the grill torn in half like it was paper. I was only sixteen. I had it all in my mother's name, and I lost it quick, but before I lost it I had every one of my relatives, and their relatives, to dinner, and I also bought that red Olds I mentioned, along with Henry.

The first time we saw it! I'll tell you when we first saw it. We had gotten a ride to Winnipeg, and both of us had money. Don't ask me why, because we never mentioned a car or anything, we just had all our money. Mine was cash, a big bankroll from the Joliet's insurance. Henry had two checks—a week's extra pay for being laid off, and his regular check from the Jewel Bearing Plant.

We were walking down Portage anyway, seeing the sights, when we saw it. There it was, parked, large as life. Really as *if* it was alive. I thought of the word *repose*, because the car wasn't simply stopped, parked, or whatever. That car reposed, calm and gleaming, a FOR SALE sign in its left front window. Then, before we had thought it over at all, the car belonged to us and our pockets were empty. We had just enough money for gas back home.

We went places in that car, me and Henry. We took off driving all one whole summer. We started off toward the Little Knife River and Mandaree in Fort Berthold and then we found ourselves down in Wakpala somehow, and then suddenly we were over in Montana on the Rocky Boy, and yet the summer was not even half over. Some people hang on to details when they travel, but we didn't let them bother us and just lived our everyday lives here to there.

I do remember this place with willows. I remember I laid under those trees and it was comfortable. So comfortable. The branches bent down all around me like a tent or a stable. And quiet, it was quiet, even though there was a powwow close enough so I could see it going on. The air was not too still, not too windy either. When the dust rises up and hangs in the air around dancers like that, I feel good. Henry was asleep with his arms thrown wide. Later on, he woke up and we started driving again. We were somewhere in Montana, or maybe on the Blood Reserve— it could have been anywhere. Anyway it was where we met the girl.

All her hair was in buns around her ears, that's the first thing I noticed about her. She was posed alongside the road with her arm out, so we stopped. That girl was short, so short her lumber shirt looked comical on her, like a nightgown. She had jeans on and fancy moccasins and she carried a little suitcase.

"Hop on in," says Henry. So she climbs in between us.

"We'll take you home," I says. "Where do you live?"

"Chicken," she says.

"Where the hell's that?" I ask her.

"Alaska."

"Okay," says Henry, and we drive.

We got up there and never wanted to leave. The sun doesn't truly set there in summer, and the night is more a soft dusk. You might doze off, sometimes, but before you know it you're up again, like an animal in nature. You never feel like you have to sleep hard or put away the world. And things would grow up there. One day just dirt or moss, the next day flowers and long grass. The girl's name was Susy. Her family really took to us. They fed us and put us up. We had our own tent to live in by their house, and the kids would be in and out of there all day and night. They couldn't get over me and Henry being brothers, we looked so different. We told them we knew we had the same mother, anyway.

One night Susy came in to visit us. We sat around in the tent talking of this and that. The season was changing. It was getting darker by that time, and the cold was even getting just a little mean. I told her it was time for us to go. She stood up on a chair.

"You never seen my hair," Susy said.

That was true. She was standing on a chair, but still, when she unclipped her buns the hair reached all the way to the ground. Our eyes opened. You couldn't tell how much hair she had when it was rolled up so neatly. Then my brother Henry did something funny. He went up to the chair and said, "Jump on my shoulders." So she did that, and her hair reached down past his waist, and he started twirling, this way and that, so her hair was flung out from side to side.

"I always wondered what it was like to have long pretty hair," Henry says. Well, we laughed. It was a funny sight, the way he did it. The next morning we got up and took leave of those people.

On to greener pastures, as they say. It was down through Spokane and across Idaho then Montana and very soon we were racing the weather right along under the Canadian border through Columbus, Des Lacs, and then were in Bottineau County and soon home. We'd made most of the trip, that summer, without putting up the car hood at all. We got home just in time.

I don't wonder that the army was so glad to get my brother that they turned him into a Marine. He was built like a brick outhouse anyway. We liked to tease him that they really wanted him for his Indian nose. He had a nose big and sharp as a hatchet, like the nose on Red Tomahawk, the Indian who killed Sitting Bull, whose profile is on signs all along the North Dakota highways. Henry went off to training camp, came home once during Christmas, then the next thing you know we got an overseas letter from him. It was 1970, and he said he was stationed up in the northern hill country. Whereabouts I did not know. He wasn't such a hot letter writer, and only got off two before the enemy caught him. I could never keep it straight, which direction those good Vietnam soldiers were from.

I wrote him back several times, even though I didn't know if those letter would get through. I kept him informed all about the car. Most of the time I had it up on blocks in the yard or half taken apart, because that long trip did a hard job on it under the hood.

I always had good luck with numbers, and never worried about the draft myself. I never even had to think about what my number was. But Henry was never lucky in the same way as me. It was at least three years before Henry came home. By then I guess the whole war was solved in the government's mind, but for him it would keep on going. In those years I'd put his car into almost perfect shape. I always thought of it as his car while he was gone, even though when he left he said, "Now it's yours," and threw me his key.

"Thanks for the extra key," I'd said. "I'll put it in your drawer just in case I need it." He laughed.

When he came home, though, Henry was very different, and I'll say this: the change was no good. You could hardly expect him to change for the better, I know. But he was quiet, so quiet, and never comfortable sitting still anywhere but always up and moving around. I thought back to times we'd sat still for whole afternoons, never moving a muscle, just shifting our weight along the ground, talking to who-ever sat with us, watching things. He'd always had a joke, then, too, and now you couldn't get him to laugh, or when he did it was more the sound of a man choking, a sound that stopped up the throats of other people around him. They got to leaving him alone most of the time, and I didn't blame them. It was a fact: Henry was jumpy and mean.

I'd bought a color TV set for my mom and the rest of us while Henry was away. Money still came very easy. I was sorry I'd ever bought it though, because of Henry. I was also sorry I'd bought color, because with black-and-white the pictures seem older and farther away. But what are you going to do? He sat in front of it, watching it, and that was the only time he was completely still. But it was the kind of stillness that you see in a rabbit when it freezes and before it will bolt. He was not easy. He sat in his chair gripping the armrests with all his might, as if the chair itself was moving at a high speed and if he let go at all he would rocket forward and maybe crash right through the set.

Once I was in the room watching TV with Henry and I heard his teeth click at something. I looked over, and he'd bitten through his lip. Blood was going down his chin. I tell you right then I wanted to smash that tube to pieces. I went over to it but Henry must have known what I was up to. He rushed from his chair and shoved me out of the way, against the wall. I told myself he didn't know what he was doing.

My mom came in, turned the set off real quiet, and told us she had made something for supper. So we went and sat down. There was still blood going down Henry's chin, but he didn't notice it and no one said anything, even though every time he took a bite of his bread his blood fell onto it until he was eating his own blood mixed in with the food.

While Henry was not around we talked about what was going to happen to him. There were no Indian doctors on the reservation, and my mom couldn't come around to trusting the old man, Moses Pillager, because he courted her long ago and was jealous of her husbands. He might take revenge through her son. We were afraid that if we brought Henry to a regular hospital they would keep him.

"They don't fix them in those places," Mom said; "they just give them drugs."

"We wouldn't get him there in the first place," I agreed, "so let's just forget about it."

Then I thought about the car.

Henry had not even looked at the car since he'd gotten home, though like I said, it was in tip-top condition and ready to drive. I thought the car might bring the old Henry back somehow. So I bided my time and waited for my chance to interest him in the vehicle.

One night Henry was off somewhere. I took myself a hammer. I went out to that car and I did a number on its underside. Whacked it up. Bent the tail pipe double. Ripped the muffler loose. By the time I was done with the car it looked worse than any typical Indian car that has been driven all its life on reservation roads, which they always say are like government promises—full of holes. It just about hurt me, I'll tell you that! I threw dirt in the carburetor and I ripped all the electric tape off the seats. I make it look just as beat up as I could. Then I sat back and waited for Henry to find it.

Still, it took him over a month. That was all right, because it was just getting warm enough, not melting, but warm enough to work outside.

"Lyman," he says, walking in one day, "that red car looks like shit."

"Well, it's old," I says. "You got to expect that."

"No way!" says Henry. "That car's a classic! But you went and ran the piss right out of it, Lyman, and you know it don't deserve that. I kept that car in A-one shape. You don't remember. You're too young. But when I left, that car was running like a watch. Now I don't even know if I can get it to start again, let alone get it anywhere near its old condition."

"Well you try," I said, like I was getting mad, "but I say it's a piece of junk."

Then I walked out before he could realize I knew he'd strung together more than six words at once.

After that I thought he'd freeze himself to death working on that car. He was out there all day, and at night he rigged up a little lamp, ran a cord out the window, and had himself some light to see by while he worked. He was better than he had been before, but that's still not saying much. It was easier for him to do the things the rest of us did. He ate more slowly and didn't jump up and down during the meal to get this or that or look out the window. I put my hand in the back of the TV set, I admit, and fiddled around with it good, so that it was almost impossible now to get a clear picture. He didn't look at it very often anyway. He was always out with that car or going off to get parts for it. By the time it was really melting outside, he had it fixed.

I had been feeling down in the dumps about Henry around this time. We had always been together before. Henry and Lyman. But he was such a loner now that I didn't know how to take it. So I jumped at the chance one day when Henry seemed friendly. It's not that he smiled or anything. He just said, "Let's take that old shit-box for a spin." Just the way he said it made me think he could be coming around.

We went out to the car. It was spring. The sun was shining very bright. My only sister, Bonita, who was just eleven years old, came out and made us stand together for a picture. Henry leaned his elbow on the red car's windshield, and he took his other arm and put it over my shoulder, very carefully, as though it was heavy for him to lift and he didn't want to bring the weight down all at once.

"Smile," Bonita said, and he did.

That picture. I never look at it anymore. A few months ago, I don't know why, I got his picture out and tacked it on the wall. I felt good about Henry at the time, close to him. I felt good having his picture on the wall, until one night when I was looking at television. I was a little drunk and stoned. I looked up at the wall and Henry was staring at me. I don't know what it was, but his smile had changed, or maybe it was gone. All I know is I couldn't stay in the same room with that picture. I was shaking. I got up, closed the door, and went into the kitchen. A little later my friend Ray came over and we both went back into that room. We put the picture in a brown bag, folded the bag over and over tightly, then put it way back in a closet.

I still see that picture now, as if it tugs at me, whenever I pass that closet door. The picture is very clear in my mind. It was so sunny that day Henry had to squint against the glare. Or maybe the camera Bonita held flashed like a mirror, blinding him, before she snapped the picture. My face is right out in the sun, big and round. But he might have drawn back, because the shadows on his face are deep as holes. There are two shadows curved like little hooks around the ends of his smile, as if to frame it and try to keep it there—that one, first smile that looked like it might have hurt his face. He has his field jacket on and the worn-in clothes he'd come back in and kept wearing ever since. After Bonita took the picture, she went into the house and we got into the car. There was a full cooler in the trunk. We started off, east, toward Pembina and the Red River because Henry said he wanted to see the high water.

The trip over there was beautiful. When everything starts changing, drying up, clearing off, you feel like your whole life is starting. Henry felt it, too. The top was down and the car hummed like a top. He'd really put it back in shape, even the tape on the seats was very carefully put down and glued back in layers. It's not that he smiled again or even joked, but his face looked to me as if it was clear, more peaceful. It looked as though he wasn't thinking of anything in particular except the bare fields and windbreaks and houses we were passing.

The river was high and full of winter trash when we got there. The sun was still out, but it was colder by the river. There were still little clumps of dirty snow here and there on the banks. The water hadn't gone over the banks yet, but it would, you could tell. It was just at its limit, hard swollen, glossy like an old gray scar. We made ourselves a fire, and we sat down and watched the current go. As I watched it I felt something squeezing inside me and tightening and trying to let go all at the same time. I knew I was not just feeling it myself; I knew I was feeling what Henry was going through at that moment. Except that I couldn't stand it, the closing and opening. I jumped to my feet. I took Henry by the shoulders and I started shaking him. "Wake up," I says, "wake up, wake up, wake up!" I didn't know what had come over me. I sat down beside him again.

His face was totally white and hard. Then it broke, like stones break all of a sudden when water boils up inside them.

"I know it," he says. "I know it. I can't help it. It's no use."

We start talking. He said he knew what I'd done with the car. It was obvious it had been whacked out of shape and not just neglected. He said he wanted to give the car to me for good now, it was no use. He said he'd fixed it just to give it back and I should take it.

"No way," I says. "I don't want it."

"That's okay," he says, "you take it."

"I don't want it, though," I says back to him, and then to emphasize, just to emphasize, you understand, I touch his shoulder. He slaps my hand off.

"Take that car," he says.

"No," I say. "Make me," I say, and then he grabs my jacket and rips the arm loose. That jacket is a class act, suede with tags and zippers. I push Henry backwards, off the log. He jumps up and bowls me over. We go down in a clinch and come up swinging hard, for all we're worth, with our fists. He socks my jaw so hard I feel like it swings loose. Then I'm at his rib cage and land a good one under his chin so his head snaps back. He's dazzled. He looks at me and I look at him and then his eyes are full of tears and blood and at first I think he's crying. But no, he's laughing. "Ha, ha!" he says. "Ha! Ha! Take good care of it."

"Okay," I says. "Okay, no problem. Ha! Ha!"

I can't help it, and I start laughing, too. My face feels fat and strange, and after a while I get a beer from the cooler in the trunk, and when I hand it to Henry he takes his shirt and wipes my germs off. "Hoof-and-mouth disease," he says. For some reason this cracks me up, and so we're really laughing for a while, and then we drink all the rest of the beers one by one and throw them in the river and see how far, how fast, the current takes them before they fill up and sink.

"You want to go on back?" I ask after a while. "Maybe we could snag a couple nice Kashpaw girls."

He says nothing. But I can tell his mood is turning again.

"They're all crazy, the girls up here, every damn one of them."

"You're crazy too," I say, to jolly him up. "Crazy Lamartine boys!"

He looks as though he will take this wrong at first. His face twists, then clears, and he jumps up on his feet. "That's right!" he says. "Crazier 'n hell. Crazy Indians!"

I think it's the old Henry again. He throws off his jacket and starts springing his legs up from the knees like a fancy dancer. He's down doing something between a grass dance and a bunny hop, no kind of dance I ever saw before, but neither has anyone else on all this green growing earth. He's wild. He wants to pitch whoopee! He's up and at me and all over. All this time I'm laughing so hard, so hard my belly is getting tied up in a knot.

"Got to cool me off!" he shouts all of a sudden. Then he runs over to the river and jumps in.

There's boards and other things in the current. It's so high. No sound comes from the river after the splash he makes, so I run right over. I look around. It's getting dark. I see he's halfway across the water already, and I know he didn't swim there but the current took him. It's far. I hear his voice, though, very clearly across it.

"My boots are filling," he says.

He says this in a normal voice, like he just noticed and he doesn't know what to think of it. Then he's gone. A branch comes by. Another branch. And I go in.

By the time I get out of the river, off the snag I pulled myself onto, the sun is down. I walk back to the car, turn on the high beams, and drive it up the bank. I put it in first gear and then I take my foot off the clutch. I get out, close the door, and watch it plough softly into the water. The headlights reach in as they go down, searching, still lighted even after the water swirls over the back end. I wait. The wires short out. It is all finally dark. And then there is only the water, the sound of it going and running and going and running and running.

CRITICAL THINKING QUESTIONS

1. The word *pariah* means outcast or outsider. When Vietnam vets returned to American society, some said they felt like pariahs. In what way does the brother demonstrate this attitude in Erdrich's story?

2. Louise Erdrich is a Native American. In what ways does that influence her story?

WRITING TOPICS

1. At the Red River, Henry and Lyman fight over their car, then laugh and joke—"pitch whoopee." When Lyman says, "Crazy Lamartine boys!", Henry responds, "Crazier 'n hell. Crazy Indians!" Is Henry crazy? Does his final act suggest that he is in control or out of control? Use evidence from the story to discuss how you arrived at your *claim of value* in judging Henry.

2. Do you know any war veterans (World War II, Korean, Vietnam, Persian Gulf War, Bosnian Conflict)? If so, interview him or her to learn about his or her war and post-war experiences. Also, contact your local veterans' affairs office to find out information about the benefits for veterans who have sustained disabilities. Do you think veterans are generally treated fairly and adequately?

Maile Meloy

Ranch Girl

If you're white, and you're not rich or poor but somewhere in the middle, it's hard to have worse luck than to be born a girl on a ranch. It doesn't matter if your dad's the foreman or the rancher—you're still a ranch girl, and you've been dealt a bad hand.

She's the foreman's daughter. She grew up on Ted Haskell's Running-H cattle ranch, in the foreman's house, on the dirt road between Haskell's place and the barn. There are two bedrooms with walls made of particleboard, one bathroom (no tub), muddy boots and jackets in the living room, and a kitchen that's never used. The front door is painted with Haskell's brand—an H slanted to the right—and for a long time she didn't know that an H normally stands up straight. No one from school ever visits the ranch, so she's kept her room the way she decorated it at ten: a pink comforter on the bed, horse posters on the walls, plastic horse models on the shelves. There's a cow dog with a ruined hip, a barn cat who sleeps in the rafters, and, until he dies, a runt calf named Minute, who cries at night outside the front door.

She helps her dad when the other hands are busy, wading after him into an irrigation ditch, or rounding up a stray cow-calf pair. Her mother used to help, too—she sits a horse better than any of the hands—but then she took an office job in town, and bought herself a house to be close to work. That was the story, anyway; her mom hasn't shown up at the ranch since junior high. Her dad works late now, comes home tired and opens a beer. She brings him cheese and crackers, and watches him fall asleep in his chair.

Down the road, at the ranch house, Ted Haskell grills steaks from his cows every night. He's been divorced for years, but he's never learned how to cook anything except grilled steak. Whenever she's there to visit Haskell's daughter Carla, who's in her class at school, Haskell tries to get her to stay for dinner. He says that she's too thin and that a good beefsteak will make her strong. But she doesn't like leaving her dad alone, and Haskell's joking embarrasses her, so she walks home hungry.

When she's sixteen and starts going out at night, Haskell's ranch house is the best place to get ready. Carla has her own bathroom, with a big mirror, where they curl their hair into ringlets and put on blue eyeshadow. She and Carla wear matching Wranglers, and when it gets cold she wears knitted gloves with rainbow-striped fingers that the boys love to look at when they get drunk out on the Hill.

The Hill is the park where everyone stands and talks after they get bored driving their cars in circles on the drag. The cowboys are always on the Hill, and there's a fight every night; on a good night, there are five or six. On a good night, someone gets slid across the asphalt on his back, T-shirt riding up over his bare skin. It doesn't matter what the fights are about—no one ever knows—all that matters is that Andy Tyler always wins. He's the one who slides the other guy into the road. Afterward, he gets casual, walks over with his cowboy-boot gait, takes a button from the school blood drive off his shirt (and he always seems to have a button), and reads it aloud: "'I Gave Blood Today,'" he says. "Looks like you did, too," and then he pins the button to the other guy's shirt. He puts his jean jacket back on and hides a beer inside it, his hand tucked in like Napoleon's, and smiles that invincible smile of his.

"Hey," he says. "Do that rainbow thing again."

She waves her gloved hands in fast arcs, fingers together so the stripes line up.

Andy laughs, and grabs her hands, and says, "Come home and fuck me."

But she doesn't. She walks away. And Andy leaves the Hill without saying goodbye, and rolls his truck in a ditch for the hundredth time, but a buddy of his dad's always tows him, and no one ever calls the cops.

Virginity is as important to rodeo boys as it is to Catholics, and she doesn't go home and fuck Andy Tyler because, when she finally gets him, she wants to keep him. But she likes his asking. Some nights, he doesn't ask. Some nights, Lacey Estrada climbs into Andy's truck, dark hair bouncing in soft curls on her shoulders, and moves close to Andy on the front seat as they drive away. Lacey's dad is a doctor, and she lives in a big white house where she can sneak Andy into her bedroom without waking anyone up. But cowboys are romantics; when they settle down they want the girl they haven't fucked.

When Haskell marries an ex-hippie, everyone on the ranch expects trouble. Suzy was a beauty once; now she's on her third husband and doesn't take any shit. Suzy reads tarot cards, and when she lays them out to answer the question of Andy Tyler, the cards say to hold out for him.

On the spring cattle drive, she shows Suzy how to ride behind the mob and stay out of the dust. Suzy talks about her life before Haskell: she has a Ph.D. in anthropology, a police record for narcotics possession, a sorority pin, and a ski-bum son in Jackson Hole. She spent her twenties throwing dinner parties for her first husband's business clients—that, she says, was her biggest mistake—and then the husband ran off with one of her sorority sisters. She married a Buddhist next. "Be interesting in your twenties," Suzy says. "Otherwise you'll want to do it in your thirties or forties, when it wreaks all kinds of havoc, and you've got a husband and kids."

She listens to Suzy talk and says nothing. What's wrong with a husband and kids? A sweet guy, a couple of brown-armed kids running around outside—it wouldn't be so bad.

There's a fall cattle drive, too, but no one ever wants to come on it. It's cold in November, and the cows have scattered in the National Forest. They're half wild from being out there for months, especially the calves, who are stupid as only calves can be. The cowboys have disappeared, gone back to college or off on binges or to other jobs. So she goes out with her dad and Haskell, the three of them sweating in their heavy coats as they chase down the calves, fighting the herd back to winter pasture before it starts to snow. But it always snows before they finish, and her dad yells at her when her horse slips on the wet asphalt and scrapes itself up.

In grade school, it's O.K. to do well. But by high school, being smart gives people ideas. Science teachers start bugging her in the halls. They tell her Eastern schools have Montana quotas, places for ranch girls who are good at math. She could get scholarships, they say. But she knows, as soon as they suggest it, that if she went to one of those schools she'd still be a ranch girl—not the Texas kind who are débutantes and just happen to have a ranch in the family, and not the horse-farm kind who ride English. Horse people are different, because horses are elegant and clean. Cows are mucusy, muddy, shitty, slobbery things, and it takes another kind of person to live with them. Even her long, curled hair won't help at a fancy college, because prep-school girls don't curl their hair. The rodeo boys like it, but there aren't any rodeo boys out East. So she comes up with a plan: she has to start flunking. She has two and a half years of straight A's, and she has to flunk quietly, not to draw attention. Western Montana College, where Andy Tyler wants to go, will take anyone who applies. She can live cheap in Dillon, and if things don't work out with Andy she already knows half the football team.

When rodeo season begins, the boys start skipping school. She'd skip, too, but the goal is to load up on D's, not to get kicked out or sent into counselling. She paints her nails in class and follows the rodeo circuit on week-ends. Andy rides saddle bronc, but his real event is bull riding. The bull riders have to be a little crazy, and Andy Tyler is a little crazy. He's crazy in other ways, too: two years of asking her to come home and fuck him have made him urgent about it. She dances with him at the all-night graduation party, and he catches her around the waist and says he doesn't know a more beautiful girl. At dawn, he leaves for spring rodeo finals in Reno, driving down with his best friend, Rick Marcille, and she goes with Carla to Country Kitchen in a happy fog. She orders a chocolate shake and thinks about dancing with Andy. Then she falls asleep on Carla's bedroom floor, watching cartoons, too tired to make it down the road to bed.

Andy Tyler calls once from Reno, at 2 A.M. She answers the phone before it wakes her dad. Andy's taken second place in the bull riding and won a silver belt buckle and three thousand dollars. He says he'll take her to dinner at the Grub Stake when he gets home. Rick Marcille shouts "Ro-*day*-o!" in the background.

There's a call the next night, too. But it's from Rick Marcille's dad. Rick and Andy rolled the truck somewhere in Idaho, and the doctors don't think Rick will make it, though Andy might. Mr. Marcille sounds angry that Andy's the one who's going to live, but he offers to drive her down there. She doesn't wake her dad; she just goes.

The doctors are wrong. It's Andy who doesn't make it. When she gets to Idaho, he's already dead. Rick Marcille is paralyzed from the neck down. The cops say the boys weren't drinking, that a wheel came loose and the truck rolled, but she guesses the cops are just being nice. It's her turn to be angry, at Mr. Marcille, because his son will live and Andy is dead. But when they leave the hospital, Mr. Marcille falls down on his knees, squeezing her hand until it hurts.

At Andy's funeral, his uncle's band plays, and his family sets white doves free. One won't go, and it hops around the grass at her feet. The morning is already hot and blue, and there will be a whole summer of days like this to get through.

Andy's obituary says he was engaged to Lacey Estrada, which only Lacey or her doctor father could have put in. If she had the guts, she'd buy every paper in town and burn them outside the big white house where Lacey took him home and fucked him. Then Lacey shows up on the Hill with an engagement ring and gives her a sad smile as if they've shared something. If she were one of the girls who gets in fights on the Hill, she'd fight Lacey. But she doesn't; she looks away. They'll all be too old for the Hill once school starts, anyway.

At Western, in the fall, in a required composition class, her professor accuses her of plagiarism because her first paper is readable. She drops his class. Carla gets an A on her biology midterm at the university in Bozeman. She's going to be a big-animal vet. Her dad tells everyone, beaming.

But the next summer, Carla quits college to marry a boy named Dale Banning. The Bannings own most of central Montana, and Dale got famous at the family's fall livestock sale. He'd been putting black bulls on Herefords when everyone wanted purebreds. They said he was crazy, but at the sale Dale's crossbred black-baldies brought twice what the purebreds did. Dale stood around grinning, embarrassed, like a guy who'd beaten his friends at poker.

Carla tells her about the engagement in Haskell's kitchen, and says she'll still be working with animals, without slogging through all those classes. "Dale's never been to vet school," Carla says. "But he can feel an embryo the size of a pea inside a cow's uterus."

She's heard Dale use that line on girls before, but never knew it to work so well. Carla's voice has a dreamy edge.

"If I don't marry him now," Carla says, "he'll find someone else."

In his head, Haskell has already added the Banning acreage to his own, and the numbers make him giddy. He forgets about having a vet for a daughter, and talks about the wedding all the time. If Carla backed out, he'd marry Dale himself. For the party, they clear the big barn and kill a cow. Carla wears a high-collared white gown that hides the scar on her neck—half a Running-H—from the time she got in the way at branding, holding a struggling calf. Dale wears a string tie and a black ten-gallon hat, and everyone dances to Andy's uncle's band.

Her mother drives out to the ranch for the wedding; it's the first time she's seen her parents together in years. Her dad keeps ordering whiskeys and her mother gets drunk and giggly. But they sober up enough not to go home together.

That winter, her dad quits his job, saying he's tired of Haskell's crap. He leaves the foreman's house and moves in with his new girlfriend, who then announces he can't stay there without a job. He hasn't done anything but ranch work for twenty-five years, so he starts day riding for Haskell again, then working full-time hourly, until he might as well be the foreman.

When she finishes Western, she moves into her mother's house in town. Stacks of paperwork for the local horse-racing board cover every chair and table, and an old leather racing saddle straddles an arm of the couch. Her mother still thinks of herself as a horsewoman, and buys unbroken thoroughbreds she doesn't have time or money to train. She doesn't have a truck or a trailer, or land for pasture, so she boards the horses and they end up as big, useless pets she never sees.

Summer evenings, she and her mother sit on the front step and eat ice cream with chocolate-peanut-butter chunks for dinner. She thinks about moving out, but then her mother might move in with her—and that would be worse.

She isn't a virgin anymore, thanks to a boy she found who wouldn't cause her trouble. He drops by from time to time, to see if things might start up again. They don't. He's nothing like Andy. He isn't the one in her head.

She drives out to see Carla's baby when Carla leaves Dale and moves back home to the Running H. It feels strange to be at the ranch now, with the foreman's house empty and Carla's little boy in the yard, and everything else the same.

"You're so lucky to have a degree and no kid," Carla says. "You can still leave."

And Carla is right: She could leave. Apply to grad school in Santa Cruz and live by the beach. Take the research job in Chicago that her chemistry professor keeps calling about. Go to Zihuatenejo with Haskell's friends, who need a nanny. They have tons of room, because in Mexico you don't have to pay property tax if you're still adding on to the house.

But none of these things seem real; what's real is the payments on her car and her mom's crazy horses, the feel of the ranch road she can drive blindfolded, and her dad needing her in November to bring in the cows.

Suzy lays out the tarot cards on the kitchen table. The cards say, Go on, go away. But, she thinks, out there in the world you get old. You don't get old here. Here you can always be a ranch girl. Suzy knows. When Haskell comes in wearing muddy boots, saying, "Hi, baby, Hi, hon," his wife stacks up the tarot cards and kisses him hello. She pours him fresh coffee and puts away the cards that say go.

CRITICAL THINKING QUESTIONS

1. What stereotypes are associated with a "ranch girl"? How do Carla and the narrator reinforce, challenge, or qualify these stereotypes?

2. Read back over the last few paragraphs, and analyze the narrator's reasoning process in deciding to stay where she is—living with her Mom and close by the ranch.

    a. What value assumptions about life "out there in the world" and about ranch life does the narrator hold?

    b. Evaluate the narrator's decision to stay rather than to "Go on, go away," as the Tarot cards say. Do you think her decision is reasonable and valid? Why or why not?

WRITING TOPIC

What does the author imply about the role of one's childhood environment in shaping individual character and one's life path choices? To what degree do you agree with this claim? Does a person's childhood environment always/often/sometimes/rarely determine his or her character and life path? What evidence can you provide to support your claim?

Tim O'Brien

On the Rainy River

This is one story I've never told before. Not to anyone. Not to my parents, not to my brother or sister, not even to my wife. To go into it, I've always thought, would only cause embarrassment for all of us, a sudden need to be elsewhere, which is the natural response to a confession. Even now, I'll admit, the story makes me squirm. For more than twenty years I've had to live with it, feeling the shame, trying to push it away, and so by this act of remembrance, by putting the facts down on paper, I'm hoping to relieve at least some of the pressure on my dreams. Still, it's a hard story to tell. All of us, I suppose, like to believe that in a moral emergency we will behave like the heroes of our youth, bravely and forthrightly, without thought of personal loss or discredit. Certainly that was my conviction back in the summer of 1968. Tim O'Brien: a secret hero. The Lone Ranger. If the stakes ever became high enough— if the evil were evil enough, if the good were good enough—I would simply tap a secret reservoir of courage that had been accumulating inside me over the years. Courage, I seemed to think, comes to us in finite quantities, like an inheritance, and by being frugal and stashing it away and letting it earn interest, we steadily increase our moral capital in preparation for that day when the account must be drawn down. It was a comforting theory. It dispensed with all those bothersome little acts of daily courage: it offered hope and grace to the repetitive coward; it justified the past while amortizing the future.

In June of 1968, a month after graduating from Macalester College, I was drafted to fight a war I hated. I was twenty-one years old. Young, yes, and politically naive, but even so the American war in Vietnam seemed to me wrong. Certain blood was being shed for uncertain reasons. I saw no unity of purpose, no consensus on matters of philosophy or history or law. The very facts were shrouded in uncertainty: Was it a civil war? A war of national liberation or simple aggression? Who started it, and when, and why? What really happened to the *USS Maddox* on that dark night in the Gulf of Tonkin? Was Ho Chi Minh a Communist stooge, or a nationalist savior, or both, or neither? What about the Geneva Accords? What about SEATO and the Cold War? What about dominoes? America was divided on these and a thousand other issues, and the debate had spilled out across the floor of the United States Senate and into the streets, and smart men in pinstripes could not agree on even the most fundamental matters of public policy. The only certainty that summer was moral confusion. It was my view then, and still is, that you don't make war without knowing why. Knowledge, of course, is always imperfect, but it seemed to me that when a nation goes to war it must have reasonable confidence in the justice and imperative of its cause. You can't fix your mistakes. Once people are dead, you can't make them undead.

In any case those were my convictions, and back in college I had taken a modest stand against the war. Nothing radical, no hothead stuff, just ringing a few doorbells for Gene McCarthy, composing a few tedious, uninspired editorials for the campus newspaper. Oddly, though, it was almost entirely an intellectual activity. I brought some energy to it, of course, but it was the energy that accompanies almost any abstract endeavor; I felt no personal danger; I felt no sense of an impending crisis in my life. Stupidly, with a kind of smug removal that I can't begin to fathom, I assumed that the problems of killing and dying did not fall within my special province.

The draft notice arrived on June 17, 1968. It was a humid afternoon, I remember, cloudy and very quiet, and I'd just come in from a round of golf. My mother and father were having lunch out in the kitchen. I remember opening up the letter, scanning the first few lines, feeling the blood go thick behind my eyes. I remember a sound in my head. It wasn't thinking, just a silent howl. A million things all at once—I was too *good* for this war. Too smart, too compassionate, too everything. It couldn't happen. I was above it. I had the world dicked—Phi Beta Kappa and summa cum laude and president of the student body and a full-ride scholarship for grad studies at Harvard. A mistake, maybe—a foul-up in the paperwork. I was no soldier. I hated Boy Scouts. I hated camping out. I hated dirt and tents and mosquitoes. The sight of blood made me queasy, and I couldn't tolerate authority, and I didn't know a rifle from a slingshot. I was a *liberal,* for Christ sake: If they needed fresh bodies, why not draft some back-to-the-stone-age hawk? Or some dumb jingo in his hard hat and Bomb Hanoi button, or one of LBJ's pretty daughters, or Westmoreland's whole handsome family—nephews and nieces and baby grandson. There should be a law, I thought. If you support a war, if you think it's worth the price, that's fine, but you have to put your own precious fluids on the line. You have to head for the front and hook up with an infantry unit and help spill the blood. And you have to bring along your wife, or your kids, or your lover. A *law,* I thought.

I remember the rage in my stomach. Later it burned down to a smoldering self-pity, then to numbness. At dinner that night my father asked what my plans were.

"Nothing," I said. "Wait."

I spent the summer of 1968 working in an Armour meat-packing plant in my hometown of Worthington, Minnesota. The plant specialized in pork products, and for eight hours a day I stood on a quarter-mile assembly line—more properly, a disassembly line—removing blood clots from the necks of dead pigs. My job title, I believe, was Declotter. After slaughter, the hogs were decapitated, split down the length of the belly, pried open, eviscerated, and strung up by the hind hocks on a high conveyer belt. Then gravity took over. By the time a carcass reached my spot on the line, the fluids had mostly drained out, everything except for thick clots of blood in the neck and upper chest cavity. To remove the stuff, I used a kind of water gun. The machine was heavy, maybe eighty pounds, and was suspended from the ceiling by a heavy rubber cord. There was some bounce to it, an elastic up-and-down give, and the trick was to maneuver the gun with your whole body, not lifting with the arms, just letting the rubber cord do the work for you. At one end was a trigger; at the muzzle end was a small nozzle and a steel roller brush. As a carcass passed by, you'd lean forward and swing the gun up against the clots and squeeze the trigger, all in one motion, and the brush would whirl and water would come shooting out and you'd hear a quick splattering sound as the clots dissolved into a fine red mist. It was not pleasant work. Goggles were a necessity, and a rubber apron, but even so it was like standing for eight hours a day under a lukewarm blood-shower. At night I'd go home smelling of pig. It wouldn't go away. Even after a hot bath, scrubbing hard, the stink was always there—like old bacon, or sausage, a dense greasy pig stink that soaked deep into my skin and hair. Among other things, I remember, it was tough getting dates that summer. I felt isolated; I spent a lot of time alone. And there was also that draft notice tucked away in my wallet.

In the evenings I'd sometimes borrow my father's car and drive aimlessly around town, feeling sorry for myself, thinking about the war and the pig factory and how my life seemed to be collapsing toward slaughter. I felt paralyzed. All around me the options seemed to be narrowing, as if I were hurtling down a huge black funnel, the whole world squeezing in tight. There was no happy way out. The government had ended most graduate school deferments; the waiting lists for the National Guard and Reserves were impossibly long; my health was solid; I didn't qualify for CO status—no religious grounds, no history as a pacifist. Moreover, I could not claim to be opposed to war as a matter of general principle. There were occasions, I believed, when a nation was justified in using military force to achieve its ends, to stop a Hitler or some comparable evil, and I told myself that in such circumstances I would've willingly marched off to the battle. The problem, though, was that a draft board did not let you choose your war.

Beyond all this, or at the very center, was the raw fact of terror. I did not want to die. Not ever. But certainly not then, not there, not in a wrong war. Driving up Main Street, past the courthouse and the Ben Franklin store, I sometimes felt the fear spreading inside me like weeds. I imagined myself dead. I imagined myself doing things I could not do—charging an enemy position, taking aim at another human being.

At some point in mid-July I began thinking seriously about Canada. The border lay a few hundred miles north, an eight-hour drive. Both my conscience and my instincts were telling me to make a break for it, just take off and run like hell and never stop. In the beginning the idea seemed purely abstract, the word Canada printing itself out in my head; but after a time I could see particular shapes and images, the sorry details of my own future—a hotel room in Winnipeg, a battered old suitcase, my father's eyes as I tried to explain myself over the telephone. I could almost hear his voice, and my mother's. Run, I'd think. Then I'd think, Impossible. Then a second later I'd think, *Run.*

It was a kind of schizophrenia. A moral split. I couldn't make up my mind. I feared the war, yes, but I also feared exile. I was afraid of walking away from my own life, my friends and my family, my whole history, everything that mattered to me. I feared losing the respect of my parents. I feared the law. I feared ridicule and censure. My hometown was a conservative little spot on the prairie, a place where tradition counted, and it was easy to imagine people sitting around a table down at the old Gobbler Café on Main Street, coffee cups poised, the conversation slowly zeroing in on the young O'Brien kid, how the damned sissy had taken off for Canada. At night, when I couldn't sleep, I'd sometimes carry on fierce arguments with those people. I'd be screaming at them, telling them how much I detested their blind, thoughtless, automatic acquiescence to it all, their simple-minded patriotism, their prideful ignorance, their love-it-or-leave-it platitudes, how they were sending me off to fight a war they didn't understand and didn't want to understand. I held them responsible. By God, yes. I *did*. All of them—I held them personally and individually responsible—the polyestered Kiwanis boys, the merchants and farmers, the pious churchgoers, the chatty housewives, the PTA and Lions club and the Veterans of Foreign Wars and the fine upstanding gentry out at the country club. They didn't know Bao Dai from the man in the moon. They didn't know history. They didn't know the first thing about Diem's tyranny, or the nature of Vietnamese nationalism, or the long colonialism of the French—this was all too damned complicated, it required some reading—but no matter, it was a war to stop the Communists, plain and simple, which was how they liked things, and you were a treasonous pussy if you had second thoughts about killing or dying for plain and simple reasons.

I was bitter, sure. But it was so much more than that. The emotions went from outrage to terror to bewilderment to guilt to sorrow and then back again to outrage. I felt a sickness inside me. Real disease.

Most of this I've told before, or at least hinted at, but what I have never told is the full truth. How I cracked. How at work one morning, standing on the pig line, I felt something break open in my chest. I don't know what it was. I'll never know. But it was real, I know that much, it was a physical rupture—a cracking-leaking-popping feeling. I remember dropping my water gun. Quickly, almost without thought, I took off my apron and walked out of the plant and drove home. It was midmorning, I remember, and the house was empty. Down in my chest there was still that leaking sensation, something very warm and precious spilling out, and I was covered with blood and hog-stink, and for a long while I just concentrated on holding myself together. I remember taking a hot shower. I remember packing a suitcase and carrying it out to the kitchen, standing very still for a few minutes, looking carefully at the familiar objects all around me. The old chrome toaster, the telephone, the pink and white Formica on the kitchen counters. The room was full of bright sunshine. Everything sparkled. My house, I thought. My life. I'm not sure how long I stood there, but later I scribbled out a short note to my parents.

What it said, exactly, I don't recall now. Something vague. Taking off, will call, love Tim.

I drove north.

It's a blur now, as it was then, and all I remember is a sense of high velocity and the feel of the steering wheel in my hands. I was riding on adrenaline. A giddy feeling, in a way, except there was the dreamy edge of impossibility to it—like running a dead-end maze—no way out—it couldn't come to a happy conclusion and yet I was doing it anyway because it was all I could think of to do. It was pure flight, fast and mindless. I had no plan. Just hit the border at high speed and crash through and keep on running. Near dusk I passed through Bemidji, then turned northeast toward International Falls. I spent the night in the car behind a closed-down gas station a half mile from the border. In the morning, after gassing up, I headed straight west along the Rainy River, which separates Minnesota from Canada, and which for me separated one life from another. The land was mostly wilderness. Here and there I passed a motel or bait shop, but otherwise the country unfolded in great sweeps of pine and birch and sumac. Though it was still August, the air already had the smell of October, football season, piles of yellow-red leaves, everything crisp and clean. I remember a huge blue sky. Off to my right was the Rainy River, wide as a lake in places, and beyond the Rainy River was Canada.

For a while I just drove, not aiming at anything, then in the late morning I began looking for a place to lie low for a day or two. I was exhausted, and scared sick, and around noon I pulled into an old fishing resort called the Tip Top Lodge. Actually it was not a lodge at all, just eight or nine tiny yellow cabins clustered on a peninsula that jutted northward into the Rainy River. The place was in sorry shape. There was a dangerous wooden dock, an old minnow tank, a flimsy tar paper boathouse along the shore. The main building, which stood in a cluster of pines on high ground, seemed to lean heavily to one side, like a cripple, the roof sagging toward Canada. Briefly, I thought about turning around, just giving up, but then I got out of the car and walked up to the front porch.

The man who opened the door that day is the hero of my life. How do I say this without sounding sappy? Blurt it out—the man saved me. He offered exactly what I needed, without questions, without any words at all. He took me in. He was there at the critical time—a silent, watchful presence. Six days later, when it ended, I was unable to find a proper way to thank him, and I never have, and so, if nothing else, this story represents a small gesture of gratitude twenty years overdue.

Even after two decades I can close my eyes and return to that porch at the Tip Top Lodge. I can see the old guy staring at me. Elroy Berdahl: eighty-one years old, skinny and shrunken and mostly bald. He wore a flannel shirt and brown work pants. In one hand, I remember, he carried a green apple, a small paring knife in the other. His eyes had the bluish gray color of a razor blade, the same polished shine, and as he peered up at me I felt a strange sharpness, almost painful, a cutting sensation, as if his gaze were somehow slicing me open. In part, no doubt, it was my own sense of guilt, but even so I'm absolutely certain that the old man took one look and went right to the heart of things—a kid in trouble. When I asked for a room, Elroy made a little clicking sound with his tongue. He nodded, led me out to one of the cabins, and dropped a key in my hand. I remember smiling at him. I also remember wishing I hadn't. The old man shook his head as if to tell me it wasn't worth the bother.

"Dinner at five-thirty," he said. "You eat fish?"

"Anything," I said.

Elroy grunted and said, "I'll bet."

*　　*　　*

We spent six days together at the Tip Top Lodge. Just the two of us. Tourist season was over, and there were no boats on the river, and the wilderness seemed to withdraw into a great permanent stillness. Over those six days Elroy Berdahl and I took most of our meals together. In the mornings we sometimes went out on long hikes into the woods, and at night we played Scrabble or listened to records or sat reading in front of his big stone fireplace. At times I felt the awkwardness of an intruder, but Elroy accepted me into his quiet routine without fuss or ceremony. He took my presence for granted, the same way he might've sheltered a stray cat—no wasted sighs or pity—and there was never any talk about it. Just the opposite. What I remember more than anything is the man's willful, almost ferocious silence. In all that time together, all those hours, he never asked the obvious questions: Why was I there? Why alone? Why so preoccupied? If Elroy was curious about any of this, he was careful never to put it into words.

My hunch, though, is that he already knew. At least the basics. After all, it was 1968, and guys were burning draft cards, and Canada was just a boat ride away. Elroy Berdahl was no hick. His bedroom, I remember, was cluttered with books and newspapers. He killed me at the Scrabble board, barely concentrating, and on those occasions when speech was necessary he had a way of compressing large thoughts into small, cryptic packets of language. One evening, just at sunset, he pointed up at an owl circling over the violet-lighted forest to the west.

"Hey, O'Brien," he said. "There's Jesus."

The man was sharp—he didn't miss much. Those razor eyes. Now and then he'd catch me staring out at the river, at the far shore, and I could almost hear the tumblers clicking in his head. Maybe I'm wrong, but I doubt it.

One thing for certain, he knew I was in desperate trouble. And he knew I couldn't talk about it. The wrong word—or even the right word—and I would've disappeared. I was wired and jittery. My skin felt too tight. After supper one evening I vomited and went back to my cabin and lay down for a few moments and then vomited again; another time, in the middle of the afternoon, I began sweating and couldn't shut it off. I went through whole days feeling dizzy with sorrow. I couldn't sleep; I couldn't lie still. At night I'd toss around in bed, half awake, half dreaming, imagining how I'd sneak down to the beach and quietly push one of the old man's boats out into the river and start paddling my way toward Canada. There were times when I thought I'd gone off the psychic edge. I couldn't tell up from down, I was just falling, and late in the night I'd lie there watching weird pictures spin through my head. Getting chased by the Border Patrol—helicopters and searchlights and barking dogs—I'd be crashing through the woods, I'd be down on my hands and knees—people shouting out my name—the law closing in on all sides—my hometown draft board and the FBI and the Royal Canadian Mounted Police. It all seemed crazy and impossible. Twenty-one years old, an ordinary kid with all the ordinary dreams and ambitions, and all I wanted was to live the life I was born to—a mainstream life—I loved baseball and hamburgers and cherry Cokes—and now I was off on the margins of exile, leaving my country forever, and it seemed so impossible and terrible and sad.

I'm not sure how I made it through those six days. Most of it I can't remember. On two or three afternoons, to pass some time, I helped Elroy get the place ready for winter, sweeping down the cabins and hauling in the boats, little chores that kept my body moving. The days were cool and bright. The nights were very dark. One morning the old man showed me how to split and stack firewood, and for several hours we just worked in silence out behind his house. At one point, I remember, Elroy put down his maul and looked at me for a long time, his lips drawn as if framing a difficult question, but then he shook his head and went back to work. The man's self-control was amazing. He never pried. He never put me in a position that required lies or denials. To an extent, I suppose, his reticence was typical of that part of Minnesota, where privacy still held value, and even if I'd been walking around with some horrible deformity—four arms and three heads—I'm sure the old man would've talked about everything except those extra arms and heads. Simple politeness was part of it. But even more than that, I think, the man understood that words were insufficient. The problem had gone beyond discussion. During that long summer I'd been over and over the various arguments, all the pros and cons, and it was no longer a question that could be decided by an act of pure reason. Intellect had come up against emotion. My conscience told me to run, but some irrational and powerful force was resisting, like a weight pushing me toward the war. What it came down to, stupidly, was a sense of shame. Hot, stupid shame. I did not want people to think badly of me. Not my parents, not my brother and sister, not even the folks down at the Gobbler Café. I was ashamed to be there at the Tip Top Lodge. I was ashamed of my conscience, ashamed to be doing the right thing.

Some of this Elroy must've understood. Not the details, of course, but the plain fact of crisis.

Although the old man never confronted me about it, there was one occasion when he came close to forcing the whole thing out into the open. It was early evening, and we'd just finished supper, and over coffee and dessert I asked him about my bill, how much I owed so far. For a long while the old man squinted down at the tablecloth.

"Well, the basic rate," he said, "is fifty bucks a night. Not counting meals. This makes four nights, right?"

I nodded. I had three hundred and twelve dollars in my wallet.

Elroy kept his eyes on the tablecloth. "Now that's an on-season price. To be fair, I suppose we should knock it down a peg or two." He leaned back in his chair. "What's a reasonable number, you figure?"

"I don't know," I said. "Forty?"

"Forty's good. Forty a night. Then we tack on food—say another hundred? Two hundred sixty total?"

"I guess."

He raised his eyebrows. "Too much?"

"No, that's fair. It's fine. Tomorrow, though . . . I think I'd better take off tomorrow."

Elroy shrugged and began clearing the table. For a time he fussed with the dishes, whistling to himself as if the subject had been settled. After a second he slapped his hands together.

"You know what we forgot?" he said. "We forgot wages. Those odd jobs you done. What we have to do, we have to figure out what your time's worth. Your last job—how much did you pull in an hour?"

"Not enough," I said.

"A bad one?"

"Yes. Pretty bad."

Slowly then, without intending any long sermon, I told him about my days at the pig plant. It began as a straight recitation of the facts, but before I could stop myself I was talking about the blood clots and the water gun and how the smell had soaked into my skin and how I couldn't wash it away. I went on for a long time. I told him about wild hogs squealing in my dreams, the sounds of butchery, slaughterhouse sounds, and how I'd sometimes wake up with that greasy pig-stink in my throat.

When I was finished, Elroy nodded at me.

"Well, to be honest," he said, "when you first showed up here, I wondered about all that. The aroma, I mean. Smelled like you was awful damned fond of pork chops." The old man almost smiled. He made a snuffling sound, then sat down with a pencil and a piece of paper. "So what'd this crud job pay? Ten bucks an hour? Fifteen?"

"Less."

Elroy shook his head. "Let's make it fifteen. You put in twenty-five hours here, easy. That's three hundred seventy-five bucks total wages. We subtract the two hundred sixty for food and lodging, I will owe you a hundred and fifteen."

He took four fifties out of his shirt pocket and laid them on the table.

"Call it even," he said.

"No."

"Pick it up. Get yourself a haircut."

The money lay on the table for the rest of the evening. It was still there when I went back to my cabin. In the morning, though, I found an envelope tacked to my door. Inside were the four fifties and a two-word note that said EMERGENCY FUND.

The man knew.

Looking back after twenty years, I sometimes wonder if the events of that summer didn't happen in some other dimension, a place where your life exists before you've lived it, and where it goes afterward. None of it ever seemed real. During my time at the Tip Top Lodge I had the feeling that I'd slipped out of my own skin, hovering a few feet away while some poor yo-yo with my name and face tried to make his way toward a future he didn't understand and didn't want. Even now I can see myself as I was then. It's like watching an old home movie: I'm young and tan and fit. I've got hair—lots of it. I don't smoke or drink. I'm wearing faded blue jeans and a white polo shirt. I can see myself sitting on Elroy Berdahl's dock near dusk one evening, the sky a bright shimmering pink, and I'm finishing up a letter to my parents that tells what I'm about to do and why I'm doing it and how sorry I am that I'd never found the courage to talk to them about it. I ask them not to be angry. I try to explain some of my feelings, but there aren't enough words, and so I just say that it's a thing that has to be done. At the end of the letter I talk about the vacations we used to take up in this north country, at a place called Whitefish Lake, and how the scenery here reminds me of those good times. I tell them I'm fine. I tell them I'll write again from Winnipeg or Montreal or wherever I end up.

On my last full day, the sixth day, the old man took me out fishing on the Rainy River. The afternoon was sunny and cold. A stiff breeze came in from the north, and I remember how the little fourteen-foot boat made sharp rocking motions as we pushed off from the dock. The current was fast. All around us, I remember, there was a vastness to the world, an unpeople rawness, just the trees and the sky and the water reaching out toward nowhere. The air had the brittle scent of October.

For ten or fifteen minutes Elroy held a course upstream, the river choppy and silver-gray, then he turned straight north and put the engine on full throttle. I felt the bow lift beneath me. I remember the wind in my ears, the sound of the old outboard Evinrude. For a time I didn't pay attention to anything, just feeling the cold spray against my face, but then it occurred to me that at some point we must've passed into Canadian waters, across the dotted line between two different worlds, and I remember a sudden tightness in my chest as I looked up and watched the far shore come at me. This wasn't a daydream. It was tangible and real. As we came in toward land, Elroy cut the engine, letting the boat fishtail lightly about twenty yards off shore. The old man didn't look at me or speak. Bending down, he opened up his tackle box and busied himself with a bobber and a piece of wire leader, humming to himself, his eyes down.

It struck me then that he must've planned it. I'll never be certain, of course, but I think he meant to bring me up against the realities, to guide me across the river and to take me to the edge and to stand a kind of vigil as I chose a life for myself.

I remember starting at the old man, then at my hands, then at Canada. The shoreline was dense with brush and timber. I could see tiny red berries on the bushes. I could see a squirrel up in one of the birch trees, a big crow looking at me from a boulder along the river. That close—twenty yards—and I could see the delicate latticework of the leaves, the texture of the soil, the browned needles beneath the pines, the configurations of geology and human history. Twenty yards. I could've done it. I could've jumped and started swimming for my life. Inside me, in my chest, I felt a terrible squeezing pressure. Even now, as I write this, I can still feel that tightness. And I want you to feel it—the wind coming off the river, the waves, the silence, the wooded frontier. You're at the bow of a boat on the Rainy River. You're twenty-one years old, you're scared, and there's a hard squeezing pressure in your chest.

What would you do?

Would you jump? Would you feel pity for yourself? Would you think about your family and your childhood and your dreams and all you're leaving behind? Would it hurt? Would it feel like dying? Would you cry, as I did?

I tried to swallow it back. I tried to smile, except I was crying.

Now, perhaps, you can understand why I've never told this story before. It's not just the embarrassment of tears. That's part of it, no doubt, but what embarrasses me much more, and always will, is the paralysis that took my heart. A moral freeze: I couldn't decide, I couldn't act, I couldn't comport myself with even a pretense of modest human dignity.

All I could do was cry. Quietly, not bawling, just the chest-chokes.

At the rear of the boat Elroy Berdahl pretended not to notice. He held a fishing rod in his hands, his head bowed to hide his eyes. He kept humming a soft, monotonous little tune. Everywhere, it seemed, in the trees and water and sky, a great worldwide sadness came pressing down on me, a crushing sorrow, sorrow like I had never known it before. And what was so sad, I realized, was that Canada had become a pitiful fantasy. Silly and hopeless. It was no longer a possibility. Right then, with the shore so close, I understood that I would not do what I should do. I would not swim away from my hometown and my country and my life. I would not be brave. That old image of myself as a hero, as a man of conscience and courage, all that was just a threadbare pipe dream. Bobbing there on the Rainy River, looking back at the Minnesota shore, I felt a sudden swell of helplessness come over me, a drowning sensation, as if I had toppled overboard and was being swept away by the silver waves. Chunks of my own history flashed by. I saw a seven-year-old boy in a white cowboy hat and a Lone Ranger mask and a pair of holstered six-shooters; I saw a twelve-year-old Little League shortstop pivoting to turn a double play; I saw a sixteen-year-old kid decked out for his first prom, looking spiffy in a white tux and a black bow tie, his hair cut short and flat, his shoes freshly polished. My whole life seemed to spill out into the river, swirling away from me, everything I had ever been or ever wanted to be. I couldn't get my breath; I couldn't stay afloat; I couldn't tell which way to swim. A hallucination, I suppose, but it was as real as anything I would ever feel. I saw my parents calling to me from the far shoreline. I saw my brother and sister, all the townsfolk, the mayor and the entire Chamber of Commerce and all my old teachers and girlfriends and high school buddies. Like some weird sporting event: everybody screaming from the sidelines, rooting me on—a loud stadium roar. Hotdogs and popcorn—stadium smells, stadium heat. A squad of cheerleaders did cartwheels along the banks of the Rainy River; they had megaphones and pompoms and smooth brown thighs. The crowd swayed left and right. A marching band played fight songs. All my aunts and uncles were there, and Abraham Lincoln, and Saint George, and a nine-year-old girl named Linda who had died of a brain tumor back in fifth grade, and several members of the United States Senate, and a blind poet scribbling notes, and LBJ, and Huck Finn, and Abbie Hoffman, and all the dead soldiers back from the grave, and the many thousands who were later to die—villagers with terrible burns, little kids without arms or legs—yes, and the Joint Chiefs of Staff were there, and a couple of popes, and a first lieutenant named Jimmy Cross, and the last surviving veteran of the American Civil War, and Jane Fonda dressed up as Barbarella, and an old man sprawled beside a pigpen, and my grandfather, and Gary Cooper, and a kind-faced woman carrying an umbrella and a copy of Plato's *Republic,* and a million ferocious citizens waving flags of all shapes and colors—people in hard hats, people in headbands—they were all whooping and chanting and urging me toward one shore or the other. I saw faces from my distant past and distant future. My wife was there. My unborn daughter waved at me, and my two sons hopped up and down, and a drill sergeant named Blyton sneered and shot up a finger and shook his head. There was a choir in bright purple robes. There was a cabbie from the Bronx. There was a slim young man I would one day kill with a hand grenade along a red clay trail outside the village of My Khe.

The little aluminum boat rocked softly beneath me. There was the wind and the sky.

I tried to will myself overboard.

I gripped the edge of the boat and leaned forward and thought, *Now.*

I did try. It just wasn't possible.

All those eyes on me—the town, the whole universe—and I couldn't risk the embarrassment. It was as if there were an audience to my life, that swirl of faces along the river, and in my head I could hear people screaming at me. Traitor! they yelled. Turncoat! Pussy! I felt myself blush. I couldn't tolerate it. I couldn't endure the mockery, or the disgrace, or the patriotic ridicule. Even in my imagination, the shore just twenty yards away, I couldn't make myself be brave. It had nothing to do with morality. Embarrassment, that's all it was.

And right then I submitted.

I would go to the war—I would kill and maybe die—because I was embarrassed not to.

That was the sad thing. And so I sat in the bow of the boat and cried.

It was loud now. Loud, hard crying.

Elroy Berdahl remained quiet. He kept fishing. He worked his line with the tips of his fingers, patiently, squinting out at his red and white bobber on the Rainy River. His eyes were flat and impassive. He didn't speak. He was simply there, like the river and the late-summer sun. And yet by his presence, his mute watchfulness, he made it real. He was the true audience. He was a witness, like God, or like the gods, who look on in absolute silence as we live our lives, as we make our choices or fail to make them.

"Ain't biting," he said.

Then after a time the old man pulled in his line and turned the boat back toward Minnesota.

I don't remember saying goodbye. That last night we had dinner together, and I went to bed early, and in the morning Elroy fixed breakfast for me. When I told him I'd be leaving, the old man nodded as if he already knew. He looked down at the table and smiled.

At some point later in the morning it's possible that we shook hands—I just don't remember—but I do know that by the time I'd finished packing the old man had disappointed. Around noon, when I took my suitcase out to the car, I noticed that his old black pickup truck was no longer parked in front of the house. I went inside and waited for a while, but I felt a bone certainty that he wouldn't be back. In a way, I thought, it was appropriate. I washed up the breakfast dishes, left his two hundred dollars on the kitchen counter, got into the car, and drove south toward home.

The day was cloudy. I passed through towns with familiar names, through the pine forests and down to the prairie, and then to Vietnam, where I was a soldier, and then home again. I survived, but it's not a happy ending. I was a coward. I went to the war.

CRITICAL THINKING QUESTION

O'Brien says he is telling this story of his moral crisis twenty years ago, in part as a tribute to "the hero of my life . . . the man saved me." But he also is evaluating the choice he made on his sixth day at the Tip Top Lodge. Here is a *Toulmin analysis* of his evaluation argument:

Warrant: Courage is taking right and moral action, "bravely and forthrightly, without fear of personal loss or discredit."

Support: It is shameful to participate in a war that is immoral and wrong.

Claim: "I was a coward. I went to the war."

O'Brien's argument is logical: the claim follows logically from the premises. Is it valid? Do you accept his claim? Why or why not?

WRITING TOPIC

Evaluate a moral choice you made in the past. What was the warrant, the support, and the claim in your case?

Ernesto Quiñonez

from Bodega Dreams

Back in Julia de Burgos Junior High, back in the days of my growing up and all that Piri Thomas kinda crap that I will spare you from, there was the English teacher, Mr. Blessington. He kept telling us boys we were all going to end up in jail and that all the girls were going to end up hooking. He would say these things right out loud and the administration wouldn't do anything. I hated Blessington and he knew it. He looked at Blanca with the eyes of a repressed rapist. He thought he was smooth but what he came out looking was creepy. He'd come to school in a suit and tell us that a man with a suit is a man that is valuable and that a man without a suit has no worth. He always did Robert Frost poems with us, which were all right, but after a while we started to hate Robert Frost. Blessington thought he was doing us a service, and that was his error. He was one of those upper-middle-class people who think highly of themselves because they could be making money or something, but no, they have taken the high road and have chosen to "help" poor kids from the ghetto.

On the other hand the science teacher, Jose Tapia, was always lecturing us on how fortunate we were because we were young and Latin. His speeches were at times so fiery and full of passion that every year the principal would try to make Tapia the gym teacher, in hopes of cutting down Tapia's influence over us. But as a science teacher Tapia was state certified and was appointed to our school so there was no way for the principal to get rid of him.

And he didn't want to be called Mr. Tapia, simply Tapia.

One day when Sapo and me were in the eighth grade, Tapia told us, "You speak two languages, you are worth two people." Sapo retorted, "What about the pope? He speaks like a hundred languages, but he ain't worth jack." The class was rolled.

"Sapo, do you think the pope would be the pope if he didn't know his hundred languages?" Tapia asked after the laughter died down.

"Nah, if he didn't speak a hundred languages he'd still be pope, because he's white. All popes are white. I ain't never seen no black pope. I ain't seen a Spanish pope, either."

"Hey, Tapia," I said, "I never even seen a black nun." Of course we were just stalling. The truth was we hadn't done our homework and wanted to kill time.

"Or a Chinese nun. All I've ever seen are white nuns," Edwin jumped in, so I figured he hadn't done his homework either. "You can't have a black pope if there are no black nuns." I hated Edwin. When he borrowed a pencil he never gave it back and when school was almost over, he always borrowed loose-leaf paper because he didn't see the point of buying a new notebook.

"Yeah, a black nun!" Sapo shouted in agreement.

"Julio, can you shut him up?" Blanca whispered to me. I always sat next to Blanca. I would leave my science book at home on purpose so I could use the excuse of sharing hers. Tapia understood this and, even though we had assigned seats, would always let me move.

"No," I whispered back at Blanca. "Sapo has a point."

"The point is Sapo hasn't done his homework."

"I haven't done mine, either," I said.

"Then this book"—she pulled the science text we were sharing toward her side of the desk—"does you no good."

"Look, forget about the pope," Tapia continued. "I don't care about the pope. The pope is not one of my students. The pope has a good job and there are black nuns and Chinese nuns, too, but that doesn't matter. All that matters is you. I care about you. And I played the same games when I was your age. If you haven't done your homework just tell me." Hands shot up.

Tapia sighed loudly. "Edwin, you didn't do your homework?"

"Yeah, I did."

"Well?"

"Well, I did it, I just didn't bring it." The class laughed and Tapia looked at his roll book.

"All right, Edwin, you live on 102nd and Third. That's three blocks from here. You better get your homework at lunchtime or you'd better have it done by then." Edwin nodded his head.

"Sapo, your homework?"

"I didn't do it."

"Why didn't you do it?"

"Because Mr. Blessington told me I was going to end up in jail, so why waste my time doing homework?" We all laughed.

"Sapo, don't you want to prove Blessington wrong?"

"Nah, I'd rather not do my homework."

Tapia got upset. He threw down the roll book and began to yell at us. "I don't care what Blessington's been telling you! If you are here it is because you want to be, right? Otherwise don't even come to school, just stay on the street. You can make more money selling pot on the stairwells than coming to my classroom, but if you come—and I want you to come, I like having you here—all I ask is that you make an effort! That's all I ask. Don't give me this nonsense about what Mr. Blessington is telling you. You guys are smart enough to know that it's up to you to become what you want to be. So why even listen to him? I've heard what he says. It's all nonsense." Tapia pointed at one of the girls. "Rita Moreno, she was once like you, is Rita Moreno hooking?" Tapia then pointed at one of the guys. "Reggie Jackson, he was once as young as you, he's half Puerto Rican, is Reggie in jail? They worked hard. That's what you have to do. Just do your work and don't pay attention to Blessington."

So we all quieted down and did our work, even Sapo, although he copied off me. Sapo always copied me but it was no big deal. The next period was English and we hated it because it was Blessington. I was in no mood for Robert Frost, that white-assed crusty old man from some cow state. But I couldn't say that to Blessington. Instead, as politely as I could, I asked, "Mr. Blessington, why do we always do Robert Frost, why can't we do someone else?"

"Because Robert Frost," he said, slowly shaking his head in disbelief as if I was asking something real stupid, "is a major American poet."

"Well, I heard that Julia de Burgos was a poet; why don't we do some of her poems?" I said, and the class jumped in with me.

"That's right," Lucy, Blanca's Pentecostal friend whom we used to call Chewbacca, chimed in, "why did they name the school after her? She must have been important."

"Yeah, they didn't name the school Robert Frost Junior High, why we always reading him?" someone else asked. Truth was, I was happy we were killing time. I wanted those forty-five minutes in his class to fly. I wanted to keep this discussion going for as long as possible.

"If any of you have noticed since September," Blessington pointed out, "this is English class, not Spanish. Julia-day-Burgos"—he pronounced her name with a thick accent—"wrote only in Spanish."

"But maybe she wrote in English too. I write in Spanish and in English sometimes," Blanca said to him. Every time Blanca spoke Blessington would leer. It was one of those cartoon monster smiles, where the monster rubs his hands as he thinks of something dastardly.

"Listen, you people"—he always called us you people—"Julia-day-Burgos is so obscure it would be hard to find a single poem of hers. In any language." I turned to Blanca and, whispering,, asked what *obscure* meant. Sapo was quietly drawing all this time. He drew terribly, but it never stopped him. He mostly did it because he was bored. But I knew he was listening and could jump in any minute.

"But if she is so unknown," I said confidently, emphasizing the word Blanca had provided to let Blessington know that I knew what *obscure* meant, "then I agree with Lucy, why did they name an entire school after her? Why not after someone famous?"

"Finally, a good question," Blessington said, adjusting his tie and buttoning up his blazer. I'll tell you why: because the people in this district are simpletons, that's why. District Four has no idea what it's doing. The name they chose for this school was probably the worst name they could choose. Why, we teachers didn't even know who she was when they renamed this place."

"Mr. Tapia did," Sapo piped up, leaving his drawing for a minute. We all knew what Blessington was saying was that none of the white teachers knew who she was, and they were the only teachers that mattered.

"Oh, him," Blessington said in a tired voice. "Him again. Well, I heard he's a good science teacher," he said with a smirk, "but we're in English now. You people need to get on with today's work." And it was all right with me because we had chopped off at least fifteen minutes of the period. Blessington then went to the board and wrote, "Analogies Between Frost's Poems and New York City." I turned around and asked Blanca what *analogies* meant. She told me. I laughed.

"What similarities?" I called out. Blessington was upset now.

"End of discussion," he said. "Get out your homework." Blessington walked over to Sapo's desk.

"Enrique, where's your homework?" Blessington asked.

"I'm going to jail, so why bother, right?" Sapo kept drawing. "Yo'r the smart guy here, right, can't you figure that out yo'self?" The class went "Oooooh," which Blessington took as a challenge.

"You'll be lucky to even make jail," he said to Sapo.

"Why you snapping at me? I said you were right."

"I know I'm right. I'm doing all you people a favor. I say these things to you so you can maybe prove me wrong. Now, it's sad to say, but I've yet to see one of my Puerto Rican students, just one, prove me wrong. And I know it's not going to be Sapo here." Blessington then leaned over and took Sapo's drawing from him and crumpled it in his hands. Sapo got so mad, he shot straight up from his seat and thrust himself at Blessington so they were face to face.

"Thass right, I won't prove you wrong b'cause I'm going to jail for jamming your wife." The class was silent because that wasn't a snap any longer but an insult. They stared each other down for a second or two before Sapo turned around and headed for the door. "Where do you think you're going?" Blessington yelled, and went after Sapo, grabbing him by the shoulder.

"Don't touch me, man!" Sapo yelled, but Blessington didn't listen. I got up from my seat and went over to Sapo.

"Yo, take a chill pill," I said to Sapo. Blessington yelled at me, "I can handle this. Sit back down!" He didn't let go of Sapo. Sapo started to pull himself away and that's when Blessington made the mistake of putting Sapo in a headlock.

"Yo, you choking him!" I yelled, but Blessington kept at it, all the while cursing at Sapo. Blanca and her friend Lucy started to run out of the room to get the teacher next door. Blessington released Sapo and went after Blanca. And that's when Sapo jumped him from behind. Sapo crawled on Blessington as if Blessington were going to give him a piggyback ride. Before Blessington could shake Sapo free, Sapo dug his teeth into the base of the teacher's neck. Blessington screamed; the blood spurted out, running down his back and staining his white shirt collar crimson. Sapo scrambled off Blessington's back as Blessington fell to his knees, pressing the wound with his hands. Then Sapo came around and grabbed Blessington's face in his hands and pulled it toward his own. Sapo spat out a chunk of Blessington's flesh, bouncing it off Blessington's left cheekbone. Covered in blood and saliva, Blessington's eyes were frozen in disbelief. He wasn't screaming. He was in shock. It was only when he saw a piece of his own flesh on the floor that he registered what had happened, and passed out.

Standing in front of the classroom Sapo smiled as only Sapo could; he slowly turned to the class, showing us his shining red teeth. He then calmly walked out of the room. Everyone was stunned. Blanca was the first one to shake herself and ran out of the room. "Help us, help us, Blessington's dying!" she kept yelling down the hall. A minute later the school nurse arrived. When she saw all that blood on the floor she took off her smock and put pressure on Blessington's neck. Meanwhile I went looking for Sapo. He had stopped by the bathroom to rinse his mouth and when he saw me he laughed.

"The nigga had that shit coming." He spat water.

"Sapo, bro, what you gonna do?"

"I could give two fucks," he said. "I never felt better. It's as if I let some fucken courier pigeon go free." At that minute Tapia walked into the bathroom, his face red with fury. It was the same anger he would show us when we let him down by not behaving, by not doing work or getting in trouble.

"Did he really have you in a headlock?" Tapia asked Sapo.

"Yeah, I saw it all, Ta—"

"Shut up! I'm asking Sapo!" I quieted down and backed away. Sapo nodded and Tapia paced the bathroom. He sighed loudly. He stopped in front of Sapo and placed both arms on top of Sapo's shoulders.

"Look at me," Tapia said. "Don't say that he had you in a headlock—"

I jumped in. "But he did, Tapia—"

"Shut up, Chino! *Coño*, just shut up!" This time I did for good. Tapia breathed hard. His eyes were watery. "Sapo, look at me. If you say he had you in a headlock, when he recovers he will deny it. And it won't matter which of your friends backs you up, they will believe Blessington. Now, you listen to me and you listen good because I don't want you to go to Juvie. The police are on their way. When they ask you why you bit Blessington, you tell them you heard voices. You got that?" Sapo nodded. "You tell them the voices said to bite Blessington. You don't say Blessington said all this bullshit to you or that he had you in a headlock, you just say you heard voices. You got that?" Sapo understood and a slow smirk began to form on his big lips as he nodded. When he had completely registered what Tapia had told him, that smirk became a full-blown smile.

That whole year Sapo saw a shrink and thus avoided juvenile detention. He must have lied, and I bet for a while he loved the opportunity to have an audience for those stories he was so good at making up. It was like getting away with biting Blessington's neck all over again. But then he got tired of it, started blowing off sessions, and ultimately he dropped out of school and moved out on his own. That year something happened to Sapo. He had always been Sapo but that year, after biting Blessington, he started turning into someone who wasn't afraid to die. It was the beginning of the adult Sapo. His was the sneaker you wouldn't want to step on because "sorry" wouldn't cut it. He became that person you wouldn't want to cut off in traffic because he'd pull a knife and slice you. He became that person you wanted on your side so you could unleash him on your enemies. Like the rest of us, Sapo was still a kid, but he was already turning into something else. He had reached that point in existence where he wasn't afraid to hurt anyone who threatened his only source of meaning, his love for himself.

CRITICAL THINKING QUESTIONS

1. In your high school experience, did you encounter a Mr. Blessington or a Mr. Tapia? What arguments did they offer their students? What arguments do the two teachers in the story offer?

2. Do you recall young people who underwent major changes? Did the forces that prompted those changes come from within or without?

WRITING TOPIC

There is much discussion of violence in our nations' high schools today. When a shooting occurs, often it is done by a student who feels like an outsider, one who does not feel integrated into the high school community. What factors contribute to such an individual who is capable of violence? Based on what you saw as a high school student, what conditions do you think push some students to the fringe? Argue for an approach high schools might take to reduce the anger within such individuals.

Kurt Vonnegut, Jr.

Harrison Bergeron

The year was 2081, and everybody was finally equal. They weren't only equal before God and the law. They were equal every which way. Nobody was smarter than anybody else. Nobody was better looking than anybody else. Nobody was stronger or quicker than anybody else. All this equality was due to the 211th, 212th, and 213th Amendments to the Constitution, and to the unceasing vigilance of agents of the United States Handicapper General.

Some things about living still weren't quite right, though. April, for instance, still drove people crazy by not being springtime. And it was in that clammy month that the H-G men took George and Hazel Bergeron's fourteen-year-old son, Harrison, away.

It was tragic, all right, but George and Hazel couldn't think about it very hard. Hazel had a perfectly average intelligence, which meant she couldn't think about anything except in short bursts. And George, while his intelligence was way above normal, had a little mental handicap radio in his ear. He was required by law to wear it at all times. It was tuned to a government transmitter. Every twenty seconds or so, the transmitter would send out some sharp noise to keep people like George from taking unfair advantage of their brains.

George and Hazel were watching television. There were tears on Hazel's cheeks, but she'd forgotten for the moment what they were about.

On the television screen were ballerinas.

A buzzer sounded in George's head. His thoughts fled in panic, like bandits from a burglar alarm.

"That was a real pretty dance, that dance they just did," said Hazel.

"Huh?" said George.

"That dance—it was nice," said Hazel.

"Yup," said George. He tried to think a little about the ballerinas. They weren't really very good—no better than anybody else would have been, anyway. They were burdened with sashweights and bags of birdshot, and their faces were masked, so that no one, seeing a free and graceful gesture or a pretty face, would feel like something the cat drug in. George was toying with the vague notion that maybe dancers shouldn't be handicapped. But he didn't get very far with it before another noise in his ear radio scattered his thoughts.

George winced. So did two out of the eight ballerinas.

Hazel saw him wince. Having no mental handicap herself, she had to ask George what the latest sound had been.

"Sounded like somebody hitting a milk bottle with a ball peen hammer," said George.

"I'd think it would be real interesting, hearing all the different sounds," said Hazel, a little envious. "All the things they think up."

"Um," said George.

"Only, if I was Handicapper General, you know what I would do?" said Hazel. Hazel, as a matter of fact, bore a strong resemblance to the Handicapper General, a woman named Diana Moon Glampers. "If I was Diana Moon Glampers," said Hazel, "I'd have chimes on Sunday—just chimes. Kind of in honor of religion."

"I could think, if it was just chimes," said George.

"Well—maybe make 'em real loud," said Hazel. "I think I'd make a good Handicapper General."

"Good as anybody else," said George.

"Who knows better'n I do what normal is?" said Hazel.

"Right," said George. He began to think glimmeringly about his abnormal son who was now in jail, about Harrison, but a twenty-one-gun salute in his head stopped that.

"Boy!" said Hazel, "that was a doozy, wasn't it?"

It was such a doozy that George was white and trembling, and tears stood on the rims of his red eyes. Two of the eight ballerinas had collapsed to the studio floor, were holding their temples.

"All of a sudden you look so tired," said Hazel. "Why don't you stretch out on the sofa, so's you can rest your handicap bag on the pillows, honeybunch." She was referring to the forty-seven pounds of birdshot in a canvas bag, which was padlocked around George's neck. "Go on and rest the bag for a little while," she said. "I don't care if you're not equal to me for a while."

George weighed the bag with his hands. "I don't mind it," he said. "I don't notice it any more. It's just a part of me."

"You been so tired lately—kind of wore out," said Hazel. "If there was just some way we could make a little hole in the bottom of the bag, and just take out a few of them lead balls. Just a few."

"Two years in prison and two thousand dollars fine for every ball I took out," said George. "I don't call that a bargain."

"If you could just take a few out when you came home from work," said Hazel. "I mean—you don't compete with anybody around here. You just set around."

"If I tried to get away with it," said George, "then other people'd get away with it—and pretty soon we'd be right back to the dark ages again, with everybody competing against everybody else. You wouldn't like that, would you?"

"I'd hate it," said Hazel.

"There you are," said George. "The minute people start cheating on laws, what do you think happens to society?"

If Hazel hadn't been able to come up with an answer to this question, George couldn't have supplied one. A siren was going off in his head.

"Reckon it'd fall all apart," said Hazel.

"What would?" said George blankly.

"Society," said Hazel uncertainly. "Wasn't that what you just said?"

"Who knows?" said George.

The television program was suddenly interrupted for a news bulletin. It wasn't clear at first as to what the bulletin was about, since the announcer, like all announcers, had a serious speech impediment. For about half a minute, and in a state of high excitement, the announcer tried to say, "Ladies and gentlemen—"

He finally gave up, handed the bulletin to a ballerina to read.

"That's all right—" Hazel said of the announcer, "he tried. That's the big thing. He tried to do the best he could with what God gave him. He should get a nice raise for trying so hard."

"Ladies and gentlemen—" said the ballerina, reading the bulletin. She must have been extraordinarily beautiful, because the mask she wore was hideous. And it was easy to see that she was the strongest and most graceful of all the dancers, for her handicap bags were as big as those worn by two-hundred-pound men.

And she had to apologize at once for her voice, which was a very unfair voice for a woman to use. Her voice was a warm, luminous, timeless melody. "Excuse me—" she said, and she began again, making her voice absolutely uncompetitive.

"Harrison Bergeron, age fourteen," she said in grackle squawk, "has just escaped from jail, where he was held on suspicion of plotting to overthrow the government. He is a genius and an athlete, is under-handicapped, and should be regarded as extremely dangerous."

A police photograph of Harrison Bergeron was flashed on the screen upside down, then sideways, upside down again, then right side up. The picture showed the full length of Harrison against a background calibrated in feet and inches. He was exactly seven feet tall.

The rest of Harrison's appearance was Halloween and hardware. Nobody had ever borne heavier handicaps. He had outgrown hindrances faster than the H-G men could think them up. Instead of a little ear radio for a mental handicap, he wore a tremendous pair of earphones, and spectacles with thick wavy lenses. The spectacles were intended to make him not only half blind, but to give him whanging headaches besides.

Scrap metal was hung all over him. Ordinarily, there was a certain symmetry, a military neatness to the handicaps issued to strong people, but Harrison looked like a walking junkyard. In the race of life, Harrison carried three hundred pounds.

And to offset his good looks, the H-G men required that he wear at all times a red rubber ball for a nose, keep his eyebrows shaved off, and cover his even white teeth with black caps at snaggle-tooth random.

"If you see this boy," said the ballerina, "do not—I repeat, do not—try to reason with him."

There was the shriek of a door being torn from its hinges.

Screams and barking cries of consternation came from the television set. The photograph of Harrison Bergeron on the screen jumped again and again, as though dancing to the tune of an earthquake.

George Bergeron correctly identified the earthquake, and well he might have—for many was the time his own home had danced to the same crashing tune. "My God—" said George, "that must be Harrison!"

The realization was blasted from his mind instantly by the sound of an automobile collision in his head.

When George could open his eyes again, the photograph of Harrison was gone. A living, breathing Harrison filled the screen.

Clanking, clownish, and huge, Harrison stood in the center of the studio. The knob of the uprooted studio door was still in his hand. Ballerinas, technicians, musicians, and announcers cowered on their knees before him, expecting to die.

"I am the Emperor!" cried Harrison. "Do you hear? I am the Emperor! Everybody must do what I say at once!" He stamped his foot and the studio shook.

"Even as I stand here—" he bellowed, "crippled, hobbled, sickened—I am a greater ruler than any man who ever lived! Now watch me become what I *can* become!"

Harrison tore the straps of his handicap harness like wet tissue paper, tore straps guaranteed to support five thousand pounds.

Harrison's scrap-iron handicaps crashed to the floor.

Harrison thrust his thumbs under the bar of the padlock that secured his head harness. The bar snapped like celery. Harrison smashed his headphones and spectacles against the wall.

He flung away his rubber-ball nose, revealed a man that would have awed Thor, the god of thunder.

"I shall now select my Empress!" he said, looking down on the cowering people. "Let the first woman who dares rise to her feet claim her mate and her throne!"

A moment passed, and then a ballerina arose, swaying like a willow.

Harrison plucked the mental handicap from her ear, snapped off her physical handicaps with marvelous delicacy. Last of all, he removed her mask.

She was blindingly beautiful.

"Now—" said Harrison, taking her hand, "shall we show the people the meaning of the word dance? Music!" he commanded.

The musicians scrambled back into their chairs, and Harrison stripped them of their handicaps, too. "Play your best," he told them, "and I'll make you barons and dukes and earls."

The music began. It was normal at first—cheap, silly, false. But Harrison snatched two musicians from their chairs, waved them like batons as he sang the music as he wanted it played. He slammed them back into their chairs.

The music began again and was much improved.

Harrison and his Empress merely listened to the music for a while—listened gravely, as though synchronizing their heartbeats with it.

They shifted their weights to their toes.

Harrison placed his big hands on the girl's tiny waist, letting her sense the weightlessness that would soon be hers.

And then, in an explosion of joy and grace, into the air they sprang!

Not only were the laws of the land abandoned, but the law of gravity and the laws of motion as well.

They reeled, whirled, swiveled, flounced, capered, gamboled, and spun.

They leaped like deer on the moon.

The studio ceiling was thirty feet high, but each leap brought the dancers nearer to it.

It became their obvious intention to kiss the ceiling.

They kissed it.

And then, neutralizing gravity with love and pure will, they remained suspended in air inches below the ceiling, and they kissed each other for a long, long time.

It was then that Diana Moon Glampers, the Handicapper General, came into the studio with a double-barreled ten-gauge shotgun. She fired twice, and the Emperor and the Empress were dead before they hit the floor.

Diana Moon Glampers loaded the gun again. She aimed it at the musicians and told them they had ten seconds to get their handicaps back on.

It was then that the Bergerons' television tube burned out.

Hazel turned to comment about the blackout to George. But George had gone out into the kitchen for a can of beer.

George came back in with the beer, paused while a handicap signal shook him up. And then he sat down again. "You been crying?" he said to Hazel.

"Yup," she said.

"What about?" he said.

"I forget," she said. "Something real sad on television."

"What was it?" he said.

"It's all kind of mixed up in my mind," said Hazel.

"Forget sad things," said George.

"I always do," said Hazel.

"That's my girl," said George. He winced. There was the sound of a rivetting gun in his head.

"Gee—I could tell that one was a doozy," said Hazel.

"You can say that again," said George.

"Gee—" said Hazel, "I could tell that one was a doozy."

CRITICAL THINKING QUESTIONS

1. Harrison is the romantic rebel who faces a very pragmatic opponent. While Vonnegut has pushed this situation to extremes, thus creating a cartoon rather than reality, do you find any parallels to Harrison in history?

2. Totalitarian governments have most often used brute force to control their citizens, yet Aldous Huxley in his novel *Brave New World* argues that through technology we will learn to love our oppressors. Do you see any ways in which contemporary individuals or groups are manipulated through technology?

3. What is Vonnegut's *claim* in this story? Rebellion is doomed so accept your place? Equality cannot be forced upon people? Write out your concept of the *claim* in a single sentence.

WRITING TOPIC

When the founders of this country talked about *equality*, surely they did not have in mind the world described in this story. When you use the term *equality* today, what exactly do you mean? Write a definition for this term.

Sherman Alexie

The Reservation Cab Driver

waits outside the Breakaway Bar
in the '65 Malibu with no windshield.

It's a beer a mile. No exceptions.

He picks up Lester FallsApart
who lives in the West End
twelve miles away, good for a half-rack.

When congress raised the minimum wage
the reservation cab driver upped his rates
made it a beer and a cigarette each mile.

HUD evicted him
so he wrapped himself in old blankets
and slept in the front seat of his cab.

When the BIA rescinded his benefits
he added a can of commodities for every mile.

Seymour climbed in the cab
said, this is a hell of a pony.
Ain't no pony, the reservation cab driver
said, it's a car.

During the powwow, he works 24 hours a day
gets paid in quilts, beads, fry bread, firewood.

3 a.m., he picks up Crazy Horse hitchhiking.
Where are you going, asks the reservation cab driver.
Same place you are, Crazy Horse answers
somewhere way up the goddamn road.

CRITICAL THINKING QUESTIONS

1. As you read the poem, you naturally compare this odd situation to the reality most of us accept. Certainly no cab driver in New York City or Los Angeles would work for beer and cigarettes. What does the author wish us to see by creating this contrast?

2. Does the situation described in the poem challenge any assumptions you hold concerning Native Americans?

WRITING TOPIC

A Justice Department report showed that during 1998, there were 110 victims of violent crime for every 1,000 Native Americans, compared with 43 victims per 1,000 blacks, 38 per 1,000 whites, and 22 per 1,000 Asians. Read about the situation on Native American reservations, and write an essay which argues that X is the cause of the disparity indicated by these figures.

Michael Cleary

Burning Dreams on the Sun

LONG BEACH, Calif. (AP)—A truck driver with 45 weather bal-
loons rigged to a lawn chair took a 45 minute ride . . . up to 16,000
feet before he got cold, shot some balloons with a BB gun and crashed
into a power line.

Were there too many turnaround loads,
distance measured by all-night diners,
hours yawning through too much coffee,
kidneys throbbing again at 3 a.m.?
Were there too many nights on your hands
that hung like chains from the wheel,
monotonous, humdrum motion
droning away the sound of your dream?
And did the darkness ever whisper,
it might not work, it might not,
nearly grounding you in mortal shame,
too foolish ever to dream again?

Icarus, too, must have felt like you,
restless with impudent wonder.
No labyrinth could hold him;
he flew on wings of feathers and wax
until he burned his dreams on the sun.
But no matter. For a time,
you dared to leave the darkful land,
rising high in wacky flight
like an uncouth god, purified by light.

CRITICAL THINKING QUESTIONS

1. What stereotypes are associated with truck drivers?
2. How does Cleary's poem refute those stereotypes?
3. What is the poet's implied *claim of value* about Icarus's and the truck driver's flights? Are you convinced?

T. S. Eliot

The Love Song of J. Alfred Prufrock

S o'io credesse che mia risposta fosse
A persona che mai tornasse al mondo,
Questa fiamma staria senza piu scosse.
Ma perciocche giammai di questo fondo
Non torno vivo alcun, s 'i'odo il vero,
Senza tema d'infamia ti rispondo.

Let us go then, you and I,
When the evening is spread out against the sky
Like a patient etherised upon a table;
Let us go, through certain half-deserted streets,
The muttering retreats
Of restless nights in one-night cheap hotels
And sawdust restaurants with oyster-shells:
Streets that follow like a tedious argument
Of insidious intent
To lead you to an overwhelming question . . .
Oh, do not ask, "What is it?"
Let us go and make our visit.

In the room the women come and go
Talking of Michelangelo.

The yellow fog that rubs its back upon the window-panes,
The yellow smoke that rubs its muzzle on the window-panes
Licked its tongue into the corners of the evening,
Lingered upon the pools that stand in drains,
Let fall upon its back the soot that falls from chimneys,
Slipped by the terrace, made a sudden leap,
And seeing that it was a soft October night,
Curled once about the house, and fell asleep.

And indeed there will be time
For the yellow smoke that slides along the street,
Rubbing its back upon the window-panes;
There will be time, there will be time

To prepare a face to meet the faces that you meet;
There will be time to murder and create,
And time for all the works and days of hands
That lift and drop a question on your plate;
Time for you and time for me,
And time yet for a hundred indecisions,
And for a hundred visions and revisions,
Before the taking of a toast and tea.

    In the room the women come and go
Talking of Michelangelo.

    And indeed there will be time
To wonder, "Do I dare?" and, "Do I dare?"
Time to turn back and descend the stair,
With a bald spot in the middle of my hair—
[They will say: "How his hair is growing thin!"]
My morning coat, my collar mounting firmly to the chin,
My necktie rich and modest, but asserted by a simple pin—
[They will say: "But how his arms and legs are thin!"]
Do I dare
Disturb the universe?
In a minute there is time
For decisions and revisions which a minute will reverse.

    For I have known them all already, known them all:—
Have known the evenings, mornings, afternoons,
I have measured out my life with coffee spoons;
I know the voices dying with a dying fall
Beneath the music from a farther room.
    So how should I presume?

    And I have known the eyes already, known them all—
The eyes that fix you in a formulated phrase,
And when I am formulated, sprawling on a pin,
When I am pinned and wriggling on the wall,
Then how should I begin
To spit out all the butt-ends of my days and ways?
    And how should I presume?

    And I have known the arms already, known them all—
Arms that are braceleted and white and bare
[But in the lamplight, downed with light brown hair!]

Is it perfume from a dress
That makes me so digress?
Arms that lie along a table, or wrap about a shawl.
    And should I then presume?
    And how should I begin?

      *   *   *

Shall I say, I have gone at dusk through narrow streets
And watched the smoke that rises from the pipes
Of lonely men in shirt-sleeves, leaning out of windows? . . .

    I should have been a pair of ragged claws
Scuttling across the floors of silent seas.

      *   *   *

And the afternoon, the evening, sleeps so peacefully!
Smoothed by long fingers,
Asleep . . . tired . . . or it malingers,
Stretched on the floor, here beside you and me.
Should I, after tea and cakes and ices,
Have the strength to force the moment to its crisis?
But though I have wept and fasted, wept and prayed,
Though I have seen my head [grown slightly bald] brought in upon a platter,
I am no prophet—and here's no great matter;
I have seen the moment of my greatness flicker,
And I have seen the eternal Footman hold my coat, and snicker,
And in short, I was afraid.

    And would it have been worth it, after all,
After the cups, the marmalade, the tea,
Among the porcelain, among some talk of you and me,
Would it have been worth while,
To have bitten off the matter with a smile,
To have squeezed the universe into a ball
To roll it toward some overwhelming question,
To say: "I am Lazarus, come from the dead,
Come back to tell you all, I shall tell you all"—
If one, settling a pillow by her head,
    Should say: "That is not what I meant at all.
    That is not it, at all."

    And would it have been worth it, after all,
Would it have been worth while,
After the sunsets and the dooryards and the sprinkled streets,
After the novels, after the teacups, after the skirts that trail along the floor—

And this, and so much more?—
It is impossible to say just what I mean!
But as if a magic lantern threw the nerves in patterns on a screen:
Would it have been worth while
If one, settling a pillow or throwing off a shawl,
And turning toward the window, should say:
    "That is not it at all,
      That is not what I meant, at all."

           *   *   *

No! I am not Prince Hamlet, nor was meant to be;
Am an attendant lord, one that will do
To swell a progress, start a scene or two,
Advise the prince; no doubt, an easy tool,
Deferential, glad to be of use,
Politic, cautious, and meticulous;
Full of high sentence but a bit obtuse;
At times, indeed, almost ridiculous—
Almost, at times, the Fool.

    I grow old . . . I grow old . . .
I shall wear the bottoms of my trousers rolled.

    Shall I part my hair behind? Do I dare to eat a peach?
I shall wear white flannel trousers, and walk upon the beach.
I have heard the mermaids singing, each to each.

    I do not think that they will sing to me.

    I have seen them riding seaward on the waves
Combing the white hair of the waves blown back
When the wind blows the water white and black.

    We have lingered in the chambers of the sea
By sea-girls wreathed with seaweed red and brown
Till human voices wake us, and we drown.

CRITICAL THINKING QUESTIONS

1. In presenting the reader with J. Alfred Prufrock, Eliot is also presenting an argument about an individual's sense of self in modern society. Articulate a claim for this argument.

2. What specific evidence is offered in the poem to support the claim you wrote in question 1?

WRITING TOPIC

Does the claim you articulated apply exclusively to Prufrock, or would you extend it to apply generally to persons today? Write your own argument that either limits or extends the poem's claim; use evidence from the poem and your own experience to support your claim.

Judy Grahn

Ella, in a Square Apron, along Highway 80

She's a copperheaded waitress,
tired and sharp-worded, she hides
her bad brown tooth behind a wicked
smile, and flicks her ass
out of habit, to fend off the pass
that passes for affection.
She keeps her mind the way men
keep a knife—keen to strip the game
down to her size. She has a thin spine,
swallows her eggs cold, and tells lies.
She slaps a wet rag at the truck drivers
if they should complain. She understands
the necessity for pain, turns away
the smaller tips, out of pride, and
keeps a flask under the counter. Once,
she shot a lover who misused her child.
Before she got out of jail, the courts had pounced
and given the child away. Like some isolated lake,
her flat blue eyes take care of their own stark
bottoms. Her hands are nervous, curled, ready to scrape.
The common woman is as common
as a rattlesnake.

CRITICAL THINKING QUESTIONS

1. Compare and contrast your response to the snake imagery in the poem's opening and closing lines.
2. What is the speaker's *claim of value* about Ella as "the common woman"?
3. On which rhetorical appeal is this poem's argument based? Is this an effective persuasive strategy?

Langston Hughes

Passing

On sunny summer Sunday afternoons in Harlem
when the air is one interminable ball game
and grandma cannot get her gospel hymns
from the Saints of God in Christ
on account of the Dodgers on the radio,
on sunny Sunday afternoons
when the kids look all new
and far too clean to stay that way,
and Harlem has its
washed-and-ironed-and-cleaned-best out,
the ones who've crossed the line
to live downtown
miss you,
Harlem of the bitter dream,
since their dream has
come true.

CRITICAL THINKING QUESTIONS

1. Who are these people who have "crossed the line/to live downtown"?
2. If the community looks so good on "sunny Sunday afternoons," why does Hughes call it "Harlem of the bitter dream"?

Etheridge Knight

Hard Rock Returns to Prison from the Hospital for the Criminal Insane

Hard Rock was "known not to take no shit
From nobody," and he had the scars to prove it:
Split purple lips, lumped ears, welts above
His yellow eyes, and one long scar that cut
Across his temple and plowed through a thick
Canopy of kinky hair.

The WORD was that Hard Rock wasn't a mean nigger
Anymore, that the doctors had bored a hole in his head,
Cut out part of his brain, and shot electricity
Through the rest. When they brought Hard Rock back,
Handcuffed and chained, he was turned loose,
Like a freshly gelded stallion, to try his new status.
And we all waited and watched, like indians at a corral,
To see if the WORD was true.

As we waited we wrapped ourselves in the cloak
Of his exploits: "Man, the last time, it took eight
Screws to put him in the Hole." "Yeah, remember when he
Smacked the captain with his dinner tray?" "He set
The record for time in the Hole—67 straight days!"
"Ol Hard Rock! man, that's one crazy nigger."
And then the jewel of a myth that Hard Rock had once bit
A screw on the thumb and poisoned him with syphilitic spit.

The testing came, to see if Hard Rock was really tame.
A hillbilly called him a black son of a bitch
And didn't lose his teeth, a screw who knew Hard Rock
From before shook him down and barked in his face.
And Hard Rock did *nothing*. Just grinned and looked silly,
His eyes empty like knot holes in a fence.

And even after we discovered that it took Hard Rock
Exactly 3 minutes to tell you his first name,
We told ourselves that he had just wised up,
Was being cool; but we could not fool ourselves for long,

And we turned away, our eyes on the ground. Crushed.
He had been our Destroyer, the doer of things
We dreamed of doing but could not bring ourselves to do,
The fears of years, like a biting whip,
Had cut grooves too deeply across our backs.

CRITICAL THINKING QUESTIONS

1. How does the poem's speaker use *pathos* appeal?
2. Describe the speaker and assess his *ethos* appeal.
3. How does this poem affect your attitude toward or feelings about prisoners?

WRITING TOPIC

The hospital procedure which Hard Rock was forced to undergo is no longer allowed; however, solitary time is a form of punishment still used in some prisons for misbehavior. Do some research on high security prisons and the treatment of individuals for infractions of prison rules, particularly, the use of solitary confinement as punishment. Based on your research, write a *claim of policy* argument on the use of solitary confinement (or other punishments) as a correction method for individual prisoners.

Claude McKay

Outcast

For the dim regions whence my fathers came
My spirit, bondaged by the body, longs.
Words felt, but never heard, my lips would frame;
My soul would sing forgotten jungle songs.
I would go back to darkness and to peace,
But the great western world holds me in fee,
And I may never hope for full release
While to its alien gods I bend my knee.
Something in me is lost, forever lost,
Some vital thing has gone out of my heart,
And I must walk the way of life a ghost
Among the sons of earth, a thing apart.

For I was born, far from my native clime,
Under the white man's menace, out of time.

CRITICAL THINKING QUESTIONS

1. Use the rhetorical triangle to analyze and evaluate this poem as an argument.
   a. How does the speaker create *ethos* appeal?
   b. How does the speaker use *logos* appeal?
   c. How does the speaker use *pathos* appeal?
2. In your view, is one appeal more persuasive?

WRITING TOPIC

Knight's character, Hard Rock, literally fights to preserve his individuality, but he loses in the end. His fellow prisoners have already lost that fight. Look at McKay's dancer and Grahn's waitress. In what ways are these two women maintaining their individuality within their environment? Are they winning the battle? Write about the pressures your environment exerts on your sense of individuality.

Dwight Okita

In Response to Executive Order 9066

All Americans of Japanese Descent Must Report to Relocation Centers

Dear Sirs:
Of course I'll come. I've packed my galoshes
and three packets of tomato seeds. Janet calls them
"love apples." My father says where we're going
they won't grow.

I am a fourteen-year-old girl with bad spelling
and a messy room. If it helps any, I will tell you
I have always felt funny using chopsticks
and my favorite food is hot dogs.
My best friend is a white girl named Denise—
we look at boys together. She sat in front of me
all through grade school because of our names:
O'Connor, Ozawa. I know the back of Denise's head very well.
I tell her she's going bald. She tells me I copy on tests.
We're best friends.

I saw Denise today in Geography class.
She was sitting on the other side of the room.
"You're trying to start a war," she said, "giving secrets away
to the Enemy, Why can't you keep your big mouth shut?"
I didn't know what to say.
I gave her a packet of tomato seeds
and asked her to plant them for me, told her
when the first tomato ripens
to miss me

CRITICAL THINKING QUESTIONS

1. Why does the author choose a fourteen-year-old girl to write this letter? What does this persona or voice offer the reader?

2. Would the letter be less convincing if it were written by the girl's father?

3. What evidence might the father select to prove that this order is unfair to inno-cent people?

WRITING TOPIC

The United States moved Americans of Japanese descent into camps during World War II. A few years ago, the government paid a settlement to these people for their mistreatment. Write an argument defending or refuting such payments.

Edwin Arlington Robinson

Richard Cory

Whenever Richard Cory went down town,
We people on the pavement looked at him:
He was a gentleman from sole to crown,
Clean favored, and imperially slim.

And he was always quietly arrayed,
And he was always human when he talked;
But still he fluttered pulses when he said;
"Good-morning," and he glittered when he walked.

And he was rich—yes, richer than a king—
And admirably schooled in every grace:
In fine, we thought that he was everything
To make us wish that we were in his place.
So on we worked, and waited for the light,
And went without the meat, and cursed the bread;
And Richard Cory, one calm summer night,
Went home, and put a bullet through his head.

CRITICAL THINKING QUESTIONS

1. What assumptions do the townspeople make about Richard Cory? On what evidence are those assumptions based?

2. The poem urges the reader to accept another generalization—money does not make people happy. Does your experience cause you to support or reject that generalization?

Muriel Rukeyser

The Lost Romans

Where are they, not those young men, not those young women
Who walked among the bullet-headed Romans with their roads, their
    symmetry, their iron rule—
We know the dust and bones they are gone to, those young Romans
Who stood against the bitter imperial, their young green life with its
    poems—
Where are the poems made music against the purple
Setting their own purple up for a living sign,
Bright fire of some forgotten future against empire,
Their poems in the beautiful Roman tongue
Sex-songs, love-poems, freedom-songs?
Not only the young, but the old and in chains,
The slaves in their singing, the fierce northern gentle blond rhythms,
The Judean cantillations, lullabies of Carthage,
Gaul with her cries, all the young Roman rebels,
Where are their songs? Who will unlock them,
Who will find them for us, in some undiscovered painted cave
For we need you, sisters, far brothers, poems of our lost Rome.

CRITICAL THINKING QUESTIONS

1. Reading this poem as an argument that is a "call to action," whom is the poet
   addressing and what action is she advocating?

2. On which rhetorical appeal does the poet's argument rely? Provide some examples and evaluate their persuasiveness.

WRITING TOPIC

Does Rukeyser's argument speak directly to you as an individual? Why or why
not?

Cathy Song

Lost Sister

1
In China,
even the peasants
named their first daughters
Jade—
the stone that in the far fields
could moisten the dry season,
could make men move mountains
for the healing green of the inner hills
glistening like slices of winter melon.

And the daughters were grateful:
They never left home.
To move freely was a luxury
stolen from them at birth.
Instead, they gathered patience;
learning to walk in shoes
the size of teacups,
without breaking—
the arc of their movements
as dormant as the rooted willow,
as redundant as the farmyard hens.
But they traveled far
in surviving,
learning to stretch the family rice,
to quiet the demons,
the noisy stomachs.

2
There is a sister
across the ocean,
who relinquished her name,
diluting jade green
with the blue of the Pacific.
Rising with a tide of locusts,
she swarmed with others

to inundate another shore.
In America,
there are many roads
and women can stride along with men.

But in another wilderness,
the possibilities,
the loneliness,
can strangulate like jungle vines
The meager provisions and sentiments
of once belonging—
fermented roots, Mah-Jong tiles and firecrackers—set but
a flimsy household
in a forest of nightless cities.
A giant snake rattles above,
spewing black clouds into your kitchen.
Dough-faced landlords
slip in and out of your keyholes,
making claims you don't understand,
tapping into your communication systems
of laundry lines and restaurant chains.

You find you need China:
your one fragile identification,
a jade link
handcuffed to your wrist.
You remember your mother
who walked for centuries,
footless—
and like her,
you have left no footprints,
but only because
there is an ocean in between,
the unremitting space of your rebellion.

CRITICAL THINKING QUESTIONS

1. What *value assumptions* about the individual and freedom does this poem challenge?

2. The poet implies that the sister should have stayed in China. Are you convinced? Why or why not?

Alma Luz Villanueva

Crazy Courage

To Michael B.

Why do I think of Michael . . .
He came to my fiction class
as a man (dressed in men's
clothes); then he came

to my poetry class
as a woman (dressed in women's
clothes; but he was still
a man under the clothes).
Was I moved in the face of
such courage (man/woman
woman/man) . . .
Was I moved by the gentleness

of his masculinity; the strength
of his femininity . . .
His presence at the class poetry
reading, dressed in a miniskirt,

high boots, bright purple tights,
a scooped-neck blouse, carrying
a single, living, red rose, in a
vase, to the podium (the visitors,

not from the class, shocked—
the young, seen-it-all MTV crowd—
into silence as he's introduced,
"Michael . . . ") And what it was, I think,

was his perfect dignity, the offering
of his living, red rose to the perceptive,
to the blind, to the amused, to the impressed,
to those who would kill him, and

to those who would love him.
And of course I remember the surprise
of his foamy breasts as we hugged
goodbye, his face blossomed

open, set apart, the pain of it,
the joy of it (the crazy courage
to be whole, as a rose is
whole, as a child is

whole before they're
punished for including
everything in their
innocence.)

CRITICAL THINKING QUESTIONS

1. In judging Michael, what is the speaker's *claim of value?* On what evidence is this claim based? Are you convinced?

2. What values underlie our attitudes about nonconformist or unconventional behavior? How do these value assumptions inform our judgments about those individuals who exhibit nonconformist behavior?

WRITING TOPIC

In the United States, we often say we value expressions of individuality, yet people who run counter to prevailing cultural norms sometimes face some degree of discrimination. Using at least two specific examples, argue that this discrimination is either justified or unjustified.

Sophocles

Antigone

An English Version by Dudley Fitts
and Robert Fitzgerald

Characters

ANTIGONE ⎱ *daughters of Oedipus*
ISMENE ⎰

EURYDICE, *wife of Creon*

CREON, *King of Thebes*

HAIMON, *son of Creon*

TEIRESIAS, *a blind seer*

A SENTRY

A MESSENGER

CHORUS

Scene: Before the palace of CREON, *King of Thebes. A central double door, and two lateral doors. A platform extends the length of the façade, and from this platform three steps lead down into the "orchestra" or chorus-ground.*

Time: Dawn of the day after the repulse of the Argive army from the assault on Thebes.

PROLOGUE

ANTIGONE *and* ISMENE *enter from the central door of the Palace.*

ANTIGONE: Ismene, dear sister,
  You would think that we had already suffered enough
  For the curse on Oedipus[1]
  I cannot imagine any grief
  That you and I have not gone through. And now—
  Have they told you of the new decree of our King Creon?

---

[1]Oedipus: Oedipus, father of Antigone, Ismene, Polyneices, and Eteocles, was King of Thebes. Unknowingly, he killed his father and married his mother. Upon learning what he had done, he put out his eyes and went into exile. Heirs to the throne, Polyneices and Eteocles eventually quarreled. Eteocles drove out Polyneices, but Polyneices returned to attack Thebes, and both brothers died in battle. Creon became king and ordered that Polyneices's body be left unburied.

ISMENE: I have heard nothing: I know
   That two sisters lost two brothers, a double death
   In a single hour; and I know that the Argive army
   Fled in the night; but beyond this, nothing.
ANTIGONE: I thought so. And that is why I wanted you
   To come out here with me. There is something we must do.
ISMENE: Why do you speak so strangely?
ANTIGONE: Listen, Ismene:
   Creon buried our brother Eteocles
   With military honors, gave him a soldier's funeral,
   And it was right that he should; but Polyneices,
   Who fought as bravely and died as miserably,—
   They say that Creon has sworn
   No one shall bury him, no one mourn for him,
   But his body must lie in the fields, a sweet treasure
   For carrion birds to find as they search for food.
   That is what they say, and our good Creon is coming here
   To announce it publicly; and the penalty—
   Stoning to death in the public square!
                                                   There it is,
   And now you can prove what you are:
   A true sister, or a traitor to your family.
ISMENE: Antigone, you are mad! What could I possibly do?
ANTIGONE: You must decide whether you will help me or not.
ISMENE: I do not understand you. Help you in what?
ANTIGONE: Ismene, I am going to bury him. Will you come?
ISMENE: Bury him! You have just said the new law forbids it.
ANTIGONE: He is my brother. And he is your brother, too.
ISMENE: But think of the danger! Think what Creon will do!
ANTIGONE: Creon is not strong enough to stand in my way.
ISMENE: Ah sister!
   Oedipus died, everyone hating him
   For what his own search brought to light, his eyes
   Ripped out by his own hand; and Iocaste died,
   His mother and wife at once: she twisted the cords
   That strangled her life; and our two brothers died,
   Each killed by the other's sword. And we are left:
   But oh, Antigone,
   Think how much more terrible than these
   Our own death would be if we should go against Creon
   And do what he has forbidden! We are only women,
   We cannot fight with men, Antigone!
   The law is strong, we must give in to the law
   In this thing, and in worse. I beg the Dead

To forgive me, but I am helpless: I must yield
To those in authority. And I think it is dangerous business
To be always meddling.
ANTIGONE: If that is what you think,
I should not want you, even if you asked to come.
You have made your choice, you can be what you want to be
But I will bury him; and if I must die,
I say that this crime is holy: I shall lie down
With him in death, and I shall be as dear
To him as he to me.
                              It is the dead,
Not the living, who make the longest demands:
We die for ever . . .
                              You may do as you like,
Since apparently the laws of the gods mean nothing to you.
ISMENE: They mean a great deal to me; but I have no strength
To break laws that were made for the public good.
ANTIGONE: That must be your excuse, I suppose. But as for me,
I will bury the brother I love.
ISMENE: Antigone,
I am so afraid for you!
ANTIGONE: You need not be:
You have yourself to consider, after all.
ISMENE: But no one must hear of this, you must tell no one!
I will keep it a secret, I promise!
ANTIGONE: Oh tell it! Tell everyone!
Think how they'll hate you when it all comes out
If they learn that you knew about it all the time!
ISMENE: So fiery! You should be cold with fear.
ANTIGONE: Perhaps. But I am doing only what I must.
ISMENE: But can you do it? I say that you cannot.
ANTIGONE: Very well: when my strength gives out, I shall do no more.
ISMENE: Impossible things should not be tried at all.
ANTIGONE: Go away, Ismene:
I shall be hating you soon, and the dead will too,
For your words are hateful. Leave me my foolish plan:
I am not afraid of the danger; if it means death,
It will not be the worst of deaths—death without
honor.
ISMENE: Go then, if you feel that you must.
You are unwise,
But a loyal friend indeed to those who love you.

Exit into the Palace. ANTIGONE *goes off, left. Enter the* CHORUS.

PARODOS[2]

Strophe[3] 1

CHORUS: Now the long blade of the sun, lying
  Level east to west, touches with glory
  Thebes of the Seven Gates. Open, unlidded
  Eye of golden day! O marching light
  Across the eddy and rush of Dirce's stream,[4]
  Striking the white shields of the enemy
  Thrown headlong backward from the blaze of morning!
CHORAGOS:[5] Polyneices their commander
  Roused them with windy phrases,
  He the wild eagle screaming
  Insults above our land,
  His wings their shields of snow,
  His crest their marshalled helms.

Antistrophe[6] 1

CHORUS: Against our seven gates in a yawning ring
  The famished spears came onward in the night;
  But before his jaws were sated with our blood,
  Or pinefire took the garland of our towers,
  He was thrown back; and as he turned, great Thebes—
  No tender victim for his noisy power—
  Rose like a dragon behind him, shouting war.
CHORAGOS: For God hates utterly
  The bray of bragging tongues;
  And when he beheld their smiling,
  Their swagger of golden helms,
  The frown of his thunder blasted
  Their first man from our walls.

Strophe 2

CHORUS: We heard his shout of triumph high in the air
  Turn to a scream; far out in a flaming arc
  He fell with his windy torch, and the earth struck him.
  And others storming in fury no less than his
  Found shock of death in the dusty joy of battle.

---

[2]Parodos: Sung by the Chorus upon entering. [3]Strophe: Sung by the chorus as they move from stage right to stage left. [4]Dirce's stream: Near Thebes. [5]Choragos: Leader of the Chorus. [6]Antistrophe: Sung by the chorus as they move from stage left to stage right.

CHORAGOS: Seven captains at seven gates
  Yielded their clanging arms to the god
  That bends the battle-line and breaks it.
  These two only, brothers in blood,
  Face to face in matchless rage,
  Mirroring each the other's death,
  Clashed in long combat.

Antistrophe 2

CHORUS: But now in the beautiful morning of victory
  Let Thebes of the many chariots sing for joy!
  With hearts for dancing we'll take leave of war:
  Our temples shall be sweet with hymns of praise,
  And the long night shall echo with our chorus.

SCENE 1

CHORAGOS: But now at last our new King is coming:
  Creon of Thebes, Menoikeus' son.
  In this auspicious dawn of his reign
  What are the new complexities
  That shifting Fate has woven for him?
  What is his counsel? Why has he summoned
  The old men to hear him?

Enter CREON *from the Palace, center. He addresses the* CHORUS *from the top step.*

CREON: Gentlemen: I have the honor to inform you that our Ship of State, which
  recent storms have threatened to destroy, has come safely to harbor at last, guided
  by the merciful wisdom of Heaven. I have summoned you here this morning because I know that I can depend upon you: your devotion to King Laios was absolute; you never hesitated in your duty to our late ruler Oedipus; and when
  Oedipus died, your loyalty was transferred to his children. Unfortunately, as you
  know, his two sons, the princes Eteocles and Polyneices, have killed each other in
  battle; and I, as the next in blood, have succeeded to the full power of the throne.
    I am aware, of course, that no Ruler can expect complete loyalty from his subjects
  until he has been tested in office. Nevertheless, I say to you at the very outset that I
  have nothing but contempt for the kind of Governor who is afraid, for whatever
  reason, to follow the course that he knows is best for the State; and as for the man
  who sets private friendship above the public welfare,—I have no use for him, either.
  I call God to witness that if I saw my country headed for ruin, I should not be afraid
  to speak out plainly; and I need hardly remind you that I would never have any dealings with an enemy of the people. No one values friendship more highly than I; but

we must remember that friends made at the risk of wrecking our Ship are not real friends at all.

These are my principles, at any rate, and that is why I have made the following decision concerning the sons of Oedipus: Eteocles, who died as a man should die, fighting for his country, is to be buried with full military honors, with all the ceremony that is usual when the greatest heroes die; but his brother Polyneices, who broke his exile to come back with fire and sword against his native city and the shrines of his fathers' gods, whose one idea was to spill the blood of his blood and sell his own people into slavery—Polyneices, I say, is to have no burial: no man is to touch him or say the least prayer for him; he shall lie on the plain, unburied; and the birds and the scavenging dogs can do with him whatever they like.

This is my command, and you can see the wisdom behind it. As long as I am King, no traitor is going to be honored with the loyal man. But whoever shows by word and deed that he is on the side of the State,—he shall have my respect while he is living, and my reverence when he is dead.

CHORAGOS: If that is your will, Creon son of Menoikeus,
  You have the right to enforce it: we are yours.
CREON: That is my will. Take care that you do your part.
CHORAGOS: We are old men: let the younger ones carry it out.
CREON: I do not mean that: the sentries have been appointed.
CHORAGOS: Then what is it that you would have us do?
CREON: You will give no support to whoever breaks this law.
CHORAGOS: Only a crazy man is in love with death!
CREON: And death it is; yet money talks, and the wisest
  Have sometimes been known to count a few coins too many.

Enter SENTRY *from left.*

SENTRY: I'll not say that I'm out of breath from running, King, because every time I stopped to think about what I have to tell you, I felt like going back. And all the time a voice kept saying, "You fool, don't you know you're walking straight into trouble?"; and then another voice: "Yes, but if you let somebody else get the news to Creon first, it will be even worse than that for you!" But good sense won out, at least I hope it was good sense, and here I am with a story that makes no sense at all; but I'll tell it anyhow, because, as they say, what's going to happen's going to happen, and—
CREON: Come to the point. What have you to say?
SENTRY: I did not do it. I did not see who did it. You must not punish me for what someone else has done.
CREON: A comprehensive defense! More effective, perhaps, If I knew its purpose. Come: what is it?
SENTRY: A dreadful thing . . . I don't know how to put it—
CREON: Out with it!
SENTRY: Well, then;

The dead man—

          Polyneices—

Pause. The SENTRY *is overcome, fumbles for words.* CREON *waits impassively.*

                 out there—

                       someone,—

New dust on the slimy flesh!

Pause. No sign from CREON.

Someone has given it burial that way, and
Gone . . .

Long pause. CREON *finally speaks with deadly control:*

CREON: And the man who dared do this?

SENTRY: I swear I

Do not know! You must believe me!

                      Listen:

The ground was dry, not a sign of digging, no,
Not a wheeltrack in the dust, no trace of anyone.
It was when they relieved us this morning: and one of them,
The corporal, pointed to it.

                  There it was,

The strangest—

        Look:

The body, just mounded over with light dust: you see?
Not buried really, but as if they'd covered it
Just enough for the ghost's peace. And no sign
Of dogs or any wild animal that had been there.

And then what a scene there was! Every man of us
Accusing the other: we all proved the other man did it,
We all had proof that we could not have done it.
We were ready to take hot iron in our hands,
Walk through fire, swear by all the gods,
It was not I
I do not know who it was, but it was not I!

CREON's *rage has been mounting steadily, but the* SENTRY *is too intent upon his story to notice it.*

And then, when this came to nothing, someone said
A thing that silenced us and made us stare
Down at the ground: you had to be told the news,
And one of us had to do it! We threw the dice,
And the bad luck fell to me. So here I am,
No happier to be here than you are to have me:
Nobody likes the man who brings bad news.

CHORAGOS: I have been wondering, King: can it be that the gods have done this?
CREON (*Furiously*): Stop!

 Must you doddering wrecks
 Go out of your heads entirely? "The gods!"
 Intolerable!
 The gods favor this corpse? Why? How had he served them?
 Tried to loot their temples, burn their images,
 Yes, and the whole State, and its laws with it!
 Is it your senile opinion that the gods love to honor bad men?
 A pious thought!—

      No, from the very beginning
 There have been those who have whispered together,
 Stiff-necked anarchists, putting their heads together,
 Scheming against me in alleys. These are the men,
 And they have bribed my own guard to do this thing.
 (*Sententiously*) Money!
 There's nothing in the world so demoralizing as money.
 Down go your cities,
 Homes gone, men gone, honest hearts corrupted,
 Crookedness of all kinds, and all for money!
 (*To* SENTRY)   But you—!
 I swear by God and by the throne of God,
 The man who has done this thing shall pay for it!
 Find that man, bring him here to me, or your death
 Will be the least of your problems: I'll string you up
 Alive, and there will be certain ways to make you
 Discover your employer before you die;
 And the process may teach you a lesson you seem to have missed:
 The dearest profit is sometimes all too dear:
 That depends on the source. Do you understand me?
 A fortune won is often misfortune.

SENTRY: King, may I speak?
CREON: Your very voice distresses me.
SENTRY: Are you sure that it is my voice, and not your conscience?
CREON: By God, he wants to analyze now!
SENTRY: It is not what I say, but what has been done, that hurts you.
CREON: You talk too much.
SENTRY: Maybe; but I've done nothing.
CREON: Sold your soul for some silver: that's all you've done.
SENTRY: How dreadful it is when the right judge judges wrong!
CREON: Your figures of speech

 May entertain you now; but unless you bring me the man,
 You will get little profit from them in the end.

Exit CREON *into the Palace.*

SENTRY: "Bring me the man"—!
   I'd like nothing better than bringing him the man!
   But bring him or not, you have seen the last of me here.
   At any rate, I am safe!

Exit SENTRY.

ODE 1

Strophe 1

CHORUS: Numberless are the world's wonders, but none
   More wonderful than man; the stormgray sea
   Yields to his prows, the huge crests bear him high;
   Earth, holy and inexhaustible, is graven
   With shining furrows where his plows have gone
   Year after year, the timeless labor of stallions.

Antistrophe 1

   The lightboned birds and beasts that cling to cover,
   The lithe fish lighting their reaches of dim water,
   All are taken, tamed in the net of his mind;
   The lion on the hill, the wild horse windy-maned,
   Resign to him; and his blunt yoke has broken
   The sultry shoulders of the mountain bull.

Strophe 2

   Words also, and thought as rapid as air,
   He fashions to his good use; statecraft is his,
   And his the skill that deflects the arrows of snow,
   The spears of winter rain: from every wind
   He has made himself secure—from all but one:
   In the late wind of death he cannot stand.

Antistrophe 2

   O clear intelligence, force beyond all measure!
   O fate of man, working both good and evil!
   When the laws are kept, how proudly his city stands!
   When the laws are broken, what of his city then?
   Never may the anarchic man find rest at my hearth,
   Never be it said that my thoughts are his thoughts.

SCENE II

Re-enter SENTRY *leading* ANTIGONE.

CHORAGOS: What does this mean: Surely this captive woman
  Is the Princess, Antigone. Why should she be taken?
SENTRY: Here is the one who did it! We caught her
  In the very act of burying him.—Where is Creon?
CHORAGOS: Just coming from the house.

Enter CREON, *center.*

CREON: What has happened?
  Why have you come back so soon?
SENTRY (*Expansively*):

                                        O King,
  A man should never be too sure of anything:
  I would have sworn
  That you'd not see me here again: your anger
  Frightened me so, and the things you threatened me with;
  But how could I tell then
  That I'd be able to solve the case so soon?
  No dice-throwing this time: I was only too glad to come!
  Here is this woman. She is the guilty one:
  We found her trying to bury him.
  Take her, then; question her; judge her as you will.
  I am through with the whole thing now, and glad of it.
CREON: But this is Antigone! Why have you brought her here?
SENTRY: She was burying him, I tell you!
CREON (*Severely*):

                                        Is this the truth?
SENTRY: I saw her with my own eyes. Can I say more?
CREON: The details: come, tell me quickly!
SENTRY: It was like this:
  After those terrible threats of yours, King,
  We went back and brushed the dust away from the body.
  The flesh was soft by now, and stinking,
  So we sat on a hill to windward and kept guard.
  No napping this time! We kept each other awake.
  But nothing happened until the white round sun
  Whirled in the center of the round sky over us:
  Then, suddenly,
  A storm of dust roared up from the earth, and the sky
  Went out, the plain vanished with all its trees
  In the stinging dark. We closed our eyes and endured it.

The whirlwind lasted a long time, but it passed;
And then we looked, and there was Antigone!
I have seen
A mother bird come back to a stripped nest, heard
Her crying bitterly a broken note or two
For the young ones stolen. Just so, when this girl
Found the bare corpse, and all her love's work wasted,
She wept, and cried on heaven to damn the hands
That had done this thing.
                              And then she brought more dust
And sprinkled wine three times for her brother's ghost.

We ran and took her at once. She was not afraid,
Not even when we charged her with what she had done.
She denied nothing.
And this was a comfort to me,
                              And some uneasiness: for it is a good thing
To escape from death, but it is no great pleasure
To bring death to a friend.
                              Yet I always say
There is nothing so comfortable as your own safe skin!
CREON (*Slowly, dangerously*): And you, Antigone,
    You with your head hanging,—do you confess this thing?
ANTIGONE: I do. I deny nothing.
creon (*To* SENTRY):   You may go.

                                                      (*Exit* SENTRY)

(*To* ANTIGONE) Tell me, tell me briefly:
    Had you heard my proclamation touching this matter?
ANTIGONE: It was public. Could I help hearing it?
CREON: And yet you dared defy the law.
ANTIGONE: I dared.
    It was not God's proclamation. That final Justice
    That rules the world below makes no such laws.

Your edict, King, was strong,
But all your strength is weakness itself against
The immortal unrecorded laws of God.
They are not merely now: they were, and shall be,
Operative for ever, beyond man utterly.

I knew I must die, even without your decree:
I am only mortal. And if I must die
Now, before it is my time to die,
Surely this is no hardship: can anyone

Living, as I live, with evil all about me,
Think Death less than a friend? This death of mine
Is of no importance; but if I had left my brother
Lying in death unburied, I should have suffered.
Now I do not.
     You smile at me. Ah Creon,
Think me a fool, if you like; but it may well be
That a fool convicts me of folly.
CHORAGOS: Like father, like daughter: both headstrong, deaf to reason!
 She has never learned to yield.
CREON: She has much to learn.
 The inflexible heart breaks first, the toughest iron
 Cracks first, and the wildest horses bend their necks
 At the pull of the smallest curb.
       Pride? In a slave?
 This girl is guilty of a double insolence,
 Breaking the given laws and boasting of it.
 Who is the man here,
 She or I, if this crime goes unpunished?
 Sister's child, or more than sister's child,
 Or closer yet in blood—she and her sister
 Win bitter death for this!
 (*To* SERVANTS)   Go, some of you,
 Arrest Ismene. I accuse her equally.
 Bring her: you will find her sniffling in the house there.

 Her mind's a traitor: crimes kept in the dark
 Cry for light, and the guardian brain shudders;
 But how much worse than this
 Is brazen boasting of barefaced anarchy!
ANTIGONE: Creon, what more do you want than my death?
CREON: Nothing.
 That gives me everything.
ANTIGONE: Then I beg you: kill me.
 This talking is a great weariness: your words
 Are distasteful to me, and I am sure that mine
 Seem so to you. And yet they should not seem so:
 I should have praise and honor for what I have done.
 All these men here would praise me
 Were their lips not frozen shut with fear of you.
 (*Bitterly*) Ah the good fortune of kings,
 Licensed to say and do whatever they please!
CREON: You are alone here in that opinion.
ANTIGONE: No, they are with me. But they keep their tongues in leash.

CREON: Maybe. But you are guilty, and they are not.

ANTIGONE: There is no guilt in reverence for the dead.

CREON: But Eteocles—was he not your brother too?

ANTIGONE: My brother too.

CREON: And you insult his memory?

ANTIGONE (*Softly*): The dead man would not say that I insult it.

CREON: He would: for you honor a traitor as much as him.

ANTIGONE: His own brother; traitor or not, and equal in blood.

CREON: He made war on his country. Eteocles defended it.

ANTIGONE: Nevertheless, there are honors due all the dead.

CREON: But not the same for the wicked as for the just.

ANTIGONE: Ah Creon, Creon,
   Which of us can say what the gods hold wicked?

CREON: An enemy is an enemy, even dead.

ANTIGONE: It is my nature to join in love, not hate.

CREON (*Finally losing patience*): Go join them, then; if you must have your love,
   Find it in hell!

CHORAGOS: But see, Ismene comes:

Enter ISMENE, *guarded.*

   Those tears are sisterly, the cloud
   That shadows her eyes rains down gentle sorrow.

CREON: You too, Ismene,
   Snake in my ordered house, sucking my blood
   Stealthily—and all the time I never knew
   That these two sisters were aiming at my throne!

                         Ismene,
   Do you confess your share in this crime, or deny it?
   Answer me.

ISMENE: Yes, if she will let me say so. I am guilty.

ANTIGONE (*Coldly*): No, Ismene. You have no right to say so.
   You would not help me, and I will not have you help me.

ISMENE: But now I know what you meant; and I am here
   To join you, to take my share of punishment.

ANTIGONE: The dead man and the gods who rule the dead
   Know whose act this was. Words are not friends.

ISMENE: Do you refuse me, Antigone? I want to die with you:
   I too have a duty that I must discharge to the dead.

ANTIGONE: You shall not lessen my death by sharing it.

ISMENE: What do I care for life when you are dead?

ANTIGONE: Ask Creon. You're always hanging on his opinions.

ISMENE: You are laughing at me. Why, Antigone?

ANTIGONE: It's a joyless laughter, Ismene.

ISMENE: But can I do nothing?

ANTIGONE: Yes, Save yourself. I shall not envy you.

There are those who will praise you; I shall have honor, too.

ISMENE: But we are equally guilty!

ANTIGONE: No more, Ismene.

You are alive, but I belong to Death.

CREON (*To the* CHORUS): Gentlemen, I beg you to observe these girls:

One has just now lost her mind; the other,

It seems, has never had a mind at all.

ISMENE: Grief teaches the steadiest minds to waver, King.

CREON: Yours certainly did, when you assumed guilt with the guilty!

ISMENE: But how could I go on living without her?

CREON: You are.

She is already dead.

ISMENE: But your own son's bride!

CREON: There are places enough for him to push his plow.

I want no wicked women for my sons!

ISMENE: O dearest Haimon, how your father wrongs you!

CREON: I've had enough of your childish talk of marriage!

CHORAGOS: Do you really intend to steal this girl from your son?

CREON: No; Death will do that for me.

CHORAGOS: Then she must die?

CREON (*Ironically*): You dazzle me.

—But enough of this talk!

(*To* GUARDS) You, there, take them away and guard them well:

For they are but women, and even brave men run

When they see Death coming.

Exeunt ISMENE, ANTIGONE, *and* GUARDS

ODE II

Strophe 1

CHORUS: Fortunate is the man who has never tasted God's vengeance!

Where once the anger of heaven has struck, that house is shaken

For ever: damnation rises behind each child

Like a wave cresting out of the black northeast,

When the long darkness under sea roars up

And bursts drumming death upon the windwhipped sand.

Antistrophe 1

I have seen this gathering sorrow from time long past

Loom upon Oedipus' children: generation from generation

Takes the compulsive rage of the enemy god.

So lately this last flower of Oedipus' line

Drank the sunlight! but now a passionate word

And a handful of dust have closed up all its beauty.

Strophe 2

What mortal arrogance
Transcends the wrath of Zeus?
Sleep cannot lull him, nor the effortless long months
Of the timeless gods; but he is young for ever,
And his house is the shining day of high Olympos.
All that is and shall be,
And all the past, is his.
No pride on earth is free of the curse of heaven.

Antistrophe 2

The straying dreams of men
May bring them ghosts of joy:
But as they drowse, the waking embers burn them;
Or they walk with fixed eyes, as blind men walk.
But the ancient wisdom speaks for our own time:
Fate works most for woe
With Folly's fairest show.
Man's little pleasure is the spring of sorrow.

SCENE III

CHORAGOS: But here is Haimon, King, the last of all your sons.
Is it grief for Antigone that brings him here,
And bitterness at being robbed of his bride?

Enter HAIMON.

CREON: We shall soon see, and no need of diviners.
—Son,
You have heard my final judgment on that girl:
Have you come here hating me, or have you come
With deference and with love, whatever I do?
HAIMON: I am your son, father. You are my guide.
You make things clear for me, and I obey you.
No marriage means more to me than your continuing wisdom.
CREON: Good. That is the way to behave: subordinate
Everything else, my son, to your father's will.
This is what a man prays for, that he may get
Sons attentive and dutiful in his house,
Each one hating his father's enemies,
Honoring his father's friends. But if his sons
Fail him, if they turn out unprofitably,
What has he fathered but trouble for himself
And amusement for the malicious?

                                             So you are right
Not to lose your head over this woman.
Your pleasure with her would soon grow cold, Haimon,
And then you'd have a hellcat in bed and elsewhere.
Let her find her husband in Hell!
Of all the people in this city, only she
Has had contempt for my law and broken it.

Do you want me to show myself weak before the people?
Or to break my sworn word? No, and I will not.
The woman dies.
I suppose she'll plead "family ties." Well, let her.
If I permit my own family to rebel,
How shall I earn the world's obedience?
Show me the man who keeps his house in hand,
He's fit for public authority.
                                    I'll have no dealings
With law-breakers, critics of the government:
Whoever is chosen to govern should be obeyed—
Must be obeyed, in all things, great and small,
Just and unjust! O Haimon,
The man who knows how to obey, and that man only,
Knows how to give commands when the time comes.
You can depend on him, no matter how fast
The spears come: he's a good soldier, he'll stick it out.
Anarchy, anarchy! Show me a greater evil!
This is why cities tumble and the great houses rain down,
This is what scatters armies!
No, no: good lives are made so by discipline.
We keep the laws then, and the lawmakers,
And no woman shall seduce us. If we must lose,
Let's lose to a man, at least! Is a woman stronger than we?
CHORAGOS: Unless time has rusted my wits,
What you say, King, is said with point and dignity.
HAIMON (*Boyishly earnest*): Father:
Reason is God's crowning gift to man, and you are right.
To warn me against losing mine. I cannot say—
I hope that I shall never want to say!—that you
Have reasoned badly. Yet there are other men
Who can reason, too; and their opinions might be helpful.
You are not in a position to know everything
That people say or do, or what they feel:
Your temper terrifies them—everyone
Will tell you only what you like to hear.

But I, at any rate, can listen; and I have heard them
Muttering and whispering in the dark about this girl.
They say no woman has ever, so unreasonably,
Died so shameful a death for a generous act:
"She covered her brother's body. Is this indecent?
She kept him from dogs and vultures. Is this a crime?
Death?—She should have all the honor that we can give her!"

This is the way they talk out there in the city.

You must believe me:
Nothing is closer to me than your happiness.
What could be closer? Must not any son
Value his father's fortune as his father does his?
I beg you, do not be unchangeable:
Do not believe that you alone can be right.
The man who thinks that,
The man who maintains that only he has the power
To reason correctly, the gift to speak, the soul—
A man like that, when you know him, turns out empty.
It is not reason never to yield to reason!

In flood time you can see how some trees bend,
And because they bend, even their twigs are safe,
While stubborn trees are torn up, roots and all.
And the same thing happens in sailing:
Make your sheet fast, never slacken,—and over you go,
Head over heels and under: and there's your voyage.
Forget you are angry! Let yourself be moved!
I know I am young; but please let me say this:
The ideal condition
Would be, I admit, that men should be right by instinct;
But since we are all too likely to go astray,
The reasonable thing is to learn from those who can teach.
CHORAGOS: You will do well to listen to him, King,
    If what he says is sensible. And you, Haimon.
    Must listen to your father.—Both speak well.
CREON: You consider it right for a man of my years and experience
    to go to school to a boy?
HAIMON: It is not right
    If I am wrong. But if I am young, and right,
    What does my age matter?
CREON: You think it right to stand up for an anarchist?
HAIMON: Not at all. I pay no respect to criminals.

CREON: Then she is not a criminal?

HAIMON: The City would deny it, to a man.

CREON: And the City proposes to teach me how to rule?

HAIMON: Ah. Who is it that's talking like a boy now?

CREON: My voice is the one voice giving orders in this City!

HAIMON: It is no City if it takes orders from one voice.

CREON: The State is the King!

HAIMON: Yes, if the State is a desert.

Pause.

CREON: This boy, it seems, has sold out to a woman.

HAIMON: If you are a woman: my concern is only for you.

CREON: So? Your "concern"! In a public brawl with your father!

HAIMON: How about you, in a public brawl with justice?

CREON: With justice, when all that I do is within my rights?

HAIMON: You have no right to trample God's right.

CREON (*Completely out of control*): Fool, adolescent fool! Taken in by a woman!

HAIMON: You'll never see me taken in by anything vile.

CREON: Every word you say is for her!

HAIMON (*Quietly, darkly*):   And for you.
   And for me. And for the gods under the earth.

CREON: You'll never marry her while she lives.

HAIMON: Then she must die.—But her death will cause another.

CREON: Another?
   Have you lost your senses? Is this an open threat?

HAIMON: There is no threat in speaking to emptiness.

CREON: I swear you'll regret this superior tone of yours!
   You are the empty one!

HAIMON: If you were not my father,
   I'd say you were perverse.

CREON: You girlstruck fool, don't play at words with me!

HAIMON: I am sorry. You prefer silence.

CREON: Now, by God—!
   I swear, by all the gods in heaven above us,
   You'll watch it, I swear you shall!
   (*To the* SERVANTS)   Bring her out!
   Bring the woman out! Let her die before his eyes!
   Here, this instant, with her bridegroom beside her!

HAIMON: Not here, no; she will not die here, King.
   And you will never see my face again.
   Go on raving as long as you've a friend to endure you.

Exit HAIMON.

CHORAGOS: Gone, gone.
   Creon, a young man in a rage is dangerous!
CREON: Let him do, or dream to do, more than a man can.
   He shall not save these girls from death.
CHORAGOS: These girls
   You have sentenced them both?
CREON: No, you are right.
   I will not kill the one whose hands are clean.
CHORAGOS: But Antigone?
CREON (*Somberly*): I will carry her far away
   Out there in the wilderness, and lock her
   Living in a vault of stone. She shall have food,
   As the custom is, to absolve the State of her death.
   And there let her pray to the gods of hell:
   They are her only gods:
   Perhaps they will show her an escape from death,
   Or she may learn,
                though late,
   That piety shown the dead is pity in vain.

Exit CREON.

ODE III

Strophe

CHORUS: Love, unconquerable
   Waster of rich men, keeper
   Of warm lights and all-night vigil
   In the soft face of a girl:
   Sea-wanderer, forest-visitor!
   Even the pure Immortals cannot escape you,
   And mortal man, in his one day's dusk,
   Trembles before your glory.

Antistrophe

   Surely you swerve upon ruin
   The just man's consenting heart,
   As here you have made bright anger
   Strike between father and son—
   And none has conquered but Love!
   A girl's glance working the will of heaven:
   Pleasure to her alone who mocks us,
   Merciless Aphrodite.

SCENE IV

CHORAGOS　　　　(*As* ANTIGONE *enters guarded*):
　　But I can no longer stand in awe of this,
　　Nor, seeing what I see, keep back my tears.
　　Here is Antigone, passing to that chamber
　　Where all find sleep at last.

Strophe 1

ANTIGONE:　Look upon me, friends, and pity me
　　Turning back at the night's edge to say
　　Good-by to the sun that shines for me no longer;
　　Now sleepy Death
　　Summons me down to Acheron, that cold shore:
　　There is no bridesong there, nor any music.
CHORUS:　Yet not unpraised, not without a kind of honor,
　　You walk at last into the underworld;
　　Untouched by sickness, broken by no sword.
　　What woman has ever found your way to death?

Antistrophe 1

ANTIGONE:　How often I have heard the story of Niobe,
　　Tantalos' wretched daughter, how the stone
　　Clung fast about her, ivy-close: and they say
　　The rain falls endlessly
　　And sifting soft snow; her tears are never done.
　　I feel the loneliness of her death in mine.
CHORUS:　But she was born of heaven, and you
　　Are woman, woman-born. If her death is yours,
　　A mortal woman's, is this not for you
　　Glory in our world and in the world beyond?

Strophe 2

ANTIGONE:　You laugh at me. Ah, friends, friends,
　　Can you not wait until I am dead? O Thebes,
　　O men many-charioted, in love with Fortune,
　　Dear springs of Dirce, sacred Theban grove,
　　Be witnesses for me, denied all pity,
　　Unjustly judged! and think a word of love
　　For her whose path turns
　　Under dark earth, where there are no more tears.

CHORUS: You have passed beyond human daring and come at last
　　Into a place of stone where Justice sits.
　　I cannot tell
　　What shape of your father's guilt appears in this.

Antistrophe 2

ANTIGONE: You have touched it at last: that bridal bed
　　Unspeakable, horror of son and mother mingling:
　　Their crime, infection of all our family!
　　O Oedipus, father and brother!
　　Your marriage strikes from the grave to murder mine.
　　I have been a stranger here in my own land:
　　All my life
　　The blasphemy of my birth has followed me.
CHORUS: Reverence is a virtue, but strength
　　Lives in established law: that must prevail.
　　You have made your choice,
　　Your death is the doing of your conscious hand.

Epode

ANTIGONE: Then let me go, since all your words are bitter,
　　And the very light of the sun is cold to me.
　　Lead me to my vigil, where I must have
　　Neither love nor lamentation; no song, but silence.

CREON *interrupts impatiently.*

CREON: If dirges and planned lamentations could put off death,
　　Men would be singing for ever.
　　(*To the* SERVANTS)　　　　　　Take her, go!
　　You know your orders: take her to the vault
　　And leave her alone there. And if she lives or dies,
　　That's her affair, not ours: our hands are clean.
ANTIGONE: O tomb, vaulted bride-bed in eternal rock,
　　Soon I shall be with my own again
　　Where Persephone welcomes the thin ghosts underground:
　　And I shall see my father again, and you, mother,
　　And dearest Polyneices—
　　　　　　　　　　　dearest indeed
　　To me, since it was my hand
　　That washed him clean and poured the ritual wine:
　　And my reward is death before my time!

　　And yet, as men's hearts know, I have done no wrong.
　　I have not sinned before God. Or if I have,

I shall know the truth in death. But if the guilt
Lies upon Creon who judged me, then, I pray,
  May his punishment equal my own.
CHORAGOS: O passionate heart,
  Unyielding, tormented still by the same winds!
CREON: Her guards shall have good cause to regret their delaying.
ANTIGONE: Ah! That voice is like the voice of death!
CREON: I can give you no reason to think you are mistaken.
ANTIGONE: Thebes, and you my fathers' gods,
  And rulers of Thebes, you see me now, the last
  Unhappy daughter of a line of kings,
  Your kings, led away to death. You will remember
  What things I suffer, and at what men's hands,
  Because I would not transgress the laws of heaven.
  (*To the* GUARDS, *simply*): Come: let us wait no longer.

Exit ANTIGONE, *left, guarded.*

ODE IV

Strophe 1

CHORUS: All Danae's beauty was locked away
  In a brazen cell where the sunlight could not come:
  A small room, still as any grave, enclosed her.
  Yet she was a princess too,
  And Zeus in a rain of gold poured love upon her.
  O child, child,
  No power in wealth or war
  Or tough sea-blackened ships
  Can prevail against untiring Destiny!

Antistrophe 1

  And Dryas' son[7] also, that furious king,
  Bore the god's prisoning anger for his pride:
  Sealed up by Dionysos in deaf stone,
  His madness died among echoes.
  So at the last he learned what dreadful power
  His tongue had mocked:
  For he had profaned the revels,
  And fired the wrath of the nine
  Implacable Sisters[8] that love the sound of the flute.

---

   [7]Dryas' son: Lycurgus, King of Thrace. [8]Implacable sisters: The nine Muses.

Strophe 2

And old men tell a half-remembered tale
Of horror done where a dark ledge splits the sea
And a double surf beats on the gray shores:
How a king's new woman[9], sick
With hatred for the queen he had imprisoned,
Ripped out his two sons' eyes with her bloody hands
While grinning Ares watched the shuttle plunge
Four times: four blind wounds crying for revenge,

Antistrophe 2

Crying, tears and blood mingled.—Piteously born,
Those sons whose mother was of heavenly birth!
Her father was the god of the North Wind
And she was cradled by gales,
She raced with young colts on the glittering hills
And walked untrammeled in the open light:
But in her marriage deathless Fate found means
To build a tomb like yours for all her job.

SCENE V

Enter blind TEIRESIAS, *led by a boy. The opening speeches of* TEIRESIAS *should be in singsong contrast to the realistic lines of* CREON.

TEIRESIAS: This is the way the blind man comes, Princes, Princes,
   Lock-step, two heads lit by the eyes of one.
CREON: What new thing have you to tell us, Old Teiresias?
TEIRESIAS: I have much to tell you: listen to the prophet, Creon.
CREON: I am not aware that I have ever failed to listen.
TEIRESIAS: Then you have done wisely, King, and ruled well.
CREON: I admit my debt to you. But what have you to say?
TEIRESIAS: This, Creon: you stand once more on the edge of fate.
CREON: What do you mean? Your words are a kind of dread.
TEIRESIAS: Listen, Creon:
   I was sitting in my chair of augury, at the place
   Where the birds gather about me. They were all a-chatter,
   As is their habit, when suddenly I heard
   A strange note in their jangling, a scream, a

---

[9]King's new woman: Reference to Eidothea, wife of King Phineas.

Whirring fury; I knew that they were fighting,
Tearing each other, dying
In a whirlwind of wings clashing. And I was afraid.
I began the rites of burnt-offering at the altar,
But Hephaistos failed me: instead of bright flame,
There was only the sputtering slime of the fat thighflesh
Melting: the entrails dissolved in gray smoke,
The bare bone burst from the welter. And no blaze!

This was a sign from heaven. My boy described it,
Seeing for me as I see for others.

I tell you, Creon, you yourself have brought
This new calamity upon us. Our hearths and altars
Are stained with the corruption of dogs and carrion birds
That glut themselves on the corpse of Oedipus' son.
The gods are deaf when we pray to them, their fire
Recoils from our offering, their birds of omen
Have no cry of comfort, for they are gorged
With the thick of the dead.
                              O my son,
These are no trifes! Think: all men make mistakes,
But a good man yields when he knows his course is wrong,
And repairs the evil. The only crime is pride.

Give in to the dead man, then: do not fight with a corpse—
What glory is it to kill a man who is dead?
Think, I beg you:
It is for your own good that I speak as I do.
You should be able to yield for your own good.
CREON: It seems that prophets have made me their special province.
   All my life long
   I have been a kind of butt for the dull arrows
   Of doddering fortune-tellers!
                              No, Teiresias:
   If your birds—if the great eagles of God himself
   Should carry him stinking bit by bit to heaven,
   I would not yield. I am not afraid of pollution:
   No man can defile the gods.
                              Do what you will,
   Go into business, make money, speculate
   In India gold or that synthetic gold from Sardis,
   Get rich otherwise than by my consent to bury him.

Teiresias, it is a sorry thing when a wise man
Sells his wisdom, lets out his words for hire!

TEIRESIAS: Ah Creon! Is there no man left in the world—

CREON: To do what?—Come, let's have the aphorism!

TEIRESIAS: No man who knows that wisdom outweighs any wealth?

CREON: As surely as bribes are baser than any baseness.

TEIRESIAS: You are sick, Creon! You are deathly sick!

CREON: As you say: it is not my place to challenge a prophet.

TEIRESIAS: Yet you have said my prophecy is for sale.

CREON: The generation of prophets has always loved gold.

TEIRESIAS: The generation of kings has always loved brass.

CREON: You forget yourself! You are speaking to your King.

TEIRESIAS: I know it. You are a king because of me.

CREON: You have a certain skill; but you have sold out.

TEIRESIAS: King, you will drive me to words that—

CREON: Say them, say them!
Only remember: I will not pay you for them.

TEIRESIAS: No, you will find them too costly.

CREON: No doubt. Speak:
Whatever you say, you will not change my will.

TEIRESIAS: Then take this, and take it to heart!
The time is not far off when you shall pay back
Corpse for corpse, flesh of your own flesh.
You have thrust the child of this world into living night,
You have kept from the gods below the child that is theirs:
The one in a grave before her death, the other,
Dead, denied the grave. This is your crime:
And the Furies and the dark gods of Hell
Are swift with terrible punishment for you.

Do you want to buy me now, Creon?
                                                 Not many days,
And your house will be full of men and women weeping.
And curses will be hurled at you from far
Cities grieving for sons unburied, left to rot
Before the walls of Thebes.

These are my arrows, Creon: they are all for you.
(*To* BOY): But come, child: lead me home.
Let him waste his fine anger upon younger men.
Maybe he will learn at last
To control a wiser tongue in a better head.

Exit TEIRESIAS.

CHORAGOS: The old man has gone, King, but his words
  Remain to plague us. I am old, too,
  But I cannot remember that he was ever false.
CREON: That is true. . . . It troubles me.
  Oh it is hard to give in! but it is worse
  To risk everything for stubborn pride.
CHORAGOS: Creon: take my advice.
CREON: What shall I do?
CHORAGOS: Go quickly: free Antigone from her vault
  And build a tomb for the body of Polyneices.
CREON: You would have me do this?
CHORAGOS: Creon, yes!
  And it must be done at once: God moves
  Swiftly to cancel the folly of stubborn men.
CREON: It is hard to deny the heart! But I
  Will do it: I will not fight with destiny.
CHORAGOS: You must go yourself, you cannot leave it to others.
CREON: I will go.
  —Bring axes, servants:
  Come with me to the tomb. I buried her, I
  Will set her free.
                Oh quickly!
  My mind misgives—
  The laws of the gods are mighty, and a man must serve them
  To the last day of his life!

Exit CREON.

PAEAN

Strophe 1

CHORAGOS: God of many names
CHORUS: O Iacchos
                              son
  of Kadmeian Semele
               O born of the Thunder!
  Guardian of the West
              Regent
  of Eleusis' plain
           O Prince of maenad Thebes
  and the Dragon Field by rippling Ismenos:

Antistrophe 1

CHORAGOS: God of many names

CHORUS: the flame of torches
    flares on our hills
                        the nymphs of Iacchos
    dance at the spring of Castalia:
    From the vine-close mountain
                            come ah come in ivy:
    Evohe evohe![10] sings through the streets of Thebes

Strophe 2

CHORAGOS: God of many names
CHORUS: Iacchos of Thebes
    heavenly Child
                        of Semele bride of the Thunderer!
    The shadow of plague is upon us:
                                            come
    with clement feet
                        oh come from Parnasos
    down the long slopes
                            across the lamenting water

Antistrophe 2

CHORAGOS: Io Fire! Chorister of the throbbing stars!
    O purest among the voices of the night!
    Thou son of God, blaze for us!
CHORUS: Come with choric rapture of circling Maenads
    Who cry *Io Iacche!*
                    God of many names!

EXODOS[11]

Enter MESSENGER, *left.*

MESSENGER: Men of the line of Kadmos, you who live
    Near Amphion's citadel.[12]
                            I cannot say
    Of any condition of human life "This is fixed,
    This is clearly good, or bad." Fate raises up,
    And Fate casts down the happy and unhappy alike:
    No man can foretell his Fate.
                        Take the case of Creon:

---

[10]Evohe evohe!: "Come forth; come forth!" [11]Exodos: Concluding scene. [12]Amphion's citadel: Thebes.

Creon was happy once, as I count happiness:
Victorious in battle, sole governor of the land,
Fortunate father of children nobly born.
And now it has all gone from him! Who can say
That a man is still alive when his life's joy fails?
He is a walking dead man. Grant him rich,
Let him live like a king in his great house:
If his pleasure is gone, I would not give
So much as the shadow of smoke for all he owns.

CHORAGOS: Your words hint at sorrow: what is your news for us?

MESSENGER: They are dead. The living are guilty of their death.

CHORAGOS: Who is guilty? Who is dead? Speak!

MESSENGER: Haimon.
Haimon is dead; and the hand that killed him
Is his own hand.

CHORAGOS: His father's? or his own?

MESSENGER: His own, driven mad by the murder his father had done.

CHORAGOS: Teiresias, Teiresias, how clearly you saw it all!

MESSENGER: This is my news: you must draw what conclusions you can from it.

CHORAGOS: But look: Eurydice, our Queen:
Has she overheard us?

Enter EURYDICE *from the Palace, center.*

EURYDICE: I have heard something, friends:
As I was unlocking the gate of Pallas' shrine,
For I needed her help today, I heard a voice
Telling of some new sorrow. And I fainted
There at the temple with all my maidens about me.
But speak again: whatever it is, I can bear it:
Grief and I are no strangers.

MESSENGER: Dearest Lady,
I will tell you plainly all that I have seen.
I shall not try to comfort you: what is the use,
Since comfort could lie only in what is not true?
The truth is always best.
                    I went with Creon
To the outer plain where Polyneices was lying,
No friend to pity him, his body shredded by dogs.
We made our prayers in that place to Hecate
And Pluto, that they would be merciful. And we bathed
The corpse with holy water, and we brought
Fresh-broken branches to burn what was left of it,
And upon the urn we heaped up a towering barrow
Of the earth of his own land.

When we were done, we ran
To the vault where Antigone lay on her couch of stone.
One of the servants had gone ahead,
And while he was yet far off he heard a voice
Grieving within the chamber, and he came back
And told Creon. And as the King went closer,
The air was full of wailing, the words lost,
And he begged us to make all haste. "Am I a prophet?"
He said, weeping, "And must I walk this road,
The saddest of all that I have gone before?
My son's voice calls me on. Oh quickly, quickly!
Look through the crevice there, and tell me
If it is Haimon, or some deception of the gods!"

We obeyed; and in the cavern's farthest corner
We saw her lying:
She had made a noose of her fine linen veil
And hanged herself. Haimon lay beside her,
His arms about her waist, lamenting her,
His love lost under ground, crying out
That his father had stolen her away from him.

When Creon saw him the tears rushed to his eyes
And he called to him: "What have you done, child?
     Speak to me.
What are you thinking that makes your eyes so strange?
O my son, my son, I come to you on my knees!"
But Haimon spat in his face. He said not a word,
Staring—
               And suddenly drew his sword
And lunged. Creon shrank back, the blade missed; and the boy,
Desperate against himself, drove it half its length
Into his own side, and fell. And as he died
He gathered Antigone close in his arms again,
Choking, his blood bright red on her white cheek.
And now he lies dead with the dead, and she is his
At last, his bride in the houses of the dead.

Exit EURYDICE *into the Palace.*

CHORAGOS: She has left us without a word. What can this mean?
MESSENGER: It troubles me, too; yet she knows what is best,
     Her grief is too great for public lamentation,
     And doubtless she has gone to her chamber to weep
     For her dead son, leading her maidens in his dirge.

Pause.

CHORAGOS: It may be so: but I fear this deep silence
MESSENGER: I will see what she is doing. I will go in.

Exit MESSENGER *into the Place.*

Enter CREON *with attendants, bearing* HAIMON's *body.*

CHORAGOS: But here is the King himself: oh look at him,
    Bearing his own damnation in his arms.
CREON: Nothing you say can touch me any more.
    My own blind heart has brought me
    From darkness to final darkness. Here you see
    The father murdering, the murdered son—
    And all my civic wisdom!

    Haimon my son, so young, so young to die,
    I was the fool, not you; and you died for me.
CHORAGOS: That is the truth; but you were late in learning it.
CREON: This truth is hard to bear. Surely a god
    Has crushed me beneath the hugest weight of heaven,
    And driven me headlong a barbaric way
    To trample out the thing I held most dear.

    The pains that men will take to come to pain!

Enter MESSENGER *from the Palace.*

MESSENGER: The burden you carry in your hands is heavy,
    But it is not all: you will find more in your house.
CREON: What burden worse than this shall I find there?
MESSENGER: The Queen is dead.
CREON: O port of death, deaf world,
    Is there no pity for me? And you, Angel of evil,
    I was dead, and your words are death again.
    Is it true, boy? Can it be true?
    Is my wife dead? Has death bred death?
MESSENGER: You can see for yourself.

The doors are opened, and the body of EURYDICE *is disclosed within.*

CREON: Oh pity!
    All true, all true, and more than I can bear!
    O my wife, my son!
MESSENGER: She stood before the altar, and her heart
    Welcomed the knife her own hand guided,
    And a great cry burst from her lips for Megareus[13] dead,

And for Haimon dead, her sons; and her last breath
Was a curse for their father, the murderer of her sons.
And she fell, and the dark flowed in through her closing eyes.
CREON: O God, I am sick with fear.
   Are there no swords here? Has no one a blow for me?
MESSENGER: Her curse is upon you for the deaths of both.
CREON: It is right that it should be. I alone am guilty.
   I know it, and I say it. Lead me in,
   Quickly, friends.
   I have neither life nor substance. Lead me in.
CHORAGOS: You are right, if there can be right in so much wrong.
   The briefest way is best in a world of sorrow.
CREON: Let it come.
   Let death come quickly, and be kind to me.
   I would not ever see the sun again.
CHORAGOS: All that will come when it will; but we, meanwhile,
   Have much to do. Leave the future to itself.
CREON: All my heart was in that prayer!
CHORAGOS: Then do not pray any more: the sky is deaf.
CREON: Lead me away. I have been rash and foolish.
   I have killed my son and my wife.
   I look for comfort; my comfort lies here dead.
   Whatever my hands have touched has come to nothing.
   Fate has brought all my pride to a thought of dust.

As CREON *is being led into the house, the* CHORAGOS *advances and speaks directly to the audience.*

CHORAGOS: There is no happiness where there is no wisdom;
   No wisdom but in submission to the gods.
   Big words are always punished,
   And proud men in old age learn to be wise.

CRITICAL THINKING QUESTIONS

1. Antigone is making a *claim of value*. State her claim in a single sentence. Creon is making a *claim of policy*. State his claim in a single sentence.

2. Creon makes an appeal to *pathos* as he tries to convince Antigone to abandon her efforts to bury her brother. Specifically, what does Creon say to play on her emotions?

---

[13]Megareus: Son of Creon, killed in the attack on Thebes.

3. Creon seems to be telling the truth when he describes the sacrifices he has made in order to create peace and prosperity for Thebes, yet Antigone refuses even to consider his position. What *inferences* do you draw from her refusal?

4. Who has more power in this play, Creon or Antigone?

WRITING TOPIC

Some legal experts argue that the law is totally sacred, that a society cannot tolerate disobedience to the law because that is an invitation to anarchy. The Nazis used this as a defense during the Nuremberg Trials after World War II, saying they were following the laws in Germany. Read about these trials and the judgments passed there. Defend or refute the Nazi defense.

John Hope Franklin

The Train from Hate

My pilgrimage from racial apprehension—read just plain confusion—to racial toler-ance was early and brief. I was 7 years old, and we lived in the all-black town of Rentiesville, Oklahoma. My father had moved to Tulsa where he hoped to have a law practice that would make it possible for him to support his family. Meanwhile, my mother, sister, and I would occasionally make the journey to Checotah, six miles away, to shop for supplies.

One day, we went down, as usual, by railroad. My mother flagged the train and we boarded. It so happened that when the train stopped, the only place we could enter was the coach reserved for white people. We did not take notice of this, and as the train picked up speed, the conductor entered and told us that we would have to move to the "colored" coach. My mother explained that we were not responsible for where the coach stopped and we had no other alternative to climbing aboard and finding seats as soon as possible. She told him that she could not risk the possible injury of her and her children by going to the "colored" coach while the train was moving. The conductor seemed to agree and said that he would signal to the engi-neer to stop the train. When the train came to a halt, the conductor did not guide us to the coach for African Americans. Instead, he commanded us to leave the train. We had no alternative to stepping off the train into the woods and beginning the trek back to Rentiesville.

As we trudged along, I began to cry. Taking notice of my sadness, my mother sought to comfort me by saying that it was not all that far to Rentiesville. I assured her that I did not mind the walk, but that man, the conductor, was so mean. Why would he not permit us to ride the train to Checotah?

My mother then gave me my first lesson in race relations. She told me that the laws required racial separation, but that they did not, could not, make us inferior in any way. She assured me that the conductor was not superior because he was white, and I was not inferior because I was black. I must always remember that simple fact, she said. Then she made a statement that is as vivid and clear to me today as the day she uttered it. Under no circumstances, she said, should I be upset or distressed be-cause someone sought to demean me. It took too much energy to hate or even to fight intolerance with one's emotions. She smiled and added that in going home we did not have far to walk.

It would be too much to claim that my mother's calm talk removed a burden from my shoulders. But it is not too much to say that her observations provided a sound basis for my attitudes and conduct from that day to this. At that early age, I had made an important journey. In the future, I remembered that I should not waste my time or energy lamenting the inability of some members of society to take me as I was. Instead, I would use my energies to make me a better person and to distance myself from the perpetrators and purveyors of hate and misunderstanding. I shall always be happy that my mother taught me that the journey to understanding and tolerance was more important than the journey to Checotah.

CRITICAL THINKING QUESTIONS

1. Through his personal experience, Franklin argues for a personal *claim of policy*. Can you articulate that claim?

2. What *assumptions* underlie the thinking of those who put the Franklins off that train?

Martin Luther King, Jr.

Letter from Birmingham Jail

April 16, 1963

My Dear Fellow Clergymen:

While confined here in the Birmingham city jail, I came across your recent statement calling my present activities "unwise and untimely." Seldom do I pause to answer criticism of my work and ideas. If I sought to answer all the criticisms that cross my desk, my secretaries would have little time for anything other than such correspondence in the course of the day, and I would have no time for constructive work. But since I feel that you are men of genuine good will and that your criticisms are sincerely set forth, I want to try to answer your statement in what I hope will be patient and reasonable terms.

I think I should indicate why I am here in Birmingham, since you have been influenced by the view which argues against "outsiders coming in." I have the honor of serving as president of the Southern Christian Leadership Conference, an organization operating in every southern state, with headquarters in Atlanta, Georgia. We have some eighty-five affiliated organizations across the South, and one of them is the Alabama Christian Movement for Human Rights. Frequently we share staff, educational and financial resources with our affiliates. Several months ago the affiliate here in Birmingham asked us to be on call to engage in a nonviolent direct-action program if such were deemed necessary. We readily consented, and when the hour came we lived up to our promise. So I, along with several members of my staff, am here because I was invited here. I am here because I have organizational ties here.

But more basically, I am in Birmingham because injustice is here. Just as the prophets of the eighth century B.C. left their villages and carried their "thus saith the Lord" far beyond the boundaries of their home towns, and just as the Apostle Paul left his village of Tarsus and carried the gospel of Jesus Christ to the far corners of the Greco-Roman world, so am I compelled to carry the gospel of freedom beyond my own home town. Like Paul, I must constantly respond to the Macedonian call for aid.

Moreover, I am cognizant of the interrelatedness of all communities and states. I cannot sit idly by in Atlanta and not be concerned about what happens in Birmingham. Injustice anywhere is a threat to justice everywhere. We are caught in an inescapable network of mutuality, tied in a single garment of destiny. Whatever affects one directly, affects all indirectly. Never again can we afford to live with the narrow, provincial "outside agitator" idea. Anyone who lives inside the United States can never be considered an outsider anywhere within its bounds.

You deplore the demonstrations taking place in Birmingham. But your statement, I am sorry to say, fails to express a similar concern for the conditions that brought about the demonstrations. I am sure that none of you would want to rest content with the superficial kind of social analysis that deals merely with effects and does not grapple with underlying causes. It is unfortunate that demonstrations are taking place in Birmingham, but it is even more unfortunate that the city's white power structure left the Negro community with no alternative.

In any nonviolent campaign there are four basic steps: collection of the facts to determine whether injustices exist; negotiation; self-purification; and direct action. We have gone through all these steps in Birmingham. There can be no gainsaying the fact that racial injustice engulfs this community. Birmingham is probably the most thoroughly segregated city in the United States. Its ugly record of brutality is widely known. Negroes have experienced grossly unjust treatment in the courts. There have been more unsolved bombings of Negro homes and churches in Birmingham than in any other city in the nation. These are the hard, brutal facts of the case. On the basis of these conditions, Negro leaders sought to negotiate with the city fathers. But the latter consistently refused to engage in good-faith negotiation.

Then, last September, came the opportunity to talk with leaders of Birmingham's economic community. In the course of the negotiations, certain promises were made by the merchants—for example, to remove the stores' humiliating racial signs. On the basis of these promises, the Reverend Fred Shuttlesworth and the leaders of the Alabama Christian Movement for Human Rights agreed to a moratorium on all demonstrations. As the weeks and months went by, we realized that we were the victims of a broken promise. A few signs, briefly removed, returned; the others remained.

As in so many past experiences, our hopes had been blasted, and the shadow of deep disappointment settled upon us. We had no alternative except to prepare for direct action, whereby we would present our very bodies as a means of laying our case before the conscience of the local and the national community. Mindful of the difficulties involved, we decided to undertake a process of self-purification. We began a series of workshops on nonviolence, and we repeatedly asked ourselves: "Are you able to accept blows without retaliating?" "Are you able to endure the ordeal of jail?" We decided to schedule our direct-action program for the Easter season, realizing that except for Christmas, this is the main shopping period of the year. Knowing that a strong economic-withdrawal program would be the by-product of direct action, we felt that this would be the best time to bring pressure to bear on the merchants for the needed change.

Then it occurred to us that Birmingham's mayoral election was coming up in March, and we speedily decided to postpone action until after election day. When we discovered that the Commissioner of Public Safety, Eugene "Bull" Connor, had piled up enough votes to be in the run-off, we decided again to postpone action until the day after the run-off so that the demonstrations could not be used to cloud the issues. Like many others, we waited to see Mr. Connor defeated, and to this end we endured postponement after postponement. Having aided in this community need, we felt that our direct action program could be delayed no longer.

You may well ask: "Why direct action? Why sit-ins, marches and so forth? Isn't negotiation a better path?" You are quite right in calling for negotiation. Indeed, this is the very purpose of direct action. Nonviolent direct action seeks to create such a crisis and foster such a tension that a community which has constantly refused to negotiate is forced to confront the issue. It seeks so to dramatize the issue that it can no longer be ignored. My citing the creation of tension as part of the work of the nonviolent-resister may sound rather shocking. But I must confess that I am not afraid of the word "tension." I have earnestly opposed violent tension, but there is a type of constructive, nonviolent tension which is necessary for growth. Just as Socrates felt that it was necessary to create a tension in the mind so that individuals could rise from the bondage of myths and half-truths to the unfettered realm of creative analysis and objective appraisal, so must we see the need for nonviolent gadflies to create the kind of tension in society that will help men rise from the dark depths of prejudice and racism to the majestic heights of understanding and brotherhood.

The purpose of our direct-action program is to create a situation so crisis-packed that it will inevitably open the door to negotiation. I therefore concur with you in your call for negotiation. Too long has our beloved Southland been bogged down in a tragic effort to live in monologue rather than dialogue.

One of the basic points in your statements is that the action that I and my associates have taken in Birmingham is untimely. Some have asked: "Why didn't you give the new city administration time to act?" The only answer that I can give to this query is that the new Birmingham administration must be prodded about as much as the outgoing one, before it will act. We are sadly mistaken if we feel that the election of Albert Boutwell as mayor will bring the millennium to Birmingham. While Mr. Boutwell is a much more gentle person than Mr. Connor, they are both segregationists, dedicated to maintenance of the status quo. I have hope that Mr. Boutwell will be reasonable enough to see the futility of massive resistance to desegregation. But he will not see this without pressure from devotees of civil rights. My friends, I must say to you that we have not made a single gain in civil rights without determined legal and nonviolent pressure. Lamentably, it is an historical fact that privileged groups seldom give up their privileges voluntarily. Individuals may see the moral light and voluntarily give up their unjust posture; but, as Reinhold Niebuhr has reminded us, groups tend to be more immoral than individuals.

We know through painful experience that freedom is never voluntarily given by the oppressor; it must be demanded by the oppressed. Frankly, I have yet to engage in a direct-action campaign that was "well timed" in the view of those who have not suffered unduly from the disease of segregation. For years now I have heard the word "Wait!" It rings in the ear of every Negro with piercing familiarity. This "Wait" has almost always meant "Never." We must come to see, with one of our distinguished jurists, that "justice too long delayed is justice denied."

We have waited for more than 340 years for our constitutional and God-given rights. The nations of Asia and Africa are moving with jetlike speed toward gaining political independence, but we still creep at horse-and-buggy pace toward gaining a cup of coffee at a lunch counter. Perhaps it is easy for those who have never felt the stinging darts of segregation to say, "Wait." But when you have seen vicious mobs lynch your mothers and fathers at will and drown your sisters and brothers at whim; when you have seen hate-filled policemen curse, kick and even kill your black brothers and sisters; when you see the vast majority of your twenty million Negro brothers smothering in an airtight cage of poverty in the midst of an affluent society; when you suddenly find your tongue twisted and your speech stammering as you seek to explain to your six-year-old daughter why she can't go to the public amusement park that has just been advertised on television, and see tears welling up in her eyes when she is told that Funtown is closed to colored children, and see ominous clouds of inferiority beginning to form in her little mental sky, and see her beginning to distort her personality by developing an unconscious bitterness toward white people; when you have to concoct an answer for a five-year-old son who is asking: "Daddy, why do white people treat colored people so mean?"; when you take a cross-country drive and find it necessary to sleep night after night in the uncomfortable corners of your automobile because no motel will accept you; when you are humiliated day in and day out by nagging signs reading "white" and "colored"; when your first name becomes "nigger," your middle name becomes "boy" (however old you are) and your last name becomes "John," and your wife and mother are never given the respected title "Mrs."; when you are harried by day and haunted by night by the fact that you are a Negro, living constantly at tiptoe stance, never quite knowing what to expect next, and are plagued with inner fears and outer resentments; when you are forever fighting a degenerating sense of "nobodiness"—then you will understand why we find it difficult to wait. There comes a time when the cup of endurance runs over, and men are no longer willing to be plunged into the abyss of despair. I hope, sirs, you can understand our legitimate and unavoidable impatience.

You express a great deal of anxiety over our willingness to break laws. This is certainly a legitimate concern. Since we so diligently urge people to obey the Supreme Court's decision of 1954 outlawing segregation in the public schools, at first glance it may seem rather paradoxical for us consciously to break laws. One may well ask: "How can you advocate breaking some laws and obeying others?" The answer lies in the fact that there are two types of laws: just and unjust. I would be the first to advocate obeying just laws. One has not only a legal but a moral responsibility to obey just laws. Conversely, one has a moral responsibility to disobey unjust laws. I would agree with St. Augustine that "an unjust law is no law at all."

Now, what is the difference between the two? How does one determine whether a law is just or unjust? A just law is a man-made code that squares with the moral law or the law of God. An unjust law is a code that is out of harmony with the moral law. To put it in the terms of St. Thomas Aquinas: An unjust law is a human law that is not rooted in eternal law and natural law. Any law that uplifts human personality is just. Any law that degrades human personality is unjust. All segregation statutes are unjust because segregation distorts the soul and damages the personality. It gives the segregator a false sense of superiority and the segregated a false sense of inferiority. Segregation, to use the terminology of the Jewish philosopher Martin Buber, substitutes an "I-it" relationship for an "I-thou" relationship and ends up relegating persons to the status of things. Hence segregation is not only politically, economically and sociologically unsound, it is morally wrong and sinful. Paul Tillich has said that sin is separation. Is not segregation an existential expression of man's tragic separation, his awful estrangement, his terrible sinfulness? Thus it is that I can urge men to obey the 1954 decision of the Supreme Court, for it is morally right; and I can urge them to disobey segregation ordinances, for they are morally wrong.

Let us consider a more concrete example of just and unjust laws. An unjust law is a code that a numerical or power majority group compels a minority group to obey but does not make binding on itself. This is *difference* made legal. By the same token, a just law is a code that a majority compels a minority to follow and that it is willing to follow itself. This is *sameness* made legal.

Let me give another explanation. A law is unjust if it is inflicted on a minority that, as a result of being denied the right to vote, had no part in enacting or devising the law. Who can say that the legislature of Alabama which set up that state's segregation laws was democratically elected? Throughout Alabama all sorts of devious methods are used to prevent Negroes from becoming registered voters, and there are some counties in which, even though Negroes constitute a majority of the population, not a single Negro is registered. Can any law enacted under such circumstances be considered democratically structured?

Sometimes a law is just on its face and unjust in its application. For instance, I have been arrested on a charge of parading without a permit. Now, there is nothing wrong in having an ordinance which requires a permit for a parade. But such an ordinance becomes unjust when it is used to maintain segregation and to deny citizens the First-Amendment privilege of peaceful assembly and protest.

I hope you are able to see the distinction I am trying to point out. In no sense do I advocate evading or defying the law, as would the rabid segregationist. That would lead to anarchy. One who breaks an unjust law must do so openly, lovingly, and with a willingness to accept the penalty. I submit that an individual who breaks a law that conscience tells him is unjust, and who willingly accepts the penalty of imprisonment in order to arouse the conscience of the community over its injustice, is in reality expressing the highest respect for law.

Of course, there is nothing new about this kind of civil disobedience. It was evidenced sublimely in the refusal of Shadrach, Meshach and Abednego to obey the laws of Nebuchadnezzar, on the ground that a higher moral law was at stake. It was practiced superbly by the early Christians, who were willing to face hungry lions and the excruciating pain of chopping blocks rather than submit to certain unjust laws of the Roman Empire. To a degree, academic freedom is a reality today because Socrates practiced civil disobedience. In our own nation, the Boston Tea party represented a massive act of civil disobedience.

We should never forget that everything Adolf Hitler did in Germany was "legal" and everything the Hungarian freedom fighters did in Hungary was "illegal." It was "illegal" to aid and comfort a Jew in Hitler's Germany. Even so, I am sure that, had I lived in Germany at the time, I would have aided and comforted my Jewish brothers. If today I lived in a Communist country where certain principles dear to the Christian faith are suppressed, I would openly advocate disobeying that country's antireligious laws.

I must make two honest confessions to you, my Christian and Jewish brothers. First, I must confess that over the past few years I have been gravely disappointed with the white moderate. I have almost reached the regrettable conclusion that the Negro's great stumbling block in his stride toward freedom is not the White Citizen's Counciler or the Ku Klux Klanner, but the white moderate, who is more devoted to "order" than to justice; who prefers a negative peace which is the absence of tension to a positive peace which is the presence of justice; who constantly says: "I agree with you in the goal you seek, but I cannot agree with your methods of direct action"; who paternalistically believes he can set the timetable for another man's freedom; who lives by a mythical concept of time and who constantly advises the Negro to wait for a "more convenient season." Shallow understanding from people of good will is more frustrating than absolute misunderstanding from people of ill will. Lukewarm acceptance is much more bewildering than outright rejection.

I had hoped that the white moderate would understand that law and order exist for the purpose of establishing justice and that when they fail in this purpose they become the dangerously structured dams that block the flow of social progress. I had hoped that the white moderate would understand that the present tension in the South is a necessary phase of the transition from an obnoxious negative peace, in which the Negro passively accepted his unjust plight, to a substantive and positive peace, in which all men will respect the dignity and worth of human personality. Actually, we who engage in nonviolent direct action are not the creators of tension. We merely bring to the surface the hidden tension that is already alive. We bring it out in the open, where it can be seen and dealt with. Like a boil that can never be cured so long as it is covered up but must be opened with all its ugliness to the natural medicines of air and light, injustice must be exposed, with all the tension its exposure creates, to the light of human conscience and the air of national opinion before it can be cured.

In your statement you assert that our actions, even though peaceful, must be condemned because they precipitate violence. But is this a logical assertion? Isn't this like condemning a robbed man because his possession of money precipitated the evil act of robbery? Isn't this like condemning Socrates because his unswerving commitment to truth and his philosophical inquiries precipitated the act by the misguided populace in which they made him drink hemlock? Isn't this like condemning Jesus because his unique God-consciousness and never-ceasing devotion to God's will precipitated the evil act of crucifixion? We must come to see that, as the federal courts have consistently affirmed, it is wrong to urge an individual to cease his efforts to gain his basic constitutional rights because the quest may precipitate violence. Society must protect the robbed and punish the robber.

I had also hoped that the white moderate would reject the myth concerning time in relation to the struggle for freedom. I have just received a letter from a white brother in Texas. He writes: "All Christians know that the colored people will receive equal rights eventually, but it is possible that you are in too great a religious hurry. It has taken Christianity almost two thousand years to accomplish what it has. The teachings of Christ take time to come to earth." Such an attitude stems from a tragic misconception of time, from the strangely irrational notion that there is something in the very flow of time that will inevitably cure all ills. Actually, time itself is neutral; it can be used either destructively or constructively. More and more I feel that the people of ill will have used time much more effectively than have the people of good will. We will have to repent in this generation not merely for the hateful words and actions of the bad people but for the appalling silence of the good people. Human progress never rolls in on wheels of inevitability; it comes through the tireless efforts of men willing to be co-workers with God, and without this hard work, time itself becomes an ally of the forces of social stagnation. We must use time creatively, in the knowledge that time is always ripe to do right. Now is the time to make real the promise of democracy and transform our pending national elegy into a creative psalm of brotherhood. Now is the time to lift our national policy from the quicksand of racial injustice to the solid rock of human dignity.

You speak of our activity in Birmingham as extreme. At first I was rather disappointed that fellow clergymen would see my nonviolent efforts as those of an extremist. I began thinking about the fact that I stand in the middle of two opposing forces in the Negro community. One is a force of complacency, made up in part of Negroes who, as a result of long years of oppression, are so drained of self-respect and a sense of "somebodiness" that they have adjusted to segregation; and in part of a few middle-class Negroes who, because of a degree of academic and economic security and because in some ways they profit by segregation, have become insensitive to the problems of the masses. The other force is one of bitterness and hatred, and it comes perilously close to advocating violence. It is expressed in the various black nationalist groups that are springing up across the nation, the largest and best-known being Elijah Muhammad's Muslim movement. Nourished by the Negro's frustration over the continued existence of racial discrimination, this movement is made up of people who have lost faith in America, who have absolutely repudiated Christianity, and who have concluded that the white man is an incorrigible "devil."

I have tried to stand between these two forces, saying that we need emulate neither the "do-nothingism" of the complacent nor the hatred and despair of the black nationalist. For there is the more excellent way of love and nonviolent protest. I am grateful to God that, through the influence of the Negro church, the way of nonviolence became an integral part of our struggle.

If this philosophy had not emerged, by now many streets of the South would, I am convinced, be flowing with blood. And I am further convinced that if our white brothers dismiss as "rabble-rousers" and "outside agitators" those of us who employ nonviolent direct action, and if they refuse to support our nonviolent efforts, millions of Negroes will, out of frustration and despair, seek solace and security in black-nationalist ideologies—a development that would inevitably lead to a frightening racial nightmare.

Oppressed people cannot remain oppressed forever. The yearning for freedom eventually manifests itself, and that is what has happened to the American Negro. Something within has reminded him of his birthright of freedom, and something without has reminded him that it can be gained. Consciously or unconsciously, he has been caught up by the *Zeitgeist,* and with his black brothers of Africa and his brown and yellow brothers of Asia, South America and the Caribbean, the United States Negro is moving with a sense of great urgency toward the promised land of racial justice. If one recognizes this vital urge that has engulfed the Negro community, one should readily understand why public demonstrations are taking place. The Negro has many pent-up resentments and latent frustrations, and he must release them. So let him march; let him make prayer pilgrimages to the city hall; let him go on freedom rides—and try to understand why he must do so. If his repressed emotions are not released in nonviolent ways, they will seek expression through violence; this is not a threat but a fact of history. So I have not said to my people: "Get rid of your discontent." Rather, I have tried to say that this normal and healthy discontent can be channeled into the creative outlet of nonviolent direct action. And now this approach is being termed extremist.

But though I was initially disappointed at being categorized as an extremist, as I continued to think about the matter I gradually gained a measure of satisfaction from the label. Was not Jesus an extremist for love: "Love your enemies, bless them that curse you, do good to them that hate you, and pray for them which despitefully use you, and persecute you." Was not Amos an extremist for justice: "Let justice roll down like waters and righteousness like an ever-flowing stream." Was not Paul an extremist for the Christian gospel: "I bear in my body the marks of the Lord Jesus." Was not Martin Luther an extremist: "Here I stand; I cannot do otherwise, so help me God." And John Bunyan: "I will stay in jail to the end of my days before I make a butchery of my conscience." And Abraham Lincoln: "This nation cannot survive half slave and half free." And Thomas Jefferson: "We hold these truths to be self-evident, that all men are created equal . . . " So the question is not whether we will be extremists, but what kind of extremists we will be. Will we be extremists for hate or for love? Will we be extremists for the preservation of injustice or for the extension of justice? In that dramatic scene on Calvary's hill three men were crucified. We must never forget that all three were crucified for the same crime—the crime of extremism. Two were extremists for immorality, and thus fell below their environment. The other, Jesus Christ, was an extremist for love, truth and goodness, and thereby rose above his environment. Perhaps the South, the nation and the world are in dire need of creative extremists.

I had hoped that the white moderate would see this need. Perhaps I was too optimistic; perhaps I expected too much. I suppose I should have realized that few members of the oppressor race can understand the deep groans and passionate yearnings of the oppressed race, and still fewer have the vision to see that injustice must be rooted out by strong, persistent and determined action. I am thankful, however, that some of our white brothers in the South have grasped the meaning of this social revolution and committed themselves to it. They are still all too few in quantity, but they are big in quality. Some—such as Ralph McGill, Lillian Smith, Harry Golden, James McBride Dabbs, Ann Braden and Sarah Patton Boyle—have written about our struggle in eloquent and prophetic terms. Others have marched with us down nameless streets of the South. They have languished in filthy, roach-infested jails, suffering the abuse and brutality of policemen who view them as "dirty nigger-lovers." Unlike so many of their moderate brothers and sisters, they have recognized the urgency of the moment and sensed the need for powerful "action" antidotes to combat the disease of segregation.

Let me take note of my other major disappointment. I have been so greatly disappointed with the white church and its leadership. Of course, there are some notable exceptions. I am not unmindful of the fact that each of you has taken some significant stands on this issue. I commend you, Reverend Stallings, for your Christian stand on this past Sunday, in welcoming Negroes to your worship service on a nonsegregated basis. I commend the Catholic leaders of this state for integrating Spring Hill College several years ago.

But despite these notable exceptions, I must honestly reiterate that I have been disappointed with the church. I do not say this as one of those negative critics who can always find something wrong with the church. I say this as a minister of the gospel, who loves the church; who was nurtured in its bosom; who has been sustained by its spiritual blessings and who will remain true to it as long as the cord of life shall lengthen.

When I was suddenly catapulted into the leadership of the bus protest in Montgomery, Alabama, a few years ago, I felt we would be supported by the white church. I felt that the white ministers, priests and rabbis of the South would be among our strongest allies. Instead, some have been outright opponents, refusing to understand the freedom movement and misrepresenting its leaders; all too many others have been more cautious than courageous and have remained silent behind the anesthetizing security of stained-glass windows.

In spite of my shattered dreams, I came to Birmingham with the hope that the white religious leadership of this community would see the justice of our cause and, with deep moral concern, would serve as the channel through which our just grievances could reach the power structure. I had hoped that each of you would understand. But again I have been disappointed.

I have heard numerous southern religious leaders admonish their worshipers to comply with a desegregation decision because it is the law, but I have longed to hear white ministers declare: "Follow this decree because integration is morally right and because the Negro is your brother." In the midst of blatant injustices inflicted upon the Negro, I have watched white churchmen stand on the sideline and mouth pious irrelevancies and sanctimonious trivialities. In the midst of a mighty struggle to rid our nation of racial and economic injustice, I have heard many ministers say: "Those are social issues, with which the gospel has no real concern." And I have watched many churches commit themselves to a completely otherworldly religion which makes a strange, un-biblical distinction between body and soul, between the sacred and the secular.

I have traveled the length and breadth of Alabama, Mississippi and all the other southern states. On sweltering summer days and crisp autumn mornings I have looked at the South's beautiful churches with their lofty spires pointing heavenward. I have beheld the impressive outlines of her massive religious-education buildings. Over and over I have found myself asking: "What kind of people worship here? Who is their God? Where were their voices when the lips of Governor Barnett dripped with words of interposition and nullification? Where were they when Governor Wallace gave a clarion call for defiance and hatred? Where were their voices of support when bruised and weary Negro men and women decided to rise from the dark dungeons of complacency to the bright hills of creative protest?"

Yes, these questions are still in my mind. In deep disappointment I have wept over the laxity of the church. But be assured that my tears have been tears of love. There can be no deep disappointment where there is not deep love. Yes, I love the church. How could I do otherwise? I am in the rather unique position of being the son, the grandson and the great-grandson of preachers. Yes, I see the church as the body of Christ. But, oh! How we have blemished and scarred that body through social neglect and through fear of being nonconformists.

There was a time when the church was very powerful—in the time when the early Christians rejoiced at being deemed worthy to suffer for what they believed. In those days the church was not merely a thermometer that recorded the ideas and principles of popular opinion; it was a thermostat that transformed the mores of society. Whenever the early Christians entered a town, the people in power became disturbed and immediately sought to convict the Christians for being "disturbers of the peace" and "outside agitators." But the Christians pressed on, in the conviction that they were "a colony of heaven," called to obey God rather than man. Small in number, they were big in commitment. They were too God-intoxicated to be "astronomically intimidated." By their effort and example they brought an end to such ancient evils as infanticide and gladiatorial contests.

Things are different now. So often the contemporary church is a weak, ineffectual voice with an uncertain sound. So often it is an arch-defender of the status quo. Far from being disturbed by the presence of the church, the power structure of the average community is consoled by the church's silent—and often even vocal—sanction of things as they are.

But the judgment of God is upon the church as never before. If today's church does not recapture the sacrificial spirit of the early church, it will lose its authenticity, forfeit the loyalty of millions, and be dismissed as an irrelevant social club with no meaning for the twentieth century. Every day I meet young people whose disappointment with the church has turned into outright disgust.

Perhaps I have once again been too optimistic. Is organized religion too inextricably bound to the status quo to save our nation and the world? Perhaps I must turn my faith to the inner spiritual church, the church within the church, as the true *ekklesia* and the hope of the world. But again I am thankful to God that some noble souls from the ranks of organized religion have broken loose from the paralyzing chains of conformity and joined us as active partners in the struggle for freedom. They have left their secure congregations and walked the streets of Albany, Georgia, with us. They have gone down the highways of the South on tortuous rides for freedom. Yes, they have gone to jail with us. Some have been dismissed from their churches, have lost the support of their bishops and fellow ministers. But they have acted in the faith that right defeated is stronger than evil triumphant. Their witness has been the spiritual salt that has preserved the true meaning of the gospel in these troubled times. They have carved a tunnel of hope through the dark mountain of disappointment.

I hope the church as a whole will meet the challenge of this decisive hour. But even if the church does not come to the aid of justice, I have no despair about the future. I have no fear about the outcome of our struggle in Birmingham, even if our motives are at present misunderstood. We will reach the goal of freedom in Birmingham and all over the nation, because the goal of America is freedom. Abused and scorned though we may be, our destiny is tied up with America's destiny. Before the pilgrims landed at Plymouth, we were here. Before the pen of Jefferson etched the majestic words of the Declaration of Independence across the pages of history, we were here. For more than two centuries our forebears labored in this country without wages; they made cotton king; they built the homes of their masters while suffering gross injustice and shameful humiliation—and yet out of a bottomless vitality they continued to thrive and develop. If the inexpressible cruelties of slavery could not stop us, the opposition we now face will surely fail. We will win our freedom because the sacred heritage of our nation and the eternal will of God are embodied in our echoing demands.

Before closing I feel impelled to mention one other point in your statement that has troubled me profoundly. You warmly commended the Birmingham police force for keeping "order" and "preventing violence." I doubt that you would have so warmly commended the police force if you had seen its dogs sinking their teeth into unarmed, nonviolent Negroes. I doubt that you would so quickly commend the policemen if you were to observe their ugly and inhumane treatment of Negroes here in the city jail; if you were to watch them push and curse old Negro women and young Negro girls; if you were to see them slap and kick old Negro men and young boys; if you were to observe them, as they did on two occasions, refuse to give us food because we wanted to sing our grace together. I cannot join you in your praise of the Birmingham Police Department.

It is true that the police have exercised a degree of discipline in handling the demonstrators. In this sense they have conducted themselves rather "nonviolently" in public. But for what purpose? To preserve the evil system of segregation. Over the past few years I have consistently preached that nonviolence demands that the means we use must be as pure as the ends we seek. I have tried to make clear that it is wrong to use immoral means to attain moral ends. But now I must affirm that it is just as wrong, or perhaps even more so, to use moral means to preserve immoral ends. Perhaps Mr. Connor and his policemen have been rather nonviolent in public, as was Chief Pritchett in Albany, Georgia, but they have used the moral means of nonviolence to maintain the immoral end of racial injustice. As T. S. Eliot has said: "The last temptation is the greatest treason: To do the right deed for the wrong reason."

I wish you had commended the Negro sit-inners and demonstrators of Birmingham for their sublime courage, their willingness to suffer and their amazing discipline in the midst of great provocation. One day the South will recognize its real heroes. They will be the James Merediths, with the noble sense of purpose that enables them to face jeering and hostile mobs, and with the agonizing loneliness that characterizes the life of the pioneer. They will be old, oppressed, battered Negro women, symbolized in a seventy-two-year-old woman in Montgomery, Alabama, who rose up with a sense of dignity and with her people decided not to ride segregated buses, and who responded with ungrammatical profundity to one who inquired about her weariness: "My feets is tired, but my soul is at rest." They will be the young high school and college students, the young ministers of the gospel and a host of their elders, courageously and nonviolently sitting in at lunch counters and willingly going to jail for conscience sake. One day the South will know that when these disinherited children of God sat down at lunch counters, they were in reality standing up for what is best in the American dream and for the most sacred values in our Judaeo-Christian heritage, thereby bringing our nation back to those great wells of democracy which were dug deep by the founding fathers in their formulation of the Constitution and the Declaration of Independence.

Never before have I written so long a letter. I'm afraid it is much too long to take your precious time. I can assure you that it would have been much shorter if I had been writing from a comfortable desk, but what else can one do when he is alone in a narrow jail cell, other than write long letters, think long thoughts and pray long prayers?

If I have said anything in this letter that overstates the truth and indicates an unreasonable impatience, I beg you to forgive me. If I have said anything that understates the truth and indicates my having a patience that allows me to settle for anything less than brotherhood, I beg God to forgive me.

I hope this letter finds you strong in the faith. I also hope that circumstances will soon make it possible for me to meet each of you, not as an integrationist or a civil-rights leader but as a fellow clergyman and a Christian brother. Let us all hope that the dark clouds of racial prejudice will soon pass away and the deep fog of misunderstanding will be lifted from our fear-drenched communities, and in some not too distant tomorrow the radiant stars of love and brotherhood will shine over our great nation with all their scintillating beauty.

Yours for the cause of Peace and Brotherhood,

Martin Luther King, Jr.

CRITICAL THINKING QUESTIONS

1. How does Martin Luther King, Jr. create an *appeal to our emotions?* Cite examples of what you consider the most effective instance of that appeal.

2. What types of *evidence* does King use in his argument? Cite examples.

3. Are there places in the letter where the argument seems to be more oral than written, places where you can *hear* the words?

WRITING TOPIC

If you were to become an activist, what cause would you support today? Write to a friend inviting that person to join you in your support, citing evidence in the form of reports, personal experience, and authority.

Plato

from Crito

SOCRATES: . . . Ought a man to do what he admits to be right, or ought he to betray the right?

CRITO: He ought to do what he thinks right.

SOCRATES: But if this is true, what is the application? In leaving the prison against the will of the Athenians, do I wrong any? Or rather do I not wrong those whom I ought least to wrong? Do I not desert the principles which are acknowledged by us to be just—what do you say?

CRITO: I cannot tell, Socrates; for I do not know.

SOCRATES: Then consider the matter in this way:—Imagine that I am about to play truant (you may call the proceeding by any name which you like), and the laws of the government come and interrogate me: "Tell us, Socrates," they say: "what are you about? Are you not going by an act of yours to overturn us—the laws, and the whole state, as far as in you lies? Do you imagine that a state can subsist and not be overthrown, in which the decisions of law have no power, but are set aside and trampled upon by individuals?" What will be our answer, Crito, to these and the like words? Any one, and especially a rhetorician, will have a good deal to say on behalf of the law which requires a sentence to be carried out. He will argue that this law should not be set aside; and shall we reply, "Yes, but the state has injured us and given an unjust sentence." Suppose I say that?

CRITO: Very good, Socrates.

SOCRATES: "And was that our agreement with you?" the law would answer; "or were you to abide by the sentence of the state?" And if I were to express my astonishment at their words, the law would probably add: "Answer, Socrates, instead of opening your eyes—you are in the habit of asking and answering questions. Tell us,—What complaint have you to make against us which justifies you in attempting to destroy us and the state? In the first place did we not bring you into existence? Your father married your mother by our aid and begat you. Say whether you have any objection to urge against those of us who regulate marriage?" None, I should reply. "Or against those of us who after birth regulate the nurture and education of children, in which you also were trained? Were not the laws, which have the charge of education, right in commanding your father to train you in music and gymnastics?" Right, I should reply. "Well then, since you were brought into the world and nurtured and educated by us, can you deny in the first place that you are our child and slave, as your fathers were before you? And if this is true you are not on equal terms with us; nor can you think that you have a right to do to us what we are doing to you. Would you have any right to strike or revile or do any other evil to your father or your master, if you had one, because you have been struck or reviled by him, or received some other evil at his hands?—you would not say this? And because we think right to destroy you, do you think that you have any right to destroy us in return, and your country as far as in you lies? Will you, O professor of true virtue, pretend that you are justified in this? Has a philosopher like you failed to discover that our country is more to be valued and higher and holier far than mother or father or any ancestor, and more to be regarded in the eyes of the gods and of men of understanding? Also to be soothed, and gently and reverently entreated when angry, even more than a father, and either to be persuaded, or if not persuaded, to be obeyed? And when we are punished by her, whether with imprisonment or stripes, the punishment is to be endured in silence, and if she leads us to wounds or death in battle, thither we follow as is right; neither may any one yield or retreat or leave his rank, but whether in battle or in a court of law, or in any other place, he must do what his city and his country order him; or he must change their view of what is just: and if he may do no violence to his father or mother, much less may he do violence to his country." What answer shall we make to this, Crito? Do the laws speak truly, or do they not?

CRITO: I think that they do.

SOCRATES: Then the laws will say, "Consider, Socrates, if we are speaking truly that in your present attempt you are going to do us an injury. For, having brought you into the world, and nurtured and educated you, and given you and every other citizen a share in every good which we had to give, we further proclaim to any Athenian by the liberty which we allow him, that if he does not like us when he has become of age and has seen the ways of the city, and made our acquaintance, he may go where he pleases and take his goods with him. None of us laws will forbid him or interfere with him. Any one who does not like us and the city, and who wants to emigrate to a colony or to any other city, may go where he likes, retaining his property. But he who has experience of the manner in which we order justice and administer the state, and still remains, has entered into an implied contract that he will do as we command him. And he who disobeys us is, as we maintain, thrice wrong; first, because in disobeying us he is disobeying his parents; secondly, because we are the authors of his education; thirdly, because he has made an agreement with us that he will duly obey our commands; and he neither obeys them nor convinces us that our commands are unjust; and we do not rudely impose them, but give him the alternative of obeying or convincing us;— that is what we offer, and he does neither.

"These are the sort of accusations to which, as we were saying, you, Socrates, will be exposed if you accomplish your intentions; you, above all other Athenians." Suppose now I ask, why I rather than anybody else? They will justly retort upon me that I above all other men have acknowledged the agreement. "There is clear proof," they will say, "Socrates, that we and the city were not displeasing to you. Of all Athenians you have been the most constant resident in the city, which, as you never leave, you may be supposed to love. For you never went out of the city either to see the games, except once when you went to the Isthmus, or to any other place unless when you were on military service; nor did you travel as other men do. Nor had you any curiosity to know other states or their laws: your affections did not go beyond us and our state; we were your special favorites, and you acquiesced in our government of you; and here in this city you begat your children, which is a proof of your satisfaction. Moreover, you might in the course of the trial, if you had liked, have fixed the penalty at banishment; the state which refuses to let you go now would have let you go then. But you pretended that you preferred death to exile, and that you were not unwilling to die. And now you have forgotten these fine sentiments, and pay no respect to us the laws, of whom you are the destroyer; and are doing what only a miserable slave would do, running away and turning your back upon the compacts and agreements which you made as a citizen. And first of all answer this very question: Are we right in saying that you agreed to be governed according to us in deed, and not in word only? Is that true or not?" How shall we answer, Crito? Must we not assent?

CRITO: We cannot help it, Socrates.

SOCRATES: Then will they not say: "You, Socrates, are breaking the covenants and agreements which you made with us at your leisure, not in any haste or under any compulsion or deception, but after you have had seventy years to think of them, during which time you were at liberty to leave the city, if we were not to your mind, or if our covenants appeared to you to be unfair. You had your choice, and might have gone either to Lacedaemon or Crete, both which states are often praised by you for their good government, or to some other Hellenic or foreign state. Whereas you, above all our Athenians, seemed to be so fond of the state, or, in other words, of us her laws (and who would care about a state which has no laws?), that you never stirred out of her; the halt, the blind, the maimed were not more stationary in her than you were. And now you run away and forsake your agreements. Not so, Socrates, if you will take our advice; do not make yourself ridiculous by escaping out of the city.

"For just consider, if you transgress and err in this sort of way, what good will you do either to yourself or to your friends? That your friends will be driven into exile and deprived of citizenship, or will lose their property, is tolerably certain; and you yourself, if you fly to one of the neighboring cities, as, for example, Thebes or Megara, both of which are well governed, will come to them as an enemy, Socrates, and their government will be against you, and all patriotic citizens will cast an evil eye upon you as a subverter of the laws, and you will confirm in the minds of the judges the justice of their own condemnation of you. For he who is a corrupter of the laws is more than likely to be a corrupter of the young and foolish portion of mankind. Will you then flee from well-ordered citizens and virtuous men? and is existence worth having on these terms? Or will you go to them without shame, and talk to them, Socrates? And what will you say to them? What you say here about virtue and justice and institutions and laws being the best things among men? Would that be decent of you? Surely not. But if you go away from well-governed states to Crito's friends in Thessaly, where there is a great disorder and licence, they will be charmed to hear the tale of your escape from prison, set off with ludicrous particulars of the manner in which you were wrapped in a goatskin or some other disguise, and metamorphosed as the manner is of runaways; but will there be no one to remind you that in your old age you were ashamed to violate the most sacred laws from a miserable desire of a little more life? Perhaps not, if you keep them in a good temper; but if they are out of temper you will hear many degrading things; you will live, but how?—as the flatterer of all men, and the servant of all men; and doing what?—eating and drinking in Thessaly, having gone abroad in order that you may get a dinner. And where will be your fine sentiments about justice and virtue? Say that you wish to live for the sake of your children—you want to bring them up and educate them—will you take them into Thessaly and deprive them of Athenian citizenship? Is this the benefit which you will confer upon them? Or are you under the impression that they will be better cared for and educated here if you are still alive, although absent from them; for your friends will take care of them? Do you fancy that if you are an inhabitant of Thessaly they will take care of them, and if you are an inhabitant of the other world that they will not take care of them? Nay: but if they who call themselves friends are good for anything, they will—to be sure they will.

"Listen, then, Socrates, to us who have brought you up. Think not of life and children first, and of justice afterwards, but of justice first, that you may be justified before the princes of the world below. For neither will you nor any that belong to you be happier or holier or juster in this life, or happier in another, if you do as Crito bids. Now you depart in innocence, a sufferer and not a doer of evil; a victim, not of the laws of men. But if you go forth, returning evil for evil, and injury for injury, breaking the covenants and agreements which you have made with us, and wronging those whom you ought least of all to wrong, that is to say, yourself, your friends, your country, and us, we shall be angry with you while you live, and our brethren, the laws in the world below, will receive you as an enemy; for they will know that you have done your best to destroy us. Listen, then, to us and not to Crito."

This, dear Crito, is the voice which I seem to hear murmuring in my ears, like the sound of the flute in the ears of the mystic; that voice, I say, is humming in my ears, and prevents me from hearing any other. And I know that anything more which you may say will be vain. Yet speak, if you have anything to say.

CRITO: I have nothing to say, Socrates.

SOCRATES: Leave me then, Crito, to fulfill the will of God, and to follow whither he leads.

CRITICAL THINKING QUESTIONS

1. Socrates rejects the argument that he should escape even though escape would be quite easily accomplished. Do you admire his willingness to adhere to his principles?

2. Socrates feels he must model appropriate behavior as a citizen despite the dire consequences. Are there any situations you can imagine where your own individual needs must be placed behind the needs of the society as a whole even when such situations demand individual sacrifice?

WRITING TOPIC

What would Dr. Martin Luther King, Jr. say in response to Socrates? Write a dialogue you imagine the two men might have as they discussed Socrates' decision.

Richard Rodriguez

The Chinese in All of Us

A Mexican American Explores Multiculturalism

The other day, the phone rang; it was a woman who identified herself as the "talent coordinator" for the "Oprah Winfrey Show." She said Oprah was planning a show on self-hating ethnics. "You know," she confided, "Norwegians who don't want to be Norwegian, Greeks who hate Greek food." Anyway, she said breezily, wouldn't I like to make an appearance?

About 10 years ago I wrote a thin book called *Hunger of Memory.* It was a book about my education, which is to say, a book about my Americanization. I wrote of losses and triumphs. And, in passing, I wrote about two issues particularly, affirmative action and bilingual education.

I was a nay-sayer. I became, because of my book, a notorious figure among the Ethnic Left in America. Consider me the brown Uncle Tom. I am a traitor, a sellout. The Spanish word is *pocho.* A *pocho* is someone who forgets his true home. (A shame.) A Richard Rodriguez.

Last year, I was being interviewed by Bill Moyers. "Do you consider yourself American or Hispanic?" he asked.

"I think of myself as Chinese," I answered.

A smart-aleck answer, but one that is true enough. I live in San Francisco, a city that has become, in my lifetime, predominantly Asian, predominantly Chinese. I am becoming like them. Do not ask me how, it is too early to tell. But it is inevitable, living side by side, that we should become like each other. So think of me as Chinese.

Oh, my critics say: Look at you Mr. Rod-ree-guess. You have lost your culture.

They mean, I think, that I am not my father, which is true enough. I did not grow up in the state of Jalisco, in the western part of Mexico. I grew up here, in this country, amongst you. I am like you.

My critics mean, when they speak of culture, something solid, something intact. You have lost your culture, they say, as though I lost it at the Greyhound bus station. You have lost your culture, as though culture is a coat I took off one warm afternoon and then forgot.

I AM MY CULTURE. Culture is not something opposite us, it is rather something we breathe and sweat and live. My culture? Lucille Ball is my culture. (I love Lucy, after all.) And Michael Jackson. And Benjamin Franklin is my culture. And Elvis Presley and Walter Cronkite. Walt Disney is my culture. The New York Yankees.

My culture is you. You created me; if you don't like it, if I make you uncomfortable now by being too much like you, too bad.

When I was a little boy in Sacramento, California, the son of Mexican immigrant parents, Spanish-speaking mainly, even then, in those years, America came at me. America was everywhere around me. America was in the pace of the traffic lights, the assertion of neon, the slouch of the crowd, the impatience of the fast food counter. America was everywhere.

I recognized America best, in those years, standing outside the culture. I recognized its power, and from the first I knew that it threatened to swallow me up. America did not feel like something to choose or not choose. America felt inevitable.

Truman Capote said somewhere that he never met a true bisexual. He meant, I think, that finally people are one thing or the other.

Well, I must tell you that I have never met a truly bicultural person. Oh, I have met people who speak two languages, and all that. But finally, their allegiance belongs more to one side of the border than the other.

And yet, I believe in multiculturalism—my kind of multiculturalism.

I think the adventure of living in a multi-racial, multi-ethnic America leaves one vulnerable to a variety of cultures, a variety of influences. Consider me, for example, Chinese. I am also Irish.

About 10 years ago, I was going to school in England. One weekend, Aer Lingus, the Irish national airline, was offering a reduced fare to Dublin. I thought, "What a lark—it'd be fun to go off to Ireland for the weekend." Strange thing, once I got off the plane, I suddenly felt myself at home. I knew these people. I recognized their faces and their irony and their wit and their sadness.

I'll tell you why. I was educated by Irish Catholic nuns. They were my first, my most important foreign culture, intruding on my Mexican soul, reshaping my soul with their voices.

Sometime after Dublin, I realized something more about myself: All of my best friends from childhood to now, the people I have been closest to, have been Irish-Americans, Irish Catholics.

How is this possible? How is it possible for a Mexican kid from Sacramento, California, to discover himself to be Irish?

In the orthodox American scheme of things, it is nonsense. America is a Protestant country. A low-church Protestant country. America was founded by Puritans who resisted the notion of the group. The most important founding idea of America was the notion of individualism—your freedom from the group, my freedom from you. A most glamorous idea.

Consider this paradox: The belief we share in common as Americans is the belief that we are separate from one another.

There is already with this paradox implied an important tension, one basic to American experience. Our culture, by which I mean our daily experience, is at war with our ideology, by which I mean our Protestant belief in separateness.

Diversity is our strength, we say. There is not an American president who would say anything else: We are a country made stronger by our individuality, by our differences. Which is, in a way, true. But only partly true.

The other truth, I call it my catholic truth about puritan America, is that America exists. America exists as a culture, a sound, an accent, a walk.

Thousands of hotel clerks in thousands of hotels around the world will tell you that America exists. There is a recognizable type. Here they come, the Americans. Bermuda shorts. High-pitched voices. Too easy familiarity. Big tip, insecure tip. A slap on the back.

And when we ourselves are far from home, when we are in the Hilton lobby in Cairo or in Paris, we, too, recognize one another immediately. Across the crowded hotel lobby Americans find one another immediately, either with relief or with slight, acknowledging embarrassment.

It is only when we are home working alongside one another and living next to one another that we wonder whether America exists. We wonder about our individuality. And we talk about our traditional Protestant virtues. We talk about respecting our diversity.

Nativist politicians are saying these days that maybe we should think twice about allowing non-European immigrants into this country. Can America, after all, sustain such diversity?

Liberal American educators end up echoing the point, in a way. They look at faces like mine and they see only what they call "diversity." They wonder, now, if the purpose of education shouldn't be diversity. We should teach our children about their separate cultures—forget the notion of a common culture.

The other day in Las Vegas I was speaking to a group of high school principals. One man, afterward, came up and told me that his school has changed in recent years. In little more than a decade the student body has changed its color, changed its complexion; the school is no longer black and white, but now suddenly Asian and Hispanic.

This principal smiled and said his school has dropped Black History Month in favor of what he calls, "Newcomers Month."

I think this is absurd. I think this is nonsense.

There isn't an American whose history is not black history. All of us, by virtue of being Americans, share in the history of black America—the oppression, the endurance, the triumph.

Do not speak to me of your diversity. My cultural forefathers are black slaves and black emancipators. I am an American.

America exists. Nothing more will I tell you, can I tell you.

Let me tell you some stories.

A friend of mine—let's call him Michael—tells me he's confused by America. Mike goes to junior high school in San Francisco. His teacher is always telling him to stand up, look up. "Speak up, Michael, we can't hear you! Look at me, Michael!"

Then Michael goes home. His Chinese father is always complaining at home. His Chinese father says that Michael is picking up American ways. "And since when have you started to look your father in the eye?"

America exists, dear Michael.

At the family picnic, the boy listens to his relatives argue and laugh. The spices are as familiar as the jokes. There are arguments about old civil wars and faceless politicians. The family is talking Greek or Chinese or Spanish. The boy grows restless; the boy gets up and wanders away from the family picnic to watch some other boys playing baseball in the distance.

America exists.

My Mexican father looks out at America from the window of his morning newspaper. After all these years in this country, he still doubts that America exists. Look at this place, he says. So many faces. So many colors. So many grandmothers and religions and memories here. This is not a real country. Not a real country like China or Germany or Mexico.

It falls to the son to say, America exists, Papa.

There is an unresolved tension between the "I" and the "we." We trust most the "I," though grudgingly we admit the necessity of the "we." The most important communal institution we have is the classroom. We build classrooms, recognize their necessity. But we don't like them.

In the most famous American novel, our greatest book about ourselves, Mark Twain's *Adventures of Huckleberry Finn,* the school marm plays the comic villain. She is always trying to tie down Huck. She tries to make him speak regular. She is always trying to civilize.

We recognize the value of having Huck Finn learn to speak regular, even if we don't like it. And we don't like it. Something in us as Americans forces us to fear the coming of fall, the chill in the woods, the starched shirt, the first day of school.

Let me tell you about my first day of school. I came to the classroom clutching a handful of English. A bilingual child?

The important distinction I want to make here is not between Spanish and English, but between private and public language.

I was the son of working class, immigrant parents. I stress working class. Too often in recent years, we have considered ethnicity and race at the expense of economic standing. Thus, we speak of "minorities" in America and we mean only certain races or so-called "non-white" groups. We use the term minority in a numerical sense. Am I a minority? Well, yes, if we mean that Hispanics generally are "under represented" in American public life. But the term minority is richer as a cultural term. There are certain people in this country who do not imagine themselves to belong to majority society. White. Black. Brown. Most of them are poor. Many of them are uneducated. All of them share a diffidence, a fear, an anxiety about public institutions.

When I walked into the classroom, I was such a minority. I remember the nun wrote my name on the black board: RICHARD RODRIGUEZ. She pronounced it. Then she said, repeat it after me.

It was not that I could not say it. Rather, I would not say it. Why should I? Who was this nun?

She said: Repeat your name after me loud enough so all the boys and girls can understand.

The nun was telling me not just to speak English, but to use language publicly. To speak in a voice loud enough to be heard by strangers. (She was calling me to the first and most crucial lesson of grammar school.)

I was a minority child. It wasn't a question of English versus Spanish. It was a question of public language. I didn't want to speak to you—*los gringos,* boys and girls.

I would not. I could not. I refused to speak up, to look up.

Half a year passed. The nuns worried over me. Speak up, Richard. Stand up, Richard. A year passed. A second year began.

Then one Saturday three nuns appeared at our door. They walked into our house and sat on our sagging blue sofa.

Would it be possible, Mrs. Rodriguez, for you and your husband to use English around the house?

Of course, my mother complied. (What would she not do for her children's public success?)

At first, it seemed a kind of game. We practiced English after dinner. But it was still your language.

Until one other Saturday. I remember my mother and father were speaking Spanish to one another in the kitchen. I did not realize they were speaking Spanish until, the moment they saw me, they switched to English.

I felt pushed away. I remember going over to the sink and turning on the water; standing there dumbly, feeling the water on my hand. I wanted to cry. The water was tepid, then warm, then scalding. I wanted to scream. But I didn't. I turned off the faucet and walked out of the room.

And now you have forgotten how I used to go after school to your house. I used to watch you. I watched television with you, there on the floor. I used to watch the way you laughed. I used to listen to the way you used words. I wanted to swallow you up, to become you. Five-thirty and your mom said, Well, Rickey, we're going to eat in half an hour. Do you want to stay? And I did. I became you.

Something happens to you in the classroom if you are a very good student. You change.

A friend of mine, who went to Bryn Mawr College in the 1950s—when she was the only black student in her class—remembers coming home to North Carolina. She remembers getting off the Greyhound bus. She remembers walking up the sidewalk on the hot early summer day.

When she got home and walked up the five steps of the front porch, her mother was waiting for her behind the screen door.

"I don't want you talkin' white in here," her mother said.

There is a sad story in America about "making it." It is the story of summer vacations. Of no longer being able to speak to one's parents. Of having your Chinese father mock your American ways. ("And since when have you started to look your father in the eye?") It is the story of the girl who learns a different kind of English at school and then is embarrassed to use it at the dinner table.

Bilinguists speak of the necessity of using what they call "family language" in the classroom. If I know anything about education, it is that such a bilingual scheme is bound to fail. Classroom language can never be family language. It is a matter not of different words, but of different contexts.

We don't like to hear such things. We don't like the school marm to change us. We want to believe that August will go on forever and that we can avoid wearing shoes. Huck Finn is America's archetypal bilingual student. He speaks one way— his way, his free way—the school marm wants him to speak another.

As Americans, we must root for Huck.

Americans have lately been searching for a new multi-cultural metaphor for America. We don't like the melting pot. Hispanic Americans particularly have been looking for a new metaphor. Our political coming of age in the late 1960s was accompanied by a stern resistance to the melting pot model of America.

America is a stew. (All of us, presumably chunks of beef in a common broth.)

Or America is a mosaic. A Mexican-American bishop recently said that to me. He pointed at a mosaic of the Virgin of Guadalupe. "That is how I think of America," he said. "We are each of us different colors, but united we produce a wonderful, a beautiful effect."

The trouble, I thought to myself, the trouble is that the tiny pieces of glass are static. In our real lives, we are not static.

America is fluid. The best metaphors of America for me are metaphors suggesting fluidity. Our lives melting into one another.

For myself, I like the metaphor of the melting pot. I like it for two reasons.

First, its suggestion of pain—and there is pain. The school teacher can put a sombrero on my head and tell me to feel proud of my heritage, but I know I am becoming a different person than my father. There is pain in the melting pot. Fall in and you are burned.

But there is to the metaphor also a suggestion of alchemy or magic. Fall into the melting pot and you become a new person, changed, like magic, to gold.

Why do we even talk about multiculturalism?

For several reasons, most of them positive. First and foremost is the influence of the great black civil rights movement of the 1950s and 1960s. We are more apt today to recognize the colors of America than perhaps we were several decades ago. On the TV ad, on the football field, in the bank, in a room like this—we have grown used to different shades of America. But that is only to say that we are more apt to be struck by our differences now that we are side by side than in earlier times when segregation legalized separation.

Less positively, the black civil rights movement was undermined by a romantic separatism. Americans were romanced by the moral authority of the outsider, and the benefits of claiming outsider status. White women. Hispanics. Asians. Suddenly, in the 1970s there was a rush to proclaim one's separate status. The benefit was clear: America confronted real social problems. But the decadence also was clear: middle class Americans ended up competing with one another to proclaim themselves society's victims.

The second factor that gives rise to this multicultural preoccupation has recently been the epic migration of non-Europeans into this country.

A friend of mine teaches at a school in Los Angeles where, she says, there are children from 54 language groups. "What possibility is there," she asks, "to teach such a diverse student body anything in common?"

These children do have something in common, however. They may be strangers to Los Angeles, but they are becoming Americans in Los Angeles. That is the beginning.

While I believe in the notion of a common culture, I believe also in the notion of a dynamic culture. Even while America changes the immigrants, the immigrants are changing us. They have always changed us. Assimilation is reciprocal.

Consider American English, for example. It is not British English. The British forced it down our throats, but the language we speak is changed. We speak American here. There are the sighs of German grandmothers and the laughter of Africans in the speech we use. There are in our speech thousands of words imported and brought unregistered through Ellis Island. Swedish words. Yiddish. Italian.

Listen to my voice and you will hear your Lithuanian grandmother. Listen to my American voice and you will hear the echoes of my Chinese neighbors.

Yes, Mr. Bill Moyers, we are all destined to become Chinese.

CRITICAL THINKING QUESTIONS

1. Richard Rodriguez has angered many advocates of bilingual education as well as those arguing for ethnic pride. Can you see why his *assertions* would stir hostility among these groups?

2. How does Rodriguez make use of personal experience, not only as evidence in support of his assertion, but also in establishing an appeal to *ethos*?

WRITING TOPIC

In what specific ways do you think our society is influenced by ethnic diversity? You might look for examples in food, music, fashion, and language. Write an essay in which you offer at least four pieces of evidence to support your claim.

Frank Chin

A Chinese-American Playwright and Novelist

"When I was a little kid, during World War II, I was raised by white folks: a retired vaudeville acrobat and a retired silent-screen bit player. We lived in a tarpaper shanty, outside Sacramento.

"A war veteran, with one eye missing and a few drinks, said to them, 'What are you doin' with that Jap kid?' I said, 'I'm no Jap kid. I'm an American of Chinese descent.' I didn't know what it was, but he didn't either. The rest of my life, I've been trying to find out exactly what it is." [Laughs.]

He later moved in with his grandmother and aunts in Oakland. "All we spoke in the family was Cantonese."

I hung out with blacks. I learned if I could make them laugh, I wouldn't get beat up and I could walk away and maintain my dignity. They actually came to respect me because I could talk my way out of fights in a way that would make them feel good. They would walk me to school.

Some people looked at this as a rejection of things Chinese. On the other hand, the blacks would say, and the whites, too, why was I talking about all this Chinese stuff? "We think of you as a member of the family." That always bothered me.

The Tower of Babel story always bothered me, too.

Oakland is the Tower of Babel. All these languages. And nobody even speaks English like everybody else. I've come to believe that monotheism encourages racism, whoever practices it. There is only one God and everyone else is an infidel, a pagan, or a goy. The Chinese look on all behavior as tactics and strategy. It's like war. You have to know the terrain. You don't destroy the terrain, you deal with it. We get along, not because we share a belief in God or Original Sin or a social contract, but because we make little deals and alliances with each other.

I like whites and blacks. I take them as individuals. I admire white culture: Shakespeare, the great ideas of Western Civilization. I also like black culture. In the sixties, it became a force in Asian-America. It always had a large presence in Oakland. I grew up with rhythm-and-blues, jazz, our original American art forms.

The fifties was still our age of innocence: the Eisenhower era. Everything was looking up: Perry Como. Since I grew up a loner, without any idea of parents, I thought Mommy and Daddy were just nicknames, like Shorty and Skinny. The idea that parents had a proprietary right over children was alien to me. A lot of the ideas of Chinese inferiority came late to me, from the outside. The one thing that

195

saved me from being raised in the stereotype was my isolation during World War II, being raised by these white folks.

The sixties and the civil-rights movement came along, and the blacks were asserting themselves and getting our attention with phrases like "Power to the People." These wonderful black-leather jackets and the shades and the black berets were new even to the blacks themselves. It was like a parade, everyone in uniform.

As for the yellows, the civil-rights movement made us aware that we had no presence, no image in American culture as men, as people. We were perceived as being bright but with less physical prowess than the blacks and whites. We were more favored than the blacks, but we lacked their manhood. So a bunch of us began to appropriate "blackness." We'd wear the clothes, we'd affect the walk and we began talking black. We'd call our selves "Bro" and began talking Southern: "Hey, man."

We started talking about the sisters in the street and the brothers in the joint. I'd been in the joint and I didn't see any yellows there. I didn't see so many of our sisters walking the streets. That wasn't our thing. If it had been, we might have had a better sex life. [*Laughs.*]

[*He imitates the Black Panther rap.*] "Brothers and sisters, we've gotta organize, get together, and fight the *pig*. Brothers and sisters, Power to the People. Right on!" I said, "*What is this?* This isn't Chinese. It's a yellow minstrel show."

At this time, the government was throwing a lot of money at the gangs. The War on Poverty was on. Chinatown gangs, whose main business was being criminals, suddenly had social significance. They were perfectly happy to collect chump change.

I was teaching a class in Asian-American studies. My students were Chinese-Americans and Japanese-Americans. They were from the suburbs, outside Chinatown. My purpose was to break down stereotypes. So I decided to do an agit-prop thing, having them *play* the stereotypes.

We were rehearsing, doing a rock-and-roll version of

Ching-chong Chinaman,
sitting on a rail,
along come a choo-choo train,
cut off his tail.

Guitars, everything. The Lum gang walks in, walks up to the singer [*Simulates a deep, menacing voice.*]: "Stop singing that song. We don't like it." Lum comes up to me, he's holding his fist down, staring a hole through my chest. A student, a quiet little girl, who'd become a militant, is behind me saying, "Don't take no shit from nobody." I'm saying, "Shhh, shhh!" Porky, who's standing behind Lum, is yelling, "Kill 'im! Kill 'im!"

Lum is growling, "Stop singing that song. It makes fun of Chinese people." I say, in my gentlest voice, "Have you ever heard of satire? We *know* it's a racist song. That's why we're singing it. We're making fun of the people who make fun of Chinese. Do you understand?" I could see I wasn't cutting it. Porky is hollering,

"Kill 'im! Kill 'im!" Finally, in frustration, because I wasn't responding to a fight, they walk out.

The gang council decides that we're too controversial. They call me to a meeting. The leader of the Chinatown Red Guard taps me on the shoulder and says, "I want to talk to you." I turn around and just like in the movies, his fist is coming toward me. He knocks me down, my glasses go flying, he punches me in the stomach. Just like in the movies, he hits me in the back of the neck. While I'm on my hands and knees, he stomps on me and starts kicking me. I'm saying [*in a whining voice*], "This is the wrong movie, guys."

He says, "Identify with China!" I say, "Wait a minute. We're in America. This is where we are, where we live and where we're going to die. There's not going to be any revolution. That's crazy." He can't hit me anymore. He's already done that and it's not working. I've interrupted his speech. This had never happened to him before. He curls his lip and says, "You cultural nationalist!" I go, "*What?* What's a cultural nationalist? Don't you know how to swear? Call me motherfucker, call me asshole, call me anything you want, but what's a cultural nationalist?" He doesn't know what to say to that, so they leave.

George Woo, a big guy, who's now teaching Asian-American Studies at San Francisco State, was pretty tight with the gangs then. He runs after the Red Guard and tells them if they ever beat me up again, he'll take it personally, that I'm his friend. All of a sudden, the leader of the gang council comes up to me and says, "I want to shake your hand. No one ever talked back to Alex that way before." We're all buddy-buddy now, because George said he'll take it personally.

The word flashes through Chinatown. Twenty-five minutes later, another gang of kids shows up. Must be fifteen, sixteen years old. One of them has a Tommy gun. "*Where are they?* We heard someone beat up a friend of George's." [*Laughs.*] I said, "No, no, that's not my style. Let's do it with words."

The civil-rights movement of the sixties affected the Chinese-American community in a number of ways. In ways that aren't very flattering to us. When I went to interview some Asian-American actors who played Charlie Chan's Number One, Two, Three, and Four sons, they were blaming the blacks for the yellows not getting more parts. "Here we've been good people, keeping our noses clean—" Suddenly they realized what I was up to and they saw *me* as a threat. I was making Chinese-Americans controversial by speaking out against racism.

It's an old story. The good Chinese were the Christian Chinese. The good Chinese were the ones who shucked all Chinese ways. They revere Pearl Buck and the missionaries that worked Chinatown. That's what bothered me, our history in Chinatown, San Francisco.

In Chinatown's twelve blocks, there are forty-two Christian churches. On the walls of Chinatown, there's a plaque honoring Ross Hunter, who produced *The Flower Drum Song*; a plaque honoring the song "Grant Avenue"; a plaque marking the birthplace of the first white child in San Francisco; a monument to the first white school. *Nothing* for the Chinese. There is one exception: a monument to Sun Yat Sen. He was a Christian.

Most in the community saw the civil-rights movement as a threat. They objected to school integration because they didn't want their children to be influenced by blacks. The fact is the mimicking of blacks that I experienced were of a few. White journalists have emphasized that aspect. As though the Chinese don't think of themselves as Chinese-Americans. As though we're an enclave, like Americans working for Aramco in Saudi Arabia.

Chinatown may be a stronghold of Chinese culture, but we're Chinese-Americans. We saw the movement as a threat because we might be identified as a minority. We were thinking of ourselves as being assimilated. We had worked so hard at being acculturated that we didn't know anything about China anymore.

During the Depression, my uncle was raised in a Chinese Baptist Home for Boys. To raise money, they put on a show. It was the first Chinese-American black-face minstrel show in the history of the world. I came across the autobiography of the founder. I showed my uncle a picture in the book; the boys in blackface. He burst into tears. He was one of the Chung-mai minstrels. He got sad and I got angry. It was humiliating.

At the same time, we thought we were above the blacks. My family owned some property in the black district of Oakland. I once went with my mother to collect the rent. I said, "These places are terrible." She says, "Yeah, but they drive Cadillacs. It's what you call nigger-rich." That struck me so hard. I had never heard my folks put down blacks, denigrate people that way. Yet we were slumlords, taking advantage, exploiting them. It was a moment of moral confusion. I was eight at the time.

We feel because we're more civilized, quote unquote, because we're more middle-class, that we deserve more acceptance than the blacks. We don't riot, we don't' make waves, we didn't protest, we're more American. We don't see that we've described ourselves as a race of Helen Kellers, mute, blind and deaf. We're the perfect minority.

We embrace Charlie Chan as an image of racist love. Most of us still think the good Chinaman is the Christian, Charlie Chan. There's a Chinese-American sociologist who said, "The Chinese, much to their credit, have never been overly bitter about racial prejudice. They have gone into jobs that reduced visibility and are moving out of population vortices of New York and San Francisco's Chinatown to outlying areas. Such a movement should be encouraged, because dispersion discourages visibility." The stereotype is embraced as a strategy for white acceptance.

The prejudice against blacks still continues, but we're smart enough to know it isn't quite civilized. We're also smart enough to use it to get our share. It happened to me. It was in the sixties. The railroads were taken to court for failing to integrate. They fell under ICC [Interstate Communication Commission] rules. So they put up a call: they were hiring brakemen. I was encouraged to apply. I was a clerk for a railroad company. It was the lowest of the low. I was fairly assured I'd be hired, implying I'd be more acceptable than a black. By default, I became the first Chinese-American brakeman on the Southern Pacific. I was the lesser of the two evils.

We believed what whites believed about blacks. We adopted all the white prejudice. The blacks adopted the same prejudices about us. David Hilliard of the Black

Panthers got up in Portsmouth Square—luckily most Chinese there didn't understand English—and said, "You Chinese are the Uncle Toms of the colored peoples." It was apt. At the same time, the solution was not for us to become black.

The new immigrants, the Indochinese, are a revelation. They still speak all the dialects of Indochina: Lao, Viet, or Cambodian. They pick up English as a matter of necessity, as a language of commerce. It's strategic. It's a white-man's world and you have to get along. Yet, all these languages are being spoken. They're using English as a dialect of Chinese and not following the rules. In Chinese-America, it is the new immigrants threatening our relationship with the whites, not the blacks. They are the unredeemed Chinese Chinese. It's an interesting, exciting time.

CRITICAL THINKING QUESTIONS

1. The narrator creates a frank discussion of his experience as a Chinese-American. What is his attitude toward assimilation by minorities in this country?

2. At the close of his piece, the narrator calls the new Chinese immigrants "unredeemed Chinese Chinese." What does he mean by that phrase?

Henry David Thoreau

Civil Disobedience

I heartily accept the motto,—"That government is best which governs least"; and I should like to see it acted up to more rapidly and systematically. Carried out, it finally amounts to this, which also I believe,—"That government is best which governs not at all;" and when men are prepared for it, that will be the kind of government which they will have. Government is at best but an expedient; but most governments are usually, and all governments are sometimes, inexpedient. The objections which have been brought against a standing army, and they are many and weighty, and deserve to prevail, may also at last be brought against a standing government. The standing army is only an arm of the standing government. The government itself, which is only the mode which the people have chosen to execute their will, is equally liable to be abused and perverted before the people can act through it. Witness the present Mexican war, the work of comparatively a few individuals using the standing government as their tool; for, in the outset, the people would not have consented to this measure.

This American government—what is it but a tradition, though a recent one, endeavoring to transmit itself unimpaired to posterity, but each instant losing some of its integrity? It has not the vitality and force of a single living man; for a single man can bend it to his will. It is a sort of wooden gun to the people themselves. But it is not the less necessary for this; for the people must have some complicated machinery or other, and hear its din, to satisfy that idea of government which they have. Governments show thus how successfully men can be imposed on, even impose on themselves, for their own advantage. It is excellent, we must all allow. Yet this government never of itself furthered any enterprise, but by the alacrity with which it got out of its way. *It* does not keep the country free. *It* does not settle the West. *It* does not educate. The character inherent in the American people has done all that has been accomplished; and it would have done somewhat more, if the government had not sometimes got in its way. For government is an expedient by which men would fain succeed in letting one another alone; and, as has been said, when it is most expedient, the governed are most let alone by it. Trade and commerce, if they were not made of India-rubber, would never manage to bounce over the obstacles which legislators are continually putting in their way; and, if one were to judge these men wholly by the effects of their actions and not partly by their intentions, they would deserve to be classed and punished with those mischievous persons who put obstructions on the railroads.

But, to speak practically and as a citizen, unlike those who call themselves no-government men, I ask for, not at once no government, but *at once* a better government. Let every man make known what kind of government would command his respect, and that will be one step toward obtaining it.

After all, the practical reason why, when the power is once in the hands of people, a majority are permitted, and for a long period continue, to rule is not because they are most likely to be in the right, nor because this seems fairest to the minority, but because they are physically the strongest. But a government in which the majority rule in all cases cannot be based on justice, even as far as men understand it. Can there not be a government in which majorities do not virtually decide right and wrong, but conscience?—in which majorities decide only those questions to which the rule of expediency is applicable? Must the citizen ever for a moment, or in the least degree, resign his conscience to the legislator? Why has every man a conscience, then? I think that we should be men first, and subjects afterward. It is not desirable to cultivate a respect for the law, so much as for the right. The only obligation which I have a right to assume is to do at any time what I think right. It is truly enough said, that a corporation has no conscience; but a corporation of conscientious men is a corporation *with* a conscience. Law never made men a whit more just; and, by means of their respect for it, even the well-disposed are daily made the agents of injustice. A common and natural result of an undue respect for law is, that you may see a file of soldiers, colonel, captain, corporal, privates, powder-monkeys, and all, marching in admirable order over hill and dale to the wars, against their will, ay, against their common sense and consciences, which makes it very steep marching indeed, and produces a palpitation of the heart. They have no doubt that it is a damnable business in which they are concerned; they are all peaceably inclined. Now, what are they? Men at all? or small movable forts and magazines, at the service of some unscrupulous man in power? Visit the Navy-Yard, and behold a marine, such a man as an American government can make, or such as it can make a man with its black arts,—a mere shadow and reminiscence of humanity, a man laid out alive and standing, and already, as one may say, buried under arms with funeral accompaniments, though it may be,—

> Not a drum was heard, not a funeral note,
>   As his corse to the rampart we hurried;
> Not a soldier discharged his farewell shot
>   O'er the grave where our hero we buried.

The mass of men serve the state thus, not as men mainly, but as machines, with their bodies. They are the standing army, and the militia, jailers, constables, posse comitatus, etc. In most cases there is no free exercise whatever of the judgment or of the moral sense; but they put themselves on a level with wood and earth and stones; and wooden men can perhaps be manufactured that will serve the purpose as well. Such command no more respect than men of straw or a lump of dirt. They have the same sort of worth only as horses and dogs. Yet such as these even are commonly esteemed good citizens. Others—as most legislators, politicians, lawyers, ministers, and office-holders—serve the state chiefly with their heads; and, as they rarely make any moral distinctions, they are as likely to serve the Devil, without *intending* it, as

God. A very few, as heroes, patriots, martyrs, reformers in the great sense, and *men*, serve the state with their consciences also, and so necessarily resist it for the most part; and they are commonly treated as enemies by it. A wise man will only be useful as a man, and will not submit to be "clay," and "stop a hole to keep the wind away," but leave that office to his dust at least:—

> I am too high-born to be propertied,
> To be a secondary at control,
> Or useful serving-man and instrument
> To any sovereign state throughout the world.

He who gives himself entirely to his fellow-men appears to them useless and selfish; but he who gives himself partially to them is pronounced a benefactor and philanthropist.

How does it become a man to behave toward this American government to-day? I answer, that he cannot without disgrace be associated with it. I cannot for an instant recognize that political organization as *my* government which is the *slave's* government also.

All men recognize the right of revolution; that is, the right to refuse allegiance to, and to resist, the government, when its tyranny or its inefficiency are great and unendurable. But almost all say that such is not the case now. But such was the case, they think, in the Revolution of '75. If one were to tell me that this was a bad government because it taxed certain foreign commodities brought to its ports, it is most probable that I should not make an ado about it, for I can do without them. All machines have their friction; and possibly this does enough good to counterbalance the evil. At any rate, it is a great evil to make a stir about it. But when the friction comes to have its machine, and oppression and robbery are organized, I say, let us not have such a machine any longer. In other words, when a sixth of the population of a nation which has undertaken to be the refuge of liberty are slaves, and a whole country is unjustly overrun and conquered by a foreign army, and subjected to military law, I think that it is not too soon for honest men to rebel and revolutionize. What makes this duty the more urgent is the fact that the country so overrun is not our own, but ours is the invading army.

Paley, a common authority with many on moral questions, in his chapter on the "Duty of Submission to Civil Government," resolves all civil obligation into expediency; and he proceeds to say, "that so long as the interest of the whole society requires it, that is, so long as the established government cannot be resisted or changed without public inconveniency, it is the will of God that the established government be obeyed, and no longer. . . . This principle being admitted, the justice of every particular case of resistance is reduced to a computation of the quantity of the danger and grievance on the one side, and of the probability and expense of redressing it on the other." Of this, he says, every man shall judge for himself. But Paley appears never to have contemplated those cases to which the rule of expediency does not apply, in which a people, as well as an individual, must do justice, cost what it may. If I have unjustly wrested a plank from a drowning man, I must restore it to him though I drown myself. This, according to Paley, would be inconvenient. But he that would save his life, in such a case, shall lose it. This people must cease to hold slaves, and to make war on Mexico, though it cost them their existence as a people.

In their practice, nations agree with Paley; but does any one think that Massachusetts does exactly what is right at the present crisis?

> A drab of state, a cloth-o'-silver slut,
> To have her train borne up, and her soul trail in the dirt.

Practically speaking, the opponents to a reform in Massachusetts are not a hundred thousand politicians at the South, but a hundred thousand merchants and farmers here, who are more interested in commerce and agriculture than they are in humanity, and are not prepared to do justice to the slave and to Mexico, *cost what it may*. I quarrel not with far-off foes, but with those who, near at home, coöperate with, and do the bidding of, those far away, and without whom the latter would be harmless. We are accustomed to say, that the mass of men are unprepared; but improvement is slow, because the few are not materially wiser or better than the many. It is not so important that many should be as good as you, as that there be some absolute goodness somewhere; for that will leaven the whole lump. There are thousands who are *in opinion* opposed to slavery and to the war, who yet in effect do nothing to put an end to them; who, esteeming themselves children of Washington and Franklin, sit down with their hands in their pockets, and say that they know not what to do, and do nothing; who even postpone the question of freedom to the question of free-trade, and quietly read the prices-current along with the latest advices from Mexico, after dinner, and, it may be, fall asleep over them both. What is the price-current of an honest man and patriot to-day? They hesitate, and they regret, and sometimes they petition; but they do nothing in earnest and with effect. They will wait, well disposed, for others to remedy the evil, that they may no longer have it to regret. At most, they give only a cheap vote, and a feeble countenance and Godspeed, to the right, as it goes by them. There are nine hundred and ninety-nine patrons of virtue to one virtuous man. But it is easier to deal with the real possessor of a thing than with the temporary guardian of it.

All voting is a sort of gaming, like checkers or backgammon, with a slight moral tinge to it, a playing with right and wrong, with moral questions; and betting naturally accompanies it. The character of the voters is not staked. I cast my vote, perchance, as I think right; but I am not vitally concerned that that right should prevail. I am willing to leave it to the majority. Its obligation, therefore, never exceeds that of expediency. Even voting *for the right* is *doing* nothing for it. It is only expressing to men feebly your desire that it should prevail. A wise man will not leave the right to the mercy of chance, nor wish it to prevail through the power of the majority. There is but little virtue in the action of masses of men. When the majority shall at length vote for the abolition of slavery, it will be because they are indifferent to slavery, or because there is but little slavery left to be abolished by their vote. *They* will then be the only slaves. Only *his* vote can hasten the abolition of slavery who asserts his own freedom by his vote.

I hear of a convention to be held at Baltimore, or elsewhere, for the selection of a candidate for the Presidency, made up chiefly of editors, and men who are politicians by profession; but I think, what is it to any independent, intelligent, and respectable man what decision they may come to? Shall we not have the advantage of his wisdom and honesty, nevertheless? Can we not count upon some independent votes? Are there not many individuals in the country who do not attend conventions? But no: I find that the respectable man, so called, has immediately drifted from his position, and despairs of his country, when his country has more reason to despair of him. He forthwith adopts one of the candidates thus selected as the only *available* one, thus proving that he is himself *available* for any purposes of the demagogue. His vote is of no more worth than that of any unprincipled foreigner or hireling native, who may have been bought. O for a man who is a *man*, and, as my neighbor says, has a bone in his back which you cannot pass your hand through! Our statistics are at fault: the population has been returned too large. How many *men* are there to a square thousand miles in his country? Hardly one. Does not America offer any inducement for men to settle here? The American has dwindled into an Odd Fellow,—one who may be known by the development of his organ of gregariousness, and a manifest lack of intellect and cheerful self-reliance; whose first and chief concern, on coming into the world, is to see that the Almshouses are in good repair; and, before yet he has lawfully donned the virile garb, to collect a fund for the support of the widows and orphans that may be; who, in short, ventures to live only by the aid of the Mutual Insurance company, which has promised to bury him decently.

It is not a man's duty, as a matter of course, to devote himself to the eradication of any, even the most enormous wrong; he may still properly have other concerns to engage him; but it is his duty, at least, to wash his hands of it, and, if he gives it no thought longer, not to give it practically his support. If I devote myself to other pursuits and contemplations, I must first see, at least, that I do not pursue them sitting upon another man's shoulders. I must get off him first, that he may pursue his contemplations too. See what gross inconsistency is tolerated. I have heard some of my townsmen say, "I should like to have them order me out to help put down an insurrection of the slaves, or to march to Mexico;—see if I would go"; and yet these very men have each, directly by their allegiance, and so indirectly, at least, by their money, furnished a substitute. The soldier is applauded who refuses to serve in an unjust war by those who do not refuse to sustain the unjust government which makes the war; is applauded by those whose own act and authority he disregards and sets at naught; as if the state were penitent to that degree that it hired one to scourge it while it sinned, but not to that degree that it left off sinning for a moment. Thus, under the name of Order and Civil Government, we are all made at last to pay homage to and support our own meanness. After the first blush of sin comes its indifference; and from immoral it becomes, as it were, *un*moral, and not quite unnecessary to that life which we have made.

The broadest and most prevalent error requires the most disinterested virtue to sustain it. The slight reproach to which the virtue of patriotism is commonly liable, the noble are most likely to incur. Those who, while they disapprove of the character and measures of a government, yield to it their allegiance and support are undoubtedly its most conscientious supporters, and so frequently the most serious obstacles to reform. Some are petitioning the state to dissolve the Union, to disregard the requisitions of the President. Why do they not dissolve it themselves,—the union between themselves and the state,—and refuse to pay their quota into its treasury? Do not they stand in the same relation to the state that the state does to the Union? And have not the same reasons prevented the state from resisting the Union which have prevented them from resisting the state?

How can a man be satisfied to entertain an opinion merely, and enjoy *it?* Is there any enjoyment in it, if his opinion is that he is aggrieved? If you are cheated out of a single dollar by your neighbor, you do not rest satisfied with knowing that you are cheated, or with saying that you are cheated, or even with petitioning him to pay you your due; but you take effectual steps at once to obtain the full amount, and see that you are never cheated again. Action from principle, the perception and the performance of right, changes things and relations; it is essentially revolutionary, and does not consist wholly with anything which was. It not only divides states and churches, it divides families; ay, it divides the *individual*, separating the diabolical in him from the divine.

Unjust laws exist: shall we be content to obey them, or shall we endeavor to amend them, and obey them until we have succeeded, or shall we transgress them at once? Men generally, under such a government as this, think that they ought to wait until they have persuaded the majority to alter them. They think that, if they should resist, the remedy would be worse than the evil. But it is the fault of the government itself that the remedy *is* worse than the evil. *It* makes it worse. Why is it not more apt to anticipate and provide for reform? Why does it not cherish its wise minority? Why does it cry and resist before it is hurt? Why does it not encourage its citizens to be on the alert to point out its faults, and *do* better than it would have them? Why does it always crucify Christ, and excommunicate Copernicus and Luther, and pronounce Washington and Franklin rebels?

One would think, that a deliberate and practical denial of its authority was the only offense never contemplated by government; else, why has it not assigned its definite, its suitable and proportionate penalty? If a man who has no property refuses but once to earn nine shillings for the state, he is put in prison for a period unlimited by any law that I know, and determined only by the discretion of those who placed him there; but if he should steal ninety times nine shillings from the state, he is soon permitted to go at large again.

If the injustice is part of the necessary friction of the machine of government, let it go, let it go; perchance it will wear smooth,—certainly the machine will wear out. If the injustice has a spring, or a pulley, or a rope, or a crank, exclusively for itself, then perhaps you may consider whether the remedy will not be worse than the evil; but if it is of such a nature that it requires you to be the agent of injustice to another, then, I say, break the law. Let your life be a counter friction to stop the machine. What I have to do is to see, at any rate, that I do not lend myself to the wrong which I condemn.

As for adopting the ways which the state has provided for remedying the evil, I know not of such ways. They take too much time, and a man's life will be gone. I have other affairs to attend to. I came into this world, not chiefly to make this a good place to live in, but to live in it, be it good or bad. A man has not everything to do, but something; and because he cannot do *everything*, it is not necessary that he should do *something* wrong. It is not my business to be petitioning the Governor or the Legislature any more than it is theirs to petition me; and if they should not hear my petition, what should I do then? But in this case the state has provided no way; its very Constitution is the evil. This may seem to be harsh and stubborn and unconciliatory; but it is to treat with the utmost kindness and consideration the only spirit that can appreciate or deserves it. So is all change for the better, like birth and death, which convulse the body.

I do not hesitate to say, that those who call themselves Abolitionists should at once effectually withdraw their support, both in person and property, from the government of Massachusetts, and not wait till they constitute a majority of one, before they suffer the right to prevail through them. I think that it is enough if they have God on their side, without waiting for that other one. Moreover, any man more right than his neighbors constitutes a majority of one already.

I meet this American government, or its representative, the state government, directly, and face to face, once a year—no more—in the person of its tax-gatherer; this is the only mode in which a man situated as I am necessarily meets it; and it then says distinctly, Recognize me; and the simplest, the most effectual, and, in the present posture of affairs, the indispensablest mode of treating with it on this head, of expressing your little satisfaction with and love for it, is to deny it then. My civil neighbor, the tax-gatherer, is the very man I have to deal with,—for it is, after all, with men and not with parchment that I quarrel,—and he has voluntarily chosen to be an agent of the government. How shall he ever know well what he is and does as an officer of the government, or as a man, until he is obliged to consider whether he shall treat me, his neighbor, for whom he has respect, as a neighbor and well-disposed man, or as a maniac and disturber of the peace, and see if he can get over this obstruction to his neighborliness without a ruder and more impetuous thought or speech corresponding with his action. I know this well, that if one thousand, if one hundred, if ten men whom I could name,—if ten *honest* men only,—ay, if *one* HONEST man, in this State of Massachusetts, *ceasing to hold slaves,* were actually to withdraw from this copartnership, and be locked up in the county jail therefor, it would be the abolition of slavery in America. For it matters not how small the beginning may seem to be; what is once well done is done forever. But we love better to talk about it: that we say is our mission. Reform keeps many scores of newspapers in its service, but not one man. If my esteemed neighbor, the State's ambassador, who will devote his days to the settlement of the question of human rights in the Council Chamber, instead of being threatened with the prisons of

Carolina, were to sit down the prisoner of Massachusetts, that State which is so anxious to foist the sin of slavery upon her sister,—though at present she can discover only an act of inhospitality to be the ground of a quarrel with her,—the Legislature would not wholly waive the subject the following winter.

Under a government which imprisons any unjustly, the true place for a just man is also a prison. The proper place to-day, the only place which Massachusetts has provided for her freer and less desponding spirits, is in her prisons, to be put out and locked out of the State by her own act, as they have already put themselves out by their principles. It is there that the fugitive slave, and the Mexican prisoner on parole, and the Indian come to plead the wrongs of his race should find them; on that separate, but more free and honorable ground, where the State places those who are not *with* her, but *against* her,—the only house in a slave State in which a free man can abide with honor. If any think that their influence would be lost there, and their voices no longer afflict the ear of the State, that they would not be as an enemy within its walls, they do not know by how much truth is stronger than error, nor how much more eloquently and effectively he can combat injustice who has experienced a little in his own person. Cast your whole vote, not a strip of paper merely, but your whole influence. A minority is powerless while it conforms to the majority; it is not even a minority then; but it is irresistible when it clogs by its whole weight. If the alternative is to keep all just men in prison, or give up war and slavery, the State will not hesitate which to choose. If a thousand men were not to pay their tax-bills this year, that would not be a violent and bloody measure, as it would be to pay them, and enable the State to commit violence and shed innocent blood. This is, in fact, the definition of a peaceable revolution, if any such is possible. If the tax-gatherer, or any other public officer, asks me, as one has done, "But what shall I do?" my answer is, "If you really wish to do anything, resign your office." When the subject has refused allegiance, and the officer has resigned his office, then the revolution is accomplished. But even suppose blood should flow. Is there not a sort of blood shed when the conscience is wounded? Through this wound a man's real manhood and immortality flow out, and he bleeds to an everlasting death. I see this blood flowing now.

I have contemplated the imprisonment of the offender, rather than the seizure of his goods,—though both will serve the same purpose,—because they who assert the purest right, and consequently are most dangerous to a corrupt State, commonly have not spent much time in accumulating property. To such the State renders comparatively small service, and a slight tax is wont to appear exorbitant, particularly if they are obliged to earn it by special labor with their hands. If there were one who lived wholly without the use of money, the State itself would hesitate to demand it of him. But the rich man—not to make any invidious comparison—is always sold to the institution which makes him rich. Absolutely speaking, the more money, the less virtue; for money comes between a man and his objects, and obtains them for him; and it was certainly no great virtue to obtain it. It puts to rest many questions which he would otherwise be taxed to answer; while the only new question which it puts is the hard but superfluous one, how to spend it. Thus his moral ground is taken from under his feet. The opportunities of living are diminished in proportion as what are called the "means" are increased. The best thing a man can do for his culture when he is rich is to endeavor to carry out those schemes which he entertained when he was poor. Christ answered to Herodians according to their condition. "Show me the tribute-money," said he;—and one took a penny out of his pocket;—if you use money which has the image of Caesar on it, and which he has made current and valuable, that is, *if you are men of the State,* and gladly enjoy the advantages of Caesar's government, then pay him back some of his own when he demands it. "Render therefore to Caesar that which is Caesar's, and to God those things which are God's,"—leaving them no wiser than before as to which was which; for they did not wish to know.

When I converse with the freest of my neighbors, I perceive that, whatever they may say about the magnitude and seriousness of the question, and their regard for the public tranquillity, the long and the short of the matter is, that they cannot spare the protection of the existing government, and they dread the consequences to their property and families of disobedience to it. For my own part, I should not like to think that I ever rely on the protection of the State. But, if I deny the authority of the State when it presents its tax-bill, it will soon take and waste all my property, and so harass me and my children without end. This is hard. This makes it impossible for a man to live honestly, and at the same time comfortably, in outward respects. It will not be worth the while to accumulate property; that would be sure to go again. You must hire or squat somewhere, and raise but a small crop, and eat that soon. You must live within yourself, and depend upon yourself always tucked up and ready for a start, and not have many affairs. A man may grow rich in Turkey even, if he will be in all respects a good subject of the Turkish government. Confucius said: "If a state is governed by the principles of reason, poverty and misery are subjects of shame; if a state is not governed by the principles of reason, riches and honors are the subjects of shame." No: until I want the protection of Massachusetts to be extended to me in some distant Southern port, where my liberty is endangered, or until I am bent solely on building up an estate at home by peaceful enterprise, I can afford to refuse allegiance to Massachusetts, and her right to my property and life. It costs me less in every sense to incur the penalty of disobedience to the State than it would to obey. I should feel as if I were worth less in that case.

Some years ago, the State met me in behalf of the Church, and commanded me to pay a certain sum toward the support of a clergyman whose preaching my father attended, but never I myself. "Pay," it said, "or be locked up in the jail." I declined to pay. But, unfortunately, another man saw fit to pay it. I did not see why the schoolmaster should be taxed to support the priest, and not the priest the schoolmaster; for I was not the State's schoolmaster, but I supported myself by voluntary subscription. I did not see why the lyceum should not present its tax-bill, and have the State to back its demand, as well as the Church. However, at the request of the selectmen, I condescended to make some such statement as this in writing:—"Know all men by these presents, that I, Henry Thoreau, do not wish to be regarded as a member of any incorporated society which I have not joined." This I gave to the town clerk; and he has it. The State, having thus learned that I did not wish to be regarded as a member of that church, has never made a like demand on me since; though it said that it must adhere to its original presumption that time. If I had known how to name them, I should then have signed off in detail from all the societies which I never signed on to; but I did not know where to find a complete list.

I have paid no poll-tax for six years. I was put into jail once on this account, for one night; and, as I stood considering the walls of solid stone, two or three feet thick, the door of wood and iron, a foot thick, and the iron grating which strained the light, I could not help being struck with the foolishness of that institution which treated me as if I were mere flesh and blood and bones, to be locked up. I wondered that it should have concluded at length that this was the best use it could put me to, and had never thought to avail itself of my services in some way. I saw that, if there was a wall of stone between me and my townsmen, there was still a more difficult one to climb or break through before they could get to be as free as I was. I did not for a moment feel confined, and the walls seemed a great waste of stone and mortar. I felt as if I alone of all my townsmen had paid my tax. They plainly did not know how to treat me, but behaved like persons who are underbred. In every threat and in every compliment there was a blunder; for they thought that my chief desire was to stand the other side of that stone wall. I could not but smile to see how industriously they locked the door on my meditations, which followed them out again without let or hindrance, and *they* were really all that was dangerous. As they could not reach me, they had resolved to punish my body; just as boys, if they cannot come at some person against whom they have a spite, will abuse his dog. I saw that the State was half-witted, that it was timid as a lone woman with her silver spoons, and that it did not know its friends from its foes, and I lost all my remaining respect for it, and pitied it.

Thus the State never intentionally confronts a man's sense, intellectual or moral, but only his body, his senses. It is not armed with superior wit or honesty, but with superior physical strength. I was not born to be forced. I will breathe after my own fashion. Let us see who is the strongest. What force has a multitude? They only can force me who obey a higher law than I. They force me to become like themselves. I do not hear of *men* being *forced* to live this way or that by masses of men. What sort of life were that to live? When I meet a government which says to me, "Your money or your life," why should I be in haste to give it my money? It may be in a great strait, and not know what to do: I cannot help that. It must help itself; do as I do. It is not worth the while to snivel about it. I am not responsible for the successful working of the machinery of society. I am not the son of the engineer. I perceive that, when an acorn and a chestnut fall side by side, the one does not remain inert to make way for the other, but both obey their own laws, and spring and grow and flourish as best they can, till one, perchance, overshadows and destroys the other. If a plant cannot live according to its nature, it dies; and so a man.

The night in prison was novel and interesting enough. The prisoners in their shirt-sleeves were enjoying a chat and the evening air in the doorway, when I entered. But the jailer said, "Come, boys, it is time to lock up;" and so they dispersed, and I heard the sound of their steps returning into the hollow apartments. My room-mate was introduced to me by the jailer as "a first-rate fellow and a clever man." When the door was locked, he showed me where to hang my hat, and how he managed matters there. The rooms were whitewashed once a month; and this one, at least, was the whitest, most simply furnished, and probably the neatest apartment in the town. He naturally wanted to know where I came from, and what brought me there; and, when I had told him, I asked him in my turn how he came there, presuming him to be an honest man, of course; and, as the world goes, I believe he was. "Why," said he, "they accuse me of burning a barn; but I never did it." As near as I could discover, he had probably gone to bed in a barn when drunk, and smoked his pipe there; and so a barn was burnt. He had the reputation of being a clever man, had been there some three months waiting for his trial to come on, and would have to wait as much longer; but he was quite domesticated and contented, since he got his board for nothing, and thought that he was well treated.

He occupied one window, and I the other; and I saw that if one stayed there long, his principal business would be to look out the window. I had soon read all the tracts that were left there, and examined where former prisoners had broken out, and where a grate had been sawed off, and heard the history of the various occupants of that room; for I found that even here there was a history and a gossip which never circulated beyond the walls of the jail. Probably this is the only house in the town where verses are composed, which are afterward printed in a circular form, but not published. I was shown quite a long list of verses which were composed by some young men who had been detected in an attempt to escape, who avenged themselves by singing them.

I pumped my fellow-prisoner as dry as I could, for fear I should never see him again; but at length he showed me which was my bed, and left me to blow out the lamp.

It was like traveling into a far country, such as I had never expected to behold, to lie there for one night. It seemed to me that I never had heard the town-clock strike before, nor the evening sounds of the village; for we slept with the windows open, which were inside the grating. It was to see my native village in the light of the Middle Ages, and our Concord was turned into a Rhine stream, and visions of knights and castles passed before me. They were the voices of old burghers that I heard in the streets. I was an involuntary spectator and auditor of whatever was done and said in the kitchen of the adjacent village-inn,—a wholly new and rare experience to me. It was a closer view of my native town. I was fairly inside of it. I never had seen its institutions before. This is one of its peculiar institutions; for it is a shire town. I began to comprehend what its inhabitants were about.

In the morning, our breakfasts were put through the hole in the door, in small oblong-square tin pans, made to fit, and holding a pint of chocolate, with brown bread, and an iron spoon. When they called for the vessels again, I was green enough to return what bread I had left; but my comrade seized it, and said that I should lay that up for lunch or dinner. Soon after he was let out to work at haying in a neighboring field, whither he went every day, and would not be back till noon; so he bade me good-day, saying that he doubted if he should see me again.

When I came out of prison,—for some one interfered, and paid that tax,—I did not perceive that great changes had taken place on the common, such as he observed who went in a youth and emerged a tottering and gray-headed man; and yet a change had to my eyes come over the scene,—the town, and State, and country,—greater than any that mere time could effect. I saw yet more distinctly the State in which I lived. I saw to what extent the people among whom I lived could be trusted as good neighbors and friends; that their friendship was for summer weather only; that they did not greatly propose to do right; that they were a distinct race from me by their prejudices and superstitions, as the Chinamen and Malays are; that in their sacrifices to humanity they ran no risks, not even to their property; that after all they were not so noble but they treated the thief as he had treated them, and hoped, by a certain outward observance and a few prayers, and by walking in a particular straight though useless path from time to time, to save their souls. This may be to judge my neighbors harshly; for I believe that many of them are not aware that they have such an institution as the jail in their village.

It was formerly the custom in our village, when a poor debtor came out of jail, for his acquaintances to salute him, looking through their fingers, which were crossed to represent the grating of a jail window, "How do ye do?" My neighbors did not thus salute me, but first looked at me, and then at one another, as if I had returned from a long journey. I was put into jail as I was going to the shoemaker's to get a shoe which was mended. When I was let out the next morning, I proceeded to finish my errand, and, having put on my mended shoe, joined a huckleberry party, who were impatient to put themselves under my conduct; and in half an hour,—for the horse was soon tackled,—was in the midst of a huckleberry field, on one of our highest hills, two miles off, and then the State was nowhere to be seen.

This is the whole history of "My Prisons."

I have never declined paying the highway tax, because I am as desirous of being a good neighbor as I am of being a bad subject; and as for supporting schools, I am doing my part to educate my fellow-countrymen now. It is for no particular item in the tax-bill that I refuse to pay it. I simply wish to refuse allegiance to the State, to withdraw and stand aloof from it effectually. I do not care to trace the course of my dollar, if I could, till it buys a man or a musket to shoot one with,—the dollar is innocent,—but I am concerned to trace the effects of my allegiance. In fact, I quietly declare war with the State, after my fashion, though I will still make what use and get what advantage of her I can, as is usual in such cases.

If others pay the tax which is demanded of me, from a sympathy with the State, they do but what they have already done in their own case, or rather they abet injustice to a greater extent than the State requires. If they pay the tax from a mistaken interest in the individual taxed, to save his property, or prevent his going to jail, it is because they have not considered wisely how far they let their private feelings interfere with the public good.

This, then, is my position at present. But one cannot be too much on his guard in such a case, lest his action be biased by obstinacy or an undue regard for the opinions of men. Let him see that he does only what belongs to himself and to the hour.

I think sometimes, Why, this people mean well, they are only ignorant; they would do better if they knew how: why give your neighbors this pain to treat you as they are not inclined to? But I think again, This is no reason why I should do as they do, or permit others to suffer much greater pain of a different kind. Again, I sometimes say to myself, When many millions of men, without heat, without ill will, without personal feeling of any kind, demand of you a few shillings only, without the possibility, such is their constitution, of retracting or altering their present demand, and without the possibility, on your side, of appeal to any other millions, why expose yourself to this overwhelming brute force? You do not resist cold and hunger, the winds and the waves, thus obstinately; you quietly submit to a thousand similar necessities. You do not put your head into the fire. But just in proportion as I regard this as not wholly a brute force, but partly a human force, and consider that I have relations to those millions as to so many millions of men, and not of mere brute or inanimate things, I see that appeal is possible, first and instantaneously, from them to the Maker of them, and, secondly, from them to themselves. But if I put my head deliberately into the fire, there is no appeal to fire or to the Maker of fire, and I have only myself to blame. If I could convince myself that I have any right to be satisfied with men as they are, and to treat them accordingly, and not according, in some respects, to my requisitions and expectations of what they and I ought to be, then, like a good Mussulman and fatalist, I should endeavor to be satisfied with things as they are, and say it is the will of God. And, above all, there is this difference between resisting this and a purely brute or natural force, that I can resist this with some effect; but I cannot expect, like Orpheus, to change the nature of the rocks and trees and beasts.

I do not wish to quarrel with any man or nation. I do not wish to split hairs, to make fine distinctions, or set myself up as better than my neighbors. I seek rather, I may say, even an excuse for conforming to the laws of the land. I am but too ready to conform to them. Indeed, I have reason to suspect myself on this head; and each year, as the tax-gatherer comes round, I find myself disposed to review the acts and position of the general and State governments, and the spirit of the people, to discover a pretext for conformity.

> We must affect our country as our parents,
> And if at any time we alienate
> Our love or industry from doing it honor,
> We must respect effects and teach the soul
> Matter of conscience and religion,
> And not desire of rule or benefit.

I believe that the State will soon be able to take all my work of this sort out of my hands, and then I shall be no better a patriot than my fellow-countrymen. Seen from a lower point of view, the Constitution, with all its faults, is very good; the law and the courts are very respectable; even this State and this American government are, in many respects, very admirable, and rare things, to be thankful for, such as a great many have described them; but seen from a point of view a little higher, they are what I have described them; seen from a higher still, and the highest, who shall say what they are, or that they are worth looking at or thinking of at all?

However, the government does not concern me much, and I shall bestow the fewest possible thoughts on it. It is not many moments that I live under a government, even in this world. If a man is thought-free, fancy-free, imagination-free, that which *is not* never *for* a long time appearing *to be* to him, unwise rulers or reformers cannot fatally interrupt him.

I know that most men think differently from myself; but those whose lives are by profession devoted to the study of these or kindred subjects content me as little as any. Statesmen and legislators, standing so completely within the institution, never distinctly and nakedly behold it. They speak of moving society, but have no resting-place without it. They may be men of a certain experience and discrimination, and have no doubt invented ingenious and even useful systems, for which we sincerely thank them; but all their wit and usefulness lie within certain not very wide limits. They are wont to forget that the world is not governed by policy and expediency. Webster never goes behind government, and so cannot speak with authority about it. His words are wisdom to those legislators who contemplate no essential reform in the existing government; but for thinkers, and those who legislate for all time, he never once glances at the subject. I know of those whose serene and wise speculations on this theme would soon reveal the limits of his mind's range and hospitality. Yet, compared with the cheap professions of most reformers, and the still cheaper wisdom and eloquence of politicians in general, his are almost the only sensible and valuable words, and we thank Heaven for him. Comparatively, he is always strong, original, and above all, practical. Still, his quality is not wisdom, but prudence. The lawyer's truth is not Truth, but consistency or a consistent expediency. Truth is always in harmony with herself, and is not concerned chiefly to reveal the justice that may consist with wrong doing. He well deserves to be called, as he has been called, the Defender of the Constitution. There are really no blows to be given by him but defensive ones. He is not a leader, but a follower. His leaders are the men of '87. "I have never made an effort," he says, "and never propose to make an effort; I have never countenanced an effort, and never mean to countenance an effort, to disturb the arrangement as originally made, by which the various States came into the Union." Still thinking of the sanction which the Constitution gives to slavery, he says, "Because it was a part of the original compact,—let it stand." Notwithstanding his special acuteness and ability, he is unable to take a fact out of its merely political relations, and behold it as it lies absolutely to be disposed of by the intellect,—what, for instance, it behooves a man to do here in America to-day with regard to slavery,—but ventures, or is driven, to make some such desperate answer as the following, while professing to speak absolutely, and as a private man,—from which what new and singular code of social duties might be inferred? "The manner," says he, "in which the governments of those States where slavery exists are to regulate it is for their own consideration, under their responsibility to their constituents, to the general laws of propriety, humanity, and justice, and to God. Associations formed elsewhere, springing from a feeling of humanity, or any other cause, have nothing whatever to do with it. They have never received any encouragement from me, and they never will."

They who know of no purer sources of truth, who have traced up its stream no higher, stand, and wisely stand, by the Bible and the Constitution, and drink at it there with reverence and humility; but they who behold where it comes trickling into this lake or that pool, gird up their loins once more, and continue their pilgrimage toward its fountain-head.

No man with a genius for legislation has appeared in America. They are rare in the history of the world. There are orators, politicians, and eloquent men, by the thousand; but the speaker has not yet opened his mouth to speak who is capable of settling the much-vexed questions of the day. We love eloquence for its own sake, and not for any truth which it may utter, or any heroism it may inspire. Our legislators have not yet learned the comparative value of free-trade and of freedom, of union, and of rectitude, to a nation. They have no genius or talent for comparatively humble questions of taxation and finance, commerce and manufactures and agriculture. If we were left solely to the wordy wit of legislators in Congress for our guidance, uncorrected by the seasonable experience and the effectual complaints of the people, America would not long retain her rank among the nations. For eighteen hundred years, though perchance I have no right to say it, the New Testament has been written; yet where is the legislator who has wisdom and practical talent enough to avail himself of the light which it sheds on the science of legislation?

The authority of government, even such as I am willing to submit to,—for I will cheerfully obey those who know and can do better than I, and in many things even those who neither know nor can do so well,—is still an impure one; to be strictly just, it must have the sanction and consent of the governed. It can have no pure right over my person and property but what I concede to it. The progress from an absolute to a limited monarchy, from a limited monarchy to a democracy, is a progress toward a true respect for the individual. Even the Chinese philosopher was wise enough to regard the individual as the basis of the empire. Is a democracy, such as we know it, the last improvement possible in government? Is it not possible to take a step further towards recognizing and organizing the rights of man? There will never be a really free and enlightened State until the State comes to recognize the individual as a higher and independent power, from which all its own power and authority are derived, and treats him accordingly. I please myself with imagining a State at last which can afford to be just to all men, and to treat the individual with respect as a neighbor; which even would not think it inconsistent with its own repose if a few were to live aloof from it, not meddling with it, nor embraced by it, who fulfilled all the duties of neighbors and fellow-men. A State which bore this kind of fruit, and suffered it to drop off as fast as it ripened, would prepare the way for a still more perfect and glorious State, which also I have imagined, but not yet anywhere seen.

CRITICAL THINKING QUESTIONS

1. Thoreau states, "The mass of men serve the state thus, not as men mainly, but as machines . . . In most cases there is not free exercise whatever of the judgment or of the moral sense. . . . " Do you think he is being too harsh on his fellow citizens?

2. "If I devote myself to other pursuits and contemplations, I must first see, at least, that I do not pursue them sitting upon another man's shoulders." If you agree with Thoreau's *assertion,* to what extent would you modify your behavior to follow this concept?

CHAPTER ACTIVITIES

1. The question of school uniforms comes up often in discussion of public schools. Advocates claim uniforms take the emphasis away from class and economic distinctions teens so often focus upon, therefore allowing scholarship to regain its rightful place in schools. On the other hand, placing people in uniforms just does not sound American somehow. Suddenly the land of the free starts sounding a lot like Chairman Mao's China, or at least so argue those against school uniforms. What do you think? Read at least two articles written on this topic and combine the facts of the articles with some *evidence* in the form of personal experience in order to support a *claim of policy* about school uniforms in public schools. Two pieces in this chapter might help you consider this argument, the poem, "Crazy Courage" by Alma Luz Villanueva and the short story, "Harrison Bergeron" by Kurt Vonnegut, Jr.

2. Puritans came to these shores seeking freedom, yet ironically created one of the most repressive societies in our country's history. Our ambivalence toward questions of freedom and conformity, therefore, go back to our very beginnings. Look at the short story, "On the Rainy River," and the poem, "The Love Song of J. Alfred Prufrock" in this chapter which might help you gain some perspective on this subject. Where do you observe or personally encounter that ambivalence today? Based on your observations, create a *claim of fact* and list at least three examples of *evidence* to support your claim.

3. Snowboarders have evoked a great deal of criticism from the skiing community over the past ten years. They do not behave like downhill skiers on the slopes, nor do they choose to wear the glitzy clothing downhill skiers typically choose. They are rebels and enjoy that role. Now, however, the sport has been recognized and accepted into the Winter Olympics, an action some say means snowboarding is becoming mainstream. In fact, societies do often absorb their rebels, co-opting their philosophies and symbols. In this chapter, read the poem, "Passing," to help you see this problem in a wider context. Are there other non-conformists presently being absorbed into mainstream society? How do their positions change as a result? What compromises are demanded? What *evidence* do you see confirming such compromises?

4. Since the American Revolutionary War, this country's flag has been a sacred symbol of our national community. However, during the war protests in the late 1960s, crowds burned the flag and through that act evoked the ire of a wide range of citizens who felt strongly that this nation's flag should not be desecrated. Since that time, the use of the American flag by social protesters and artists has continued to elicit an emotional response from citizen groups who oppose such actions. In Washington, Congress regularly considers an amendment to the Constitution, making the unconventional use of the flag for artistic expression or protests illegal. To gain some insight into restrictive, and some-

times unjust, laws, read the essay, "Letter from Birmimgham Jail," and the poem, "In Response to Executive Order 9066," found in this chapter. Also, read about laws governing the use of the American flag and form a *claim of policy* concerning this topic.

5. What is a hero? How do others define this concept? How do you define it? Think about some of the characters in the selections you have just read; do they fit a definition of hero? Think about real people you have encountered in your life; do any of them fit the definition? How does a hero relate to his or her society? Broaden your understanding of a hero by reading this chapter's play *Antigone,* the short selection "from *Bodega Dreams,*" and the poem, "Hard Rock Returns to Prison from the Hospital for the Criminal Insane." Do some research in the library in order to broaden your understanding of the concept of a hero. Using your research, argue that a particular character within this chapter is or is not a hero. Don't hedge; take a stand and offer support.

Chapter Four

Nature and Place

This land is your land, this land is my land
From California to the New York Island
From the redwood forest to the gulfstream water,
This land was made for you and me.

Woodie Guthrie's 1950s' folk ballad celebrates the American people's proud possession of the continent. In the last half of the twentieth century, the responsibility which that possession imposes on us became starkly apparent in the form of clear-cut mountainsides, smog-ridden cities, and fouled waterways. Entering the twenty-first century, we accept our role as custodians of the earth, water, and sky; in some ways the "state" of the environment is healthier than it was fifty years ago. We recognize, too, the complexities of our stewardship as we wrestle with finding a balance between the economic and aesthetic values of our natural resources. Moreover, research shows that preserving species of plants and animals is intrinsically related to the preservation of our own viability as a species. Preservationist advocates also argue that humankind's connection to nature, our sense of community with other living things on this earth—whether in an urban or a rural setting—nurtures our humanity and, likewise, the well-being of the human community. Adding to this ethical argument, they underscore our moral imperative to preserve this legacy of the land for our children. To understand the urgency of these arguments, we need look only to our past.

Only two hundred years ago, the continent of North America was largely uncharted wilderness area. In 1803, President Thomas Jefferson enlisted the services of Meriwether Lewis to follow the Missouri River and its tributaries westward to the Pacific Ocean in order to chart a transcontinental water route. And in May 1804, Lewis, William Clark, and a small party of men set off on their historical journey. Following is an excerpt from *The Journals of Lewis and Clark*, dated Friday, June 3, 1805:

Capt. C. & myself stroled out to the top of the hights in the fork of the rivers from whence we had an extensive and most inchanting view; the country in every derection around us was one vast plain in which innumerable herds of Buffalow were seen attended by their shepperds the wolves; the solatary antelope were distributed over it's face; some herds of Elk were also seen; . . . to the South we saw a range of lofty mountains . . . these were partially covered with snow;. . . . [1]

Although the explorers failed to discover a continuous transcontinental water route, they did document the bounty and beauty of the American West and, thus, inspired a century of westward expansion. European and American settlers pushed westward throughout the 1800s, forcing Native Americans from their lands; acres of virgin forests were cleared, and wild animals slaughtered and displaced. By the end of the nineteenth century, the transformation of the continent was well underway.

In addition to a transcontinental railroad, factories, and metropolises, the nineteenth century spawned some of America's best-known nature writers, notably, Henry David Thoreau and Ralph Waldo Emerson. Whether or not we have read Thoreau in a book, many of us can recite some Thoreau lines, popularized on posters and notecards: "Simplicity, simplicity, simplicity!"; "Time is but the stream I go a-fishing in"; "in Wildness is the preservation of the World." In his celebrated book, *Walden, or Life in the Woods* (1854), Thoreau writes, "I went to the woods because I wished to live deliberately, . . . to live deep and suck out the marrow of life . . . " Inspiring Thoreau was his contemporary Emerson. Emerson's first published book, *Nature,* launched the transcendentalist movement in nineteenth-century America, a philosophy that spiritualized nature, equating it with the soul of the individual:

Standing on the bare ground,—my head bathed by the blithe air, and uplifted into infinite space,—all mean egotism vanishes. I become a transparent eye-ball. I am nothing. I see all. The currents of the Universal Being circulate through me; I am part or particle of God. . . . In the wilderness, I find something more dear and connate than in streets or villages. In the tranquil landscape, and especially in the distant line of the horizon, man beholds somewhat as beautiful as his own nature. (*Nature,* Chapter 1)

Singing his praises of nature, poet Walt Whitman contributed to Emerson's and Thoreau's legacy—the elevation of nature to a mystical experience, a spiritual communion between the self and nature:

I believe a leaf of grass is no less than the journey-work of the stars,
And the pismire is equally perfect, and a grain of sand, and the egg of the wren,
And the tree-toad is a chief-d'oeuvre for the highest,
And the running blackberry would adorn the parlors of heaven,

---

[1] *The Journals of Lewis and Clark,* ed. Bernard DeVoto (Boston: Houghton Mifflin, Co.), p.125.

And the narrowest hinge in my hand puts to scorn all machinery,
And the cow crunching with depress'd head surpasses any statue,
And a mouse is miracle enough to stagger sextillions of infidels.
(*Song of Myself,* 31)

Observing the world of nature, Whitman celebrates its simple yet celestial beauty.

The spiritual concept of nature is neither uniquely American nor uniquely nineteenth century. Its roots reach back to pre-Christian times and span the globe. However, Thoreau and his contemporaries were instrumental in resurrecting and renewing the spiritual concept of nature for nineteenth- and twentieth-century readers and authors. Indeed, Annie Dillard's 1974 Pulitzer Prize-winning book, *Pilgrim at Tinker Creek,* is a direct literary descendant of Thoreau's *Walden.* Dillard's first-person narrative is rendered with minute, descriptive details and laced with meditative musings:

> Trees stir memories; live waters heal them. The creek is the mediator, benevolent, impartial, subsuming my shabbiest evils and dissolving them, transforming them into live moles, and shiners, and sycamore leaves. It is a place even my faithfulness hasn't offended; it still flashes for me, now and tomorrow, that intricate, innocent face. It waters an undeserving world, saturating cells with lodes of light. I stand by the creek over rock under trees. ("The Present")

In the 1970s, Dillard's book found a highly receptive audience. As the protest causes of the 1960s (the Vietnam War and civil rights) cooled, the call to "save the environment" helped fill the vacuum for a new decade of protesters.

Environmental causes became central themes in popular culture—in art, literature, music, and movies. Most of us know Dr. Suess's modern children's classics, *The Cat in the Hat* and *Green Eggs and Ham.* In 1971, he published *The Lorax,* the story of the destruction of an ecosystem—the chopping down of the Truffula Trees to build a factory to produce Thneeds: "and BIGGERING and BIGGERING and BIGGERING, turning MORE Truffula Trees into Thneeds which everyone, EVERYONE, EVERYONE needs!" Singer Randy Newman took up the cause of urban pollution in his 1972 song, "Burn on":

> There's a red moon rising
> On the Cuyahoga River
> Rolling into Cleveland to the lake
>
> · · · ·
> And the Lord can make you overflow
> But the Lord can't make you burn
> Burn on, big river, burn on

And raising the banner of endangered species for moviegoers in *Star Trek IV: The Voyage Home,* Captain Kirk and the crew of the Enterprise travel back in time to 1988 to save the humpback whale from extinction. Today, as we enter the new millennium, interest in the environment is mainstream, central to the lives of individuals of all economic and ethnic backgrounds and a potent issue at the local community level as well as national and global levels. We share a common concern about our planet's environmental quality.

This chapter presents readings that invite you to explore different ways of seeing, feeling, and thinking about the themes of nature and place. For Emerson and Thoreau, for example, nature provides a place for a spiritual cleansing, the path to a higher state of being. However, for the narrator in Jack London's "To Build a Fire" and for Phoenix Jackson in Eudora Welty's "A Worn Path," nature presents physical challenges, throwing out obstacles that may even prove to be deadly. Several selections focus on human relationships to animals. Specifically, the slaying of wildlife is featured in James Fenimore Cooper's "The Slaughter of the Pigeons" and Sarah Orne Jewett's short story, "A White Heron." Ursula K. Le Guin's "May's Lion" depicts a mystical communion between an old woman and a dying mountain lion. However, the poem, "The Panther" by Rainer Maria Rilke, dramatizes the disquieting disharmony between animals and humans, when an animal is caged as an exotic creature, on view for humans. In William Stafford's poem, "Traveling through the Dark," the speaker confronts a dilemma that illustrates the inherent conflict between the human and wilderness communities: "I stood in the glare of the warm exhaust turning red;/ around our group, I could hear the wilderness sing." In contrast, poet James Wright's "A Blessing" displays a harmonious and tranquil moment of contact between humans and animals.

Furthermore, the literature in this chapter presents varying perspectives on one's sense of place, the values an individual associates with his or her physical setting. N. Scott Momaday, for example, weaves together the vibrant threads of his Kiowa heritage—its myths, legends, histories—to create a sense of place as palpable as the mountain which titles his book, *The Way to Rainy Mountain.* But Alice Walker, even as she admires the view from her deck in Northern California, declares, "I am a displaced person. . . . there are days when my view of mountains and redwoods makes me nostalgic for small rounded hills . . . the look of big leaf poplar and the scent of pine and firs." For poet Theodore Roethke, in "Meditation at Oyster River," a rocky ledge above a river quite literally provides a seat for reflection: "Water's my will, and my way/ And the spirit runs, intermittently." On the other hand, as we suggested in Chapter One, for the speaker of Lucille Clifton's poem, "For de Lawd," an urban setting, "the inner city," is "home" where she is "happy to be alive." And in Virginia Woolf's short story, "Kew Gardens," the details about the flowers and insects of a formal botanic garden in suburban London overshadow the human element, the garden's visitors.

Finally, as readers, we bring the authority of our particular experiences and ideas to our readings of the story, poem, play, or essay text. Before reading the selections that follow, let's explore our personal perspectives on nature and on place.

PREWRITING AND DISCUSSION

1. a. What is *nature?* Spend several minutes thinking about your views on nature. Write about your own personal experiences with nature and about images of nature you can recall from movies, songs, photographs, paintings, or books.

In reading back over your writing, does anything surprise you? Write a sentence or two that sums up the most important impression or ideas that emerge in your writing.

b. Spend several minutes writing about *place,* an actual, physical setting, or landscape, that has particular meaning or value for you as an individual. What makes this place special? How do you relate to it? Is it a part of your self-identity—of who you are? How so?

2. In groups of three or four, discuss your writings. Look for common ground, for shared values and attitudes, and note different viewpoints or ideas. Drawing from each group member's writings, list key impressions and ideas for both *nature* and *place,* and be prepared to report your findings to the rest of the class.

Rick Bass

Antlers

Halloween brings us all closer, in the valley. The Halloween party at the saloon is when we all, for the first time since last winter, realize why we are all up here—all three dozen of us—living in this cold, blue valley. Sometimes there are a few tourists through the valley in the high green grasses of summer, and the valley is opened up a little. People slip in and out of it; it's almost a regular place. But in October the snows come, and it closes down. It becomes our valley again, and the tourists and less hardy-of-heart people leave.

Everyone who's up here is here because of the silence. It is eternity up here. Some are on the run, and others are looking for something; some are incapable of living in a city, among people, while others simply love the wildness of new un-touched country. But our lives are all close enough, our feelings, that when winter comes in October there's a feeling like a sigh, a sigh after the great full meal of sum-mer, and at the Halloween party everyone shows up, and we don't bother with cos-tumes because we all know one another so well, if not through direct contact then through word of mouth—what Dick said Becky said about Don, and so forth—knowing more in this manner, sometimes. And instead of costumes, all we do is strap horns on our heads—moose antlers, or deer antlers, or even the high throw-back of elk antlers—and we have a big potluck supper and get drunk as hell, even those of us who do not drink, that one night a year, and we dance all night long, putting nickels in the jukebox (Elvis, the Doors, Marty Robbins) and clomping around in the bar as if it were a dance floor, tables and stools set outside in the falling snow to make room, and the men and women bang their antlers against each other in mock battle. Then around two or three in the morning we all drive home, or ski home, or snowshoe home, or ride back on horses—however we got to the party is how we'll return.

It usually snows big on Halloween—a foot, a foot and a half. Sometimes who-ever drove down to the saloon will give the skiers a ride home by fastening a long rope to the back bumper, and we skiers will hold on to that rope, still wearing our antlers, too drunk or tired to take them off, and we'll ride home that way, being pulled up the hill by the truck, gliding silently over the road's hard ice across the new snow, our heads tucked against the wind, against the falling snow . . .

Like children being let off at a bus stop, we'll let go of the rope when the truck passes our dark cabins. It would be nice to leave a lantern burning in the window, for coming home, but you don't ever go to sleep or leave with a lantern lit like that—it can burn your cabin down in the night and leave you in the middle of win-ter with nothing. We come home to dark houses, all of us. The antlers feel natural after having been up there for so long. Sometimes we bump them against the door going in and knock them off. We wear them only once a year: only once a year do we become the hunted.

We believe in this small place, this valley. Many of us have come here from other places and have been running all our lives from other things, and I think that everyone who is up here has decided not to run anymore.

There is a woman up here, Suzie, who has moved through the valley with a regularity, a rhythm, that is all her own and has nothing to do with our—the men's—pleadings or desires. Over the years, Suzie has been with all the men in this valley. All, that is, except Randy. She won't have anything to do with Randy. He still wishes very much for his chance, but because he is a bowhunter—he uses a strong compound bow and wicked, heart-gleaming aluminum arrows with a whole spindle of razor blades at one end for the killing point—she will have nothing to do with him.

Sometimes I wanted to defend Randy, even though I strongly disagreed with bowhunting. Bowhunting, it seemed to me, was wrong—but Randy was just Randy, no better or worse than any of the rest of us who had dated Suzie. Bowhunting was just something he did, something he couldn't help; I didn't see why she had to take it so personally.

Wolves eviscerate their prey; it's a hard life. Dead's dead, isn't it? And isn't pain the same everywhere?

I would say that Suzie's boyfriends lasted, on the average, three months. Nobody ever left her. Even the most sworn bachelors among us enjoyed her company—she worked at the bar every evening—and it was always Suzie who left the men, who left us, though I thought it was odd and wonderful that she never left the valley.

Suzie has sandy-red hair, high cold cheeks, and fury-blue eyes; she is short, no taller than anyone's shoulders. But because most of us had known her for so long—and this is what the other men had told me after she'd left them—it was fun, and even stirring, but it wasn't really that *great*. There wasn't a lot of heat in it for most of them—not the dizzying, lost feeling kind you get sometimes when you meet someone for the first time, or even glimpse them in passing, never to meet. . . . That kind of heat was missing, said most of the men, and it was just comfortable, they said—*comfortable*.

When it was my turn to date Suzie, I'm proud to say that we stayed together for five months—longer than she's ever stayed with anyone—long enough for people to talk, and to kid her about it.

Our dates were simple enough; we'd go for long drives to the tops of snowy mountains and watch the valley. We'd drive into town, too, seventy miles away down a one-lane, rutted, cliff-hanging road, just for dinner and a movie. I could see how there was not heat and wild romance in it for some of the other men, but for me it was warm, and *right*, while it lasted.

When she left, I did not think I would ever eat again, drink again. It felt like my heart had been torn from my chest, like my lungs were on fire; every breath burned. I couldn't understand why she had to leave; I didn't know why she had to do that to me. I'd known it was coming, someday, but still it hurt. But I got over it; I lived. She's lovely. She's a nice girl. For a long time, I wished she would date Randy.

Besides being a bowhunter, Randy was carpenter. He did odd jobs for people in the valley, usually fixing up old cabins rather than ever building any new ones. He kept his own schedule, and stopped working entirely in the fall so that he could hunt to his heart's content. He would roam the valley for days, exploring all of the wildest places, going all over the valley. He had hunted everywhere, had seen everything in the valley. We all hunted in the fall—grouse, deer, elk, though we left the moose and bear alone because they were rarer and we liked seeing them—but none of us were clever or stealthy enough to bowhunt. You had to get so close to the animal, with a bow.

Suzie didn't like any form of hunting. "That's what cattle are for," she'd say. "Cattle are like city people. Cattle expect, even deserve, what they've got coming. But wild animals are different. Wild animals enjoy life. They live in the woods on purpose. It's cruel to go in after them and kill them. It's cruel."

We'd all hoo-rah her and order more beers, and she wouldn't get angry, then—she'd understand that it was just what everyone did up here, the men and the women alike, that we loved the animals, loved seeing them, but that for one or two months out of the year we loved to hunt them. She couldn't understand it, but she knew that was how it was.

Randy was so good at what he did that we were jealous, and we admired him for it, tipped our hats to his talent. He could crawl right up to within thirty yards of wild animals when they were feeding, or he could sit so still that they would walk right past him. And he was good with his bow—he was deadly. The animal he shot would run a short way with the arrow stuck through it. An arrow wouldn't kill the way a bullet did, and the animal always ran at least a little way before dying—bleeding to death, or dying from trauma—and no one liked for that to happen, but the blood trail was easy to follow, especially in the snow. There was nothing that could be done about it; that was just the way bowhunting was. The men looked at it as being much fairer than hunting with a rifle, because you had to get so close to the animal to get a good shot—thirty-five, forty yards was the farthest away you could be—but Suzie didn't see it that way.

She would serve Randy his drinks and would chat with him, would be polite, but her face was a mask, her smiles were stiff.

What Randy did to try to gain Suzie's favor was to build her things. Davey, the bartender—the man she was dating that summer—didn't really mind. It wasn't as if there were any threat of Randy stealing her away, and besides, he liked the objects Randy built her; and, too, I think it might have seemed to add just the smallest bit of that white heat to Davey and Suzie's relationship—though I can't say that for sure.

Randy built her a porch swing out of bright larch wood and stained it with tung oil. It was as pretty as a new truck; he brought it up to her at the bar one night, having spent a week sanding it and getting it just right. We all gathered around, admiring it, running our hands over its smoothness. Suzie smiled a little—a polite smile, which was, in a way, worse than if she had looked angry—and said nothing, not even "thank you," and she and Davey took it home in the back of Davey's truck. This was in June.

Randy built her other things, too—small things, things she could fit on her dresser: a little mahogany box for her earrings, of which she had several pairs, and a walking stick with a deer's antler for the grip. She said she did not want the walking stick, but would take the earring box.

Some nights I would lie awake in my cabin and think about how Suzie was with Davey, and then I would feel sorry for Davey, because she would be leaving him eventually. I'd lie there on my side and look out my bedroom window at the northern lights flashing above the snowy mountains, and their strange light would be reflected on the river that ran past my cabin, so that the light seemed to be coming from beneath the water as well. On nights like those I'd feel like my heart was never going to heal—in fact, I was certain that it never would. I didn't love Suzie anymore—didn't think I did, anyway—but I wanted to love someone, and to be loved. Life, on those nights, seemed shorter than anything in the world, and so important, so precious, that it terrified me.

Perhaps Suzie was right about the bowhunting, and about all hunters.

In the evenings, back when we'd been together, Suzie and I would sit out on the back porch after she got in from work—still plenty of daylight left, the sun not setting until very late—and we'd watch large herds of deer, their antlers covered with summer velvet, wade out into the cool shadows of the river to bathe, like ladies. The sun would finally set, and those deer bodies would take on the dark shapes of the shadows, still out in the shallows of the rapids, splashing and bathing. Later, well into the night, Suzie and I would sit in the same chair, wrapped up in a single blanket, and nap. Shooting stars would shriek and howl over the mountains as if taunting us.

This past July, Randy, who lives along a field up on the side of the mountains at the north end of the valley up against the brief foothills, began practicing: standing out in the field at various marked distances—ten, twenty, thirty, forty yards—and shooting arrow after arrow into the bull's-eye target that was stapled to bales of hay. It was unusual to drive past in July and not see him out there in the field, practicing—even in the middle of the day, shirtless, perspiring, his cheeks flushed. He lived by himself, and there was probably nothing else to do. The bowhunting season began in late August, months before the regular gun season.

Too many people up here, I think, just get comfortable and lazy and lose their real passions—for whatever it is they used to get excited about. I've been up here only a few years, so maybe I have no right to say that, but it's what I feel.

It made Suzie furious to see Randy out practicing like that. She circulated a petition in the valley, requesting that bowhunting be banned.

But we—the other men, the other hunters—would have been doing the same thing, hunting the giant elk with bows for the thrill of it, luring them in with calls and rattles, right in to us, hidden in the bushes, the bulls wanting to fight, squealing madly and rushing in, tearing at trees and brush with their great dark antlers. If we could have gotten them in that close before killing them, we would have, and it would be a thing we would remember longer than any other thing. . . .

We just weren't good enough. We couldn't sign Suzie's petition. Not even Davey could sign it.

"It's wrong," she'd say.

"It's personal choice," Davey would say. "If you use the meat, and apologize to the spirit right before you do it and right after—if you give thanks—it's okay. It's a man's choice, honey," he'd say—and if there was one thing Suzie hated, it was that man-woman stuff.

"He's trying to prove something," she said.

"He's just doing something he cares about, dear," Davey said.

"He's trying to prove his manhood—to me, to all of us," she said. "He's dangerous."

"No," said Davey, "that's not it. He likes it and hates it both. It fascinates him is all."

"It's sick," Suzie said. "He's dangerous."

I could see that Suzie would not be with Davey much longer. She moved from man to man almost with the seasons. There was a wildness, a flightiness, about her—some sort of combination of strength and terror—that made her desirable. To me, anyway, though I can only guess for the others.

I'd been out bowhunting with Randy once to see how it was done. I saw him shoot an elk, a huge bull, and I saw the arrow go in behind the bull's shoulder where the heart and lungs were hidden—and I saw, too, the way the bull looked around in wild-eyed surprise, and then went galloping off through the timber, seemingly uninjured, running hard. For a long time Randy and I sat there, listening to the clack-clack of the aluminum arrow banging against trees as the elk ran away with it.

"We sit and wait," Randy said. "We just wait." He was confident and did not seem at all shaky, though I was. It was a record bull, a beautiful bull. We sat there and waited. I did not believe we would ever see that bull again. I studied Randy's cool face, tiger-striped and frightening with the camouflage painted on it, and he seemed so cold, so icy.

After a couple of hours we got up and began to follow the blood trail. There wasn't much of it at all, at first—just a drop or two, drops in the dry leaves, already turning brown and cracking, drops that I would never have seen—but after about a quarter of a mile, farther down the hill, we began to see more of it, until it looked as if entire buckets of blood had been lost. We found two places where the bull had lain down beneath a tree to die, but had then gotten up and moved on again. We found him by the creek, a half mile away, down in the shadows, but with his huge antlers rising into a patch of sun and gleaming. He looked like a monster from another world; even after his death, he looked noble. The creek made a beautiful trickling sound. It was very quiet. But as we got closer, as large as he was, the bull looked like someone's pet. He looked friendly. The green-and-black arrow sticking out of him looked as if it had hurt his feelings more than anything; it did not look as if such a small arrow could kill such a large and strong animal.

We sat down beside the elk and admired him, studied him. Randy, who because of the scent did not smoke during the hunting season—not until he had his elk—pulled out a pack of cigarettes, shook one out, and lit it.

"I'm not sure why I do it," he admitted, reading my mind. "I feel kind of bad about it each time I see one like this, but I keep doing it." He shrugged. I listened to the sound of the creek. "I know it's cruel, but I can't help it. I have to do it," he said.

"What do you think it must feel like?" Suzie had asked me at the bar. "What do you think it must feel like to run around with an arrow in your heart, knowing you're going to die for it?" She was furious and righteous, red-faced, and I told her I didn't know. I paid for my drink and left, confused because she was right. The animal had to be feeling pain—serious, continuous pain. It was just the way it was.

In July, Suzie left Davey, as I'd predicted. It was gentle and kind—amicable—and we all had a party down at the saloon to celebrate. We roasted a whole deer that Holger Jennings had hit with his truck the night before while coming back from town with supplies, and we stayed out in front of the saloon and ate steaming fresh meat on paper plates with barbecue sauce and crisp apples from Idaho, and watched the lazy little river that followed the road that ran through town. We didn't dance or play loud music or anything—it was too mellow. There were children and dogs. This was back when Don Terlinde was still alive, and he played his accordion: a sad, sweet sound. We drank beer and told stories.

All this time, I'd been uncertain about whether it was right or wrong to hunt if you used the meat and said those prayers. And I'm still not entirely convinced, one way or the other. But I do have a better picture of what it's like now to be the elk or deer. And I understand Suzie a little better, too: I no longer think of her as cruel for hurting Randy's proud heart, for singling out, among all the other men in the valley, only Randy to shun, to avoid.

She wasn't cruel. She was just frightened. Fright—sometimes plain fright, even more than terror—is every bit as bad as pain, and maybe worse.

What I am getting at is that Suzie went home with me that night after the party; she had made her rounds through the men of the valley, had sampled them all (except for Randy and a few of the more ancient ones), and now she was choosing to come back to me.

"I've got to go somewhere," she said. "I hate being alone. I can't stand to be alone." She slipped her hand in mine as we were walking home. Randy was still sitting on the picnic table with Davey when we left, eating slices of venison. The sun still hadn't quite set. Ducks flew down the river.

"I guess that's as close to 'I love you' as I'll get," I said.

"I'm serious," she said, twisting my hand. "You don't understand. It's *horrible*. I can't *stand* it. It's not like other people's loneliness. It's worse."

"Why?" I asked.

"No reason," Suzie said. "I'm just scared, is all. Jumpy. Spooky. Some people are that way. I can't help it."

"It's okay," I said.

We walked down the road like that, holding hands, walking slowly in the dusk. It was about three miles down the gravel road to my cabin. Suzie knew the way. We heard owls as we walked along the river and saw lots of deer. Once, for no reason, I turned and looked back, but I saw nothing, saw no one.

If Randy can have such white-hot passion for a thing—bowhunting—he can, I understand full well, have just as much heat in his hate. It spooks me the way he doesn't bring Suzie presents anymore in the old, hopeful way. The flat looks he gives me could mean anything: they rattle me.

"It's like I can't *see* him.

Sometimes I'm afraid to go into the woods.

But I do anyway. I go hunting in the fall and cut wood in the fall and winter, fish in the spring, and go for walks in the summer, walks and drives up to the tops of the high snowy mountains—and there are times when I feel someone or something is just behind me, following at a distance, and I'll turn around, frightened and angry both, and I won't see anything, but still, later on into the walk, I'll feel it again.

But I feel other things, too: I feel my happiness with Suzie. I feel the sun on my face and on my shoulders. I like the way we sit on the porch again, the way we used to, with drinks in hand, and watch the end of day, watch the deer come slipping down into the river.

I'm frightened, but it feels delicious.

This year at the Halloween party, it dumped on us; it began snowing the day before and continued on through the night and all through Halloween day and then Halloween night, snowing harder than ever. The roof over the saloon groaned that night under the load of new snow, but we had the party anyway and kept dancing, all of us leaping around and waltzing, drinking, proposing toasts, and arm-wrestling, then leaping up again and dancing some more, with all the antlers from all the animals in the valley strapped to our heads—everyone. It looked pagan. We all whooped and danced. Davey and Suzie danced in each other's arms, swirled and pirouetted; she was so light and so free, and I watched them and grinned. Randy sat on the porch and drank beers and watched, too, and smiled. It was a polite smile.

All of the rest of us drank and stomped around. We shook our heads at each other and pretended we were deer, pretended we were elk.

We ran out of beer around three in the morning, and we all started gathering up our skis, rounding up rides, people with trucks who could take us home. The rumble of trucks being warmed up began, and the beams of headlights crisscrossed the road in all directions, showing us just how hard it really was snowing. The flakes were as large as the biggest goose feathers. Because Randy and I lived up the same road, Davey drove us home, and Suzie took hold of the tow rope and skied with us.

Davey drove slowly because it was hard to see the road in such a storm.

Suzie had had a lot to drink—we all had—and she held on to the rope with both hands, her deer antlers slightly askew, and she began to ask Randy some questions about his hunting—not razzing him, as I thought she would, but simply questioning him—things she'd been wondering for a long time, I supposed, but had been too angry to ask. We watched the brake lights in front of us, watched the snow spiraling into our faces and concentrated on holding on to the rope. As usual, we all seemed to have forgotten the antlers that were on our heads.

"What's it like?" Suzie kept wanting to know. "I mean, what's it *really* like?"

We were sliding through the night, holding on to the rope, being pulled through the night. The snow was striking our faces, caking our eyebrows, and it was so cold that it was hard to speak.

"You're a real asshole, you know?" Suzie said, when Randy wouldn't answer. "You're too cold-blooded for me," she said. "You scare me, mister."

Randy just stared straight ahead, his face hard and flat and blank, and he held on to the rope.

I'd had way too much to drink. We all had. We slid over some rough spots in the road.

"Suzie, honey," I started to say—I have no idea what I was going to say after that—something to defend Randy, I think—but then I stopped, because Randy turned and looked at me, for just a second, with fury, terrible fury, which I could *feel* as well as see, even in my drunkenness. But then the mask, the polite mask, came back down over him, and we continued down the road in silence, the antlers on our heads bobbing and weaving, a fine target for anyone who might not have understood that we weren't wild animals.

CRITICAL THINKING QUESTIONS

1. Explain what the narrator means when he says, "We believe in this small place, this valley."

2. Why does Suzie object to Randy's bowhunting? How does the narrator view bowhunting? What are some of the other men's viewpoints?

3. Randy declines to defend or explain his choice to bowhunt. Based on what you know about Randy, why do you think he bowhunts?

4. Why is Suzie frightened? What does the narrator mean when he says, "I'm frightened, but it feels delicious"?

WRITING TOPICS

1. Identify the different viewpoints that are presented about the ethics of hunting. Which viewpoint do you support and why?

2. Examine the significance of the title. In your study, consider what the narrator says early on about the annual Halloween party costume: "The antlers feel natural after having been up there for so long. . . . We wear them only once a year: only once a year do we become the hunted." Also, read carefully the closing scene when Suzie questions Randy about his bowhunting; note, in particular, the images in the last sentence.

James Fenimore Cooper

The Slaughter of the Pigeons

from *The Pioneers*

"Men, boys, and girls.
Desert th' unpeopled village; and wild crowds
Spread o'er the plain, by the sweet frenzy driven."

—SOMERVILLE

From this time to the close of April, the weather continued to be a succession of great and rapid changes. One day, the soft airs of spring would seem to be stealing along the valley, and, in unison with an invigorating sun, attempting, covertly, to rouse the dormant powers of the vegetable world; while on the next, the surly blasts from the north would sweep across the lake, and erase every impression left by their gentle adversaries. The snow, however, finally disappeared, and the green wheat fields were seen in every direction, spotted with the dark and charred stumps that had, the preceding season, supported some of the proudest trees of the forest. Ploughs were in motion, wherever those useful implements could be used, and the smokes of the sugarcamps were no longer seen issuing from the summits of the woods of maple. The lake had lost all the characteristic beauty of a field of ice, but still a dark and gloomy covering concealed its waters, for the absence of currents left them yet hid under a porous crust, which, saturated with the fluid, barely retained enough of its strength to preserve the contiguity of its parts. Large flocks of wild geese were seen passing over the country, which would hover, for a time, around the hidden sheet of water, apparently searching for an opening, where they might obtain a resting-place; and then, on finding themselves excluded by the chill covering, would soar away to the north, filling the air with their discordant screams, as if venting their complaints at the tardy operations of nature.

For a week, the dark covering of the Otsego was left to the undisturbed possession of two eagles, who alighted on the centre of its field, and sat proudly eyeing the extent of their undisputed territory. During the presence of these monarchs of the air, the flocks of migrating birds avoided crossing the plain of ice, by turning into the hills, and apparently seeking the protection of the forests, while the white and bald heads of the tenants of the lake were turned upward, with a look of majestic contempt, as if penetrating to the very heavens, with the acuteness of their vision. But the time had come, when even these kings of birds were to be dispossessed. An opening had been gradually increasing, at the lower extremity of the lake, and around the dark spot where the current of the river had prevented the formation of ice, during even the coldest weather; and the fresh southerly winds, that now breathed freely up the valley, obtained an impression on the waters. Mimic waves begun to curl over the margin of the frozen field, which exhibited an outline of crystallizations, that slowly receded towards the north. At each step the power of the winds and the waves increased, until, after a struggle of a few hours, the turbulent little billows succeeded in setting the whole field in an undulating motion, when it was driven beyond the reach of the eye, with a rapidity, that was as magical as the change produced in the scene by this expulsion of the lingering remnant of winter. Just as the last sheet of agitated ice was disappearing in the distance, the eagles rose over the border of crystals, and soared with a wide sweep far above the clouds, while the waves tossed their little caps of snow into the air, as if rioting in their release from a thraldom of five months duration.

The following morning Elizabeth was awakened by the exhilarating sounds of the martins, who were quarrelling and chattering around the little boxes which were suspended above her windows, and the cries of Richard, who was calling, in tones as animating as the signs of the season itself—

"Awake! awake! my lady fair! the gulls are hovering over the lake already, and the heavens are alive with the pigeons. You may look an hour before you can find a hole, through which, to get a peep at the sun. Awake! awake! lazy ones! Benjamin is overhauling the ammunition, and we only wait for our breakfasts, and away for the mountains and pigeon-shooting."

There was no resisting this animated appeal, and in a few minutes Miss Temple and her friend descended to the parlour. The doors of the hall were thrown open, and the mild, balmy air of a clear spring morning was ventilating the apartment, where the vigilance of the ex-steward had been so long maintaining an artificial heat, with such unremitted diligence. All of the gentlemen, we do not include Monsieur Le Quoi, were impatiently waiting their morning's repast, each being equipt in the garb of a sportsman. Mr. Jones made many visits to the southern door, and would cry—

"See, cousin Bess! see, 'duke! the pigeon-roosts of the south have broken up! They are growing more thick every instant. Here is a flock that the eye cannot see the end of. Three is food enough in it to keep the army of Xerxes for a month, and feathers enough to make beds for the whole county. Xerxes, Mr. Edwards, was a Grecian king, who—no, he was a Turk, or a Persian, who wanted to conquer Greece, just the same as these rascals will overrun our wheat-fields, when they come back in the fall.—Away! away! Bess; I long to pepper them from the mountain."

In this wish both Marmaduke and young Edwards seemed equally to participate, for really the sight was most exhilarating to a sportsman; and the ladies soon dismissed the party, after a hasty breakfast.

If the heavens were alive with pigeons, the whole village seemed equally in motion, with men, women, and children. Every species of fire-arms, from the French ducking-gun, with its barrel of near six feet in length, to the common horseman's pistol, was to be seen in the hands of the men and boys; while bows and arrows, some made of the simple stick of a walnut sapling, and others in a rude imitation of the ancient cross-bows, were carried by many of the latter.

The houses, and the signs of life apparent in the village, drove the alarmed birds from the direct line of their flight, towards the mountains, along the sides and near the bases of which they were glancing in dense masses, that were equally wonderful by the rapidity of their motion, as by their incredible numbers.

We have already said, that across the inclined plane which fell from the steep ascent of the mountain to the banks of the Susquehanna, ran the highway, on either side of which a clearing of many acres had been made, at a very early day. Over those clearings, and up the eastern mountain, and along the dangerous path that was cut into its side, the different individuals posted themselves, as suited their inclinations; and in a few moments the attack commenced.

Amongst the sportsmen was to be seen the tall, gaunt form of Leatherstocking, who was walking over the field, with his rifle hanging on his arm, his dogs following close at his heels, now scenting the dead or wounded birds, that were beginning to tumble from the flocks, and then crouching under the legs of their master, as if they participated in his feelings, at this wasteful and unsportsmanlike execution.

The reports of the fire-arms became rapid, whole volleys rising from the plain, as flocks of more than ordinary numbers darted over the opening, covering the field with darkness, like an interposing cloud; and then the light smoke of a single piece would issue from among the leafless bushes on the mountain, as death was hurled on the retreat of the affrighted birds, who would rise from a volley, for many feet into the air, in a vain effort to escape the attacks of man. Arrows, and missiles of every kind, were seen in the midst of the flocks; and so numerous were the birds, and so low did they take their flight, that even long poles, in the hands of those on the sides of the mountain, were used to strike them to the earth.

During all this time, Mr. Jones, who distained the humble and ordinary means of destruction used by his companions, was busily occupied, aided by Benjamin, in making arrangements for an assault of a more than ordinarily fatal character. Among the relics of the old military excursions, that occasionally are discovered throughout the different districts of the western part of New York, there had been found in Templeton, at its settlement, a small swivel, which would carry a ball of a pound weight. It was thought to have been deserted by a war-party of the whites, in one of their inroads into the Indian settlements, when, perhaps, their convenience or their necessities induced them to leave such an encumbrance to the rapidity of their march, behind them in the woods. This miniature cannon had been released from the rust, and mounted on little wheels, in a state for actual service. For several years, it was the sole organ for extraordinary rejoicings that was used in those mountains. On the mornings of the Fourth of July, it would be heard, with its echoes ringing among the hills, and telling forth its sounds, for thirteen times, with all the dignity of a two-and-thirty pounder; and even Captain Hollister, who was the highest authority in that part of the country on all such occasions, affirmed that, considering its dimensions, it was no despicable gun for a salute. It was somewhat the worse for the service it had performed, it is true, there being but a trifling difference in size between the touch-hole and the muzzle. Still, the grand conceptions of

Richard had suggested the importance of such an instrument, in hurling death at his nimble enemies. The swivel was dragged by a horse into a part of the open space, that the sheriff thought most eligible for planting a battery of the kind, and Mr. Pump proceeded to load it. Several handfuls of duck-shot were placed on top of the powder, and the Major-domo soon announced that his piece was ready for service.

The sight of such an implemented collected all the idle spectators to the spot, who, being mostly boys, filled the air with their cries of exultation and delight. The gun was pointed on high, and Richard, holding a coal of fire in a pair of tongs, patiently took his seat on a stump, awaiting the appearance of a flock that was worthy of his notice.

So prodigious was the number of the birds, that the scattering fire of the guns, with the hurling of missiles, and the cries of the boys, had no other effect than to break off small flocks from the immense masses that continued to dart along the valley, as if the whole creation of the feathered tribe were pouring through that one pass. None pretended to collect the game, which lay scattered over the fields in such profusion, as to cover the very ground with the fluttering victims.

Leather-stocking was a silent, but uneasy spectator of all these proceedings, but was able to keep his sentiments to himself until he saw the introduction of the swivel into the sports.

"This comes of settling a country" he said—"here have I known the pigeons to fly for forty long years, and, till you made your clearings, there was nobody to scare or to hurt them. I loved to see them come into the woods, for they were company to a body; hurting nothing; being, as it was, as harmless as a garter-snake. But now it gives me sore thoughts when I hear the frighty things whizzing through the air, for I know it's only a motion to bring out all the brats in the village at them. Well! the Lord won't see the waste of his creaters for nothing, and right will be done to the pigeons, as well as others, by-and-by.—There's Mr. Oliver, as bad as the rest of them, firing into the flocks as if he was shooting down nothing but the Mingo warriors."

Among the sportsmen was Billy Kirby, who, armed with an old musket, was loading, and, without even looking into the air, was firing, and shouting as his victims fell even on his own person. He heard the speech of Natty, and took upon himself to reply—

"What's that, old Leather-stocking!" he cried; "grumbling at the loss of a few pigeons! If you had to sow your wheat twice, and three times, as I have done, you wouldn't be so massyfully feeling'd to'ards the divils.—Hurrah, boys! scatter the feathers. This is better than shooting at a turkey's head and neck, old fellow."

"It's better for you, maybe, Billy Kirby," returned the indignant old hunter, "and all them as don't know how to put a ball down a rifle-barrel, or how to bring it up ag'in with a true aim; but it's wicked to be shooting into flocks in this wastey manner; and none do it, who know how to knock over a single bird. If a body has a craving for pigeon's flesh, why! it's made the same as all other creaters, for man's eating, but not to kill twenty and eat one. When I want such a thing, I go into the woods till I find one to my liking, and then I shoot him off the branches without touching a feather of another, though there might be a hundred on the same tree. But you couldn't do such a thing, Billy Kirby—you couldn't do it if you tried."

"What's that you say, you old, dried cornstalk! you sapless stub!" cried the wood-chopper. "You've grown mighty boasting, sin you killed the turkey; but if you're for a single shot, here goes at that bird which comes on by himself."

The fire from the distant part of the field had driven a single pigeon below the flock to which it had belonged, and, frightened with the constant reports of the muskets, it was approaching the spot where the disputants stood, darting first from one side, and then to the other, cutting the air with the swiftness of lightning, and making a noise with its wings, not unlike the rushing of a bullet. Unfortunately for the wood-chopper, notwithstanding his vaunt, he did not see his bird until it was too late for him to fire as it approached, and he pulled his trigger at the unlucky moment when it was darting immediately over his head. The bird continued its course with incredible velocity.

Natty had dropped his piece from his arm, when the challenge was made, and, waiting a moment, until the terrified victim had got in a line with his eyes, and had dropped near the bank of the lake, he raised his rifle with uncommon rapidity, and fired. It might have been chance, or it might have been skill, that produced the result; it was probably a union of both; but the pigeon whirled over in the air, and fell into the lake, with a broken wing. At the sound of his rifle, both his dogs started from his feet, and in a few minutes the "slut" brought out the bird, still alive.

The wonderful exploit of Leather-stocking was noised through the field with great rapidity, and the sportsmen gathered in to learn the truth of the report.

"What," said young Edwards, "have you really killed a pigeon on the wing, Natty, with a single ball?"

"Haven't I killed loons before now, lad, that dive at the flash?" returned the hunter. "It's much better to kill only such as you want, without wasting your powder and lead, than to be firing into God's creaters in such a wicked manner. But I come out for a bird, and you know the reason why I like small game, Mr. Oliver, and now I have got one I will go home, for I don't like to see these wasty ways that you are all practysing, as if the least thing was not made for use, and not to destroy."

"Thou sayest well, Leather-stocking," cried Marmaduke, "and I begin to think it time to put an end to this work of destruction."

"Put an ind, Judge, to your clearings. An't the woods his work as well as the pigeons? Use, but don't waste. Wasn't the woods made for the beasts and birds to harbour in? and when man wanted their flesh, their skins, or their feathers, there's the place to seek them. But I'll go to the hut with my own game, for I wouldn't touch one of the harmless things that kiver the ground here, looking up with their eyes at me, as if they only wanted tongues to say their thoughts."

With this sentiment in his mouth, Leather-stocking threw his rifle over his arm, and, followed by his dogs, stepped across the clearing with great caution, taking care not to tread on one, of the hundreds of the wounded birds that lay in his path. He soon entered the bushes on the margin of the lake, and was hid from view.

Whatever might be the impression the morality of Natty made on the Judge, it was utterly lost on Richard. He availed himself of the gathering of the sportsmen, to lay a plan for one "fell swoop" of destruction. The musket-men were drawn up in battle array, in a line extending on each side of his artillery, with orders to await the signal of firing from himself.

"Stand by, my lads," said Benjamin, who acted as an aid-de-camp on this momentous occasion, "stand by, my hearties, and when Squire Dickens heaves out the signal for to begin the firing, d'ye see, you may open upon them in a broadside. Take care and fire low, boys, and you'll be sure to hull the flock."

"Fire low!" shouted Kirby—"hear the old fool! If we fire low, we may hit the stumps, but not ruffle a pigeon."

"How should you know, you lubber?" cried Benjamin, with a very unbecoming heat, for an officer on the eve of battle—"how should you know, you grampus? Havn't I sailed aboard of the Boadishy for five years? and wasn't it a standing order to fire low, and to hull your enemy? Keep silence at your guns, boys, and mind the order that is passed."

The loud laughs of the musketmen were silenced by the authoritative voice of Richard, who called to them for attention and obedience to his signals.

Some millions of pigeons were supposed to have already passed, that morning, over the valley of Templeton; but nothing like the flock that was now approaching had been seen before. It extended from mountain to mountain in one solid blue mass, and the eye looked in vain over the southern hills to find its termination. The front of this living column was distinctly marked by a line, but very slightly indented, so regular and even was the flight. Even Marmaduke forgot the morality of Leather-stocking as it approached, and, in common with the rest, brought his musket to his shoulder.

"Fire!" cried the Sheriff, clapping his coal to the priming of the cannon. As half of Benjamin's charge escaped through the touch-hole, the whole volley of the musketry preceded the report of the swivel. On receiving this united discharge of small-arms, the front of the flock darted upward, while, at the same instant, myriads of those in their rear rushed with amazing rapidity into their places, so that when the column of white smoke gushed from the mouth of the little cannon, an accumulated mass of objects was gliding over its point of direction. The roar of the gun echoed along the mountains, and died away to the north, like distant thunder, while the whole flock of alarmed birds seemed, for a moment, thrown into one disorderly and agitated mass. The air was filled with their irregular flights, layer rising over layer, far above the tops of the highest pines, none daring to advance beyond the dangerous pass; when, suddenly, some of the leaders of the feathered tribe shot across the valley, taking their flight directly over the village, and the hundreds of thousands in their rear followed their example, deserting the eastern side of the plain to their persecutors and the fallen.

"Victory!" shouted Richard, "victory! we have driven the enemy from the field."

"Not so, Dickon," said Marmaduke; "the field is covered with them; and, like the Leather-stocking, I see nothing but eyes, in every direction, as the innocent sufferers turn their heads in terror, to examine my movements. Full one half of those that have fallen are yet alive: and I think it is time to end the sport; if sport it be."

"Sport!" cried the Sheriff; "it is princely sport. There are some thousands of the blue-coated boys on the ground, so that every old woman in the village may have a pot-pie for the asking."

"Well, we have happily frightened the birds from this pass," said Marmaduke, "and our carnage must of necessity end, for the present.—Boys, I will give thee six-pence a hundred for the pigeons' heads only; so go to work, and bring them into the village, when I will pay thee."

This expedient produced the desired effect, for every urchin on the ground went industriously to work to wring the necks of the wounded birds. Judge Temple retired towards his dwelling with that kind of feeling, that many a man has experi-enced before him, who discovers, after the excitement of the moment has passed, that he has purchased pleasure at the price of misery to others. Horses were loaded with the dead; and, after this first burst of sporting, the shooting of pigeons became a business, for the remainder of the season, more in proportion to the wants of the people. Richard, however, boasted for many a year, of his shot with the "cricket;" and Benjamin gravely asserted, that he thought that they killed nearly as many pi-geons on that day, as there were Frenchmen destroyed on the memorable occasion of Rodney's victory.

CRITICAL THINKING QUESTIONS

1. What is the author's claim about the ethics of hunting?
2. Point out specific wording and details that the author uses to *stack the evidence* (see Glossary) for his claim.
3. Which *rhetorical appeal* is most prevalent?

WRITING TOPIC

What is Leather-stocking's viewpoint on the ethics of hunting? Compare Leather-stocking's viewpoint to Davey's in Bass's "Antlers." Both characters use similar ethical standards to justify hunting; however, Leather-stocking lived in early-nineteenth-century America while Davey lives in contemporary Amer-ica. Is Davey's position on the ethics of hunting defensible as a *Rogerian argu-ment claim?*

Pam Houston

A Blizzard under Blue Sky

The doctor said I was clinically depressed. It was February, the month in which depression runs rampant in the inversion-cloaked Salt Lake Valley and the city dwellers escape to Park City, where the snow is fresh and the sun is shining and everybody is happy, except me. In truth, my life was on the verge of more spectacular and satisfying discoveries than I had ever imagined, but of course I couldn't see that far ahead. What I saw was work that wasn't getting done, bills that weren't getting paid, and a man I'd given my heart to weekending in the desert with his ex.

The doctor said, "I can give you drugs."

I said, "No way."

She said, "The machine that drives you is broken. You need something to help you get it fixed."

I said, "Winter camping."

She said, "Whatever floats your boat."

One of the things I love the most about the natural world is the way it gives you what's good for you even if you don't know it at the time. I had never been winter camping before, at least not in the high country, and the weekend I chose to try and fix my machine was the same weekend the air mass they called the Alaska Clipper showed up. It was thirty-two degrees below zero in town on the night I spent in my snow cave. I don't know how cold it was out on Beaver Creek. I had listened to the weather forecast, and to the advice of my housemate, Alex, who was an experienced winter camper.

"I don't know what you think you're going to prove by freezing to death," Alex said, "but if you've got to go, take my bivvy sack; it's warmer than anything you have."

"Thanks," I said.

"If you mix Kool-Aid with your water it won't freeze up," he said, "and don't forget lighting paste for your stove."

"Okay," I said.

"I hope it turns out to be worth it," he said, "because you are going to freeze your butt."

When everything in your life is uncertain, there's nothing quite like the clarity and precision of fresh snow and blue sky. That was the first thought I had on Saturday morning as I stepped away from the warmth of my truck and let my skis slap the snow in front of me. There was no wind and no clouds that morning, just still

239

air and cold sunshine. The hair in my nostrils froze almost immediately. When I took a deep breath, my lungs only filled up halfway.

I opened the tailgate to excited whines and whimpers. I never go skiing without Jackson and Hailey: my two best friends, my yin and yang of dogs. Some of you might know Jackson. He's the oversized sheepdog-and-something-else with the great big nose and the bark that will shatter glass. He gets out and about more than I do. People I've never seen before come by my house daily and call him by name. He's all grace, and he's tireless; he won't go skiing with me unless I let him lead. Hailey is not so graceful, and her body seems in constant indecision when she runs. When we ski she stays behind me, and on the downhills she tries to sneak rides on my skis.

The dogs ran circles in the chest-high snow while I inventoried my backpack one more time to make sure I had everything I needed. My sleeping bag, my Thermarest, my stove, Alex's bivvy sack, matches, lighting paste, flashlight, knife. I brought three pairs of long underwear—tops and bottoms—so I could change once before I went to bed, and once again in the morning, so I wouldn't get chilled by my own sweat. I brought paper and pen, and Kool-Aid to mix with my water. I brought Mountain House chicken stew and some freeze-dried green peas, some peanut butter and honey, lots of dried apricots, coffee and Carnation instant breakfast for morning.

Jackson stood very still while I adjusted his backpack. He carries the dog food and enough water for all of us. He takes himself very seriously when he's got his pack on. He won't step off the trail for any reason, not even to chase rabbits, and he gets nervous and angry if I do. That morning he was impatient with me. "Miles to go, Mom," he said over his shoulder. I snapped my boots into my skis and we were off.

There are not too many good things you can say about temperatures that dip past twenty below zero, except this: They turn the landscape into a crystal palace and they turn your vision into Superman's. In the cold thin morning air the trees and mountains, even the twigs and shadows, seemed to leap out of the background like a 3-D movie, only it was better than 3-D because I could feel the sharpness of the air.

I have a friend in Moab who swears that Utah is the center of the fourth dimension, and although I know he has in mind something much different and more complicated than subzero weather, it was there, on that ice-edged morning, that I felt on the verge of seeing something more than depth perception in the brutal clarity of the morning sun.

As I kicked along the first couple of miles, I notice the sun crawling higher in the sky and yet the day wasn't really warming, and I wondered if I should have brought another vest, another layer to put between me and the cold night ahead.

It was utterly quiet out there, and what minimal noise we made intruded on the morning like a brass band: the squeaking of my bindings, the slosh of the water in Jackson's pack, the whoosh of nylon, the jangle of dog tags. It was the bass line and percussion to some primal song, and I kept wanting to sing to it, but I didn't know the words.

Jackson and I crested the top of a hill and stopped to wait for Hailey. The trail stretched out as far as we could see into the meadow below us and beyond, a double track and pole plants carving through softer trails of rabbit and deer.

"Nice place," I said to Jackson, and his tail thumped the snow underneath him without sound.

We stopped for lunch near something that looked like it could be a lake in its other life, or maybe just a womb-shaped meadow. I made peanut butter and honey sandwiches for all of us, and we opened the apricots.

"It's fabulous here," I told the dogs. "But so far it's not working."

There had never been anything wrong with my life that a few good days in the wilderness wouldn't cure, but there I sat in the middle of all those crystal-coated trees, all that diamond-studded sunshine, and I didn't feel any better. Apparently clinical depression was not like having a bad day, it wasn't even like having a lot of bad days, it was more like a house of mirrors, it was like being in a room full of one-way glass.

"Come on, Mom," Jackson said. "Ski harder, go faster, climb higher."

Hailey turned her belly to the sun and groaned.

"He's right," I told her. "It's all we can do."

After lunch the sun had moved behind our backs, throwing a whole different light on the path ahead of us. The snow we moved through stopped being simply white and became translucent, hinting at other colors, reflections of blues and purples and grays. I thought of Moby Dick, you know, the whiteness of the whale, where white is really the absence of all color, and whiteness equals truth, and Ahab's search is finally futile, as he finds nothing but his own reflection.

"Put your mind where your skis are," Jackson said, and we made considerably better time after that.

The sun was getting quite low in the sky when I asked Jackson if he thought we should stop to build the snow cave, and he said he'd look for the next good bank. About one hundred yards down the trail we found it, a gentle slope with eastern exposure that didn't look like it would cave in under any circumstances. Jackson started to dig first.

Let me make one thing clear. I knew only slightly more about building snow caves than Jackson, having never built one, and all my knowledge coming from disaster tales of winter camping fatalities. I knew several things *not* to do when building a snow cave, but I was having a hard time knowing what exactly to do. But Jackson helped, and Hailey supervised, and before too long we had a little cave built, just big enough for three. We ate dinner quite pleased with our accomplishments and set the bivvy sack up inside the cave just as the sun slipped away and dusk came over Beaver Creek.

The temperature, which hadn't exactly soared during the day, dropped twenty degrees in as many minutes, and suddenly it didn't seem like such a great idea to change my long underwear. The original plan was to sleep with the dogs inside the bivvy sack but outside the sleeping bag, which was okay with Jackson the super-metabolizer, but not so with Hailey, the couch potato. She whined and wriggled and managed to stuff her entire fat body down inside my mummy bag, and Jackson stretched out full-length on top.

One of the unfortunate things about winter camping is that it has to happen when the days are so short. Fourteen hours is a long time to lie in a snow cave under the most perfect of circumstances. And when it's thirty-two below, or forty, fourteen hours seems like weeks.

I wish I could tell you I dropped right off to sleep. In truth, fear crept into my spine with the cold and I never closed my eyes. Cuddled there, amid my dogs and water bottles, I spent half of the night chastising myself for thinking I was Wonder Woman, not only risking my own life but the lives of my dogs, and the other half trying to keep the numbness in my feet from crawling up to my knees. When I did doze off, which was actually more like blacking out than dozing off, I'd come back to my senses wondering if I had frozen to death, but the alternating pain and numbness that started in my extremities and worked its way into my bones convinced me I must still be alive.

It was a clear night, and every now and again I would poke my head out of its nest of down and nylon to watch the progress of the moon across the sky. There is no doubt that it was the longest and most uncomfortable night of my life.

But then the sky began to get gray, and then it began to get pink, and before too long the sun was on my bivvy sack, not warm, exactly, but holding the promise of warmth later in the day. And I ate apricots and drank Kool-Aid-flavored coffee and celebrated the rebirth of my fingers and toes, and the survival of many more important parts of my body. I sang "Rocky Mountain High" and "If I Had a Hammer," and yodeled and whistled, and even danced the two-step with Jackson and let him lick my face. And when Hailey finally emerged from the sleeping bag a full hour after I did, we shared a peanut butter and honey sandwich and she said nothing ever tasted so good.

We broke camp and packed up and kicked in the snow cave with something resembling glee.

I was five miles down the trail before I realized what had happened. Not once in that fourteen-hour night did I think about deadlines, or bills, or the man in the desert. For the first time in many months I was happy to see a day beginning. The morning sunshine was like a present from the gods. What really happened, of course, is that I remembered about joy.

I know that one night out at thirty-two below doesn't sound like much to those of you who have climbed Everest or run the Iditarod or kayaked to Antarctica, and I won't try to convince you that my life was like the movies where depression goes away in one weekend, and all of life's problems vanish with a moment's clear sight. The simple truth of the matter is this: On Sunday I had a glimpse outside of the house of mirrors, on Saturday I couldn't have seen my way out of a paper bag. And while I was skiing back toward the truck that morning, a wind came up behind us and swirled the snow around our bodies like a blizzard under blue sky. And I was struck by the simple perfection of the snowflakes, and startled by the hopefulness of sun on frozen trees.

CRITICAL THINKING QUESTIONS

1. Write a *claim of policy* that this story suggests for an individual who is battling depression. Does the claim have merit?

2. In the closing paragraph, the narrator anticipates and attempts to rebut readers' objections. How effective is this strategy?

WRITING TOPIC

Compare and contrast Houston's narrator and the man in London's "To Build a Fire." Specifically, examine their value assumptions about their place in nature and their relationship to their canine companions. Which character's assumptions do you think are generally representative of many people today? On what evidence—observations, examples—do you base your conclusion?

Sarah Orne Jewett

A White Heron

I

The woods were already filled with shadows one June evening, just before eight o'clock, though a bright sunset still glimmered faintly among the trunks of the trees. A little girl was driving home her cow, a plodding, dilatory, provoking creature in her behavior, but a valued companion for all that. They were going away from whatever light there was, and striking deep into the woods, but their feet were familiar with the path, and it was no matter whether their eyes could see it or not.

There was hardly a night the summer through when the old cow could be found waiting at the pasture bars; on the contrary, it was her greatest pleasure to hide herself away among the huckleberry bushes, and though she wore a loud bell she had made the discovery that if one stood perfectly still it would not ring. So Sylvia had to hunt for her until she found her, and call Co'! Co'! with never an answering Moo, until her childish patience was quite spent. If the creature had not given good milk and plenty of it, the case would have seemed very different to her owners. Besides, Sylvia had all the time there was, and very little use to make of it. Sometimes in pleasant weather it was a consolation to look upon the cow's pranks as an intelligent attempt to play hide and seek, and as the child had no playmates she lent herself to this amusement with a good deal of zest. Though this chase had been so long that the wary animal herself had given an unusual signal of her whereabouts, Sylvia had only laughed when she came upon Mistress Moolly at the swampside, and urged her affectionately homeward with a twig of birch leaves. The old cow was not inclined to wander farther, she even turned in the right direction for once as they left the pasture, and stepped along the road at a good pace. She was quite ready to be milked now, and seldom stopped to browse. Sylvia wondered what her grandmother would say because they were so late. It was a great while since she had left home at half-past five o'clock, but everybody knew the difficulty of making this errand a short one. Mrs. Tilley had chased the hornéd torment too many summer evenings herself to blame any one else for lingering, and was only thankful as she waited that she had Sylvia, nowadays, to give such valuable assistance. The good woman suspected that Sylvia loitered occasionally on her own account; there never was such a child for straying about out-of-doors since the world was made! Everybody said that it was a good change for a little maid who had tried to grow for eight years in a crowded manufacturing town, but as for Sylvia herself, it seemed as if she never had been alive at all before she came to live at the farm. She thought often with wistful compassion of a wretched geranium that belonged to a town neighbor.

"'Afraid of folks,'" old Mrs. Tilley said to herself, with a smile, after she had made the unlikely choice of Sylvia from her daughter's houseful of children, and was returning to the farm. "'Afraid of folks,' they said! I guess she won't be troubled no great with 'em up to the old place!" When they reached the door of the lonely house and stopped to unlock it, and the cat came to purr loudly, and rub against them, a deserted pussy, indeed, but fat with young robins, Sylvia whispered that this was a beautiful place to live in, and she never should wish to go home.

The companions followed the shady woodroad, the cow taking slow steps and the child very fast ones. The cow stopped long at the brook to drink, as if the pasture were not half a swamp, and Sylvia stood still and waited, letting her bare feet cool themselves in the shoal water, while the great twilight moths struck softly against her. She waded on through the brook as the cow moved away, and listened to the thrushes with a heart that beat fast with pleasure. There was a stirring in the great boughs overhead. They were full of little birds and beasts that seemed to be wide awake, and going about their world, or else saying goodnight to each other in sleepy twitters. Sylvia herself felt sleepy as she walked along. However, it was not much farther to the house, and the air was soft and sweet. She was not often in the woods so late as this, and it made her feel as if she were a part of the gray shadows and the moving leaves. She was just thinking how long it seemed since she first came to the farm a year ago, and wondering if everything went on in the noisy town just the same as when she was there; the thought of the great red-faced boy who used to chase and frighten her made her hurry along the path to escape from the shadow of the trees.

Suddenly this little woods-girl is horror-stricken to hear a clear whistle not very far away. Not a bird's-whistle, which would have a sort of friendliness, but a boy's whistle, determined, and somewhat aggressive. Sylvia left the cow to whatever sad fate might await her, and stepped discreetly aside into the brushes, but she was just too late. The enemy had discovered her, and called out in a very cheerful and persuasive tone, "Halloa, little girl, how far is it to the road?" and trembling Sylvia answered almost inaudibly, "A good ways."

She did not dare to look boldly at the tall young man, who carried a gun over his shoulder, but she came out of her bush and again followed the cow, while he walked alongside.

"I have been hunting for some birds," the stranger said kindly, "and I have lost my way, and need a friend very much. Don't be afraid," he added gallantly. "Speak up and tell me what your name is, and whether you think I can spend the night at your house, and go out gunning early in the morning."

Sylvia was more alarmed than before. Would not her grandmother consider her much to blame? But who could have foreseen such an accident as this? It did not seem to be her fault, and she hung her head as if the stem of it were broken, but managed to answer "Sylvy," with much effort when her companion again asked her name.

Mrs. Tilley was standing in the doorway when the trio came into view. The cow gave a loud moo by way of explanation.

"Yes, you'd better speak up for yourself, you old trial! Where'd she tucked herself away this time, Sylvy?" But Sylvia kept an awed silence; she knew by instinct that her grandmother did not comprehend the gravity of the situation. She must be mistaking the stranger for one of the farmer-lads of the region.

The young man stood his gun beside the door, and dropped a lumpy game-bag beside it; then he bade Mrs. Tilley good-evening, and repeated his wayfarer's story, and asked if he could have a night's lodging.

"Put me anywhere you like," he said. "I must be off early in the morning, before day; but I am very hungry, indeed. You can give me some milk at any rate, that's plain."

"Dear sakes, yes," responded the hostess, whose long slumbering hospitality seemed to be easily awakened. "You might fare better if you went out to the main road a mile or so, but you're welcome to what we've got. I'll milk right off, and you make yourself at home. You can sleep on husks or feathers," she proffered graciously. "I raised them all myself. There's good pasturing for geese just below here towards the ma'sh. Now step round and set a plate for the gentleman, Sylvy!" And Sylvia promptly stepped. She was glad to have something to do, and she was hungry herself.

It was a surprise to find so clean and comfortable a little dwelling in this New England wilderness. The young man had known the horrors of its most primitive housekeeping, and the dreary squalor of that level of society which does not rebel at the companionship of hens. This was the best thrift of an old-fashioned farmstead, though on such a small scale that it seemed like a hemitage. He listened eagerly to the old woman's quaint talk, he watched Sylvia's pale face and shining gray eyes with ever growing enthusiasm, and insisted that this was the best supper he had eaten for a month, and afterward the new-made friends sat down in the door-way together while the moon came up.

Soon it would be berry-time, and Sylvia was a great help at picking. The cow was a good milker, though a plaguy thing to keep track of, the hostess gossiped frankly, adding presently that she had buried four children, so Sylvia's mother, and a son (who might be dead) in California were all the children she had left. "Dan, my boy, was a great hand to go gunning," she explained sadly. "I never wanted for pa'tridges or gray squer'ls while he was to home. He's been a great wand'rer, I expect, and he's no hand to write letters. There, I don't blame him, I'd ha' seen the world myself if it had been so I could."

"Sylvy takes after him," the grandmother continued affectionately, after a minute's pause. "There ain't a foot o' ground she don't know her way over, and the wild creatures counts her one o' themselves. Squer'ls she'll tame to come an' feed right out o' her hands, and all sorts o' birds. Last winter she got the jay-birds to bangeing here, and I believe she'd 'a' scanted herself of her own meals to have plenty to throw out amongst 'em, if I had n't kep' watch. Anything but crows, I tell her, I'm willin' to help support—though Dan he had a tamed one o' them that did seem to have reason same as folks. It was round here a good spell after he went away. Dan an' his father they didn't hitch,—but he never held up his head ag'in after Dan had dared him an' gone off."

The guest did not notice this hint of family sorrows in his eager interest in something else.

"So Sylvy knows all about birds, does she?" he exclaimed, as he looked round at the little girl who sat, very demure but increasingly sleepy, in the moonlight. "I am making a collection of birds myself. I have been at it ever since I was a boy." (Mrs. Tilley smiled.) "There are two or three very rare ones I have been hunting for these five years. I mean to get them on my own ground if they can be found."

"Do you cage 'em up?" asked Mrs. Tilley doubtfully, in response to this enthusiastic announcement.

"Oh no, they're stuffed and preserved, dozens and dozens of them," said the ornithologist, "and I have shot or snared every one myself. I caught a glimpse of a white heron a few miles from here on Saturday, and I have followed it in this direction. They have never been found in this district at all. The little white heron, it is," and he turned again to look at Sylvia with the hope of discovering that the rare bird was one of her acquaintances.

But Sylvia was watching a hop-toad in the narrow footpath.

"You would know the heron if you saw it," the stranger continued eagerly. "A queer tall white bird with soft feathers and long thin legs. And it would have a nest perhaps in the top of a high tree, made of sticks, something like a hawk's nest."

Sylvia's heart gave a wild beat; she knew that strange white bird, and had once stolen softly near where it stood in some bright green swamp grass, away over at the other side of the woods. There was an open place where the sunshine always seemed strangely yellow and hot, where tall, nodding rushes grew, and her grandmother had warned her that she might sink in the soft black mud underneath and never be heard of more. Not far beyond were the salt marshes just this side the sea itself, which Sylvia wondered and dreamed much about, but never had seen, whose great voice could sometimes be heard above the noise of the woods on storm nights.

"I can't think of anything I should like so much as to find that heron's nest," the handsome stranger was saying. "I would give ten dollars to anybody who could show it to me," he added desperately, "and I mean to spend my whole vacation hunting for it if need be. Perhaps it was only migrating, or had been chased out of its own region by some bird of prey."

Mrs. Tilley gave amazed attention to all this, but Sylvia still watched the toad, not divining, as she might have done at some calmer time, that the creature wished to get to its hole under the door-step, and was much hindered by the unusual spectators at that hour of the evening. No amount of thought, that night, could decide how many wished-for treasures the ten dollars, so lightly spoken of, would buy.

The next day the young sportsman hovered about the woods, and Sylvia kept him company, having lost her first fear of the friendly lad, who proved to be most kind and sympathetic. He told her many things about the birds and what they knew and where they lived and what they did with themselves. And he gave her a jack-knife, which she thought as great a treasure as if she were a desert-islander. All day long he did not once make her troubled or afraid except when he brought down some unsuspecting singing creature from its bough. Sylvia would have liked him vastly better without his gun; she could not understand why he killed the very birds he seemed to like so much. But as the day waned, Sylvia still watched the young man with loving admiration. She had never seen anybody so charming and delightful; the woman's heart, asleep in the child, was vaguely thrilled by a dream of love. Some premonition of that great power stirred and swayed these young creatures who traversed the solemn woodlands with soft-footed silent care. They stopped to listen to a bird's song; they pressed forward again eagerly, parting the branches—speaking to each other rarely and in whispers; the young man going first and Sylvia following, fascinated, a few steps behind, with her gray eyes dark with excitement.

She grieved because the longed-for white heron was elusive, but she did not lead the guest, she only followed, and there was no such thing as speaking first. The sound of her own unquestioned voice would have terrified her—it was hard enough to answer yes or no when there was need of that. At last evening began to fall, and they drove the cow home together, and Sylvia smiled with pleasure when they came to the place where she heard the whistle and was afraid only the night before.

II

Half a mile from home, at the farther edge of the woods, where the land was highest, a great pine-tree stood, the last of its generation. Whether it was left for a boundary mark, or for what reason, no one could say; the woodchoppers who had felled its mates were dead and gone long ago, and a whole forest of sturdy trees, pines and oaks and maples, had grown again. But the stately head of this old pine towered above them all and made a landmark for sea and shore miles and miles away. Sylvia knew it well. She had always believed that whoever climbed to the top of it could see the ocean; and the little girl had often laid her hand on the great rough trunk and looked up wistfully at those dark boughs that the wind always stirred, no matter how hot and still the air might be below. Now she thought of the tree with a new excitement, for why, if one climbed it at break of day could not one see all the world, and easily discover from whence the white heron flew, and mark the place, and find the hidden nest?

What a spirit of adventure, what wild ambition! What fancied triumph and delight and glory for the later morning when she could make known the secret! It was almost too real and too great for the childish heart to bear.

All night the door of the little house stood open and the whippoorwills came and sang upon the very step. The young sportsman and his old hostess were sound asleep, but Sylvia's great design kept her broad awake and watching. She forgot to think of sleep. The short summer night seemed as long as the winter darkness, and at last when the whippoorwills ceased, and she was afraid the morning would after all come too soon, she stole out of the house and followed the pasture path through the woods, hastening toward the open ground beyond, listening with a sense of comfort and companionship to the drowsy twitter of a half-awakened bird, whose perch she had jarred in passing. Alas, if the great wave of human interest which flooded for the first time this dull little life should sweep away the satisfactions of an existence heart to heart with nature and the dumb life of the forest!

There was the huge tree asleep yet in the paling moonlight, and small and silly Sylvia began with utmost bravery to mount to the top of it, with tingling, eager blood coursing the channels of her whole frame, with her bare feet and fingers, that pinched and held like bird's claws to the monstrous ladder reaching up, up, almost to the sky itself. First she must mount the white oak tree that grew alongside, where she was almost lost among the dark branches and the green leaves heavy and wet with dew; a bird fluttered off its nest, and a red squirrel ran to and fro and scolded pettishly at the harmless housebreaker. Sylvia felt her way easily. She had often climbed there, and knew that higher still one of the oak's upper branches chafed against the pine trunk, just where its lower boughs were set close together. There, when she made the dangerous pass from one tree to the other, the great enterprise would really begin.

She crept out along the swaying oak limb at last, and took the daring step across into the old pine-tree. The way was harder than she thought; she must reach far and hold fast, the sharp dry twigs caught and held her and scratched her like angry talons, the pitch made her thin little fingers clumsy and stiff as she went round and round the tree's great stem, higher and higher upward. The sparrows and robins in the woods below were beginning to wake and twitter to the dawn, yet it seemed much lighter there aloft in the pine-tree, and the child knew she must hurry if her project were to be of any use.

The tree seemed to lengthen itself out as she went up, and to reach farther and farther upward. It was like a great main-mast to the voyaging earth; it must truly have been amazed that morning though all its ponderous frame as it felt this determined spark of human spirit wending its way from higher branch to branch. Who knows how steadily the least twigs held themselves to advantage this light, weak creature on her way! The old pine must have loved his new dependent. More than all the hawks, and bats, and moths, and even the sweet voiced thrushes, was the brave, beating heart of the solitary gray-eyed child. And the tree stood still and frowned away the winds that June morning while the dawn grew bright in the east.

Sylvia's face was like a pale star, if one had seen it from the ground, when the last thorny bough was past, and she stood trembling and tired but wholly triumphant, high in the treetop. Yes, there was the sea with the dawning sun making a golden dazzle over it, and toward that glorious east flew two hawks with slow-moving pinions. How low they looked in the air from that height when one had only seen them before far up, and dark against the blue sky. Their gray feathers were as soft as moths; they seemed only a little way from the tree, and Sylvia felt as if she too could go flying away among the clouds. Westward, the woodlands and farms reached miles and miles into the distance; here and there were church steeples, and white villages, truly it was a vast and awesome world!

The birds sang louder and louder. At last the sun came up bewilderingly bright. Sylvia could see the white sails of ships out at sea, and the clouds that were purple and rose-colored and yellow at first began to fade away. Where was the white heron's nest in the sea of green branches, and was this wonderful sight and pageant of the world the only reward for having climbed to such a giddy height? Now look down again, Sylvia, where the green marsh is set among the shining birches and dark hemlocks; there where you saw the white heron once you will see him again; look, look! a white spot of him like a single floating feather comes up from the dead hemlock and grows larger, and rises, and comes close at last, and goes by the land-mark pine with steady sweep of wing and outstretched slender neck and crested head. And wait! wait! do not move a foot or a finger, little girl, do not send an arrow of light and consciousness from your two eager eyes, for the heron has perched on a pine bough not far beyond yours, and cries back to his mate on the nest and plumes his feathers for the new day!

The child gives a long sigh a minute later when a company of shouting cat-birds comes also to the tree, and vexed by their fluttering and lawlessness the solemn heron goes away. She knows his secret now, the wild, light, slender bird that floats and wavers, and goes back like an arrow presently to his home in the green world beneath. Then Sylvia, well satisfied, makes her perilous way down again, not daring to look far below the branch she stands on, ready to cry sometimes because her fingers ache and her lamed feet slip. Wondering over and over again what the stranger would say to her, and what he would think when she told him how to find his way straight to the heron's nest.

"Sylvy, Sylvy!" called the busy old grandmother again and again, but nobody answered, and the small husk bed was empty and Sylvia had disappeared.

The guest waked from a dream, and remembering his day's pleasure hurried to dress himself that might it sooner begin. He was sure from the way the shy little girl looked once or twice yesterday that she had at least seen the white heron, and now she must really be made to tell. Here she comes now, paler than ever, and her worn old frock is torn and tattered, and smeared with pine pitch. The grandmother and the sportsman stand in the door together and question her, and the splendid mo-ment has come to speak of the dead hemlock-tree by the green marsh.

But Sylvia does not speak after all, though the old grandmother fretfully re-bukes her, and the young man's kind, appealing eyes are looking straight in her own. He can make them rich with money; he has promised it, and they are poor now. He is so well worth making happy, and he waits to hear the story she can tell.

No, she must keep silence! What is it that suddenly forbids her and makes her dumb? Has she been nine years growing and now, when the great world for the first time puts out a hand to her, must she thrust it aside for a bird's sake? The murmur of the pine's green branches is in her ears, she remembers how the white heron came fly-ing through the golden air and how they watched the sea and the morning together, and Sylvia cannot speak; she cannot tell the heron's secret and give its life away.

Dear loyalty, that suffered a sharp pang as the guest went away disappointed later in the day, that could have served and followed him and loved him as a dog loves! Many a night Sylvia heard the echo of his whistle haunting the pasture path as she came home with the loitering cow. She forgot even her sorrow at the sharp report of his gun and the sight of thrushes and sparrow's dropping silent to the ground, their songs hushed and their pretty feathers stained and wet with blood.

Were the birds better friends than their hunter might have been,—who can tell? Whatever treasures were lost to her, woodlands and summer-time, remember! Bring your gifts and graces and tell your secrets to this lonely country child!

CRITICAL THINKING QUESTIONS

1. In the pre-dawn, Sylvia slips out of her grandmother's home to locate the white heron's nesting place, so she can tell the young man and earn his gratitude and a monetary reward. But when the moment arrives for her to reveal the heron's nest location, she decides "she must keep silence." What *value assumptions* about nature enter into Sylvia's decision?

2. Like Sylvia, the young man seems to regard the natural world with reverence. However, carrying a gun, "the ornithologist" has a distinctly different purpose. What values motivate the young man's pursuit of nature?

3. In the depiction of the two opposing views toward nature, represented by Sylvia and the young man, does the author seem to favor one or the other? Find specific passages that may reveal the author's underlying *bias*. Is the language primarily emotional (*pathos* appeal) or logical (*logos* appeal)?

4. What is the author's *implied claim* about the value of wilderness? How does the closing paragraph qualify the claim?

Ursula K. Le Guin

May's Lion

Jim remembers it as a bobcat, and he was May's nephew, and ought to know. It probably was a bobcat. I don't think May would have changed her story, though you can't trust a good story-teller not to make the story suit herself, or get the facts to fit the story better. Anyhow she told it to us more than once, because my mother and I would ask for it; and the way I remember it, it was a mountain lion. And the way I remember May telling it is sitting on the edge of the irrigation tank we used to swim in, cement rough as a lava flow and hot in the sun, the long cracks tarred over. She was an old lady then with a long Irish upper lip, kind and wary and balky. She liked to come sit and talk with my mother while I swam; she didn't have all that many people to talk to. She always had chickens, in the chickenhouse very near the back door of the farmhouse, so the whole place smelled pretty strong of chickens, and as long as she could she kept a cow or two down in the old barn by the creek. The first of May's cows I remember was Pearl, a big handsome Holstein who gave fourteen or twenty-four or forty gallons or quarts of milk at a milking, whichever is right for a prize milker. Pearl was beautiful in my eyes when I was four or five years old; I loved and admired her. I remember how excited I was, how I reached upward to them, when Pearl or the workhorse Prince, for whom my love amounted to worship, would put an immense and sensitive muzzle through the three-strand fence to whisk a cornhusk from my fearful hand; and then the munching and the sweet breath and the big nose would be at the barbed wire again: the offering is acceptable. . . . After Pearl there was Rosie, a purebred Jersey. May got her either cheap or free because she was a runt calf, so tiny that May brought her home on her lap in the back of the car, like a fawn. And Rosie always looked like she had some deer in her. She was a lovely, clever little cow and even more willful than old May. She often chose not to come in to be milked. We would hear May calling and then see her trudging across our lower pasture with the bucket, going to find Rosie wherever Rosie had decided to be milked today on the wild hills she had to roam in, a hundred acres of our and Old Jim's land. Then May had a fox terrier named Pinky, who yipped and nipped and turned me against fox terriers for life, but he was long gone when the mountain lion came; and the black cats who lived in the barn kept discreetly out of the story. As a matter of fact now I think of it the chickens weren't in it either. It might have been quite different if they had been. May had quit keeping chickens after old Mrs. Walter died. It was just her all alone there, and Rosie and the cats down in the barn, and nobody else within sight or sound of the old farm. We were in our house up the hill only in the summer, and Jim lived in town, those

252

years. What time of year it was I don't know, but I imagine the grass still green or just turning gold. And May was in the house, in the kitchen, where she lived entirely unless she was asleep or outdoors, when she heard this noise.

Now you need May herself, sitting skinny on the edge of the irrigation tank, seventy or eighty or ninety years old, nobody knew how old May was and she had made sure they couldn't find out, opening her pleated lips and letting out this noise—a huge, awful yowl, starting soft with a nasal hum and rising slowly into a snarling gargle that sank away into a sobbing purr. . . . It got better every time she told the story.

"It was some meow," she said.

So she went to the kitchen door, opened it, and looked out. Then she shut the kitchen door and went to the kitchen window to look out, because there was a mountain lion under the fig tree.

Puma, cougar, catamount; *Felis concolor,* the shy, secret, shadowy lion of the New World, four or five feet long plus a yard of black-tipped tail, weighs about what a woman weighs, lives where the deer live from Canada to Chile, but always shyer, always fewer, the color of dry leaves, dry grass.

There were plenty of deer in the Valley in the forties, but no mountain lion had been seen for decades anywhere near where people lived. Maybe way back up in the canyons; but Jim, who hunted, and knew every deer-trail in the hills, had never seen a lion. Nobody had, except May, now, alone in her kitchen.

"I thought maybe it was sick," she told us. "It wasn't acting right. I don't think a lion would walk right into the yard like that if it was feeling well. If I'd still had the chickens it'd be a different story maybe! But it just walked around some, and then it lay down there," and she points between the fig tree and the decrepit garage. "And then after a while it kind of meowed again, and got up and come into the shade right there." The fig tree, planted when the house was built, about the time May was born, makes a great, green, sweet-smelling shade. "It just laid there looking around. It wasn't well," says May.

She had lived with and looked after animals all her life; she had also earned her living for years as a nurse.

"Well, I didn't know exactly what to do for it. So I put out some water for it. It didn't even get up when I come out the door. I put the water down there, not so close to it that we'd scare each other, see, and it kept watching me, but it didn't move. After I went back in it did get up and tried to drink some water. Then it made that kind of meowowow. I do believe it come here because it was looking for help. Or just for company, maybe."

The afternoon went on, May in the kitchen, the lion under the fig tree.

But down in the barnyard by the creek was Rosie the cow. Fortunately the grate was shut, so she could not come wandering up to the house and meet the lion; but she would be needing to be milked, come six or seven o'clock, and that got to worrying May. She also worried how long a sick mountain lion might hang around, keeping her shut in the house. May didn't like being shut in.

"I went out a time or two, and went shoo!"

Eyes shining amidst fine wrinkles, she flaps her thin arms at the lion. "Shoo! Go on home now!"

But the silent wild creature watches her with yellow eyes and does not stir.

"So when I was talking to Miss Macy on the telephone, she said it might have rabies, and I ought to call the sheriff. I was uneasy then. So finally I did that, and they come out, those county police, you know. Two carloads."

Her voice is dry and quiet.

"I guess there was nothing else they knew how to do. So they shot it."

She looks off across the field Old Jim, her brother, used to plow with Prince the horse and irrigate with the water from this tank. Now wild oats and black-berry grow there. In another thirty years it will be a rich man's vineyard, a tax write-off.

"He was seven feet long, all stretched out, before they took him off. And so thin! They all said, 'Well, Aunt May, I guess you were scared there! I guess you were some scared!' But I wasn't. I didn't want him shot. But I didn't know what to do for him. And I did need to get to Rosie."

I have told this true story which May gave to us as truly as I could, and now I want to tell it as fiction, yet without taking it from her: rather to give it back to her, if I can do so. It is a tiny part of the history of the Valley, and I want to make it part of the Valley outside history. Now the field that the poor man plowed and the rich man harvested lies on the edge of a little town, houses and workshops of timber and fieldstone standing among almond, oak, and eucalyptus trees; and now May is an old woman with a name that means the month of May: Rains End. An old woman with a long, wrinkled-pleated upper lip, she is living alone for the summer in her summer place, a meadow a mile or so up in the hills above the little town. Sinshan. She took her cow Rose with her, and since Rose tends to wander she keeps her on a long tether down by the tiny creek, and moves her into fresh grass now and then. The summerhouse is what they call a nine-pole house, a mere frame of poles stuck in the ground—one of them is a live digger-pine sapling—with stick and matting walls, and mat roof and floors. It doesn't rain in the dry season, and the roof is just for shade. But the house and its little front yard where Rains End has her camp stove and clay oven and matting loom are well shaded by a fig tree that was planted there a hundred years or so ago by her grandmother.

Rains End herself has no grandchildren; she never bore a child, and her one or two marriages were brief and very long ago. She has a nephew and two grandnieces, and feels herself an aunt to all children, even when they are afraid of her and rude to her because she has got so ugly with old age, smelling as musty as a chickenhouse. She considers it natural for children to shrink away from somebody part way dead, and knows that when they're a little older and have got used to her they'll ask her for stories. She was for sixty years a member of the Doctors Lodge, and though she doesn't do curing any more people still ask her to help with nursing sick children, and the children come to long for the kind, authoritative touch of her hands when she bathes them to bring a fever down, or changes a dressing, or combs out bed-tangled hair with witch hazel and great patience.

So Rains End was just waking up from an early afternoon nap in the heat of the day, under the matting roof, when she heard a noise, a huge, awful yowl that started soft with a nasal hum and rose slowly into a snarling gargle that sank away into a sobbing purr. . . . And she got up and looked out from the open side of the house of sticks and matting, and saw a mountain lion under the fig tree. She looked at him from her house; he looked at her from his.

And this part of the story is much the same: the old woman; the lion; and, down by the creek, the cow.

It was hot. Crickets sang shrill in the yellow grass on all the hills and canyons, in all the chaparral. Rains End filled a bowl with water from an unglazed jug and came slowly out of the house. Halfway between the house and the lion she set the bowl down on the dirt. She turned and went back to the house.

The lion got up after a while and came and sniffed at the water. He lay down again with a soft, querulous groan, almost like a sick child, and looked at Rains End with the yellow eyes that saw her in a different way than she had ever been seen before.

She sat on the matting in the shade of the open part of her house and did some mending. When she looked up at the lion she sang under her breath, tunelessly; she wanted to remember the Puma Dance Song but could only remember bits of it, so she made a song for the occasion:

You are there, lion.
You are there, lion. . . .

As the afternoon wore on she began to worry about going down to milk Rose. Unmilked, the cow would start tugging at her tether and making a commotion. That was likely to upset the lion. He lay so close to the house now that if she came out that too might upset him, and she did not want to frighten him or to become frightened of him. He had evidently come for some reason, and it behooved her to find out what the reason was. Probably he was sick; his coming so close to a human person was strange, and people who behave strangely are usually sick or in some kind of pain. Sometimes, though, they are spiritually moved to act strangely. The lion might be a messenger, or might have some message of his own for her or her townspeople. She was more used to seeing birds as messengers; the four-footed people go about their own business. But the lion, dweller in the Seventh House, comes from the place dreams come from. Maybe she did not understand. Maybe someone else would understand. She could go over and tell Valiant and her family, whose summerhouse was in Gahheya meadow, farther up the creek; or she could go over to Buck's, on Baldy Knoll. But there were four or five adolescents there, and one of them might come and shoot the lion, to boast that he'd saved old Rains End from getting clawed to bits and eaten.

Mooooooo! said Rose, down by the creek, reproachfully.

The sun was still above the southwest ridge, but the branches of pines were across it and the heavy heat was out of it, and shadows were welling up in the low fields of wild oats and blackberry.

Moooooo! said Rose again, louder.

The lion lifted up his square, heavy head, the color of dry wild oats, and gazed down across the pastures. Rains End knew from that weary movement that he was very ill. He had come for company in dying, that was all.

"I'll come back, lion," Rains End sang tunelessly. "Lie still. Be quiet. I'll come back soon." Moving softly and easily, as she would move in a room with a sick child, she got her milking pail and stool, slung the stool on her back with a woven strap so as to leave a hand free, and came out of the house. The lion watched her at first very tense, the yellow eyes firing up for a moment, but then put his head down again with that little grudging, groaning sound. "I'll come back, lion," Rains End said. She went down to the creekside and milked a nervous and indignant cow. Rose could smell lion, and demanded in several ways, all eloquent, just what Rains End intended to *do?* Rains End ignored her questions and sang milking songs to her: "Su bonny, su bonny, be still my grand cow . . ." Once she had to slap her hard on the hip. "Quit that, you old fool! Get over! I am *not* going to untie you and have you walking into trouble! I won't let him come down this way."

She did not say how she planned to stop him.

She retethered Rose where she could stand down in the creek if she liked. When she came back up the rise with the pail of milk in hand, the lion had not moved. The sun was down, the air above the ridges turning clear gold. The yellow eyes watched her, no light in them. She came to pour milk into the lion's bowl. As she did so, he all at once half rose up. Rains End started, and spilled some of the milk she was pouring. "Shoo! Stop that!" she whispered fiercely, waving her skinny arm at the lion. "Lie down now! I'm afraid of you when you get up, can't you see that, stupid? Lie down now, lion. There you are. Here I am. It's all right. You know what you're doing." Talking softly as she went, she returned to her house of stick and matting. There she sat down as before, in the open porch, on the grass mats.

The mountain lion made the grumbling sound, ending with a long sigh, and let his head sink back down on his paws.

Rains End got some cornbread and a tomato from the pantry box while there was still daylight left to see by, and ate slowly and neatly. She did not offer the lion food. He had not touched the milk, and she thought he would eat no more in the House of Earth.

From time to time as the quiet evening darkened and stars gathered thicker overhead she sang to the lion. She sang the five songs of *Going Westward to the Sunrise,* which are sung to human beings dying. She did not know if it was proper and appropriate to sing these songs to a dying mountain lion, but she did not know his songs.

Twice he also sang: once a quavering moan, like a house cat challenging another tom to battle, and once a long, sighing purr.

Before the Scorpion had swung clear of Sinshan Mountain, Rains End had pulled her heavy shawl around herself in case the fog came in, and had gone sound asleep in the porch of her house.

She woke with the grey light before sunrise. The lion was a motionless shadow, a little farther from the trunk of the fig tree than he had been the night before. As the light grew, she saw that he had stretched himself out full length. She knew he had finished his dying, and sang the fifth song, the last song, in a whisper, for him:

The doors of the Four Houses
are open.
Surely they are open.

Near sunrise she went to milk Rose, and to wash in the creek. When she came back up to the house she went closer to the lion, though not so close as to crowd him, and stood for a long time looking at him stretched out in the long, tawny, delicate light. "As thin as I am!" she said to Valiant, when she went up to Gahheya later in the morning to tell the story and to ask help carrying the body of the lion off where the buzzards and coyotes could clean it.

It's still your story, Aunt May; it was your lion. He came to you. He brought his death to you, a gift; but the men with the guns won't take gifts, they think they own death already. And so they took from you the honor he did you, and you felt that loss. I wanted to restore it. But you don't need it. You followed the lion where he went, years ago now.

CRITICAL THINKING QUESTION

In the closing paragraph, Le Guin's narrator is fairly explicit in condemning the county police, "the men with guns," who shoot the lion. May, however, says, "I guess there was nothing else for them to do." Do you side with May's or the narrator's assessment of the situation?

WRITING TOPIC

Consider the saying, "Fiction is a lie that tells the truth." In Le Guin's story, the narrator says, "I have told this true story which May gave to us as truly as I could, and now I want to tell it as fiction, yet without taking it from her: rather to give it back to her, if I can do so. It is a tiny part of the history of the Valley, and I want to make it part of the Valley outside history." By retelling May's story as "fiction," what "truth" is the narrator attempting to express? Do you agree with the narrator that the fictionalized version of this tiny part of the Valley's history contains more truth than the factual account?

Jack London

To Build a Fire

Day had broken cold and grey, exceedingly cold and grey, when the man turned aside from the main Yukon trail and climbed the high earthbank, where a dim and little-travelled trail led eastward through the fat spruce timberland. It was a steep bank, and he paused for breath at the top, excusing the act to himself by looking at his watch. It was nine o'clock. There was no sun nor hint of sun, though there was not a cloud in the sky. It was a clear day, and yet there seemed an intangible pall over the face of things, a subtle gloom that made the day dark, and that was due to the absence of sun. This fact did not worry the man. He was used to the lack of sun. It had been days since he had seen the sun, and he knew that a few more days must pass before that cheerful orb, due south, would just peep above the skyline and dip immediately from view.

The man flung a look back along the way he had come. The Yukon lay a mile wide and hidden under three feet of ice. On top of this ice were as many feet of snow. It was all pure white, rolling in gentle undulations where the ice jams of the freeze-up had formed. North and south, as far as his eye could see, it was unbroken white, save for a dark hairline that curved and twisted from around the spruce-covered island to the south, and that curved and twisted away into the north, where it disappeared behind another spruce-covered island. This dark hairline was the trail—the main trail—that led south five hundred miles to the Chilcoot Pass, Dyea, and salt water; and that led north seventy miles to Dawson, and still on to the north a thousand miles to Nulato, and finally to St. Michael, on Bering Sea, a thousand miles and half a thousand more.

But all this—the mysterious, far-reaching hairline trail, the absence of sun from the sky, the tremendous cold, and the strangeness and weirdness of it all—made no impression on the man. It was not because he was long used to it. He was a newcomer in the land, a *chechaquo,* and this was his first winter. The trouble with him was that he was without imagination. He was quick and alert in the things of life, but only in the things, and not in the significances. Fifty degrees below zero meant eighty-odd degrees of frost. Such fact impressed him as being cold and uncomfortable, and that was all. It did not lead him to meditate upon his frailty as a creature of temperature, and upon man's frailty in general, able only to live within certain narrow limits of heat and cold; and from there on it did not lead him to the conjectural field of immortality and man's place in the universe. Fifty degrees below zero stood for a bite of frost that hurt and that must be guarded against by the use of mittens, ear flaps, warm moccasins, and thick socks. Fifty degrees below zero. That there should be anything more to it than that was a thought that never entered his head.

As he turned to go on, he spat speculatively. There was a sharp explosive crackle that startled him. He spat again. And again, in the air, before it could fall to the snow, the spittle crackled. He knew that at fifty below spittle crackled on the snow, but this spittle had crackled in the air. Undoubtedly it was colder than fifty below—how much colder he did not know. But the temperature did not matter. He was bound for the old claim on the left fork of Henderson Creek, where the boys were already. They had come over across the divide from the Indian Creek country, while he had come the roundabout way to take a look at the possibilities of getting out logs in the spring from the islands in the Yukon. He would be in to camp by six o'clock; a bit after dark, it was true, but the boys would be there, a fire would be going, and a hot supper would be ready. As for lunch, he pressed his hand against the protruding bundle under his jacket. It was also under his shirt, wrapped up in a handkerchief and lying against the naked skin. It was the only way to keep the biscuits from freezing. He smiled agreeably to himself as he thought of those biscuits, each cut open and sopped in bacon grease, and each enclosing a generous slice of fried bacon.

He plunged in among the big spruce trees. The trail was faint. A foot of snow had fallen since the last sled had passed over, and he was glad he was without a sled, travelling light. In fact, he carried nothing but the lunch wrapped in the handkerchief. He was surprised, however, at the cold. It certainly was cold, he concluded, as he rubbed his numb nose and cheekbones with his mittened hand. He was a warm-whiskered man, but the hair on his face did not protect the high cheekbones and the eager nose that thrust itself aggressively into the frosty air.

At the man's heels trotted a dog, a big native husky, the proper wolfdog, grey-coated and without any visible or temperamental difference from its brother, the wild wolf. The animal was depressed by the tremendous cold. It knew that it was no time for travelling. Its instinct told it a truer tale than was told to the man by the man's judgment. In reality, it was not merely colder than fifty below zero; it was colder than sixty below, than seventy below. It was seventy-five below zero. Since the freezing point is thirty-two above zero, it meant that one hundred and seven degrees of frost obtained. The dog did not know anything about thermometers. Possibly in its brain there was no sharp consciousness of a condition of very cold such as was in the man's brain. But the brute had its instinct. It experienced a vague but menacing apprehension that subdued it and made it slink along at the man's heels, and that made it question eagerly every unwonted movement of the man as if expecting him to go into camp or to seek shelter somewhere and build a fire. The dog had learned fire, and it wanted fire, or else to burrow under the snow and cuddle its warmth away from the air.

The frozen moisture of its breathing had settled on its fur in a fine powder of frost, and especially were its jowls, muzzle, and eyelashes whitened by its crystal breath. The man's red beard and moustache were likewise frosted, but more solidly, the deposit taking the form of ice and increasing with every warm, moist breath he exhaled. Also, the man was chewing tobacco, and the muzzle of ice held his lips so rigidly that he was unable to clear his chin when he expelled the juice. The result was a crystal beard of the color and solidity of amber that was increasing its length on his chin. If he fell down it would shatter itself, like glass, into brittle fragments. But he did not mind the appendage. It was the penalty all tobacco chewers paid in that country, and he had been out before in two cold snaps. They had not been so cold as this, he knew, but by the spirit thermometer at Sixty Mile he knew they had been registered at fifty below and at fifty-five.

He held on through the level stretch of woods for several miles, crossed a wide flat of nigger heads, and dropped down a bank to the frozen bed of a small stream. This was Henderson Creek, and he knew he was ten miles from the forks. He looked at his watch. It was ten o'clock. He was making four miles an hour, and he calculated that he would arrive at the forks at half-past twelve. He decided to celebrate that event by eating his lunch there.

The dog dropped in again at his heels, with a tail drooping discouragement, as the man swung along the creek bed. The furrow of the old sled trail was plainly visible, but a dozen inches of snow covered up the marks of the last runners. In a month no man had come up or down that silent creek. The man held steadily on. He was not much given to thinking, and just then particularly he had nothing to think about save that he would eat lunch at the forks and that at six o'clock he would be in camp with the boys. There was nobody to talk to; and, had there been, speech would have been impossible because of the ice muzzle on his mouth. So he continued monotonously to chew tobacco and to increase the length of his amber beard.

Once in a while the thought reiterated itself that it was very cold and that he had never experienced such cold. As he walked along he rubbed his cheekbones and nose with the back of his mittened hand. He did this automatically, now and again changing hands. But, rub as he would, the instant he stopped his cheekbones went numb, and the following instant the end of his nose went numb. He was sure to frost his cheeks; he knew that, and experienced a pang of regret that he had not devised a nose strap of the sort Bud wore in cold snaps. Such a strap passed across the cheeks, as well, and saved them. But it didn't matter much, after all. What were frosted cheeks? A bit painful, that was all; they were never serious.

Empty as the man's mind was of thoughts, he was keenly observant, and he noticed the changes in the creeks, the curves and bends and timber jams, and always he sharply noted where he placed his feet. Once, coming round a bend, he shied abruptly, like a startled horse, curved away from the place where he had been walking, and retreated several places back along the trail. The creek he knew was frozen clear to the bottom—no creek could contain water in that arctic winter—but he knew also that there were springs that bubbled out from the hillsides and ran along under the snow and on top of the ice of the creek. He knew that the coldest snaps never froze these springs, and he knew likewise their danger. They were traps. They hid pools of water under the snow that might be three inches deep, or three feet. Sometimes a skin of ice half an inch thick covered them, and in turn was covered by the snow. Sometimes there were alternate layers of water and ice skin, so that when one broke through he kept on breaking through for a while, sometimes wetting himself to the waist.

That was why he had shied in such a panic. He had felt the give under his feet and heard the crackle of a snow-hidden ice skin. And to get his feet wet in such a temperature meant trouble and danger. At the very least it meant delay, for he would be forced to stop and build a fire, and under its protection to bare his feet while he dried his socks and moccasins. He stood and studied the creek bed and its banks, and decided that the flow of water came from the right. He reflected awhile, rubbing his nose and cheeks, then skirted to the left, stepping gingerly and testing the footing for each step. Once clear of the danger, he took a fresh chew of tobacco and swung along at his four-mile gait.

In the course of the next two hours he came upon several similar traps. Usually the snow above the hidden pools had a sunken, candied appearance that advertised the danger. Once again, however, he had a close call; and once, suspecting danger, he compelled the dog to go on in front. The dog did not want to go. It hung back until the man shoved it forward, and then it went quickly across the white, unbroken surface. Suddenly it broke through, floundered to one side, and got away to firmer footing. It had wet its forefeet and legs, and almost immediately the water that clung to it turned to ice. It made quick efforts to lick the ice off its legs, then dropped down in the snow and began to bite out the ice that had formed between the toes. This was a matter of instinct. To permit the ice to remain would mean sore feet. It did not know this. It merely obeyed the mysterious prompting that arose from the deep crypts of its being. But the man knew, having achieved a judgment on the subject, and he removed the mitten from his right hand and helped to tear out the ice particles. He did not expose his fingers more than a minute, and was astonished at the swift numbness that smote them. It certainly was cold. He pulled on the mitten hastily, and beat the hand savagely across his chest.

At twelve o'clock the day was at its brightest. Yet the sun was too far south on its winter journey to clear the horizon. The bulge of the earth intervened between it and Henderson Creek, where the man walked under a clear sky at noon and cast no shadow. At half-past twelve, to the minute, he arrived at the forks of the creek. He was pleased at the speed he had made. If he kept it up, he would certainly be with the boys by six. He unbuttoned his jacket and shirt and drew forth his lunch. The action consumed no more than a quarter of a minute, yet in that brief moment the numbness laid hold of the exposed fingers. He did not put the mitten on, but, instead, struck the fingers a dozen sharp smashes against his leg. Then he sat down on a snow-covered log to eat. The sting that followed upon the striking of his fingers against his leg ceased so quickly that he was startled. He had had no chance to take a bite of biscuit. He struck the fingers repeatedly and returned them to the mitten, baring the other hand for the purpose of eating. He tried to take a mouthful, but the ice muzzle prevented. He had forgotten to build a fire and thaw out. He chuckled at his foolishness, and as he chuckled he noted the numbness creeping into the exposed fingers. Also, he noted that the stinging which had first come to his toes when he sat down was already passing away. He wondered whether the toes were warm or numb. He moved them inside the moccasins and decided that they were numb.

He pulled the mitten on hurriedly and stood up. He was a bit frightened. He stamped up and down until the stinging returned into the feet. It certainly was cold, was his thought. That man from Sulphur Creek had spoken the truth when telling how cold it sometimes got in the country. And he had laughed at him at the time! That showed one must not be too sure of things. There was no mistake about it, it *was* cold. He strode up and down, stamping his feet and threshing his arms, until reassured by the returning warmth. Then he got out matches and proceeded to make a fire. From the undergrowth, where high water of the previous spring had lodged a supply of seasoned twigs, he got his firewood. Working carefully from a small beginning, he soon had a roaring fire, over which he thawed the ice from his face and in the protection of which he ate his biscuits. For the moment the cold of space was outwitted. The dog took satisfaction in the fire, stretching out close enough for warmth and far enough away to escape being singed.

When the man had finished, he filled his pipe and took his comfortable time over a smoke. Then he pulled on his mittens, settled the ear flaps of his cap firmly about his ears, and took the creek trail up the left fork. The dog was disappointed and yearned back towards the fire. This man did not know cold. Possibly all the generations of his ancestry had been ignorant of cold, of real cold, of cold one hundred and seven degrees below freezing point. But the dog knew; all its ancestry knew, and it had inherited the knowledge. And it knew that it was not good to walk abroad in such fearful cold. It was the time to lie snug in a hole in the snow and wait for a curtain of cloud to be drawn across the face of outer space whence this cold came. On the other hand, there was no keen intimacy between the dog and the man. The one was the toil slave of the other, and the only caresses it had ever received were the caresses of the whip lash and of harsh and menacing throat sounds that threatened the whip lash. So the dog made no effort to communicate its apprehension to the man. It was not concerned in the welfare of the man; it was for its own sake that it yearned back towards the fire. But the man whistled, and spoke to it with the sound of whip lashes, and the dog swung in at the man's heels and followed after.

The man took a chew of tobacco and proceeded to start a new amber beard. Also, his moist breath quickly powdered with white his moustache, eyebrows, and lashes. There did not seem to be so many springs on the left fork of the Henderson, and for half an hour the man saw no signs of any. And then it happened. At a place where there were no signs, where the soft, unbroken snow seemed to advertise solidity beneath, the man broke through. It was not deep. He wet himself half-way to the knees before he floundered out of the firm crust.

He was angry, and cursed his luck aloud. He had hoped to get into camp with the boys at six o'clock, and this would delay him an hour, for he would have to build a fire and dry out his footgear. This was imperative at that low temperature—he knew that much; and he turned aside to the bank, which he climbed. On top, tangled in the underbrush about the trunks of several small spruce trees, was a high-water deposit of dry firewood—sticks and twigs, principally, but also larger portions of seasoned branches and fine, dry, last year's grasses. He threw down several large pieces on top of the snow. This served for a foundation and prevented the young flame from drowning itself in the snow it otherwise would melt. The flame he got by touching a match to a small shred of birch bark that he took from his pocket. This burned even more readily than paper. Placing it on the foundation, he fed the young flame with wisps of dry grass and with the tiniest dry twigs.

He worked slowly and carefully, keenly aware of his danger. Gradually, as the flame grew stronger, he increased the size of the twigs with which he fed it. He squatted in the snow pulling the twigs out from their entanglement in the brush and feeding directly to the flame. He knew there must be no failure. When it is seventy-five below zero, a man must not fail in his first attempt to build a fire—that is, if his feet are wet. If his feet are dry, and he fails, he can run along the trail for half a mile and restore his circulation. But the circulation of wet and freezing feet cannot be restored by running when it is seventy-five below. No matters how fast he runs, the wet feet will freeze the harder.

All this the man knew. The old-timer on Sulphur Creek had told him about it the previous fall, and now he was appreciating the advice. Already all sensation had gone out of his feet. To build the fire he had been forced to remove his mittens, and the fingers had quickly gone numb. His pace of four miles an hour had kept his heart pumping blood to the surface of his body and to all the extremities. But the instant he stopped, the action of the pump eased down. The cold of space smote the unprotected tip of the planet, and he, being on that unprotected tip, received the full force of the blow. The blood of his body recoiled before it. The blood was alive, like the dog, and like the dog it wanted to hide away and cover itself up from the fearful cold. So long as he walked four miles an hour, he pumped that blood, willy-nilly, to the surfaces; but not it ebbed away and sank down into the recesses of his body. The extremities were the first to feel its absence. His wet feet froze the faster, and his exposed fingers numbed the faster, though they had not yet begun to freeze. Nose and cheeks were already freezing, while the skin of all his body chilled as it lost its blood.

But he as safe. Toes and nose and cheeks would be only touched by the frost, for the fire was beginning to burn with strength. He was feeding it with twigs the size of his finger. In another minute he would be able to feed it with branches the size of his wrist, and then he could remove his wet footgear, and, while it dried, he could keep his naked feet warm by the fire, rubbing them at first, of course, with snow. The fire was a success. He was safe. He remembered the advice of the old-timer on Sulphur Creek, and smiled. The old-timer had been very serious in laying down the law that no man must travel alone in the Klondike after fifty below. Well, here he was; he had had the accident; he was alone; and he had saved himself. Those old-timers were rather womanish, some of them, he thought. All a man had to do was to keep his head, and he was all right. Any man who was a man could travel alone. But it was surprising, the rapidity with which his cheeks and nose were freezing. And he had not thought his fingers could go lifeless in so short a time. Lifeless they were, for he could scarcely make them move together to grip a twig, and they seemed remote from his body and from him. When he touched a twig, he had to look and see whether or not he had hold of it. The wires were pretty well down between him and his finger ends.

All of which counted for little. There was the fire, snapping and crackling and promising life with every dancing flame. He started to untie his moccasins. They were coated with ice; the thick German socks were like sheaths of iron halfway to the knees; and the moccasin strings were like rods of steel all twisted and knotted as by some conflagration. For a moment he tugged with his numb fingers, then, realizing the folly of it, he drew his sheath knife.

But before he could cut the strings, it happened. It was his own fault or, rather, his mistake. He should not have built the fire under the spruce tree. He should have built it in the open. But it had been easier to pull the twigs from the brush and drop them directly on the fire. Now the tree under which he had done this carried a weight of snow on its boughs. No wind had blown for weeks, and each bough was fully freighted. Each time he had pulled a twig he had communicated a slight agitation to the tree—an imperceptible agitation, so far as he was concerned, but an agitation sufficient to bring about the disaster. High up in the tree one bough capsized its load of snow. This fell on the boughs beneath, capsizing them. This process continued, spreading out and involving the whole tree. It grew like an avalanche, and it descended without warning upon the man and the fire, and the fire was blotted out! Where it had burned was a mantle of fresh and disordered snow.

The man was shocked. It was as though he had just heard his own sentence of death. For a moment he sat and stared at the spot where the fire had been. Then he grew very calm. Perhaps the old-timer on Sulphur Creek was right. If he had only had a trail mate he would have been in no danger now. The trail mate could have built the fire. Well, it was up to him to build the fire over again, and this second time there must be no failure. Even if he succeeded, he would most likely lose some toes. His feet must be badly frozen by now, and there would be some time before the second fire was ready.

Such were his thoughts, but he did not sit and think them. He was busy all the time they were passing through his mind. He made a new foundation for a fire, this time in the open, where no treacherous tree could blot it out. Next he gathered dry grasses and tiny twigs from the high-water flotsam. He could not bring his fingers together to pull them out, but he was able to gather them by the handful. In this way he got many rotten twigs and bits of green moss that were undesirable, but it was the best he could do. He worked methodically, even collecting an armful of the larger branches to be used later when the fire gathered strength. And all the while the dog sat and watched him, a certain yearning wistfulness in its eyes, for it looked upon him as the fire provider, and the fire was slow in coming.

When all was ready, the man reached in his pocket for a second piece of birch bark. He knew the bark was there, and, though he could not feel it with his fingers, he could hear its crisp rustling as he fumbled for it. Try as he would, he could not clutch hold of it. And all the time, in his consciousness, was the knowledge that each instant his feet were freezing. This thought tended to put him in a panic, but he fought against it and kept calm. He pulled on his mittens with his teeth, and threshed his arms back and forth, beating his hands with all his might against his sides. He did this sitting down, and he stood up to do it; and all the while the dog sat in the snow, its wolf brush of a tail curled around warmly over its forefront, its sharp wolf ears pricked forward intently as it watched the man. And the man, as he beat and threshed with his arms and hands, felt a great surge of envy as he regarded the creature that was warm and secure in its natural covering.

After a time he was aware of the first faraway signals of sensation in his beaten fingers. The faint tingling grew stronger till it evolved into a stinging ache that was excruciating, but which the man hailed with satisfaction. He stripped the mitten from his right hand and fetched forth the birch bark. The exposed fingers were quickly going numb again. Next he brought out his bunch of sulphur matches. But the tremendous cold had already driven the life out of his fingers. In his effort to separate one match from the others, the whole bunch fell in the snow. He tried to pick it out of the snow, but failed. The dead fingers could neither touch nor clutch. He was very careful. He drove the thought of his freezing feet, and nose, and cheeks, out of his mind, devoting his whole soul to the matches. He watched, using the sense of vision in place of that touch, and when he saw his fingers on each side of the bunch, he closed them—that is, he willed to close them, for the wires were down, and the fingers did not obey. He pulled the mitten on the right hand, and beat it fiercely against his knee. Then with both mittened hands, he scooped the bunch of matches, along with much snow, into his lap. Yet he was no better off.

After some manipulation he managed to get the bunch between the heels of his mittened hands. In his fashion he carried it to his mouth. The ice crackled and snapped when by a violent effort he opened his mouth. He drew the lower jaw in, curled the upper lip out of the way, and scraped the bunch with his upper teeth in order to separate a match. He succeeded in getting one, which he dropped on his lap. He was no better off. He could not pick it up. Then he devised a way. He picked it up in his teeth and scratched it on his leg. Twenty times he scratched before he succeeded in lighting it. As it flamed he held it with his teeth to the birch bark. But the burning brimstone went up his nostrils and into his lungs, causing him to cough spasmodically. The match fell into the snow and went out.

The old-timer on Sulphur Creek was right, he thought in the moment of controlled despair that ensued: after fifty below, a man should travel with a partner. He beat his hands, but failed in exciting any sensation. Suddenly he bared both hands, removing the mittens with his teeth. He caught the whole bunch between the heels of his hands. His arm muscles not being frozen enabled him to press the hand heels tightly against the matches. Then he scratched the bunch along his leg. It flared into flame, seventy sulphur matches at once! There was no wind to blow them out. He kept his head to one side to escape the strangling fumes, and held the blazing bunch to the birch bark. As he so held it, he became aware of sensation in his hand. His flesh was burning. He could smell it. Deep down below the surface he could feel it. The sensation developed into pain that grew acute. And still he endured it, holding the flame of the matches clumsily to the bark that would not light readily because his own burning hands were in the way, absorbing most of the flame.

At last, when he could endure no more, he jerked his hands apart. The blazing matches fell sizzling into the snow, but the birch bark was alight. He began laying dry grasses and the tiniest twigs on the flame. He could not pick and choose, for he had to lift the fuel between the heels of his hands. Small pieces of rotten wood and green moss clung to the twigs, and he bit them off as well as he could with his teeth. He cherished the flame carefully and awkwardly. It meant life, and it must not perish. The withdrawal of blood from the surface of his body now made him begin to shiver, and he grew more awkward. A large piece of green moss fell squarely on the little fire. He tried to poke it out with his fingers, but his shivering frame made him poke too far, and he disrupted the nucleus of the little fire, the burning grasses and tiny twigs separating and scattering. He tried to poke them together again, but in spite of the tenseness of the effort, his shivering got away with him, and the twigs were hopelessly scattered. Each twig gushed a puff of smoke and went out. The fire provider had failed. As he looked apathetically about him, his eyes chanced on the dog, sitting across the ruins of the fire from him, in the snow, making restless, hunching movements, slightly lifting one forefoot and then the other, shifting its weight back and forth on them with wistful eagerness.

The sight of the dog put a wild idea into his head. He remembered the tale of the man, caught in a blizzard, who killed a steer and crawled inside the carcass, and so was saved. He would kill the dog and bury his hands in the warm body until the numbness went out of them. Then he could build another fire. He spoke to the dog, calling it to him; but in his voice was a strange note of fear that frightened the animal, who had never known the man to speak in such a way before. Something was the matter, and its suspicious nature sensed danger—it knew not what danger, but somewhere, somehow, in its brain arose an apprehension of the man. It flattened its ears down at the sound of the man's voice, and its restless, hunching movements and the liftings and shiftings of its forefeet became more pronounced; but it would not come to the man. He got on his hands and knees and crawled towards the dog. This unusual posture again excited suspicion, and the animal sidled mincingly away.

The man sat up in the snow for a moment and struggled for calmness. Then he pulled on his mittens, by means of his teeth, and got upon his feet. He glanced down at first in order to assure himself that he was really standing up, for the absence of sensation in his feet left him unrelated to the earth. His erect position in itself started to drive the webs of suspicion from the dog's mind; and when he spoke peremptorily, with the sound of whip lashes in his voice, the dog rendered its customary allegiance and came to him. As it came within reaching distance, the man lost his control. His arms flashed out to the dog, and he experienced genuine surprise when he discovered that his hands could not clutch, that there was neither bend nor feeling in the fingers. He had forgotten for the moment that they were frozen and that they were freezing more and more. All this happened quickly, and before the animal could get away, he encircled its body with his arms. He sat down in the snow, and in this fashion held the dog, while it snarled and whined and struggled.

But it was all he could do, hold its body encircled in his arms and sit there. He realized he could not kill the dog. There was no way to do it. With his helpless hands he could neither draw nor hold his sheath knife nor throttle the animal. He released it, and it plunged wildly away, with tail between its legs, and still snarling. It halted forty feet away and surveyed him curiously, with ears sharply pricked forward.

The man looked down at his hands in order to locate them, and found them hanging on the ends of his arms. It struck him as curious that one should have to use his eyes in order to find out where his hands were. He began threshing his arms back and forth, beating the mittened hands against his sides. He did this for five minutes, violently, and his heart pumped enough blood up to the surface to put a stop to his shivering. But no sensation was aroused in the hands. He had an impression that they hung like weights on the ends of his arms, but when he tried to run the impression down, he could not find it.

A certain fear of death, dull and oppressive, came to him. This fear quickly became poignant as he realized that it was no longer a mere matter of freezing his fingers and toes, or of losing his hands and feet, but that it was a matter of life and death with the chances against him. This threw him into a panic, and he turned and ran up the creek bed along the old, dim trail. The dog joined in behind him and kept up with him. He ran blindly, without intention, in fear such as he had never known in his life. Slowly, as be ploughed and floundered through the snow, he began to see things again—the banks of the creek, the old timber jams, the leafless aspens, and the sky. The running made him feel better. He did not shiver. Maybe, if he ran on, his feet would thaw out; and, anyway, if he ran far enough, he would reach camp and the boys. Without doubt he would lose some fingers and toes and some of his face; but the boys would take care of him, and save the rest of him when he got there. And at the same time there was another thought in his mind that said he would never get to the camp and the boys; that it was too many miles away, that the freezing had too great a start on him, and that he would soon be stiff and dead. This thought he kept in the background and refused to consider. Sometimes it pushed itself forward and demanded to be heard, but he thrust it back and strove to think of other things.

It struck him as curious that he could run at all on feet so frozen that he could not feel them when they struck the earth and took the weight of his body. He seemed to himself to skim along above the surface, and to have no connection with the earth. Somewhere he had once seen a winged Mercury, and he wondered if Mercury felt as he felt when skimming over the earth.

His theory of running until he reached camp and the boys had one flaw in it: he lacked the endurance. Several times he stumbled, and finally he tottered, crumpled up, and fell. When he tried to rise, he failed. He must sit and rest, he decided, and next time he would merely walk and keep on going. As he sat and regained his breath, he noted that he was feeling quite warm and comfortable. He was not shivering, and it even seemed that a warm glow had come to his chest and trunk. And yet, when he touched his nose or cheeks, there was no sensation. Running would not thaw them out. Nor would it thaw out his hands and feet. Then the thought came to him that the frozen portions of his body must be extending. He tried to keep this thought down, to forget it, to think of something else; he was aware of the panicky feeling that it caused, and he was afraid of the panic. But the thought asserted itself, and persisted, until it produced a vision of his body totally frozen. This was too much, and he made another wild run along the trail. Once he slowed down to a walk, but the thought of the freezing extending itself made him run again.

And all the time the dog ran with him, at his heels. When he fell down a second time, it curled its tail over its forefeet and sat in front of him, facing him, curiously eager and intent. The warmth and security of the animal angered him, and he cursed it till it flattened down its ears appeasingly. This time the shivering came more quickly upon the man. He was losing in his battle with the frost. It was creeping into his body from all sides. The thought of it drove him on, but he ran no more than a hundred feet, when he staggered and pitched headlong. It was his last panic. When he had recovered his breath and control, he sat up and entertained in his mind the conception of meeting death with dignity. However, the conception did not come to him in such terms. His idea of it was that he had been making a fool of himself, running around like a chicken with its head cut off—such was the simile that occurred to him. Well, he was bound to freeze anyway, and he might as well take it decently. With this new-found peace of mind came the first glimmerings of drowsiness. A good idea, he thought, to sleep off to death. It was like taking an anaesthetic. Freezing was not so bad as people thought. There were lots worse ways to die.

He pictured the boys finding his body next day. Suddenly he found himself with them, coming along the trail looking for himself. And, still with them, he came around a turn in the trail and found himself lying in the snow. He did not belong with himself any more, for even then he was out of himself, standing with the boys and looking at himself in the snow. It certainly was cold, was his thought. When he got back to the States he could tell the folks what real cold was. He drifted on from this to a vision of the old-timer on Sulphur Creek. He could see him quite clearly, warm and comfortable, and smoking a pipe.

"You were right, old hoss; you were right," the man mumbled to the old-timer of Sulfur Creek.

Then the man drowsed off into what seemed to him the most comfortable and satisfying sleep he had ever known. The dog sat facing him and waiting. The brief day drew to a close in a long, slow twilight. There were no signs of a fire to be made, and, besides, never in the dog's experience had it known a man to sit like that in the snow and make no fire. As the twilight drew on, its eager yearning for the fire mastered it, and with a great lifting and shifting of forefeet, it whined softly, then flattened its ears down in anticipation of being chidden by the man. But the man remained silent. Later the dog whined loudly. And still later it crept close to the man and caught the scent of death. This made the animal bristle and back away. A little longer it delayed, howling under the stars that leaped and danced and shone brightly in the cold sky. Then it turned and trotted up the trail in the direction of the camp it knew, where were the other food providers and fire providers.

CRITICAL THINKING QUESTIONS

1. Dismissing the old-timer's warning—"no man must travel alone in the Klondike below fifty degrees"—the man sets out alone on his journey along the Yukon. Later, after his "accident" of breaking through some ice and then saving himself, the man thought, "Those old-timers were rather womanish, some of them. . . . Any man who was a man could travel alone." Evaluate the man's reasoning in *jumping to the conclusion* that the old-timer was wrong:

   a. On what evidence does he base his conclusion? How do logic and emotion influence his reasoning?

   b. What *warrant* informs his definition of a man?

2. What value assumptions about animals inform the man's interaction with the dog? How does the story's plot challenge those assumptions?

WRITING TOPIC

What is London's *claim* about the individual person and nature? Can you think of evidence—examples from your own experience and knowledge—that supports this claim? In what ways have we attempted to alter the relationship between humans and nature? What warrant underlies these efforts? What is your perspective on these topics? Do you think there is a natural order among living things that should be respected by science and technology? Is there a middle-ground (*Rogerian*) position?

Leslie Marmon Silko

The Man to Send Rain Clouds

One

They found him under a big cottonwood tree. His Levi jacket and pants were faded light blue so that he had been easy to find. The big cottonwood tree stood apart from a small grove of winterbare cottonwoods which grew in the wide, sandy arroyo. He had been dead for a day or more, and the sheep had wandered and scattered up and down the arroyo. Leon and his brother-in-law, Ken, gathered the sheep and left them in the pen at the sheep camp before they returned to the cottonwood tree. Leon waited under the tree while Ken drove the truck through the deep sand to the edge of the arroyo. He squinted up at the sun and unzipped his jacket—it sure was hot for this time of year. But high and northwest the blue mountains were still deep in snow. Ken came sliding down the low, crumbling bank about fifty yards down, and he was bringing the red blanket.

Before they wrapped the old man, Leon took a piece of string out of his pocket and tied a small gray feather in the old man's long white hair. Ken gave him the paint. Across the brown wrinkled forehead he drew a streak of white, and along the high cheekbones he drew a strip of blue paint. He paused and watched Ken throw pinches of corn meal and pollen into the wind that fluttered the small gray feather. Then Leon painted with yellow under the old man's broad nose; and finally, when he had painted green across the chin, he smiled.

"Send us rain clouds, Grandfather." They laid the bundle in the back of the pickup and covered it with a heavy tarp before they started back to the pueblo.

They turned off the highway onto the sandy pueblo road. Not long after they passed the store and post office they saw Father Paul's car coming toward them. When he recognized their faces he slowed his car and waved for them to stop. The young priest rolled down the car window.

"Did you find old Teofilo?" he asked loudly.

Leon stopped the truck. "Good morning, Father. We were just out to the sheep camp. Everything is O.K. now."

"Thank God for that. Teofilo is a very old man. You really shouldn't allow him to stay at the sheep camp alone."

"No, he won't do that any more now."

"Well, I'm glad you understand. I hope I'll be seeing you at Mass this week— we missed you last Sunday. See if you can get old Teofilo to come with you." The priest smiled and waved at them as they drove away.

Two

Louise and Teresa were waiting. The table was set for lunch, and the coffee was boiling on the black iron stove. Leon looked at Louise and then at Teresa.

"We found him under a cottonwood tree in the big arroyo near sheep camp. I guess he sat down to rest in the shade and never got up again." Leon walked toward the old man's bed. The red plaid shawl had been shaken and spread carefully over the bed, and a new brown flannel shirt and pair of stiff new Levis were arranged neatly beside the pillow. Louise held the screen door open while Leon and Ken carried in the red blanket. He looked small and shriveled, and after they dressed him in the new shirt and pants he seemed more shrunken.

It was noontime now because the church bells rang the Angelus. They ate the beans with hot bread, and nobody said anything until after Teresa poured the coffee.

Ken stood up and put on his jacket. "I'll see about the gravediggers. Only the top layer of soil is frozen. I think it can be ready before dark."

Leon nodded his head and finished his coffee. After Ken had been gone for a while, the neighbors and clanspeople came quietly to embrace Teofilo's family and to leave food on the table because the gravediggers would come to eat when they were finished.

Three

The sky in the west was full of pale-yellow light. Louise stood outside with her hands in the pockets of Leon's green army jacket that was too big for her. The funeral was over, and the old men had taken their candles and medicine bags and were gone. She waited until the body was laid into the pickup before she said anything to Leon. She touched his arm, and he noticed that her hands were still dusty from the corn meal that she had sprinkled around the old man. When she spoke, Leon could not hear her.

"What did you say? I didn't hear you."

"I said that I had been thinking about something."

"About what?"

"About the priest sprinkling holy water for Grandpa. So he won't be thirsty."

Leon stared at the new moccasins that Teofilo had made for the ceremonial dances in the summer. They were nearly hidden by the red blanket. It was getting colder, and the wind pushed gray dust down the narrow pueblo road. The sun was approaching the long mesa where it disappeared during the winter. Louise stood there shivering and watching his face. Then he zipped up his jacket and opened the truck door. "I'll see if he's there."

Four

Ken stopped the pickup at the church, and Leon got out; and then Ken drove down the hill to the graveyard where people were waiting. Leon knocked at the old carved door with its symbols of the Lamb. While he waited he looked up at the twin bells from the king of Spain with the last sunlight pouring around them in their tower.

The priest opened the door and smiled when he saw who it was. "Come in! What brings you here this evening?"

The priest walked toward the kitchen, and Leon stood with his cap in his hand, playing with the earflaps and examining the living room—the brown sofa, the green armchair, and the brass lamp that hung down from the ceiling by links of chain. The priest dragged a chair out of the kitchen and offered it to Leon.

"No thank you, Father. I only came to ask you if you would bring your holy water to the graveyard."

The priest turned away from Leon and looked out the window at the patio full of shadows and the dining-room windows of the nuns' cloister across the patio. The curtains were heavy, and the light from within faintly penetrated; it was impossible to see the nuns inside eating supper. "Why didn't you tell me he was dead? I could have brought the Last Rites anyway."

Leon smiled. "It wasn't necessary, Father."

The priest stared down at his scuffed brown loafers and the worn hem of his cassock. "For a Christian burial it was necessary."

His voice was distant, and Leon thought that his blue eyes looked tired.

"It's O.K. Father, we just want him to have plenty of water."

The priest sank down into the green chair and picked up a glossy missionary magazine. He turned the colored pages full of lepers and pagans without looking at them.

"You know I can't do that, Leon. There should have been the last Rites and a funeral Mass at the very least."

Leon put on his green cap and pulled the flaps down over his ears. "It's getting late, Father. I've got to go."

When Leon opened the door Father Paul stood up and said, "Wait." He left the room and came back wearing a long brown overcoat. He followed Leon out the door and across the dim churchyard to the adobe steps in front of the church. They both stooped to fit through the low adobe entrance. And when they started down the hill to the graveyard only half of the sun was visible above the mesa.

The priest approached the grave slowly, wondering how they had managed to dig into the frozen ground; and then he remembered that this was New Mexico, and saw the pile of cold loose sand beside the hole. The people stood close to each other with little clouds of steam puffing from their faces. The priest looked at them and saw a pile of jackets, gloves, and scarves in the yellow, dry tumbleweeds that grew in the graveyard. He looked at the red blanket, not sure that Teofilo was so small, wondering if it wasn't some perverse Indian trick—something they did in March to ensure a good harvest—wondering if maybe old Teofilo was actually at sheep camp corralling the sheep for the night. But there he was, facing into a cold dry wind and squinting at the last sunlight, ready to bury a red wool blanket while the faces of his parishioners were in shadow with the last warmth of the sun on their backs.

His fingers were stiff, and it took him a long time to twist the lid off the holy water. Drops of water fell on the red blanket and soaked into dark icy spots. He sprinkled the grave and the water disappeared almost before it touched the dim, cold sand; it reminded him of something—he tried to remember what it was, because he thought if he could remember he might understand this. He sprinkled more water; he shook the container until it was empty, and the water fell through the light from sundown like August rain that fell while the sun was still shining, almost evaporating before it touched the wilted squash flowers.

The wind pulled at the priest's brown Franciscan robe and swirled away the corn meal and pollen that had been sprinkled on the blanket. They lowered the bundle into the ground, and they didn't bother to untie the stiff pieces of new rope that were tied around the ends of the blanket. The sun was gone, and over on the highway the eastbound lane was full of headlights. The priest walked away slowly. Leon watched him climb the hill, and when he had disappeared within the tall, thick walls, Leon turned to look up at the high blue mountains in the deep snow that reflected a faint red light from the west. He felt good because it was finished, and he was happy about the sprinkling of the holy water; now the old man could send them big thunderclouds for sure.

CRITICAL THINKING QUESTIONS

1. In this story, the author notes specific colors and lighting frequently in depicting characters and setting. List details that include color or lighting and speculate on their thematic significance.

2. Explain how this story leaves you feeling.

3. What is Silko's *implied claim* about Native Americans' spiritual heritage in late twentieth-century America? What evidence in the story supports your interpretation of her claim?

WRITING TOPIC

Why do you think Father Paul decides to bend the rules of his religion and accompany Leon to the graveyard to sprinkle holy water for Teofilo? Another mystery in Father Paul's character is suggested in the next to last paragraph: "He sprinkled the grave and the water disappeared almost before it touched the dim, cold sand; it reminded him of something—he tried to remember what it was, because he thought if he could remember he might understand this." Using evidence from the story and your own ideas and speculation, write a brief character sketch of Father Paul.

Eudora Welty

A Worn Path

It was December—a bright frozen day in the early morning. Far out in the country there was an old Negro woman with her head tied in a red rag, coming along a path through the pinewoods. Her name was Phoenix Jackson. She was very old and small and she walked slowly in the dark pine shadows, moving a little from side to side in her steps, with the balanced heaviness and lightness of a pendulum in a grandfather clock. She carried a thin, small cane made from an umbrella, and with this she kept tapping the frozen earth in front of her. This made a grave and persistent noise in the still air, that seemed meditative like the chirping of a solitary little bird.

She wore a dark striped dress reaching down to her shoe tops, and an equally long apron of bleached sugar sacks, with a full pocket: all neat and tidy, but every time she took a step she might have fallen over her shoe-laces, which dragged from her unlaced shoes. She looked straight ahead. Her eyes were blue with age. Her skin had a pattern all its own of numberless branching wrinkles and as though a whole little tree stood in the middle of her forehead, but a golden color ran underneath, and the two knobs of her cheeks were illuminated by a yellow burning under the dark. Under the red rag her hair came down on her neck in the frailest of ringlets, still black, and with an odor like copper.

Now and then there was a quivering in the thicket. Old Phoenix said, "Out of my way, all you foxes, owls, beetles, jack rabbits, coons, and wild animals! . . . Keep out from under these feet, little bob-whites. . . . Keep the big wild hogs out of my path. Don't let none of those come running my direction. I got a long way." Under her small black-freckled hand her cane, limber as a buggy whip, would switch at the brush as if to rouse up any hiding things.

On she went. The woods were deep and still. The sun made the pine needles almost too bright to look at, up where the wind rocked. The cones dropped as light as feathers. Down in the hollow was the mourning dove—it was not too late for him.

The path ran up a hill. "Seem like there is chains about my feet, time I get this far," she said, in the voice of argument old people keep to use with themselves. "Something always takes a hold of me on this hill—pleads I should stay."

After she got to the top she turned and gave a full, severe look behind her where she had come. "Up through pines," she said at length. "Now down through oaks."

Her eyes opened their widest, and she started down gently. But before she got to the bottom of the hill a bush caught her dress.

Her fingers were busy and intent, but her skirts were full and long, so that before she could pull them free in one place they were caught in another. It was not possible to allow the dress to tear. "I in the thorny bush," she said. "Thorns, you doing your appointed work. Never want to let folks pass—no sir. Old eyes thought you was a pretty little *green* bush."

Finally, trembling all over, she stood free, and after a moment dared to stoop for her cane.

"Sun so high!" she cried, leaning back and looking, while the thick tears went over her eyes, "The time getting all gone here."

At the foot of this hill was a place where a log was laid across the creek.

"Now comes the trial," said Phoenix.

Putting her right foot out, she mounted the log and shut her eyes. Lifting her skirt, levelling her cane fiercely before her, like a festival figure in some parade, she began to march across. Then she opened her eyes and she was safe on the other side.

"I wasn't as old as I thought," she said.

But she sat down to rest. She spread her skirts on the bank around her and folded her hands over her knees. Up above her was a tree in a pearly cloud of mistletoe. She did not dare to close her eyes, and when a little boy brought her a little plate with a slice of marble-cake on it she spoke to him. "That would be acceptable," she said. But when she went to take it there was just her own hand in the air.

So she left that tree, and had to go through a barbed-wire fence. There she had to creep and crawl, spreading her knees and stretching her fingers like a baby trying to climb the steps. But she talked loudly to herself: she could not let her dress be torn now, so late in the day, and she could not pay for having her arm or her leg sawed off if she got caught fast where she was.

At last she was safe through the fence and risen up out in the clearing. Big dead trees, like black men with one arm, were standing in the purple stalks of the withered cotton field. There sat a buzzard.

"Who you watching?"

In the furrow she made her way along.

"Glad this not the season for bulls," she said, looking sideways, "and the good Lord made his snakes to curl up and sleep in the winter. A pleasure I don't see no two-headed snake coming around that tree, where it come once. It took a while to get by him, back in the summer."

She passed through the old cotton and went into a field of dead corn. It whispered and shook and was taller than her head. "Through the maze now," she said, for there was no path.

Then there was something tall, black, and skinny there, moving before her.

At first she took it for a man. It could have been a man dancing in the field. But she stood still and listened, and it did not make a sound. It was as silent as a ghost.

"Ghost," she said sharply, "who be you the ghost of? For I have heard of nary death close by."

But there was no answer—only the ragged dancing in the wind.

She shut he eyes, reached out her hand, and touched a sleeve. She found a coat and inside that an emptiness, cold as ice.

"You scarecrow," she said. Her face lighted. "I ought to be shut up for good," she said with laughter. "My senses is gone. I too old. I the oldest people I ever know. Dance, old scarecrow," she said, "while I dancing with you."

She kicked her foot over the furrow, and with mouth drawn down, shook her head once or twice in a little strutting way. Some husks blew down and whirled in streamers about her skirts.

Then she went on, parting her way from side to side with the cane, through the whispering field. At last she came to the end, to a wagon track where the silver grass blew between the red ruts. The quail were walking around like pullets, seeming all dainty and unseen.

"Walk pretty," she said. "This the easy place. This the easy going."

She followed the track, swaying through the quiet bare fields, through the little strings of tree silver in their dead leaves, past cabins silver from weather, with the doors and windows boarded shut, all like old women under a spell sitting there. "I walking in their sleep," she said, nodding her head vigorously.

In a ravine she went where a spring was silently flowing through a hollow log. Old Phoenix bent and drank. "Sweet-gum makes the water sweet," she said, and drank more. "Nobody know who made this well, for it was here when I was born."

The track crossed a swampy part where the moss hung as white as lace from every limb. "Sleep on, alligators, and blow your bubbles." Then the track went into the road.

Deep, deep the road went down between the high green-colored banks. Overhead the live-oaks met, and it was as dark as a cave.

A black dog with a lolling tongue came up out of the weeds by the ditch. She was meditating, and not ready, and when he came at her she only hit him a little with her cane. Over she went in the ditch, like a little puff of milk-weed.

Down there, her senses drifted away. A dream visited her, and she reached her hand up, but nothing reached down and gave her a pull. So she lay there and presently went to talking. "Old woman," she said to herself, "that black dog came up out of the weeds to stall you off, and now there he sitting on his fine tail, smiling at you."

A white man finally came along and found her—a hunter, a young man, with his dog on a chain.

"Well, Granny!" he laughed. "What are you doing there?"

"Lying on my back like a June-bug waiting to be turned over, mister," she said, reaching up her hand.

He lifted her up, gave her a swing in the air, and set her down, "Anything broken, Granny?"

"No sir, them old dead weeds is springy enough," said Phoenix, when she had got her breath. "I thank you for your trouble."

"Where do you live, Granny?" he asked, while the two dogs were growling at each other.

"Away back yonder, sir, behind the ridge. You can't even see it from here."

"On your way home?"

"No, sir, I going to town."

"Why, that's too far! That's as far as I walk when I come out myself, and I get something for my trouble." He patted the stuffed bag he carried, and there hung down a little closed claw. It was one of the bob-whites, with its beak hooked bitterly to show it was dead. "Now you go on home, Granny!"

"I bound to go to town, mister," said Phoenix. "The time come around."

He gave another laugh, filling the whole landscape. "I know you old colored people! Wouldn't miss going to town to see Santa Claus!"

But something held Old Phoenix very still. The deep lines in her face went into a fierce and different radiation. Without warning, she had seen with her own eyes a flashing nickel fall out of the man's pocket onto the ground.

"How old are you, Granny?" he was saying.

"There is no telling, mister," she said, "no telling."

Then she gave a little cry and clapped her hands and said, "Git on away from here, dog! Look! Look at that dog!" She laughed as if in admiration. "He ain't scared of nobody. He a big black dog." She whispered, "Sic him!"

"Watch me get rid of that cur," said the man. "Sic him, Pete! Sic him!"

Phoenix heard the dogs fighting, and heard the man running and throwing sticks. She even heard a gunshot. But she was slowly bending forward by that time, further and further forward, the lids stretched down over her eyes, as if she were doing this in her sleep. Her chin was lowered almost to her knees. The yellow palm of her hand came out from the fold of her apron. Her fingers slid down and along the ground under the piece of money with the grace and care they would have in lifting an egg from under a sitting hen. Then she slowly straightened up, she stood erect, and the nickel was in her apron pocket. A bird flew by. Her lips moved. "God watching me the whole time. I come to stealing."

The man came back, and his own dog panted about them. "Well, I scared him off that time," he said, and then he laughed and lifted his gun and pointed it at Phoenix.

She stood straight and faced him.

"Doesn't the gun scare you?" he said, still pointing it.

"No, sir, I seen plenty go off closer by, in my day, and for less than what I done," she said, holding utterly still.

He smiled, and shouldered the gun. "Well, Granny," he said, "you must be a hundred years old, and scared of nothing. I'd give you a dime if I had any money with me. But you take my advice and stay home, and nothing will happen to you."

"I bound to go on my way, mister," said Phoenix. She inclined her head in the red rag. Then they went in different directions, but she could hear the gun shooting again and again over the hill.

She walked on. The shadows hung from the oak trees to the road like curtains. Then she smelled wood-smoke, and smelled the river, and she saw a steeple and the cabins on their steep steps. Dozens of little black children whirled around her. There ahead was Natchez shining. Bells were ringing. She walked on.

In the paved city it was Christmas time. There were red and green electric lights strung and crisscrossed everywhere, and all turned on in the daytime. Old Phoenix would have been lost if she had not distrusted her eyesight and depended on her feet to know where to take her.

She paused quietly on the sidewalk where people were passing by. A lady came along in the crowd, carrying an armful of red-, green-, and silver-wrapped presents; she gave off perfume like the red roses in hot summer, and Phoenix stopped her.

"Please, missy, will you lace up my shoe?" She held up her foot.

"What do you want, Grandma?"

"See my shoe," said Phoenix. "Do all right for out in the country, but wouldn't look right to go in a big building."

"Stand still then, Grandma," said the lady. She put her packages down on the sidewalk beside her and laced and tied both shoes tightly.

"Can't lace 'em with a cane," said Phoenix. "Thank you, missy. I doesn't mind asking a nice lady to tie up my shoe, when I gets out on the street."

Moving slowly and from side to side, she went into the big building and into a tower of steps, where she walked up and around and around until her feet knew to stop.

She entered a door, and there she saw nailed up on the wall the document that had been stamped with the gold seal and framed in the gold frame, which matched the dream that was hung up in her head.

"Here I be," she said. There was a fixed and ceremonial stiffness over her body.

"A charity case, I suppose," said an attendant who sat at the desk before her.

But Phoenix only looked above her head. There was sweat on her face, the wrinkles in her skin shone like a bright net.

"Speak up, Grandma," the woman said. "What's your name? We must have your history, you know. Have you been here before? What seems to be the trouble with you?"

Old Phoenix only gave a twitch to her face as if a fly were bothering her.

"Are you deaf?" cried the attendant.

But then the nurse came in.

"Oh, that's just old Aunt Phoenix," she said. "She doesn't come for herself—she has a little grandson. She makes these trips just as regular as clockwork. She lives away back off the Old Natchez Trace." She bent down. "Well, Aunt Phoenix, why don't you just take a seat? We won't keep you standing after your long trip." She pointed.

The old woman sat down, bolt upright in the chair.

"Now, how is the boy?" asked the nurse.

Old Phoenix did not speak.

"I said, how is the boy?"

But Phoenix only waited and stared straight ahead, her face very solemn and withdrawn into rigidity.

"Is his throat any better?" asked the nurse. "Aunt Phoenix, don't you hear me? Is your grandson's throat any better since the last time you came for the medicine?"

With her hands on her knees, the old woman waited, silent, erect and motionless, just as if she were in amour.

"You mustn't take up our time this way, Aunt Phoenix," the nurse said. "Tell us quickly about your grandson, and get it over with. He isn't dead, is he?"

At last there came a flicker and then a flame of comprehension across her face, and she spoke.

"My grandson. It was my memory had left me. There I sat and forgot why I made my long trip."

"Forgot?" The nurse frowned. "After you came so far?"

Then Phoenix was like an old woman begging a dignified forgiveness for waking up frightened in the night. "I never did go to school, I was too old at the Surrender," she said in a soft voice. "I'm an old woman without an education. It was my memory fail me. My little grandson, he is just the same, and I forgot it in the coming."

"Throat never heals, does it?" said the nurse, speaking in a loud, sure voice to Old Phoenix. By now she had a card with something written on it, a little list. "Yes. Swallowed lye. When was it—January—two-three years ago—"

Phoenix spoke unasked now. "No, missy, he not dead, he just the same. Every little while his throat begin to close up again, and he not able to swallow. He not get his breath. He not able to help himself. So the time come around, and I go on another trip for the soothingmedicine."

"All right. The doctor said as long as you came to get it, you could have it," said the nurse. "But it's an obstinate case."

"My little grandson, he sit up there in the house all wrapped up, waiting by himself," Phoenix went on. "We is the only two left in the world. He suffer and it don't seem to put him back at all. He got a sweet look. He going to last. He wear a little patch quilt and peep out holding his mouth open like a little bird. I remembers so plain now. I not going to forget him again, no, the whole enduring time. I could tell him from all the others in creation."

"All right." The nurse was trying to hush her now. She brought her a bottle of medicine. "Charity," she said, making a check mark in a book.

Old Phoenix held the bottle close to her eyes and then carefully put it into her pocket.

"I thank you," she said.

"It's Christmas time, Grandma," said the attendant. "Could I give you a few pennies out of my purse?"

"Five pennies is a nickel," said Phoenix stiffly.

"Here's a nickel," said the attendant.

Phoenix rose carefully and held out her hand. She received the nickel and then fished the other nickel out of her pocket and laid it beside the new one. She stared at her palm closely, with her head on one side.

Then she gave a tap with her cane on the floor.

"That is what come to me to do," she said. "I going to the store and buy my child a little windmill they sells, made out of paper. He going to find it hard to believe there such a thing in the world. I'll march myself back where he waiting, holding it straight up in this hand."

She lifted her free hand, gave a little nod, turned round, and walked out of the doctor's office. Then her slow step began on the stairs, going down.

CRITICAL THINKING QUESTIONS

1. a. When Phoenix arrives at the clinic, the attendant makes the *inference* that she is "a charity case." On what evidence is her inference based?
   b. What value assumptions underlie her inference?
   c. Do you think the attendant has "jumped to a conclusion," or is her conclusion valid?
   d. Later, when Phoenix is leaving, what do you think is the attendant's motive in offering Phoenix a few pennies?

2. Phoenix chats amiably with all she encounters along her path from the woods, across the fields, and into town. Arriving at the clinic, she announces, "Here I be," and then she seems to become temporarily mute. Why this sudden loss of speech?

3. What is the significance of the title?

WRITING TOPIC

What is wisdom? Write a claim statement that defines wisdom, and use evidence from this story and your own experience to illustrate and support your definition.

Virginia Woolf

Kew Gardens

From the oval-shaped flower-bed there rose perhaps a hundred stalks spreading into heart-shaped or tongue-shaped leaves halfway up and unfurling at the tip red or blue or yellow petals marked with spots of colour raised upon the surface; and from the red, blue or yellow gloom of the throat emerged a straight bar, rough with gold dust and slightly clubbed at the end. The petals were voluminous enough to be stirred by the summer breeze, and when they moved, the red, blue and yellow lights passed one over the other, staining an inch of the brown earth beneath with a spot of the most intricate colour. The light fell either upon the smooth, grey back of a pebble, or, the shell of a snail with its brown, circular veins, or falling into a raindrop, it expanded with such intensity of red, blue and yellow the thin walls of water that one expected them to burst and disappear. Instead, the drop was left in a second silver grey once more, and the light now settled upon the flesh of a leaf, revealing the branching thread of fibre beneath the surface, and again it moved on and spread its illumination in the vast green spaces beneath the dome of the heart-shaped and tongue-shaped leaves. Then the breeze stirred rather more briskly overhead and the colour was flashed into the air above, into the eyes of the men and women who walk in Kew Gardens in July.

The figures of these men and women straggled past the flower-bed with a curiously irregular movement not unlike that of the white and blue butterflies who crossed the turf in zig-zag flights from bed to bed. The man was about six inches in front of the woman, strolling carelessly, while she bore on with greater purpose, only turning her head now and then to see that the children were not too far behind. The man kept this distance in front of the woman purposely, though perhaps unconsciously, for he wished to go on with his thoughts.

"Fifteen years ago I came here with Lily," he thought. "We sat somewhere over there by a lake and I begged her to marry me all through the hot afternoon. How the dragonfly kept circling round us: how clearly I see the dragonfly and her shoe with the square silver buckle at the toe. All the time I spoke I saw her shoe and when it moved impatiently I knew without looking up what she was going to say: the whole of her seemed to be in her shoe. And my love, my desire, were in the dragonfly; for some reason I thought that if it settled there, on that leaf, the broad one with the red flower in the middle of it, if the dragonfly settled on the leaf she would say 'Yes' at once. But the dragonfly went round and round: it never settled anywhere—of course not, happily not, or I shouldn't be walking here with Eleanor and the children. Tell me, Eleanor. D'you ever think of the past?"

"Why do you ask, Simon?"

"Because I've been thinking of the past. I've been thinking of Lily, the woman I might have married. . . . Well, why are you silent? Do you mind my thinking of the past?"

"Why should I mind, Simon? Doesn't one always think of the past, in a garden with men and women lying under the trees. Aren't they one's past, all that remains of it, those men and women, those ghosts lying under the trees . . . one's happiness, one's reality?"

"For me, a square silver shoe buckle and a dragonfly—"

"For me, a kiss. Imagine six little girls sitting before their easels twenty years ago, down by the side of a lake, painting the water-lilies, the first red water-lilies I'd ever seen. And suddenly a kiss, there on the back of my neck. And my hand shook all the afternoon so that I couldn't paint. I took out my watch and marked the hour when I would allow myself to think of the kiss for five minutes only—it was so precious—the kiss of an old grey-haired woman with a wart on her nose, the mother of all my kisses all my life. Come, Caroline, come, Hubert."

They walked on past the flower-bed, now walking four abreast, and soon diminished in size among the trees and looked half transparent as the sunlight and shade swam over their backs in large trembling irregular patches.

In the oval flower-bed the snail, whose shell had been stained red, blue and yellow for the space of two minutes or so, now appeared to be moving very slightly in its shell, and next began to labour over the crumbs of loose earth which broke away and rolled down as it passed over them. It appeared to have a definite goal in front of it, differing in this respect from the singular high stepping angular green insect who attempted to cross in front of it, and waited for a second with its antennae trembling as if in deliberation, and then stepped off as rapidly and strangely in the opposite direction. Brown cliffs with deep green lakes in the hollows, flat, blade-like trees that waved from root to tip, round boulders of grey stone, vast crumpled surfaces of a thin crackling texture—all these objects lay across the snail's progress between one stalk and another to his goal. Before he had decided whether to circumvent the arched tent of a dead leaf or to breast it there came past the bed the feet of other human beings.

This time they were both men. The younger of the two wore an expression of perhaps unnatural calm; he raised his eyes and fixed them very steadily in front of him while his companion spoke, and directly his companion had done speaking he looked on the ground again and sometimes opened his lips only after a long pause and sometimes did not open them at all. The elder man had a curiously uneven and shaky method of walking, jerking his hand forward and throwing up his head abruptly, rather in the manner of an impatient carriage horse tired of waiting outside a house; but in the man these gestures were irresolute and pointless. He talked almost incessantly; he smiled to himself and again began to talk, as if the smile had been an answer. He was talking about spirits—the spirits of the dead, who, according to him, were even now telling him all sorts of odd things about their experiences in Heaven.

"Heaven was known to the ancients as Thessaly, William, and now, with this war, the spirit matter is rolling between the hills like thunder." He paused, seemed to listen, smiled, jerked his head and continued:

"You have a small electric battery and a piece of rubber to insulate the wire—isolate?—insulate?—well, we'll skip the details, no good going into details that wouldn't be understood—and in short the little machine stands in any convenient position by the head of the bed, we will say, on a neat mahogany stand. All arrangements being properly fixed by workmen under my direction, the widow applies her ear and summons the spirit by sign as agreed. Women! Widows! Women in black—"

Here he seemed to have caught sight of a woman's dress in the distance, which in the shade looked a purple black. He took off his hat, placed his hand upon his heart, and hurried towards her muttering and gesticulating feverishly. But William caught him by the sleeve and touched a flower with the tip of his walking stick in order to divert the old man's attention. After looking at it for a moment in some confusion the old man bent his ear to it and seemed to answer a voice speaking from it, for he began talking about the forests of Uruguay which he had visited hundreds of years ago in company with the most beautiful young woman in Europe. He could be heard murmuring about forests of Uruguay blanketed with the wax petals of tropical roses, nightingales, sea beaches, mermaids, and women drowned at sea, as he suffered himself to be moved on by William, upon whose face the look of stoical patience grew slowly deeper and deeper.

Following his steps so closely as to be slightly puzzled by his gestures came two elderly women of the lower middle class, one stout and ponderous, the other rosy cheeked and nimble. Like most people of their station they were frankly fascinated by other signs of eccentricity betokening a disordered brain, especially in the well-to-do; but they were too far off to be certain whether the gestures were merely eccentric or genuinely mad. After they had scrutinized the old man's back in silence for a moment and given each other a queer, sly look, they went on energetically piecing together their very complicated dialogue:

"Nell, Bert, Lot, Cess, Phil, Pa, he says, I says, she says, I says, I says—"

"My Bert, Sis, Bill, Grandad, the old man, sugar,
     Sugar, flour, kippers, greens,
     Sugar, sugar, sugar."

The ponderous woman looked through the pattern of falling words at the flowers standing cool, firm, and upright in the earth, with a curious expression. She saw them as a sleeper waking from a heavy sleep sees a brass candlestick reflecting the light in an unfamiliar way, and closes his eyes and opens them, and seeing the brass candlestick again, finally starts broad awake and stares at the candlestick with all his powers. So the heavy woman came to a standstill opposite the oval-shaped flower-bed, and ceased even to pretend to listen to what the other woman was saying. She stood there letting the words fall over her, swaying the top part of her body slowly backwards and forwards, looking at the flowers. Then she suggested that they should find a seat and have their tea.

The snail had now considered every possible method of reaching his goal without going round the dead leaf or climbing over it. Let alone the effort needed for climbing a leaf, he was doubtful whether the thin texture which vibrated with such an alarming crackle when touched even by the tips of his horns would bear his weight; and this determined him finally to creep beneath it, for there was a point where the leaf curved high enough from the ground to admit him. He had just inserted his head in the opening and was taking stock of the high brown roof and was getting used to the cool brown light when two other people came past outside on the turf. This time they were both young, a young man and a young woman. They were both in the prime of youth, the season before the smooth pink folds of the flower have burst their gummy case, when the wings of the butterfly, though fully grown, are motionless in the sun.

"Lucky it isn't Friday," he observed.

"Why? D'you believe in luck?"

"They make you pay sixpence on Friday."

"What's a sixpence anyway? Isn't it worth sixpence?"

"What's 'it'—what do you mean by 'it'?"

"O, anything—I mean—you know what I mean."

Long pauses came between each of these remarks: they were uttered in toneless and monotonous voices. The couple stood still on the edge of the flower-bed, and together pressed the end of her parasol deep down into the soft earth. The action and the fact that his hand rested on the top of hers expressed their feelings in a strange way, as these short insignificant words also expressed something, words with short wings for their heavy body of meaning, inadequate to carry them far and thus alighting awkwardly upon the very common objects that surrounded them, and were to their inexperienced touch so massive; but who knows (so they thought as they pressed the parasol into the earth) what precipices aren't concealed in them, or what slopes of ice don't shine in the sun on the other side? Who knows? Who has ever seen this before? Even when she wondered what sort of tea they gave you at Kew, he felt that something loomed up behind her words, and stood vast and solid behind them; and the mist very slowly rose and uncovered—O, Heavens, what were those shapes?—little white tables, and waitresses who looked first at her and then at him; and there was a bill that he would pay with a real two-shilling piece, and it was real, all real, he assured himself, fingering the coin in his pocket, real to everyone except to him and to her; even to him it began to seem real; and then—but it was too exciting to stand and think any longer, and he pulled the parasol out of the earth with a jerk and was impatient to find the place where one had tea with other people, like other people.

"Come along, Trissie; it's time we had our tea."

"Wherever *does* one have one's tea?" she asked with the oddest thrill of excitement in her voice, looking vaguely round and letting herself be drawn on down the grass path, trailing her parasol; turning her head this way and that way forgetting her tea, wishing to go down there and then down there, remembering orchids and cranes among wild flowers, a Chinese pagoda and a crimson crested bird; but he bore her on.

Thus one couple after another with much the same irregular and aimless movement passed the flower-bed and were enveloped in layer after layer of green-blue vapour, in which at first their bodies had substance and a dash of colour, but later both substance and colour dissolved in the green-blue atmosphere. How hot it was! So hot that even the thrush chose to hop, like a mechanical bird, in the shadow of the flowers, with long pauses between one movement and the next; instead of rambling vaguely the white butterflies danced one above another, making with their white shifting flakes the outline of a shattered marble column above the tallest flowers; the glass roofs of the palm house shone as if a whole market full of shiny green umbrellas had opened in the sun; and in the drone of the aeroplane the voice of the summer sky murmured its fierce soul. Yellow and black, pink and snow white, shapes of all these colours, men, women, and children were spotted for a second upon the horizon, and then, seeing the breadth of yellow that lay upon the grass, they wavered and sought shade beneath the trees, dissolving like drops of water in the yellow and green atmosphere, staining it faintly with red and blue. It seemed as if all gross and heavy bodies had sunk down in the heat motionless and lay huddled upon the ground, but their voices went wavering from them as if they were flames lolling from the thick waxen bodies of candles. Voices. Yes, voices. Wordless voices, breaking the silence suddenly with such depth of contentment, such passion of desire, or, in the voices of children, such freshness of surprise; breaking the silence? But there was no silence; all the time the motor omnibuses were turning their wheels and changing their gear; like a vast nest of Chinese boxes all of wrought steel turning ceaselessly one within another the city murmured; on the top of which the voices cried aloud and the petals of myriads of flowers flashed their colours into the air.

CRITICAL THINKING QUESTIONS

1. Who are the characters, nonhuman and human, in this story? Does one character seem more significant than others?

2. Examine the story's dialogue, which includes snippets of conversation involving four separate pairs of human visitors. What does each conversation reveal?

3. What do the nonhuman characters—the flowers, the snail, the dragonfly, and butterflies—contribute to the story?

WRITING TOPIC

This story records the minute details of a particular time in a particular place, Kew Gardens—from the progress of a snail with "a definite goal in front of it" to the remarks and actions of a young couple who "together pressed the end of her parasol deep down into the soft earth." With its symphony of sights and sounds, the classic plot question—what happens next?—seems to play second string to setting. However, turning to theme questions—Why? For what purpose?—construct a response. What does this story imply about reality, the meaning of lives in a time and place? What evidence supports your response? To what extent do you accept this conception of reality?

Lucille Clifton

For de Lawd

people say they have a hard time
understanding how I
go on about my business
playing my Ray Charles
hollering at my kids—
seem like my Afro
cut off in some old image
would show I got a long memory
and I come from a line
of black and going on women
who got used to making it through murdered sons
and who kept on pushing
who fried chicken
ironed
swept off the back steps
who grief kept
for their still alive sons
for their sons coming
for their sons gone
just pushing
in the inner city
or
like we call it
home
we think a lot about uptown
and the silent nights
and the houses straight as
dead men
and the pastel lights
and we hang on to our no place
happy to be alive
and in the inner city
or
like we call it
home

CRITICAL THINKING QUESTIONS

1. Has the speaker persuaded you that the inner city is a home where one can feel "happy to be alive"? Why?
2. What is Clifton's implied claim about life in the suburbs?

James Dickey

Deer among Cattle

Here and there in the searing beam
Of my hand going through the night meadow
They all are grazing

With pins of human light in their eyes.
A wild one also is eating
The human grass,

Slender, graceful, domesticated
By darkness, among the bred-
for-slaughter,

Having bounded their paralyzed fence
And inclined his branched forehead onto
Their green frosted table,

The only live thing in this flashlight
Who can leave whenever he wishes,
Turn grass into forest,

Foreclose inhuman brightness from his eyes
But stands here still, unperturbed,
In their wide-open country,

The sparks from my hand in his pupils
Unmatched anywhere among cattle,

Grazing with them the night of the hammer
As one of their own who shall rise.

CRITICAL THINKING QUESTIONS

1. What *value assumptions* about animals does Dickey's poem address?
2. What *value judgments* about animals does Dickey imply?
3. Make an *inference* about the claim of value implicit in the poem's last four lines. What evidence in the poem supports your conclusion?

Carolyn Forché

Dulcimer Maker

Calf-deep in spruce dust
wood curls off his knife
blade wet bare bulb light.

The finish of his hands
shows oil, grain, knots
where his growth scarred him.

Planing black oak
thin to flow sounds.
Tones of wind filling
bottle lips.

It is his work tying strings
across fresh-cut pine.

He sings into wood, listens:
tree rings, water!

The wood drinks his cloth,
its roots going to the depths of him,
spreading.

He wants to build a lute for music
carved on Sumerian stones, a music
no one has heard for three thousand years.

For this he will work
the oldest wood he can find.
It will not be as far away,
as unfamiliar.

CRITICAL THINKING QUESTIONS

1. What values does the dulcimer maker's work represent?
2. What do you think the last two lines may mean?

WRITING TOPIC

Do you know any artisans such as this dulcimer maker? How does our society value artisans and their work?

Robert Frost

A Young Birch

The birch begins to crack its outer sheath
Of baby green and show the white beneath,
As whosoever likes the young and slight
May well have noticed. Soon entirely white
To double day and cut in half the dark
It will stand forth, entirely white in bark,
And nothing but the top a leafy green—
The only native tree that dares to lean,
Relying on its beauty, to the air.
(Less brave perhaps than trusting are the fair.)
And someone reminiscent will recall
How once in cutting brush along the wall
He spared it from the number of the slain,
At first to be no bigger than a cane,
And then no bigger than a fishing pole,
But now at last so obvious a bole
The most efficient help you ever hired
Would know that it was there to be admired,

And zeal would not be thanked that cut it down
When you were reading books or out of town.
It was a thing of beauty and was sent
To live its life out as an ornament.

CRITICAL THINKING QUESTIONS

1. Read and compare Forché's "Dulcimer Maker" and Frost's "A Young Birch."
   a. Presumably, the "oldest wood" that the dulcimer maker desires for building his instrument would require cutting down a tree, possibly from a virgin forest. What *warrant/value assumption* justifies this action?
   b. What is Frost's *claim* about the value of trees?
   c. Are the values you articulated above consistent and complementary or incompatible and contradictory? Why?

Linda Hogan

Heartland

There are few moments of silence
but it comes
through little pores in the skin.
Between traffic and voices
it comes
and I begin to understand those city poems,
small prayers
where we place our palms together
and feel the heart
beating in a handful of nothing.

City poems
about yellow hard hats
and brotherly beggars
Wasn't Lazarus one of these?
And now Saint Pigeon of the Railroad Tracks
paces across a child's small handprint,
human acids etching themselves into metal.

We are all the least of these,
beggars, almsmen,
listening hard to the underground language
of the wrist.
Through the old leather of our feet
city earth with fossils and roots
breathes the heart of soil upward,
the voice of our gods beneath concrete.

CRITICAL THINKING QUESTIONS

1. What do you think the poet means by "city poems"?
2. In stanza 3, what is the "underground language" we all are "listening hard to"?

WRITING TOPIC

Read the prose piece, "Time and the Machine," by Aldous Huxley, written in the first half of the twentieth century. Huxley claims that urbanism and industrialism have changed our consciousness of time; we are "inhabitant[s] of an artificial universe that is, to a great extent, walled off from the world of nature." Hogan's poem, written in the latter part of the twentieth century, presents an implicit argument for us to penetrate this wall of separation. In a sense, the poet offers a solution to the problem Huxley presents. Are you convinced by Hogan's argument? Why or why not?

Galway Kinnell

Saint Francis and the Sow

The bud
stands for all things,
even for those things that don't flower,
for everything flowers, from within, of self-blessing;
though sometimes it is necessary
to reteach a thing its loveliness,
to put a hand on its brow
of the flower
and retell it in words and in touch
it is lovely
until it flowers again from within, of self-blessing;
as Saint Francis
put his hand on the creased forehead
of the sow, and told her in words and in touch
blessings of earth on the sow, and the sow
began remembering all down her thick length,
from the earthen snout all the way
through the fodder and slops to the spiritual curl of the tail,
from the hard spininess spiked out from the spine
down through the great broken heart
to the sheer blue milken dreaminess spurting and shuddering
from the fourteen teats into the fourteen mouths sucking and blowing
    beneath them:
the long, perfect loveliness of sow.

CRITICAL THINKING QUESTIONS

1. In one or two sentences, summarize Kinnell's claim.

2. On which rhetorical appeal does the poet rely? Point out and evaluate specific examples of this appeal.

3. Examine the *diction* in the second half of the poem. How does language contribute to the persuasive effect of the poet's argument?

Denise Levertov

The Victors

In June the bush we call
alder was heavy, listless,
its leaves studded with galls,

growing wherever we didn't
want it. We cut it
savagely, hunted it from the pasture, chopped it

away from the edge of the wood.
In July, still everywhere, it appeared
wearing green berries.

Anyway it must go. It takes
the light and air and the good of the earth
from flowers and young trees.

But now in August
its berries are red. Do the birds
eat them? Swinging

clusters of red, the hedges are full of them,
red-currant red, a graceful
ornament or a merry smile.

CRITICAL THINKING QUESTIONS

1. In the last line, the poet says the berries can be "a merry smile"? How do you interpret the metaphor?

2. Who or what are the victors?

3. Describe the poet's tone. How does tone influence your assessment of her *ethos?*

Rainer Maria Rilke

The Panther

TRANSLATED BY STEPHEN MITCHELL

His vision, from the constantly passing bars,
has grown so weary that it cannot hold
anything else. It seems to him there are
a thousand bars; and behind the bars, no world.

As he paces in cramped circles, over and over,
the movement of his powerful soft strides
is like a ritual dance around a center
in which a mighty will stands paralyzed.

Only at times, the curtain of the pupils
lifts, quietly—. An image enters in,
rushes down through the tensed, arrested muscles,
plunges into the heart and is gone.

CRITICAL THINKING QUESTIONS

1. On which of the rhetorical appeals does the poet rely?
2. What value assumptions about animals are suggested? How would these values factor into the debate over the use of animals for medical research?
3. Articulate a claim for the poem. Extend or qualify the claim to apply to today's zoos.

Theodore Roethke

Meditation at Oyster River

1

Over the low, barnacled, elephant-colored rocks,
Come the first tide-ripples, moving, almost without sound, toward me,
Running along the narrow furrows of the shore, the rows of dead clam
    shells;
Then a runnel behind me, creeping closer,
Alive with tiny striped fish, and young crabs climbing in and out of the
    water.

No sound from the bay. No violence.
Even the gulls quiet on the far rocks,
Silent, in the deepening light,
Their cat-mewing over,
Their child-whimpering.

At last one long undulant ripple,
Blue-black from where I am sitting,
Makes almost a wave over a barrier of small stones,
Slapping lightly against a sunken log.
I dabble my toes in the brackish foam sliding forward,
Then retire to a rock higher up on the cliff-side.
The wind slackens, light as a moth fanning a stone:
A twilight wind, light as a child's breath
Turning not a leaf, not a ripple.
The dew revives on the beach-grass;
The salt-soaked wood of a fire crackles;
A fish raven turns on its perch (a dead tree in the rivermouth),
Its wings catching a last glint of the reflected sunlight.

2

The self persists like a dying star,
In sleep, afraid. Death's face rises afresh,
Among the shy beasts, the deer at the salt-lick,
The doe with its sloped shoulders loping across the highway,
The young snake, poised in green leaves, waiting for its fly,

The hummingbird, whirring from quince-blossom to morning-glory—
With these I would be.
And with water: the waves coming forward, without cessation,
The waves, altered by sand-bars, beds of kelp, miscellaneous driftwood,
Topped by cross-winds, tugged at by sinuous undercurrents
The tide rustling in, sliding between the ridges of stone,
The tongues of water, creeping in, quietly.

3

In this hour,
In this first heaven of knowing,
The flesh takes on the pure poise of the spirit,
Acquires, for a time, the sandpiper's insouciance,
The hummingbird's surety, the kingfisher's cunning—
I shift on my rock, and I think:
Of the first trembling of a Michigan brook in April,
Over a lip of stone, the tiny rivulet;
And that wrist-thick cascade tumbling from a cleft rock,
Its spray holding a double rain-bow in early morning,
Small enough to be taken in, embraced, by two arms,—
Or the Tittebawasee, in the time between winter and spring,
When the ice melts along the edges in early afternoon.
And the midchannel begins cracking and heaving from the pressure
    beneath,
The ice piling high against the iron-bound spiles,
Gleaming, freezing hard again, creaking at midnight—
And I long for the blast of dynamite,
The sudden sucking roar as the culvert loosens its debris of branches and
    sticks,
Welter of tin cans, pails, old bird nests, a child's shoe riding a log,
As the piled ice breaks away from the battered spiles,
And the whole river begins to move forward, its bridges shaking.

4

Now, in this waning of light,
I rock with the motion of morning;
In the cradle of all that is,
I'm lulled into half-sleep
By the lapping of water,
Cries of the sandpiper.
Water's my will, and my way,
And the spirit runs, intermittently,
In and out of the small waves,

Runs with the intrepid shorebirds—
How graceful the small before danger!

In the first of the moon,
All's a scattering,
A shining.

WRITING TOPIC

Roethke's poem implies that a natural world setting is vital to *his* meditative experience. In the debate over public funding for preserving nature areas, some persons might generalize from Roethke's experience to make a case for preserving these areas. Others, however, might reject such a generalization, arguing that only a small group seeks out nature areas for meditation. Based on your experience and observation, which side of the debate to you support?

Pattiann Rogers

Rolling Naked
in the Morning Dew

Out among the wet grasses and wild barley-covered
Meadows, backside, frontside, through the white clover
And feather peabush, over spongy tussocks
And shaggy-mane mushrooms, the abandoned nests
Of larks and bobolinks, face to face
With vole trails, snail niches, jelly
Slug eggs; or in a stone-walled garden, level
With the stemmed bulbs of orange and scarlet tulips,
Cricket carcasses, the bent blossoms of sweet william,
Shoulder over shoulder, leg over leg, clear
To the ferny edge of the goldfish pond—some people
Believe in the rejuvenating powers of this act—naked
As a toad in the forest, belly and hips, thighs
And ankles drenched in the dew-filled gulches
Of oak leaves, in the soft fall beneath yellow birches,
All of the skin exposed directly to the *killy* cry
Of the kingbird, the buzzing of grasshopper sparrows,
Those calls merging with the dawn-red mists
Of crimson steeplebush, entering the bare body then
Not merely through the ears but through the skin
Of every naked person willing every event and potentiality
Of a damp transforming dawn to enter.

Lillie Langtry practiced it, when weather permitted,
Lying down naked every morning in the dew,
With all of her beauty believing the single petal
Of her white skin could absorb and assume
That radiating purity of liquid and light.
And I admit to believing myself, without question,
In the magical powers of dew on the cheeks
And breasts of Lillie Langtry believing devotedly
In the magical powers of early morning dew on the skin

Of her body lolling in purple beds of bird's-foot violets,
Pink prairie mimosa. And I believe, without doubt,
In the mystery of the healing energy coming
From that wholehearted belief in the beneficent results
Of the good delights of the naked body rolling
And rolling through all the silked and sun-filled,
Dusky-winged, sheathed and sparkled, looped
And dizzied effluences of each dawn
Of the rolling earth.

Just consider how the mere idea of it alone
Has already caused me to sing and sing
This whole morning long.

CRITICAL THINKING QUESTIONS

1. a. What is Rogers attempting to persuade her readers to do?
   b. How do the last lines *qualify* her claim? Does this qualifier strengthen or weaken the persuasive effect of her claim?

2. a. List the evidence Rogers provides for her claim. On which *rhetorical appeal* does she rely, and how effective is this strategy?
   b. What *testimonial evidence* does Rogers provide?

WRITING TOPIC

What value appeals are implicit in Rogers's argument? In a broader context, Rogers seems to advocate that an individual adopt an outlook on his or her daily living experience. How would you articulate this outlook? Do many people you know endorse this outlook and attitude towards their lives? How does it compare and contrast with your personal outlook on your daily experience?

Carl Sandburg

Chicago

Hog Butcher for the World,
Tool Maker, Stacker of Wheat,
Player with Railroads and the Nation's Freight Handler;
Stormy, husky, brawling,
City of the Big Shoulders:

They tell me you are wicked and I believe them, for I have seen your painted
    women under the gas lamps luring the farm boys.
And they tell me you are crooked and I answer: Yes, it is true I have seen the
    gunman kill and go free to kill again.
And they tell me you are brutal and my reply is: On the faces of women and
    children I have seen the marks of wanton hunger.
And having answered so I turn once more to those who sneer at this my city,
    and I give them back the sneer and say to them:
Come and show me another city with lifted head singing so proud to be
    alive and coarse and strong and cunning.
Flinging magnetic curses amid the toil of piling job on job, here is a tall bold
    slugger set vivid against the little soft cities;
Fierce as a dog with tongue lapping for action, cunning as a savage pitted
    against the wilderness,
        Bareheaded,
        Shoveling,
        Wrecking,
        Planning,
        Building, breaking, rebuilding,
Under the smoke, dust all over his mouth, laughing with white teeth,
Under the terrible burden of destiny laughing as a young man laughs,
Laughing even as an ignorant fighter laughs who has never lost a battle,
Bragging and laughing that under his wrist is the pulse, and under his ribs
    the heart of the people,
        Laughing!
Laughing the stormy, husky, brawling laughter of Youth, half-naked,
    sweating, proud to be Hog butcher, Tool Maker, Stacker of Wheat,
    Player with Railroads and Freight Handler to the Nation.

CRITICAL THINKING QUESTIONS

1. In personifying Chicago as "Youth," what values or characteristics does the poet attribute to youth? Do you agree or disagree with the poet's generalizations about the nature of youth?

2. Based on the poet's depiction of Chicago in the early twentieth century, articulate a *claim of value* about the city at that time. How would you modify this claim to apply to today's larger metropolitan cities? Or, write a *claim of value* that specifies a city you know firsthand, either as a resident or a visitor.

Anne Sexton

The Fury of Flowers and Worms

Let the flowers make a journey
on Monday so that I can see
ten daisies in a blue vase
with perhaps one red ant
crawling to the gold center.
A bit of the field on my table,
close to the worms
who struggle blindly,
moving deep into their slime,
moving deep into God's abdomen,
moving like oil through water,
sliding through the good brown.

The daisies grow wild
like popcorn.
They are God's promise to the field.
How happy I am, daisies, to love you.
How happy you are to be loved
and found magical, like a secret
from the sluggish field.
If all the world picked daisies
wars would end, the common cold would stop,
unemployment would end, the monetary market
would hold steady and no money would float.
Listen world,
if you'd just take the time to pick
the white fingers, the penny heart,
all would be well.
They are so unexpected.

They are as good as salt.
If someone had brought them
to van Gogh's room daily
his ear would have stayed on.
I would like to think that no one would die anymore
if we all believed in daisies

but the worms know better, don't they?
They slide into the ear of a corpse
and listen to his great sigh.

CRITICAL THINKING QUESTIONS

1. Examining the poem stanza by stanza, describe the poet's varying tone. How do these shifts affect your assessment of the poet's *ethos* appeal?

2. Do the flowers or the worms dominate? What do you think is this poem's implied claim? Do you agree or disagree?

Gary Snyder

The Call of the Wild

The heavy old man in his bed at night
Hears the Coyote singing
                 in the back meadow.
All the years he ranched and mined and logged.
A Catholic.
A native Californian.
    and the Coyotes howl in his
Eightieth year.
He will call the Government
Trapper
Who uses iron leg-traps on Coyotes,
Tomorrow.
My sons will lose this
Music they have just started
To love.

The ex acid-heads from the cities
Converted to Guru or Swami,
Do penance with shiny
Dopey eyes, and quit eating meat.
In the forests of North America,
The land of Coyote and Eagle,
They dream of India, of
    forever blissful sexless highs.
And sleep in oil-heated
Geodesic domes, that
Were stuck like warts
In the woods.

And the Coyote singing
    is shut away
    for they fear
    the call
    of the wild.

And they sold their virgin cedar trees,
    the tallest trees in miles,
To a logger
Who told them,

"Trees are full of bugs."
The Government finally decided
To wage the war   all-out. Defeat is Un-American.
And they took to the air,
Their women beside them
    in bouffant hairdos
    putting nail-polish on the
    gunship cannon-buttons.
And they never came down,
    for they found,
    the ground
is pro-Communist. And dirty.
And the insects side with the Viet Cong.
So they bomb and they bomb
Day after day, across the planet
    blinding sparrows
    breaking the ear-drums of owls
    splintering trunks of cherries
    twining and looping
    deer intestines
    in the shaken, dusty, rocks.
All these Americans up in special cities in the sky
Dumping poisons and explosives
Across Asia first,
And next North America,

A war against earth.
When it's done there'll be
    no place

A Coyote could hide.

    envoy

I would like to say
Coyote is forever
Inside you.

But it's not true.

CRITICAL THINKING QUESTIONS

1. According to Snyder, who is responsible for "a war against earth"?
2. Give examples of the poet's use of *pathos* appeal. Are some examples more effective than others in persuading you to accept the poet's viewpoint?

WRITING TOPIC

Reading the poem's last nine lines from today's perspective, what is your viewpoint of Snyder's foreboding statement? Defend or refute his assertion that the Coyote is *not* "forever/Inside you."

William Stafford

Traveling through the Dark

Traveling through the dark I found a deer
dead on the edge of the Wilson River road.
It is usually best to roll them into the canyon:
that road is narrow; to swerve might make more dead.

By glow of the tail-light I stumbled back of the car
and stood by the heap, a doe, a recent killing;
she had stiffened already, almost cold.
I dragged her off; she was large in the belly.

My fingers touching her side brought me the reason—
her side was warm; her fawn lay there waiting,
alive, still, never to be born.
Beside that mountain road I hesitated.

The car aimed ahead its lowered parking lights;
under the hood purred the steady engine.
I stood in the glare of the warm exhaust turning red;
around our group I could hear the wilderness listen.

I thought hard for us all—my only swerving—,
then pushed her over the edge into the river.

CRITICAL THINKING QUESTIONS

1. Use the rhetorical triangle to examine this poem.
   a. How does the poet create *ethos* appeal?
   b. How does the poet use *logos* appeal?
   c. How does the poet use *pathos* appeal?
2. Evaluate the persuasive effect of each rhetorical appeal. In your view, is one more effective (or less effective) than the other two appeals? Why?

WRITING TOPIC

We generally agree that freedom is inextricably linked to an individual's right to choose. And we generally agree that the freedom to make choices carries with it the mantle of responsibility for the consequences of one's choices. Also, other persons judge us—assess our character or *ethos*—by the choices we make. Examine this poem in the context of these ethical principles. What choice confronts the speaker? Does he accept or shirk the mantle of responsibility? Finally, how do you judge him?

Robert Penn Warren

from Audubon

I. *Was Not the Lost Dauphin*

[A]

Was not the lost dauphin, though handsome was only
Base-born and not even able
To make a decent living, was only
Himself, Jean Jacques, and his passion—what
Is man but his passion?

                    Saw,
Eastward and over the cypress swamp, the dawn,
Redder than meat, break;
And the large bird,
Long neck outthrust, wings crooked to scull air, moved
In a slow calligraphy, crank, flat, and black against
The color of God's blood spilt, as though
Pulled by a string.

                   Saw
It proceed across the inflamed distance.

Moccasins set in hoar frost, eyes fixed on the bird,
Thought: "On that sky it is black."
Thought: "In my mind it is white."
Thinking: "*Ardea occidentalis,* heron, the great one."

[B]

October: and the bear,
Daft in the honey-light, yawns.

The bear's tongue, pink as a baby's, out-crisps to the curled tip,
It bleeds the black blood of the blueberry.

The teeth are more importantly white
Than has ever been imagined.

The bear feels his own fat
Sweeten, like a drowse, deep to the bone.

Bemused, above the fume of ruined blueberries,
The last bee hums.

The wings, like mica, glint
In the sunlight.

He leans on his gun. Thinks
How thin is the membrane between himself and the world.

VI. *Love and Knowledge*

Their footless dance
Is of the beautiful liability of their nature.
Their eyes are round, boldly convex, bright as a jewel,
And merciless. They do not know
Compassion, and if they did,
We should not be worthy of it. They fly
In air that glitters like fluent crystal
And is hard as perfectly transparent iron, they cleave it
With no effort. They cry
In a tongue multitudinous, often like music.

He slew them, at surprising distances, with his gun.
Over a body held in his hand, his head was bowed low,
But not in grief.

He put them where they are, and there we see them:
In our imagination.

What is love?

Our name for it is knowledge.

Dawn: his heart shook in the tension of the world.

Dawn: and what is your passion?

VII. *Tell Me a Story*

[A]

Long ago, in Kentucky, I, a boy, stood
By a dirt road, in first dark, and heard
The great geese hoot northward.

I could not see them, there being no moon
And the stars sparse. I heard them.

I did not know what was happening in my heart.

It was the season before the elderberry blooms,
Therefore they were going north.

The sound was passing northward.

[B]

Tell me a story.

In this century, and moment, of mania,
Tell me a story.

Make it a story of great distances, and starlight.

The name of the story will be Time,
But you must not pronounce its name.

Tell me a story of deep delight.

CRITICAL THINKING QUESTIONS

1. John James Audubon (1785–1851), an ornithologist, is famous for his paintings of North American birds. In these excerpts, the poet shows Audubon shooting those birds he would later represent in masterful paintings. In "VI. Love and Knowledge," how does the poet explain Audubon's actions? How do you judge Audubon?

2. Hunters and wildlife preservationists often have much more in common than their emotions allow them to acknowledge. What value assumptions (*warrants*) might the two factions share?

Walt Whitman

from Song of Myself

14

The wild gander leads his flock through the cool night,
Ya-honk he says, and sounds it down to me like an invitation,
The pert may suppose it meaningless, but I listening close,
Find its purpose and place up there toward the wintry sky.

The sharp-hoof'd moose of the north, the cat on the house-sill, the
    chickadee, the prairie-dog,
The litter of the grunting sow as they tug at her teats,
The brood of the turkey-hen and she with her half-spread wings,
I see in them and myself the same old law.

The press of my foot to the earth springs a hundred affections,
They scorn the best I can do to relate them.

I am enamour'd of growing out-doors.
Of men that live among cattle or taste of the ocean or woods,
Of the builders and steerers of ships and the wielders of axes and mauls,
    and the drivers of horses,
I can eat and sleep with them week in and week out.

What is commonest, cheapest, nearest, easiest, is Me,
Me going in for my chances, spending for vast returns,
Adorning myself to bestow myself on the first that will take me,
Not asking the sky to come down to my good will,
Scattering it freely forever.

CRITICAL THINKING QUESTIONS

1. Describe the *ethos* Whitman creates. Point out evidence from the poem that suggests those character qualities.
2. What values does Whitman assign to "growing out-doors"? From your perspective as a twenty-first-century reader, are the values Whitman, a late nineteenth-century poet, celebrates still valid?

Walt Whitman

from Song of Myself

31

I believe a leaf of grass is no less than the journey-work of the stars,
And the pismire is equally perfect, and a grain of sand, and the egg of the
    wren,
And the tree-toad is a chief-d'œuvre for the highest,
And the running blackberry would adorn the parlors of heaven,
And the narrowest hinge in my hand puts to scorn all machinery,
And the cow crunching with depress'd head surpasses any statue,
And a mouse is miracle enough to stagger sextillions of infidels.

I find I incorporate gneiss, coal, long-threaded moss, fruits, grains, esculent
    roots,
And am stucco'd with quadrupeds and birds all over,
And have distanced what is behind me for good reasons,
But call any thing back again when I desire it.

In vain the speeding or shyness,
In vain the plutonic rocks send their old heat against my approach,
In vain the mastodon retreats beneath its powder'd bones,
In vain objects stand leagues off and assume manifold shapes,
In vain the ocean settling in hollows and the great monsters lying low,
In vain the buzzard houses herself with the sky,
In vain the snake slides through the creepers and logs,
In vain the elk takes to the inner passes of the woods,
In vain the razor-bill'd auk sails far north to Labrador,
I follow quickly, I ascend to the nest in the fissure of the cliff.

CRITICAL THINKING QUESTIONS

1. Articulate a *claim of value* for stanza one.

2. How does stanza one support and/or qualify Whitman's implied argument for
   an enlarged sense of self?

3. What is your attitude toward the *ethos* the poet creates?

William Wordsworth

To My Sister

It is the first mild day of March:
Each minute sweeter than before,
The redbreast sings from the tall larch
that stands beside our door.

There is a blessing in the air,
Which seems a sense of joy to yield
To the bare trees, and mountains bare,
And grass in the green field.

My sister! ('tis a wish of mine)
Now that our morning meal is done,
Make haste, your morning task resign;
Come forth and feel the sun.

Edward will come with you;—and, pray,
Put on with speed your woodland dress;
And bring no book: for this one day
We'll give to idleness.

No joyless forms shall regulate
Our living calendar:
We from to-day, my Friend, will date
The opening of the year.

Love, now a universal birth,
From heart to heart is stealing,
From earth to man, from man to earth:
—It is the hour of feeling.

One moment now may give us more
Than years of toiling reason:
Our minds shall drink at every pore
The spirit of the season.

Some silent laws our hearts will make,
Which they shall long obey:
We for the year to come may take
Our temper from to-day.

And from the blessed power that rolls
About, below, above,
We'll frame the measure of our souls:
They shall be tuned to love.

Then come, my Sister! come, I pray,
With speed put on your woodland dress;
And bring no book: for this one day
We'll give to idleness.

CRITICAL THINKING QUESTIONS

1. The poet is making a direct argument to his sister. What is his claim?
2. Examine the supporting evidence—his reasoning. How persuasive is it?
3. Has the poet convinced you to "give to idleness"? Why or why not?

James Wright

A Blessing

Just off the highway to Rochester, Minnesota,
Twilight bounds softly forth on the grass.
And the eyes of those two Indian ponies
Darken with kindness.
They have come gladly out of the willows
To welcome my friend and me.
We step over the barbed wire into the pasture
Where they have been grazing all day, alone.
They ripple tensely, they can hardly contain their happiness
That we have come.
They bow shyly as wet swans. They love each other.
There is no loneliness like theirs.
At home once more,
They begin munching the young tufts of spring in the darkness.
I would like to hold the slenderer one in my arms,
For she has walked over to me
And nuzzled my left hand.
She is black and white,
Her mane falls wild on her forehead,
And the light breeze moves me to caress her long ear
That is delicate as the skin over a girl's wrist.
Suddenly I realize
That if I stepped out of my body I would break
Into blossom.

WRITING TOPIC

Read and compare Wright's poem with Rogers's "Rolling Naked in the Morning Dew." Drawing on these poems and your own imagination and experience, write an argument targeting older adults that gives vitality to the cliché, "take time to stop and smell the roses."

Edward Abbey

The Heat of Noon:
Rock and Tree and Cloud

from *Desert Solitaire*

At lunchtime I leave my post at the entrance station, hurrying from its shade through the blaze to the housetrailer, where I take a pitcher from the refrigerator and still in a hurry gulp down about a pint of fruit juice without stopping for breath. There are times in this hot and arid place when my thirst becomes so intense I cannot seem to drink any liquid fast enough to quench it.

July. Though all the windows are wide open and the blinds rattle in a breeze the heat is terrific. The inside of the trailer is like the inside of a kiln, a fierce dry heat that warps the loose linoleum on the floor, turns an exposed slice of bread into something like toast within half an hour, makes my papers crackle like parchment.

I take off my shirt and hang it over a chair; the sweat-soaked armpits will dry within five minutes, leaving a rime of salt along the seams. Hastily I assemble a couple of sandwiches: lettuce, leftover bacon from breakfast, sliced ham, peanut butter, salami, longhorn cheese, cashews, raisins, horseradish, anything else that will fit comfortably between two slices of bread—and take the dewy-cold pitcher of juice and hasten outside and through the storm of sunlight over the baking sandstone of the 33,000-acre terrace to the shade and relative coolness of the ramada.

The thermometer nailed to a post reads 110° F., but in the shade, with a breeze and almost no humidity, such a temperature is comfortable, even pleasant. I sit down at the table, pull off my boots and socks, dig my toes into the gritty, cleansing sand. Fear no more the heat of the sun. This is comfort. More, this is bliss, pure smug animal satisfaction. I relax beneath the sheltering canopy of juniper boughs and gaze out squinting and blinking at a pink world being sunburned to death.

Yes, July. The mountains are almost bare of snow except for patches within the couloirs on the northern slopes. Consoling nevertheless, those shrunken snowfields, despite the fact that they're twenty miles away by line of sight and six to seven thousand feet higher than where I sit. They comfort me with the promise that if the heat down here becomes less endurable I can escape for at least two days each week to the refuge of the mountains—those islands in the sky surrounded by a sea of desert. The knowledge that refuge is available, when and if needed, makes the silent inferno of the desert more easily bearable. Mountains complement desert as desert complements city, as wilderness complements and completes civilization.

A man could be a lover and defender of the wilderness without ever in his lifetime leaving the boundaries of asphalt, powerlines, and right-angled surfaces. We need wilderness whether or not we ever set foot in it. We need a refuge even though we may never need to go there. I may never in my life get to Alaska, for example, but I am grateful that it's there. We need the possibility of escape as surely as we need hope; without it the life of the cities would drive all men into crime or drugs or psychoanalysis.

A familiar and plaintive admonition; I would like to introduce here an entirely new argument in what has now become a stylized debate: the wilderness should be preserved for political reasons. We may need it someday not only as a refuge from excessive industrialism but also as a refuge from authoritarian government, from political oppression. Grand Canyon, Big Bend, Yellowstone and the High Sierras may be required to function as bases for guerrilla warfare against tyranny. What reason have we Americans to think that our own society will necessarily escape the world-wide drift toward the totalitarian organization of men and institutions?

This may seem, at the moment, like a fantastic thesis. Yet history demonstrates that personal liberty is a rare and precious thing, that all societies tend toward the absolute until attack from without or collapse from within breaks up the social machine and makes freedom and innovation again possible. Technology adds a new dimension to the process by providing modern despots with instruments far more efficient than any available to their classical counterparts. Surely it is no accident that the most thorough of tyrannies appeared in Europe's most thoroughly scientific and industrialized nation. If we allow our own country to become as densely populated, overdeveloped and technically unified as modern Germany we may face a similar fate.

The value of wilderness, on the other hand, as a base for resistance to centralized domination is demonstrated by recent history. In Budapest and Santo Domingo, for example, popular revolts were easily and quickly crushed because an urbanized environment gives the advantage to the power with the technological equipment. But in Cuba, Algeria and Vietnam the revolutionaries, operating in mountain, desert and jungle hinterlands with the active or tacit support of a thinly dispersed population, have been able to overcome or at least fight to a draw official establishment forces equipped with all of the terrible weapons of twentieth century militarism. Rural insurrections can then be suppressed only by bombing and burning villages and countryside so thoroughly that the mass of the population is forced to take refuge in the cities, there the people are then policed and if necessary starved into submission. The city, which should be the symbol and center of civilization, can also be made to function as a concentration camp. This is one of the significant discoveries of contemporary political science.

How does this theory apply to the present and future of the famous United States of North America? Suppose we were planning to impose a dictatorial regime upon the American people—the following preparations would be essential:

1. Concentrate the populace in megalopolitan masses so that they can be kept under close surveillance and where, in case of trouble, they can be bombed, burned, gassed or machine-gunned with a minimum of expense and waste.

2. Mechanize agriculture to the highest degree of refinement, thus forcing most of the scattered farm and ranching population into the cities. Such a policy is desirable because farmers, woodsmen, cowboys, Indians, fishermen and other relatively self-sufficient types are difficult to manage unless displaced from their natural environment.

3. Restrict the possession of firearms to the police and the regular military organizations.

4. Encourage or at least fail to discourage population growth. Large masses of people are more easily manipulated and dominated than scattered individuals.

5. Continue military conscription. Nothing excels military training for creating in young men an attitude of prompt, cheerful obedience to officially constituted authority.

6. Divert attention from deep conflicts within the society by engaging in foreign wars; make support of these wars a test of loyalty, thereby exposing and isolating potential opposition to the new order.

7. Overlay the nation with a finely reticulated network of communications, airlines and interstate *autobahns*.

8. *Raze the wilderness.* Dam the rivers, flood the canyons, drain the swamps, log the forests, strip-mine the hills, bulldoze the mountains, irrigate the deserts and improve the national parks into national parking lots.

Idle speculations, feeble and hopeless protest. It was all foreseen nearly half a century ago by the most cold-eyed and clear-eyed of our national poets, on California's shore, at the end of the open road. Shine, perishing republic.

The sun reigns, I am drowned in light. At this hour, sitting alone at the focal point of the universe, surrounded by a thousand square miles of largely uninhabited no-man's-land—or all-men's-land—I cannot seriously be disturbed by any premonitions of danger to my vulnerable wilderness or my all-too-perishable republic. All dangers seem equally remote. In this glare of brilliant emptiness, in this arid intensity of pure heat, in the heart of a weird solitude, great silence and grand desolation, all things recede to distances out of reach, reflecting light but impossible to touch, annihilating all thought and all that men have made to a spasm of whirling dust far out on the golden desert.

The flowers that graced the red dunes in April and May have withered now, all gone to seed except for a few drooping sunflowers. The cliffrose has faded, the yucca stalks have bloomed, blown, died, cracked and dried, the seedpods now only empty husks. Under the daily sweep of the parching May winds almost everything that was green has been burned to soft, sere tones of saffron and auburn. But the summer thunderstorms have not yet begun. When they come, as they soon will, we'll see a resurgence of hairy green across the land—the succulent scratchy allergenic tumbleweed, that exotic import from the Mongolian steppes.

The majority of living things retreat before the stunning glare and heat of midday. A snake or lizard exposed to the noon sun for more than ten minutes would die; having no internal cooling mechanism the reptiles must at all costs avoid

extremes of temperature, especially in the desert where the temperature on the surface of the ground is much higher than it is in the air a few feet above. The snakes
therefore seek shade, waiting until sundown to come out to hunt for supper. The
insect-eating lizards dart from shelter to shelter, never lingering for more than a few
moments in the open blaze.

The other creatures do the same. Like myself, they stay in the shade as much as
possible. To conserve bodily moisture and energy the rodents remain in their bur-
rows during the day. Scorpions and spiders go underground for the duration. Deer,
antelope, bighorn sheep, bobcats, foxes and coyotes all shade up beneath rock
ledges, oakbrush, pinyon and juniper trees, till the sun goes down.

Even the red ants keep to the inside of their evil nests at noon, though they will
come spilling out eager to fight if riled with a stick—I've tried it, naturally.

Flowers curl up. Leaves fold inward. Everything shrinks, contracts, shrivels;
somewhere a desiccated limb on an ancient dying cottonwood tree splits off from
the trunk, and the rending fibers make a sound like the shriek of a woman.

The birds are muted, inactive. Now and then I can hear the faraway call of a
mourning dove—a call that always sounds far away. A few gray desert sparrows fly
from one tree to the next, stop there, do not reappear. The ravens and magpies stay
in the shade, the former up on the rimrock, the latter in the trees. The owls, of
course, and the nighthawks keep to holes and crevices during the day.

Insect life, sparse to begin with on the open desert, diminishes to near total
invisibility and inaudibility during the heat of the day, although at times, during
the very hottest and stillest hour, you may hear the eerie ticking noise of a
sun-demented cricket or locust, a small sad music that seems to have—like a Bach
partita—a touch of something ageless, out of time, eternal in its primeval vibrations.

In this static period even the domestic livestock—horses, sheep, goats, cattle—
have sense enough to take it easy, relaxing in the shade. Of all the featherless beasts
only man, chained by his self-imposed slavery to the clock, denies the elemental fire
and proceeds as best he can about his business, suffering quietly, martyr to his madness. Much to learn.

Among the wild things only the hawks, vultures and eagles seem to remain fully
active during the hottest days and hottest hours of the desert. I have seen them circling
and soaring far in the sky at high noon, dark wings against the blue, above the heat.

What are they doing up there in the middle of the sky at the apex of the day? I
watch them for hour after hour with the naked eye and with binoculars and never
see either hawk or eagle stoop and strike at such a time. And no wonder, for there's
precious little fresh meat abroad. Nor does the buzzard descend for lunch or make
any effort of any kind. The hawks appear most frequently and most briefly, gliding
overhead on some invisible stream in the air. The golden eagle does not come into
sight often but stays longer than the hawk, floating toward the horizon in overlapping circles until out of sight.

The vulture or buzzard, master of soaring flight, is most common and most
often seen. He stays aloft for hours at a time without ever stirring his long black

white-trimmed wings, recognizable at a great distance by their dihedral inclination. Never in a hurry to get anywhere or do anything, an indolent and contemplative bird, he hovers on a thermal, rocking slightly, rising slowly, slips off, sails forward and upward without lifting a feather, primaries extended like fingers at his wingtips. He soars around and around in expanding spirals, lingering at a thousand feet above the landscape, bleak eyes missing nothing that moves below. Or maybe—who can be sure?—he is fast asleep up there, dreaming of a previous incarnation when wings were only a dream. Still without a stroke the vulture rises higher, higher, in ever wider circles, until nothing can be seen of this gaunt, arrogant, repellent bird but the coal-dark V-sign of his wings against the blue dome of heaven.

Around noon the heat waves begin flowing upward from the expanses of sand and bare rock. They shimmer like transparent, filmy veils between my sanctuary in the shade and all the sun-dazzled world beyond. Objects and forms viewed through this tremulous flow appear somewhat displaced or distorted, as a stick seems bent when half-immersed in water.

The great Balanced Rock floats a few inches above its pedestal, supported by a layer of superheated air. The buttes, pinnacles and fins in the Windows area bend and undulate beyond the middle ground like a painted backdrop stirred by a draft of air. The peaks of the Sierra La Sal—Mount Nass, Mount Tomaski, Mount Peale, Mount Tukuhnikivats and the others—seem to melt into one another, merging like cloud forms so that the profile of one mountain cannot be distinguished from that of another closer or farther away.

In the foreground the dwarf trees of pinyon pine and juniper waver like algae under water without, however, losing any of their sharpness of detail. There is in fact no illusion of the sort called mirage, only the faint deception of motion where nothing is actually moving but the overheated air. You are not likely to see a genuine mirage on the high desert of canyon and mesa country; for that spectacle we must go west or southwest into the basin-and-range provinces of Arizona, Nevada, Southern California and Sonora. There the dry lake beds between the parallel mountain ranges fill with planes of hot air which reflect sky and mountains in mirror fashion, creating the illusory lakes of blue water, the inverted mountains, the strange vision of men and animals walking through or upon water—Palestinian miracles.

Dehydration: the desert air sucks moisture from every pore. I take a drink from the canvas water-bag dangling near my head, the water cooled by evaporation. Noontime here is like a drug. The light is psychedelic, the dry electric air narcotic. To me the desert is stimulating, exciting, exacting; I feel no temptation to sleep or to relax into occult dreams but rather an opposite effect which sharpens and heightens vision, touch, hearing, taste and smell. Each stone, each plant, each grain of sand exists in and for itself with a clarity that is undimmed by any suggestion of a different realm. *Claritas, integritas, veritas.* Only the sunlight holds things together. Noon is the crucial hour: the desert reveals itself nakedly and cruelly, with no meaning but its own existence.

My lone juniper stands half-alive, half-dead, the silvery wind-rubbed claw of wood projected stiffly at the sun. A single cloud floats in the sky to the northeast, motionless, a magical coalescence of vapor where a few minutes before there was nothing visible but the hot, deep, black-grained blueness of infinity.

Life has come to a standstill, at least for the hour. In this forgotten place the tree and I wait on the shore of time, temporarily free from the force of motion and process and the surge toward—what? Something called the *future?* I am free, I am compelled, to contemplate the world which underlies life, struggle, thought, ideas, the human labyrinth of hope and despair.

Through half-closed eyes, for the light would otherwise be overpowering, I consider the tree, the lonely cloud, the sandstone bedrock of this part of the world and pray—in my fashion—for a vision of truth. I listen for signals from the sun— but that distant music is too high and pure for the human ear. I gaze at the tree and receive no response. I scrape my bare feet against the sand and rock under the table and am comforted by their solidity and resistance. I look at the cloud.

CRITICAL THINKING QUESTIONS

1. Abbey writes, "A man could be a lover and defender of the wilderness without ever in his lifetime leaving the boundaries of asphalt, powerlines, and right-angled surfaces. We need wilderness whether or not we ever set foot in it." Examine the reasoning Abbey provides to support his claim. Do you accept his stated warrant about the consequence of *not* having wilderness?

2. Abbey introduces "an entirely new argument" in the debate over the value of wilderness. He claims, " . . . the wilderness should be preserved for political reasons." How effectively does Abbey support this claim? Are you convinced? Why or why not?

Rachel Carson

The Obligation to Endure

from *Silent Spring*

The history of life on earth has been a history of interaction between living things and their surroundings. To a large extent, the physical form and the habits of the earth's vegetation and its animal life have been molded by the environment. Considering the whole span of earthly time, the opposite effect, in which life actually modifies its surroundings, has been relatively slight. Only within the moment of time represented by the present century has one species—man—acquired significant power to alter the nature of his world.

During the past quarter century this power has not only increased to one of disturbing magnitude but it has changed in character. The most alarming of all man's assaults upon the environment is the contamination of air, earth, rivers, and sea with dangerous and even lethal materials. This pollution is for the most part irrecoverable; the chain of evil it initiates not only in the world that must support life but in living tissues is for the most part irreversible. In this now universal contamination of the environment, chemicals are the sinister and little-recognized partners of radiation in changing the very nature of the world—the very nature of its life. Strontium 90, released through nuclear explosions into the air, comes to earth in rain or drifts down as fallout, lodges in soil, enters into the grass or corn or wheat grown there, and in time takes up its abode in the bones of a human being, there to remain until his death. Similarly, chemicals sprayed on croplands or forests or gardens lie long in soil, entering into living organisms, passing from one to another in a chain of poisoning and death. Or they pass mysteriously by underground streams until they emerge and, through the alchemy of air and sunlight, combine into new forms that kill vegetation, sicken cattle, and work unknown harm on those who drink from once pure wells. As Albert Schweitzer has said, "Man can hardly even recognize the devils of his own creation."

It took hundreds of millions of years to produce the life that now inhabits the earth—eons of time in which that developing and evolving and diversifying life reached a state of adjustment and balance with its surroundings. The environment, rigorously shaping and directing the life it supported, contained elements that were hostile as well as supporting. Certain rocks gave out dangerous radiation; even within the light of the sun, from which all life draws its energy, there were shortwave radiations with power to injure. Given time—time not in years but in millennia—life adjusts, and a balance has been reached. For time is the essential ingredient; but in the modern world there is no time.

The rapidity of change and the speed with which new situations are created follow the impetuous and heedless pace of man rather than the deliberate pace of nature. Radiation is no longer merely the background radiation of rocks, the bombardment of cosmic rays, the ultraviolet of the sun that have existed before there was any life on earth; radiation is now the unnatural creation of man's tampering with the atom. The chemicals to which life is asked to make its adjustment are no longer merely the calcium and silica and copper and all the rest of the minerals washed out of the rocks and carried in rivers to the sea; they are the synthetic creations of man's inventive mind, brewed in his laboratories, and having no counterparts in nature.

To adjust to these chemicals would require time on the scale that is nature's; it would require not merely the years of a man's life but the life of generations. And even this, were it by some miracle possible, would be futile, for the new chemicals come from our laboratories in an endless stream; almost 500 annually find their way into actual use in the United States alone. The figure is staggering and its implications are not easily grasped—500 new chemicals to which the bodies of men and animals are required somehow to adapt each year, chemicals totally outside the limits of biologic experience.

Among them are many that are used in man's war against nature. Since the mid-1940s over 200 basic chemicals have been created for use in killing insects, weeds, rodents, and other organisms described in the modern vernacular as "pests"; and they are sold under several thousand different brand names.

These sprays, dusts, and aerosols are now applied almost universally to farms, gardens, forests, and homes—nonselective chemicals that have the power to kill every insect, the "good" and the "bad," to still the song of birds and the leaping of fish in the streams, to coat the leaves with a deadly film, and to linger on in soil—all this though the intended target may be only a few weeds or insects. Can anyone believe it is possible to lay down such a barrage of poisons on the surface of the earth without making it unfit for all life? They should not be called "insecticides," but "biocides."

The whole process of spraying seems caught up in an endless spiral. Since DDT was released for civilian use, a process of escalation has been going on in which ever more toxic materials must be found. This has happened because insects, in a triumphant vindication of Darwin's principle of the survival of the fittest, have evolved super races immune to the particular insecticide used, hence a deadlier one has always to be developed—and then a deadlier one than that. It has happened also because, for reasons to be described later, destructive insects often undergo a "flareback," or resurgence, after spraying, in numbers greater than before. Thus the chemical war is never won, and all life is caught in its violent crossfire.

Along with the possibility of the extinction of mankind by nuclear war, the central problem of our age has therefore become the contamination of man's total environment with such substances of incredible potential for harm—substances that accumulate in the tissues of plants and animals and even penetrate the germ cells to shatter or alter the very material of heredity upon which the shape of the future depends.

Some would-be architects of our future look toward a time when it will be possible to alter the human germ plasm by design. But we may easily be doing so now by inadvertence, for many chemicals, like radiation, bring about gene mutations. It is ironic to think that man might determine his own future by something so seemingly trivial as the choice of an insect spray.

All this has been risked—for what? Future historians may well be amazed by our distorted sense of proportion. How could intelligent beings seek to control a few unwanted species by a method that contaminated the entire environment and brought the threat of disease and death even to their own kind? Yet this is precisely what we have done. We have done it, moreover, for reasons that collapse the moment we examine them. We are told that the enormous and expanding use of pesticides is necessary to maintain farm production. Yet is our real problem not one of *overproduction?* Our farms, despite measures to remove acreages from production and to pay farmers *not* to produce, have yielded such a staggering excess of crops that the American taxpayer in 1962 is paying out more than one billion dollars a year as the total carrying cost of the surplus-food storage program. And is the situation helped when one branch of the Agriculture Department tries to reduce production while another states, as it did in 1958, "It is believed generally that reduction of crop acreages under provisions of the Soil Bank will stimulate interest in use of chemicals to obtain maximum production on the land retained in crops."

All this is not to say there is no insect problem and no need of control. I am saying, rather, that control must be geared to realities, not to mythical situations, and that the methods employed must be such that they do not destroy us along with the insects.

The problem whose attempted solution has brought such a train of disaster in its wake is an accompaniment of our modern way of life. Long before the age of man, insects inhabited the earth—a group of extraordinarily varied and adaptable beings. Over the course of time since man's advent, a small percentage of the more than half a million species of insects have come into conflict with human welfare in two principal ways: as competitors for the food supply and as carriers of human disease.

Disease-carrying insects become important where human beings are crowded together, especially under conditions where sanitation is poor, as in time of natural disaster or war or in situations of extreme poverty and deprivation. Then control of some sort becomes necessary. It is a sobering fact, however . . . that the method of massive chemical control has had only limited success, and also threatens to worsen the very conditions it is intended to curb.

Under primitive agricultural conditions the farmer had few insect problems. These arose with the intensification of agriculture—the devotion of immense acreages to a single crop. Such a system set the stage for explosive increases in specific insect populations. Single-crop farming does not take advantage of the principles by which nature works; it is agriculture as an engineer might conceive it to be. Nature has introduced great variety into the landscape, but man has displayed a passion for simplifying it. Thus he undoes the built-in checks and balances by which nature holds the species within bounds. One important natural check is a limit on the amount of suitable habitat for each species. Obviously then, an insect that lives on wheat can build up its population to much higher levels on a farm devoted to wheat than on one in which wheat is intermingled with other crops to which the insect is not adapted.

The same thing happens in other situations. A generation or more ago, the towns of large areas of the United States lined their streets with the noble elm tree. Now the beauty they hopefully created is threatened with complete destruction as disease sweeps through the elms, carried by a beetle that would have only limited chance to build up large populations and to spread from tree to tree if the elms were only occasional trees in a richly diversified planting.

Another factor in the modern insect problem is one that must be viewed against a background of geologic and human history: the spreading of thousands of different kinds of organisms from their native homes to invade new territories. This worldwide migration has been studied and graphically described by the British ecologist Charles Elton in his recent book *The Ecology of Invasions*. During the Cretaceous Period, some hundred million years ago, flooding seas cut many land bridges between continents and living things found themselves confined in what Elton calls "colossal separate nature reserves." There, isolated from others of their kind, they developed many new species. When some of the land masses were joined again, about fifteen million years ago, these species began to move out into new territories—a movement that is not only still in progress but is now receiving considerable assistance from man.

The importation of plants is the primary agent in the modern spread of species, for animals have almost invariably gone along with the plants, quarantine being a comparatively recent and not completely effective innovation. The United States Office of Plant Introduction alone has introduced almost 200,000 species and varieties of plants from all over the world. Nearly half of the 180 or so major insect enemies of plants in the United States are accidental imports from abroad, and most of them have come as hitchhikers on plants.

In new territory, out of reach of the restraining hand of the natural enemies that kept down its numbers in its native land, an invading plant or animal is able to become enormously abundant. Thus it is no accident that our most troublesome insects are introduced species.

These invasions, both the naturally occurring and those dependent on human assistance, are likely to continue indefinitely. Quarantine and massive chemical campaigns are only extremely expensive ways of buying time. We are faced, according to Dr. Elton, "with a life-and-death need not just to find new technological means of suppressing this plant or that animal"; instead we need the basic knowledge of animal populations and their relations to their surroundings that will "promote an even balance and damp down the explosive power of outbreaks and new invasions."

Much of the necessary knowledge is now available but we do not use it. We train ecologists in our universities and even employ them in our governmental agencies but we seldom take their advice. We allow the chemical death rain to fall as though there were no alternative, whereas in fact there are many, and our ingenuity could soon discover many more if given opportunity.

Have we fallen into a mesmerized state that makes us accept as inevitable that which is inferior or detrimental, as though having lost the will or the vision to demand that which is good? Such thinking, in the words of the ecologist Paul Shepard, "idealizes life with only its head out of water, inches above the limits of toleration of the corruption of its own environment. . . . Why should we tolerate a diet of weak poisons, a home in insipid surroundings, a circle of acquaintances who are not quite our enemies, the noise of motors with just enough relief to prevent insanity? Who would want to live in a world which is just not quite fatal?"

Yet such a world is pressed upon us. The crusade to create a chemically sterile, insect free world seems to have engendered a fanatic zeal on the part of many specialists and most of the so-called control agencies. On every hand there is evidence that those engaged in spraying operations exercise a ruthless power. "The regulatory entomologists . . . function as prosecutor, judge and jury, tax assessor and collector and sheriff to enforce their own orders," said Connecticut entomologist Neely Turner. The most flagrant abuses go unchecked in both state and federal agencies.

It is not my contention that chemical insecticides must never be used. I do contend that we have put poisonous and biologically potent chemicals indiscriminately into the hands of persons largely or wholly ignorant of their potentials for harm. We have subjected enormous numbers of people to contact with these poisons, without their consent and often without their knowledge. If the Bill of Rights contains no guarantee that a citizen shall be secure against lethal poisons distributed either by private individuals or by public officials, it is surely only because our forefathers, despite their considerable wisdom and foresight, could conceive of no such problem.

I contend, furthermore, that we have allowed these chemicals to be used with little or no advance investigation of their effect on soil, water, wildlife, and man himself. Future generations are unlikely to condone our lack of prudent concern for the integrity of the natural world that supports all life.

There is still very limited awareness of the nature of the threat. This is an era of specialists, each of whom sees his own problem and is unaware of or intolerant of the larger frame into which it fits. It is also an era dominated by industry, in which the right to make a dollar at whatever cost is seldom challenged. When the public protests, confronted with some obvious evidence of damaging results of pesticide applications, it is fed little tranquilizing pills of half truth. We urgently need an end to these false assurances, to the sugar coating of unpalatable facts. It is the public that is being asked to assume the risks that the insect controllers calculate. The public must decide whether it wishes to continue on the present road, and it can do so only when in full possession of the facts. In the words of Jean Rostand, "The obligation to endure gives us the right to know."

CRITICAL THINKING QUESTIONS

1. What is Carson's claim?

2. What types of evidence does the author provide to support her claim? Does she rely more heavily on *logos* or *pathos* appeal?

3. This essay is from her 1962 book, *Silent Spring*. How does the author build *ethos* appeal with her audience?

RESEARCH/WRITING TOPIC

Reread this essay's closing paragraph. From your perspective as a reader today, consider the implications of Carson's warnings and call to action— "The public must decide. . . ." Choose a specific issue area to research, for example, genetically modified foods. Are we demanding and are we receiving the facts we need to make choices about the short- and long-term health and environmental impacts of genetically modified foods?

Annie Dillard

from "The Present" *in* Pilgrim at Tinker Creek

III

Live water heals memories. I look up the creek and here it comes, the future, being borne aloft as on a winding succession of laden trays. You may wake and look from the window and breathe the real air, and say, with satisfaction or with longing, "This is it." But if you look up the creek, if you look up the creek in any weather, your spirit fills, and you are saying, with an exulting rise of the lungs, "Here it comes!"

Here it comes. In the far distance I can see the concrete bridge where the road crosses the creek. Under that bridge and beyond it the water is flat and silent, blued by distance and stilled by depth. It is so much sky, a fallen shred caught in the cleft of banks. But it pours. The channel here is straight as an arrow; grace itself is an archer. Between the dangling wands of bankside willows, beneath the overarching limbs of tulip, walnut, and Osage orange, I see the creek pour down. It spills toward me streaming over a series of sandstone tiers, down, and down, and down. I feel as though I stand at the foot of an infinitely high staircase, down which some exuberant spirit is flinging tennis ball after tennis ball, eternally, and the one thing I want in the world is a tennis ball.

There must be something wrong with a creekside person who, all things being equal, chooses to face downstream. It's like fouling your own nest. For this and a leather couch they pay fifty dollars an hour? Tinker Creek doesn't back up, pushed up its own craw, from the Roanoke River; it flows down, easing, from the northern, unseen side of Tinker Mountain. "Gravity, to Copernicus, is the nostalgia of things to become spheres." This is a curious, tugged version of the great chain of being. Ease is the way of perfection, letting fall. But, as in the classic version of the great chain, the pure trickle that leaks from the unfathomable heart of Tinker Mountain, this Tinker Creek, widens, taking shape and cleaving banks, weighted with the live and intricate impurities of time, as it descends to me, to where I happen to find myself, in this intermediate spot, halfway between here and there. Look upstream. Just simply turn around; have you no will? The future is a spirit, or a distillation of *the* spirit, heading my way. It is north. The future is the light on the water; it comes, mediated, only on the skin of the real and present creek. My eyes can stand no brighter light than this; nor can they see without it, if only the undersides of leaves.

Trees are tough. They last, taproot and bark, and we soften at their feet. "For we are strangers before thee, and sojourners, as were all our fathers: our days on the earth are as a shadow, and there is none abiding." We can't take the lightning, the scourge of high places and rare airs. But we can take the light, the reflected light that shines up the valleys on creeks. Trees stir memories; live waters heal them. The creek is the mediator, benevolent, impartial, subsuming my shabbiest evils and dissolving them, transforming them into live moles, and shiners, and sycamore leaves. It is a place even my faithlessness hasn't offended; it still flashes for me, now and tomorrow, that intricate, innocent face. It waters an undeserving world, saturating cells with lodes of light. I stand by the creek over rock under trees.

It is sheer coincidence that my hunk of the creek is strewn with boulders. I never merited this grace, that when I face upstream I scent the virgin breath of mountains, I feel a spray of mist on my cheeks and lips, I hear a ceaseless splash and susurrus, a sound of water not merely poured smoothly down air to fill a steady pool, but tumbling live about, over, under, around, between, through an intricate speckling of rock. It is sheer coincidence that upstream from me the creek's bed is ridged in horizontal croppings of sandstone. I never merited this grace, that when I face upstream I see the light on the water careening towards me, inevitably, freely, down a graded series of terraces like the balanced winged platforms on an infinite, inexhaustible font. "Ho, if you are thirsty, come down to the water; ho, if you are hungry, come and sit and eat." This is the present, at last. I can pat the puppy any time I want. This is the now, this flickering, broken light, this air that the wind of the future presses down my throat, pumping me buoyant and giddy with praise.

My God, I look at the creek. It is the answer to Merton's prayer, "Give us time!" It never stops. If I seek the senses and skill of children, the information of a thousand books, the innocence of puppies, even the insights of my own city past, I do so only, solely, and entirely that I might look well at the creek. You don't run down the present, pursue it with baited hooks and nets. You wait for it, empty-handed, and you are filled. You'll have fish left over. The creek is the one great giver. It is, by definition, Christmas, the incarnation. This old rock planet gets the present for a present on its birthday every day.

Here is the word from a subatomic physicist: "Everything that has already happened is particles, everything in the future is waves." Let me twist his meaning. Here it comes. The particles are broken; the waves are translucent, laving, roiling with beauty like sharks. The present is the wave that explodes over my head, flinging the air with particles at the height of its breathless unroll; it is the live water and light that bears from undisclosed sources the freshest news, renewed and renewing, world without end.

WRITING TOPIC

We know that water is vital to life, and we generally acknowledge its value as an energy source and appreciate its recreational values. However, Dillard's excerpt from *Pilgrim at Tinker Creek* and Roethke's poem, "Meditation at Oyster River," celebrate an intangible and less obvious value of water—moving water as a source of reflection and for rejuvenation. Would our quality of life be diminished without places where we can observe freely moving water? Must these places be private or, at least, conducive to solitary visitations? Using Roethke's poem, Dillard's prose selection, and your own experiences and ideas, write an essay that examines and assesses the intangible value of water.

Ralph Waldo Emerson

from Nature

To go into solitude, a man needs to retire as much from his chamber as from society. I am not solitary whilst I read and write, though nobody is with me. But if a man would be alone, let him look at the stars. The rays that come from those heavenly worlds, will separate between him and vulgar things. One might think the atmosphere was made transparent with this design, to give man, in the heavenly bodies, the perpetual presence of the sublime. Seen in the streets of cities, how great they are! If the stars should appear one night in a thousand years, how would men believe and adore; and preserve for many generations the remembrance of the city of God which had been shown! But every night come out these preachers of beauty, and light the universe with their admonishing smile.

The stars awaken a certain reverence, because though always present, they are always inaccessible; but all natural objects make a kindred impression, when the mind is open to their influence. Nature never wears a mean appearance. Neither does the wisest man extort all her secret, and lose his curiosity by finding out all her perfection. Nature never became a toy to a wise spirit. The flowers, the animals, the mountains, reflected all the wisdom of his best hour, as much as they had delighted the simplicity of his childhood.

When we speak of nature in this manner, we have a distinct but most poetical sense in the mind. We mean the integrity of impression made by manifold natural objects. It is this which distinguishes the stick of timber of the woodcutter, from the tree of the poet. The charming landscape which I saw this morning, is indubitably made up of some twenty or thirty farms. Miller owns this field, Locke that, and Manning the woodland beyond. But none of them owns the landscape. There is a property in the horizon which no man has but he whose eye can integrate all the parts, that is, the poet. This is the best part of these men's farms, yet to this their land-deeds give them no title.

To speak truly, few adult persons can see nature. Most persons do not see the sun. At least they have a very superficial seeing. The sun illuminates only the eye of the man, but shines into the eye and the heart of the child. The lover of nature is he whose inward and outward senses are still truly adjusted to each other; who has retained the spirit of infancy even into the era of manhood. His intercourse with heaven and earth, becomes part of his daily food. In the presence of nature, a wild delight runs through the man, in spite of real sorrows. Nature says,—he is my creature, and maugre all his impertinent griefs, he shall be glad with me. Not the sun or the summer alone, but every hour and season yields its tribute of delight; for every hour and change corresponds to and authorizes a different state of the mind, from breathless noon to grimmest midnight. Nature is a setting that fits equally well a comic or a mourning piece. In good health, the air is a cordial of incredible virtue. Crossing a bare common, in snow puddles, at twilight, under a clouded sky, without unaffecting, the landscape which they compose, is round and symmetrical. And as the eye is the best composer, so light is the first of painters. There is no object so foul that intense light will not make beautiful. And the stimulus it affords to the sense, and a sort of infinitude which it hath, like space and time, make all matter gay. Even the corpse hath its own beauty. But beside this general grace diffused over nature, almost all the individual forms are agreeable to the eye, as is proved by our endless imitations of some of them, as the acorn, the grape, the pine-cone, the wheat-ear, the egg, the wings and forms of most birds, the lion's claw, the serpent, the butterfly, sea-shells, flames, clouds, buds, leaves, and the forms of many trees, as the palm.

For better consideration, we may distribute the aspects of Beauty in a threefold manner.

1. First, the simple perception of natural forms is a delight. The influence of the forms and actions in nature, is so needful to man, that, in its lowest functions, it seems to lie on the confines of commodity and beauty. To the body and mind which have been cramped by noxious work or company, nature is medicinal and restores their tone. The tradesman, the attorney comes out of the din and craft of the street, and sees the sky and the woods, and is a man again. In their eternal calm, he finds himself. The health of the eye seems to demand a horizon. We are never tired, so long as we can see far enough.

But in other hours, Nature satisfies the soul purely by its loveliness, and without any mixture of corporeal benefit. I have seen the spectacle of morning from the hill-top over against my house, from day-break to sun-rise, with emotions which an angel might share. The long slender bars of cloud float like fishes in the sea of crimson light. From the earth, as a shore, I look out into that silent sea. I seem to partake its rapid transformations: the active enchantment reaches my dust, and I dilate and conspire with the morning wind. How does Nature deify us with a few and cheap elements! Give me health and a day, and I will make the pomp of emperors ridiculous. The dawn is my Assyria; the sun-set and moon-rise my Paphos, and unimaginable realms of faerie, broad noon shall be my England of the senses and the understanding; the night shall be my Germany of mystic philosophy and dreams.

Not less excellent, except for our less susceptibility in the afternoon, was the charm, last evening, of a January sunset. The western clouds divided and subdivided themselves into pink flakes modulated with tints of unspeakable softness; and the air had so much life and sweetness, that it was a pain to come within doors. What was it that nature would say? Was there no meaning in the live repose of the valley behind the mill, and which Homer or Shakespeare could not re-form for me in words? The leafless trees become spires of flame in the sunset, with the blue east for their background, and the stars of the dead calices of flowers, and every withered stem and stubble rimed with frost, contribute something to the mute music.

The inhabitants of cities suppose that the country landscape is pleasant only half the year. I please myself with observing the graces of the winter scenery, and believe that we are as much touched by it as by the genial influences of summer. To the attentive eye, each moment of the year has its own beauty, and in the same field, it beholds, every hour, a picture which was never seen before, and which shall never be seen again. The heavens change every moment, and reflect their glory or gloom on the plains beneath. The state of the crop in the surrounding farms alters the expression of the earth from week to week. The succession of native plants in the pastures and roadsides, which make the silent clock by which time tells the summer hours, will make even the divisions of the day sensible to a keen observer. The tribes of birds and insects, like the plants punctual to their time, follow each other, and the year has room for all. By water-courses, the variety is greater. In July, the blue pontederia or pickerel-weed blooms in large beds in the shallow parts of our pleasant river, and swarms with yellow butterflies in continual motion. Art cannot rival this pomp of purple and gold. Indeed the river is a perpetual gala, and boasts each month a new ornament.

But this beauty of Nature which is seen and felt as beauty, is the least part. The shows of day, the dewy morning, the rainbow, mountains, orchards in blossom, stars, moonlight, shadows in still water, and the like, if too eagerly hunted, become shows merely, and mock us with their unreality. Go out of the house to see the moon, and 't is mere tinsel; it will not please as when its light shines upon your necessary journey. The beauty that shimmers in the yellow afternoons of October, who ever could clutch it? Go forth to find it, and it is gone: 't is only a mirage as you look from the windows of the diligence.

2. The presence of a higher, namely, of the spiritual element is essential to its perfection. The high and divine beauty which can be loved without effeminacy, is that which is found in combination with the human will, and never separate. Beauty is the mark God sets upon virtue. Every natural action is graceful. Every heroic act is also decent, and causes the place and the bystanders to shine. We are taught by great actions that the universe is the property of every individual in it. Every rational creature has all nature for his dowry and estate. It is his, if he will. He may divest himself of it; he may creep into a corner, and abdicate his kingdom, as most men do, but he is entitled to the world by his constitution. In proportion to the energy of his thought and will, he takes up the world into himself. "All those things for which men plough, build, or sail, obey virtue;" said an ancient historian. "The winds and waves," said Gibbon, "are always on the side of the ablest navigators." So are the sun and moon and all the stars of heaven. When a noble act is done,—perchance in a scene of great natural beauty; when Leonidas and his three hundred martyrs consume one day in dying, and the sun and moon come each and look at them once in the steep defile of Thermopylæ; when Arnold Winkelried, in the high Alps, under the shadow of the avalanche, gathers in his side a sheaf of Austrian spears to break the line for his comrades; are not these

heroes entitled to add the beauty of the scene to the beauty of the deed? When the bark of Columbus nears the shore of America;—before it, the beach lined with savages, fleeing out of all their huts of cane; the sea behind; and the purple mountains of the Indian Archipelago around, can we separate the man from the living picture? Does not the New World clothe his form with her palm-groves and savannahs as fit drapery? Ever does natural beauty steal in like air, and envelope great actions. When Sir Harry Vane was dragged up the Tower-hill, sitting on a sled, to suffer death, as the champion of the English laws, one of the multitude cried out to him, "You never sate on so glorious a seat." Charles II., to intimidate the citizens of London, caused the patriot Lord Russel to be drawn in an open coach, through the principal streets of the city, on his way to the scaffold. "But," to use the simple narrative of his biographer, "the multitude imagined they saw liberty and virtue sitting by his side." In private places, among sordid objects, an act of truth or heroism seems at once to draw to itself the sky as its temple, the sun as its candle. Nature stretcheth out her arms to embrace man, only let his thoughts be of equal greatness. Willingly does she follow his steps with the rose and the violet, and bend her lines of grandeur and grace to the decoration of her darling child. Only let his thoughts be of equal scope, and the frame will suit the picture. A virtuous man, is in unison with her works, and makes the central figure of the visible sphere. Homer, Pindar, Socrates, Phocion, associate themselves fitly in our memory with the whole geography and climate of Greece. The visible heavens and earth sympathize with Jesus. And in common life, whosoever has seen a person of powerful character and happy genius, will have remarked how easily he took all things along with him,—the persons, the opinions, and the day, and nature became ancillary to a man.

3. There is still another aspect under which the beauty of the world may be viewed, namely, as it becomes an object of the intellect. Beside the relation of things to virtue, they have a relation to thought. The intellect searches out the absolute order of things as they stand in the mind of God, and without the colors of affection. The intellectual and the active powers seem to succeed each other in man, and the exclusive activity of the one, generates the exclusive activity of the other. There is something unfriendly in each to the other, but they are like the alternate periods of feeding and working in animals; each prepares and certainly will be followed by the other. Therefore does beauty, which, in relation to actions, as we have seen comes unsought, and comes because it is unsought, remain for the apprehension and pursuit of the intellect; and then again, in its turn, of the active power. Nothing divine dies. All good is eternally reproductive. The beauty of nature reforms itself in the mind, and not for barren contemplation, but for new creation.

All men are in some degree impressed by the face of the world. Some men even to delight. This love of beauty is Taste. Others have the same love in such excess, that, not content with admiring, they seek to embody it in new forms. The creation of beauty is Art.

The production of a work of art throws a light upon the mystery of humanity. A work of art is an abstract or epitome of the world. It is the result or expression of nature, in miniature. For although the works of nature are innumerable and all different, the result or the expression of them all is similar and single. Nature is a sea of forms radically alike and even unique. A leaf, a sunbeam, a landscape, the ocean, make an analogous impression on the mind. What is common to them all,—that perfectness and harmony, is beauty. Therefore the standard of beauty, is the entire circuit of natural forms,—the totality of nature; which the Italians expressed by defining beauty "il piu nell' uno." Nothing is quite beautiful alone: nothing but is beautiful in the whole. A single object is only so far beautiful as it suggests this universal grace. The poet, the painter, the sculptor, the musician, the architect seek each to concentrate this radiance of the world on one point, and each in his several work to satisfy the love of beauty which stimulates him to produce. Thus is Art, a nature passed through the alembic of man. Thus in art, does nature work through the will of a man filled with the beauty of her first works.

The world thus exists to the soul to satisfy the desire of beauty. Extend this element to the uttermost, and I call it an ultimate end. No reason can be asked or given why the soul seeks beauty. Beauty, in its largest and profoundest sense, is one expression for the universe. God is the all-fair. Truth, and goodness, and beauty, are but different faces of the same All. But beauty in nature is not ultimate. It is the herald of inward and eternal beauty, and is not alone a solid and satisfactory good. It must therefore stand as a part and not as yet the last or highest expression of the final cause of Nature.

CRITICAL THINKING QUESTION

Does Emerson's prose have stronger *logos* or *pathos* appeal? Can you find examples of each?

WRITING TOPIC

Copy five or six passages from the *Nature* excerpt that seemed important or interesting to you. Select two or three and freewrite about each for five or ten minutes; record your personal reflection and reaction, questions or confusions. Be prepared to share your writings with a small group in class.

Aldous Huxley

Time and the Machine

from *The Olive Tree*

Time, as we know it, is a very recent invention. The modern time-sense is hardly older than the United States. It is a by-product of industrialism—a sort of psychological analogue of synthetic perfumes and aniline dyes.

Time is our tyrant. We are chronically aware of the moving minute hand, even of the moving second hand. We have to be. There are trains to be caught, clocks to be punched, tasks to be done in specified periods, records to be broken by fractions of a second, machines that set the pace and have to be kept up with. Our consciousness of the smallest units of time is now acute. To us, for example, the moment 8:17 A.M. means something—something very important, if it happens to be the starting time of our daily train. To our ancestors, such an odd eccentric instant was without significance—did not even exist. In inventing the locomotive, Watt and Stevenson were part inventors of time.

Another time-emphasizing entity is the factory and its dependent, the office. Factories exist for the purpose of getting certain quantities of goods made in a certain time. The old artisan worked as it suited him with the result that consumers generally had to wait for the goods they had ordered from him. The factory is a device for making workmen hurry. The machine revolves so often each minute; so many movements have to be made, so many pieces produced each hour. Result: the factory worker (and the same is true, *mutatis mutandis,* of the office worker) is compelled to know time in its smallest fractions. In the hand-work age there was no such compulsion to be aware of minutes and seconds.

Our awareness of time has reached such a pitch of intensity that we suffer acutely whenever our travels take us into some corner of the world where people are not interested in minutes and seconds. The unpunctuality of the Orient, for example, is appalling to those who come freshly from a land of fixed meal-times and regular train services. For a modern American or Englishman, waiting is a psychological torture. An Indian accepts the blank hours with resignation, even with satisfaction. He has not lost the fine art of doing nothing. Our notion of time as a collection of minutes, each of which must be filled with some business or amusement, is wholly alien to the Oriental, just as it was wholly alien to the Greek. For the man who lives in a pre-industrial world, time moves at a slow and easy pace; he does not care about each minute, for the good reason that he has not been made conscious of the existence of minutes.

This brings us to a seeming paradox. Acutely aware of the smallest constituent particles of time—of time, as measured by clock-work and train arrivals and the revolutions of machines—industrialized man has to a great extent lost the old awareness of time in its larger divisions. The time of which we have knowledge is artificial, machine-made time. Of natural, cosmic time, as it is measured out by sun and moon, we are for the most part almost wholly unconscious. Pre-industrial people know time in its daily, monthly and seasonal rhythms. They are aware of sunrise, noon and sunset; of the full moon and the new; of equinox and solstice; of spring and summer, autumn and winter. All the old religions, including Catholic Christianity, have insisted on this daily and seasonal rhythm. Pre-industrial man, was never allowed to forget the majestic movement of cosmic time.

Industrialism and urbanism have changed all this. One can live and work in a town without being aware of the daily march of the sun across the sky; without ever seeing the moon and stars. Broadway and Piccadilly are our Milky Way; our constellations are outlined in neon tubes. Even changes of season affect the townsman very little. He is the inhabitant of an artificial universe that is, to a great extent, walled off from the world of nature. Outside the walls, time is cosmic and moves with the motion of sun and stars. Within, it is an affair of revolving wheels and is measured in seconds and minutes—at its longest, in eight-hour days and six-day weeks. We have a new consciousness; but it has been purchased at the expense of the old consciousness.

CRITICAL THINKING QUESTION

Huxley explicitly blames industrialism and urbanism for our loss of awareness of cosmic time and our separation from the world of nature. Is Huxley's indictment valid? For debate purposes, be prepared to defend or to refute Huxley's claim.

WRITING TOPIC

Today's computer technology has given us digital time and virtual reality. Has this technology created yet a "new consciousness"? How would you explain this twenty-first-century consciousness? Do you agree or disagree that (like Huxley's townsman) we are "inhabitant[s] of an artificial universe that is, to a great extent, walled off from the world of nature"?

Aldo Leopold

Thinking Like a Mountain

A deep chesty bawl echoes from rimrock to rimrock, rolls down the mountain, and fades into the far blackness of the night. It is an outburst of wild defiant sorrow, and of contempt for all the adversities of the world.

Every living thing (and perhaps many a dead one as well) pays heed to that call. To the deer it is a reminder of the way of all flesh, to the pine a forecast of midnight scuffles and of blood upon the snow, to the coyote a promise of gleanings to come, to the cowman a threat of red ink at the bank, to the hunter a challenge of fang against bullet. Yet behind these obvious and immediate hopes and fears there lies a deeper meaning, known only to the mountain itself. Only the mountain has lived long enough to listen objectively to the howl of a wolf.

Those unable to decipher the hidden meaning know nevertheless that it is there, for it is felt in all wolf country, and distinguishes that country from all other land. It tingles in the spine of all who hear wolves by night, or who scan their tracks by day. Even without sight or sound of wolf, it is implicit in a hundred small events: the midnight whinny of a pack horse, the rattle of rolling rocks, the bound of a flee-ing deer, the way shadows lie under the spruces. Only the ineducable tyro can fail to sense the presence or absence of wolves, or the fact that mountains have a secret opinion about them.

My own conviction on this score dates from the day I saw a wolf die. We were eating lunch on a high rimrock, at the foot of which a turbulent river elbowed its way. We saw what we thought was a doe fording the torrent, her breast awash in white water. When she climbed the bank toward us and shook out her tail, we real-ized our error: it was a wolf. A half-dozen others, evidently grown pups, sprang from the willows and all joined in a welcoming mêlée of wagging tails and playful maulings. What was literally a pile of wolves writhed and tumbled in the center of an open flat at the foot of our rimrock.

In those days we had never heard of passing up a chance to kill a wolf. In a second we were pumping lead into the pack, but with more excitement than accu-racy: how to aim a steep downhill shot is always confusing. When our rifles were empty, the old wolf was down, and a pup was dragging a leg into impassable slide-rocks.

We reached the old wolf in time to watch a fierce green fire dying in her eyes. I realized then, and have known ever since, that there was something new to me in those eyes—something known only to her and to the mountain. I was young then, and full of trigger-itch; I thought that because fewer wolves meant more deer, that no wolves would mean hunters' paradise. But after seeing the green fire die, I sensed that neither the wolf nor the mountain agreed with such a view.

*   *   *

Since then I have lived to see state after state extirpate its wolves. I have watched the face of many a newly wolfless mountain, and seen the south-facing slopes wrinkle with a maze of new deer trails. I have seen every edible bush and seedling browsed, first to anaemic desuetude, and then to death. I have seen every edible tree defoliated to the height of a saddlehorn. Such a mountain looks as if someone had given God a new pruning shears, and forbidden Him all other exercise. In the end the starved bones of the hoped-for deer herd, dead of its own toomuch, bleach with the bones of the dead sage, or molder under the high-lined junipers.

I now suspect that just as a deer herd lives in mortal fear of its wolves, so does a mountain live in mortal fear of its deer. And perhaps with better cause, for while a buck pulled down by wolves can be replaced in two or three years, a range pulled down by too many deer may fail of replacement in as many decades.

So also with cows. The cowman who cleans his range of wolves does not realize that he is taking over the wolf's job of trimming the herd to fit the range. He has not learned to think like a mountain. Hence we have dust-bowls, and rivers washing the future into the sea.

*   *   *

We all strive for safety, prosperity, comfort, long life, and dullness. The deer strives with his supple legs, the cowman with trap and poison, the statesman with pen, the most of us with machines, votes, and dollars, but it all comes to the same thing: peace in our time. A measure of success in this is all well enough, and perhaps is a requisite to objective thinking, but too much safety seems to yield only danger in the long run. Perhaps this is behind Thoreau's dictum: In wildness is the salvation of the world. Perhaps this is the hidden meaning in the howl of the wolf, long known among mountains, but seldom perceived among men.

CRITICAL THINKING QUESTION

Use the three rhetorical appeals—*ethos, logos, pathos*—to analyze and evaluate Leopold's argument for preserving wolves.

WRITING TOPIC

In his closing paragraph, Leopold warns that "too much safety seems to yield only danger in the long run," a statement that would seem to be contradictory and counterintuitive. What does his warning mean to you? Do you agree or disagree?

Joyce Carol Oates

Against Nature

We soon get through with Nature. She excites an expectation which she cannot satisfy.

—Thoreau, *Journal*, 1854

Sir, if a man has experienced the inexpressible, he is under no obligation to attempt to express it.

—Samuel Johnson

The writer's resistance to Nature.

It has no sense of humor: in its beauty, as in its ugliness, or its neutrality, there is no laughter.

It lacks a moral purpose.

It lacks a satiric dimension, registers no irony.

Its pleasures lack resonance, being accidental; its horrors, even when premeditated, are equally perfunctory, "red in tooth and claw," et cetera.

It lacks a symbolic subtext—excepting that provided by man.

It has no (verbal) language.

It has no interest in ours.

It inspires a painfully limited set of responses in "nature writers"—REVERENCE, AWE, PIETY, MYSTICAL ONENESS.

It eludes us even as it prepares to swallow us up, books and all.

I was lying on my back in the dirt gravel of the towpath beside the Delaware and Raritan Canal, Titusville, New Jersey, staring up at the sky and trying, with no success, to overcome a sudden attack of tachycardia that had come upon me out of nowhere—such attacks are always "out of nowhere," that's their charm—and all around me Nature thrummed with life, the air smelling of moisture and sunlight, the canal reflecting the sky, red-winged blackbirds testing their spring calls; the usual. I'd become the jar in Tennessee, a fictitious center, or parenthesis, aware beyond my erratic heartbeat of the numberless heartbeats of the earth, its pulsing, pumping life, sheer life, incalculable. Struck down in the midst of motion—I'd been jogging a minute before—I was "out of time" like a fallen, stunned boxer, privileged (in an abstract manner of speaking) to be an involuntary witness to the random, wayward, nameless motion on all sides of me.

Paroxysmal tachycardia can be fatal, but rarely; if the heartbeat accelerates to 250–270 beats a minute you're in trouble, but the average attack is about 100–150 beats and mine seemed about average; the trick now was to prevent it from getting worse. Brainy people try brainy strategies, such as thinking calming thoughts, pseudo-mystic thoughts, *If I die now it's a good death,* that sort of thing, *if I die this is a good place and good time;* the idea is to deceive the frenzied heartbeat that, really, you don't care: you hadn't any other plans for the afternoon. The important thing with tachycardia is to prevent panic! you must prevent panic! otherwise you'll have to be taken by ambulance to the closest emergency room, which is not so very nice a way to spend the afternoon, really. So I contemplated the blue sky overhead. The earth beneath my head. Nature surrounding me on all sides; I couldn't quite see it but I could hear it, smell it, sense it, there is something *there,* no mistake about it. Completely oblivious to the predicament of the individual but that's only "natural," after all, one hardly expects otherwise.

When you discover yourself lying on the ground, limp and unresisting, head in the dirt, and, let's face it, helpless, the earth seems to shift forward as a presence; hard, emphatic, not mere surface but a genuine force—there is no other word for it but *presence.* To keep in motion is to keep in time, and to be stopped, stilled, is to be abruptly out of time, in another time dimension perhaps, an alien one, where human language has no resonance. Nothing to be said about it expresses it, nothing touches it, it's an absolute against which nothing human can be measured. . . . Moving through space and time by way of your own volition you inhabit an interior consciousness, a hallucinatory consciousness, it might be said, so long as breath, heartbeat, the body's autonomy hold; when motion is stopped you are jarred out of it. The interior is invaded by the exterior. The outside wants to come in, and only the self's fragile membrane prevents it.

The fly buzzing at Emily's death.

Still, the earth *is* your place. A tidy grave site measured to your size. Or, from another angle of vision, one vast democratic grave.

Let's contemplate the sky. Forget the crazy hammering heartbeat, don't listen to it, don't start counting, remember that there is a clever way of breathing that conserves oxygen as if you're lying below the surface of a body of water breathing through a very thin straw but you *can* breathe through it if you're careful, if you don't panic; one breath and then another and then another, isn't that the story of all lives? careers? Just a matter of breathing. Of course it is. But contemplate the sky, it's there to be contemplated. A mild shock to see it so blank, blue, a thin airy ghostly blue, no clouds to disguise its emptiness. You are beginning to feel not only weightless but near-bodiless, lying on the earth like a scrap of paper about to be blown off. Two dimensions and you'd imagined you were three! And there's the sky rolling away forever, into infinity—if "infinity" can be "rolled into"—and the forlorn truth is, that's where you're going too. And the lovely blue isn't even blue, is it? isn't even there, is it? a mere optical illusion, isn't it? no matter what art has urged you to believe.

Early Nature memories. Which it's best not to suppress.

. . . Wading, as a small child, in Tonawanda Creek near our house, and afterward trying to tear off, in a frenzy of terror and revulsion, the sticky fat black bloodsuckers that had attached themselves to my feet, particularly between my toes.

. . . Coming upon a friend's dog in a drainage ditch, dead for several days, evidently the poor creature had been shot by a hunter and left to die, bleeding to death, and we're stupefied with grief and horror but can't resist sliding down to where he's lying on his belly, and we can't resist squatting over him, turning the body over.

. . . The raccoon, mad with rabies, frothing at the mouth and tearing at his own belly with his teeth, so that his intestines spill out onto the ground . . . a sight I seem to remember though in fact I did not see. I've been told I did not see.

Consequently, my chronic uneasiness with Nature mysticism; Nature adoration; Nature-as-(moral)-instruction-for-mankind. My doubt that one can, with philosophical validity, address "Nature" as a single coherent noun, anything other than a Platonic, hence discredited, is-ness. My resistance to "Nature writing" as a genre, except when it is brilliantly fictionalized in the service of a writer's individual vision—Thoreau's books and *Journal;* of course, but also, less known in this country, the miniaturist prose poems of Colette (*Flowers and Fruit*) and Ponge (*Taking the Side of Things*)—in which case it becomes yet another, and ingenious, form of storytelling. The subject is *there* only by the grace of the author's language.

Nature has no instructions for mankind except that our pool beleaguered humanist-democratic way of life, our fantasies of the individual's high worth, our sense that the weak, no less than the strong, have a right to survive, are absurd. When Edmund of *King Lear* said excitedly, "Nature, be thou my goddess!" he knew whereof he spoke.

In any case, where *is* Nature, one might (skeptically) inquire. Who has looked upon her/its face and survived?

But isn't this all exaggeration, in the spirit of rhetorical contentiousness? Surely Nature is, for you, as for most reasonably intelligent people, a "perennial" source of beauty, comfort, peace, escape from the delirium of civilized life; a respite from the ego's ever-frantic strategies of self-promotion, as a way of ensuring (at least in fantasy) some small measure of immortality? Surely Nature, as it is understood in the usual slapdash way, as human, if not dilettante, *experience* (hiking in a national park, jogging on the beach at dawn, even tending, with the usual comical frustrations, a suburban garden), is wonderfully consoling; a place where, when you go there, it has to take you in?—a palimpsest of sorts you choose to read, layer by layer, always with care, always cautiously, in proportion to your psychological strength?

Nature: as in Thoreau's upbeat Transcendentalist mode ("The indescribable innocence and beneficence of Nature,—such health, such cheer, they afford forever! and such sympathy have they ever with our race, that all Nature would be affected . . . if any man should ever for a just cause grieve"), and not in Thoreau's grim mode ("Nature is hard to be overcome but she must be overcome").

Another way of saying, not *Nature-in-itself* but *Nature-as-experience.*

The former, Nature-in-itself, is, to allude slantwise to Melville, a blankness ten times blank; the latter is what we commonly, or perhaps always, mean, when we speak of Nature as a noun, a single entity—something of *ours.* Most of the time it's just an activity, a sort of hobby, a weekend, a few days, perhaps a few hours, staring out the window at the mind-dazzling autumn foliage of, say, northern Michigan, being rendered speechless—temporarily—at the sight of Mr. Shasta, the Grand Canyon, Ansel Adams's West. Or Nature writ small, contained in the back yard. Nature filtered through our optical nerves, our "senses," our fiercely romantic expectations. Nature that pleases us because it mirrors our souls, or gives the comforting illusion of doing so.

Nature as the self's (flattering) mirror, but not ever, no, never, Nature-in-itself.

Nature is mouths, or maybe a single mouth. Why glamorize it, romanticize it?—well, yes, but we must, we're writers, poets, mystics (of a sort) aren't we, precisely what else are we to do but glamorize and romanticize and generally exaggerate the significance of anything we focus the white heat of our "creativity" upon? And why not Nature, since it's there, common property, mute, can't talk back, allows us the possibility of transcending the human condition for a while, writing prettily of mountain ranges, white-tailed deer, the purple crocuses outside this very window, the thrumming dazzling "life force" we imagine we all support. Why not?

Nature *is* more than a mouth—it's a dazzling variety of mouths. And it pleases the senses, in any case, as the physicists' chill universe of numbers certainly does not.

Oscar Wilde, on our subject:

> Nature is no great mother who has borne us. She is our creation. It is in our brain that she quickens to life. Things are because we see them, and what we see, and how we see it, depends on the Arts that have influenced us. To look at a thing is very different from seeing a thing. . . . At present, people see fogs, not because there are fogs, but because poets and painters have taught them the mysterious loveliness of such effects. There may have been fogs for centuries in London. I dare say there were. But no one saw them. They did not exist until Art had invented them. . . . Yesterday evening Mrs. Arundel insisted on my going to the window and looking at the glorious sky, as she called it. And so I had to look at it. . . . And what was it? It was simply a very second-rate Turner, a Turner of a bad period, with all the painter's worst faults exaggerated and over-emphasized.
>
> *"The Decay of Lying,"* 1889

(If we were to put it to Oscar Wilde that he exaggerates, his reply might well be, "Exaggeration? I don't know the meaning of the word.")

Walden, that most artfully composed of prose fictions, concludes, in the rhapsodic chapter "Spring," with Henry David Thoreau's contemplation of death, decay, and regeneration as it is suggested to him, or to his protagonist, by the spectacle of vultures feeding off carrion. Three is a dead horse close by his cabin, and the stench of its decomposition, in certain winds, is daunting. Yet "the assurance it gave me of the strong appetite and inviolable health of Nature was my compensation for this. I love to see that Nature is so rife with life that myriads can be afforded to be sacrificed and suffered to prey upon one another; that tender organizations can be so serenely squashed out of existence like pulp,—tadpoles which herons gobble up, and tortoises and toads run over in the road; and that sometimes it has rained flesh and blood! . . . The impression made on a wise man is that of universal innocence."

Come off it, Henry David. You've grieved these many years for your elder brother, John, who died a ghastly death of lockjaw; you've never wholly recovered from the experience of watching him die. And you know, or must know, that you're fated too to die young of consumption. . . . But this doctrinaire Transcendentalist passage ends *Walden* on just the right note. It's as impersonal, as coolly detached, as the Oversoul itself: a "wise man" filters his emotions through his brain.

Or through his prose.

Nietzsche: "We all pretend to ourselves that we are more simpleminded than we are: that is how we get a rest from our fellow men."

> Once out of nature I shall never take
> My bodily form from any natural thing,
> But such a form as Grecian goldsmiths make
> Of hammered gold and gold enamelling
> To keep a drowsy Emperor awake;
> Or set upon a golden bough to sing
> To lords and ladies of Byzantium
> Of what is past, or passing, or to come.
>
> William Butler Yeats, "Sailing to Byzantium"

Yet even the golden bird is a "bodily form [taken from a] natural thing." No, it's impossible to escape!

The writer's resistance to Nature.
Wallace Stevens: "In the presence of extraordinary actuality, consciousness takes the place of imagination."

Once, years ago, in 1972 to be precise, when I seemed to have been another person, related to the person I am now as one is related, tangentially, sometimes embarrassingly, to cousins not seen for decades—once, when we were living in London, and I was very sick, I had a mystical vision. That is, I "had" a "mystical vision"—the heart sinks: such pretension—or something resembling one. A fever dream, let's call it. It impressed me enormously and impresses me still, though I've long since lost the capacity to see it with my mind's eye, or even, I suppose, to believe in it. There is a statue of limitations on "mystical visions," as on romantic love.

I was very sick, and I imagined my life as a thread, a thread of breath, or heartbeat, or pulse, or light—yes, it was light, radiant light; I was burning with fever and

I ascended to that plane of serenity that might be mistaken for (or *is,* in fact) Nirvana, where I had a waking dream of uncanny lucidity:

> My body is a tall column of light and heat.
> My body is not "I" but "it."
> My body is not one but many.

My body, which "I" inhabit is inhabited as well by other creatures, unknown to me, imperceptible—the smallest of them mere sparks of light.

My body, which I perceive as substance, is in fact an organization of infinitely complex, overlapping, imbricated structures, radiant light their manifestation, the "body" a tall column of light and blood heat, a temporary agreement among atoms, like a high-rise building with numberless rooms, corridors, corners, elevator shafts, windows. . . . In this fantastical structure the "I" is deluded as to its sovereignty, let alone its autonomy in the (outside) world; the most astonishing secret is that the "I" doesn't exist!—but it behaves as if it does, as if it were one and not many.

In any case, without the "I" the tall column of light and heat would die, and the microscopic life particles would die with it . . . will die with it. The "I," which doesn't exist, is everything.

> But Dr. Johnson is right, the inexpressible need not be expressed.
> And what resistance, finally? There is none.

This morning, an invasion of tiny black ants. One by one they appear, out of nowhere—that's their charm too!—moving single file across the white Parsons table where I am sitting, trying without much success to write a poem. A poem of only three or four lines is what I want, something short, tight, mean; I want it to hurt like a white-hot wire up the nostrils, small and compact and turned in upon itself with the density of a hunk of rock from the planet Jupiter. . . .

But here come the black ants: harbingers, you might say, of spring. One by one by one they appear on the dazzling white table and one by one I kill them with a forefinger, my deft right forefinger, mashing each against the surface of the table and then dropping it into a wastebasket at my side. Idle labor, mesmerizing, effortless, and I'm curious as to how long I can do it—sit here in the brilliant March sunshine killing ants with my right forefinger—how long I, and the ants, can keep it up.

After a while I realize that I can do it a long time. And that I've written my poem.

CRITICAL THINKING QUESTION

Describe the author's tone. How do you assess her *ethos* appeal?

WRITING TOPIC

Using selections in this chapter, defend, refute, and/or qualify Oates's argument against nature and nature writers.

N. Scott Momaday

from The Way to Rainy Mountain

Headwaters

Noon in the intermountain plain:
There is scant telling of the marsh—
A log, hollow and weather-stained,
An insect at the mouth, and moss—
Yet waters rise against the roots,
Stand brimming to the stalks. What moves?
What moves on this archaic force
Was wild and welling at the source.

Introduction

A single knoll rises out of the plain in Oklahoma, north and west of the Wichita Range. For my people, the Kiowas, it is an old landmark, and they gave it the name Rainy Mountain. The hardest weather in the world is there. Winter brings blizzards, hot tornadic winds arise in the spring, and in summer the prairie is an anvil's edge. The grass turns brittle and brown, and it cracks beneath your feet. There are green belts along the rivers and creeks, linear groves of hickory and pecan, willow and witch hazel. At a distance in July or August the steaming foliage seems almost to writhe in fire. Great green and yellow grasshoppers are everywhere in the tall grass, popping up like corn to string the flesh, and tortoises crawl about on the red earth, going nowhere in the plenty of time. Loneliness is an aspect of the land. All things in the plain are isolate; there is no confusion of objects in the eye, but *one* hill or *one* tree or *one* man. To look upon that landscape in the early morning, with the sun at your back, is to lose the sense of proportion. Your imagination comes to life, and this, you think, is where Creation was begun.

I returned to Rainy Mountain in July. My grandmother had died in the spring, and I wanted to be at her grave. She had lived to be very old and at last infirm. Her only living daughter was with her when she died, and I was told that in death her face was that of a child.

I like to think of her as a child. When she was born, the Kiowas were living the last great moment of their history. For more than a hundred years they had controlled the open range from the Smoky Hill River to the Red, from the headwaters of the Canadian to the fork of the Arkansas and Cimarron. In alliance with the Comanches, they had ruled the whole of the southern Plains. War was their sacred business, and they were among the finest horsemen the world has ever known. But

349

warfare for the Kiowas was preeminently a matter of disposition rather than of survival, and they never understood the grim, unrelenting advance of the U.S. Cavalry. When at last, divided and ill-provisioned, they were driven onto the Staked Plains in the cold rains of autumn, they fell into panic. In Palo Duro Canyon they abandoned their crucial stores to pillage and had nothing then but their lives. In order to save themselves, they surrendered to the soldiers at Fort Sill and were imprisoned in the old stone corral that now stands as a military museum. My grandmother was spared the humiliation of those high gray walls by eight or ten years, but she must have known from birth the affliction of defeat, the dark brooding of old warriors.

Her name was *Aho,* and she belonged to the last culture to evolve in North America. Her forebears came down from the high country in western Montana nearly three centuries ago. They were a mountain people, a mysterious tribe of hunters whose language has never been positively classified in any major group. In the late seventeenth century they began a long migration to the south and east. It was a journey toward the dawn, and it led to a golden age. Along the way the Kiowas were befriended by the Crows, who gave them the culture and religion of the Plains. They acquired horses, and their ancient nomadic spirit was suddenly free of the ground. They acquired Tai-me, the sacred Sun Dance doll, from that moment the object and symbol of their worship, and so shared in the divinity of the sun. Not least, they acquired the sense of destiny, therefore courage and pride. When they entered upon the southern Plains they had been transformed. No longer were they slaves to the simple necessity of survival; they were a lordly and dangerous society of fighters and thieves, hunters and priests of the sun. According to their origin myth, they entered the world through a hollow log. From one point of view, their migration was the fruit of an old prophecy, for indeed they emerged from a sunless world.

Although my grandmother lived out her long life in the shadow of Rainy Mountain, the immense landscape of the continental interior lay like memory in her blood. She could tell of the Crows, whom she had never seen, and of the Black Hills, where she had never been. I wanted to see in reality what she had seen more perfectly in the mind's eye, and traveled fifteen hundred miles to begin my pilgrimage.

Yellowstone, it seemed to me, was the top of the world, a region of deep lakes and dark timber, canyons and waterfalls. But, beautiful as it is, one might have the sense of confinement there. The skyline in all directions is close at hand, the high wall of the woods and deep cleavages of shade. There is a perfect freedom in the mountains, but it belongs to the eagle and the elk, the badger and the bear. The Kiowas reckoned their stature by the distance they could see, and they were bent and blind in the wilderness.

Descending eastward, the highland meadows are a stairway to the plain. In July the inland slope of the Rockies is luxuriant with flax and buckwheat, stonecrop and larkspur. The earth unfolds and the limit of the land recedes. Clusters of trees, and animals grazing far in the distance, cause the vision to reach away and wonder to build upon the mind. The sun follows a longer course in the day, and the sky is immense beyond all comparison. The great billowing clouds that sail upon it are shadows that move upon the grain like water, dividing light. Farther down, in the land of the Crows and Blackfeet, the plain is yellow. Sweet clover takes hold of the hills and bends upon itself to cover and seal the soil. There the Kiowas paused on their way; they had come to the place where they must change their lives. The sun is at home on the plains. Precisely there does it have the certain character of a god. When the Kiowas came to the land of the Crows, they could see the dark lees of the hills at dawn across the Bighorn River, the profusion of light on the grain shelves, the oldest deity ranging after the solstices. Not yet would they veer southward to the caldron of the land that lay below; they must wean their blood from the northern winter and hold the mountains a while longer in their view. They bore Tai-me in procession to the east.

A dark mist lay over the Black Hills, and the land was like iron. At the top of a ridge I caught sight of Devil's Tower upthrust against the gray sky as if in the birth of time the core of the earth had broken through its crust and the motion of the world was begun. There are things in nature that engender an awful quiet in the heart of man; Devil's Tower is one of them. Two centuries ago, because they could not do otherwise, the Kiowas made a legend at the base of the rock. My grandmother said:

> Eight children were there at play, seven sisters and their brother. Suddenly the boy was struck dumb; he trembled and began to run upon his hands and feet. His fingers became claws, and his body was covered with fur. Directly there was a bear where the boy had been. The sisters were terrified; they ran, and the bear after them. They came to the stump of a great tree, and the tree spoke to them. It bade them climb upon it, and as they did so it began to rise into the air. The bear came to kill them, but they were just beyond its reach. It reared against the tree and scored the bark all around with its claws. The seven sisters were borne into the sky, and they became the stars of the Big Dipper.

From that moment, and so long as the legend lives, the Kiowas have kinsmen in the night sky. Whatever they were in the mountains, they could be no more. However tenuous their well-being, however much they had suffered and would suffer again, they had found a way out of the wilderness.

My grandmother had a reverence for the sun, a holy regard that now is all but gone out of mankind. There was a wariness in her, and an ancient awe. She was a Christian in her later years, but she had come a long way about, and she never forgot her birthright. As a child she had been to the Sun Dances, she had taken part in those annual rites, and by them she had learned the restoration of her people in the presence of Tai-me. She was about seven when the last Kiowa Sun Dance was held in 1887 on the Washita River above Rainy Mountain Creek. The buffalo were gone. In order to consummate the ancient sacrifice—to impale the head of a buffalo bull upon the medicine tree—delegation of old men journeyed into Texas, there to beg and barter for an animal from the Goodnight herd. She was ten when the Kiowas came together for the last time as a living Sun Dance culture. They could find no buffalo; they had to hang an old hide from the sacred tree. Before the dance could begin, a company of soldiers rode out from Fort Sill under orders to disperse the tribe. Forbidden without cause the essential act of their faith, having seen the wild herds slaughtered and left to rot upon the ground, the Kiowas backed away forever from the medicine tree. That was July 20, 1890, at the great bend of the Washita. My grandmother was there. Without bitterness, and for as long as she lived, she bore a vision of deicide.

Now that I can have her only in memory, I see my grandmother in the several postures that were peculiar to her: standing at the wood stove on a winter morning and turning meat in a great iron skillet; sitting at the south window, bent above her beadwork, and afterwards, when her vision failed, looking down for a long time into the fold of her hands; going out upon a cane, very slowly as she did when the weight of age came upon her; praying. I remember her most often at prayer. She made long, rambling prayers out of suffering and hope, having seen many things. I was never sure that I had the right to hear, so exclusive were they of all mere custom and company. The last time I saw her she prayed standing by the side of her bed at night, naked to the waist, the light of a kerosene lamp moving upon her dark skin. Her long, black hair, always drawn and braided in the day, lay upon her shoulders and against her breasts like a shawl. I do not speak Kiowa, and I never understood her prayers, but there was something inherently sad in the sound, some merest hesitation upon the syllables of sorrow. She began in a high and descending pitch, exhausting her breath to silence; then again and again—and always the same intensity of effort, of something that is, and is not, like urgency in the human voice. Transported so in the dancing light among the shadows of her room, she seemed beyond the reach of time. But that was illusion; I think I knew then that I should not see her again.

Houses are like sentinels in the plain, old keepers of the weather watch. There, in a very little while, wood takes on the appearance of great age. All colors wear soon away in the wind and rain, and then the wood is burned gray and the grain appears and the nails turn red with rust. The windowpanes are black and opaque; you imagine there is nothing within, and indeed there are many ghosts, bones given up to the land. They stand here and there against the sky, and you approach them for a longer time than you expect. They belong in the distance; it is their domain.

Once there was a lot of sound in my grandmother's house, a lot of coming and going, feasting and talk. The summers there were full of excitement and reunion. The Kiowas are a summer people; they abide the cold and keep to themselves, but when the season turns and the land becomes warm and vital they cannot hold still; an old love of going returns upon them. The aged visitors who came to my grandmother's house when I was a child were made of lean and leather, and they bore themselves upright. They wore great black hats and bright ample shirts that shook in the wind. They rubbed fat upon their hair and wound their braids with strips of colored cloth. Some of them painted their faces and carried the scars of old and cherished enmities. They were an old council of warloads, come to remind and be reminded of who they were. Their wives and daughters served them well. The women might indulge themselves; gossip was at once the mark and compensation of their servitude. They made loud and elaborate talk among themselves, full of jest and gesture, fright and false alarm. They went abroad in fringed and flowered shawls, bright beadwork and German silver. They were at home in the kitchen, and they prepared meals that were banquets.

There were frequent prayer meetings, and great nocturnal feasts. When I was a child I played with my cousins outside, where the lamplight fell upon the ground and the singing of the old people rose up around us and carried away into the darkness. There were a lot of good things to eat, a lot of laughter and surprise. And afterwards, when the quiet returned, I lay down with my grandmother and could hear the frogs away by the river and feel the motion of the air.

Now there is a funeral silence in the rooms, the endless wake of some final word. The walls have closed in upon my grandmother's house. When I returned to it in mourning, I saw for the first time in my life how small it was. It was late at night, and there was a white moon, nearly full. I sat for a long time on the stone steps by the kitchen door. From there I could see out across the land; I could see the long row of trees by the creek, the low light upon the rolling plains, and the stars of the Big Dipper. Once I looked at the moon and caught sight of a strange thing. A cricket had perched upon the handrail, only a few inches away from me. My line of vision was such that the creature filled the moon like a fossil. It had gone there, I thought, to live and die, for there, of all places, was its small definition made whole and eternal. A warm wind rose up and purled like the longing within me.

The next morning I awoke at dawn and went out on the dirt road to Rainy Mountain. It was already hot, and the grasshoppers began to fill the air. Still, it was early in the morning, and the birds sang out of the shadows. The long yellow grass on the mountain shone in the bright light, and a scissortail hied above the land. There, where it ought to be, at the end of a long and legendary way, was my grandmother's grave. Here and there on the dark stones were ancestral names. Looking back once, I saw the mountain and came away.

CRITICAL THINKING QUESTIONS

1. How does the author create *ethos* appeal?

2. After reading this excerpt, how are you left feeling about Native American cultural heritage—e.g., with a sense of sorrow and loss of acknowledgment and affirmation? You can extend your thinking by reading Leslie Marmon Silko's story, "The Man to Send Rain Clouds" (page 269).

Henry David Thoreau

Solitude

from *Walden, or Life in the Woods*

This is a delicious evening, when the whole body is one sense, and imbibes delight through every pore. I go and come with a strange liberty in Nature, a part of herself. As I walk along the stony shore of the pond in my shirt-sleeves, though it is cool as well as cloudy and windy, and I see nothing special to attract me, all the elements are unusually congenial to me. The bullfrogs trump to usher in the night, and the note of the whip-poor-will is borne on the rippling wind from over the water. Sympathy with the fluttering alder and poplar leaves almost takes away my breath; yet, like the lake, my serenity is rippled but not ruffled. These small waves raised by the evening wind are as remote from storm as the smooth reflecting surface. Though it is now dark, the wind blows and roars in the wood, the waves still dash, and some creatures lull the rest with their notes. The repose is never complete. The wildest animals do not repose, but seek their prey now; the fox, and skunk, and rabbit, now roam the fields and woods without fear. They are Nature's watchmen—links which connect the days of animated life.

When I return to my house I find that visitors have been there and left their cards, either a bunch of flowers, or a wreath of evergreen, or a name in pencil on a yellow walnut leaf or a chip. They who come rarely to the woods take some little piece of the forest into their hands to play with by the way, which they leave, either intentionally or accidentally. One has peeled a willow wand, woven it into a ring, and dropped it on my table. I could always tell if visitors had called in my absence, either by the bended twigs or grass, or the print of their shoes, and generally of what sex or age or quality they were by some slight trace left, as a flower dropped, or a bunch of grass plucked and thrown away, even as far off as the railroad, half a mile distant, or by the lingering odor of a cigar or pipe. Nay, I was frequently notified of the passage of a traveller along the highway sixty rods off by the scent of his pipe.

There is commonly sufficient space about us. Our horizon is never quite at our elbows. The thick wood is not just at our door, nor the pond, but somewhat is always clearing, familiar and worn by us, appropriated and fenced in some way, and reclaimed from Nature. For what reason have I this vast range and circuit, some square miles of unfrequented forest, for my privacy, abandoned to me by men? My nearest neighbor is a mile distant, and no house is visible from any place but the hill-tops within half a mile of my own. I have my horizon bounded by woods all to myself; a distant view of the railroad where it touches the pond on the one hand,

and of the fence which skirts the woodland road on the other. But for the most part it is as solitary where I live as on the prairies. It is as much Asia or Africa as New England. I have, as it were, my own sun and moon and stars, and a little world all to myself. At night there was never a traveller passed my house, or knocked at my door, more than if I were the first or last man; unless it were in the spring, when at long intervals some came from the village to fish for pouts—they plainly fished much more in the Walden Pond of their own natures, and baited their hooks with darkness—but they soon retreated, usually with light baskets, and left "the world to darkness and to me," and the black kernel of the night was never profaned by any human neighborhood. I believe that men are generally still a little afraid of the dark, though the witches are all hung, and Christianity and candles have been introduced.

Yet I experienced sometimes that the most sweet and tender, the most innocent and encouraging society may be found in any natural object, even for the poor misanthrope and most melancholy man. There can be no very black melancholy to him who lives in the midst of nature and has his senses still. There was never yet such a storm but it was Æolian music to a healthy and innocent ear. Nothing can rightly compel a simple and brave man to a vulgar sadness. While I enjoy the friendship of the seasons I trust that nothing can make life a burden to me. The gentle rain which waters my beans and keeps me in the house today is not drear and melancholy, but good for me too. Though it prevents my hoeing them, it is of far more worth than my hoeing. If it should continue so long as to cause the seeds to rot in the ground and destroy the potatoes in the low lands, it would still be good for the grass on the uplands, and, being good for the grass, it would be good for me. Sometimes, when I compare myself with other men, it seems as if I were more favored by the gods than they, beyond any deserts that I am conscious of; as if I had a warrant and surety at their hands which my fellows have not, and were especially guided and guarded. I do not flatter myself, but if it be possible they flatter me. I have never felt lonesome, or in the least oppressed by a sense of solitude, but once, and that was a few weeks after I came to the woods, when, for an hour, I doubted if the near neighborhood of man was not essential to a serene and healthy life. To be alone was something unpleasant. But I was at the same time conscious of a slight insanity in my mood, and seemed to foresee my recovery. In the midst of a gentle rain while these thoughts prevailed, I was suddenly sensible of such sweet and beneficent society in Nature, in the very pattering of the drops, and in every sound and sight around my house, an infinite and unaccountable friendliness all at once like an atmosphere sustaining me, as made the fancied advantages of human neighborhood insignificant, and I have never thought of them since. Every little pine needle expanded and swelled with sympathy and befriended me. I was so distinctly made aware of the presence of something kindred to me, even in scenes which we are accustomed to call wild and dreary, and also that the nearest of blood to me and humanest was not a person nor a villager, that I thought no place could ever be strange to me again.

Mourning untimely consumes the sad;
Few are their days in the land of the living,
Beautiful daughter of Toscar.

Some of my pleasantest hours were during the long rain-storms in the spring or fall, which confined me to the house for the afternoon as well as the forenoon, soothed by their ceaseless roar and pelting; when an early twilight ushered in a long evening in which many thoughts had time to take root and unfold themselves. In those driving northeast rains which tried the village houses so, when the maids stood ready with mop and pail in front entries to keep the deluge out, I sat behind my door in my little house, which was all entry, and thoroughly enjoyed its protection. In one heavy thunder-shower the lightning struck a large pitch pine across the pond, making a very conspicuous and perfectly regular spiral groove from top to bottom, an inch or more deep, and four or five inches wide, as you would groove a walking-stick. I passed it again the other day, and was struck with awe on looking up and beholding that mark, now more distinct than ever, where a terrific and resistless bolt came down out of the harmless sky eight years ago. Men frequently say to me, "I should think you would feel lonesome down there, and want to be nearer to folks, rainy and snowy days and nights especially." I am tempted to reply to such—This whole earth which we inhabit is but a point in space. How far apart, think you, dwell the two most distant inhabitants of yonder star, the breadth of whose disk cannot be appreciated by our instruments? Why should I feel lonely? is not our planet in the Milky Way? This which you put seems to me not to be the most important question. What sort of space is that which separates a man from his fellows and makes him solitary? I have found that no exertion of the legs can bring two minds much nearer to one another. What do we want most to dwell near to? Not to many men surely, the depot, the post-office, the bar-room, the meeting-house, the school-house, the grocery, Beacon Hill, or the Five Points, where men most congregate, but to the perennial source of our life, whence in all our experience we have found that to issue, as the willow stands near the water and sends out its roots in that direction. This will vary with different natures, but this is the place where a wise man will dig his cellar. . . . I one evening overtook one of my townsmen, who has accumulated what is called "a handsome property"—though I never got a *fair* view of it—on the Walden road, driving a pair of cattle to market, who inquired of me how I could bring my mind to give up so many of the comforts of life. I answered that I was very sure I liked it passably well; I was not joking. And so I went home to my bed, and left him to pick his way through the darkness and the mud to Brighton—or Bright-town—which place he would reach some time in the morning.

Any prospect of awakening or coming to life to a dead man makes indifferent all times and places. The place where that may occur is always the same, and indescribably pleasant to all our senses. For the most part we allow only outlying and transient circumstances to make our occasions. They are, in fact, the cause of our distraction.

Nearest to all things is that power which fashions their being. *Next* to us the grandest laws are continually being executed. *Next* to us is not the workman whom we have hired, with whom we love so well to talk, but the workman whose work we are.

"How vast and profound is the influence of the subtile powers of Heaven and of Earth!"

"We seek to perceive them, and we do not see them; we seek to hear them, and we do not hear them; identified with the substance of things, they cannot be separated from them."

"They cause that in all the universe men purify and sanctify their hearts, and clothe themselves in their holiday garments to offer sacrifices and oblations to their ancestors. It is an ocean of subtile intelligences. They are everywhere, above us, on our left, on our right; they environ us on all sides."

We are the subjects of an experiment which is not a little interesting to me. Can we not do without the society of our gossips a little while under these circumstances—have our own thoughts to cheer us? Confucius says truly, "Virtue does not remain as an abandoned orphan; it must of necessity have neighbors."

With thinking we may be beside ourselves in a sane sense. By a conscious effort of the mind we can stand aloof from actions and their consequences; and all things, good and bad, go by us like a torrent. We are not wholly involved in Nature. I may be either the driftwood in the stream, or Indra in the sky looking down on it. I *may* be affected by a theatrical exhibition; on the other hand, I *may not* be affected by an actual event which appears to concern me much more. I only know myself as a human entity; the scene, so to speak, of thoughts and affections; and am sensible of a certain doubleness by which I can stand as remote from myself as from another. However intense my experience, I am conscious of the presence and criticism of a part of me, which, as it were, is not a part of me, but spectator, sharing no experience, but taking note of it, and that is no more I than it is you. When the play, it may be the tragedy, of life is over, the spectator goes his way. It was a kind of fiction, a work of the imagination only, so far as he was concerned. This doubleness may easily make us poor neighbors and friends sometimes.

I find it wholesome to be alone the greater part of the time. To be in company, even with the best, is soon wearisome and dissipating. I love to be alone. I never found the companion that was so companionable as solitude. We are for the most part more lonely when we go abroad among men than when we stay in our chambers. A man thinking or working is always alone, let him be where he will. Solitude is not measured by the miles of space that intervene between a man and his fellows. The really diligent student in one of the crowded hives of Cambridge College is as solitary as a dervis in the desert. The farmer can work alone in the field or the woods all day, hoeing or chopping, and not feel lonesome, because he is employed; but when he comes home at night he cannot sit down in a room alone, at the mercy of his thoughts, but must be where he can "see the folks," and recreate, and, as he thinks, remunerate himself for his day's solitude; and hence he wonders how the student can sit alone in the house all night and most of the day without ennui and "the blues"; but he does not realize that the student, though in the house, is still at work in *his* field, and chopping in *his* woods, as the farmer in his, and in turn seeks the same recreation and society that the latter does, though it may be a more condensed form of it.

Society is commonly too cheap. We meet at very short intervals, not having had time to acquire any new value for each other. We meet at meals three times a day, and give each other a new taste of that old musty cheese that we are. We have had to agree on a certain set of rules, called etiquette and politeness, to make this frequent meeting tolerable and that we need not come to open war. We meet at the post-office, and at the sociable, and about the fireside every night; we live thick and are in each other's way, and stumble over one another, and I think that we thus lose some respect for one another. Certainly less frequency would suffice for all important and hearty communications. Consider the girls in a factory—never alone, hardly in their dreams. It would be better if there were but one inhabitant to a square mile, as where I live. The value of a man is not in his skin, that we should touch him.

I have heard of a man lost in the woods and dying of famine and exhaustion at the foot of a tree, whose loneliness was relieved by the grotesque visions with which, owing to bodily weakness, his diseased imagination surrounded him, and which he believed to be real. So also, owing to bodily and mental health and strength, we may be continually cheered by a like but more normal and natural society, and come to know that we are never alone.

I have a great deal of company in my house; especially in the morning, when nobody calls. Let me suggest a few comparisons, that some one may convey an idea of my situation. I am no more lonely than the loon in the pond that laughs so loud, or than Walden Pond itself. What company has that lonely lake, I pray? And yet it has not the blue devils, but the blue angels in it, in the azure tint of its waters. The sun is alone, except in thick weather, when there sometimes appear to be two, but one is a mock sun. God is alone—but the devil, he is far from being alone; he sees a great deal of company; he is legion. I am no more lonely than a single mullein or dandelion in a pasture, or a bean leaf, or sorrel, or a horse-fly, or a humblebee. I am no more lonely than the Mill Brook, or a weathercock, or the north star, or the southwind, or an April shower, or a January thaw, or the first spider in a new house.

I have occasional visits in the long winter evenings, when the snow falls fast and the wind howls in the wood, from an old settler and original proprietor, who is reported to have dug Walden Pond, and stoned it, and fringed it with pine woods; who tells me stories of old time and of new eternity; and between us we manage to pass a cheerful evening with social mirth and pleasant views of things, even without apples or cider—a most wise and humorous friend, whom I love much, who keeps himself more secret than ever did Goffe or Whalley; and though he is thought to be dead, none can show where he is buried. An elderly dame, too, dwells in my neighborhood, invisible to most persons, in whose odorous herb garden I love to stroll sometimes, gathering simples and listening to her fables; for she has a genius of unequalled fertility, and her memory runs back farther than mythology, and she can tell me the original of every fable, and on what fact every one is founded, for the incidents occurred when she was young. A ruddy and lusty old dame, who delights in all weathers and seasons, and is likely to outlive all her children yet.

The indescribable innocence and beneficence of Nature—of sun and wind and rain, of summer and winter—such health, such cheer, they afford forever! and such sympathy have they ever with our race, that all Nature would be affected, and the sun's brightness fade, and the winds would sigh humanely, and the clouds rain tears, and the woods shed their leaves and put on mourning in midsummer, if any man should ever for a just cause grieve. Shall I not have intelligence with the earth? Am I not partly leaves and vegetable mould myself?

What is the pill which will keep us well, serene, contented? Not my or thy great-grandfather's, but our great-grandmother Nature's universal, vegetable, botanic medicines, by which she has kept herself young always, outlived so many old Parrs in her day, and fed her health with their decaying fatness. For my panacea, instead of one of those quack vials of a mixture dipped from Acheron and the Dead Sea, which come out of those long shallow black-schooner looking wagons which we sometimes see made to carry bottles, let me have a draught of undiluted morning air. Morning air! If men will not drink of this at the fountainhead of the day, why, then, we must even bottle up some and sell it in the shops, for the benefit of those who have lost their subscription ticket to morning time in this world. But remember, it will not keep quite till noonday even in the coolest cellar, but drive out the stopples long ere that and follow westward the steps of Aurora. I am no worshipper of Hygeia, who was the daughter of that old herb-doctor Æsculapius, and who is represented on monuments holding a serpent in one hand, and in the other a cup out of which the serpent sometimes drinks; but rather of Hebe, cup-bearer to Jupiter, who was the daughter of Juno and wild lettuce, and who had the power of restoring gods and men to the vigor of youth. She was probably the only thoroughly sound-conditioned, healthy, and robust young lady that ever walked the globe, and wherever she came it was spring.

CRITICAL THINKING QUESTION

"I find it wholesome to be alone the greater part of the time," Thoreau declares. List some reasons the author provides in arguing for the virtue of solitude. How does Nature contribute to his argument?

WRITING TOPICS

1. Write an essay that defends, refutes, and/or qualifies Thoreau's argument for solitude.

2. Read Oates's essay, "Against Nature." Acting as Thoreau's spokesperson, write a response to Oates's critique.

Alice Walker

The Place Where I Was Born

I am a displaced person. I sit here on a swing on the deck of my house in Northern California admiring how the fog has turned the valley below into a lake. For hours nothing will be visible below me except this large expanse of vapor; then slowly, as the sun rises and gains in intensity, the fog will start to curl up and begin its slow rolling drift toward the ocean. People here call it the dragon; and, indeed, a dragon is what it looks like, puffing and coiling, winged, flaring and in places thin and discreet, as it races before the sun, back to its ocean coast den. Mornings I sit here in awe and great peace. The mountains across the valley come and go in the mist; the redwoods and firs, oaks and giant bays appear as clumpish spires, enigmatic shapes of green, like the stone forests one sees in Chinese paintings of Guilin.

It is incredibly beautiful where I live. Not fancy at all, or exclusive. But from where I sit on my deck I can look down on the backs of hawks, and the wide, satiny wings of turkey vultures glistening in the sun become my present connection to ancient Egyptian Africa. The pond is so still below me that the trees reflected in it seem, from this distance, to be painted in its depths.

All this: the beauty, the quiet, the cleanliness, the peace, is what I love. I realize how lucky I am to have found it here. And yet, there are days when my view of the mountains and redwoods makes me nostalgic for small rounded hills easily walked over, and for the look of big leaf poplar and the scent of pine.

I am nostalgic for the land of my birth, the land I left forever when I was thirteen—moving first to the town of Eatonton, and then, at seventeen, to the city of Atlanta.

I cried one day as I talked to a friend about a tree I loved as a child. A tree that had sheltered my father on his long cold walk to school each morning: it was midway between his house and the school and because there was a large cavity in its trunk, a fire could be made inside it. During my childhood, in a tiny, overcrowded house in a tiny dell below it, I looked up at it frequently and felt reassured by its age, its generosity despite its years of brutalization (the fires, I knew, had to hurt), and its tall, old-growth pine nobility. When it was struck by lightning and killed, and then was cut down and made into firewood, I grieved as if it had been a person. Secretly. Because who among the members of my family would not have laughed at my grief?

I have felt entirely fortunate to have had this companion, and even today remember it with gratitude. But why the tears? my friend wanted to know. And it suddenly dawned on me that perhaps it *was* sad that it was a tree and not a member of my family to whom I was so emotionally close.

As a child I assumed I would always have the middle Georgia landscape to live in, as Brer Rabbit, a native also, and relative, had his brier patch. It was not to be. The pain of racist oppression, and its consequence, economic impoverishment, drove me to the four corners of the earth in search of justice and peace, and work that affirmed my whole being. I have come to rest here, weary from travel, on a deck—not a southern front porch—overlooking another world.

I am content; and yet, I wonder what my life would have been like if I had been able to stay home?

I remember early morning fogs in Georgia, not so dramatic as California ones, but magical too because out of the Southern fog of memory tramps my dark father, smiling and large, glowing with rootedness, and talking of hound dogs, biscuits and coons. And my equally rooted mother bustles around the corner of our house preparing to start a wash, the fire under the black wash pot extending a circle of warmth in which I, a grave-eyed child, stand. There is my sister Ruth, beautiful to me and dressed elegantly for high school in gray felt skirt and rhinestone brooch, hurrying up the road to catch the yellow school bus which glows like a large glow worm in the early morning fog.

> O, landscape of my birth
> because you were so good to me as I grew
> I could not bear to lose you.
>   O, landscape of my birth
> because when I lost you, a part of my soul died.
>   O, landscape of my birth
> because to save myself I pretended it was *you*
> who died.
>   You that now did not exist
> because I could not see you.
>   But O, landscape of my birth
> now I can confess how I have lied.
>   Now I can confess the sorrow
> of my heart
>   as the tears flow
> and I see again with memory's bright eye
> my dearest companion cut down
> and can bear to resee myself
> so lonely and so small
> there in the sunny meadows
> and shaded woods
> of childhood
> where my crushed spirit
> and stricken heart
> ran in circles
> looking for a friend.
>
> Soon I will have known fifty summers.
> Perhaps that is why

my heart
an imprisoned tree
so long clutched tight
inside its core
insists
on shedding
like iron leaves
the bars
from its cell.

You flow into me.
And like the Aborigine or Bushperson or Cherokee
who braves everything
to stumble home to die
no matter that cowboys
are herding cattle where the ancestors slept
I return to you, my earliest love.

Weeping in recognition at the first trees
I ever saw, the first hills I ever climbed and rested my unbearable cares
upon, the first rivers I ever dreamed myself across,
the first pebbles I ever lifted up, warm from the sun, and put into
my mouth.

   O landscape of my birth
you have never been far from my heart.
It is *I* who have been far.
   If you will take me back
   Know that I
   Am yours.

CRITICAL THINKING QUESTION

According to Walker's essay, what makes a place a home? What value assumptions or *warrants* underlie her definition? Do you accept them?

CHAPTER ACTIVITIES

1. What makes a place a home? How does an individual form a connection with a geographical location or physical environment that marks this place as his or her home? Also, why do some places, despite years of one's residence, never feel like a home? Based on your reading of several literature selections and your own experience and observations, write a personal perspective argument about place and home (literature suggestions: Bass's "Antlers," Clifton's "For de Lawd," Walker's "The Place Where I Was Born").

2. a. What is the value of a tree? Read several literature selections to explore various perspectives on the issue question, and write a Rogerian argument that addresses the issue (literature suggestions: Forché's "The Dulcimer Maker," Frost's "A Young Birch," Oliver's "A Black Walnut Tree").

   b. For a longer writing project, research land management policies involving America's woodlands and national forests. In the summer 2000, for example, a rash of wildfires destroyed more than four million acres of land; in one area alone, Los Alamos, New Mexico, wildfires caused an estimated $1 billion in damage.[2] Foresters and conservationists point their fingers at conflicting land management policies—from the extreme of clear-cutting, on the one hand, to the extreme of "zero-cutting," on the other hand. Meanwhile, foresters, commercial groups, and conservation groups are asking what we want from our forests and how policies can be designed to promote what some have called "compatible forestry." Based on your research and evaluation of the issue, write a *claim of policy* argument.

3. Do we *need* wilderness? In the essay, "The Heat of Noon: Rock and Tree and Cloud," Edward Abbey asserts this *warrant:* "We need the possibility of escape [to wilderness] as surely as we need hope; without it, life in the cities would drive all men into crime or drugs or psychoanalysis." However, some supporters of wilderness preservation would dispute Abbey's warrant. They contend that the idea of wilderness should be a natural element in our rhythm of living, a place we view as an integral part of our perspective on our daily lives—not as a place for running away from the problems of daily living. Consider several literature selections in this chapter and your own experience and observations, and write an argument to defend, refute, or qualify Abbey's warrant.

4. What value do zoos serve? Today's zoos do not enclose animals in small cages such as Rainer Maria Rilke's poem, "The Panther," describes. Animals are provided with habitats, modeled after their native habitats. From the zoo visitor's perspective, the animals appear to roam freely. Yet some animal welfare groups claim that it is unethical to remove an animal from its native habitat. Regard-

---

[2]Joseph B. Verrengia, "Some Ecologists Yielding to Nature's Logic," *The Tallahassee Democrat*, August 20, 2000, sec. A, p. 7.

less of the aesthetic qualities of the zoo's environment, the animal is still captive—denied its right to freedom. Also, zoo critics contend that efforts to breed animals in captivity are both costly and unsuccessful. In contrast, advocates argue that zoos provide opportunities for important research that contributes to species' viability. Moreover, zoos bring the general public in direct contact with wild and exotic animals, therefore, fostering public support for preserving endangered species. Conduct research on the economic, ethical, and scientific issues in the debate over zoos. Based on some readings in this chapter and your research findings, write a *claim of value* argument about zoos (literature suggestions: Bass's "Antlers," Jewett's "A White Heron," LeGuin's "May's Lion," Dickey's "Deer among Cattle," Rilke's "The Panther").

5. What efforts should we make to maintain wild animal populations? In making his argument for the preservation of wolves in "Thinking Like a Mountain," Aldo Leopold concludes with a reference to "Thoreau's dictum: In wildness is the salvation of the world." Two symbols of "wildness" popularized by environmental groups have been the wolf and the grizzly, species whose numbers were greatly diminished throughout the twentieth century. Ongoing efforts to restore wolf populations in the lower forty-eight states have been highly controversial. More recently, in July 2000, a proposed experimental program to restore grizzly populations in some wilderness areas in the western mountain states has engendered an emotional debate. Research the issue of wolf and/or grizzly habitat restoration efforts. Based on your research, take a position on the issue and defend it.

6. Unlike Thoreau in the mid-nineteenth century, most of us cannot walk out our back doors and into a wilderness area, yet many of us continue to seek out some kind of wilderness experience. Meanwhile, the millions of visitors to national parks and wilderness areas "run the risk of loving them to death," according to a *Nature Conservancy* article.[3] Granted, the national parks and nature preserves exist for the enjoyment of their human visitors; after all, public funding (tax revenue) contributes to their maintenance. But the value of these parks and preserves resides in their integrity as natural resources—in their wildness and pristine qualities. Meanwhile, biologists, park officials, and conservation groups are struggling to balance the demands of the human population and the demands of resource protection. Research this issue area and write a claim of policy argument. You probably will need to narrow this issue. For example, you can research management policies at a specific national park, perhaps one you have visited; or you can research the guidelines or restrictions on the use of automobiles, helicopters, horses, or snowmobiles in national forests or parks. (Related literature selections: Houston's "A Blizzard under Blue Sky," Snyder's "The Call of the Wild," Emerson's excerpt from *Nature*)

---

[3]"Whose Woods These Are?" *Nature Conservancy,* July/Aug. 1998, p. 3.

Chapter Five

Family and Identity

"Mickey and Minnie sitting in a tree, k-i-s-s-i-n-g; first comes love, then comes marriage, then comes baby in the baby carriage." And then the house, the car, the dog, and we have The Family. This schoolyard jingle taunts the young girl or boy who dares to smile at a child of the opposite sex. Though childhood play, it reflects a long-standing cultural norm: you fall in love, you get married, you have children . . . you "live happily ever after." Of course, the well-documented reality is that many couples neither live happily together nor ever after. In fact, couples are choosing cohabitation without marriage and, increasingly, without children. Meanwhile, a parent may be pushing the baby in the stroller without a partner or, perhaps, with a partner of the same sex. Some applaud these variations on The Family; after all, they argue, a loving family is a healthy one, and neither laws nor social custom should attempt to dictate the bonds of love. Equally passionate are those who decry these variations. They claim that the collapse of the traditional (heterosexual, two-parent) family structure has eroded "family values," instigated a contagion of social illnesses, and fed into a moral decrepitude that threatens to bring down the country. Clearly, no single definition of The Family can be agreed upon; however, most of us do agree upon the primary importance of family in our individual lives and, as adults, aspire to create a family of our own.

Looking back to the first half of the twentieth century, we see the model of the family evolve from the extended family to the nuclear family as people abandoned the working farm and moved to the city. By the end of the twentieth century, however, extended families were reemerging, although in an updated guise from earlier times: divorced parents were remarrying and creating families made up of stepsiblings and step-parents. And crossing into the twenty-first century, we witness more and more young adults choosing to postpone (or reject) marriage and children. As an alternative to the traditional family centered on a husband and wife, they are forging families of friends, peer groups of individuals, who may or may not share living space, but who do share emotional intimacies and traditional family rituals and holidays such as Thanksgiving and birthday celebrations.

Not surprisingly, TV programs, notably sitcoms, reflect the metamorphosis of the family. In the early 1960s, shows such as *Father Knows Best* and *Leave it to Beaver* featured the then, so-called ideal family: the wise, bread-winner Dad (always smiling); the docile, homemaker Mom (also smiling); and a pair of mischievous but dutiful children. The post–civil rights movement and Vietnam War generation of the 1970s, however, added to its list of grievances the image of the perfect family of the '60s sitcom. In response, TV unleashed sitcoms featuring the likes of the hapless and gratingly flawed Archie Bunker family. In place of ingratiating smiles and niceties, they berated each other relentlessly. Also, in keeping with the women's equal rights movement of the 1970s, *The Mary Tyler Moore Show* validated the presence of women in the working world; women had moved out of the home and into the workplace. Then in the 1980s with the inauguration of Ronald Reagan as president, the pendulum of family sentiment swung back toward the right: Mom and Dad and children, the nuclear family, again took center stage on the TV sitcom (*Family Ties*), although with a dose of diversity on *The Cosby Show*. Even though the Cosby family seemed to represent a feel-good return to the "perfect" family of the '60s, the show featured an African-American (upper-middle-class) family and the new Superwoman, Clair Huxtable, a loving and nurturing mom and wife who also was a well-respected, successful attorney. On the other hand, shows such as *Roseanne* and *The Simpsons* featured lower-working-class families, a refreshing antidote to the near-perfect Cosby family. And in the 1990s, TV sitcoms introduced the hyper-extended family of friends, adults forming families with their peers, in shows such as *Seinfeld* and *Friends*. Even though the friends in Monica's apartment don't live together, they drop in on each other spontaneously and regularly, somewhat like college students in a dormitory. Living independently, these characters, however, are sustained by an emotional interdependency—a sort of family "on call."

In reporting statistics that document the single-adult lifestyle dramatized on current TV sitcoms, one newspaper declared, "Married couples are the new endangered species." Data collected by the U.S. Census Bureau in the 1990s showed that married couples with children younger than eighteen fell from 50 percent of all households in 1970 to an estimated 36 percent in 1997.[1] Even so, every June, the fashion industry's self-proclaimed wedding month, advertisers saturate the market with images of the perfect wedding; clearly, these advertisers are not playing to an unreceptive audience. The ideal of marriage and family seems to reign supreme, in our dreams if not in reality.

Looking to the past and to our future, how do we assess the "state" of the family? And how does each of us shape our personal identity as an individual in response to our experiences and our attitudes about family? As suggested above, popular culture, in particular, the TV sitcom, tends to reflect current trends or fads.

---

[1] Martha Irvine, "Married Couples Are the New Endangered Species," *Tallahassee Democrat*, November 25, 1999, sec. B, p. 6.

Authors of literature, however, for the most part, are less beholden to commercial interests than TV producers; they need not please a projected audience—or keep up with Nielsen ratings.

Rather than reinforcing socially popular attitudes and assumptions, the stories, poems, plays, and essays in this chapter are more likely to shake up our sensibilities and provoke us to question assumptions and examine underlying values and beliefs. For example, in the poem, "Cinderella," Anne Sexton playfully lampoons the happily-ever-after myth. Kate Chopin's story, "The Storm," dares to suggest that a wife's moment of spontaneous infidelity may rejuvenate rather than wreck her marriage. Although statistics suggest that divorce is fairly commonplace, John Updike's story, "Separating," reminds us that the emotional reality of a marital breakup still stuns its family members. Meanwhile, Harvey Fierstein's play, *On Tidy Endings,* brings to center stage a homosexual relationship and family dynamics. One of the play's characters, Marion, says she married right after college and "settled down for a nice quiet life of Kids and Careers . . . Talk about life's little surprises!" Reading Fierstein's play, we hear the voices of individuals who, despite differences in sexual preferences, share a basic human need for love.

In contrast to the TV sitcom image of homogenized, middle-class families, Alice Walker's "Everyday Use" presents the perspective of an African American woman rearing her daughters in the rural South: ". . . I am a large, big-boned woman with rough, man-working hands. . . . I can kill and clean a hog as mercilessly as a man." In "Red Moccasins," author Susan Power takes us to the Standing Rock Sioux Reservation, where a mother's love for her son is challenged by powerful forces. On the other hand, the poems, "Advice to My Son" by Peter Meinke and "Not Leaving the House" by Gary Snyder, feature different aspects of a father's love. And Genaro González's story, "Too Much His Father's Son," shows a young boy torn between his loyalty to both his mother and his father.

In our search for answers to the question, who am I?, we can look to our parents and grandparents and ask, who were they? A number of authors' works present the perspective of the adult looking back on his or her parents or forebears to ponder the identity question. In a retrospective poem, "I Go Back to May, 1937," Sharon Olds's speaker arrives at a somewhat grim conclusion; however, in "Mothers," Nikki Giovanni's reflections lead her to celebrate the bond among generations. Essayists Scott Russell Sanders and Harper Stevens focus on their fathers' role in shaping their values and personal identities. And Pauli Murray's chapter from her memoir about growing up in the first part of the twentieth century testifies to the value of family stories and the protective bond of the extended family.

Seeking love and approval, we may "look homeward" to our family. But what if the family roots have been stretched across national borders or half way around the globe? When children grow up in a nation that is not their parents' homeland, what are the effects on the family members' identities and their sense of home? And can those who leave their homeland as adults ever reclaim that home in their new nations? Bharati Mukherjee's story, "A Father," portrays the inner disharmony that, some 20 years after moving from Bombay to Detroit, gnaws at the father and finally erupts. On the other hand, in "Safe," Cherylene Lee shows how Chinese immigrants endure and prevail as a family living in San Francisco. Describing her parents' perspective, Lee's narrator says, "Only the family home felt safe to them and this is what they tried to impart on both my brother and me." Crossing cultural and ethnic lines is the assumption that the "family home" provides a refuge, a safe haven from the dangers beyond its (locked) doors. Several works in this chapter prompt us to ask if this notion is based on reality or wishful thinking.

In the story, "A Red Sweater," Fae Myenne Ng's narrator says, "Family exists only because somebody has a story, and knowing that story connects us to a history." As we read the works that follow, we may ask ourselves what story we have to tell and how it "connects us to a history" that informs our identity.

PREWRITING AND DISCUSSION

1. Write about your concept of *family*. Describe specific experiences, observations, or ideas that inform your definition.

2. Describe your role as a member of a family. How is your sense of self-identity defined by your experiences with family? What personal values do you attribute directly to your experience with family?

Kate Chopin

The Storm

I

The leaves were so still that even Bibi thought it was going to rain. Bobinôt, who was accustomed to converse on terms of perfect equality with his little son, called the child's attention to certain sombre clouds that were rolling with sinister intention from the west, accompanied by a sullen, threatening roar. They were at Friedheimer's store and decided to remain there till the storm had passed. They sat within the door on two empty kegs. Bibi was four years old and looked very wise.

"Mama'll be 'fraid, yes," he suggested with blinking eyes.

"She'll shut the house. Maybe she got Sylvie helpin' her this evening'," Bobinôt responded reassuringly.

"No; she ent got Sylvie. Sylvie was helpin' her yistiday," piped Bibi.

Bobinôt arose and going across to the counter purchased a can of shrimps, of which Calixta was very fond. Then he returned to his perch on the keg and sat stolidly holding the can of shrimps while the storm burst. It shook the wooden store and seemed to be ripping great furrows in the distant field. Bibi laid his little hand on his father's knee and was not afraid.

II

Calixta, at home, felt no uneasiness for their safety. She sat at a side window sewing furiously on a sewing machine. She was greatly occupied and did not notice the approaching storm. But she felt very warm and often stopped to mop her face on which the perspiration gathered in beads. She unfastened her white sacque at the throat. It began to grow dark, and suddenly realizing the situation she got up hurriedly and went about closing windows and doors.

Out on the small front gallery she had hung Bobinôt's Sunday clothes to air and she hastened out to gather them before the rain fell. As she stepped outside, Alcée Laballière rode in at the gate. She had not seen him very often since her marriage, and never alone. She stood there with Bobinôt's coat in her hands, and the big rain drops began to fall. Alcée rode his horse under the shelter of a side projection where the chickens had huddled and there were plows and a harrow piled up in the corner.

"May I come and wait on your gallery till the storm is over, Calixta?" he asked.

"Come 'long in, M'sieur Alcée."

His voice and her own startled her as if from a trance, and she seized Bobinôt's vest. Alcée, mounting to the porch, grabbed the trousers and snatched Bibi's braided jacket that was about to be carried away by a sudden gust of wind. He expressed an intention to remain outside, but it was soon apparent that he might as well have been out in the open: the water beat in upon the boards in driving sheets, and he went inside, closing the door after him. It was even necessary to put something beneath the door to keep the water out.

"My! what a rain! It's good two years sence it rain' like that," exclaimed Calixta as she rolled up a piece of bagging and Alcée helped her to thrust it beneath the crack.

She was a little fuller of figure than five years before when she married; but she had lost nothing of her vivacity. Her blue eyes still retained their melting quality; and her yellow hair, dishevelled by the wind and rain, kinked more stubbornly than ever about her ears and temples.

The rain beat upon the low, shingled roof with a force and clatter that threatened to break an entrance and deluge them there. They were in the dining room—the sitting room—the general utility room. Adjoining was her bed room, with Bibi's couch along side her own. The door stood open, and the room with its white, monumental bed, its closed shutters, looked dim and mysterious.

Alcée flung himself into a rocker and Calixta nervously began to gather up from the floor the lengths of a cotton sheet which she had been sewing.

"If this keeps up, *Dieu sait* if the levees goin' to stan' it!" she exclaimed.

"What have you got to do with the levees?"

"I got enough to do! An' there's Bobinôt with Bibi out in that storm—if he only didn' left Friedheimer's!"

"Let us hope, Calixta, that Bobinôt's got sense enough to come in out of a cyclone."

She went and stood at the window with a greatly disturbed look on her face. She wiped the frame that was clouded with moisture. It was stiflingly hot. Alcée got up and joined her at the window, looking over her shoulder. The rain was coming down in sheets obscuring the view of far-off cabins and enveloping the distant wood in a gray mist. The playing of the lighting was incessant. A bolt struck a tall chinaberry tree at the edge of the field. It filled all visible space with a blinding glare and the crash seemed to invade the very boards they stood upon.

Calixta put her hands to her eyes, and with a cry, staggered backward. Alcée's arm encircled her, and for an instant he drew her close and spasmodically to him.

"Bonté!" she cried, releasing herself from his encircling arm and retreating from the window, "the house'll go next! If I only knew w'ere Bibi was!" She would not compose herself; she would not be seated. Alcée clasped her shoulders and looked into her face. The contact of her warm, palpitating body when he had unthinkingly drawn her into his arms, had aroused all the old-time infatuation and desire for her flesh.

"Calixta," he said, "don't be frightened. Nothing can happen. The house is too low to be struck, with so many tall trees standing about. There! aren't you going to be quiet? say, aren't you?" He pushed her hair back from her face that was warm and steaming. Her lips were as red and moist as pomegranate seed. Her white neck and a glimpse of her full, firm bosom disturbed him powerfully. As she glanced up at him the fear in her liquid blue eyes had given place to a drowsy gleam that unconsciously betrayed a sensuous desire. He looked down into her eyes and there was nothing for him to do but to gather her lips in a kiss. It reminded him of Assumption.

"Do you remember—in Assumption, Calixta?" he asked in a low voice broken by passion. Oh! she remembered; for in Assumption he had kissed her and kissed and kissed her; until his senses would well nigh fail, and to save her he would resort to a desperate flight. If she was not an immaculate dove in those days, she was still inviolate; a passionate creature whose very defenselessness had made her defense, against which his honor forbade him to prevail. Now—well, now—her lips seemed in a manner free to be tasted, as well as her round, white throat and her whiter breasts.

They did not heed the crashing torrents, and the roar of the elements made her laugh as she lay in his arms. She was a revelation in that dim, mysterious chamber; as white as the couch she lay upon. Her firm, elastic flesh that was knowing for the first time its birthright, was like a creamy lily that the sun invites to contribute its breath and perfume to the undying life of the world.

The generous abundance of her passion, without guile or trickery, was like a white flame which penetrated and found response in depths of his own sensuous nature that had never yet been reached.

When he touched her breasts they gave themselves up in quivering ecstasy, inviting his lips. Her mouth was a fountain of delight. And when he possessed her, they seemed to swoon together at the very borderland of life's mystery.

He stayed cushioned upon her, breathless, dazed, enervated, with his heart beating like a hammer upon her. With one hand she clasped his head, her lips lightly touching his forehead. The other hand stroked with a soothing rhythm his muscular shoulders.

The growl of the thunder was distant and passing away. The rain beat softly upon the shingles, inviting them to drowsiness and sleep. But they dared not yield.

The rain was over; and the sun was turning the glistening green world into a palace of gems. Calixta, on the gallery, watched Alcée ride away. He turned and smiled at her with a beaming face; and she lifted her pretty chin in the air and laughed aloud.

III

Bobinôt and Bibi, trudging home, stopped without at the cistern to make themselves presentable.

"My! Bibi, w'at will yo' mama say! You ought to be ashame'. You oughtn' put on those good pants. Look at 'em! An' that mud on yo' collar! How you got that mud on yo' collar, Bibi? I never saw such a boy!" Bibi was the picture of pathetic resignation. Bobinôt was the embodiment of serious solicitude as he strove to remove from his own person and his son's the signs of their tramp over heavy roads and through wet fields. He scraped the mud off Bibi's bare legs and feet with a stick and carefully removed all traces from his heavy brogans. Then, prepared for the worst—the meeting with an over-scrupulous housewife, they entered cautiously at the back door.

Calixta was preparing supper. She had set the table and was dripping coffee at the hearth. She sprang up as they came in.

"Oh! Bobinôt! You back! My! but I was uneasy. W'ere you been during the rain? An' Bibi? he ain't wet? he ain't hurt?" She had clasped Bibi and was kissing him effusively. Bobinôt's explanations and apologies which he had been composing all along the way, died on his lips as Calixta felt him to see if he were dry, and seemed to express nothing but satisfaction at their safe return.

"I brought you some shrimps, Calixta," offered Bobinôt, hauling the can from his ample side pocket and laying it on the table.

"Shrimps! Oh, Bobinôt! you too good fo' anything!" and she gave him a smacking kiss on the cheek that resounded. *"J'vous réponds,* we'll have a feas' to night! umph-umph!"

Bobinôt and Bibi began to relax and enjoy themselves, and when the three seated themselves at table they laughed much and so loud that anyone might have heard them as far away as Laballière's.

IV

Alcée Laballière wrote to his wife, Clarisse, that night. It was a loving letter, full of tender solicitude. He told her not to hurry back, but if she and the babies liked it at Biloxi, to stay a month longer. He was getting on nicely; and though he missed them, he was willing to bear the separation a while longer—realizing that their health and pleasure were the first things to be considered.

V

As for Clarisse, she was charmed upon receiving her husband's letter. She and the babies were doing well. The society was agreeable; many of her old friends and acquaintances were at the bay. And the first free breath since her marriage seemed to restore the pleasant liberty of her maiden days. Devoted as she was to her husband, their intimate conjugal life was something which she was more than willing to forego for a while.

So the storm passed and everyone was happy.

CRITICAL THINKING QUESTIONS

1. How does Bobinôt's role as a husband inform his self-identity? How does Calixta's role as a wife inform hers?

2. What is Chopin's implied *claim of value* about marriage? What evidence in the story supports this claim? Are you convinced? Why or why not?

WRITING TOPIC

The story's closing line asserts, "So the storm passed and everyone was happy." Is this a "happy" ending? What assumptions about happiness underlie the narrator's assertion? Do you accept or reject those assumptions? Why?

Genaro González

Too Much His Father's Son

In the middle of the argument, without warning, Arturo's mother confronted her husband point-blank: "Is it another woman?"

"For heaven's sake, Carmela, not in front of—"

"Nine is old enough to know. You owe both of us that much."

Sitting in the room, Arturo could not help but overhear. Usually he could dissimulate with little effort—being a constant chaperone on his cousin Anita's dates had made him a master at fading into the background. But at that moment he was struggling hard to control a discomfort even more trying than those his cousin and her boyfriends put him through.

The argument had already lasted an hour and, emotionally, his mother had carried its brunt. Trying to keep her voice in check was taking more out of her than if she had simply vented her tension.

His father, though, lay fully clothed in bed, shirt half-buttoned and hands locked under his head. From his closed eyes and placid breathing, one would have thought that her frustration was simply lulling him into a more profound relaxation. Only an occasional gleam from those perfect, white teeth told Arturo he was still listening, and even then with bemused detachment.

"Is it another woman, Raúl?"

His father batted open his eyes only to look away, as though the accusation did not even merit the dignity of a defense. His gaze caught Arturo and tried to lock him into the masculine intimacy they often shared, an unspoken complicity between father and son. But at that instant it simply aggravated Arturo's shame.

"Who is she, Raúl?"

His smile made it clear that if there were another woman, he was not saying. "You tell me. You're the one who made her up."

Arturo had seen that smile in all its shadings—sometimes with disarming candor, but more often full of arrogance. When his father wished, his smile could become a gift of pearls, invigorating all who saw his teeth shining with their special luster.

Yet other times his father needed only to curl his lips, and those same teeth turned into a sadistic show of strength. Well aware of his power over others, the father seemed indifferent to whether the end effect exalted or belittled.

Out of nowhere, perhaps to add to the confusion he ordered, "Bring *abuelo's* belt, Arturo."

Instead of strapping it on, he pretended to admire what had once been his own father's gun belt. The holster was gone, but a bullet that had remained rusted inside a middle clasp added a certain authority. The hand-tooled leather, a rich dark brown, had delicate etchings now too smooth to decipher. His grandfather Edelmiro had been a large, mean-looking man in life, and Arturo still remembered the day his father received the belt. He had strapped it on for only a moment, over his own belt. Later that day Arturo opened the closet for a closer inspection and had come upon his father, piercing another notch for his smaller waist.

His mother continued to confront his father, who idly looped the belt, grabbed it at opposite ends and began whipping it with a solemn force. At first the rhythmic slaps disconcerted her, until she turned their tension into punctuations for her own argument. Suddenly the belt cracked so violently that Arturo thought the ancient cartridge had fired. He was startled, as much from the noise as from the discovery that his father's legendary control had snapped. For an instant both parents, suddenly realizing how far things had gone, appeared paralyzed.

No, his father would never strike her, he was sure of that. But nobody had ever pushed him that far, least of all his mother, whose own strength had always been her patience.

He wondered why his eyes were suddenly brimming. Perhaps trespassing into the unknown terrified him, or perhaps he was ashamed of his father's indifference. That confusion—crying without knowing why—frightened him even more.

"See, Carmela? Now you've got the boy blubbering."

He was hoping to hide his weakness from his father, and the unmasking only added to the disgrace. Desperate to save face, he yelled, "I'm leaving!"

As always his father turned the threat in his favor. "That's good, son. Wait outside and let me handle this."

"I'm going to *papá grande's* house!"

Arturo had never been that close to his mother's family, and that made his decision all the more surprising. But if his father felt betrayed he did not show it. "Fine, then. You're on your own."

It took him a while to catch his father's sarcasm and his own unthinking blunder; he did not know the way to his grandparents' house. He had walked there only once—last Sunday—and that time his mother had disoriented him with a different route from the one his father took.

But now, standing there facing his father, he had no choice. Rushing out the kitchen door, he ran across the back yard, expecting at any moment to be stopped in his tracks. When his arms brushed against a clothesline, he almost tripped as if his father had lassoed him with his belt. Not until he reached the alley did he realize he had been hoping his father would indeed stop him, even with a word.

He crossed the alley into an abandoned lot. There he matted a patch of grass and weeds reaching his waist and settled in, so as to give his heart time to hush. He sat for a long time, wondering whether to gather his thoughts or let them scramble until nothing mattered.

From Doña Chole's house came the blare of a Mexican radio station. Two announcers were sandwiching every song with a frenzied assault. Farther away David's father continued working on his pet project—a coop and flypen for his game cocks:

four or five swift whacks into wood . . . silence . . . then another volley. For a while he lost himself in the hammering. If he listened closer he could hear the cursing and singing that gave the neighborhood life. Only his own home remained absolutely still.

Soon the sun began to get in his eyes whenever he looked homeward. A cool breeze was blowing at his back, and as he waited in the weeds a sun-toasted aroma penetrated his corduroy shirt.

Someone was coming up the path, making soft lashing sounds in the weeds. His intuition told him that the person was Fela the *curandera* and when he finally dared peek he immediately dove back into his hiding place, wondering whether to congratulate or curse himself.

A part of him scrambled for a rational explanation: who else could it be? Fela the healer was the only grown-up unconcerned about snakes in the undergrowth. In her daily forages for herbs she was used to cutting swaths through the weeds. Yet another side of him was forced to side with the barrio lore—that she had special powers, that she appeared and disappeared at will, that she could think your thoughts before they occurred to you.

The brushing got closer, so he lay very still, trying to imitate his father's self-discipline. When the rustling suddenly stopped, he swore the waft of his corduroy shirt had given him away.

A voice called out: "Since when do little boys live in the wild?"

His heart began beating wildly, but her tone carried enough teasing that he half-raised his head.

"You're hiding from someone?"

All at once, he had a clear image of his father sprawled across the bed, amused, almost bored. Arturo answered her question with a nod, afraid that if he spoke, his rage might leap out and injure them both.

"You did something bad?"

He managed a hoarse, determined vow: "I'm going to smash my father's teeth."

He expected the violence in his words to stun her, but instead she disarmed him with a kind smile. "Whatever for? He has such nice teeth. Some day yours will look just like his."

For a moment, in place of the familiar habit of his own body, he experienced an undefined numbness, followed by the fascinated terror of someone who has inherited a gleaming crown with awesome responsibilities. He stood speechless, repulsed yet tempted by the thought of turning into his father.

"Anyway," she added, "before you know it he'll be old and toothless like me."

She picked a row of burrs clinging to her faded dress, then said as she left, "And tell your mother she's in my thoughts and prayers." Watching her walk away, he tried without success to retrace the route he and his mother had taken to her father's house at the time of their secret visit last Sunday.

That Sunday morning, while his mother talked to Fela in the living room, he had sat on a wicker chair on Fela's porch, entertained by Cuco, an ancient caged parrot with colorful semi-circles under his eyes. Arturo was feeding him chile from a nearby plant to make him talk. "Say it," he urged between bribes: *"Chinga tu madre."* But the chile only agitated Cuco's whistling.

"Come on, you stupid bird. *Chinga tu madre.* Screw your mother."

Suddenly there was a raucous squawk. "Screw your *padre* instead!"

As he wheeled about and felt the blood rush to his face, Fela was already raising her arms in innocence. "Who says he's stupid? That's an exotic, bilingual bird you're talking to."

From there, he and his mother had gone to his grandparents' house. Her route through alleys and unfenced back yards led him to ask, "How do you know all these shortcuts?"

She had paused to dry her forehead on her sleeve, and for the first time in days he had seen her smile. "I grew up in this barrio. This is where I used to play."

Trying to imagine her at the same age he now was, he had to smile to himself.

When they got to his grandfather's house, they had to wait until his grandfather Marcelo finished his *radionovela.* Then, after hearing where they had been and why, his grandfather shook his head. "I knew your marriage would come to this. But going to Fela was a mistake. If he finds out he'll claim you're trying to win him back through witchcraft."

"I had to know if he's seeing another woman."

"And what if he is?"

Arturo had never seen her as serene and as serious when she answered, "Then he's not worth winning back."

"But a *curandera* . . . Why not see a priest?"

Arturo's grandmother took her side. "What for, Marcelo? He'd only give her your advice: accept him as your cross in life."

"I wouldn't in this case. An unfaithful husband is one thing, an arrogant s.o.b. is another. Still, a priest could say a few prayers in your behalf."

"Fela offered to do that herself."

"And no doubt offered good advice," his grandmother added.

His mother's fist clenched his own. "Yes," she said, and her firmness made it obvious that was the last word.

His grandfather, deep in thought, held his breath without taking his eyes off him. Then he closed them and exhaled a stale rush of cigarette smoke, as if unclouding his thoughts. "I've always said your father was a *cabrón.*"

"Now, Marcelo. Don't turn him against his own father," his grandmother interjected.

"Mamá's right. None of this is Arturo's fault. He's going through enough as it is."

"True. But I still wouldn't give a kilo of crap for the whole de la O family, starting with Edelmiro."

"May he rest in peace," said his grandmother.

His grandfather stood up. "Not if there's a devil down below."

"Marcelo! He was your *compadre.*"

"I had as much choice in the matter as the boy had in being his grandson." He turned to Arturo's mother. "Remember, if there's a falling out, don't ask that family for anything. Your place is here."

His grandmother added, "And of course that includes Arturo. He's as much a part of the family as the rest of us."

His grandfather had simply said, "Let's hope he's not too much is father's son."

By now the late afternoon sun was slanting long, slender shadows his way, but he was determined to spend the night there if need be. He began counting in cycles of hundreds to keep his uncertainty in check.

Suddenly the rear screen door opened and his father leaned against it, his belt slung over his chest and shoulder like a bandoliered and battle-weary warrior.

"Arturo, come inside." Whenever he wanted to conceal something from the neighbors, he used that phrase.

Arturo slowly stood up but held his ground, as much from stubbornness as dread.

"It's all right, son." His father sounded final yet forgiving, like a king who had put down a castle uprising, regained control and had decided to pardon the traitors.

Arturo blinked but once, but his pounding heart made even something that small seem a life-and-death concession.

Then his mother appeared alongside his father, and for an instant, framed by the doorway, their pose reminded him of their newlywed portrait in the living room: his hands at his sides, her own clasped in front, both heads slightly tilted as if about to rest on each other's shoulder. In that eye blink of an interval before she stepped outside, he felt like an outsider looking in.

She was halfway between him and the house when his father said, "Your mother's bringing you back."

He could not believe her betrayal. After all that, she had surrendered and was bringing him in as well. He wanted to cry out at her for having put him through so much. But another part of him understood he shared the blame, for not helping her, for being too much his father's son.

"I forgot the way," he said. Although she was quite close he could not tell whether she heard—much less accepted—his timid apology. He managed his first step homeward when she blocked his path, gently took his hand and guided him in the opposite direction.

He heard, or perhaps only imagined, his father: "Come back." He tugged her arm in case she had not heard. She tightened her grasp to show that she had. Then, intuiting his dilemma, she paused, saying nothing but still gazing away from the house. He realized then and there that the decision was for him alone to make. Hers had already been made.

Unable to walk back or away, he felt like the only living thing in the open. Then his father called out, "Son," and he knew it was his last call. His spine shivered as though a weapon had been sighted at his back, and he imagined his father removing from his belt the cartridge reserved for the family traitor.

There was no way of telling how long he braced himself for whatever was coming, until he finally realized that the moment of reckoning was already behind him. It was then that he felt his father's defeat in his own blood. With it came the glorious fear of a fugitive burning his bridges into the unknown, or a believer orphaned from a false faith. And in that all-or-nothing instant that took so little doing and needed even less understanding, his all-powerful father evaporated into the myth he had always been.

He felt a flesh-and-blood grasp that both offered and drew strength. He began to walk away, knowing there was no turning back.

CRITICAL THINKING QUESTIONS

1. When Arturo chooses his mother over his father, he acknowledges that "his all-powerful father" had been a "myth." Describe this myth. What ideals and values inform it? Do you agree or disagree with Arturo's rejection of those values?

2. Disregarding your personal opinion, make a case for Arturo's mother to stay with her husband. What *warrant* about marriage informs this argument? In anticipating the opposing argument, what *warrant* may inform that argument?

Cherylene Lee

Safe

My brother sets himself on fire every summer. He's not a pyromaniac and it's not a political statement. He does it in front of people at Worlds of Water, U.S.A. My brother is a flame diver—a stuntman on a high diving platform who douses himself in flammable liquid, has someone light a torch to him, then launches himself into a cool blue pool, toes pointed, form correct—though that is hard to make out through all the flame and smoke. He says the crowds go wild because they feel afraid. He makes them feel safe.

Safe. That is the most important consideration for our family. Perhaps there is a Chinese gene encoded with a protein for caution. Or perhaps it's because my father's tailor shop is not doing so well or because of my mother's blindness. Perhaps it's because my mother and father married late in life and weren't sure how to protect their children.

We try to take precautions. My mother won't go out at night for fear of what the darkness holds. She doesn't like me to take a shower after dinner for fear I might get a cramp and somehow drown in the shower's spray. She doesn't like me to walk home from school alone, nor does she like me to walk home with boys. She'd rather I walked home with girls, at least three for maximum protection so one can always run for help. I've tried to explain to her, I like walking alone, it's not always possible to walk in female threes, I don't even have that many girlfriends. "You have to watch out at your age, you can't be too safe," she warns, "but don't hang around with the fast ones."

My father is just as bad. He's so afraid someone will dent his car, he won't park in a lot that doesn't have two spaces side by side for his ten-year-old station wagon. He refuses to go into a grocery store if he could be the first or last customer— "That's when the robbers are most likely to come." He won't eat in restaurants without first wiping the chopsticks, rice bowl, tea cup, or plate, silverware, and glass—"So many germs everywhere." He has more locks and alarms on his tailor shop door than the bank that's two doors down. It takes him ten minutes to open them up each day, turn off the alarms, before calling my mother to let her know that he has arrived safely.

We live in San Francisco—a city with its share of dangers though my parents have done their best to shield my brother and me from having to face most of them. More than from just physical harm, they've tried to protect us from loss—loss of face, loss of happiness, loss of innocence. So far we have been protected by their constant vigilance. Not that I have been sheltered so much I can't go places on my own or do things without my parents' consent, but their warnings, cautions, and dire predictions have had an effect. While I have always felt safe and have never wanted for anything, neither can I say that I've ever wanted at all. I have never been in danger, never known a need for risk. That's why I was so shocked when my brother announced he wanted to become a flame diver.

It isn't as risky as it seems, at least according to my brother who claims he could do the dive in his sleep. He wears a special flame-retardant suit. It protects him head to foot from the flames that consume him three times a day, six days a week, three months of the year. His summer job—his only job—hasn't changed him much except that he has no facial hair. The suit shields him from burns, but the wind sometimes blows flames under his protective helmet, singeing the hair off his face. The first summer he started doing this work, it took me awhile to recognize what was different about him when he sat down to dinner. He had no eyebrows, no eye lashes, just eyes, big brown eyes that seemed too large for the rest of his face. Since then he's taken to drawing in eyebrows with an eyebrow pencil because he doesn't want people to worry. Otherwise he's normal, though for a while I admit I was afraid of my brother. Who was this guy who grew up with me and suddenly became a flame diver? I thought maybe he would turn into some awful monster with scarred flesh and a swollen head from the fire and adulation. But my brother remains the same—shy, soft-spoken, introverted. Maybe he's happier these days or maybe I just think that because I am relieved. After hearing so much about danger, all he's lost are his eyebrows.

I've never seen my brother actually do his stunt though our father has many pictures of his dives hanging on the walls of his tailor shop. My brother won't let any of us watch him. He thinks we'll jinx him and we don't want to do that. He hasn't let us watch him since a high school diving meet three years ago when he made the varsity swim team. On his final and hardest dive of that meet, his foot slipped during his preparation jump causing him to start his backward twist out of control and his head to nick the edge of the platform. Our mother, already nearly blind, became hysterical even before the blood began oozing up in the water. By instinct she started screaming, "My boy, my boy!" the instant his head made contact, before anyone else knew something was wrong. Her screams echoed like a wailing gull inside the indoor swim gym. Luckily my brother wasn't badly hurt, ten stitches closed him up, but he was so embarrassed by our mother's shrieking that he asked us not to attend anymore, our presence brought him bad luck. That's why we all stay away now and only look at the pictures of his dives after he's already done them. When we know he's safe.

According to my mother, her eyesight started going bad because my father's eyes wandered. Years ago, when his tailor shop was in Chinatown, his clients were mostly women. He made cheongsams, the tight-fitting Chinese dresses the girls in the Miss Chinatown contest wear. He also did special occasion clothes, Chinese jackets, western-style wedding dresses, men's suits and such, but his busiest time of the year used to be the months before Chinese New Year when the Miss Chinatown contest was held. He would carefully take the measurements of each eager contestant, help her choose material that brought out her best coloring—mostly variations on fire-engine red—and cut the gowns so that they showed off each girl to her best advantage. My mother used to help my father by doing the embroidery on the dresses. Dragons and phoenixes were her favorite and my mother's embroidery was beautiful, small stitches of metallic thread, so fine they looked like brush strokes. She never needed a pattern, the dragons and phoenixes appeared in her head, she saw their outlines, their wings outstretched, their images flying on satin or silk which guided her hands as if by magic.

Her embroidery made my father's work much sought after, but one day she claimed her husband of 12 years was taking too much time getting the measurements of a young girl. His hands lingered a bit too long over the tape encircling her hips. After that my mother refused to do any more embroidery. She said her eyesight was failing, though she saw with bitter sharpness all the times my father's eyes seem to pause over a young girl's figure. My mother refused to see a doctor. She claimed her vision was a gift of the gods, just like her dragons and phoenixes, and my father must be up to something very bad to make it become so blurry. She became so enraged at women entering the shop, she insisted on taking their measurements herself, though indeed her eyesight was very poor and she often mistook the numbers on the tape causing much grief during the fitting sessions. Without her special embroidery and because of her mistaken measurements, my father's business suffered. He became just another tailor, his prices were considered high, his patterns a bit old-fashioned. My father decided to move his shop away from Chinatown, to a neighborhood where he would have more men for clients, not young girls seeking the Miss Chinatown crown, and thereby give my mother some peace.

But the neighborhood he chose did not give them peace. The taquerias and salsa music, the easy gatherings of young men at street corners, the rapid Spanish spoken in shops made both my father and mother feel out of place. My mother stopped going to work with my father and preferred to stay at home. She spent her time making "frogs"—Chinese buttons of thin braid twisted into three circles forming the bulges of a frog's head and eyes. She didn't have to see in order to make these buttons, she could feel her way along. She knew by instinct the exact place where stitches were needed to hold the button's shape. But Chinese buttons were not popular items in my father's new location. My parents' caution toward the outside world increased with my father's diminishing income. Only the family home felt safe to them and this is what they tried to impart to both my brother and me.

Of course my parents didn't want my brother to become a flame diver. They didn't even want him to join the swim team in high school—"too many accidents happen in pools"—but my brother didn't tell them he joined until after he'd already done it. I helped him forge our parents' signatures on the school release form, as he had done for me whenever I cut class. He didn't tell them the truth until after his first competition when he won first place for the platform swan dive. That gave them something to brag about and brag my father did. None of his customers could ever leave his shop without some comment on the first-place ribbon hanging on my father's wall. Our parents didn't like that my brother had gone behind their backs— my father never mentioned that part or my role in the conspiracy—but their pride in my brother's accomplishment did mollify some of their fear. I suppose the possibility of a college scholarship also helped. My father couldn't afford to send my brother to college—he'd used his life savings moving his shop—and since my brother wasn't too academic, his talent for diving, risky as it was, seemed the best path toward the safety of college. My father thought my brother would get a diving scholarship, learn a risk-free well-paying profession, give up his high diving ways after graduation, and live a safe life ever after.

My brother didn't get a scholarship. Although he had a spectacular swan dive, he couldn't seem to master any other. Something happened to his orientation when he tried to perform twists and somersaults. Maybe that time he hit his head made him fearful of hitting the platform again. He couldn't seem to get the spin of going head over heels quite right. When he tried a half twist or a backward gainer, his body went over too far or sometimes not far enough. He suffered spectacular belly flops. He was such a perfectionist though, he practiced diving for hours, but usually only his favorite one—the elegant and beautiful swan dive. A repertory of one dive wasn't enough to impress college recruiters, who thought my brother odd in his singular passion for swan dives. He was looked at and passed over many times during his senior year. Our parents were crushed that my brother wasn't asked to try out for any college team, but my brother didn't seem to mind. He told me one night he thought he could perform swan dives for a living.

"Look at these guys," he showed me a magazine that advertised tours to Mexico displaying muscular men in skimpy bathing suits diving off impossibly high cliffs. "Nothing but swan dives. People pay to see this."

"But you're not Mexican. And those cliffs are so high."

"It doesn't matter, I'm not going to do cliffs. There are other ways to make dives exciting. Look at this." He pulled out another magazine showing tours to Puerto Rico. This ad pictured tourists outside a fancy hotel looking entranced at the sight of a man, encased in flames, diving into a deep blue pool. The tourists clutched at their drinks, their mouths and eyes open in amazement. The caption read: "Thrills everywhere, with comfort you can't compare. Come to the island that has it all—Puerto Rico."

"This is more what I had in mind."

"Puerto Rico?"

"No, I'm going to become a flame diver. I can do it better than this guy. Look, he's not even vertical going in."

"But how can you, where can you—" I could hardly ask a question. None of us had ever been out of state, let alone leave home for such far off lands as Mexico or unimaginably, Puerto Rico.

"I can do it here."

"We don't have a swimming pool."

"God you're so dumb. I'm talking about Worlds of Water, U.S.A. It's only 30 miles from here. It's the perfect place. People are tired of watching animals do tricks for them. They feel guilty about it. They would rather see a man on fire than dolphins going through flaming hoops."

"Wait till mom and dad hear this." I could already imagine their torrents of protests. They hated candles on birthday cakes, their fear of fire was so great.

"They'll come around," my brother assured me. "It's what I want to do."

When I was thirteen, my mother asked for her embroidery basket to see if I possessed her talent. She sat me down with scraps of cloth, a packet of needles, and spools of thread though her eyesight was so poor by then, she could no longer thread the needles. She told me to close my eyes and picture a mighty dragon. She told me to feel its power, feel the flames shooting from the mouth. "Let this image guide your hands, the needle will follow the flames."

I closed my eyes and tried to see her dragon. I tried to feel its heat and let the needle follow. But I was constantly pricking myself, the thread tangled, the cloth bunched up. When I looked at my clumsy stitches all I saw were chicken scratches, uneven threads, unraveling patterns, my mother's nerves frayed at the edge. I had no dragons and phoenixes in me. My mother told me to go wash my hands and be careful putting away the scissors. She knew I hadn't inherited her gift, but she protected me just the same. She said such embroidery was not in fashion, not important anymore. We never tried again.

"I didn't raise my son to perform silly tricks for strangers," was my father's first reaction. "You are not a trained animal."

"I'm not a caged one either," I'd never heard my brother use that tone, especially in front of our father. "I can do it, dad. I've been practicing diving for years."

"High school meets, this is different."

"What's wrong with going to city college?" mother asked. "You can learn a trade, meet a nice girl. Who will you meet at this water world? Nobody there but fish."

"Ma, I have learned a trade. I know how to dive."

"Trying to kill yourself is no way for my son to make a living."

"Diving isn't trying to kill myself, dad. It feels like flying to me."

"Didn't you hear how many people were killed in that plane crash over Mexico? Flying isn't safe anymore." Our mother knew how to change the subject.

"I'm talking about diving, Ma. Swan dives."

"So why do you have to set yourself on fire?"

"Because I need a gimmick to make it look exciting. Dangerous."

There it was—the D-word. They'll never go for it, I thought. How could he expect their support when he played on their worst fears? I felt sorry for my brother then. All his diving dreams and he had to choose the wrong word.

"But it only has to look dangerous, dad. Really it's very safe."

I don't think my father was always so cautious. He was quite the gambler once. He used to go to weekly poker games in Chinatown before he moved his shop. He used to talk about opening a factory or a specialty store featuring mom's embroidery. But that was before the trouble began, before she started accusing him.

When I look at my father now, sighing as he hems a pair of trousers, replaces a zipper, or watches my mother making her buttons, I don't think he ever had a wandering eye. I think my mother must have made it up because her vision was blurred. I think she was afraid without her embroidery, my father would no longer need her. She thought he would find a younger woman, leave her with two children, middle-aged, blind, and alone.

But that never happened. I think my father felt embarrassed that he had no dragon in his head. My mother was the one with the gift. She had the visions that spread to his cloth. She had the instinct that knew just how to hold buttons and things together. He was afraid he would lose her. They didn't know how to reassure themselves, so they moved the shop to a new location and tried to shield my brother and me from further loss in a dangerous world.

Three nights after my brother made his announcement that he was going to become a flame diver, my father brought home this special material—something like rubber only more flexible—and spent hours gluing it together with a special flame retardant glue. He placed a glued piece over our kitchen stove testing to see if it melted, putting his hand on the burner to see how hot it grew. He timed how long it took before the material grew too hot for his hand. He glued squares of it together to see if he could take more heat. My mother insisted my father not risk his sewing hands and stuck her own into the makeshift glove holding it over the gas flame, turning the stove to high, staring with unseeing eyes at the blue circle of heat, patiently daring it to burn her. My parents experimented for a month with different materials, different glues, different thicknesses, different flames before deciding a suit could indeed be made that would protect their flesh and blood. Engulfed by my brother's passion, only they could make him safe.

I haven't told my parents yet, not even my brother though maybe he would understand. I see a man after school. He lives two blocks from the school and I go to his house everyday before I walk home alone. He is an older white man, not as old as my father. He called to me from his window one day as I was walking home and asked if I could bring in his paper and check his mail box for him. When I brought in his paper and mail, he was very polite and apologized for troubling me, but he couldn't get out of bed. He asked if I had a few minutes and would I mind reading something to him, he wanted to hear another voice. He asked me to read Ann Landers' column. I think he was very lonely. I read to him and he thanked me and that's how it began. Now I read to him for 15 minutes everyday, sometimes things from the newspaper, sometimes things from magazines, mostly magazines about sex that he gets delivered in the mail. The magazines are the type my parents would never approve of me reading. I sit at the foot of his bed and read and he listens to me with closed eyes. Sometimes his body tenses and I see sweat break out on his forehead. He listens so intently, I feel heat coming off his body. He's always very polite to me. He says that I am a gift. He says that when he hears my voice, it helps him to feel alive.

My brother tells me what a rush it is to be a sponge for everyone's fear. To be so focused on what he does, he only hears his own heart beat. He's vaguely aware of the ladder he climbs to the platform hanging above the pool. He doesn't hear the roll of the drum, he doesn't hear his name announced, he doesn't hear the height of the platform called out, he doesn't see the water. Encased in his protective suit, glued with familial pride, he feels which way the wind blows by the way it buffets his body. He tells me the exact routine. The number of deep breaths he takes, the number of sprays of butane needed to coat him from head to foot, the sound of the torch which explodes with a roar, the moment he holds his flaming hands outstretched before closing his eyes and flying. He tells me he opens his eyes at the peak of his arch—a dragon sailing through pure blue silk before tucking his head and splashing into the satin smooth mouth of the pool.

And I have imagined the crowd's awe building up with the flames, the tightening nerves with the drum roll, the fearful split second of silence, the collective breath for this human torch against blue sky, the lesser sun god, this crazy kid. And then I've imagined the plunge, a blurred arch of orange and smoke, a curve straightening to a lightning shaft, a sizzling hiss as he breaks the water, the cheers welling up like ocean waves sweeping aside stunned silence. I imagine when my brother surfaces and swims to the side of the pool, the audience sees a phoenix rising, their fears melt, the smiles grow, the celebration is complete. And as he doffs his helmet, waving his arms and smiling broadly, he reassures the crowd that all is well, nothing bad has happened, no loss has occurred. He dove through fire and survived. He lives to dive again. Everything is normal.

CRITICAL THINKING QUESTIONS

1. a. Expressing shock over her brother's wanting to be a flame diver, the narrator says, "I've never been in danger, never known a need for risk." Later in the story, however, she tells about her daily reading sessions with "an older white man, not as old as my father." She says she reads from newspapers and magazines, "mostly magazines about sex. . . . He's always very polite to me. He says that I am a gift." How have reason and emotion factored into the narrator's decision to read to this man?

   b. The narrator says she has not even told her brother that she is seeing this man after school, "though maybe he would understand." What is it she thinks he might understand? Do you think she should continue her visits?

2. Read Peter D. Kramer's essay, "Divorce and Our National Values," included later in this chapter. How does this story suggest a different cultural perspective on Kramer's claim about the divorce rate and American values?

WRITING TOPICS

1. Early on, the narrator says, "Safe. That is the most important consideration for our family. Perhaps there is a Chinese gene encoded with a protein for caution." The narrator suggests that the focus on the safety of one's family members may be particularly strong for her Chinese family, especially when the family has transplanted itself in a foreign culture. An assumption held by the narrator's parents is that family must provide a safe haven, a barrier from the destructive influence of outsiders. What do your experiences and observations suggest about the concept of family as protection, a safeguard for its members?

2. Does family provide a safety net that protects its members or a net that entraps them? As you formulate a claim for this family issue, you could choose to construct a Rogerian argument that posits a middle-ground perspective (other literature suggestions: Mukherjee's "A Father," Fierstein's *On Tidy Endings*).

Bharati Mukherjee

A Father

One Wednesday morning in mid-May Mr. Bhowmick woke up as he usually did at 5:43 A.M., checked his Rolex against the alarm clock's digital readout, punched down the alarm (set for 5:45), then nudged his wife awake. She worked as a claims investigator for an insurance company that had an office in a nearby shopping mall. She didn't really have to leave the house until 8:30, but she liked to get up early and cook him a big breakfast. Mr. Bhowmick had to drive a long way to work. He was a naturally dutiful, cautious man, and he set the alarm clock early enough to accommodate a margin for accidents.

While his wife, in a pink nylon negligee she had paid for with her own Master-Card card, made him a new version of French toast from a clipping ("Eggs-cellent Recipes!") Scotchtaped to the inside of a kitchen cupboard, Mr. Bhowmick brushed his teeth. He brushed, he gurgled with the loud, hawking noises that he and his brother had been taught as children to make in order to flush clean not merely teeth but also tongue and palate.

After that he showered, then, back in the bedroom again, he recited prayers in Sanskrit to Kali, the patron goddess of his family, the goddess of wrath and vengeance. In the pokey flat of his childhood in Ranchi, Bihar, his mother had given over a whole bedroom to her collection of gods and goddesses. Mr. Bhowmick couldn't be that extravagant in Detroit. His daughter, twenty-six and an electrical engineer, slept in the other of the two bedrooms in his apartment. But he had done his best. He had taken Woodworking I and II at a nearby recreation center and built a grotto for the goddess. Kali-Mata was eight inches tall, made of metal and painted a glistening black so that the metal glowed like the oiled, black skin of a peasant woman. And though Kali-Mata was totally nude except for a tiny gilt crown and a garland strung together from sinners' chopped off heads, she looked warm, cozy, *pleased*, in her makeshift wooden shrine in Detroit. Mr. Bhowmick had gathered quite a crowd of admiring, fellow woodworkers in those final weeks of decoration.

"Hurry it up with the prayers," his wife shouted from the kitchen. She was an agnostic, a believer in ambition, not grace. She frequently complained that his prayers had gotten so long that soon he wouldn't have time to go to work, play duplicate bridge with the Ghosals, or play the tabla in the Bengali Association's one Sunday per month musical soirees. Lately she'd begun to drain him in a wholly new way. He wasn't praying, she nagged; he was shutting her out of his life. There'd be no peace in the house until she hid Kali-Mata in a suitcase.

She nagged, and he threatened to beat her with his shoe as his father had threatened his mother: it was the thrust and volley of marriage. There was no question of actually taking off a shoe and applying it to his wife's body. She was bigger than he was. And, secretly, he admired her for having the nerve, the agnosticism, which as a college boy in backward Bihar he too had claimed.

"I have time," he shot at her. He was still wrapped in a damp terry towel.

"You have time for everything but domestic life."

It was the fault of the shopping mall that his wife had started to buy pop psychology paperbacks. These paperbacks preached that for couples who could sit down and talk about their "relationship," life would be sweet again. His engineer daughter was on his wife's side. She accused him of holding things in.

"Face it, Dad," she said. "You have an affect deficit."

But surely everyone had feelings they didn't want to talk about or talk over. He definitely did not want to blurt out anything about the sick-in-the-guts sensations that came over him most mornings and that he couldn't bubble down with Alka-Seltzer or smother with Gas-X. The women in his family were smarter than him. They were cheerful, outgoing, more American somehow.

How could he tell these bright, mocking women that, in the 5:43 A.M. darkness, he sensed invisible presences: gods and snakes frolicked in the master bedroom, little white sparks of cosmic static crackled up the legs of his pajamas. Something was out there in the dark, something that could invent accidents and coincidences to remind mortals that even in Detroit they were no more than mortal. His wife would label his paranoia and dismiss it. Paranoia, premonition: whatever it was, it had begun to undermine his composure.

Take this morning, Mr. Bhowmick has woken up from a pleasant dream about a man taking a Club Med vacation, and the postdream satisfaction had lasted through the shower, but when he'd come back to the shrine in the bedroom, he'd noticed all at once how scarlet and saucy was the tongue that Kali-Mata stuck out at the world. Surely he had not lavished such alarming detail, such admonitory colors on that flap of flesh.

Watch out, ambulatory sinners. Be careful out there, the goddess warned him, and not with the affection of Sergeant Esterhaus, either.

"French toast must be eaten hot-hot," his wife nagged. "Otherwise they'll taste like rubber."

Mr. Bhowmick laid the trousers of a two-trouser suit he had bought on sale that winter against his favorite tweed jacket. The navy stripes in the trousers and the small, navy tweed flecks in the jacket looked quite good together. So what if the Chief Engineer had already started wearing summer cottons?

"I am coming, I am coming," he shouted back. "You want me to eat hot-hot, you start the frying only when I am sitting down. You didn't learn anything from Mother in Ranchi?"

"Mother cooked French toast from fancy recipes? I mean French Sandwich Toast with complicated filling?"

He came into the room to give her his testiest look. "You don't know the meaning of complicated cookery. And mother had to get the coal fire of the *chula* going first."

His daughter was already at the table. "Why don't you break down and buy her a microwave oven? That's what I mean about sitting down and talking things out." She had finished her orange juice. She took a plastic measure of Slim-Fast out of its can and poured the powder into a glass of skim milk. "It's ridiculous."

Babli was not the child he would have chosen as his only heir. She was brighter certainly than the sons and daughters of the other Bengalis he knew in Detroit, and she had been the only female student in most of her classes at Georgia Tech, but as she sat there in her beige linen business suit, her thick chin dropping into a polka-dotted cravat, he regretted again that she was not the child of his dreams. Babli would be able to help him out moneywise if something happened to him, something so bad that even his pension plans and his insurance policies and his money market schemes wouldn't be enough. But Babli could never comfort him. She wasn't womanly or tender the way that unmarried girls had been in the wistful days of his adolescence. She could sing Hindi film songs, mimicking exactly the high, artificial voice of Lata Mungeshkar, and she had taken two years of dance lessons at Sona Devi's Dance Academy in Southfield, but these accomplishments didn't add up to real femininity. Not the kind that had given him palpitations in Ranchi.

Mr. Bhowmick did his best with his wife's French toast. In spite of its filling of marshmallows, apricot jam and maple syrup, it tasted rubbery. He drank two cups of Darjeeling tea, said, "Well, I'm off," and took off.

All might have gone well if Mr. Bhowmick hadn't fussed longer than usual about putting his briefcase and his trenchcoat in the backseat. He got in behind the wheel of his Oldsmobile, fixed his seatbelt and was just about to turn the key in the ignition when his neighbor, Al Stazniak, who was starting up his Buick Skylark, sneezed. A sneeze at the start of a journey brings bad luck. Al Stazniak's sneeze was fierce, made up of five short bursts, too loud to be ignored.

Be careful out there! Mr. Bhowmick could see the goddess's scarlet little tongue tip wagging at him.

He was a modern man, an intelligent man. Otherwise he couldn't have had the options in life that he did have. He couldn't have given up a good job with perks in Bombay and found a better job with General Motors in Detroit. But Mr. Bhowmick was also a prudent enough man to know that some abiding truth lies bunkered within each wanton Hindu superstition. A sneeze was more than a sneeze. The heedless are carried off in ambulances. He had choices to make. He could ignore the sneeze, and so challenge the world unseen by men. Perhaps Al Staznick had hayfever. For a sneeze to be a potent omen, surely it had to be unprovoked and terrifying, a thunderclap cleaving the summer skies. Or he could admit the smallness of mortals, undo the fate of the universe by starting over, and go back inside the apartment, sit for a second on the sofa, then re-start his trip.

Al Staznick rolled down his window. "Everything okay?"

Mr. Bhowmick nodded shyly. They weren't really friends in the way neighbors can sometimes be. They talked as they parked or pulled out of their adjacent parking stalls. For all Mr. Bhowmick knew, Al Stazniak had no legs. He had never seen the man out of his Skylark.

He let the Buick back out first. Everything was okay, yes, please. All the same he undid his seatbelt. Compromise, adaptability, call it what you will. A dozen times a day he made these small trade-offs between new-world reasonableness and old-world beliefs.

While he was sitting in his parked car, his wife's ride came by. For fifty dollars a month, she was picked up and dropped off by a hard up, newly divorced woman who worked at a florist's shop in the same mall. His wife came out the front door in brown K-Mart pants and a burgundy windbreaker. She waved to him, then slipped into the passenger seat of the florist's rusty Japanese car.

He was a metallurgist. He knew about rust and ways of preventing it, secret ways, thus far unknown to the Japanese.

Babli's fiery red Mitsubishi was still in the lot. She wouldn't leave for work for another eight minutes. He didn't want her to know he'd been undone by a sneeze. Babli wasn't tolerant of superstitions. She played New Wave music in her tapedeck. If asked about Hinduism, all she'd ever said to her American friends was that "it's neat." Mr. Bhowmick had heard her on the phone years before. The cosmos balanced on the head of a snake was like a beach ball balanced on the snout of a circus seal. "This Hindu myth stuff," he'd heard her say, "is like a series of super graphics."

He'd forgiven her. He could probably forgive her anything. It was her way of surviving high school in a city that was both native to her, and alien.

There was no question of going back where he'd come from. He hated Ranchi. Ranchi was no place for dreamers. All through his teenage years, Mr. Bhowmick had dreamed of success abroad. What form that success would take he had left vague. Success had meant to him escape from the constant plotting and bitterness that wore out India's middle class.

Babli should have come out of the apartment and driven off to work by now. Mr. Bhowmick decided to take a risk, to dash inside and pretend he'd left his briefcase on the coffee table.

When he entered the living room, he noticed Babli's spring coat and large vinyl pocketbook on the sofa. She was probably sorting through the junk jewelry on her dresser to give her business suit a lift. She read hints about dressing in women's magazines and applied them to her person with seriousness. If his luck held, he could sit on the sofa, say a quick prayer and get back to the car without her catching on.

It surprised him that she didn't shout out from her bedroom, "Who's there?" What if he had been a rapist?

Then he heard Babli in the bathroom. He heard unladylike squawking noises. She was throwing up. A squawk, a spitting, then the horrible gurgle of a waterfall.

A revelation came to Mr. Bhowmick. A woman vomiting in the privacy of the bathroom could mean many things. She was coming down with the flu. She was nervous about a meeting. But Mr. Bhowmick knew at once that his daughter, his untender, unloving daughter whom he couldn't love and hadn't tried to love, was not, in the larger world of Detroit, unloved. Sinners are everywhere, even in the bosom of an upright, unambitious family like the Bhowmicks. It was the goddess sticking out her tongue at him.

The father sat heavily on the sofa, shrinking from contact with her coat and pocketbook. His brisk, bright engineer daughter was pregnant. Someone had taken time to make love to her. Someone had thought her tender, feminine. Someone even now was perhaps mooning over her. The idea excited him. It was so grotesque and wondrous. At twenty-six Babli had found the man of her dreams; whereas at twenty-six Mr. Bhowmick had given up on truth, beauty, and poetry and exchanged them for two years at Carnegie Tech.

Mr. Bhowmick's tweed-jacketed body sagged against the sofa cushions. Babli would abort, of course. He knew his Babli. It was the only possible option if she didn't want to bring shame to the Bhowmick family. All the same, he could see a chubby baby boy on the rug, crawling to his granddaddy. Shame like that was easier to hide in Ranchi. There was always a barren womb sanctified by marriage that could claim sudden fructifying by the goddess Parvati. Babli would do what she wanted. She was headstrong and independent and he was afraid of her.

Babli staggered out of the bathroom. Damp stains ruined her linen suit. It was the first time he had seen his daughter look ridiculous, quite unprofessional. She didn't come into the living room to investigate the noises he'd made. He glimpsed her shoeless stockinged feet flip-flop on collapsed arches down the hall to her bedroom.

"Are you all right?" Mr. Bhowmick asked, standing in the hall. "Do you need Sinutab?"

She wheeled around. "What're you doing here?"

He was the one who should be angry. "I'm feeling poorly too," he said. "I'm taking the day off."

"I feel fine," Babli said.

Within fifteen minutes Babli had changed her clothes and left. Mr. Bhowmick had the apartment to himself all day. All day for praising or cursing the life that had brought him along with its other surprises an illegitimate grandchild.

It was his wife that he blamed. Coming to America to live had been his wife's idea. After the wedding, the young Bhowmicks had spent two years in Pittsburgh on his student visa, then gone back home to Ranchi for nine years. Nine crushing years. Then the job in Bombay had come through. All during those nine years his wife had screamed and wept. She was a woman of wild, progressive ideas—she'd called them her "American" ideas—and she'd been martyred by her neighbors for them. American *memsahib. Markin mem, Markin mem.* In bazaars the beggar boys had trailed her and hooted. She'd done provocative things. She'd hired a *chamar* woman who by caste rules was forbidden to cook for higher caste families, especially for widowed mothers of decent men. This had caused a blowup in the neighborhood. She'd made other, lesser errors. While other wives shopped and cooked every day, his wife had cooked the whole week's menu on weekends.

"What's the point of having a refrigerator, then?" She'd been scornful of the Ranchi women.

His mother, an old-fashioned widow, had accused her of trying to kill her by poisoning. "You are in such a hurry? You want to get rid of me quick-quick so you can go back to the States?"

Family life had been turbulent.

He had kept aloof, inwardly siding with his mother. He did not love his wife now, and he had not loved her then. In any case, he had not defended her. He felt some affection, and he felt guilty for having shunned her during those unhappy years. But he had thought of it then as revenge. He had wanted to marry a beautiful woman. Not being a young man of means, only a young man with prospects, he had had no right to yearn for pure beauty. He cursed his fate and after a while, settled for a barrister's daughter, a plain girl with a wide, flat plank of a body and myopic eyes. The barrister had sweetened the deal by throwing in an all-expenses-paid two years' study at Carnegie Tech to which Mr. Bhowmick had been admitted. Those two years had changed his wife from pliant girl to ambitious woman. She wanted America, nothing less.

It was his wife who had forced him to apply for permanent resident status in the U.S. even though he had a good job in Ranchi as a government engineer. The putting together of documents for the immigrant visa had been a long and humbling process. He had had to explain to a chilly clerk in the Embassy that, like most Indians of his generation, he had no birth certificate. He had to swear out affidavits, suffer through police checks, bribe orderlies whose job it was to move his dossier from desk to desk. The decision, the clerk had advised him, would take months, maybe years. He hadn't dared hope that merit might be rewarded. Merit could collapse under bad luck. It was for grace that he prayed.

While the immigration papers were being processed, he had found the job in Bombay. So he'd moved his mother in with his younger brother's family, and left his hometown for good. Life in Bombay had been lighthearted, almost fulfilling. His wife had thrown herself into charity work with the same energy that had offended the Ranchi women. He was happy to be in a big city at last. Bombay was the Rio de Janeiro of the East; he'd read that in a travel brochure. He drove out to Nariman Point at least once a week to admire the necklace of municipal lights, toss coconut shells into the dark ocean, drink beer at the Oberoi-Sheraton where overseas Indian girls in designer jeans beckoned him in sly ways. His nights were full. He played duplicate bridge, went to the movies, took his wife to Bingo nights at his club. In Detroit he was a lonelier man.

Then the green card had come through. For him, for his wife, and for the daughter who had been born to them in Bombay. He sold what he could sell, and put in his brother's informal trust what he couldn't to save on taxes. Then he had left for America, and one more start.

All through the week, Mr. Bhowmick watched his daughter. He kept furtive notes on how many times she rushed to the bathroom and made hawking, wrenching noises, how many times she stayed late at the office, calling her mother to say she'd be taking in a movie and pizza afterwards with friends.

He had to tell her that he knew. And he probably didn't have much time. She shouldn't be on Slim-Fast in her condition. He had to talk things over with her. But what would he say to her? What position could he take? He had to choose between public shame for the family, and murder.

For three more weeks he watched her and kept his silence. Babli wore shifts to the office instead of business suits, and he liked her better in those garments. Perhaps she was dressing for her young man, not from necessity. Her skin was pale and blotchy by turn. At breakfast her fingers looked stiff, and she had trouble with silverware.

Two Saturdays running, he lost badly at duplicate bridge. His wife scolded him. He had made silly mistakes. When was Babli meeting this man? Where? He must be American; Mr. Bhowmick prayed only that he was white. He pictured his grandson crawling to him, and the grandson was always fat and brown and buttery-skinned, like the infant Krishna. An American son-in-law was a terrifying notion. Why was she not mentioning men, at least, preparing the way for the major announcement? He listened sharply for men's names, rehearsed little lines like, "Hello, Bob, I'm Babli's old man," with a cracked little laugh. Bob, Jack, Jimmy, Tom. But no names surfaced. When she went out for pizza and a movie it was with the familiar set of Indian girls and their strange, unpopular, American friends, all without men. Mr. Bhowmick tried to be reasonable. Maybe she had already gotten married and was keeping it secret. "Well, Bob, you and Babli sure had Mrs. Bhowmick and me going there, heh-heh," he mumbled one night with the Sahas and Ghosals, over cards. "Pardon?" asked Pronob Saha. Mr. Bhowmick dropped two tricks, and his wife glared. "Such stupid blunders," she fumed on the drive back. A new truth was dawning; there would be no marriage for Babli. Her young man probably was not so young and not so available. He must be already married. She must have yielded to passion or been raped in the office. His wife seemed to have noticed nothing. Was he a murderer, or a conspirator? He kept his secret from his wife; his daughter kept her decision to herself.

Nights, Mr. Bhowmick pretended to sleep, but as soon as his wife began her snoring—not real snores so much as loud, gaspy gulpings for breath—he turned on his side and prayed to Kali-Mata.

In July, when Babli's belly had begun to push up against the waistless dresses she'd bought herself, Mr. Bhowmick came out of the shower one weekday morning and found the two women screaming at each other. His wife had a rolling pin in one hand. His daughter held up a *National Geographic* as a shield for her head. The crazy look that had been in his wife's eyes when she'd shooed away beggar kids was in her eyes again.

"Stop it!" His own boldness overwhelmed him. "Shut up! Babli's pregnant, so what? It's your fault, you made us come to the States."

Girls like Babli were caught between rules, that's the point he wished to make. They were too smart, too impulsive for a backward place like Ranchi, but not tough nor smart enough for sex-crazy places like Detroit.

"My fault?" his wife cried. "I told her to do hanky-panky with boys? I told her to shame us like this?"

She got in one blow with the rolling pin. The second glanced off Babli's shoulder and fell on his arm which he had stuck out for his grandson's sake.

"I'm calling the police," Babli shouted. She was out of the rolling pin's range. "This is brutality. You can't do this to me."

"Shut up! Shut your mouth, foolish woman." He wrenched the weapon from his wife's fist. He made a show of taking off his shoe to beat his wife on the face.

"What do you know? You don't know anything." She let herself down slowly on a dining chair. Her hair, curled overnight, stood in wild whorls around her head. "Nothing."

"And you do!" He laughed. He remembered her tormentors, and laughed again. He had begun to enjoy himself. Now *he* was the one with the crazy, progressive ideas.

"Your daughter is pregnant, yes," she said, "any fool knows that. But ask her the name of the father. Go, ask."

He stared at his daughter who gazed straight ahead, eyes burning with hate, jaw clenched with fury.

"Babli?"

"Who needs a man?" she hissed. "The father of my baby is a bottle and a syringe. Men louse up your lives. I just want a baby. Oh, don't worry—he's a certified fit donor. No diseases, college graduate, above average, and he made the easiest twenty-five dollars of his life—"

"Like animals," his wife said. For the first time he heard horror in her voice. His daughter grinned at him. He saw her tongue, thick and red, squirming behind her row of perfect teeth.

"Yes, yes, yes," she screamed, "like livestock. Just like animals. You should be happy—that's what marriage is all about, isn't it? Matching bloodlines, matching horoscopes, matching castes, matching, matching, matching . . ." and it was difficult to know if she was laughing or singing, or mocking and like a madwoman.

Mr. Bhowmick lifted the rolling pin high above his head and brought it down hard on the dome of Babli's stomach. In the end, it was his wife who called the police.

CRITICAL THINKING QUESTIONS

1. How do Mr. Bhowmick's cultural ideology and beliefs shape his identity and direct his relationships with his wife and daughter?

2. When Mr. Bhowmick's neighbor sneezes, the narrator notes, "Mr. Bhowmick could see the goddess's scarlet little tongue tip wagging at him." After some consideration, Mr. Bhowmick decides on a compromise response: "Compro-

mise, adaptability, call it what you will. A dozen times a day, he made these small trade-offs between new-world reasonableness and old-world beliefs." How does the story support or refute Mr. Bhowmick's self-evaluation?

3. What is a claim that Mukherjee's story implies about an individual's ability to live internally according to one cultural paradigm, while living externally according to a conflicting cultural paradigm?

WRITING TOPIC

Have you heard a classmate proclaim (or thought to yourself), "Why don't any of these stories have happy endings?" Record your reaction to the endings of several short stories (suggestions: Mukherjee's "A Father," Power's "Red Moccasins"). Reflect on your responses and also consider this assertion by British author, Horace Walpole (1717–1797): "The world is a comedy to those that think, a tragedy to those that feel." Then do some freewriting about the function or value of the (un)happy ending. Now, formulate a *claim of value* about the endings of short stories and write an argument that addresses the question, "Why don't any of these stories have happy endings?"

Fae Myenne Ng

A Red Sweater

I chose red for my sister. Fierce, dark red. Made in Hong Kong. Hand Wash Only because it's got that skin of fuzz. She'll look happy. That's good. Everything's perfect, for a minute. That seems enough.

Red. For Good Luck. Of course. This fire-red sweater is swollen with good cheer. Wear it, I will tell her. You'll look lucky.

We're a family of three girls. By Chinese standards, that's not lucky. "Too bad," outsiders whisper, ". . . nothing but daughters. A failed family."

First, Middle, and End girl. Our order of birth marked us. That came to tell more than our given names.

My eldest sister, Lisa, lives at home. She quit San Francisco State, one semester short of a psychology degree. One day she said, "Forget about it, I'm tired." She's working full time at Pacific Telephone now. Nine hundred a month with benefits. Mah and Deh think it's a great deal. They tell everybody, "Yes, our Number One makes good pay, but that's not even counting the discount. If we call Hong Kong, China even, there's forty percent off!" As if anyone in their part of China had a telephone.

Number Two, the in-between, jumped off the 'M' floor three years ago. Not true! What happened? Why? Too sad! All we say about that is, "It was her choice."

We sent Mah to Hong Kong. When she left Hong Kong thirty years ago, she was the envy of all: "Lucky girl! You'll never have to work." To marry a sojourner was to have a future. Thirty years in the land of gold and good fortune, and then she returned to tell the story: three daughters, one dead, one unmarried, another who-cares-where, the thirty years in sweatshops, and the prince of the Golden Mountain turned into a toad. I'm glad I didn't have to go with her. I felt her shame and regret. To return, seeking solace and comfort, instead of offering banquets and stories of the good life.

I'm the youngest. I started flying with Pan Am the year Mah returned to Hong Kong, so I got her a good discount. She thought I was good for something then. But when she returned, I was pregnant.

"Get an abortion," she said. "Drop the baby," she screamed.

"No."

"Then get married."

"No. I don't want to."

I was going to get an abortion all along. I just didn't like the way they talked about the whole thing. They made me feel like dirt, that I was a disgrace. Now I can see how I used it as an opportunity. Sometimes I wonder if there wasn't another way. Everything about those years was so steamy and angry. There didn't seem to be any answers.

"I have no eyes for you," Mah said.

"Don't call us," Deh said.

They wouldn't talk to me. They ranted idioms to each other for days. The apartment was filled with images and curses I couldn't perceive. I got the general idea: I was a rotten, no-good, dead thing. I would die in a gutter without rice in my belly. My spirit—if I had one—wouldn't be fed. I wouldn't see good days in this life or the next.

My parents always had a special way of saying things.

Now I'm based in Honolulu. When our middle sister jumped, she kind of closed the world. The family just sort of fell apart. I left. Now, I try to make up for it, but the folks still won't see me, but I try to keep in touch with them through Lisa. Flying cuts up your life, hits hardest during the holidays. I'm always sensitive then. I feel like I'm missing something, that people are doing something really important while I'm up in the sky, flying through time zones.

So I like to see Lisa around the beginning of the year. January, New Year's, and February, New Year's again, double luckiness with our birthdays in between. With so much going on, there's always something to talk about.

"You pick the place this year," I tell her.

"Around here?"

"No," I say. 'Around here' means the food is good and the living hard. You eat a steaming rice plate, and then you feel like rushing home to sew garments or assemble radio parts or something. We eat together only once a year, so I feel we should splurge. Besides, at the Chinatown places, you have nothing to talk about except the bare issues. In American restaurants, the atmosphere helps you along. I want nice light and a view and handsome waiters.

"Let's go somewhere with a view," I say.

We decide to go to FOLLOWING SEA, a new place on the Pier 39 track. We're early, the restaurant isn't crowded. It's been clear all day, so I think the sunset will be nice. I ask for a window table. I turn to talk to my sister, but she's already talking to a waiter. He's got that dark island tone that she likes. He's looking her up and down. My sister does not blink at it. She holds his look and orders two Johnny Walkers. I pick up a fork, turn it around in my hand. I seldom use chopsticks now. At home, I eat my rice in a plate, with a fork. The only chopsticks I own, I wear in my hair. For a moment, I feel strange sitting here at this unfamiliar table. I don't know this tablecloth, this linen, these candles. Everything seems foreign. It feels like we should be different people. But each time I look up, she's the same. I know this person. She's my sister. We sat together with chopsticks, mismatched bowls, braids, and braces, across the formica tabletop.

"I like three pronged forks," I say, pressing my thumb against the sharp points.

My sister rolls her eyes. She lights a cigarette.

I ask for one.

I finally say, "So, what's new?"

"Not much." Her voice is sullen. She doesn't look at me. Once a year, I come in, asking questions. She's got the answers, but she hates them. For me, I think she's got the peace of heart, knowing that she's done her share for Mah and Deh. She thinks I have the peace, not caring. Her life is full of questions, too, but I have no answers.

I look around the restaurant. The sunset is not spectacular and we don't comment on it. The waiters are lighting candles. Ours is bringing the drinks. He stops very close to my sister, seems to breathe her in. She raises her face toward him. "Ready?" he asks. My sister orders for us. The waiter struts off.

"Tight ass," I say.

"The best," she says.

My scotch tastes good. It reminds me of Deh. Johnny Walker or Seagrams 7, that's what they served at Chinese banquets. Nine courses and a bottle. No ice. We learned to drink it Chinese style, in teacups. Deh drank from his rice bowl, sipping it like hot soup. By the end of the meal, he took it like cool tea, in bold mouthfuls. We sat watching, our teacups of scotch in our laps, his three giggly girls.

Relaxed, I'm thinking there's a connection. Johnny Walker then and Johnny Walker now. I ask for another cigarette and this one I enjoy. Now my Johnny Walker pops with ice. I twirl the glass to make the ice tinkle.

We clink glasses. Three times for good luck. She giggles. I feel better.

"Nice sweater," I say.

"Michael Owyang," she says. She laughs. The light from the candle makes her eyes shimmer. She's got Mah's eyes. Eyes that make you want to talk. Lisa is reed-thin and tall. She's got a body that clothes look good on. My sister slips something on and it wraps her like skin. Fabric has pulse on her.

"Happy birthday, soon," I say.

"Thanks, and to yours too, just as soon."

"Here's to Johnny Walker in shark's fin soup," I say.

"And squab dinners."

"I LOVE LUCY," I say.

We laugh. It makes us feel like children again. We remember how to be sisters. I raise my glass. "To I LOVE LUCY, squab dinners, and brown bags."

"To bones," she says.

"Bones," I repeat. This is a funny that gets sad, and knowing it, I keep laughing. I am surprised how much memory there is in one word. Pigeons. Only recently did I learn they're called squab. Our word for them was pigeon—on a plate or flying over Portsmouth Square. A good meal at 40 cents a bird. In line by dawn, we waited at the butcher's listening for the slow, churning motor of the trucks. We watched the live fish flushing out of the tanks into the garbage pails. We smelled the honey-brushed cha sui bows baking. When the white laundry truck turned onto Wentworth, there was a puffing tail of feathers following it. A stench filled the alley. The crowd squeezed in around the truck. Old ladies reached into the crates, squeezing and tugging for the plumpest pigeons.

My sister and I picked the white ones, those with the most expressive eyes. Dove birds, we called them. We fed them leftover rice in water, and as long as they stayed plump, they were our pets, our baby dove birds. And then one day we'd come home from school and find them cooked. They were a special, nutritious treat. Mah let us fill our bowls high with little pigeon parts: legs, breasts, and wings, and take them out to the front room to watch I LOVE LUCY. We took brown bags for the bones. We balanced our bowls on our laps and laughed at Lucy. We leaned forward, our chopsticks crossed in mid-air, and called out, "Mah! Mah! Come watch! Watch Lucy cry!"

But she always sat alone in the kitchen sucking out the sweetness of the lesser parts: necks, backs, and the head. "Bones are sweeter than you know," she always said. She came out to check the bags. "Clean bones," she said, shaking the bags. "No waste," she said.

Our dinners come with a warning. "Plate's hot. Don't touch." My sister orders a carafe of house white. "Enjoy," he says, smiling at my sister. She doesn't look up.

I can't remember how to say scallops in Chinese. I ask my sister, she doesn't know either. The food isn't great. Or maybe we just don't have the taste buds in us to go crazy over it. Sometimes I get very hungry for Chinese flavors: black beans, garlic and ginger, shrimp paste and sesame oil. These are tastes we grew up with, still dream about. Crave. Run around town after. Duck liver sausage, beancurd, jook, salted fish, and fried dace with black beans. Western flavors don't stand out, the surroundings do. Three pronged forks. Pink tablecloths. Fresh flowers. Cute waiters. An odd difference.

"Maybe we should have gone to Sun Hung Heung. At least the vegetables are real," I say.

"Hung toh-vee-foo-won-tun!" she says.

"Yeah, yum!" I say.

I remember Deh teaching us how to pick bok choy, his favorite vegetable. "Stick your fingernail into the stem. Juicy and firm, good. Limp and tough, no good." The three of us followed Deh, punching our thumbnails into every stem of bok choy we saw.

"Deh still eating bok choy?"

"Breakfast, lunch and dinner." My sister throws her head back, and laughs. It is Deh's motion. She recites in a mimic tone. "Your Deh, all he needs is a good hot bowl of rice and a plate full of greens. A good monk."

There was always bok choy. Even though it was nonstop for Mah—rushing to the sweatshop in the morning, out to shop on break, and then home to cook by evening—she did this for him. A plate of bok choy, steaming with the taste of ginger and garlic. He said she made good rice. Timed full-fire until the first boil, medium until the grains formed a crust along the sides of the pot, and then low-flammed to let the rice steam. Firm, that's how Deh liked his rice.

The waiter brings the wine, asks if everything is alright.

"Everything," my sister says.

There's something else about this meeting. I can hear it in the edge of her voice. She doesn't say anything and I don't ask. Her lips make a contorting line; her face looks sour. She lets out a breath. It sounds like she's been holding it in too long.

"Another fight. The bank line," she says. "He waited four times in the bank line. Mah ran around outside shopping. He was doing her a favor. She was doing him a favor. Mah wouldn't stop yelling. 'Get out and go die! Useless Thing! Stinking Corpse!'"

I know he answered. His voice must have had that fortune teller's tone to it. You listened because you knew it was a warning.

He always threatened to disappear, jump off the Golden Gate. His thousand-year-old threat. I've heard it all before. "I will go. Even when dead, I won't be far enough away. Curse the good will that blinded me into taking you as wife!"

I give Lisa some of my scallops. "Eat," I tell her.

She keeps talking. "Of course, you know how Mah thinks, that nobody should complain because she's been the one working all these years."

I nod. I start eating, hoping she'll follow.

One bite and she's talking again. "You know what shopping with Mah is like, either you stand outside with the bags like a servant, or inside like a marker, holding a place in line. You know how she gets into being frugal—saving time because it's the one free thing in her life. Well, they're at the bank and she had him hold her place in line while she runs up and down Stockton doing her quick shopping maneuvers. So he's in line, and it's his turn, but she's not back. So he has to start all over at the back again. Then it's his turn but she's still not back. When she finally comes in, she's got bags in both hands, and he's going through the line for the fourth time. Of course she doesn't say sorry or anything."

I interrupt. "How do you know all this?" I tell myself not to come back next year. I tell myself to apply for another transfer, to the East Coast.

"She told me. Word for word." Lisa spears the scallops, puts it in her mouth. I know it's cold by now. "Word for word," she repeats. She cuts a piece of chicken. "Try," she says.

I think about how we're sisters. We eat slowly, chewing carefully, like old people. A way to make things last, to fool the stomach.

Mah and Deh both worked too hard; it's as if their marriage was a marriage of toil—of toiling together. The idea is that the next generation can marry for love.

In the old country, matches were made, strangers were wedded, and that was fate. Those days, sojourners like Deh were considered princes. To become the wife to such a man was to be saved from the war-torn villages.

Saved to work. After dinner, with the rice still in between her teeth, Mah sat down at her Singer. When we pulled out the wall-bed, she was still there, sewing. The street noises stopped long before she did. The hot lamp made all the stitches blur together. And in the mornings, long before any of us awoke, she was already there, sewing again.

His work was hard, too. He ran a laundry on Polk Street. He sailed with the American President Lines. Things started to look up when he owned the take-out place in Vallejo, and then his partner ran off. So he went to Alaska and worked the canneries.

She was good to him too. We remember. How else would we have known him all those years he worked in Guam, in the Fiji islands, in Alaska? Mah always gave him majestic welcomes home. It was her excitement that made us remember him.

I look around. The restaurant is full. The waiters move quickly.

I know Deh. His words are ugly. I've heard him. I've listened. And I've always wished for the street noises, as if in the traffic of sound, I believe I can escape. I know the hard color of his eyes and the tightness in his jaw. I can almost hear his teeth grind. I know this. Years of it.

Their lives weren't easy. So is their discontent without reason?

What about the first one? You didn't even think to come to the hospital. The first one, I say! Son or daughter, dead or alive, you didn't even come!

What about living or dying? Which did you want for me that time you pushed me back to work before my back brace was off?

Money! Money!! Money to eat with, to buy clothes with, to pass this life with!

Don't start that again! Everything I make at that dead place I hand . . .

How come . . .
What about . . .
So . . .

It was obvious. The stories themselves meant little. It was how hot and furious they could become.

Is there no end to it? What makes their ugliness so alive, so thick and impossible to let go of?

"I don't want to think about it anymore." The way she says it surprises me. This time I listen. I imagine what it would be like to take her place. It will be my turn one day.

"Ron," she says, wiggling her fingers above the candle. "A fun thing."

The opal flickers above the flame. I tell her that I want to get her something special for her birthday, ". . . next trip I get abroad." She looks up at me, smiles.

For a minute, my sister seems happy. But she won't be able to hold onto it. She grabs at things out of despair, out of fear. Gifts grow old for her. Emotions never ripen, they sour. Everything slips away from her. Nothing sustains her. Her beauty has made her fragile.

We should have eaten in Chinatown. We could have gone for coffee in North Beach, then for jook at Sam Wo's.

"No work, it's been like that for months, just odd jobs," she says.

I'm thinking, it's not like I haven't done my share. I was a kid once, I did things because I felt I should. I helped fill out forms at the Chinatown employment agencies. I went with him to the Seaman's Union. I waited too, listening and hoping for those calls: "Busboy! Presser! Prep Man!" His bags were packed, he was always ready to go. "On standby," he said.

Every week. All the same. Quitting and looking to start all over again. In the end, it was like never having gone anywhere. It was like the bank line, waiting for nothing.

How many times did my sister and I have to hold them apart? The flat ting! sound as the blade slapped onto the linoleum floors, the wooden handle of the knife slamming into the corner. Was it she or I who screamed, repeating all their ugliest words? Who shook them? Who made them stop?

The waiter comes to take the plates. He stands by my sister for a moment. I raise my glass to the waiter.

"You two Chinese?" he asks.

"No," I say, finishing off my wine. I roll my eyes. I wish I had another Johnny Walker. Suddenly I don't care.

"We're two sisters," I say. I laugh. I ask for the check, leave a good tip. I see him slip my sister a box of matches.

Outside, the air is cool and brisk. My sister links her arm into mine. We walk up Bay onto Chestnut. We pass Galileo High School and then turn down Van Ness to head toward the pier. The bay is black. The foghorns sound far away. We walk the whole length of the pier without talking.

The water is white where it slaps against the wooden stakes. For a long time Lisa's wanted out. She can stay at that point of endurance forever. Desire that becomes old feels too good, it's seductive. I know how hard it is to go.

The heart never travels. You have to be heartless. My sister holds that heart, too close and for too long. This is her weakness, and I like to think, used to be mine. Lisa endures too much.

We're lucky, not like the bondmaids growing up in service, or the new-born daughters whose mouths were stuffed with ashes. Courtesans with the three-inch foot, beardless, soft-shouldered eunuchs, and the frightened child-brides, they're all stories to us. We're the lucky generation. Our parents forced themselves to live through the humiliation in this country so that we could have it better. We know so little of the old country. We repeat the names of Grandmothers and Uncles, but they will always be strangers to us. Family exists only because somebody has a story, and knowing the story connects us to a history. To us, the deformed man is oddly compelling, the forgotten man is a good story. A beautiful woman suffers.

I want her beauty to buy her out.

The sweater cost two weeks' pay. Like the 40-cent birds that are now a delicacy, this is a special treat. The money doesn't mean anything. It is, if anything, time. Time is what I would like to give her.

A red sweater. 100%. The skin of fuzz will be a fierce rouge on her naked breasts.

Red. Lucky. Wear it. Find that man. The new one. Wrap yourself around him. Feel the pulsing between you. Fuck him and think about it. 100% angora. Hand Wash Only. Worn Once.

CRITICAL THINKING QUESTIONS

1. What *claim of value* about family does this story suggest to you?
2. List *evidence* from the story that supports this claim.

WRITING TOPICS

Select one of the following quotations from Ng's story. First, discuss its significance within the dramatic context of the story. Next, extend your reflections beyond the boundaries of the story and discuss its broader implications.

a. "Desire that becomes old feels too good, it's seductive."

b. "The heart never travels. You have to be heartless."

c. "Family exists only because somebody has a story to tell, and knowing that story connects us to a history."

Grace Paley

A Conversation with My Father

My father is eighty-six years old and in bed. His heart, that bloody motor, is equally old and will not do certain jobs any more. It still floods his head with brainy light. But it won't let his legs carry the weight of his body around the house. Despite my metaphors, this muscle failure is not due to his old heart, he says, but to a potassium shortage. Sitting on one pillow, leaning on three, he offers last-minute advice and makes a request.

"I would like you to write a simple story just once more," he says, "the kind de Maupassant wrote, or Chekhov, the kind you used to write. Just recognizable people and then write down what happened to them next."

I say, "Yes, why not? That's possible." I want to please him, though I don't remember writing that way. I *would* like to try to tell such a story, if he means the kind that begins: "There was a woman . . ." followed by plot, the absolute line between two points which I've always despised. Not for literary reasons, but because it takes all hope away. Everyone, real or invented, deserves the open destiny of life.

Finally I thought of a story that had been happening for a couple of years right across the street. I wrote it down, then read it aloud. "Pa," I said, "how about this? Do you mean something like this?"

> Once in my time there was a woman and she had a son. They lived nicely, in a small apartment in Manhattan. This boy at about fifteen became a junkie, which is not unusual in our neighborhood. In order to maintain her close friendship with him, she became a junkie too. She said it was part of the youth culture, with which she felt very much at home. After a while, for a number of reasons, the boy gave it all up and left the city and his mother in disgust. Hopeless and alone, she grieved. We all visit her.

"O.K., Pa, that's it," I said. "An unadorned and miserable tale."

"But that's not what I mean," my father said. "You misunderstood me on purpose. You know there's a lot more to it. You know that. You left everything out. Turgenev wouldn't do that. Chekhov wouldn't do that. There are in fact Russian writers you never heard of, you don't have an inkling of, as good as anyone, who can write a plain ordinary story, who would not leave out what you have left out. I object not to facts but to people sitting in trees talking senselessly, voices from who knows where. . . ."

"Forget that one, Pa, what have I left out now? In this one?"

"Her looks, for instance."

"Oh. Quite handsome, I think. Yes."

"Her hair?"

"Dark, with heavy braids, as though she were a girl or a foreigner."

"What were her parents like, her stock? That she became such a person. It's interesting, you know."

"From out of town. Professional people. The first to be divorced in their country. How's that? Enough?" I asked.

"With you, it's all a joke," he said. "What about the boy's father? Why didn't you mention him? Who was he? Or was the boy born out of wedlock?"

"Yes," I said. "He was born out of wedlock."

"For Godsakes, doesn't anyone in your stories get married? Doesn't anyone have the time to run down to City Hall before they jump into bed?"

"No," I said. "In real life, yes. But in my stories, no."

"Why do you answer me like that?"

"Oh, Pa, this is a simple story about a smart woman who came to N.Y.C. full of interest love trust excitement very up to date, and about her son, what a hard time she had in this world. Married or not, it's of small consequence."

"It is of great consequence," he said.

"O.K.," I said.

"O.K. O.K. yourself," he said, "but listen. I believe you that she's good-looking, but I don't think she was so smart."

"That's true," I said. "Actually that's the trouble with stories. People start out fantastic. You think they're extraordinary, but it turns out as the work goes along, they're just average with a good education. Sometimes the other way around, the person's kind of dumb innocent, but he outwits you and you can't even think of an ending good enough."

"What do you do then?" he asked. He had been a doctor for a couple of decades and he's still interested in details, craft, technique.

"Well, you just have to let the story lie around till some agreement can be reached between you and the stubborn hero."

"Aren't you talking silly now?" he asked. "Start again," he said. "It so happens I'm not going out this evening. Tell the story again. See what you can do this time."

"O.K.," I said. "But it's not a five-minute job." Second attempt:

Once, across the street from us, there was a fine handsome woman, our neighbor. She had a son whom she loved because she'd known him since birth (in helpless chubby infancy, and in the wrestling, hugging ages, seven to ten, as well as earlier and later). This boy, when he fell into the fist of adolescence, became a junkie. He was not a hopeless one. He was in fact hopeful, an ideologue and successful converter. With his busy brilliance, he wrote persuasive articles for his high-school newspaper. Seeking a wide audience, using important connections, he drummed into Lower Manhattan newsstand distribution a periodical called *Oh! Golden Horse!*

In order to keep him from feeling guilty (because guilt is the stony heart of nine tenths of all clinically diagnosed cancers in America today, she said), and because she had always believed in giving bad habits room at home where one could keep an eye on them, she too became a junkie. Her kitchen was famous for a while—a center for intellectual addicts who knew what they were doing. A few felt artistic like Coleridge and others were scientific and revolutionary like Leary. Although she was often high herself, certain good mothering reflexes remained, and she saw to it that there was lots of orange juice around and honey and milk and vitamin pills. However, she never cooked anything but chili, and that no more than once a week. She explained, when we talked to her, seriously, with neighborly concern, that it was her part in the youth culture and she would rather be with the young, it was an honor, than with her own generation.

One week, while nodding through an Antonioni film, this boy was severely jabbed by the elbow of a stern and proselytizing girl, sitting beside him. She offered immediate apricots and nuts for his sugar level, spoke to him sharply, and took him home.

She had heard of him and his work and she herself published, edited, and wrote a competitive journal called *Man Does Live by Bread Alone.* In the organic heat of her continuous presence he could not help but become interested once more in his muscles, his arteries, and nerve connections. In fact he began to love them, treasure them, praise them with funny little songs in *Man Does Live. . . .*

> the fingers of my flesh transcend
> my transcendental soul
> the tightness in my shoulders end
> my teeth have made me whole

To the mouth of his head (that glory of will and determination) he brought hard apples, nuts, wheat germ, and soybean oil. He said to his old friends, From now on, I guess I'll keep my wits about me. I'm going on the natch. He said he was about to begin a spiritual deep-breathing journey. How about you too, Mom? he asked kindly.

His conversion was so radiant, splendid, that neighborhood kids his age began to say that he had never been a real addict at all, only a journalist along for the smell of the story. The mother tried several times to give up what had become without her son and his friends a lonely habit. This effort only brought it to supportable levels. The boy and his girl took their electronic mimeograph and moved to the bushy edge of another borough. They were very strict. They said they would not see her again until she had been off drugs for sixty days.

At home alone in the evening, weeping, the mother read and reread the seven issues of *Oh! Golden Horse!* They seemed to her as truthful as ever. We often crossed the street to visit and console. But if we mentioned any of our children who were at college or in the hospital or dropouts at home, she would cry out, My baby! My baby! and burst into terrible, face-scarring, time-consuming tears. The End.

First my father was silent, then he said, "Number One: You have a nice sense of humor. Number Two: I see you can't tell a plain story. So don't waste time." Then he said sadly, "Number Three: I suppose that means she was alone, she was left like that, his mother. Alone. Probably sick?"

I said, "Yes."

"Poor woman. Poor girl, to be born in a time of fools, to live among fools, The end. The end. Your were right to put that down. The end."

I didn't want to argue, but I had to say, "Well, it is not necessarily the end, Pa."
Yes," he said, "what a tragedy. The end of a person."

"No, Pa," I begged him. "It doesn't have to be. She's only about forty. She could be a hundred different things in this world as time goes on. A teacher or a social worker. An ex-junkie! Sometimes it's better than having a master's in education."

"Jokes," he said. "As a writer that's your main trouble. You don't want to recognize it. Tragedy! Plain tragedy? Historical tragedy? No hope. The end."

"Oh, Pa," I said. "She could change."

"In your own life, too, you have to look it in the face." He took a couple of nitroglycerin. "Turn to five," he said, pointing to the dial on the oxygen tank. He inserted the tubes into his nostrils and breathed deep. He closed his eyes and said, "No."

I had promised the family to always let him have the last word when arguing, but in this case I had a different responsibility. That woman lives across the street. She's my knowledge and my invention. I'm sorry for her. I'm not going to leave her there in that house crying. (Actually neither would Life, which unlike me has no pity.)

Therefore: She did change. Of course her son never came home again. But right now, she's the receptionist in a storefront community clinic in the East Village. Most of the customers are young people, some old friends. The head doctor has said to her, "If we only had three people in this clinic with your experiences. . . ."

"The doctor said that?" My father took the oxygen tubes out of his nostrils and said, "Jokes. Jokes again."

"No, Pa, it could really happen that way, it's a funny world nowadays."

"No," he said. "Truth first. She will slide back. A person must have character. She does not."

"No, Pa," I said. "That's it. She's got a job. Forget it. She's in that storefront working."

"How long will it be?" he asked. "Tragedy! You too. When will you look it in the face?"

CRITICAL THINKING QUESTIONS

1. To analyze this "conversation" as an argument, identify at least two *issues*. Choose the issue that seems most significant or interesting to you and write out the *position* that each character, the father and the daughter, argues.

2. In evaluating the argument, would you declare a winner? If so, who? And if not, why? Do you support the father's or the daughter's viewpoint? Why?

WRITING TOPIC

How do you define character? What *value assumptions* influence your perspective on character and individual identity? What evidence—personal experiences, observations, specific individuals (family members, peers, teachers, coaches, etc.)—has contributed to your value assumptions about character? Based on your reflections on Paley's story and your own experience, write an argument about the significance of character as a factor in shaping an individual's identity.

Susan Power

Red Moccasins

My niece Bernardine Blue Kettle, the one I called Dina, was thirteen—too old to be sitting on my lap. But there she was, her long legs draped over mine and her feet scraping the ground. Our fingers were laced together, both sets of arms wrapped around her pole waist. My four-year-old son, Chaske, was sitting on the floor, drumming a pillow with my long wooden cooking spoon. He covered one ear with his hand and twisted his face to imitate the Sioux singers he worshiped, old men who singed their vocal cords on high notes. He pounded his song into the pillow, making the Sioux lullaby sound energetic as a powwow song.

"Dance for me," I told Dina. I wanted her to play along with Chaske. Dina left my lap and danced around her cousin as if he were a drummer at the powwow grounds. She was serious, aware of her posture, light on her feet, tucking sharp elbows into her sides. Max, my son's pet owlet, watched Dina circle the room. He bobbed forward on the offbeat from his perch atop the mantel clock. My husband had discovered him wandering through a prairie dog town.

"Look at Max," I told the children. "You've got him dancing, too." But Max quickly tired of the game and used his long legs to turn himself around, so all we could see were his feathered back and hunched shoulders.

I clapped and clapped when the song ended, and Chaske gave up the spoon so I could stir his supper, another batch of the watery potato soup we'd been eating for weeks.

It was 1935 and a good portion of North Dakota had dried up and blown away. Grit peppered our food, coated our teeth, and silted our water. We heard that cities as distant as Chicago and New York were sprinkled with Plains topsoil. I thought it was fitting, somehow. I imagined angry ancestors fed up with Removal grabbing fistfuls of parched earth to fling toward Washington, making the president choke on dust and ashes. We prayed for rain, and when it did not come, when instead we were strangled by consumption, many people said the end of the world had come to the Standing Rock Sioux Reservation. I was not a doomsday disciple. I wouldn't let the world end while my son, Chaske, still had so much living to do.

"Bet you can't guess what's for supper," I teased Chaske, who was perched on Dina's shoulders.

"Potato soup!" he shouted, delighted to be suddenly taller than me. Dina rolled her eyes but didn't say anything. She bounced Chaske up and down, stooped over and then lifted on her toes like a horse rearing on its hind legs.

They looked like two opposites, like people with blood running from separate rivers. Chaske, whose baptism name was Emery Bauer, Jr., after his German father,

was sturdy and tall for his age, his powerful calf muscles bulging like little crab apples under the skin. His hair was creamy yellow, the color of beeswax, and his eyes
were a silvery gray, so pale they were almost white.

I couldn't trace Chaske's Sioux blood or find evidence of his father in his features and coloring. It was as if he came from his own place, having sidestepped all
the family tracks laid out before him. Dina, on the other hand, was a blueprint of
the women in our family, long-legged and graceful, thick braids grazing her narrow
hips. Her little heart-shaped face was dark brown, the color of a full-blood, and her
eyes black as onyx studs. Dina had been with me when I delivered Chaske, holding
my hand while old women assisted me. Dina was the one who placed him in my
arms, and I remember thinking, as she held him, that he looked like a bundle of
sunflowers, yellow against her dusky skin. I placed the children together in my
mind, couldn't imagine one without the other.

After supper Dina washed the dishes. It was so easy it was like a game to her
because in my modern house, fit for a white woman, she could pump water directly
into my kitchen sink and watch it drain away. She didn't have to go outside and
haul buckets. I pulled out my sewing basket and let Chaske play with a jar full of
buttons.

"Have you finished my costume?" Dina called over her shoulder.

"You'll be the first to know," I said. I laughed because she was so impatient,
more impatient every day. I was sewing Dina her first complete Sioux costume. Ordinarily a mother would do this, but Dina's was the next thing to useless. Joyce Blue
Kettle had never gotten close enough to a needle to stick herself, let alone sew a costume. As a child she'd been restless and boy-crazy, so she never learned to tan hides
or do beadwork. If her mother scolded her, saying, "Look at your little cousin. Look
at her fine beadwork," Joyce would puff out her bottom lip and squeeze round tears
onto her flat cheeks. She would say, "You know I can't see right," pointing to her
left eye, which was crossed, permanently focused on her nose. Of course, she managed to see well enough to paint her face and read movie magazines she swiped
from the Lugers' store. Joyce and I were first cousins, which in our tribe made us
sisters, despite our differences.

When Dina finished stacking the clean plates, I called her into the sitting
room. "I'm almost ready to start your moccasins," I said. I traced the outline of her
foot onto a scrap of cardboard so that the soles would match perfectly her fine narrow feet.

"Will you make me rattlesnake hair ties?" Dina asked. I dropped the paring
knife I was using to cut the pattern from cardboard.

"Where did you see hair ties like that?" I was careful to leave the blade in my
lap because my hands were shaking.

"I've dreamt about the Red Dress woman," she whispered. "And she had rattlesnake rattles tied in her hair. She shook them at me. She told me I could wear my
hair like that."

"You can't," I said. I knew I sounded too angry. "When she comes after you,
you should turn the other way."

"Have you seen her?" asked Dina, staring at me.

"Yes. But I discouraged her from coming." I didn't tell my niece that at her age I had dreamt about Čuwígnaka Ša, Red Dress, my dead grandmother. I had heard her insistent voice, crackling with energy, whispering promises of a deadly power passed on through the bloodlines from one woman to the next. I had seen her kneeling beside a fire, feeding it with objects stolen from her victims: buttons, letters, twists of hair. She sang her spells, replacing the words of an ancient honor song with those of her own choosing. She doused the flames.

"Could she really control people?" Dina asked.

"That's what they say. But it didn't do her any good. She spelled one too many and he killed her."

My niece held her unfinished costume in her hands. She stroked the blue trade cloth material and pinched the cowrie shells sprinkled across the dress and leggings. I'd hidden the beaded belt and the flour-sack cape covered with inch-long bugle beads to surprise her with later.

There was a knock at the kitchen door. Dina's father, Clifford Blue Kettle, poked his head into the kitchen and waved at me.

"Come on in," I said. He shook his head and twisted the doorknob like he was trying to wring it loose. Black bangs hid his eyes.

"Dina here?" he asked me, so whispery he had to clear his throat and ask me again. Dina stepped into the doorway between the sitting room and kitchen. "Your ma says to get home now," he told her.

"He's so shy around you," Dina said, laughing softly.

I waved off her comment as if I disagreed, but she was right; my cousin's husband had feelings for me. When we were children, he had followed me everywhere, helping me with my chores and bringing me little treasures he'd discovered: seashells, fool's gold, ripe chokecherries. One time he brought me a round glass eye he'd poked from the socket of his sister's doll. It was too much for Joyce. She intercepted the gift, snatched it from the palm of my hand as I studied the green iris. She took Clifford over the same way, ordering him around, demanding his attention, and because I didn't love Clifford, I let her keep him. It never seemed to occur to him that he could protest. He was amiable and slow-minded. He longed to please. Even now he brought me little gifts or fashioned toys for Chaske, like my son's first baby rattle, and I could see he had something for me. One hand was hidden behind his back.

"What have you got there?" I asked. I walked to the door and tried to peek over his shoulder, which made him grin.

"Got these in a giveaway. Know Joyce can't use them." He handed me a mason jar full of red beads tiny as poppy seeds. I poured a few of them into my hand and admired their rich color, scarlet as a fresh wound sliced into my palm. I spilled them back into the jar.

"Thank you. I can put these to good use."

Having given me the gift, Clifford relaxed. He kicked the back steps with the toe of his boot. "Come on now," he called to his daughter.

Dina kissed Chaske's plump cheek before she left, and he smiled at her, kissing his fist and popping it against her arm.

I meant to stay up late to finish sewing Dina's leggings, but Chaske started coughing. He clenched his hands over his chest as if he had captured something between them, a sawing cricket or fluttering moth. I knew the odd gesture was a way he dealt with pain, trying to hammer it down. I carried Chaske to my lumpy brass bed and curled beside him. His coughing finally tapered off and he murmured. "Max."

"Max is fine," I said. "Go to sleep." I rubbed Chaske's back, my hand moving in circles, unable to relax while I listened to his breathing. His hair smelled like sweet grass, and his little body, changing too quickly from plump to wiry, warmed the bed. I guarded his sleep, forcing my breath into a perfect rhythm as if I could breathe for him, and in the morning I was weary but triumphant, having kept the world in orbit.

I had been a widow for two months, since the end of November. Dr. Kessler, a notorious alcoholic but the only doctor on the reservation, had diagnosed Emery as consumptive and told him he should go to the white sanatorium in Rapid City, South Dakota.

"I better not," my husband said, terse as always. But after seven years of marriage, I could practically read Emery's mind. He didn't want to split up our family. If I became ill, I would never be admitted to the hospital Dr. Kessler had suggested; I would be sent to the inferior Sioux sanatorium where few patients recovered. And our son Chaske wasn't really an appropriate candidate for either place. Who knew where he would end up?

"We'll take our chance," Emery said, and so we did. Emery remained at home where I was to keep him well fed and well rested. Consumption was rampant by this time, hitting nearly every family on our reservation, and no attempts were made to quarantine the sick from the healthy. My husband was a successful rancher, in partnership with his two brothers, and I couldn't keep him from work for very long. In the end it wasn't consumption that killed him but a wild horse he called Lutheran. Emery's two brothers brought my husband's body to me, stumbling beneath his bear weight. They were crying, promising me they would shoot that devil horse who had thrown Emery and broken his neck.

"No!" I said, and they looked suddenly wary. They grabbed my arms as if they expected me to pitch forward. "That horse did him a kindness." I wanted them to leave so I could comb Emery's hair and wash his face. "He didn't waste away from the consumption. He went quickly."

Later that night I sat on the edge of Chaske's cot. I told him that his sleeping father, laid out in the next room on our brass bed, was having such good dreams he didn't want to wake up.

"Is he dreaming about Max?" Chaske asked me.

"Yes," I said. "He's dreaming about all of us."

I panicked that night when I realized I didn't own a single photograph of my husband. It wasn't my memory I worried about, but Chaske's. He was so young I couldn't trust that he would remember Emery, the shape of his black beard, his tremendous wingspan and silent laugh. As Chaske slept I told him about his father, chanting our history until it became a song-story I hoped he would follow in his dreams.

I told him about the day I met Emery Bauer. It was the winter of 1928, and I was eighteen years old. I had been snowbound for several days in my family's cabin and was desperate to be outdoors where I could work the cramps out of my legs and fill my lungs with fresh air. I went for a long walk, fighting through high drifts, pausing only to search for landmarks.

I wandered onto the leased land of the Bauer ranch, thinking I was heading toward town. I came to a shallow frozen pond. The ice was uneven, marred by tangled clumps of weeds, but I noticed a man skimming across it as if on a smooth pane of glass. He balanced on silver blades slim as butter knives, propelling his barrel body forward and then magically backward, skirting the weeds and chiseling the ice with his skates. I had heard about ice-skating, but I'd never seen it done. I'd never seen a man spin like a top. I hunched beside a frozen bush, hoping he wouldn't notice me. But I was framed in white and difficult to miss. The graceful man suddenly skated toward me, stopping so quickly his blades spit a spray of ice. He towered over me, smiling, alternately fingering his black beard and tapping the heavy workboots slung around his neck.

"You like to dance on water?" he asked me. I shook my head. I didn't know what else to do. "I'm Emery," he said. He waited, staring directly into my eyes, which made me uncomfortable.

"I'm Anna Thunder," I finally answered.

"Now *that's* a name to live up to." He clapped his large hands together. "Come here, this will be fun." Emery removed his skates, which I saw were metal blades screwed onto a pair of workboots. He donned the shoes he'd been carrying and knelt in the snow. Even down on one knee he was tall.

"Give me your foot," he said. He was the only white man other than the doctor and reservation priest I had ever spoken to, but I trusted him completely. Ironically, I think it was his size that calmed me. He was such a giant he seemed uncomfortable in his body; his posture, an accommodating stoop, and his gestures, apologetic. Off the ice he shambled awkwardly. So I did as he requested. I watched him stuff one of his mittens in the toe of each boot and then fit the skates on my feet. He held my hands and pulled me across the ice. At first I was rigid and tottered on the slippery surface, but eventually I relaxed and pushed off the blades, cutting the ice with confident strokes.

"God made you to skate," Emery breathed in my ear.

Our courtship was an ice dance, and Emery's wedding present to me was my own set of silver blades he'd ordered from the Sears catalogue. He attached them to a new pair of ankle-high laced boots cut out of fancy thin leather.

Emery and I married despite disapproval from both sides. Joyce Blue Kettle protested the loudest, flapping her tongue so much I thought she might wear it thin as a hair ribbon. Joyce had been married for several years by that time and was already a mother, but she was jealous.

"People will say you're greedy," Joyce confided to me the night before my wedding.

"What do you mean?" I only half listened, distracted as I was by the last minute details of polishing my shoes and combing my damp hair with a clump of sage to scent it.

"They say you're marrying him to get things. What about the seven new dresses, one for each day of the week, he bought you? What about the horsehair sofa and the brass bed? Didn't he even build you a house?"

Earlier that day I had taken Joyce on a tour of the new house, a neat clapboard structure made of planed lumber. I felt guilty as we moved through the rooms, the number of my possessions suddenly overwhelming me. All my life I had been taught that material goods were dispensable, things to be shared with friends and family. We were not supposed to have more than we needed, so there were endless rounds of giveaways at our dances, where people unburdened themselves of accumulated objects. But Emery was not Sioux, and his affection for me resulted in lavish offerings.

Let them say what they want, I decided. I repeated this aloud to my cousin Joyce, who was pinching the ivory-colored velvet fabric of my wedding cap.

"They know Emery has different ways," I said.

"Whatever you say." Joyce shrugged her shoulders, and the next day when I pinned the elegant cap to my newly bobbed black hair, I noticed sharp creases in the pile that no amount of smoothing could repair.

On our first wedding anniversary, Emery and I gave a feast for my Sioux relatives. I'd thought time would set things right for Joyce, but she remained bitter about the match. She trailed after me at the feast, pretending to help me in the kitchen where she sat idle, letting her mouth do all the work.

"Čuwígnaka Ša was really looking out for you," she said, fighting a sly smile. She was referring to our grandmother, Red Dress. Joyce liked to tell people that Emery hadn't fallen for me, but for the old magic I had used to spell him. I ignored her, knowing that I'd never tested these powers. If they really existed, I figured they must have atrophied like an unused muscle. Besides, I'd heard people say the same thing about Joyce and her conquest of Clifford. I struggled for something pleasant to say.

"That Bernardine's getting smarter every day, and Clifford looks like he's doing real good."

"That's because I keep him happy." Joyce smoothed a narrow hand across her wiry hair.

"You know, it works differently in my house," I said. "Emery comes up with so many ways to please me." I ran my own narrow hand from my waist to the round edge of my hip.

Later, I forgave Joyce because when she heard about my husband's sudden death she sent Bernardine to the house to watch over Chaske. Clifford accompanied his daughter, offering to take Emery's personal stock of two horses and one cow to his own place where he could tend them. I was grateful to my cousin for letting her family assist me.

Before his brothers buried him, I bathed Emery's face and trimmed his beard. I filled his pockets with the lemon drop candies he favored and the deck of cards we used to play gin rummy. Then I packed both pairs of ice skates in the coffin so that he would be waiting for me by a shallow frozen pond, ready to strap skates on my feet and take me ice-dancing.

The first day of February was mild, so I opened the windows to air out the house. I'd traded two of my dresses for a scrawny chicken, and I was relieved to be cooking something other than potato soup. Max pecked at the chicken's liver, winking at me from his perch beside the stove.

I overheard Chaske talking to Max. "Atéwaye," my father, he called the young owl. I understood then that this was Chaske's way of keeping his father alive. "Atéwaye, look at this," he said, holding up a blue-and-white-swirled marble. He chattered for a long time, disturbing Max's sleep, until he started coughing. I moved to hold him, murmuring, "You aren't sick," because his eyes looked afraid, round as the owlet's.

He was racked by coughing fits most of the day, and his cheeks were flushed. By the time we finished supper, I considered bundling him up and trying to get him to Dr. Kessler's place, three miles away. But the wind changed. The sky was suddenly a heavy gray, and it seemed to be lowering itself, ready to flatten our reservation. Without the horses, I was afraid to set out on foot.

"Close the windows!" I shouted and felt foolish. I was the only one who could heed the command. So I sealed our house against a kicking wind and a crushing mantle of snow. Chaske and I went to bed early. I slept through the night for the first time in many weeks.

Chaske was worse the next day. The pain in his chest made him cry. I gave him castor oil, which Dr. Kessler had recommended for my husband, but it didn't seem to help. No one I knew had a phone, so I put on several layers of clothes and started to walk the half mile to Dina's place, thinking someone there could contact the doctor. But I realized it would take a long time to make it through such deep snow. I couldn't leave Chaske alone for very long.

I told him stories to take his mind off the pain. I even unpacked the baby rattle he'd given up years before, the rattlesnake rattle Clifford had made for him. I shook it beside his ear, punctuating my singing with its sliding rasp. I sang him funny songs, even dirty songs, and when the pain had exhausted him, I sang the Sioux lullaby he had so recently performed. He was too weak to raise his own voice, but he wielded the wooden cooking spoon in his hand and banged it against the wall. The brass bed rocked with our desperate rhythm, we churned the air with our noise. For a moment, I wondered if I could save Chaske myself, summon a healing magic. But I remembered Joyce's futile attempts to cure her crossed eye, the hours she spent as a child pointing her finger at the offending organ while staring at her reflection in a cracked mirror. I knew we did not have the healing touch.

The house was dark and my voice was almost gone when I heard a knock at the front door.

"Coming!" I croaked.

It was my cousin Joyce, standing on my porch. I could see Emery's sorrel mare at the gate and Dina seated on my slender palomino. I waved to her.

"I come about the costume," Joyce said. At first I didn't know what she was talking about. "There's that powwow tonight," she continued, "up at the hall. Dina was hoping her costume was ready so she could wear it."

"Chaske is real sick. He needs the doctor. Could you stop at Kessler's place and tell him to come?"

Joyce promised to fetch him. She patted my arm.

I returned to Chaske warm with confidence. "Everything will be okay," I crooned, my voice clear and strong again. I rocked Chaske in the brass bed, held his body against mine as if I could absorb the tearing coughs. At least an hour passed. I was sinking into the dark and feeling hope drain away. I could actually *feel* it, a trickle of heat on my hands.

All this time I had pictured Joyce driving the horse through wet snow as high as its chest. I could see the horse swimming across snowfields to reach Dr. Kessler. But the picture changed. I saw my cousin and her daughter break through snow walls, pound the flakes to slush beneath the horses' hooves, but only as far as the community hall. They were inside the flat building, their cheeks pink and fingers warming in their jacket pockets. They were dancing together around the drum, their feet moving in a perfect mother-daughter symmetry. Then it was Dina, dancing alone as her mother watched from the sidelines, tracking the girl with the eye she could control. Her lips were pinched with satisfaction, she held herself stiff and straight in the wooden folding chair, proud. The picture dazzled my eyes as I sat in the dark room, burned itself against the backs of my eyelids. I imagined I could even hear the song that moved Bernardine's feet. It swept across the snow and spilled its notes against the bedroom window. The glass shrieked.

Finally I lit the lamp. I saw my reflection in the windowpane and noticed new lines etched in my face, drawn from nose to chin. I lifted the lamp high to regard the rest of the room. I nearly dropped it. Patches of brilliant red speckled the walls beside my bed and the faded quilts. My own hands were covered with blood from Chaske's lungs. His eyes were truly white now, as if his spirit were the only thing that had given them pigmentation. I knew I had lost him. But before I moved to wash his body, I poked my finger in his mouth, deep in a pool of black blood. I swallowed the fluid because wherever he had gone I wanted to follow close behind.

My son's coffin was carried to town and stored in an icehouse. The ground was frozen, so we couldn't bury him just yet. Joyce Blue Kettle showed up at my door with small pails of food and wet eyes. She said Dina was so upset she couldn't get out of bed. I didn't let her inside the house.

"Get away," I said. I refused to open the door wider than an inch.

"I'm just sick about it. I didn't know how bad he was."

"You were dancing, weren't you? You were dancing."

Her eyes sparked and lit like a flash fire. "Who do you think you are? If Dina was sick you know that doctor wouldn't lift a finger to make it over here. He'd tell me to bring her in. What makes you think he'd come for yours? Is yours better than mine?"

I left the door cracked open and went to my room. I removed every dress from the wardrobe, even stepped out of the blue calico I was wearing. I rushed down the stairs in my cotton slip.

"Here!" I said, throwing the dresses at my cousin who waited, curious, on my front porch. "You always wanted them. Take them! Take them!"

Joyce backed down the steps and hurried away. She nearly tripped over the skirt of one dress, the one I wore at my wedding. I watched her run across the frozen yard, my five remaining dresses clutched to her chest.

I was as frozen as the ground, frost on my upper lip, my tongue a chunk of ice. My mind was numb, but my fingers still worked. I dug out the red beads Clifford had given me. Originally I'd planned to find dark blue beads as well, intending to decorate Dina's moccasins with the two contrasting colors. But now I just wanted to finish the slippers.

It took me three full days to bead the moccasins. I beaded the upper half, the sides, the leather tongue, even the soles, using all but a handful of beads. The moccasins were pure red. In those three days, I didn't eat a single morsel of food. I kept my stomach filled with water. The pump had frozen so I had to drink gritty, melted snow. I let Max pick at the meals the community had cooked for me.

I remember the night I finished beading Dina's moccasins the way I remember stories I have read in books—from a distance, from behind a barrier, perhaps a sheet of ice. I folded Dina's costume and placed the moccasins on top. Then I wrapped the bundle in a pillowcase. I dressed to go outdoors, wearing Emery's workboots, and I fastened Chaske's baby rattle to my braid with a leather thong. I tossed the braid over my shoulder and heard its warning rasp. It was after midnight, but I didn't take a lantern; the moon was a chilly night-light. I picked up the package and was about to set off when something stopped me, a sudden prick of heat deep inside my body. The snow attracted my gaze as I paused in the doorway. It looked clean, as though it could deaden the spark. So I covered my head and arms with snow, molding it to my thighs. I didn't feel the chill or the moisture. I moved on like a snow queen.

I can still hear my footsteps crackling through the drifts. I stopped several feet from the door of the Blue Kettle place.

"Čuwígnaka Ša, you help me now," I implored. I hunched in the snow.

Bernardine, I called with my mind. *Bernardine.* I didn't speak aloud, but my head buzzed with her name, the syllables filled my throat. My teeth clicked her name. *Bernardine.*

She was wearing the flannel nightdress I'd given her for Christmas, and she was barefoot. She came right up to me. *We must dress you,* I said, still silent. She was obedient, her eyes glazed and swollen from crying. She lifted her arms so I could remove the nightdress. Her skin shriveled in the cold, but she didn't shiver. I dressed her then, in the trade cloth dress and leggings. I tied the belt around her waist and slipped the cape over her head. I smoothed her thick braids. Finally I knelt before her and fit the beaded moccasins on her feet. I tied the laces.

"You dance," I hissed. The words were white smoke in the air.

No one will ever know how many hours Bernardine danced in the snow. She danced herself into another world. Clifford found her the next day about a mile from their house, at the edge of a circular track she'd worn through high snowdrifts. People said she was frozen to a young hackberry tree, embracing it as if she had given up on her powwow steps and commenced waltzing.

I heard Joyce wanted someone to remove the shreds of leather and beads, all that remained of Dina's red moccasins. But the pieces were fused to her daughter's skin. One old woman started to cut them off, slicing into flesh, which was the moment Joyce stumbled out of her mind. So they left them on Dina's feet.

For two months she and my son, Chaske, rested side by side in the icehouse. People avoided me and my cousin after an initial round of visits. But everyone turned out for the joint burial.

Joyce and Clifford and I stood near the open graves. I noticed everyone else had pulled back. I don't remember a single word uttered by the Catholic priest. I don't even remember walking to the tiny cemetery behind the church. But I can hear the sound of Joyce's laughter. She giggled into a white handkerchief, tears rolling down her flat cheeks. Her short hair was patchy, singed in several places, and I guessed that Clifford had tried to set her hair with a curling iron. She looked years younger, her face smooth and empty, so different from my own face, which I hardly recognized anymore. My skin was parched and lined as the bottom of a dry creek bed.

That spring, after the children were buried, I discovered that magic let loose can take on a life of its own. I had made my niece dance, and there was no one to tell her to stop. Bernardine Blue Kettle was still dancing, this time around my pretty clapboard house. I didn't actually see her; I was too afraid to look, afraid I would see Chaske riding on her shoulders. But I heard the stamp and shuffle of her steps. She never visited at the same time, teasing me with her unpredictability, and there were no footprints in the dirt. But each time the noise ended and I found the courage to step onto my porch, I saw the flash of red beads that had fallen on the ground. I didn't touch them. I kicked the dirt to hide their gleam.

I noticed that even the magpies, always greedy for shimmering objects, scavenged in some other yard. They did not covet the sparkling red beads scattered outside my house.

CRITICAL THINKING QUESTIONS

1. Discuss the *ethos* of the narrator.
2. What *claim* does this story make about the power of a mother's love?

3. Imagine that the narrator has been charged with her niece Bernardine's murder.
    a. Cast yourself in the role of her defense attorney. What arguments would you make to defend her?
    b. Cast yourself in the role of the prosecuting attorney. What arguments would you make to convict her?
    c. Cast yourself in the role of a juror. Would you vote to acquit or to convict the narrator of her niece's murder?

John Updike

Separating

The day was fair. Brilliant. All that June the weather had mocked the Maples' internal misery with solid sunlight—golden shafts and cascades of green in which their conversations had wormed unseeing, their sad murmuring selves the only stain in Nature. Usually by this time of the year they had acquired tans; but when they met their elder daughter's plane on her return from a year in England they were almost as pale as she, though Judith was too dazzled by the sunny opulent jumble of her native land to notice. They did not spoil her homecoming by telling her immediately. Wait a few days, let her recover from jet lag, had been one of their formulations, in that string of gray dialogues—over coffee, over cocktails, over Cointreau—that had shaped the strategy of their dissolution, while the earth performed its annual stunt of renewal unnoticed beyond their closed windows. Richard had thought to leave at Easter; Joan had insisted they wait until the four children were at last assembled, with all exams passed and ceremonies attended, and the bauble of summer to console them. So he had drudged away, in love, in dread, repairing screens, getting the mowers sharpened, rolling and patching their new tennis court.

The court, clay, had come through its first winter pitted and windswept bare of redcoat. Years ago the Maples had observed how often, among their friends, divorce followed a dramatic home improvement, as if the marriage were making one last twitchy effort to live; their own worst crisis had come amid the plaster dust and exposed plumbing of a kitchen renovation. Yet, a summer ago, as canary-yellow bulldozers gaily churned a grassy, daisy-dotted knoll into a muddy plateau, and a crew of pigtailed young men raked and tamped clay into a plane, this transformation did not strike them as ominous, but festive in its impudence; their marriage could rend the earth for fun. The next spring, waking each day at dawn to a sliding sensation as if the bed were being tipped, Richard found the barren tennis court, its net and tapes still rolled in the barn, an environment congruous with his mood of purposeful desolation, and the crumbling of handfuls of clay into cracks and holes (dogs had frolicked on the court in a thaw; rivulets had evolved trenches) an activity suitably elemental and interminable. In his sealed heart he hoped the day would never come.

Now it was here. A Friday. Judith was reacclimated; all four children were assembled, before jobs and camps and visits again scattered them. Joan thought they should be told one by one. Richard was for making an announcement at the table. She said, "I think just making an announcement is a cop-out. They'll start quarrelling and playing to each other instead of focusing. They're each individuals, you know, not just some corporate obstacle to your freedom."

"O.K., O.K. I agree." Joan's plan was exact. That evening, they were giving Judith a belated welcome-home dinner, of lobster and champagne. Then, the party over, they, the two of them, who nineteen years before would push her in a baby carriage along Tenth Street to Washington Square, were to walk her out of the house, to the bridge across the salt creek, and tell her, swearing her to secrecy. Then Richard Jr., who was going directly from work to a rock concert in Boston, would be told, either late when he returned on the train or early Saturday morning before he went off to his job; he was seventeen and employed as one of a golf-course maintenance crew. Then the two younger children, John and Margaret, could, as the morning wore on, be informed.

"Mopped up, as it were," Richard said.

"Do you have any better plan? That leaves you the rest of Saturday to answer any questions, pack, and make your wonderful departure."

"No," he said, meaning he had no better plan, and agreed to hers, though it had an edge of false order, a plea for control in the semblance of its achievement, like Joan's long chore lists and financial accountings and, in the days when he first knew her, her too copious lecture notes. Her plan turned one hurdle for him into four—four knife-sharp walls, each with a sheer blind drop on the other side.

All spring he had been morbidly conscious of insides and outsides, of barriers and partitions. He and Joan stood as a thin barrier between the children and the truth. Each moment was a partition, with the past on one side and the future on the other, a future containing this unthinkable *now*. Beyond four knifelike walls a new life for him waited vaguely. His skull cupped a secret, a white face, a face both frightened and soothing, both strange and known, that he wanted to shield from tears, which he felt all about him, solid as the sunlight. So haunted, he had become obsessed with battening down the house against his absence, replacing screens and sash cords, hinges and latches—a Houdini making things snug before his escape.

The lock. He had still to replace a lock on one of the doors of the screened porch. The task, like most such, proved more difficult than he had imagined. The old lock, aluminum frozen by corrosion, had been deliberately rendered obsolete by manufacturers. Three hardware stores had nothing that even approximately matched the mortised hole its removal (surprisingly easy) left. Another hole had to be gouged, with bits too small and saws too big, and the old hole fitted with a block of wood—the chisels dull, the saw rusty, his fingers thick with lack of sleep. The sun poured down, beyond the porch, on a world of neglect. The bushes already needed pruning, the windward side of the house was shedding flakes of paint, rain would get in when he was gone, insects, rot, death. His family, all those he would lose, filtered through the edges of his awareness as he struggled with screw holes, splinters, opaque instructions, minutiae of metal.

Judith sat on the porch, a princess returned from exile. She regaled them with stories of fuel shortages, of bomb scares in the Underground, of Pakistani workmen loudly lusting after her as she walked past on her way to dance school. Joan came and went, in and out of the house, calmer than she should have been, praising his struggles with the lock as if this were one more and not the last of their chain of shared chores. The younger of his sons, John, now at fifteen suddenly, unwittingly handsome, for a few minutes held the rickety screen door while his father clumsily hammered and chiseled, each blow a kind of sob in Richard's ears. His younger daughter, having been at a slumber party, slept on the porch hammock through all the noise—heavy and pink, trusting and forsaken. Time, like the sunlight, continued relentlessly; the sunlight slowly slanted. Today was one of the longest days. The lock clicked, worked. He was through. He had a drink; he drank it on the porch, listening to his daughter. "It was so sweet," she was saying, "during the worst of it, how all the butcher's and bakery shops kept open by candlelight. They're all so plucky and cute. From the papers, things sounded so much worse here—people shooting people in gas lines, and everybody freezing."

Richard asked her, "Do you still want to live in England forever?" *Forever:* the concept, now a reality upon him, pressed and scratched at the back of his throat.

"No," Judith confessed, turning her oval face to him, its eyes still childishly far apart, but the lips set as over something succulent and satisfactory. "I was anxious to come home. I'm an American." She was a woman. They had raised her; he and Joan had endured together to raise her, alone of the four. The others had still some raising left in them. Yet it was the thought of telling Judith—the image of her, their first baby, walking between them arm in arm to the bridge—that broke him. The partition between himself and the tears broke. Richard sat down to the celebratory meal with the back of his throat aching; the champagne, the lobster seemed phases of sunshine; he saw them and tasted them through tears. He blinked, swallowed, croakily joked about hay fever. The tears would not stop leaking through; they came not through a hole that could be plugged but through a permeable spot in a membrane, steadily, purely, endlessly, fruitfully. They became, his tears, a shield for himself against these others—their faces, the fact of their assembly, a last time as innocents, at a table where he sat the last time as head. Tears dropped from his nose as he broke the lobster's back; salt flavored his champagne as he sipped it; the raw clench at the back of his throat was delicious. He could not help himself.

His children tried to ignore his tears. Judith on his right, lit a cigarette, gazed upward in the direction of her too energetic, too sophisticated exhalation; on her other side, John earnestly bent his face to the extraction of the last morsels—legs, tail segments—from the scarlet corpse. Joan, at the opposite end of the table, glanced at him surprised, her reproach displaced by a quick grimace, of forgiveness, or of salute to his superior gift of strategy. Between them, Margaret, no longer called Bean, thirteen and large for her age, gazed from the other side of his pane of tears as if into a shopwindow at something she coveted—at her father, a crystalline heap of splinters and memories. It was not she, however, but John who, in the kitchen, as they cleared the plates and carapaces away, asked Joan the question: *"Why is Daddy crying?"*

Richard heard the question but not the murmured answer. Then he heard Bean cry, "Oh, no-oh!"—the faintly dramatized exclamation of one who had long expected it.

John returned to the table carrying a bowl of salad. He nodded tersely at his father and his lips shaped the conspiratorial words "She told."

"Told what?" Richard asked aloud, insanely.

The boy sat down as if to rebuke his father's distraction with the example of his own good manners and said quietly, "The separation."

Joan and Margaret returned; the child, in Richard's twisted vision, seemed diminished in size, and relieved, relieved to have had the boogeyman at last proved real. He called out to her—the distances at the table had grown immense—"You knew, you always knew," but the clenching at the back of his throat prevented him from making sense of it. From afar he heard Joan talking, levelly, sensibly, reciting what they had prepared: it was a separation for the summer, an experiment. She and Daddy both agreed it would be good for them; they needed space and time to think; they liked each other but did not make each other happy enough, somehow.

Judith, imitating her mother's factual tone, but in her youth off-key, too cool, said, "I think it's silly. You should either live together or get divorced."

Richard's crying, like a wave that has crested and crashed, had become tumultuous; but it was overtopped by another tumult, for John, who had been so reserved, now grew larger and larger at the table. Perhaps his younger sister's being credited with knowing set him off. "Why didn't you *tell* us?" he asked, in a large round voice quite unlike his own. "You should have *told* us you weren't getting along."

Richard was startled into attempting to force words through his tears. "We *do* get along, that's the trouble, so it doesn't show even to us—" "That we do not love each other" was the rest of the sentence; he couldn't finish it.

Joan finished for him, in her style. "And we've always, *especially*, loved our children."

John was not mollified. "What do you care about *us?*" he boomed. "We're just little things you *had*." His sisters' laughing forced a laugh from him, which he turned hard and parodistic: "Ha ha *ha*." Richard and Joan realized simultaneously that the child was drunk, on Judith's homecoming champagne. Feeling bound to keep the center of the stage, John took a cigarette from Judith's pack, poked it into his mouth, let it hang from his lower lip, and squinted like a gangster.

"You're not little things we had," Richard called to him. "You're the whole point. But you're grown. Or almost."

The boy was lighting matches. Instead of holding them to his cigarette (for they had never seen him smoke; being "good" had been his way of setting himself apart), he held them to his mother's face, closer and closer, for her to blow out. Then he lit the whole folder—a hiss and then a torch, held against his mother's face. Prismed by tears, the flame filled Richard's vision; he didn't know how it was extinguished. He heard Margaret say, "Oh stop showing off," and saw John, in response, break the cigarette in two and put the halves entirely into his mouth and chew, sticking out his tongue to display the shreds to his sister.

Joan talked to him, reasoning—a fountain of reason, unintelligible. "Talked about it for years . . . our children must help us . . . Daddy and I both want . . ." As the boy listened, he carefully wadded a paper napkin into the leaves of his salad, fashioned a ball of paper and lettuce, and popped it into his mouth, looking around the table for the expected laughter. None came. Judith said, "Be mature," and dismissed a plume of smoke.

Richard got up from this stifling table and led the boy outside. Though the house was in twilight, the outdoors still brimmed with light, the long waste light of high summer. Both laughing, he supervised John's spitting out the lettuce and paper and tobacco into the pachysandra. He took him by the hand—a square gritty hand, but for its softness a man's. Yet, it held on. They ran together up into the field, past the tennis court. The raw banking left by the bulldozers was dotted with daisies. Past the court and a flat stretch where they used to play family baseball stood a soft green rise glorious in the sun, each weed and species of grass distinct as illumination on parchment. "I'm sorry, so sorry." Richard cried. "You were the only one who ever tried to help me with all the goddam jobs around this place."

Sobbing, safe within his tears and the champagne, John explained, "It's not just the separation, it's the whole crummy year, I *hate* that school, you can't make any friends, the history teacher's a scud."

They sat on the crest of the rise, shaking and warm from their tears but easier in their voices, and Richard tried to focus on the child's sad year—the weekdays long with homework, the weekends spent in his room with model airplanes, while his parents murmured down below, nursing their separation. How selfish, how blind, Richard thought; his eyes felt scoured. He told his son, "We'll think about getting you transferred. Life's too short to be miserable."

They had said what they could, but did not want the moment to heal, and talked on, about the school, about the tennis court, whether it would ever again be as good as it had been that first summer. They walked to inspect it and pressed a few more tapes more firmly down. A little stiltedly, perhaps trying to make too much of the moment, to prolong it, Richard led the boy to the spot in the field where the view was best, of the metallic blue river, the emerald marsh, the scattered islands velvet with shadow in the low light, the white bits of beach far away. "See," he said. "It goes on being beautiful. It'll be here tomorrow."

"I know," John answered, impatiently. The moment had closed.

Back in the house, the others had opened some white wine, the champagne being drunk, and still sat at the table, the three females, gossiping. Where Joan sat had become the head. She turned, showing him a tearless face, and asked, "All right?"

"We're fine," he said, resenting it, though relieved, that the party went on without him.

In bed she explained, "I couldn't cry I guess because I cried so much all spring. It really wasn't fair. It's your idea, and you made it look as though I was kicking you out."

"I'm sorry," he said. "I couldn't stop. I wanted to but couldn't."

"You *didn't* want to. You loved it. You were having your way, making a general announcement."

"I love having it over," he admitted. "God, those kids were great. So brave and funny," John, returned to the house, had settled to a model airplane in his room, and kept shouting down to them, "I'm O.K. No sweat." "And the way," Richard went on, cozy in his relief, "they never questioned the reasons we gave. No thought of a third person. Not even Judith."

"That *was* touching," Joan said.

He gave her a hug. "You were great too. Thank you." Guiltily, he realized he did not feel separated.

"You still have Dickie to do," she told him. These words set before him a black mountain in the darkness; its cold breath, its near weight affected his chest. Of the four children Dickie was most nearly his conscience. Joan did not need to add, "That's one piece of your dirty work I won't do for you."

"I know. I'll do it. You go to sleep."

Within minutes, her breathing slowed, became oblivious and deep. It was quarter to midnight. Dickie's train from the concert would come in at one-fourteen. Richard set the alarm for one. He had slept atrociously for weeks. But whenever he closed his lids some glimpse of the last hours scorched them—Judith exhaling toward the ceiling in a kind of aversion, Bean's mute staring, the sunstruck growth of the field where he and John had rested. The mountain before him moved closer, moved within him; he was huge, momentous. The ache at the back of his throat felt stale. His wife slept as if slain beside him. When, exasperated by his hot lids, his crowded heart, he rose from bed and dressed, she awoke enough to turn over. He told her then, "If I could undo it all, I would."

"Where would you begin?" she asked. There was no place. Giving him courage, she was always giving him courage. He put on shoes without socks in the dark. The children were breathing in their rooms, the downstairs was hollow. In their confusion they had left lights burning. He turned off all but one, the kitchen overhead. The car started. He had hoped it wouldn't. He met only moonlight on the road; it seemed a diaphanous companion, flickering in the leaves along the roadside, haunting his rearview mirror like a pursuer, melting under his headlights. The center of town, not quite deserted, was eerie at this hour. A young cop in uniform kept company with a gang of T-shirted kids on the steps of the bank. Across from the railroad station, several bars kept open. Customers, mostly young, passed in and out of the warm night, savoring summer's novelty. Voices shouted from cars as they passed; an immense conversation seemed in progress. Richard parked and in his weariness put his head on the passenger seat, out of the commotion and wheeling lights. It was as when, in the movies, an assassin grimly carries his mission through the jostle of a carnival—except the movies cannot show the precipitous, palpable slope you cling to within. You cannot climb back down; you can only fall. The synthetic fabric of the car seat, warmed by his cheek, confided to him an ancient, distant scent of vanilla.

A train whistle caused him to lift his head. It was on time; he had hoped it would be late. The slender drawgates descended. The bell of approach tingled happily. The great metal body, horizontally fluted, rocked to a stop, and sleepy teenagers disembarked, his son among them. Dickie did not show surprise that his father was meeting him at this terrible hour. He sauntered to the car with two friends, both taller than he. He said "Hi" to his father and took the passenger's seat with an exhausted promptness that expressed gratitude. The friends got into the back, and Richard was grateful; a few more minutes' postponement would be won by driving them home.

He asked. "How was the concert?"

"Groovy," one boy said from the back seat.

"It bit," the other said.

"It was O.K.," Dickie said, moderate by nature, so reasonable that in his childhood the unreason of the world had given him headaches, stomach aches, nausea. When the second friend had been dropped off at his dark house, the boy blurted, "Dad, my eyes are killing me with hay fever! I'm out there cutting that mothering grass all day!"

"Do we still have those drops?"

"They didn't do any good last summer."

"They might this." Richard swung a U-turn on the empty street. The drive home took a few minutes. The mountain was here, in his throat. "Richard," he said, and felt the boy, slumped and rubbing his eyes, go tense at his tone, "I didn't come to meet you just to make your life easier. I came because your mother and I have some news for you, and you're a hard man to get ahold of these days. It's sad news."

"That's O.K." The reassurance came out soft, but quick, as if released from the tip of a spring.

Richard had feared that his tears would return and choke him, but the boy's manliness set an example, and his voice issued forth steady and dry. "It's sad news, but it needn't be tragic news, at least for you. It should have no practical effect on your life, though it's bound to have an emotional effect. You'll work at your job, and go back to school in September. Your mother and I are really proud of what you're making of your life; we don't want that to change at all."

"Yeah," the boy said lightly, on the intake of his breath, holding himself up. They turned the corner; the church they went to loomed like a gutted fort. The home of the woman Richard hoped to marry stood across the green. Her bedroom light burned.

"Your mother and I," he said, "have decided to separate. For the summer. Nothing legal, no divorce yet. We want to see how it feels. For some years now, we haven't been doing enough for each other, making each other as happy as we should be. Have you sensed that?"

"No," the boy said. It was an honest, unemotional answer: true or false in a quiz.

Glad for the factual basis, Richard pursued, even garrulously, the details. His apartment across town, his utter accessibility, the split vacation arrangements, the advantages to the children, the added mobility and variety of the summer. Dickie listened, absorbing. "Do the others know?"

Richard described how they had been told.

"How did they take it?"

"The girls pretty calmly. John flipped out; he shouted and ate a cigarette and made a salad out of his napkin and told us how much he hated school."

His brother chuckled. "He did?"

"Yeah. The school issue was more upsetting for him than Mom and me. He seemed to feel better for having exploded."

"He did?" The repetition was the first sign that he was stunned.

"Yes. Dickie, I want to tell you something. This last hour, waiting for your train to get in, has been about the worst of my life. I hate this. *Hate* it. My father would have died before doing it to me." He felt immensely lighter, saying this. He had dumped the mountain on the boy. They were home. Moving swiftly as a shadow, Dickie was out of the car, through the bright kitchen. Richard called after him, "Want a glass of milk or anything?"

"No thanks."

"Want us to call the course tomorrow and say you're too sick to work?"

"No, that's all right." The answer was faint, delivered at the door to his room; Richard listened for the slam of a tantrum. The door closed normally. The sound was sickening.

Joan had sunk into that first deep trough of sleep and was slow to awake. Richard had to repeat, "I told him."

"What did he say?"

"Nothing much. Could you go say good night to him? Please."

She left their room, without putting on a bathrobe. He sluggishly changed back into his pajamas and walked down the hall. Dickie was already in bed, Joan was sitting beside him, and the boy's bedside clock radio was murmuring music. When she stood, an inexplicable light—the moon?—outlined her body through the nightie. Richard sat on the warm place she had indented on the child's narrow mattress. He asked him, "Do you want the radio on like that?"

"It always is."

"Doesn't it keep you awake? It would me."

"No."

"Are you sleepy?"

"Yeah."

"Good. Sure you want to get up and go to work? You've had a big night."

"I want to."

Away at school this winter he had learned for the first time that you can go short of sleep and live. As an infant he had slept with an immobile, sweating intensity that had alarmed his babysitters. As the children aged, he became the first to go to bed, earlier for a time than his younger brother and sister. Even now, he would go slack in the middle of a television show, his sprawled legs hairy and brown. "O.K. Good boy. Dickie, listen. I love you so much, I never knew how much until now. No matter how this works out, I'll always be with you. Really."

Richard bent to kiss an averted face but his son, sinewy, turned and with wet cheeks embraced him and gave him a kiss, on the lips, passionate as a woman's. In his father's ear he moaned one word, the crucial, intelligent word: *"Why?"*

Why. It was a whistle of wind in a crack, a knife thrust, a window thrown open on emptiness. The white face was gone, the darkness was featureless. Richard had forgotten why.

CRITICAL THINKING QUESTIONS

1. Explaining the separation to the children, Joan recites her and Richard's prepared lines: "it was a separation for the summer, an experiment; . . . they liked each other but did not make each other happy enough, somehow." What *warrant* about happiness in a marriage underlies Joan's explanation? Discuss why you accept or do not accept this warrant.

2. List gender stereotypes regarding emotions and expressiveness that are associated with boys/men and girls/women. How do the characters in this story support or challenge those stereotypes?

WRITING TOPIC

In telling the children about their separation, Richard and Joan have agreed to call it "an experiment . . . for the summer." Are they protecting the children or themselves? Is withholding the full truth the same as a lie, and if so, can a lie be justified (see also Chopin's "The Storm")?

Alice Walker

Everyday Use

for your grandmama

I will wait for her in the yard that Maggie and I made so clean and wavy yesterday afternoon. A yard like this is more comfortable than most people know. It is not just a yard. It is like an extended living room. When the hard clay is swept clean as a floor and the fine sand around the edges lined with tiny, irregular grooves, anyone can come and sit and look up into the elm tree and wait for the breezes that never come inside the house.

Maggie will be nervous until after her sister goes: she will stand hopelessly in corners, homely and ashamed of the burn scars down her arms and legs, eyeing her sister with a mixture of envy and awe. She thinks her sister has held life always in the palm of one hand, that "no" is a word the world never learned to say to her.

You've no doubt seen those TV shows where the child who has "made it" is confronted, as a surprise, by her own mother and father, tottering in weakly from backstage. (A pleasant surprise, of course: What would they do if parent and child came on the show only to curse out and insult each other?) On TV mother and child embrace and smile into each other's faces. Sometimes the mother and father weep, the child wraps them in her arms and leans across the table to tell how she would not have made it without their help. I have seen these programs.

Sometimes I dream a dream in which Dee and I are suddenly brought together on a TV program of this sort. Out of a dark and soft-seated limousine I am ushered into a bright room filled with many people. There I meet a smiling, gray, sporty man like Johnny Carson who shakes my hand and tells me what a fine girl I have. Then we are on the stage and Dee is embracing me with tears in her eyes. She pins on my dress a large orchid, even though she has told me once that she thinks orchids are tacky flowers.

In real life I am a large, big-boned woman with rough, man-working hands. In the winter I wear flannel nightgowns to bed and overalls during the day. I can kill and clean a hog as mercilessly as a man. My fat keeps me hot in zero weather. I can work outside all day, breaking ice to get water for washing; I can eat pork liver cooked over the open fire minutes after it comes steaming from the hog. One winter I knocked a bull calf straight in the brain between the eyes with a sledge hammer and had the meat hung up to chill before nightfall. But of course all this does not show on television. I am the way my daughter would want me to be: a hundred pounds lighter, my skin like an uncooked barley pancake. My hair glistens in the hot bright lights. Johnny Carson has much to do to keep up with my quick and witty tongue.

But that is a mistake. I know even before I wake up. Who ever knew a Johnson with a quick tongue? Who can even imagine me looking a strange white man in the eye? It seems to me I have talked to them always with one foot raised in flight, with my head turned in whichever way is farthest from them. Dee, though. She would always look anyone in the eye. Hesitation was no part of her nature.

"How do I look, Mama?" Maggie says, showing just enough of her thin body enveloped in pink skirt and red blouse for me to know she's there, almost hidden by the door.

"Come out into the yard," I say.

Have you ever seen a lame animal, perhaps a dog run over by some careless person rich enough to own a car, sidle up to someone who is ignorant enough to be kind to him? That is the way my Maggie walks. She has been like this, chin on chest, eyes on ground, feet in shuffle, ever since the fire that burned the other house to the ground.

Dee is lighter than Maggie, with nicer hair and a fuller figure. She's a woman now, though sometimes I forget. How long ago was it that the other house burned? Ten, twelve years? Sometimes I can still hear the flames and feel Maggie's arms sticking to me, her hair smoking and her dress falling off her in little black papery flakes. Her eyes seemed stretched open, blazed open by the flames reflected in them. And Dee. I see her standing off under the sweet gum tree she used to dig gum out of; a look of concentration on her face as she watched the last dingy gray board of the house fall in toward the red-hot brick chimney. Why don't you do a dance around the ashes? I'd wanted to ask her. She had hated the house that much.

I used to think she hated Maggie, too. But that was before we raised the money, the church and me, to send her to Augusta to school. She used to read to us without pity; forcing words, lies, other folks' habits, whole lives upon us two, sitting trapped and ignorant underneath her voice. She washed us in a river of make-believe, burned us with a lot of knowledge we didn't necessarily need to know. Pressed us to her with the serious way she read, to shove us away at just the moment, like dimwits, we seemed about to understand.

Dee wanted nice things. A yellow organdy dress to wear to her graduation from high school; black pumps to match a green suit she'd made from an old suit somebody gave me. She was determined to stare down any disaster in her efforts. Her eyelids would not flicker for minutes at a time. Often I fought off the temptation to shake her. At sixteen she had a style of her own: and knew what style was.

I never had an education myself. After second grade the school was closed down. Don't ask me why: in 1927 colored asked fewer questions than they do now. Sometimes Maggie reads to me. She stumbles along good-naturedly but can't see well. She knows she is not bright. Like good looks and money, quickness passed her by. She will marry John Thomas (who has mossy teeth in an earnest face) and then

I'll be free to sit here and I guess just sing church songs to myself. Although I never was a good singer. Never could carry a tune. I was always better at a man's job. I used to love to milk till I was hooked in the side in '49. Cows are soothing and slow and don't bother you, unless you try to milk them the wrong way.

I have deliberately turned my back on the house. It is three rooms, just like the one that burned, except the roof is tin; they don't make shingle roofs any more. There are no real windows, just some holes cut in the sides, like the portholes in a ship, but not round and not square, with rawhide holding the shutters up on the outside. This house is in a pasture, too, like the other one. No doubt when Dee sees it she will want to tear it down. She wrote me once that no matter where we "choose" to live, she will manage to come see us. But she will never bring her friends. Maggie and I thought about this and Maggie asked me, "Mama, when did Dee ever *have* any friends?"

She had a few. Furtive boys in pink shirts hanging about on washday after school. Nervous girls who never laughed. Impressed with her they worshiped the well-turned phrase, the cute shape, the scalding humor that erupted like bubbles in lye. She read to them.

When she was courting Jimmy T she didn't have much time to pay to us, but turned all her fault finding power on him. He *flew* to marry a cheap city girl from a family of ignorant flashy people. She hardly had time to recompose herself.

When she comes I will meet—but there they are!

Maggie attempts to make a dash for the house, in her shuffling way, but I stay her with my hand. "Come back here," I say. And she stops and tries to dig a well in the sand with her toe.

It is hard to see them clearly through the strong sun. But even the first glimpse of leg out of the car tells me it is Dee. Her feet were always neat-looking, as if God himself had shaped them with a certain style. From the other side of the car comes a short, stocky man. Hair is all over his head a foot long and hanging from his chin like a kinky mule tail. I hear Maggie suck in her breath. "Uhnnnh," is what it sounds like. Like when you see the wriggling end of a snake just in front of your foot on the road. "Uhnnnh."

Dee next. A dress down to the ground, in this hot weather. A dress so loud it hurts my eyes. There are yellows and oranges enough to throw back the light of the sun. I feel my whole face warming from the heat waves it throws out. Earrings gold, too, and hanging down to her shoulders. Bracelets dangling and making noises when she moves her arm up to shake the folds of the dress out of her armpits. The dress is loose and flows, and as she walks closer, I like it. I hear Maggie go "Uhnnnh" again. It is her sister's hair. It stands straight up like the wool on a sheep. It is black as night and around the edges are two long pigtails that rope about like small lizards disappearing behind her ears.

"Wa-su-zo-Tean-o!" she says, coming on in that gilding way the dress makes her move. The short stocky fellow with the hair to his navel is all grinning and he follows up with "Asalamalakim, my mother and sister!" He moves to hug Maggie but she falls back, right up against the back of my chair. I feel her trembling there and when I look up I see the perspiration falling off her chin.

"Don't get up," says Dee. Since I am stout it takes something of a push. You can see me trying to move a second or two before I make it. She turns, showing white heels through her sandals, and goes back to the car. Out she peeks next with a Polaroid. She stoops down quickly and lines up picture after picture of me sitting there in front of the house with Maggie cowering behind me. She never takes a shot without making sure the house is included. When a cow comes nibbling around the edge of the yard she snaps it and me and Maggie *and* the house. Then she puts the Polaroid in the back seat of the car, and comes up and kisses me on the forehead.

Meanwhile Asalamalakim is going through motions with Maggie's hand. Maggie's hand is as limp as a fish, and probably as cold, despite the sweat, and she keeps trying to pull it back. It looks like Asalamalakim wants to shake hands but wants to do it fancy. Or maybe he don't know how people shake hands. Anyhow, he soon gives up on Maggie.

"Well," I say. "Dee."

"No, Mama," she says. "Not 'Dee,' Wangero Leewanika Kemanjo!"

"What happened to 'Dee'?" I wanted to know.

"She's dead," Wangero said. "I couldn't bear it any longer, being named after the people who oppress me."

"You know as well as me you was named after your aunt Dicie," I said. Dicie is my sister. She named Dee. We called her "Big Dee" after Dee was born.

"But who was *she* named after?" asked Wangero.

"I guess after Grandma Dee," I said.

"And who was she named after?" asked Wangero.

"Her mother," I said, and saw Wangero was getting tired. "That's about as far back as I can trace it," I said. Though, in fact, I probably could have carried it back beyond the Civil War through the branches.

"Well," said Asalamalakim, "there you are."

"Uhnnnh," I heard Maggie say.

"There I was not," I said, "before 'Dicie' cropped up in our family, so why should I try to trace it that far back?"

He just stood there grinning, looking down on me like somebody inspecting a Model A car. Every once in a while he and Wangero sent eye signals over my head.

"How do you pronounce this name?" I asked.

"You don't have to call me by it if you don't want to," said Wangero.

"Why shouldn't I?" I asked. "If that's what you want us to call you, we'll call you."

"I know it might sound awkward at first," said Wangero.

"I'll get used to it," I said. "Ream it out again."

Well, soon we got the name out of the way. Asalamalakim had a name twice as long and three times as hard. After I tripped over it two or three times he told me to just call him Hakim-a-barber. I wanted to ask him was he a barber, but I didn't really think he was, so I didn't ask.

"You must belong to those beef-cattle peoples down the road," I said. They said "Asalamalakim" when they met you, too, but they didn't shake hands. Always too busy: feeding the cattle, fixing the fences, putting up salt-lick shelters, throwing down hay. When the white folks poisoned some of the herd the men stayed up all night with rifles in their hands. I walked a mile and a half just to see the sight.

Hakim-a-barber said, "I accept some of their doctrines, but farming and raising cattle is not my style." (They didn't tell me, and I didn't ask, whether Wangero (Dee) had really gone and married him.)

We sat down to eat and right away he said he didn't eat collards and pork was unclean. Wangero, though, went on through the chitlins and corn bread, the greens and everything else. She talked a blue streak over the sweet potatoes. Everything delighted her. Even the fact that we still used the benches her daddy made for the table when we couldn't afford to buy chairs.

"Oh, Mama!" she cried. Then turned to Hakim-a-barber. "I never knew how lovely these benches are. You can feel the rump prints," she said, running her hands underneath her and along the bench. Then she gave a sigh and her hand closed over Grandma Dee's butter dish. "That's it!" she said. "I knew there was something I wanted to ask you if I could have." She jumped up from the table and went over in the corner where the churn stood, the milk in it clabber by now. She looked at the churn and looked at it.

"This churn top is what I need," she said. "Didn't Uncle Buddy whittle it out of a tree you all used to have?"

"Yes," I said.

"Uh huh," she said happily. "And I want the dasher, too."

"Uncle Buddy whittle that, too?" asked the barber.

Dee (Wangero) looked up at me.

"Aunt Dee's first husband whittled the dash," said Maggie so low you almost couldn't hear her. "His name was Henry, but they called him Stash."

"Maggie's brain is like an elephant's," Wangero said, laughing. "I can use the churn top as a centerpiece for the alcove table," she said, sliding a plate over the churn, "and I'll think of something artistic to do with the dasher."

When she finished wrapping the dasher the handle stuck out. I took it for a moment in my hands. You didn't even have to look close to see where hands pushing the dasher up and down to make butter had left a kind of sink in the wood. In fact, there were a lot of small sinks; you could see where thumbs and fingers had sunk into the wood. It was beautiful light yellow wood, from a tree that grew in the yard where Big Dee and Stash had lived.

After dinner Dee (Wangero) went to the trunk at the foot of my bed and started rifling through it. Maggie hung back in the kitchen over the dishpan. Out came Wangero with two quilts. They had been pieced by Grandma Dee and then Big Dee and me had hung them on the quilt frames on the front porch and quilted them. One was in the Lone Star pattern. The other was Walk Around the Mountain. In both of them were scraps of dresses Grandma Dee had worn fifty and more years ago. Bits and pieces of Grandpa Jarrell's Paisley shirts. And one teeny faded blue piece, about the size of a penny matchbox, that was from Great Grandpa Ezra's uniform that he wore in the Civil War.

"Mama," Wangero said sweet as a bird. "Can I have these old quilts?"

I heard something fall in the kitchen, and a minute later the kitchen door slammed.

"Why don't you take one or two of the others?" I asked. "These old things was just done by me and Big Dee from some tops your grandma pieced before she died."

"No," said Wangero. "I don't want those. They are stitched around the borders by machine."

"That'll make them last better," I said.

"That's not the point," said Wangero. "These are all pieces of dresses Grandma used to wear. She did all this stitching by hand. Imagine!" She held the quilts securely in her arms, stroking them.

"Some of the pieces, like those lavender ones, come from old clothes her mother handed down to her," I said, moving up to touch the quilts. Dee (Wangero) moved back just enough so that I couldn't reach the quilts. They already belonged to her.

"Imagine!" she breathed again, clutching them closely to her bosom.

"The truth is," I said, "I promised to give them quilts to Maggie, for when she marries John Thomas."

She gasped like a bee had stung her.

"Maggie can't appreciate these quilts!" she said. "She'd probably be backward enough to put them to everyday use."

"I reckon she would," I said. "God knows I been saving 'em for long enough with nobody using 'em. I hope she will!" I didn't want to bring up how I had offered Dee (Wangero) a quilt when she went away to college. Then she had told me they were old-fashioned, out of style.

"But they're *priceless!*" she was saying now, furiously; for she has a temper. "Maggie would put them on the bed and in five years they'd be in rags. Less than that!"

"She can always make some more," I said. "Maggie knows how to quilt."

Dee (Wangero) looked at me with hatred. "You just will not understand. The point is these quilts, *these* quilts!"

"Well," I said, stumped. "What would *you* do with them?"

"Hang them," she said. As if that was the only thing you *could* do with quilts.

Maggie by now was standing in the door. I could almost hear the sound her feet made as they scraped over each other.

"She can have them, Mama," she said, like somebody used to never winning anything, or having anything reserved for her. "I can 'member Grandma Dee without the quilts."

I looked at her hard. She had filled her bottom lip with checkerberry snuff and it gave her face a kind of dopey, hangdog look. It was Grandma Dee and Big Dee who taught her how to quilt herself. She stood there with her scarred hands hidden in the folds of her skirt. She looked at her sister with something like fear but she wasn't mad at her. This was Maggie's portion. This was the way she knew God to work.

When I looked at her like that something hit me in the top of my head and ran down to the soles of my feet. Just like when I'm in church and the spirit of God touches me and I get happy and shout. I did something I never had done before: hugged Maggie to me, then dragged her on into the room, snatched the quilts out of Miss Wangero's hands and dumped them into Maggie's lap. Maggie just sat there on my bed with her mouth open.

"Take one or two of the others," I said to Dee.

But she turned without a word and went out to Hakim-a-barber.

"You just don't understand," she said, as Maggie and I came out to the car.

"What don't I understand?" I wanted to know.

"Your heritage," she said. And then she turned to Maggie, kissed her, and said, "You ought to try to make something of yourself, too, Maggie. It's really a new day for us. But from the way you and Mama still live you'd never know it."

She put on some sunglasses that hid everything above the tip of her nose and her chin.

Maggie smiled; maybe at the sunglasses. But a real smile, not scared. After we watched the car dust settle I asked Maggie to bring me a dip of snuff. And then the two of us sat there just enjoying, until it was time to go in the house and go to bed.

CRITICAL THINKING QUESTIONS

1. What is Walker's implied *claim of value* about family heritage? What evidence in the story supports this claim? Do you agree or disagree with this claim?

2. When the mother refuses Dee's demand for the quilts and hands them over to Maggie, how did you react? What values informed your reaction?

3. In the closing scene, how is the author using *pathos* appeal?

WRITING TOPIC

In a classic rock song, the Rolling Stones sing, "You can't always get what you want, but if you try sometimes, you just might find you get what you need." Relating this quote to Walker's "Everyday Use" and your personal experience/observations, develop your own claim about getting what you *want* . . . trying, and finding what you *need*. Using evidence from the story and your experience, write an essay defending your claim.

Gwendolyn Brooks

The Mother

Abortions will not let you forget.
You remember the children you got that you did not get,
The damp small pulps with a little or with no hair,
The singers and workers that never handled the air.
You will never neglect or beat
Them, or silence or buy with a sweet.
You will never wind up the sucking-thumb
Or scuttle off ghosts that come.
You will never leave them, controlling your luscious sigh,
Return for a snack of them, with gobbling mother-eye.

I have heard in the voices of the wind the voices of my dim
    killed children.
I have contracted. I have eased
My dim dears at the breasts they could never suck.
I have said, Sweets, if I sinned, if I seized
Your luck
And your lives from your unfinished reach,
If I stole your births and your names,
Your straight baby tears and your games,
Your stilted or lovely loves, your tumults, your marriages, aches,
    and your deaths,
If I poisoned the beginnings of your breaths,
Believe that even in my deliberateness I was not deliberate.
Though why should I whine,
Whine that the crime was other than mine?—
Since anyhow you are dead.
Or rather, or instead,
You were never made.

But that too, I am afraid,
Is faulty: oh, what shall I say, how is the truth to be said?
You were born, you had body, you died.
It is just that you never giggled or planned or cried.

Believe me, I loved you all.
Believe me, I knew you, though faintly, and I loved, I loved you
All.

CRITICAL THINKING QUESTIONS

1. Beginning with line 21, when the speaker says, "Believe . . . ," she seems to be sorting through her conscience in trying to articulate "the truth." How do you interpret lines 21 to 30? How do you think she is judging herself, assessing herself as "the mother"? Working with three or four classmates, read and compare your interpretations and then collaborate on a statement that your group will present to the rest of the class. Be prepared to point to specific evidence from the poem to defend your interpretation.

2. What is the effect of repetition in the poem's closing stanza? Whom is the speaker, the mother, trying to convince?

3. Examining this poem as an implied argument, what is its *issue question?* What is its *claim?* What *evidence* in the poem supports your statement of the claim?

4. Assess the speaker's *ethos.*

Nikki Giovanni

Mothers

the last time i was home
to see my mother we kissed
exchanged pleasantries
and unpleasantries pulled a warm
comforting silence around
us and read separate books

i remember the first time
i consciously saw her
we were living in a three room
apartment on burns avenue
mommy always sat in the dark
i don't know how i knew that but she did

that night i stumbled into the kitchen
maybe because i've always been
a night person or perhaps because i had wet the bed
she was sitting on a chair
the room was bathed in moonlight diffused through
those thousands of panes landlords who rented
to people with children were prone to put in windows

she may have been smoking but maybe not
her hair was three-quarters her height
which made me a strong believer in the samson myth
and very black

i'm sure i just hung there by the door
i remember thinking: what a beautiful lady

she was very deliberately waiting
perhaps for my father to come home
from his night job or maybe for a dream
that had promised to come by
"come here" she said "i'll teach you

a poem: *i see the moon*
             the moon sees me
             god bless the moon
             and god bless me"
i taught it to my son
who recited it for her
just to say we must learn
to bear the pleasures
as we have borne the pains

CRITICAL THINKING QUESTIONS

1. Examine the details of the speaker's depiction of her childhood memory and draw some inferences about the mother's life at this time.

2. In teaching the poem, what message is the mother imparting to her daughter?

3. The speaker also has taught the poem to her son, and it is he who now recites it for his grandmother. In light of the poem's title, how is this detail significant?

WRITING TOPIC

Some social critics argue that the failure of parents (and some add, schools) to teach values to children is a primary cause for increasing problems among youth—from rude and boorish behavior to drug use and violence. What is the poet's implied claim about the teaching of values? Reflecting on your childhood, can you recall a moment when you learned a lesson about values? How do you think children should be taught values?

Thomas Hardy

The Ruined Maid

"O 'Melia, my dear, this does everything crown!
Who could have supposed I should meet you in Town?
And whence such fair garments, such prosperi-ty?"
"O didn't you know I'd been ruined?" said she.

"You left us in tatters, without shoes or socks,
Tired of digging potatoes, and spudding up docks;
And now you've gay bracelets and bright feathers three!"
"Yes: that's how we dress when we're ruined," said she.

"At home in the barton you said 'thee' and 'thou,'
And 'thik oon,' and 'theäs oon,' and 't'other'; but now
Your talking quite fits 'ee for high compa-ny!"
"Some polish is gained with one's ruin," said she.

"Your hands were like paws then, your face blue and bleak
But now I'm bewitched by your delicate cheek,
And your little gloves fit as on any la-dy!"
"We never do work when we're ruined," said she.

"You used to call home-life a hag-ridden dream,
And you'd sigh, and you'd sock; but at present you seem
To know not of megrims° or melancho-ly!"
"True. One's pretty lively when ruined," said she.

"I wish I had feathers, a fine sweeping gown,
And a delicate face, and could strut about Town!"
"My dear—a raw country girl, such as you be,
Cannot quite expect that. You ain't ruined," said she.

CRITICAL THINKING QUESTIONS

1. By leaving her home-life on the farm, what has 'Melia left behind? What has
she gained in her new life in Town?

2. Compare and contrast the values associated with her previous lifestyle and with her present one.

3. Her former acquaintance, who still lives in the country, seems to think that 'Melia has found prosperity and happiness in Town. How does this *inference* represent flawed reasoning?

Seamus Heaney

Digging

Between my finger and my thumb
The squat pen rests; snug as a gun.

Under my window, a clean rasping sound
When the spade sinks into gravelly ground:
My father, digging. I look down

Till his straining rump among the flowerbeds
Bends low, comes up twenty years away
Stooping in rhythm through potato drills
Where he was digging.

The coarse boot nestled on the lug, the shaft
Against the inside knee was levered firmly.
He rooted out tall tops, buried the bright edge deep
To scatter new potatoes that we picked
Loving their cool hardness in our hands.

By God, the old man could handle a spade.
Just like his old man.

My grandfather cut more turf in a day
Than any other man on Toner's bog.
Once I carried him milk in a bottle
Corked sloppily with paper. He straightened up
To drink it, then fell to right away

Nicking and slicing neatly, heaving sods
Over his shoulder, going down and down
For the good turf. Digging.

The cold smell of potato mould, the squelch and slap
Of soggy peat, the curt cuts of an edge
Through living roots awaken in my head.
But I've no spade to follow men like them.

Between my finger and my thumb
The squat pen rests.
I'll dig with it.

CRITICAL THINKING QUESTIONS

1. What common assumptions about the differences between mental labor and physical labor are challenged in this poem?

2. What is the poet's claim about the relationship between his work as a writer and his father's and grandfather's work as farmers?

3. List the evidence Heaney provides for his claim. On which rhetorical appeal does he rely?

WRITING TOPIC

What value assumption about family heritage informs Heaney's argument? Reflecting on your own experience and observations, how important is family heritage today?

Peter Meinke

Advice to My Son

—FOR TIM

The trick is, to live your days
as if each one may be your last
(for they go fast, and young men lose their lives
in strange and unimaginable ways)
but at the same time, plan long range
(for they go slow: if you survive
the shattered windshield and the bursting shell
you will arrive
at our approximation here below
of heaven or hell).

To be specific, between the peony and the rose
plant squash and spinach, turnips and tomatoes;
beauty is nectar
and nectar, in a desert, saves—
but the stomach craves stronger sustenance
than the honied vine.
Therefore, marry a pretty girl
after seeing her mother;
speak truth to one man,
work with another;
and always serve bread with your wine.

But, son,
always serve wine.

CRITICAL THINKING QUESTIONS

1. In lines 17 to 18, the speaker makes the claim, "Therefore, marry a pretty girl,"
   with this *qualifier* phrase, "after seeing her mother." What *warrants* or *value assumptions* underlie that statement? Are they valid?

WRITING TOPIC

Meinke is giving advice to his son, "—for Tim." Working with several other students (preferably in mixed gender groups), create a female version of Meinke's poem, "Advice to My Daughter." Be prepared to present your poem to the rest of the class.

Naomi Shihab Nye

Arabic Coffee

It was never too strong for us:
make it blacker, Papa,
thick in the bottom,
tell again how the years will gather
in small white cups,
how luck lives in a spot of grounds.
Leaning over the stove, he let it
boil to the top, and down again.
Two times. No sugar in his pot.
And the place where men and women
break off from one another
was not present in that room.
The hundred disappointments,
fire swallowing olive-wood beads
at the warehouse, and the dreams
tucked like pocket handkerchiefs
into each day, took their places
on the table, near the half-empty
dish of corn. And none was
more important than the others,
and all were guests. When
he carried the tray into the room,
high and balanced in his hands,
it was an offering to all of them,
stay, be seated, follow the talk
wherever it goes. The coffee was
the center of the flower.
Like clothes on a line saying
you will live long enough to wear me,
a motion of faith. There is this,
and there is more.

WRITING TOPIC

Compare this poem to Mark Strand's "The Continuous Life." Both poems reflect
on the meaning of human life. Compare and contrast the two poets' viewpoints.
Articulate each poet's central claim. Which claim do you support? Drawing on
evidence from the poems and your own experience, defend your position.

Sharon Olds

I Go Back to May, 1937

I see them standing at the formal gates of their colleges,
I see my father strolling out
under the ochre sandstone arch, the
red tiles glinting like bent
plates of blood behind his head, I
see my mother with a few light books at her hip
standing at the pillar made of tiny bricks with the
wrought-iron gate still open behind her, its
sword-tips black in the May air,
they are about to graduate, they are about to get married,
they are kids, they are dumb, all they know is they are
innocent, they would never hurt anybody.
I want to go up to them and say Stop,
don't do it—she's the wrong woman,
he's the wrong man, you are going to do things
you cannot imagine you would ever do,
you are going to do bad things to children,
you are going to suffer in ways you never heard of,
you are going to want to die. I want to go
up to them there in the late May sunlight and say it,
her hungry pretty blank face turning to me,
her pitiful beautiful untouched body,
his arrogant handsome blind face turning to me,
his pitiful beautiful untouched body,
but I don't do it. I want to live. I
take them up like the male and female
paper dolls and bang them together
at the hips like chips of flint as if to
strike sparks from them, I say
Do what you are going to do, and I will tell about it.

CRITICAL THINKING QUESTIONS

1. Olds's poem addresses the *issue question*—should the daughter try to stop her
   parents from marrying each other?

2. List the evidence the speaker provides in examining the question. Why does she decide not to stop her parents from marrying?

RESEARCH/WRITING TOPIC

Consider Olds's poem from a broad perspective: What if we could see into the future—how our lives will play out? Would this be a good thing? You can expand your thinking on this topic by researching biotechnology (the Human Genome Project) which may open the door—or many critics say, Pandora's box—for us to program our genes and, thus, "predict" our future.

Mary Oliver

The Black Walnut Tree

My mother and I debate:
we could sell
the black walnut tree
to the lumberman,
and pay off the mortgage.
Likely some storm anyway
will churn down its dark boughs,
smashing the house. We talk
slowly, two women trying
in a difficult time to be wise.
Roots in the cellar drains,
I say, and she replies
that the leaves are getting heavier
every year, and the fruit
harder to gather away.
But something brighter than money
moves in our blood—an edge
sharp and quick as a trowel
that wants us to dig and sow.
So we talk, but we don't do
anything. That night I dream
of my fathers out of Bohemia
filling the blue fields
of fresh and generous Ohio
with leaves and vines and orchards.
What my mother and I both know
is that we'd crawl with shame
in the emptiness we'd made
in our own and our fathers' backyard.
So the black walnut tree
swings through another year
of sun and leaping winds,
of leaves and bounding fruit,
and, month after month, the whip-
crack of the mortgage.

CRITICAL THINKING QUESTIONS

1. In debating the sale of the black walnut tree, how does the speaker appeal to *pathos?*

2. How does she appeal to *logos?*

3. What *warrant* supports the women's decision to preserve the tree? Is it valid? Can you think of issues you have debated where this warrant entered into the argument?

WRITING TOPIC

Do you think the mother's and daughter's fathers would agree or disagree with the women's decision? Why?

Dudley Randall

Ballad of Birmingham

(On the Bombing of a Church in Birmingham, Alabama, 1963)

"Mother dear, may I go downtown
Instead of out to play,
And march the streets of Birmingham
In a Freedom March today?"

"No, baby, no, you may not go,
For the dogs are fierce and wild,
And clubs and hoses, guns and jails
Aren't good for a little child."

"But, mother, I won't be alone.
Other children will go with me,
And march the streets of Birmingham
To make our country free."

"No, baby, no, you may not go,
For I fear those guns will fire.
But you may go to church instead
And sing in the children's choir."

She has combed and brushed her night-dark hair.
And bathed rose petal sweet.
And drawn white gloves on her small brown hands,
And white shoes on her feet.

The mother smiled to know her child
Was in the sacred place,
But that smile was the last smile
To come upon her face.

For when she heard the explosion,
Her eyes grew wet and wild.

She raced through the streets of Birmingham
Calling for her child.

She clawed through bits of glass and brick.
Then lifted out a shoe.
"Oh, here's the shoe my baby wore,
But, baby, where are you?"

CRITICAL THINKING QUESTIONS

1. Working in small groups, write out at least two *implied claims* for this poem. List *evidence* for each claim.

2. In committing an act of terrorism, what *value assumption* does the terrorist use to justify his or her act?

3. How does Randall's poem refute the terrorist's assumption?

WRITING TOPIC

Randall's poem and Power's story, "Red Moccasins," feature the depth and power of maternal love. Compare and contast the perspectives that each piece of literature presents. Based on your study, write a *Rogerian argument* about the conflicting powers of maternal love.

Adrienne Rich

Aunt Jennifer's Tigers

Aunt Jennifer's tigers prance across a screen,
Bright topaz denizens of a world of green.
They do not fear the men beneath the tree;
They pace in sleek chivalric certainty.

Aunt Jennifer's fingers fluttering through her wool
Find even the ivory needle hard to pull.
The massive weight of Uncle's wedding band
Sits heavily upon Aunt Jennifer's hand.

When Aunt is dead, her terrified hands will lie
Still ringed with ordeals she was mastered by.
The tigers in the panel that she made
Will go on prancing, proud and unafraid.

Anne Sexton

Cinderella

You always read about it:
the plumber with twelve children
who wins the Irish Sweepstakes.
From toilets to riches.
That story.

Or the nursemaid,
some luscious sweet from Denmark
who captures the oldest son's heart.
From diapers to Dior.
That story.

Or a milkman who serves the wealthy,
eggs, cream, butter, yogurt, milk,
the white truck like an ambulance
who goes into real estate
and makes a pile.
From homogenized to martinis at lunch.

Or the charwoman
who is on the bus when it cracks up
and collects enough from the insurance.
From mops to Bonwit Teller.
That story.

Once
the wife of a rich man was on her deathbed
and she said to her daughter Cinderella:
Be devout. Be good. Then I will smile
down from heaven in the seam of a cloud.
The man took another wife who had
two daughters, pretty enough
but with hearts like blackjacks.
Cinderella was their maid.
She slept on the sooty hearth each night
and walked around looking like Al Jolson.
Her father brought presents home from town,
jewels and gowns for the other women
but the twig of a tree for Cinderella.

She planted that twig on her mother's grave
and it grew to a tree where a white dove sat.
Whenever she wished for anything the dove
would drop it like an egg upon the ground.
The bird is important, my dears, so heed him.

Next came the ball, as you all know.
It was a marriage market.
The prince was looking for a wife.
All but Cinderella were preparing
and gussying up for the big event.
Cinderella begged to go too.
Her stepmother threw a dish of lentils
into the cinders and said: Pick them
up in an hour and you shall go.
The white dove brought all his friends;
all the warm wings of the fatherland came,
and picked up the lentils in a jiffy.
No, Cinderella, said the stepmother,
you have no clothes and cannot dance.
That's the way with stepmothers.

Cinderella went to the tree at the grave
and cried forth like a gospel singer:
Mama! Mama! My turtledove,
send me to the prince's ball!
The bird dropped down a golden dress
and delicate little gold slippers.
Rather a large package for a simple bird.
So she went. Which is no surprise.
Her stepmother and sisters didn't
recognize her without her cinder face
and the prince took her hand on the spot
and danced with no other the whole day.

As nightfall came she thought she'd better
get home. The prince walked her home
and she disappeared into the pigeon house
and although the prince took an axe and broke
it open she was gone. Back to her cinders.
These events repeated themselves for three days.
However on the third day the prince
covered the palace steps with cobbler's wax
and Cinderella's gold shoe stuck upon it.
Now he would find whom the shoe fit
and find his strange dancing girl for keeps.

He went to their house and the two sisters
were delighted because they had lovely feet.
The eldest went into a room to try the slipper on
but her big toe got in the way so she simply
sliced it off and put on the slipper.
The prince rode away with her until the white dove
told him to look at the blood pouring forth.
That is the way with amputations.
They don't just heal up like a wish.
The other sister cut off her heel
but the blood told as blood will.
The prince was getting tired.
He began to feel like a shoe salesman.
But he gave it one last try.
This time Cinderella fit into the shoe
like a love letter into its envelope.
At the wedding ceremony
the two sisters came to curry favor
and the white dove pecked their eyes out.
Two hollow spots were left
like soup spoons.

Cinderella and the prince
lived, they say, happily ever after,
like two dolls in a museum case
never bothered by diapers or dust,
never arguing over the timing of an egg,
never telling the same story twice,
never getting a middle-aged spread,
their darling smiles pasted on for eternity
Regular Bobbsey Twins.
That story.

CRITICAL THINKING QUESTIONS

1. Sexton's poem mocks the fantasy of happiness forever. Besides fairytales, which by definition are fantasies, how do popular culture and the media feed our fantasies of the "happily-ever-after" life?

2. Related to the myth of the happily-ever-after life is the quest for eternal youth and beauty. In the Walt Disney version of *Cinderella,* Cinderella is beautiful, and the prince, handsome. What *value assumption* is reinforced by their physical perfection?

WRITING TOPIC

Defend the place of the myth of happily-ever-after in our culture. In what ways might the fantasy of everlasting happiness be a positive force?

Gary Snyder

Not Leaving the House

When Kai is born
I quit going out

Hang around the kitchen—make cornbread
Let nobody in.
Mail is flat.
    Masa lies on her side, Kai sighs,
    Non washes and sweeps
We sit and watch
    Masa nurse, and drink green tea.

Navajo turquoise beads over the bed
A peacock tail feather at the head
A badger pelt from Nagano-ken
For a mattress; under the sheet;
A pot of yogurt setting
Under the blankets, at his feet.

Masa, Kai,
And Non, our friend
In the green garden light reflected in
Not leaving the house.
From dawn til late at night
    making a new world of ourselves
    around this life.

CRITICAL THINKING QUESTION

What view of a father does this poem present?

WRITING TOPIC

Some career women are choosing single motherhood by using sperm donors to conceive a child. Implicit in this choice is a *warrant* or value assumption about the father's role and the family. What is this warrant? How does Snyder's poem implicitly refute this warrant? Using this poem and other literature selections in this chapter, as well as your own primary evidence (personal experience and observations), write and defend a *claim of value* about the father's role in a family. (See Chapter Activity #3, for a longer, research-based paper on this topic.)

Mark Strand

The Continuous Life

What of the neighborhood homes awash
In a silver light, of children hunched in the bushes,
Watching the grownups for signs of surrender,
Signs the irregular pleasures of moving
From day to day, of being adrift on the swell of duty
Have run their course? O parents, confess
To your little ones the night is a long way off
And your taste for the mundane grows; tell them
Your worship of household chores has barely begun;
Describe the beauty of shovels and rakes, brooms and mops;
Say there will always be cooking and cleaning to do,
That one thing leads to another, which leads to another;
Explain that you live between two great darks, the first
With an ending, the second without one, that the luckiest
Thing is having been born, that you live in a blur
Of hours and days, months and years, and believe
It has meaning, despite the occasional fear
You are slipping away with nothing completed, nothing
To prove you existed. Tell the children to come inside,
That your search goes on for something you lost: a name,
A book of the family that fell from its own small matter
Into another, a piece of the dark that might have been yours—
You don't really know. Say that each of you tries
To keep busy, learning to lean down close and hear
The careless breathing of earth and feel its available
Languor come over you, wave after wave, sending
Small tremors of love through your brief,
Undeniable selves, into your days, and beyond.

CRITICAL THINKING QUESTIONS

1. Analyze this poem as a *Rogerian argument:*
   a. State the *issue question* that is implied in the poem's first six lines.
   b. Examine the evidence in lines 6 to 22. Describe the speaker's tone as he postulates responses to the issue question. What words or phrases contribute to a Rogerian tone?

   c. Reading the last six lines (23 to 28) as the conclusion to the poet's argument, write out a Rogerian argument claim statement—a *qualified position* in response to the issue question.

2. Reflecting on your experiences and your observations of the lives of parents, defend or refute the claim you articulated in 1c.

Margaret Walker

Lineage

My grandmothers were strong.
They followed plows and bent to toil.
They moved through fields sowing seed.

They touched earth and grain grew.
They were full of sturdiness and singing.
My grandmothers were strong.

My grandmothers are full of memories.
Smelling of soap and onions and wet clay
With veins rolling roughly over quick hands
They have many clean words to say.
My grandmothers were strong.
Why am I not as they?

CRITICAL THINKING QUESTIONS

1. What qualities does the speaker imply she has lost that her grandmothers possessed?
2. How does this poem define "strong"?
3. What value assumptions does the speaker make about the rewards of physical toil? Do you accept them?

WRITING TOPIC

Compare and contrast Heaney's "Digging" and Walker's "Lineage." Although both poems examine similar situations and share the warrant—family heritage is valuable—, the poems' two speakers arrive at opposing claims about their "lineage." Do you think Heaney's or Walker's speaker is more representative of people today when they assess their role in continuing the family lineage?

Richard Wilbur

The Writer

In her room at the prow of the house
Where light breaks, and the windows are tossed with linden,
My daughter is writing a story.

I pause in the stairwell, hearing
From her shut door a commotion of typewriter-keys
Like a chain hauled over a gunwale.

Young as she is, the stuff
Of her life is a great cargo, and some of it heavy:
I wish her a lucky passage.

But now it is she who pauses,
As if to reject my thought and its easy figure.
A stillness greatens, in which

The whole house seems to be thinking,
And then she is at it again with a bunched clamor
Of strokes, and again is silent.

I remember the dazed starling
Which was trapped in that very room, two years ago,
How we stole in, lifted a sash

And retreated, not to affright it;
And how for a helpless hour, through the crack of the door,
We watched the sleek, wild, dark

And iridescent creature
Batter against the brilliance, drop like a glove
To the hard floor, or the desk-top,

And wait then, humped and bloody,
For the wits to try it again; and how our spirits
Rose when, suddenly sure,

It lifted off from a chair-back,
Beating a smooth course for the right window
And clearing the sill of the world.

It is always a matter, my darling,
Of life or death, as I had forgotten. I wish
What I wished you before, but harder.

CRITICAL THINKING QUESTIONS

1. Who is the teacher, and who is the learner in this poem?
2. What claim does this poem imply about the process of learning?
3. Compare and contrast this poem and Meinke's "Advice to My Son." How do the two fathers illustrate different styles of parental counseling? Does the child's gender influence a father's style?

Harvey Fierstein

On Tidy Endings

SCENE

The curtain rises on a deserted, modern Upper West Side apartment. In the bright day-light that pours in through the windows we can see the living room of the apartment. Far Stage Right is the galley kitchen, next to it the multilocked front door with intercom. Stage Left reveals a hallway that leads to the two bedrooms and baths.

Though the room is still fully furnished (couch, coffee table, etc.), there are boxes stacked against the wall and several photographs and paintings are on the floor leaving shadows on the wall where they once hung. Obviously someone is moving out. From the way the boxes are neatly labeled and stacked, we know that this is an organized person.

From the hallway just outside the door we hear the rattling of keys and two arguing voices:

JIM (*Offstage*): I've got to be home by four. I've got practice.

MARION (*Offstage*): I'll get you to practice, don't worry.

JIM (*Offstage*): I don't want to go in there.

MARION (*Offstage*): Jimmy, don't make Mommy crazy, alright? We'll go inside, I'll call Aunt Helen and see if you can go down and play with Robbie.

(*The door opens.* MARION *is a handsome woman of forty. Dressed in a business suit, her hair conservatively combed, she appears to be going to a business meeting.* JIM *is a boy of eleven. His playclothes are typical, but someone has obviously just combed his hair.* MARION *recovers the key from the lock.*)

JIM: Why can't I just go down and ring the bell?

MARION: Because I said so.

(*As* MARION *steps into the room she is struck by some unexpected emotion. She freezes in her path and stares at the empty apartment.* JIM *lingers by the door.*)

JIM: I'm going downstairs.

MARION: Jimmy, please

JIM: This place gives me the creeps.

MARION: This was your father's apartment. There's nothing creepy about it.

JIM: Says you.

MARION: You want to close the door, please?

(JIM *reluctantly obeys.*)

MARION: Now, why don't you go check your room and make sure you didn't leave
    anything.
JIM: It's empty.
MARION: Go look.
JIM: I looked last time.
MARION (*Trying to be patient*): Honey, we sold the apartment. You're never going
    to be here again. Go make sure you have everything you want.
JIM: But Uncle Arthur packed everything.
MARION (*Less patiently*): Go make sure.
JIM: There's nothing in there.
MARION (*Exploding*): I said make sure!

(JIM *jumps, then realizing that she's not kidding, obeys.*)

MARION: Everything's an argument with that one. (*She looks around the room and
    breathes deeply. There is sadness here. Under her breath:*) I can still smell you. (*Sud-
    denly not wanting to be alone*) Jimmy? Are you okay?
JIM (*Returning*): Nothing. Told you so.
MARION: Uncle Arthur must have worked very hard. Make sure you thank him.
JIM: What for? Robbie says, (*Fey mannerisms*) "They love to clean up things!"
MARION: Sometimes you can be a real joy.
JIM: Did you call Aunt Helen?
MARION: Do I get a break here? (*Approaching the boy understandingly*) Wouldn't you
    like to say good-bye?
JIM: To who?
MARION: To the apartment. You and your daddy spent a lot of time here together.
    Don't you want to take one last look around?
JIM: Ma, get a real life.
MARION: "Get a real life." (*Going for the phone*) Nice. Very nice.
JIM: Could you call already?
MARION (*Dialing*): Jimmy, what does this look like I'm doing?

(JIM *kicks at the floor impatiently. Someone answers the hone at the other end.*)

MARION (*Into the phone*): Helen? Hi, we're upstairs. . . . No, we just walked in the
    door. Jimmy wants to know if he can come down. . . . Oh, thanks.

(*Hearing that,* JIM *breaks for the door.*)

MARION (*Yelling after him*): Don't run in the halls! And don't play with the elevator
    buttons!

(*The door slams shut behind him.*)

MARION (*Back to the phone*): Hi. . . . No, I'm okay. It's a little weird being here. . . .
    No. Not since the funeral, and then there were so many people. Jimmy told me to

get "a real life." I don't think I could handle anything realer. . . . No, please. Stay where you are. I'm fine. The doorman said Arthur would be right back and my lawyer should have been here already. . . . Well, we've got the papers to sign and a few other odds and ends to clean up. Shouldn't take long.

(*The intercom buzzer rings.*)

MARION: Hang on, that must be her.
    (MARION *goes to the intercom and speaks*) Yes? . . . Thank you.
    (*Back to the phone*) Helen? Yeah, it's the lawyer. I'd better go. . . . Well, I could use a stiff drink, but I drove down. Listen, I'll stop by on my way out. Okay? Okay. 'Bye.

(*She hangs up the phone, looks around the room. That uncomfortable feeling returns to her quickly. She gets up and goes to the front door; opens it and looks out. No one there yet. She closes the door, shakes her head knowing that she's being silly and starts back into the room. She looks around, can't make it and retreats to the door. She opens it, looks out, closes it, but stays right there, her hand on the doorknob.*
    The bell rings. She throws open the door.)

MARION: That was quick.

(JUNE LOWELL *still has her finger on the bell. Her arms are loaded with contracts.* MARION's *contemporary,* JUNE *is less formal in appearance and more hyper in her manner.*)

JUNE: *That* was quicker. What, were you waiting by the door?
MARION (*Embarrassed*): No. I was just passing it. Come on in.
JUNE: Have you got your notary seal?
MARION: I think so.
JUNE: Great. Then you can witness. I left mine at the office and thanks to gentrifi-
    cation I'm double-parked downstairs. (*Looking for a place to dump her load*)
    Where?
MARION (*Definitely pointing to the coffee table*): Anywhere. You mean you're not
    staying?
JUNE: If you really think you need me I can go down and find a parking lot. I think
    there's one over on Columbus. So, I can go down, park the car in the lot and take
    a cab back if you really think you need me.
MARION: Well . . . ?
JUNE: But you shouldn't have any problems. The papers are about as straightfor-
    ward as papers get. Arthur is giving you power of attorney to sell the apartment
    and you're giving him a check for half the purchase price. Everything else is just
    signing papers that state that you know that you signed the other papers. Any-
    way, he knows the deal, his lawyers have been over it all with him, it's just a mat-
    ter of signatures.
MARION (*Not fine*): Oh, fine.
JUNE: Unless you just don't want to be alone with him. . . . ?
MARION: With Arthur? Don't be silly.

JUNE (*Laying out the papers*): Then you'll handle it solo? Great. My car thanks you, the parking lot thanks you, and the cab driver that wouldn't have gotten a tip thanks you. Come have a quick look-see.

MARION (*Joining her on the couch*): There are a lot of papers here.

JUNE. Copies. Not to worry. Start here.

(MARION *starts to read.*)

JUNE: I ran into Jimmy playing Elevator Operator.

(MARION *jumps.*)

JUNE: I got him off at the sixth floor. Read on.

MARION: This is definitely not my day for dealing with him.

(JUNE *gets up and has a look around.*)

JUNE: I don't believe what's happening in this neighborhood. You made quite an investment when you bought this place.

MARION: Collin was always very good at figuring out those things.

JUNE: Well, he sure figured this place right. What, have you tripled your money in ten years?

MARION: More.

JUNE: It's a shame to let it go.

MARION: We're not ready to be a two-dwelling family.

JUNE: So, sublet it again.

MARION: Arthur needs the money from the sale.

JUNE: Arthur got plenty already. I'm not crying for Arthur.

MARION: I don't hear you starting in again, do I?

JUNE: Your interests and your wishes are my only concern.

MARION: Fine.

JUNE: I still say we should contest Collin's will.

MARION: June! . . .

JUNE: You've got a child to support.

MARION: And a great job, and a husband with a great job. Tell me what Arthur's got.

JUNE: To my thinking, half of everything that should have gone to you. And more. All of Collin's personal effects, his record collection. . . .

MARION: And I suppose their three years together meant nothing.

JUNE: When you compare them to your sixteen-year marriage? Not nothing, but not half of everything.

MARION (*Trying to change the subject*): June, who gets which copies?

JUNE: Two of each to Arthur. One you keep. The originals and anything else come back to me. (*Looking around*) I till say you should've sublet the apartment for a year and then sold it. You would've gotten an even better price. Who wants to buy an apartment when they know someone died in it. No one. And certainly no one wants to buy an apartment when they know the person died of AIDS.

MARION (*Snapping*): June. Enough!

JUNE (*Catching herself*): Sorry. That was out of line. Sometimes my mouth does that to me. Hey, that's why I'm a lawyer. If my brain worked as fast as my mouth I would have gotten a real job.

MARION (*Holding out a stray paper*): What's this?

JUNE: I forgot. Arthur's lawyer sent that over yesterday. He found it in Collin's safety-deposit box. It's an insurance policy that came along with some consulting job he did in Japan. He either forgot about it when he made out his will or else he wanted you to get the full payment. Either way, it's yours.

MARION: Are you sure we don't split this?

JUNE: Positive.

MARION: But everything else . . . ?

JUNE: Hey, Arthur found it, his lawyer sent it to me. Relax, it's all yours. Minus my commission, of course. Go out and buy yourself something. Anything else before I have to use my cut to pay the towing bill?

MARION: I guess not.

JUNE (*Starting to leave*): Great. Call me when you get home. (*Stopping at the door and looking back*) Look, I know that I'm attacking this a little coldly. I am aware that someone you loved has just died. But there's a time and place for everything. This is about tidying up loose ends, not holding hands. I hope you'll remember that when Arthur gets here. Call me.

(*And she's gone.*

MARION *looks ill at ease to be alone again. She nervously straightens the papers into neat little piles, looks at them and then remembers:*)

MARION: Pens. We're going to need pens.

(*At last a chore to be done. She looks in her purse and finds only one. She goes to the kitchen and opens a drawer where she finds two more. She starts back to the table with them but suddenly remembers something else. She returns to the kitchen and begins going through the cabinets until she finds what she's looking for: a blue Art Deco teapot. Excited to find it, she takes it back to the couch.*

Guilt strikes. She stops, considers putting it back, wavers, then:)

MARION (*To herself*): Oh, he won't care. One less thing to pack.

(*She takes the teapot and places it on the couch next to her purse. She is happier. Now she searches the room with her eyes for any other treasures she may have overlooked. Nothing here. She wanders off into the bedroom.*

We hear keys outside the front. ARTHUR *lets himself into the apartment carrying a load of empty cartons and a large shopping bag.*

ARTHUR *is in his mid-thirties, pleasant looking though sloppily dressed in work clothes and slightly overweight.*

ARTHUR *enters the apartment just as* MARION *comes out of the bedroom carrying a framed watercolor painting. They jump at the sight of each other.*)

MARION: Oh, hi, Arthur. I didn't hear the door.

ARTHUR (*Staring at the painting*): Well hello, Marion.

MARION (*Guiltily*): I was going to ask you if you were thinking of taking this painting because if you're not going to then I'll take it. Unless, of course, you want it.

ARTHUR: No. You can have it.

MARION: I never really liked it, actually. I hate cats. I didn't even like the show. I
needed something for my college dorm room. I was never the rock star poster
type. I kept it in the back of a closet for years until Collin moved in here and took
it. He said he liked it.

ARTHUR: I do too.

MARION: Well, then you keep it.

ARTHUR: No. Take it.

MARION: We've really got no room for it. You keep it.

ARTHUR: I don't want it.

MARION: Well, if you're sure.

ARTHUR (*Seeing the teapot*): You want the teapot?

MARION: If you don't mind.

ARTHUR: One less thing to pack.

MARION: Funny, but that's exactly what I thought. One less thing to pack. You
know, my mother gave it to Collin and me when we moved in to our first apartment. Silly sentimental piece of junk, but you know.

ARTHUR: That's not the one.

MARION: Sure it is. Hall used to make them for Westinghouse back in the thirties.
I see them all the time at antiques shows and I always wanted to buy another, but
they ask such a fortune for them.

ARTHUR: We broke the one your mother gave you a couple of years ago. That's a
reproduction. You can get them almost anywhere in the Village for eighteen
bucks.

MARION: Really? I'll have to pick one up.

ARTHUR: Take this one. I'll get another.

MARION: No, it's yours. You bought it.

ARTHUR: One less thing to pack.

MARION: Don't be silly. I didn't come here to raid the place.

ARTHUR: Well, was there anything else of Collin's that you thought you might like
to have?

MARION: Now I feel so stupid, but actually I made a list. Not for me. But I started
thinking about different people; friends, relatives, you know, that might want to
have something of Collin's to remember him by. I wasn't sure just what you were
taking and what you were throwing out. Anyway, I brought the list. (*Gets it from
her purse*) Of course these are only suggestions. You probably thought of a few of
these people yourself. But I figured it couldn't hurt to write it all down. Like I
said, I don't know what you are planning on keeping.

ARTHUR (*Taking the list*): I was planning on keeping it all.

MARION: Oh, I know. But most of these things are silly. Like his high school year-
books. What would you want with them?

ARTHUR: Sure. I'm only interested in his Gay period.

MARION: I didn't mean it that way. Anyway, you look it over. They're only suggestions. Whatever you decide to do is fine with me.

ARTHUR (*Folding the list*): It would have to be, wouldn't it. I mean, it's all mine
now. He did leave this all to me.

(MARION *is becoming increasingly nervous, but tries to keep a light approach as she takes a
small bundle of papers from her bag.*)

MARION: While we're on the subject of what's yours. I brought a batch of condolence cards that were sent to you care of me. Relatives mostly.

ARTHUR (*Taking them*): More cards? I'm going to have to have another printing of
thank-you notes done.

MARION: I answered these last week, so you don't have to bother. Unless you want to.

ARTHUR: Forge my signature?

MARION: Of course not. They were addressed to both of us and they're mostly distant relatives or friends we haven't seen in years. No one important.

ARTHUR: If they've got my name on them, then I'll answer them myself.

MARION: I wasn't telling you not to, I was only saying that you don't have to.

ARTHUR: I understand.

(MARION *picks up the teapot and brings it to the kitchen.*)

MARION: Let me put this back.

ARTHUR: I ran into Jimmy in the lobby.

MARION: Tell me you're joking.

ARTHUR: I got him to Helen's.

MARION: He's really racking up the points today.

ARTHUR: You know, he still can't look me in the face.

MARION: He's reacting to all of this in strange ways. Give him time. He'll come
around. He's really very fond of you.

ARTHUR: I know. But he's at that awkward age: under thirty. I'm sure in twenty
years we'll be the best of friends.

MARION: It's not what you think.

ARTHUR: What do you mean?

MARION: Well, you know.

ARTHUR: No I don't know. Tell me.

MARION: I thought that you were intimating something about his blaming you for
Collin's illness and I was just letting you know that it's not true. (*Foot in mouth,
she braves on.*) We discussed it a lot and . . . uh . . . he understands that his father
was sick before you two ever met.

ARTHUR: I don't believe this.

MARION: I'm just trying to say that he doesn't blame you.

ARTHUR: First of all, who asked you? Second of all, that's between him and me.
And third and most importantly, of course he blames me. Marion, he's eleven

years old. You can discuss all you want, but the fact is that his father died of a "fag" disease and I'm the only fag around to finger.

MARION: My son doesn't use that kind of language.

ARTHUR: Forget the language. I'm talking about what he's been through. Can you imagine the kind of crap he's taken from his friends? That poor kid's been chased and chastised from one end of town to the other. He's got to have someone to blame just to survive. He can't blame you, you're all he's got. He can't blame his father; he's dead. So, Uncle Arthur gets the shaft. Fine, I can handle it.

MARION: You are so wrong, Arthur. I know my son and that is not the way his mind works.

ARTHUR: I don't know what you know. I only know what I know. And all I know is what I hear and see. The snide remarks, the little smirks . . . And it's not just the illness. He's been looking for a scapegoat since the day you and Collin first split up. Finally he has one.

MARION (*Getting very angry now*): Wait. Are you saying that if he's going to blame someone it should be me?

ARTHUR: I think you should try to see things from his point of view.

MARION: Where do you get off thinking you're privy to my son's point of view?

ARTHUR: It's not that hard to imagine. Life's rolling right along, he's having a happy little childhood, when suddenly one day his father's moving out. No explanations, no reasons, none of the fights that usually accompany such things. Divorce is hard enough for a kid to understand when he's listened to years of battles, but yours?

MARION: So what should we have done? Faked a few months' worth of fights before Collin moved out?

ARTHUR: You could have told him the truth, plain and simple.

MARION: He was seven years old at the time. How the hell do you tell a seven-year-old that his father is leaving his mother to go sleep with other men?

ARTHUR: Well, not like that.

MARION: You know, Arthur, I'm going to say this as nicely as I can: Butt out. You're not his mother and you're not his father.

ARTHUR: Thank you. I wasn't acutely aware of that fact. I will certainly keep that in mind from now on.

MARION: There's only so much information a child that age can handle.

ARTHUR: So it's best that he reach his capacity on the street.

MARION: He knew about the two of you. We talked about it.

ARTHUR: Believe me, he knew before you talked about it. He's young, not stupid.

MARION: It's very easy for you to stand here and criticize, but there are aspects that you will just never be able to understand. You weren't there. You have no idea what it was like for me. You're talking to someone who thought that a girl went to college to meet a husband. I went to protest rallies because I liked the music. I bought a guitar because I thought it looked good on the bed! This lifestyle, this knowledge that you take for granted, was all a little out of left field for me.

ARTHUR: I can imagine.

MARION: No. I don't think you can. I met Collin in college, married him right after graduation and settled down for a nice quiet life of Kids and Careers. You think I had any idea about this? Talk about life's little surprises. You live with someone for sixteen years, you share your life, your bed, and have a child together, and then you wake up one day and he tells you that to him it's all been a lie. A lie. Try that on for size. Here you are the happiest couple you know, fulfilling your every life fantasy and he tells you he's living a lie.

ARTHUR: I'm sure he never said that.

MARION: Don't be so sure. There was a lot of new ground being broken back then and plenty of it was muddy.

ARTHUR: You know that he loved you.

MARION: What's that supposed to do, make things easier? It doesn't. I was brought up to believe, among other things, that if you had love that was enough. So what if I wasn't everything he wanted. Maybe he wasn't exactly everything I wanted either. So, you know what? You count your blessings and you settle.

ARTHUR: No one has to settle. Not him. Not you.

MARION: Of course not. You can say, "Up yours!" to everything and everyone who depends on and needs you, and go off to make yourself happy.

ARTHUR: It's not that simple.

MARION: No. This is simpler. Death is simpler. (*Yelling out*) Happy now?

(*They stare at each other.* MARION *calms the rage and catches her breath.* ARTHUR *holds his emotions in check.*)

ARTHUR: How about a nice hot cup of coffee? Tea with lemon? Hot cocoa with a marshmallow floating in it?

MARION (*Laughs*): I was wrong. You *are* a mother.

(ARTHUR *goes into the kitchen and starts preparing things.* MARION *loafs by the doorway.*)

MARION: I lied before. He *was* everything I ever wanted.

(ARTHUR *stops, looks at her, and then changes the subject as he goes on with his work.*)

ARTHUR: When I came into the building and saw Jimmy in the lobby I absolutely freaked for a second. It's amazing how much they look alike. It was like seeing a little miniature Collin standing there.

MARION: I know. He's like Collin's clone. There's nothing of me in him.

ARTHUR: I always kinda hoped that when he grew up he'd take after me. Not much chance, I guess.

MARION: Don't do anything fancy in there.

ARTHUR: Please. Anything we can consume is one less thing to pack.

MARION: So you've said.

ARTHUR: So *we've* said.

MARION: I want to keep seeing you and I want you to see Jim. You're still part of this family. No one's looking to cut you out.

ARTHUR: Ah, who'd want a kid to grow up looking like me anyway. I had enough trouble looking like this. Why pass on the misery?

MARION: You're adorable.

ARTHUR: Is that like saying I have a good personality?

MARION: I think you are one of the most naturally handsome men I know.

ARTHUR: Natural is right, and the bloom is fading.

MARION: All you need is a few good nights' sleep to kill those rings under your eyes.

ARTHUR: Forget the rings under my eyes, (*Grabbing his middle*) . . . how about the rings around my moon?

MARION: I like you like this.

ARTHUR: From the time that Collin started using the wheelchair until he died, about six months, I lost twenty-three pounds. No gym, no diet. In the last seven weeks I've gained close to fifty.

MARION: You're exaggerating.

ARTHUR: I'd prove it on the bathroom scale, but I sold it in working order.

MARION: You'd never know.

ARTHUR: Marion, *you'd* never know, but ask my belt. Ask my pants. Ask my underwear. Even my stretch socks have stretch marks. I called the ambulance at five A.M., he was gone at nine and by nine-thirty, I was on a first-name basis with Sara Lee. I can quote the business hours of every ice-cream parlor, pizzeria and bakery on the island of Manhattan. I know the location of every twenty-four-hour grocery in the greater New York area, and I have memorized the phone numbers of every Mandarin, Szechuan and Hunan restaurant with free delivery.

MARION: At least you haven't wasted your time on useless hobbies.

ARTHUR: Are you kidding? I'm opening my own Overeater's Hotline. We'll have to start small, but expansion is guaranteed.

MARION: You're the best, you know that? If I couldn't be everything that Collin wanted then I'm grateful that he found someone like you.

ARTHUR (*Turning on her without missing a beat*): Keep your goddamned gratitude to yourself. I didn't go through any of this for you. So your thanks are out of line. And he didn't find "someone like" me. It was me.

MARION (*Frightened*): I didn't mean. . . .

ARTHUR: And I wish you'd remember one thing more: He died in my arms, not yours.

(MARION *is totally caught off guard. She stares disbelieving, openmouthed.* ARTHUR *walks past her as he leaves the kitchen with place mats. He puts them on the coffee table. As he arranges the papers and place mats he speaks, never looking at her.*)

ARTHUR: Look, I know you were trying to say something supportive. Don't waste your breath. There's nothing you can say that will make any of this easier for me.

There's no way for you to help me get through this. And that's your fault. After three years you still have no idea or understanding of who I am. Or maybe you do know but refuse to accept it. I don't know and I don't care. But at least understand, from my point of view, who you are: You are my husband's *ex*-wife. If you like, the mother of *my* stepson. Don't flatter yourself into thinking you're any more than that. And whatever you are, you're certainly not my friend.

(*He stops, looks up at her; then passes her again as he goes back to the kitchen.* MARION *is shaken, working hard to control herself. She moves toward the couch.*)

MARION: Why don't we just sign these papers and I'll be out of your way.

ARTHUR: Shouldn't you say *I'll* be out of *your* way? After all, I'm not just signing papers. I'm signing away my home.

MARION (*Resolved not to fight, she gets her purse*): I'll leave the papers here. Please have them notarized and returned to my lawyer.

ARTHUR: Don't forget my painting.

MARION (*Exploding*): What do you want from me, Arthur?

ARTHUR (*Yelling back*): I want you the hell out of my apartment! I want you out of my life! And I want you to leave Collin alone!

MARION: The man's dead. I don't know how much more alone I can leave him.

(ARTHUR *laughs at the irony, but behind the laughter is something much more desperate.*)

ARTHUR: Lots more, Marion. You've got to let him go.

MARION: For the life of me, I don't know what I did, or what you think I did, for you to treat me like this. But you're not going to get away with it. You will not take your anger out on me. I will not stand here and be badgered and insulted by you. I know you've been hurt and I know you're hurting but you're not the only one who lost someone here.

ARTHUR (*Topping her*): Yes I am! You didn't just lose him. I did! You lost him five years ago when he divorced you. This is not your moment of grief and loss, it's mine! (*Picking up the bundle of cards and throwing it toward her*) These condolences do not belong to you, they're mine. (*Tossing her list back to her*) His things are not yours to give away, they're mine! This death does not belong to you, it's mine! Bought and paid for outright. I suffered for it, I bled for it. I was the one who cooked his meals. I was the one who spoon-fed them. I pushed his wheelchair. I carried and bathed him. I wiped his backside and changed his diapers. I breathed life into and wrestled fear out of his heart. I kept him alive for two years longer than any doctor thought possible and when it was time I was the one who prepared him for death.

I paid in full for my place in his life and I will *not* share it with you. We are not the two widows of Collin Redding. Your life was not here. Your husband didn't just die. You've got a son and a life somewhere else. Your husband's sitting, waiting for you at home, wondering, as I am, what the hell you're doing here and why you can't let go.

(MARION *leans back against the couch. She's blown away.* ARTHUR *stands staring at her.*)

ARTHUR (*Quietly*): Let him go, Marion. He's mine. Dead or alive; mine.

(*The teakettle whistles.* ARTHUR *leaves the room, goes to the kitchen and pours the water as* MARION *pulls herself together.*

ARTHUR *carries the loaded tray back into the living room and sets it down on the coffee table. He sits and pours a cup.*)

ARTHUR: One marshmallow or two?

(MARION *stares, unsure as to whether the attack is really over or not.*)

ARTHUR: (*Placing them in her cup*). Take three, they're small.

(MARION *smiles and takes the offered cup.*)

ARTHUR: (*Campily*). Now let me tell you how I *really* feel.

(MARION *jumps slightly, then they share a small laugh. Silence as they each gather themselves and sip their refreshments.*)

MARION (*Calmly*): Do you think that I sold the apartment just to throw you out?
ARTHUR: I don't care about the apartment . . .
MARION: . . . Because I really didn't. Believe me.
ARTHUR: I know.
MARION: I knew the expenses here were too much for you, and I knew you couldn't afford to buy out my half . . . I figured if we sold it, that you'd at least have a nice chunk of money to start over with.
ARTHUR: You could've given me a little more time.
MARION: Maybe. But I thought the sooner you were out of here, the sooner you could go on with your life.
ARTHUR: Or the sooner you could go on with yours.
MARION: Maybe. (*Pauses to gather her thoughts*) Anyway, I'm not going to tell you that I have no idea what you're talking about. I'd have to be worse than deaf and blind not to have seen the way you've been treated. Or mistreated. When I read Collin's obituary in the newspaper and saw my name and Jimmy's name and no mention of you . . . (*Shakes her head, not knowing what to say*) You know that his secretary was the one who wrote that up and sent it in. Not me. But I should have done something about it and I didn't. I know.
ARTHUR: Wouldn't have made a difference. I wrote my own obituary for him and sent it to the smaller papers. They edited me out.
MARION: I'm sorry. I remember, at the funeral, I was surrounded by all of Collin's family and business associates while you were left with your friends. I knew it was wrong. I knew I should have said something but it felt good to have them around me and you looked like you were holding up . . . Wrong. But saying that it's all my fault for not letting go? . . . There were other people involved.
ARTHUR: Who took their cue from you.

MARION: Arthur, you don't understand. Most people that we knew as a couple had no idea that Collin was Gay right up to his death. And even those that did know only found out when he got sick and the word leaked out that it was AIDS. I don't think I have to tell you how stupid and ill-informed most people are about homosexuality. And AIDS . . . ? The kinds of insane behavior that word inspires? . . .

Those people at the funeral, how many times did they call to see how he was doing over these years? How many of them ever went to see him in the hospital? Did any of them even come here? So, why would you expect them to act any differently after his death?

So, maybe that helps to explain their behavior, but what about mine, right? Well, maybe there is no explanation. Only excuses. And excuse number one is that you're right, I have never really let go of him. And I am jealous of you. Hell, I was jealous of anyone that Collin ever talked to, let alone slept with . . . let alone loved.

The first year, after he moved out, we talked all the time about the different men he was seeing. And I always listened and advised. It was kind of fun. It kept us close. It kept me a part of his intimate life. And the bottom line was always that he wasn't happy with the men he was meeting. So, I was always allowed to hang on to the hope that one day he'd give it all up and come home. Then he got sick.

He called me, told me he was in the hospital and asked if I'd come see him. I ran. When I got to his door there was a sign, INSTRUCTIONS FOR VISITORS OF AN AIDS PATIENT. I nearly died.

ARTHUR: He hadn't told you?

MARION: No. And believe me, a sign is not the way to find these thing out. I was so angry . . . And he was so sick . . . I was sure that he'd die right then. If not from the illness then from the hospital staff's neglect. No one wanted to go near him and I didn't bother fighting with them because I understood that they were scared. I was scared. That whole month in the hospital I didn't let Jimmy visit him once.

You learn.

Well, as you know, he didn't die. And he asked if he could come stay with me until he was well. And I said yes. Of course, yes. Now, here's something I never thought I'd ever admit to anyone: had he asked to stay with me for a few weeks I would have said no. But he asked to stay with me until he was well and knowing there was no cure I said yes. In my craziness I said yes because to me that meant forever. That he was coming back to me forever. Not that I wanted him to die, but I assumed from everything I'd read . . . And we'd be back together for whatever time he had left. Can you understand that?

(ARTHUR *nods.*)

MARION (*Gathers her thoughts again*): Two weeks later he left. He moved in here. Into this apartment that we had bought as an investment. Never to live in. Certainly never to live apart in. Next thing I knew, the name Arthur starts appearing in every phone call, every dinner conversation.

"Did you see the doctor?"

"Yes. Arthur made sure I kept the appointment."

"Are you going to your folks for Thanksgiving?"

"No. Arthur and I are having some friends over."

I don't know which one of us was more of a coward, he for not telling or me for not asking about you. But eventually you became a given. Then, of course, we met and became what I had always thought of as friends.

(ARTHUR *winces in guilt.*)

MARION: I don't care what you say, how could we not be friends with something so great in common: love for one of the most special human beings there ever was. And don't try and tell me there weren't times when you enjoyed my being around as an ally. I can think of a dozen occasions when we ganged up on him, teasing him with our intimate knowledge of his personal habits.

(ARTHUR *has to laugh.*)

MARION: Blanket stealing? Snoring? Excess gas, no less? (*Takes a moment to enjoy this truce*) I don't think that my loving him threatened your relationship. Maybe I'm not being truthful with myself. But I don't. I never tried to step between you. Not that I ever had the opportunity. Talk about being joined at the hip! And that's not to say I wasn't jealous. I was. Terribly. Hatefully. But always lovingly. I was happy for Collin because there was no way to deny that he was happy. With everything he was facing, he was happy. Love did that. You did that.

He lit up with you. He came to life. I envied that and all the time you spent together, but more, I watched you care for him (sometimes *overcare* for him), and I was in awe. I could never have done what you did. I never would have survived. I really don't know how you did.

ARTHUR: Who said I survived?

MARION: Don't tease. You did an absolutely incredible thing. It's not as if you met him before he got sick. You entered a relationship that you knew in all probability would end this way and you never wavered.

ARTHUR: Of course I did. Don't have me sainted, Marion. But sometimes you have no choice. Believe me, if I could've gotten away from him I would've. But I was a prisoner of love.

(*He makes a campy gesture and pose.*)

MARION: Stop.

ARTHUR: And there were lots of pluses. I got to quit a job I hated, stay home all day and watch game shows. I met a lot of doctors and learned a lot of big words. (ARTHUR *jumps up and goes to the pile of boxes where he extracts one and brings it back to the couch.*) And then there was all the exciting traveling I got to do. This box has a souvenir from each one of our trips. Wanna see?

(MARION *nods. He opens the box and pulls things out one by one.*)

ARTHUR (*Continues*) (*Holding up an old bottle*): This from the house we rented in Reno when we went to clear out his lungs. (*Holding handmade potholders*) This is from the hospital in Reno. Collin made them. They had a great arts and crafts program. (*Copper bracelets*) These are from a faith healer in Philly. They don't do much for a fever, but they look great with a green sweater. (*Glass ashtrays*) These are from our first visit to the clinic in France. Such lovely people. (*A Bible*) This is from our second visit to the clinic in France. (*A bead necklace*) A Voodoo doctor in New Orleans. Next time we'll have to get there earlier in the year. I think he sold all the pretty ones at Mardi Gras. (*A tiny piñata*) Then there was Mexico. Black market drugs and empty wallets. (*Now pulling things out at random*) L.A., San Francisco, Houston, Boston . . . We traveled everywhere they offered hope for sale and came home with souvenirs. (ARTHUR *quietly pulls a few more things out and then begins to put them all back into the box slowly. Softly as he works:*)

Marion, I would have done anything, traveled anywhere to avoid . . . or delay . . . Not just because I loved him so desperately, but when you've lived the way we did for three years . . . the battle becomes your life. (*He looks at her and then away.*)

His last few hours were beyond any scenario I had imagined. He hadn't walked in nearly six months. He was totally incontinent. If he spoke two words in a week I was thankful. Days went by without his eyes ever focusing on me. He just stared out at I don't know what. Not the meals as I fed him. Not the TV I played constantly for company. Just out. Or maybe in.

It was the middle of the night when I heard his breathing become labored. His lungs were filling with fluid again. I knew the sound. I'd heard it a hundred times before. So, I called the ambulance and got him to the hospital. They hooked him up to the machines, the oxygen, shot him with morphine and told me that they would do what they could to keep him alive.

But, Marion, it wasn't the machines that kept him breathing. He did it himself. It was that incredible will and strength inside him. Whether it came from his love of life or fear of death, who knows. But he'd been counted out a hundred times and a hundred times he fought his way back.

I got a magazine to read him, pulled a chair up to the side of his bed and holding his hand, I wondered whether I should call Helen to let the cleaning lady in or if he'd fall asleep and I could sneak home for an hour. I looked up from the page and he was looking at me. Really looking right into my eyes. I patted his cheek and said, "Don't worry, honey, you're going to be fine."

But there was something else in his eyes. He wasn't satisfied with that. And I don't know why, I have no idea where it came from, I just heard the words coming out of my mouth, "Collin, do you want to die?" His eyes filled and closed, he nodded his head.

I can't tell you what I was thinking, I'm not sure I was. I slipped off my shoes, lifted his blanket and climbed into bed next to him. I helped him to put his arms around me, and mine around him, and whispered as gently as I could into his ear, "It's alright to let go now. It's time to go on." And he did.

   Marion, you've got your life and his son. All I have is an intangible place in a man's history. Leave me that. Respect that.

MARION: I understand.

(ARTHUR *suddenly comes to life, running to get the shopping bag that he'd left at the front door.*)

ARTHUR: Jeez! With all the screamin' and sad storytelling I forget something. (*He extracts a bouquet of flowers from the bag.*) I brung you flowers and everything.

MARION: You brought *me* flowers?

ARTHUR: Well, I knew you'd never think to bring me flowers and I felt that on an occasion such as this somebody oughta get flowers from somebody.

MARION: You know, Arthur, you're really making me feel like a worthless piece of garbage.

ARTHUR: So what else is new? (*He presents the flowers.*) Just promise me one thing: Don't press one in a book. Just stick them in a vase and when they fade just toss them out. No more memorabilia.

MARION: Arthur, I want to do something for you and I don't know what. Tell me what you want.

ARTHUR: I want little things. Not much. I want to be remembered. If you get a Christmas card from Collin's mother, make sure she sent me one too. If his friends call to see how you are, ask if they've called me. Have me to dinner so I can see Jimmy. Let me take him out now and then. Invite me to his wedding.

(*They both laugh.*)

MARION: You've got it.

ARTHUR (*Clearing the table*): Let me get all this cold cocoa out of the way. We still have the deed to do.

MARION (*Checking her watch*): And I've got to get Jimmy home in time for practice.

ARTHUR: Band practice?

MARION: Baseball. (*Picking her list off the floor*) About this list, you do what you want.

ARTHUR: Believe me, I will. But I promise to consider your suggestions. Just don't rush me. I'm not ready to give it all away. (ARTHUR *is off to the kitchen with his tray and the phone rings. He answers it in the kitchen.*) Hello? . . . Just a minute. (*Calling out*) It's your eager Little Leaguer.

(MARION *picks up the living room extension and* ARTHUR *hangs his up.*)

MARION (*Into the phone*): Hello, honey. . . . I'll be down in five minutes. No. You know what? You come up here and get me. . . . NO, I said you should come up here. . . . I said I want you to come up here. . . . Because I said so. . . . Thank you.

(*She hangs up the receiver.*)

ARTHUR (*Rushing to the papers*): Alright, where do we start on these?

MARION (*Getting out her seal*): I guess you should just start signing everything and I'll stamp along with you. Keep one of everything on the side for yourself.

ARTHUR: Now I feel so rushed. What am I signing?

MARION: You want to do this another time?

ARTHUR: No. Let's get it over with. I wouldn't survive another session like this.

(*He starts to sign and she starts her job.*)

MARION: I keep meaning to ask you; how are you?

ARTHUR (*At first puzzled and then*): Oh, you mean my health? Fine. No, I'm fine. I've been tested, and nothing. We were very careful. We took many precautions. Collin used to make jokes about how we should invest in rubber futures.

MARION: I'll bet.

ARTHUR (*Stops what he's doing*): It never occurred to me until now. How about you?

MARION: (*Not stopping*). Well, we never had sex after he got sick.

ARTHUR: But before?

MARION (*Stopping but not looking up*): I have the antibodies in my blood. No signs that it will ever develop into anything else. And it's been five years so my chances are pretty good that I'm just a carrier.

ARTHUR: I'm so sorry. Collin never told me.

MARION: He didn't know. In fact, other than my husband and the doctors, you're the only one I've told.

ARTHUR: You and your husband . . . ?

MARION: Have invested in rubber futures. There'd only be a problem if we wanted to have a child. Which we do. But we'll wait. Miracles happen every day.

ARTHUR: I don't know what to say.

MARION: Tell me you'll be there if I ever need you.

(ARTHUR *gets up, goes to her and puts his arms around her. They hold each other. He gently pushes her away to make a joke.*)

ARTHUR: Sure! Take something else that should have been mine.

MARION: Don't even joke about things like that.

(*The doorbell rings. They pull themselves together.*)

ARTHUR: You know we'll never get these done today.

MARION: So, tomorrow.

(ARTHUR *goes to open the door as* MARION *gathers her things. He opens the door and* JIMMY *is standing in the hall.*)

JIM: C'mon, Ma. I'm gonna be late.

ARTHUR: Would you like to come inside?

JIM: We've gotta go.

MARION: Jimmy, come on.

JIM: Ma!

(*She glares. He comes in.* ARTHUR *closes the door.*)

MARION (*Holding out the flowers*): Take these for Mommy.

JIM (*Taking them*): Can we go?

MARION (*Picking up the painting*): Say good-bye to your Uncle Arthur.

JIM: 'Bye, Arthur. Come on.

MARION: Give him a kiss.

ARTHUR: Marion, don't.

MARION: Give your uncle a kiss good-bye.

JIM: He's not my uncle.

MARION: No. He's a hell of a lot more than your uncle.

ARTHUR (*Offering his hand*): A handshake will do.

MARION: Tell Uncle Arthur what your daddy told you.

JIM: About what?

MARION: Stop playing dumb. You know.

ARTHUR: Don't embarrass him.

MARION: Jimmy, please.

JIM (*He regards his* MOTHER'*s softer tone and then speaks*): He said that after me and Mommy he loved you the most.

MARION (*Standing behind him*): Go on.

JIM: And that I should love you too. And make sure that you're not lonely or very sad.

ARTHUR: Thank you.

(ARTHUR *reaches down to the boy and they hug.* JIM *gives him a little peck on the cheek and then breaks away.*)

MARION (*Going to open the door*): Alright, kid, you done good. Now let's blow this joint before you muck it up.

(JIM *rushes out the door.* MARION *turns to* ARTHUR)

MARION: A child's kiss is magic. Why else would they be so stingy with them. I'll call you.

(ARTHUR *nods understanding.* MARION *pulls the door closed behind her.* ARTHUR *stands quietly as the lights fade to black.*)

THE END

NOTE: *If being performed on film, the final image should be of* ARTHUR *leaning his back against the closed door on the inside of the apartment and* MARION *leaning on the outside of the door. A moment of thought and then they both move on.*

CRITICAL THINKING QUESTIONS

1. a. Speaking for Arthur, define "family."
   b. Speaking for Marion, define "family."

2. What *connotative* meanings are associated with "tidy"? Explain the significance of the play's title. Does *On Tidy Endings* present a "happy ending"? Emotionally exhausted, have Arthur and Marion given into a temporary truce between eternal rivals or found the roots for nurturing family bonds? Use evidence from the play to justify your viewpoint.

WRITING TOPIC

What claim about the definition of family does *On Tidy Endings* imply? Write an essay that explains the play's claim about family and then, using evidence from other literature selections and your own experience and observations, defend, refute, and/or qualify the claim.

Peter D. Kramer

Divorce and Our National Values

How shall we resolve a marital crisis? Consider an example from the advice column of Ann Landers. An "Iowa Wife" wrote to ask what she should do about her husband's habit, after 30 years of marriage, of reading magazines at table when the couple dined out. Ann Landers advised the wife to engage her husband by studying subjects of interest to him.

Readers from around the country protested. A "14-Year-Old Girl in Pennsylvania" crystallized the objections: "You told the wife to read up on sports or business, whatever he was interested in, even though it might be boring to her. Doesn't that defeat the basic idea of being your own self?" Chastened, Ann Landers changed course, updated her stance: Reading at table is a hostile act, perhaps even grounds for divorce.

When it comes to marriage, Ann Landers seems a reasonable barometer of our values. In practical terms, reading the sports pages might work for some Iowa wife—but we do not believe that is how spouses ought to behave. Only the second response, consider divorce, expresses our overriding respect for autonomy, for the unique and separate self.

Look south now from Iowa and Pennsylvania to Louisiana, where a new law allows couples to opt for a "covenant marriage"—terminable only after a lengthy separation or because of adultery, abandonment, abuse or imprisonment. The law has been praised by many as an expedient against the epidemic of divorce and an incarnation of our "traditional values."

Whether the law will lower the divorce rate is an empirical question to be decided in the future, but it is not too soon to ask: Does covenant marriage express the values we live by?

History seems to say no. American literature's one great self-help book is "Walden," a paean to self-reliance and an homage to Henry David Thoreau's favorite preacher, Ralph Waldo Emerson, who declaimed: "Say to them, O father, O mother, O wife, O brother, O friend, I have lived with you after appearances hitherto. Henceforward, I am the truth's. . . . I must be myself. I cannot break my self any longer for you, or you."

The economic philosophy we proudly export, fundamentalist capitalism, says that society functions best when members act in a self-interested manner. The nation's founding document is a bill of divorcement. Autonomy is the characteristic American virtue.

As a psychiatrist, I see this value embedded in our psychotherapy, the craft that both shapes and expresses the prevailing common sense. In the early 1970's, Carl Rogers, known as the "Psychologist of America," encapsulated the post-World War II version of our ideals: A successful marriage is one that increases the "self-actualization" of each member. Of a failed union, he wrote: "If Jennifer had from the first insisted on being her true self, the marriage would have had much more strife and much more hope."

Rogers was expressing the predominant viewpoint; for most of the past 50 years, enhanced autonomy has been a goal of psychotherapy. Erik Erikson began the trend by boldly proclaiming that the search for identity had become as important in his time as the study of sexuality was in Freud's. Later, Murray Bowen, a founder of family therapy, invoked a scale of maturity whose measure is a person's ability to maintain his or her beliefs in the face of family pressures. The useful response to crises within couples, Bowen suggested, is to hold fast to your values and challenge your partner to rise to meet your level of maturity.

But autonomy was a value for men only, and largely it was pseudoautonomy, the successful man propped up by the indentured wife and overburdened mother. (No doubt Thoreau sent his clothes home for laundering.)

The self-help movement, beginning in the 1970's, extended this American ideal to women. Once both partners are allowed to be autonomous, the continuation of marriage becomes more truly voluntary. In this sense, an increase in divorce signals social progress.

It signals social progress, except that divorce is itself destructive. So it seems to me the question is whether any other compelling value counterbalances the siren song of self-improvement.

Turning again to psychotherapy, we do hear arguments for a different type of American value. Answering Erikson's call for individual identity, Helen Merrell Lynd, a sociologist at Sarah Lawrence College, wrote, "Nor must complete finding of one-self . . . precede finding oneself in and through other persons."

Her belief entered psychiatry through the writings of her pupil, Jean Baker Miller. A professor of psychiatry at Boston University, Dr. Miller faults most psychotherapy for elevating autonomy at the expense of qualities important to women, such as mutuality. To feel connected (when there is genuine give-and-take) is to feel worth. Miller wants a transformed culture in which mutuality "is valued as highly as, or more highly than, self-enhancement."

Mutuality is an ideal the culture believes it should honor but does not quite. Ours is a society that does a half-hearted job of inculcating compromise, which is to say that we still teach these skills mainly to women. Much of psychotherapy addresses the troubles of those who make great efforts at compromise only to be taken advantage of by selfish partners.

Often the more vulnerable spouse requires rescue through the sort of move Ann Landers recommends, vigorous self-assertion, and even divorce.

Mutuality is a worthy ideal, one that might serve as a fit complement and counterbalance to our celebration of the self. But if we do not reward it elsewhere—if in the school and office and marketplace, we celebrate self-assertion—it seems worrisome to ask the institution of marriage to play by different rules.

What is insidious about Louisiana's covenant marriage is that, contrary to claims on its behalf, it is out of touch with our traditional values: self-expression, self-fulfillment, self-reliance.

The Louisiana law invites couples to lash themselves to a morality the broader culture does not support, an arrangement that creates a potential for terrible tensions.

Though we profess abhorrence of divorce, I suspect that the divorce rate reflects our national values with great exactness, and that conventional modern marriage—an eternal commitment with loopholes galore—expresses precisely the degree of loss of autonomy that we are able to tolerate.

WRITING TOPICS

1. Kramer suggests that, on the one hand, we Americans celebrate the individual, autonomy, and self-fulfillment, and, on the other hand, we honor marriage as the centerpiece of social stability. Must these values be competitive and destructive, or can they be complementary and empowering? Why?

2. Read Updike's "Separating" in the context of Kramer's discussion of values and the marital crisis. How does Richard's and Joan's impending separation provide evidence for Kramer's claim?

Pauli Murray

The Inheritance of Values

There was pride on both sides of the Fitzgerald family, but my greatest inheritance, perhaps, was a dogged persistence, a granite quality of endurance in the face of calamity. There was pride in family background, of course, but my folks took greater pride in doing any kind of honest work to earn a living and remain independent. Some people thought this trait was peculiarly Grandfather's, that Grandmother was flighty and contentious. They did not know the inside story: how she had struggled to keep her home together and bring up six children with her husband going blind and losing ground most of the way. Her tenacity, like that of Grandfather, sprang partly from her deep religious faith and partly from a mulishness which refused to countenance despair.

"There's more ways to kill a dog beside choking him on butter," she used to say.

She was remembering those uncertain years when the children were growing up and Grandfather was fighting for his pension while trying to build a home. He had bought an acre of ground in Durham, planned his house on the edge of his line and used the rest of the land to dig clay for his brickyard. He made bricks by hand, the hard kind used for outer walls and guaranteed to withstand all kinds of weather. It was a slow and costly process full of setbacks and failures. His hired men were often careless and took advantage of his blindness. They'd fire the kilns with raw green wood or go to sleep on the job in the middle of a burning and let the fires go out. Grandfather's bricks would come out crumbling and useless and he'd have to start all over again.

Then there were his lonely pilgrimages from place to place, guided only by his cane and a kind passerby, in search of old army comrades to help reconstruct his war record twenty years after his discharge. His search frequently ended in disappointment and he'd come home discouraged to make bricks for a while before starting out again. It took him almost ten years to prove his eligibility for pension payments.

During those years Grandmother was trying to educate their children. Fortunately, she came into a small inheritance when Mary Ruffin Smith died around 1885. Miss Mary had not forgotten the four Smith daughters. She left each of them one hundred acres of land with provision that a house be built upon it not to cost more than $150. To ensure that the land remained free from their husbands' debts or control, she gave them only a life interest in it and provided that it should pass to their children when they died. She also left her household goods and furnishings to be divided equally among the four.

Grandmother's hundred acres came out of the old Smith plantation near Chapel Hill. She was never entirely satisfied with this bequest; she felt Miss Mary had robbed her of the full inheritance her father had intended for her, and the restrictions of "heir property" which she did not own outright rankled. It served, however, as vindication of her own claims and was Miss Mary's backhanded recognition of their relationship. Aside from a twenty-five-acre gift to their half-brother, Julius, who was not of Smith blood, and a few small cash bequests, the four Smith daughters and their children were the only individuals remembered in Mary Ruffin Smith's will.

Whatever Grandmother's dissatisfactions, which increased as years passed, she made the most of her farm. She lived there with the children and worked the land while Grandfather was building his house in Durham. From time to time she sold off timber to help him in his brick business. She used whatever cash she could raise from her crops and fruit to send the children off to school. When she had no crops or fruit, she'd sell the chickens, the hogs or whatever else she could lay her hands on.

Aunt Sallie would never forget the time Grandmother sent Aunt Maria to Hampton Institute to take up the tailoring trade. When time came for tuition, Grandmother had no money so she decided to sell her cow. Grandfather was away from home working on his pension, Aunt Pauline was off teaching and Uncle Tommie was away at school. Grandmother had no one to send to market except Sallie and Agnes, who were about twelve and eleven years old at the time, but she was not dismayed.

"Children," she told them, "I want you to drive this cow down to Durham and take her to Schwartz' market. Tell Mr. Schwartz that Cornelia Smith sent her and that she's a fine milk cow. I want a good price on her and I'm depending on you to get it."

It was a huge undertaking for two little girls—Durham was fifteen miles away and the cow was none too manageable—but it would never have occurred to them that they could not deliver the cow. They started out early in the morning on a trip which took all day. The cow strayed off the road from time to time to graze in the meadows or lie down to rest and they had to pull and tug at her to get her started again. They arrived at the market in Durham near nightfall, somewhat frightened, their clothes torn and spattered with mud. When Mr. Schwartz heard all the commotion outside and came to find two bedraggled little girls standing guard over a huge cow, he listened to their story in disbelief.

"You don't mean to tell me you drove that cow all the way from Chapel Hill?" he asked.

"Yes sir, we did."

"Well, I never. And you say you're Robert Fitzgerald's daughters?"

"Yes sir, we are."

"How do I know you didn't steal that cow?"

The little girls stood their ground.

"If you doubt our word, you send for our Uncle Richard Fitzgerald."

Mr. Schwartz finally sent for Uncle Richard, who came, took one look at them and laughed.

"They're my brother's children all right, and if they say their mother sent the cow to market, you can take their word for it," he told Mr. Schwartz. So the butcher bought the cow on the spot and Aunt Maria stayed in school another few months.

It was also part of Grandfather's creed not to coddle his daughters. He expected them to make their way in life as he had done. I found a letter he had written to Aunt Maria on September 25, 1895. She had finished her work at Hampton and gone to Philadelphia to find employment as a dressmaker, without success. She wrote to Grandfather for money to come home. He replied.

> You must not depend upon sewing. I'd go into service. You can get $12 to $15 per month and stick to work for two months without taking up your money, and you can come home independent. . . . I find many a fine mechanic tramping through the state because he cannot work at his trade. Too many people make this great mistake. You must do as I did when I first went to Philadelphia, then a boy 16. I couldn't get the kind of employment I sought so I took whatever I could get to do and stuck at it until I had accumulated enough to carry me where I wanted to go with money in my pocket. Now you are young and as able as you ever will be. You can live anywhere on the face of the earth as other people can. Take my advice, getting your board and lodging and $15 per month and you will soon be able to come home.

Thrift was another household god in Grandfather's home. It was not only a strong ingredient of his own children's training but it was expected of all prospective sons-in-law. When young Leon B. Jeffers wrote my grandparents for consent to marry Aunt Maria in 1901, they replied in the affirmative, saying, "From earliest acquaintance with you, you have been held in highest esteem by us. Although you may not have money and riches to bestow upon her now, if you have that pure and undefiled love to present to her, with thrift and good management you can soon accumulate some property."

Only three of my grandparents' children were still living when I was coming along—Aunt Pauline, Aunt Maria (who preferred to be called Marie) and Aunt Sallie—all schoolteachers and all having a hand in my upbringing. Their brother, Uncle Tommie, had left home before he was twenty and was never heard from again. Some thought he was lost at sea and others that he died of smallpox during the Spanish-American War. The youngest sister, Roberta, succumbed to typhoid fever when she was barely nineteen. My own mother, Agnes, who had departed from the teaching tradition to become a registered nurse, died suddenly when I was three, leaving six children and my father, who was ill. I saw him only once after that before he died.

Having no parents of my own, I had in effect three mothers, each trying to impress upon me those traits of character expected of a Fitzgerald—stern devotion to duty, capacity for hard work, industry and thrift, and above all honor and courage in all things. Grandfather, of course, was their standard bearer for most of the virtues, but sometimes they talked of my own mother, who was a woman of beauty and courage and whose spirit became a guiding force in my own life although I was too young to remember her.

What happened on my mother's wedding night seemed typical of her courage. Her wedding to William H. Murray, a brilliant young schoolteacher from Baltimore, was scheduled for nine o'clock on the evening of July 1, 1903, at Emanuel A.M.E. Church on Chapel Hill Road in Durham, after which the reception was to be held at Grandfather's house. Engraved invitations were sent out to numerous relatives and friends and the five Fitzgerald daughters were as excited as if all of them were brides. Will Murray was the most popular of their brothers-in-law. He had come down from Baltimore in grand style, flanked by a troupe of young men to attend him.

Preparations were in full swing; everybody was scurrying about all day long. There had never been such a big wedding in the Fitzgerald household. Aunt Marie Jeffers, who was expecting a child, was putting the finishing touches on my mother's wedding gown. As family modiste, she wouldn't think of letting Aggie get married until her skillful fingers had supervised each tuck and fold.

It had been a stiflingly hot day and toward evening a thunderstorm threatened. The bride was almost ready and Aunt Marie stepped back to survey her handiwork when her face went deadly pale, she screamed and fell upon her knees in her first sharp labor pains. The wedding preparations were thrown into bedlam; everything came to a standstill. People gathered at the church and the groom was waiting impatiently, but there was no bride.

At Grandfather's house Aunt Marie's screams could be heard all over the neighborhood. To add to the confusion the thunderstorm struck with terrifying intensity. It was the worst of all times for a child to be born in the Fitzgerald home, but if my mother was frightened she gave no sign. She slipped quietly out of her wedding clothes, put on her uniform and took her place beside the doctor who came to attend Aunt Marie. She was all nurse, coolheaded and composed. Childbirth was hazardous in those days and for a while it looked as if Aunt Marie would not make it. At the height of the storm, between sharp flashes of lightning and rolls of thunder which shook the house, the baby came. My mother's trained eye saw that the doctor's forceps were askew in the emergency and she quickly readjusted them, saving the baby's life. Even so, his head and neck were severely bruised and cut in the delivery and nobody expected him to live. He was thrown aside while doctor and nurse worked frantically to save the mother's life.

Somebody suggested that Agnes call off her wedding, but she shook her head and stuck to her post. When it finally appeared that Aunt Marie would survive the crisis, my mother turned to the neglected infant, bathed and bandaged him, treated his wounds, hovered over him, smacked him and almost breathed life into him. She did not turn him loose until he let out a lusty cry and she felt that he would live. She then calmly washed her hands, put on her wedding dress once more and went out into a downpour to meet her groom. Everything went off as planned, except that it was several hours later and very much subdued. The reception was switched to Uncle Richard's house and the bride received her guests as graciously as if nothing untoward had happened. The baby, Gerald, celebrated his fifty-second birthday not long ago and Aunt Marie reached eighty-one before she died.

It was through these homespun stories, each with its own moral, that my elders sought to build their family traditions. In later years I realized how very much their wealth had consisted of intangibles. They had little of the world's goods and less of its recognition but they had forged enduring values for themselves which they tried to pass on to me. I would have need of these resources when I left the rugged security of Grandfather's house and found myself in a maze of terrifying forces which I could neither understand nor cope with. While my folks could not shield me from the impact of these forces, through their own courage and strength they could teach me to withstand them. My first experience with this outer world came the summer I was nearly seven.

CRITICAL THINKING QUESTIONS

1. What is Murray's *claim* about the definition of wealth?
2. What *evidence* does she offer in support?
3. What is your viewpoint about Murray's definition?

Scott Russell Sanders

The Men We Carry in Our Minds

This must be a hard time for women," I say to my friend Anneke. "They have so many paths to choose from, and so many voices calling them."

"I think it's a lot harder for men," she replies.

"How do you figure that?"

"The women I know feel excited, innocent, like crusaders in a just cause. The men I know are eaten up with guilt."

We are sitting at the kitchen table drinking sassafras tea, our hands wrapped around the mugs because this April morning is cool and drizzly. "Like a Dutch morning," Anneke told me earlier. She is Dutch herself, a writer and midwife and peacemaker, with the round face and sad eyes of a woman in a Vermeer painting who might be waiting for the rain to stop, for a door to open. She leans over to sniff a sprig of lilac, pale lavender, that rises from a vase of cobalt blue.

"Women feel such pressure to be everything, do everything," I say. "Career, kids, art, politics. Have their babies and get back to the office a week later. It's as if they're trying to overcome a million years' worth of evolution in one lifetime."

"But we help one another. We don't try to lumber on alone, like so many wounded grizzly bears, the way men do." Anneke sips her tea. I gave her the mug with owls on it, for wisdom. "And we have this deep-down sense that we're in the *right*—we've been held back, passed over, used—while men feel they're in the wrong. Men are the ones who've been discredited, who have to search their souls."

I search my soul. I discover guilty feelings aplenty—toward the poor, the Vietnamese, Native Americans, the whales, an endless list of debts—a guilt in each case that is as bright and unambiguous as a neon sign. But toward women I feel something more confused, a snarl of shame, envy, wary tenderness, and amazement. This muddle troubles me. To hide my unease I say, "You're right, it's tough being a man these days."

"Don't laugh." Anneke frowns at me, mournful-eyed, through the sassafras steam. "I wouldn't be a man for anything. It's much easier being the victim. All the victim has to do is break free. The persecutor has to live with his past."

How deep is that past? I find myself wondering after Anneke has left. How much of an inheritance do I have to throw off? Is it just the beliefs I breathed in as a child? Do I have to scour memory back through father and grandfather? Through St. Paul? Beyond Stonehenge and into the twilit caves? I'm convinced the past we must contend with is deeper even than speech. When I think back on my childhood, on how I learned to see men and women, I have a sense of ancient, dizzying depths. The back roads of Tennessee and Ohio where I grew up were probably

489

closer, in their sexual patterns, to the campsites of Stone Age hunters than to the genderless cities of the future into which we are rushing.

The first men, besides my father, I remember seeing were black convicts and white guards, in the cottonfield across the road from our farm on the outskirts of Memphis. I must have been three or four. The prisoners wore dingy gray-and-black zebra suits, heavy as canvas, sodden with sweat. Hatless, stooped, they chopped weeds in the fierce heat, row after row, breathing the acrid dust of boll-weevil poison. The overseers wore dazzling white shirts and broad shadowy hats. The oiled barrels of their shotguns flashed in the sunlight. Their faces in memory are utterly blank. Of course those men, white and black, have become for me an emblem of racial hatred. But they have also come to stand for the twin poles of my early vision of manhood—the brute toiling animal and the boss.

When I was a boy, the men I knew labored with their bodies. They were marginal farmers, just scraping by, or welders, steelworkers, carpenters; they swept floors, dug ditches, mined coal, or drove trucks, their forearms ropy with muscle; they trained horses, stoked furnaces, built tires, stood on assembly lines wrestling parts onto cars and refrigerators. They got up before light, worked all day long whatever the weather, and when they came home at night they looked as though somebody had been whipping them. In the evenings and on weekends they worked on their own places, tilling gardens that were lumpy with clay, fixing broken-down cars, hammering on houses that were always too drafty, too leaky, too small.

The bodies of the men I knew were twisted and maimed in ways visible and invisible. The nails of their hands were black and split, the hands tattooed with scars. Some had lost fingers. Heavy lifting had given many of them finicky backs and guts weak from hernias. Racing against conveyor belts had given them ulcers. Their ankles and knees ached from years of standing on concrete. Anyone who had worked for long around machines was hard of hearing. They squinted, and the skin of their faces was creased like the leather of old work gloves. There were times, studying them, when I dreaded growing up. Most of them coughed, from dust or cigarettes, and most of them drank cheap wine or whiskey, so their eyes looked bloodshot and bruised. The fathers of my friends always seemed older than the mothers. Men wore out sooner. Only women lived into old age.

As a boy I also knew another sort of men, who did not sweat and break down like mules. They were soldiers, and so far as I could tell they scarcely worked at all. During my early school years we lived on a military base, an arsenal in Ohio, and every day I saw GIs in the guardshacks, on the stoops of barracks, at the wheels of olive drab Chevrolets. The chief fact of their lives was boredom. Long after I left the Arsenal I came to recognize the sour smell the soldiers gave off as that of souls in limbo. They were all waiting—for wars, for transfers, for leaves, for promotions, for the end of their hitch—like so many braves waiting for the hunt to begin. Unlike the warriors of older tribes, however, they would have no say about when the battle would start or how it would be waged. Their waiting was broken only when they practiced for war. They fired guns at targets, drove tanks across the churned-up fields of the military reservation, set off bombs in the wrecks of old fighter planes. I knew this was all play. But I also felt certain that when the hour for killing arrived, they would kill. When the real shooting started, many of them would die. This was what soldiers were *for,* just as a hammer was for driving nails.

Warriors and toilers: those seemed, in my boyhood vision, to be the chief destinies for men. They weren't the only destinies, as I learned from having a few male teachers, from reading books, and from watching television. But the men on television—the politicians, the astronauts, the generals, the savvy lawyers, the philosophical doctors, the bosses who gave orders to both soldiers and laborers—seemed as remote and unreal to me as the figures in tapestries. I could no more imagine growing up to become one of these cool, potent creatures than I could imagine becoming a prince.

A nearer and more hopeful example was that of my father, who had escaped from a red-dirt farm to a tire factory, and from the assembly line to the front office. Eventually he dressed in a white shirt and tie. He carried himself as if he had been born to work with his mind. But his body, remembering the earlier years of slogging work, began to give out on him in his fifties, and it quit on him entirely before he turned sixty-five. Even such a partial escape from man's fate as he had accomplished did not seem possible for most of the boys I knew. They joined the Army, stood in line for jobs in the smoky plants, helped build highways. They were bound to work as their fathers had worked, killing themselves or preparing to kill others.

A scholarship enabled me not only to attend college, a rare enough feat in my circle, but even to study in a university meant for the children of the rich. Here I met for the first time young men who had assumed from birth that they would lead lives of comfort and power. And for the first time I met women who told me that men were guilty of having kept all the joys and privileges of the earth for themselves. I was baffled. What privileges? What joys? I thought about the maimed, dismal lives of most of the men back home. What had they stolen from their wives and daughters? The right to go five days a week, twelve months a year, for thirty or forty years to a steel mill or a coal mine? The right to drop bombs and die in war? The right to feel every leak in the roof, every gap in the fence, every cough in the engine, as a wound they must mend? The right to feel, when the lay-off comes or the plant shuts down, not only afraid but ashamed?

I was slow to understand the deep grievances of women. This was because, as a boy, I had envied them. Before college, the only people I had ever known who were interested in art or music or literature, the only ones who read books, the only ones who ever seemed to enjoy a sense of ease and grace were the mothers and daughters. Like the menfolk, they fretted about money, they scrimped and made-do. But, when the pay stopped coming in, they were not the ones who had failed. Nor did they have to go to war, and that seemed to me a blessed fact. By comparison with the narrow, ironclad days of fathers, there was an expansiveness, I thought, in the days of mothers. They went to see neighbors, to shop in town, to run errands at school, at the library, at church. No doubt, had I looked harder at their lives, I would have envied them less. It was not my fate to become a woman, so it was easier for me to see the graces. Few of them held jobs outside the home, and those who did filled thankless roles as clerks and waitresses. I didn't see, then, what a prison a house could be, since houses seemed to me brighter, handsomer places than any factory. I did not realize—because such things were never spoken of—how often women suffered from men's bullying. I did learn about the wretchedness of abandoned wives, single mothers, widows; but I also learned about the wretchedness of lone men. Even then I could see how exhausting it was for a mother to cater all day to the needs of young children. But if I had been asked, as a boy, to choose between tending a baby and tending a machine, I think I would have chosen the baby. (Having now tended both, I know I would choose the baby.)

So I was baffled when the women at college accused me and my sex of having cornered the world's pleasures. I think something like my bafflement has been felt by other boys (and by girls as well) who grew up in dirt-poor farm country, in mining country, in black ghettos, in Hispanic barrios, in the shadows of factories, in Third World nations—any place where the fate of men is as grim and bleak as the fate of women. Toilers and warriors. I realize now how ancient these identities are, how deep the tug they exert on men, the undertow of a thousand generations. The miseries I saw, as a boy, in the lives of nearly all men I continue to see in the lives of many—the body-breaking toil, the tedium, the call to be tough, the humiliating powerlessness, the battle for a living and for territory.

When the women I met at college thought about the joys and privileges of men, they did not carry in their minds the sort of men I had known in my childhood. They thought of their fathers, who were bankers, physicians, architects, stockbrokers, the big wheels of the big cities. These fathers rode the train to work or drove cars that cost more than any of my childhood houses. They were attended from morning to night by female helpers, wives and nurses and secretaries. They were never laid off, never short of cash at month's end, never lined up for welfare. These fathers made decisions that mattered. They ran the world.

The daughters of such men wanted to share in this power, this glory. So did I. They yearned for a say over their future, for jobs worthy of their abilities, for the right to live at peace, unmolested, whole. Yes, I thought, yes yes. The difference between me and these daughters was that they saw me, because of my sex, as destined from birth to become like their fathers, and therefore as an enemy to their desires. But I knew better. I wasn't an enemy, in fact or in feeling. I was an ally. If I had known, then, how to tell them so, would they have believed me? Would they now?

CRITICAL THINKING QUESTIONS

1. Rewrite Sanders's first paragraph (the essay's first two sentences) as a *claim statement*, followed by *because: Women must have . . . because they. . . .*

2. What *warrant* links the support clause (*because . . .*) to the claim? Do you accept the warrant?

WRITING TOPIC

Sanders concludes that the women he met at college should have regarded him as an ally rather than an enemy. How does Sanders's assertion reframe the issue question—who has it better, men or women? Write out the question that frames the argument for Sanders's assertion. Based on the images of men and women that you carry in your mind, which issue question has more relevance and validity? Write an essay defending your claim.

Harper Stevens

Frankenstein's Daughter

Most parents will tell you that children are natural born liars when it comes to protecting themselves. I had to be taught. My first lesson came when my sixth grade lab partner, a girl I came to loathe heartily, asked me what my father did for a living, which was not a simple question. He taught biology at the high school up the road. He coached the junior varsity football squad every afternoon until it was too dark to see the receivers post their patterns. He regularly filled in at the presbytery pulpit. My would-be suitors were certain he was a cop. . . .

"A taxidermist," I announced proudly, for I was proud of him. He took lifeless, twisted things and made them whole. He brought back the dead with sawdust and coat hangers. No one else's father that I knew could do that.

Well, perhaps a few could, but their kids weren't telling. They knew better than to declare such talents to a world that didn't believe in magic. That was the moment I learned that knowing when to lie was far more vital to surviving junior high than wearing the right jeans. I also learned that my concept of a stuffed animal collection was substantially different from other kids.

From that day on, I sat by myself until an Indian girl transferred into our class. I don't know what caste she was from, but she wasn't afraid of pariahs. I suppose that compared to her own religion, which called for ritual sacrifices from the produce section, taxidermy didn't seem all that weird. I never did learn to spell her name.

My father had been a taxidermist for as long as I could remember. He took up the pursuit because of his own father, who was an ornithologist out of Cornell. He mounted his first specimen, a hapless meadowlark, to catch his father's attention—anything with feathers and a beak did. It was a kind of crude barter, an offering to his father's god in return for the acknowledgement that he was alive. But it was a bitterly one-sided arrangement. He realized this rather quickly and turned his affections to God the Father instead, with imminently more satisfying results.

His interest in taxidermy did not fade, however, nor did his knack for bartering. My mother rarely let him take me anywhere unsupervised, perhaps afraid that he would come back with a used trolling motor but no daughter. One night just before my fourth birthday, he returned from helping fix an acquaintance's car, carrying a bundle under his jacket. There had been no cash to pay for his time, he explained. But, "Her name is Tinkerbell," he declared, lifting the skunk out of the sack.

To my knowledge, the Southern Baptists have not yet taken up the practice of canonization, but when they do, my mother will be first in line.

My father had conveniently forgotten to ask if Tinkerbell was "defused" and, taking a page out of the U.S. Guide to Israeli Diplomatic Relations, decided that we would simply give the skunk whatever it wanted and never make it angry. Eventually, we discovered that Tinkerbell was leash trained, which opened whole worlds for me. Until then, I had been confined to the sandy expanse beside our lot, studded with sweetgum balls and pecan hulls, but now I had the freedom to roam. There is nothing safer in this world than a four-year-old walking a skunk on a leash through a trailer park. My mother repeatedly warned me not to get too attached to Tinkerbell. I think she suspected the skunk was just a taxidermy project "in development," but before we could find out, my father traded her at a garage sale for a shotgun, which seemed redundant to me.

My father did not actually collect his own specimens, but had a small, faithful clientele of watery-eyed, camouflage-clad, baseball-capped runty little men. They came to the back step at odd hours with small, compact packages wrapped in newspapers that had suspicious dark brown stains at the corners. I would nod solemnly at them and accept the parcels, as if taking a heroin payoff, and recede slowly back into the house, lest they think I was trying to steal their prize and come at me, jaws snapping.

It was understood that the bodies, birds exclusively, were to be placed in the refrigerator for my father. This created a logistical crisis for my mother at times, one which she bore with remarkable fortitude. But one night, after having spent a good twenty minutes trying to secure a spot for a tray of deviled eggs that was destined for an AΔK reception, she snapped. Gathering up a half dozen of the parcels in her arms, she ran out into the backyard and began burying them like a demented squirrel, then refused to tell my father where she had hidden the bodies.

It was a unique marriage, to say the least. My mother had a severe phobia of birds, so it was a mystery that she could love him at all, but God has a wicked sense of humor as she was fond of saying. I suppose in comparison with the rest of his clan of mad scientists (in particular his youngest brother, a vertebrate zoologist whose chief hobby was releasing sand sharks into the pond at the local park), my father seemed practically normal. Most of the time.

Though his specimens were provided for him, my father still spent as many hours in the woods as he could, which was as necessary for him as it was for a fish to move its gills. We called these expeditions, "going on a date with Bambi." I said as much once to an uninitiated friend who had come over to study and asked where he was. She looked about carefully, then leaned close. *"Doesn't your mother mind?"*

"No," I replied, straight-faced. "She knew about Bambi when they got married."

There was always a distinct air about my father's return from the woods—not the fresh, crisp scent of pine and brush, but the muddy brown, turgid smell of swamp. Inevitably, he would manage to land himself in the dark, tannic water up to his knees and come squelching through the door, sneakers squeaking on the linoleum. As he wanted to be back out that door again as soon as possible, he couldn't afford to wait for his shoes to dry naturally, so he took to putting them in the oven: preheat to 250, then bake for 20 minutes. The kitchen would smell like faintly scorched rubber and end of the semester gym clothes for hours afterwards.

Even though I had a lifetime to observe him, I was remarkably dense at times about my father's ways. I knew that he hadn't shot a bird in years, but somehow we ate duck twice a week. Only when a dental filling met with birdshot for the third time in a single meal did the pieces click, and I understood how he could work for hours in his studio but never have to take out the trash. They're not lying—ignorance really is bliss sometimes.

But I shouldn't have been shocked. My father never wasted anything in his life; why should this be any different? He had a way of appropriating whatever was at hand for use in his taxidermy, modifying household items to save the cost of ordering from catalogs. For nearly two decades, I thought that sticky, silvery substance was called "duck tape" for obvious reasons. I often found my clothes crumpled on the floor as their hanger skeletons had been drafted for a higher calling. I retaliated by stealing his prized bottle of "wood duck orange" and using it for nail polish, striking back on two fronts. The next week, I came home to find my hairdryer whirring merrily, embedded in the body cavity of a Canadian goose. I think he won.

At that time, he initiated me into the fraternal rites. I wasn't so much interested in the science of it as I was fascinated by the accessories: straight probes, surgical needles, modeling clay, tiny envelopes of glass eyes, tubs of sawdust, acrylic paints, and T-pins (which could double for toothpicks in a pinch). I learned to hold a razor without cutting myself, run the wires through delicate wing bones, sew skin shut with neat, precise stitches, paint the intricate pattern of a wood duck's bill with a rock-steady hand, and mix the proportions to achieve the distinctive shade of muddy, mossy mallard green.

It was way better than Barbie.

My father was considered one of the better taxidermists in the region, but he never charged half of what he was worth. In particular, he had a reputation for being able to restore birds that had been blasted in the head at close range, sort of like Marlon Perkins meets Martha Stewart. I discovered his secret one night when I padded out to the kitchen for a drink and found him working late. I stood there in mismatched Garfield slippers and his old football jersey, looking slowly from the two headless ducks on the table to his hands, which he kept behind his back.

"You switched the heads," I intoned heavily. My father—Joe Bob Frankenstein.

He looked sheepishly at me but did not deny it. Instead, he let me stay up and assist with the procedure as we drank orange juice spiked with Coke. I felt very, very adult, and my induction into the clan was complete.

I finished my first solo mount, a drake wood duck, the summer I turned eleven, and we fenced it to one of his contacts for the regal sum of thirty-five dollars. I promptly went to the bookstore and blew it all on a hardback collection of Ray Bradbury stories.

"D'you think I c'ld have a c'reer in this?" I mused on the way home, doing my best clench-jawed Holly Hunter.

"Don't do that!" he cautioned. "Your voice might get stuck that way." But reluctantly, he supposed I could, if I didn't mind working hard for no recognition and even less money.

I had meant writing not taxidermy, but the principle was the same. I saw no point in correcting him as it would do no good. He regarded me with the kind of blind, stubborn devotion found only in golden retrievers and battered wives: what he did not see was not there. Ironically, my father tried for years to change things about me with little to no success. Though he knew he could do nothing about the inside, he always did his damnedest to do what he could about the outside. This was fueled primarily by a realization he had when I was five that I was, in fact, a girl. (I had been doing a very good impersonation of a boy up until then.) I was presented with a schedule of suitably feminine outfits that he had drawn up from an inventory of my closet. Each selection was neatly labeled with a day of the month. He taped this beside my dresser, and for the first time I knew what hate felt like. It was intoxicating.

I was also just smart enough to know there was nothing I could do to change his mind. Instead, I kept a jacket in the classroom coat closet—the multi-colored nylon kind with synthetic filling and a plastic zipper—which I put on the instant I arrived each morning. I looked like Nanook of the Trailer Park, but at least my skin was my own. The scam was working pretty well until class pictures went home. My mother held the photo at arm's length, then brought it in close, asking who in the world that child in the parka was. I said nothing, but as I was one of only four white girls, process of elimination drew the noose tight about me.

I was forbidden to wear the jacket again, barring a sudden blizzard, which in North Florida was highly improbable, and was sent back to school feeling as ugly and naked as one of the ducks on the work table. At least he dressed them nicely, combing their plumage, restoring their colors, while I waddled off, feeling awkward and unfinished.

My father had an irresistible urge to build, change, and fix things, but at times lacked any balancing aesthetic sense. He would remain true to his vision though and proceed accordingly, like some latter day Noah, as my mother and I politely averted our eyes. When we finally moved to a "real" house, he constructed a special sloping desk for his taxidermy work out of grade C plywood, covered in oak finish contact paper. The drawers never quite set properly on their runners, and opening one was no guarantee that it would close again. Still, details never deterred a good vision.

Spurred on, perhaps by some repressed schoolboy urge to periodically produce a science fair project, my father then constructed what I came to refer to as the Diorama of Death. It was a rectangular glass case, roughly one foot by three and nearly two feet high. The floor of the case was covered in a layer of dirt upon which he had fashioned a passable replica of rural marshland, complete with reeds and grasses studded around a small glass surface painted to resemble a mud puddle. There, he lovingly placed four ducks—two mated pairs, green wing and cinnamon teal—gathered together to feed and drink.

At least that's what he told us when my mother regained the capacity to speak and was able to ask him just what in God's name he had done. Why couldn't we just have a normal coffee table? she whispered. That would be ridiculous, he insisted. He didn't even like coffee. Visitors would stare, wide-eyed, and ask why there was a display case sitting in the middle of our living room. What could I tell them, that he routinely knocked over the museum of natural history? It was like living inside a Hitchcock film, but the lights never came up.

Still, his willingness to build what we could not buy was a much cherished trait, even though it led to bizarre results at times. Once I was sorely tempted by my younger cousin's Sit'n Spin™, although I knew better than to ask for things that were beyond us. It was a ludicrous toy, designed to play upon a child's innate fascination with anything that makes her dizzy and unable to stand. Naturally, I was hooked. I described the device in great detail that night, hoping perhaps that my father might know someone who had an extra one lying about the spare bedroom. He listened attentively, brows slightly knotted, and hmmmed in all the right spots, but said nothing to raise my hopes.

Two days later, he called me outside and showed me a small white board that had been bolted to half of a Jeep Wagoneer fan clutch. If a very small person—for instance, me—were to sit carefully on the board and shove off with her knuckles, it would be possible to attain an amazing rate of revolution, far faster than a store-bought Sit'n Spin™. (I later learned this was because the suits at Playskool had determined that if a child spins at more than *xyz* rpm, that child will become violently ill. My father had not consulted their research.) I was instantly the envy of every kid in the trailer park. Especially my cousin. I finally traded it to him for the Bionic Man transport and repair station, a 15 dollar retail value.

My father had a certain knack for that, assembling discarded, broken pieces into something that was never quite what you had originally envisioned, but sometimes better. This talent had a way of straying into the realm of the living and he had an endless string of projects who dragged themselves through our lives. He did the best he could to patch them back together—alcoholics, drug addicts, the molested and abused—and then send them on their way. My mother wholeheartedly approved of his use of the guest room to this end, but preferred to have some role in the interviewing process. This stipulation came after he brought home an unemployed karate instructor in the midst of a nasty divorce while my mother was out of town. But Jack would only be staying for the weekend, he pointed out. Thirty-eight of them to be precise, not that I was counting.

The only time I ever had any real fear as to how my father might employ his skills came when we went out to a local steak house for my fourteenth birthday. I was ravenous, having skipped lunch in anticipation of a thick rib-eye. As I slashed into the steak, he calmly informed me that he would be perfectly comfortable giving me a tracheotomy with his ballpoint pen should I choke. But though he could be ill-timed, he was always well-intentioned. One night as I sat wrestling with the mysteries of point of view, he looked up from his newspaper and said very seriously, "If you were ever in a plane crash, like that rugby team in the Andes . . . I would understand." I've never been in a position where cannibalism was an option (unless you count nearly gnawing my own leg off to escape one exceptionally bad secretarial job), but I've always been oddly comforted in the knowledge that I would have his support.

Despite his quirks, or perhaps because of them, he was an openly loving man and an excellent provider. I never wanted for anything and often received things I had no idea I wanted in the first place. His devotion to me was rivaled only by, of all things, his cat. It was a gigantic orange tabby, a freak of nature, that he had scooped from a garbage heap one winter night to combat a surging invasion of Norwegian ship rats, the steroid-fed kind with squinty little Eastwood eyes, that had eaten half the Christmas decorations in the attic. The cat had squinty eyes too, a whip-like tail, and the look of a defeated heavyweight boxer. If he had a neck, I certainly never saw it.

At first the cat had no name because he wasn't going to be staying. Then one morning, as my father let him drink straight from the cereal bowl, he asked how I liked the sound of "Terminator." I immediately launched a nasty and ultimately victorious campaign to call him Puff instead, though Igor would have been more fitting. And just like the boy named Sue, Puff turned into the most vicious, pugnacious tom for sixteen city blocks in each direction.

The cat eradicated not only the rat population but took on squirrel suppression duties as well, which he managed with Gestapo-like efficiency. He even besieged the Diorama for two full days, lunging at the glass without success. But as he aged and hobbled about, snarling in a cataract-misted fury, the tell-tale tails appeared less frequently on the back step. My father felt it was vitally important for the cat to have fresh protein, but I had no idea how far he had taken the notion until I found him one day with the barrel of a .22 poking out of a slit in the backdoor. The cat stood beside him with a shocked expression that seemed to say: Hallelujah, it's raining squirrels! It was only when I pulled out a map to demonstrate that yes, we *did* live within the city limits that he switched to a more dubious, if completely legal, plan.

Simply put, a dead squirrel was a dead squirrel to my father's mind, and it did not matter if it had been hit by a bullet or, oh say, a 1978 Toyota longbed. He would methodically scan the median line of every road he traveled, and when a fresh carcass was spotted, he would slow the vehicle, open the door without stopping, and scoop the body inside. It was my job to shift gears as he did this. It was a little like *Bonnie and Clyde,* but if David Lynch had directed it. Only once did my father misjudge in his harvesting and select a squirrel that was, in fact, not dead at all, but merely stunned. He examined the situation from a Darwinian perspective and with a shrug threw the cat in the truck, locked the doors, and let nature take its course. When I wrote stories about our misadventures, I was either chastised for lying or sent to the school counselor for telling the truth. I saw this as a less than hopeful sign for my aspirations as a writer.

But even as my father's eccentricities left me with certain misconceptions about how the food chain operated, I acquired a degree of maturity. Death was not some abstract concept that only visited elderly relatives or strangers on the national news.

It made house calls. I signed for its deliveries. Being a mortician seemed like a viable career for a time. The dead were quiet and peaceful. They did not ask me what I *really* wanted to be when I grew up. (My mother told me to be grateful that people considered a girl might want to do anything at all; no one had ever asked her.) I knew instinctively how to treat a person's grief, how to incline my head at a slight angle, and tense my eyebrows in concern. My collection of black clothing was beyond reproach. I knew what to do with the dead; it was the living I couldn't manage.

I changed my mind when one of my dearest friends killed himself shortly after we graduated from college. There was not supposed to be a viewing—he had put a .45 in his mouth—but they were making an exception for close friends, his fiancée informed me. I thought of him, a great, strapping Illinois farm boy with a shock of rusty hair and a laugh that deafened the cafeteria, and shook my head numbly. I had prepared too many corpses; I knew what they had done to him.

After college, however, slowly, like the lichen dripping down the oak trees my father loved so much, a divide grew between us. I stopped keeping company with him as he worked late nights and lazy Saturday afternoons with college football playing in the background. I no longer perched on the sloping work desk to talk to him for hours, my feet stuck in an extended drawer to keep myself from sliding off. I had traded my fascination with his work for my own, just as he had left his father for another.

Somehow though, this distance brought me closer to him. I understood the cycle now. I had never felt confined by any expectations that I would follow him. If anything, I was expected to live along my own lines and not allow myself to be molded and posed like those lifeless birds. And I *was* alive, alive in ways most women never dreamed of being, because the tenacity of his love for me was so pure and unquestionable, attested to in a dozen ways each hour, that I couldn't help but live. Like the Velveteen Rabbit, he had loved me to life, painful though the process was.

Then I hopped away. Children are like that.

I had my own experiments and passions to tend to. I collected words instead, watching, listening, and rummaging among the discarded and forgotten. I gathered the dead and nearly dead, taking pieces of their stories and souls, stitching them together in my basement apartment laboratory. And patiently I waited for the lightning to strike.

CRITICAL THINKING QUESTIONS

1. In the previous essay, Sanders divides men into two primary categories: "toilers and warriors" and bosses and decision makers. How does Stevens's father fit into or challenge Sanders's categorization?

2. Compare this essay to Heaney's poem, "Digging." Both authors arrive at similar claims about the relationship between their work as writers and their fathers' work. What *warrant* about their work underlies both Heaney's and Stevens's claims?

CHAPTER ACTIVITIES

1. What is "marital bliss"? Should you expect to experience self-development and equality within a marriage? What does it mean to choose a marriage partner in the twenty-first century? Should engaged couples create and sign a prenuptial contract? Do some background research on prenuptial contracts. Then conduct primary research on the state of marriage in the twenty-first century: interview peers, friends, and family members and ask them their views on the above questions. (For a representative sample, be sure to talk with persons representing different age groups and to include an even gender mix in your sample.) Based on your research findings and several chapter readings, write an argument that advocates or disputes prenuptial contracts. Or write a Rogerian argument that advocates a rethinking of the conventional concept of marriage (literature suggestions: Chopin's "The Storm," Updike's "Separating," Fierstein's *On Tidy Endings,* Kramer's "Divorce and Our National Values").

2. The nineteenth century Russian writer Leo Tolstoy opens Chapter One of his novel, *Anna Karenina,* with this two-part assertion: "All happy families are like one another; each unhappy family is unhappy in its own way."[2] What assumptions or warrants are implied in his assertion about "happy families"? What assumptions are implied about "unhappy" families? Extend your thinking beyond Tolstoy's assertions to your own experience, observations, and several readings in this chapter. Write an essay that defends, refutes, and/or qualifies Tolstoy's assertions about happy and unhappy families (literature suggestions: Mukherjee's "A Father," Snyder's "Not Leaving the House," Murray's "The Inheritance of Values").

3. What is the role of a father? Is a father's participation in a child's growing up more significant in a son's or in a daughter's long-term well-being? If a parent's personal income is sufficient, can a single parent (Mom or Dad) be "good enough" for child-rearing? How important is it for a child to have regular daily contact with both his or her mom and dad? Conduct research to find out what family therapists and sociologists are saying about these parenting issues; also, ask friends for their viewpoints. Based on your research findings and several literature selections, argue a position on an aspect of parenting (literature suggestions: González's "Too Much His Father's Son," Updike's "Separating," Wilbur's "The Writer," Stevens's "Frankenstein's Daughter").

4. How do family traditions and cultural legacies contribute to and/or inhibit an individual's self-identity? What do you know about your family history? How is this history shared, and how is it valued among individual family members? Beyond its literal meaning, what are the broader implications of the cliché, "keeping the

---

[2]Leo Tolstoy, *Anna Karenina* (New York: Signet Classics, 1961), p. 17.

family name alive"? Or has this cliché outlived its validity? A number of readings in this chapter address an aspect of family tradition/cultural heritage and individual identity and fulfillment—for example, Lee's "Safe," Ng's "A Red Sweater," Walker's "Everyday Use," Heaney's "Digging," Walker's "Lineage." Drawing on evidence from several readings and your own experience and observations, write a claim of value argument about an aspect of family heritage and individual identity.

5. What are the long-term effects of divorce on children? According to Census Bureau statistics, the divorce rate peaked in the late 1970s and early 1980s, and even though the rate has been declining for the past twenty years, the United States's divorce rate still stands at 49% of all marriages.[3] Now that the children of the recent divorce boom are adults themselves, some are speaking out about the lasting effects of their parents' divorces. In a *Time* magazine cover story, Walter Kirn reported the research findings and conclusions of therapist Judith Wallerstein. Wallerstein's research, based on interviews with adult children of divorce, suggests that divorce has significant and lasting negative impacts on children. And most significantly, Wallerstein argues that parents should stick it out and stay married for their children's sake. However, other experts vigorously dispute Wallerstein's conclusions. Author Katha Pollitt, for example, contends, "America doesn't need more 'good enough' marriages full of depressed and bitter people. . . . The 'good enough' divorce—why isn't that ever the cover story?"[4] Conduct some research on the issue of children and divorce, and reflect on several readings in this chapter. Based on your findings, take a stand on Wallerstein's claim that parents should stay together for their children's long-term welfare (literature suggestions: González's "Too Much His father's Son," Updike's "Separating," Olds's "I Go Back to May, 1937").

6. Poet Ogden Nash, well-known for his limericks, wrote this verse, "Children aren't happy with nothing to ignore,/And that's what parents were created for,"[5] implying that parents are like flies—annoyances to be swatted. Are parents to blame for their children's troubles? How accountable should parents be for their children's misbehaviors? Recently, a number of states have passed laws that punish parents with fines or sometimes even imprisonment if their child is found guilty of criminal assault, property crimes, drug or gun violations. Opponents of these laws argue that threatening parents with fines and punishment does not address the deeper layers of juvenile crime issues. Rather than punishment, these parents need proactive support, such as community-based, early intervention programs for their children. Meanwhile, purveyors of popular culture thrive on images of wanton violence to sell their products to a youthful audience. Research the issue of children and violent behavior, and based on your findings, argue a position on the accountability of parents for their children's misbehavior.

---

[3]Walter Kirn, "Should You Stay Together for the Kids?" *Time,* September 25, 2000, pp. 75–82.
[4]Katha Pollitt, "Is Divorce Getting a Bum Rap?" *Time,* September 25, 2000, p. 82.
[5]Ogden Nash, *The Parents,* in *The Macmillan Dictionary of Quotations* (Edison, NJ: Chartwell Books, Inc., 2000), p. 207.

Chapter Six

Power and Responsibility

Do you recall a playground bully from your childhood, that child whose strength and physical power made him intimidating? However, what was frightening was not merely his strength but how he chose to use that strength. He was threatening because sometimes he did not act responsibly and, thus, might hurt you. On the other hand, not all threatening children were physically powerful; some gained control through manipulation. They, too, could exert a power over you, potentially harming you by irresponsibly starting rumors and exploiting gossip to achieve their goals.

As adults, we continue to witness the abuse of power by individuals who seek to influence and control others for their own gain. In our eyes, such individuals act irresponsibly when they buy votes in our government, create insider-stock deals on Wall Street, or merely forget to consider the feelings of others as they pursue their goals. The hard truth is that with power comes responsibility, for we are all answerable, eventually accountable, for our actions.

Are you familiar with Shakespeare's play *Macbeth?* Lady Macbeth and her husband are ruthless in their acquisition of power and become intoxicated with it once they have it. The price for their irresponsibility is death, and for four hundred years now the world has found the story of their downfall instructive. Literature has examined this relationship between power and responsibility since the earliest time. The Greeks understood it well, as can be seen in the plays of Sophocles, Aeschylus, and Euripedes. The Roman playwrights Plautus and Terrence clearly understood it, as later did the poets Dante and Milton. The modern novelist F. Scott Fitzgerald explored this idea in his famous novel *The Great Gatsby,* as the fabulously wealthy Gatsby eventually pays dearly for his cavalier treatment of others.

But it is not only the rich and famous among us who struggle with the relationship between power and responsibility. At all levels of society, the theme of power and responsibility is reflected in our literature. Look at this poem by Maxine Kumin:

Woodchucks

Gassing the woodchucks didn't turn out right.
The knockout bomb from the Feed and Grain Exchange
was featured as merciful, quick at the bone
and the case we had against them was airtight,
both exits shoehorned shut with puddingstone,
but they had a sub-sub-basement out of range.

Next morning they turned up again, no worse
for the cyanide than we for our cigarettes
and state-store Scotch, all of us up to scratch.
They brought down the marigolds as a matter of course
and then took over the vegetable patch
nipping the broccoli shoots, beheading the carrots.

The food from our mouths, I said, righteously thrilling
to the feel of the .22, the bullets' neat noses.
I, a lapsed pacifist fallen from grace
puffed with Darwinian pieties for killing,
now drew a bead on the littlest woodchuck's face.
He died down in the everbearing roses.

Ten minutes later I dropped the mother. She
flipflopped in the air and fell, her needle teeth
still hooked in a leaf of Swiss chard.
Another baby next. O one-two-three
the murderer inside me rose up hard,
the hawkeye killer came on stage forthwith.

There's one chuck left. Old wily fellow, he keeps
me cocked and ready day after day after day.
All night I hunt his humped-up form. I dream
I sight along the barrel in my sleep.
If only they'd all consented to die unseen
Gassed underground the quiet Nazi way.

The poet certainly understands the conflicts surrounding the use of power. With the .22 in hand, the speaker is able to deal out death to these creatures who are merely pursuing their natural instincts and mean no personal harm. Notice the line, "puffed with Darwinian pieties for killing" in the third stanza. *The survival of the fittest* is the phrase from Darwin everyone knows, and in this case what qualifies the speaker as the *fittest?* The ability to use the .22, of course. In fact, Darwin's ideas about evolution and the hierarchy of living things have been used to justify many exertions of power in the twentieth century; some of these instances you may deem abusive. Later in this chapter, you can read the essay, "Religion and Animal Rights" by Tom Regan, in which he discusses the issue of power and responsibility as it relates to our treatment of animals as a food source.

Saying, "I thought the time had come when a few boundaries ought to be moved," Henrik Ibsen, a Norwegian playwright, wrote *The Doll's House* in 1879 and certainly ignited some controversies that continue to resonate in our contemporary world. In this play, which has seen several modern revivals on Broadway, a lawyer's wife named Nora chafes against the reins of power held firmly in the hands of her husband. As a result, she rebels, first in small ways, but eventually as scandal threatens to destroy their social position, Nora sees the reality of her situation:

NORA: . . . when I lived at home with Papa, he used to tell me his opinion about everything, and so I had the same opinion. If I thought differently, I had to hide it from him, or he wouldn't have liked it. He called me his little doll, and he used to play with me just as I played with my dolls. Then I came to live in your house—

HELMER: That's no way to talk about our marriage!

NORA (*undisturbed*): I mean when I passed out of Papa's hands into yours. You arranged everything to suit your own tastes, and so I came to have the same tastes as yours . . .

*   *   *

[*Briefly, they discuss the idea of happiness.*]

HELMER (NORA's husband): Haven't you been happy here?

NORA: No, that's something I've never been. I thought I had, but really I've never been happy.

HELMER: Never . . . happy?

NORA: No, only gay. And you've always been so kind to me. But our home has been nothing but a play-room. I've been your doll-wife here, just as at home I was Papa's doll-child . . .

You can be certain that in 1879 this play, focusing as it does on the acquisition and use of power within a marriage, "moved a few boundaries," as Ibsen said. Since Nora's unwillingness to bend to her husband's influence so obviously conflicted with traditional gender roles, many people in the original audience were outraged. Yet that is what literature so often does: it prods us to look beyond the status quo, beyond those values and social configurations we so readily accept.

In the 1970s and 1980s, *A Doll's House* found great favor among the members of the women's movement. The late 1990s saw yet another successful Broadway revival of this play, not because the idea of a woman demanding independence was any longer so shocking but because its theme of power and responsibility continues to appeal to audiences. In a reversal of roles, the 1999 film *American Beauty* portrays a husband rebelling against the powerless situation in which he finds himself, first quitting his job in advertising and then completely altering his marriage. The struggle over power and the consequences of responsibility for the use of that power are themes we are sure to see played out in the literature of the twenty-first century.

In this chapter, you will have the opportunity to examine this theme in the works of early-American writers, Herman Melville and Nathaniel Hawthorne, both of whom were quite ready to teach their readers about the use and abuse of power. Today, some psychologists argue that teenage girls sometimes choose to exert power in one of the only areas in which they have control, their intake of food; thus, they become anorexic. Similarly, Melville's character, Bartleby, a poor, powerless clerk, chooses to no longer do the work required of him and, through this choice, manipulates his boss who feels responsible. On the other hand, Hawthorne's characters wield power over their community in an effort to enforce values they deem good for everyone. As we read literature, we continually see characters struggle with the issues of power and responsibility and, in some cases, learn from their mistakes.

In a modern setting, Nadine Gordimer has centered her short story, "Terminal," on the promises and responsibilities two people share when one is stricken with illness. In this case, no one is acting selfishly or for personal gain; however, an important choice must be made, and the decision tests the bounds of commitment. As readers, we watch, consider, and learn.

PREWRITING AND DISCUSSION

1. What do people mean when they talk about *power?* Focus on a particular context, such as state government, the family, the schools, or the community. Who has power and who does not? Is power related to money? To respect?

2. Consider the saying, "Power corrupts, and absolute power corrupts absolutely." Can you think of examples where that phrase has proven to be true? Can you think of examples of powerful people who are above corruption, people who forego personal benefits in order to work for the good of others? Does Ralph Nader fall into this category?

3. Write for a few minutes about responsibility? What responsibility do we as individuals have to our families, communities, or nation? In small groups, discuss your ideas of power and responsibility.

Toni Cade Bambara

The Lesson

Back in the days when everyone was old and stupid or young and foolish and me and Sugar were the only ones just right, this lady moved on our block with nappy hair and proper speech and no makeup. And quite naturally we laughed at her, laughed the way we did at the junk man who went about his business like he was some big-time president and his sorry-ass horse his secretary. And we kinda hated her too, hated the way we did the winos who cluttered up our parks and pissed on our handball walls and stank up our hallways and stairs so you couldn't halfway play hide-and-seek without a goddamn gas mask. Miss Moore was her name. The only woman on the block with no first name. And she was black as hell, cept for her feet, which were fish-white and spooky. And she was always planning these boring-ass things for us to do, us being my cousin, mostly, who lived on the block cause we all moved North the same time and to the same apartment then spread out gradual to breathe. And our parents would yank our heads into some kinda shape and crisp up our clothes so we'd be presentable for travel with Miss Moore, who always looked like she was going to church, though she never did. Which is just one of the things the grownups talked about when they talked behind her back like a dog. But when she came calling with some sachet she'd sewed up or some gingerbread she'd made or some book, why then they'd all be too embarrassed to turn her down and we'd get handed over all spruced up. She'd been to college and said it was only right that she should take responsibility for the young ones' education, and she not even related by marriage or blood. So they'd go for it. Specially Aunt Gretchen. She was the main gofer in the family. You got some ole dumb shit foolishness you want somebody to go for, you send for Aunt Gretchen. She been screwed into the go-along for so long, it's a blood-deep natural thing with her. Which is how she got saddled with me and Sugar and Junior in the first place while our mothers were in a la-de-da apartment up the block having a good ole time.

So this one day Miss Moore rounds us all up at the mailbox and it's puredee hot and she's knockin herself out about arithmetic. And school suppose to let up in summer I heard, but she don't never let up. And the starch in my pinafore scratching the shit outta me and I'm really hating this nappy-head bitch and her goddamn college degree. I'd much rather go to the pool or to the show where it's cool. So me and Sugar leaning on the mailbox being surly, which is a Miss Moore word. And Flyboy checking out what everybody brought for lunch. And Fat Butt already wasting his peanut-butter-and-jelly sandwhich like the pig he is. And Junebug punching on Q.T.'s arm for potato chips. And Rosie Giraffe shifting from one hip to the other waiting for somebody to step on her foot or ask her if she from Georgia so she can kick ass, preferably Mercedes'. And Miss Moore asking us do we know what money is, like we a bunch of retards. I mean real money, she say, like it's only poker chips or monopoly papers we lay on the grocer. So right away I'm tired of this and say so. And would much rather snatch Sugar and go to the Sunset and terrorize the West Indian kids and take their hair ribbons and their money too. And Miss Moore files that remark away for next week's lesson on brotherhood, I can tell. And finally I say we oughta get to the subway cause it's cooler and besides we might meet some cute boys. Sugar done swiped her mama's lipstick, so we ready.

So we heading down the street and she's boring us silly about what things cost and what our parents make and how much goes for rent and how money ain't divided up right in this country. And then she gets to the part about we all poor and live in the slums, which I don't feature. And I'm ready to speak on that, but she steps out in the street and hails two cabs just like that. Then she hustles half the crew in with her and hands me a five-dollar bill and tells me to calculate 10 percent tip for the driver. And we're off. Me and Sugar and Junebug and Flyboy hangin' out the window and hollering to everybody, putting lipstick on each other cause Flyboy a faggot anyway, and making farts with our sweaty armpits. But I'm mostly trying to figure how to spend this money. But they all fascinated with the meter ticking and Junebug starts laying bets as to how much it'll read when Flyboy can't hold his breath no more. Then Sugar lays bets as to how much it'll be when we get there. So I'm stuck. Don't nobody want to go for my plan, which is to jump out at the next light and run off to the first bar-b-que we can find. Then the driver tells us to get the hell out cause we there already. And the meter reads eighty-five cents. And I'm stalling to figure out the tip and Sugar say give him a dime. And I decide he don't need it bad as I do, so later for him. But then he tries to take off with Junebug foot still in the door so we talk about his mama something ferocious. Then we check out that we on Fifth Avenue and everybody dressed up in stockings. One lady in a fur coat, hot as it is. White folks crazy.

"This is the place," Miss Moore say, presenting it to us in the voice she uses at the museum. "Let's look in the windows before we go in."

"Can we steal?" Sugar asks very serious like she's getting the ground rules squared away before she plays. "I beg your pardon," say Miss Moore, and we fall out. So she leads us around the windows of the toy store and me and Sugar screaming', "This is mine, that's mine, I gotta have that, that was made for me, I was born for that," till Big Butt drowns us out.

"Hey, I'm going to buy that there."

"That there? You don't even know what it is, stupid."

"I do so," he say punchin on Rosie Giraffe. "It's a microscope."

"Whatcha gonna do with a microscope, fool?"

"Look at things."

"Like what, Ronald?" ask Miss Moore. And Big Butt ain't got the first notion. So here go Miss Moore gabbing about the thousands of bacteria in a drop of water and the somethinorother in a speck of blood and the million and one living things in the air around us is invisible to the naked eye. And what she say that for? Junebug go to town on that "naked" and we rolling. Then Miss Moore ask what it cost. So we all jam into the window smudgin it up and the price tag say $300. So then she ask how long'd take for Big Butt and Junebug to save up their allowances. "Too long," I say. "Yeh," adds Sugar, "outgrown it by that time." And Miss Moore say no, you never outgrow learning instruments. "Why, even medical students and interns and," blah, blah, blah. And we ready to choke Big Butt for bringing it up in the first damn place.

"This here costs four hundred eighty dollars," say Rosie Giraffe. So we pile up all over her to see what she pointin out. My eyes tell me it's a chunk of glass cracked with something heavy, and different-color inks dripped into the splits, then the whole thing put into a oven or something. But for $480 it don't make sense.

"That's a paperweight made of semi-precious stones fused together under tremendous pressure," she explains slowly, with her hands doing the mining and all the factory work.

"So what's a paperweight?" asks Rosie Giraffe.

"To weigh paper with, dumbbell," say Flyboy, the wise man from the East.

"Not exactly," say Miss Moore, which is what she say when you warm or way off too. "It's to weigh paper down so it won't scatter and make your desk untidy." So right away me and Sugar curtsy to each other and then to Mercedes who is more the tidy type.

"We don't keep paper on top of the desk in my class," say Junebug, figuring Miss Moore crazy or lyin one.

"At home, then," she say. "Don't you have a calendar and a pencil case and a blotter and a letter-opener on your desk at home where you do your homework?" And she know damn well what our homes look like cause she nosys around in them every chance she gets.

"I don't even have a desk," say Junebug. "Do we?"

"No. And I don't get no homework neither," say Big Butt.

"And I don't even have a home," say Flyboy like he do at school to keep the white folks off his back and sorry for him. Send this poor kid to camp posters, is his specialty.

"I do," says Mercedes. "I have a box of stationery on my desk and a picture of my cat. My godmother bought the stationery and the desk. There's a big rose on each sheet and the envelopes smell like roses."

"Who wants to know about your smelly-ass stationery," say Rosie Giraffe fore I can get my two cents in.

"It's important to have a work area all your own so that . . ."

"Will you look at this sailboat, please," say Flyboy, cuttin her off and pointin to the thing like it was his. So once again we tumble all over each other to gaze at this magnificent thing in the toy store which is just big enough to maybe sail two kittens across the pond if you strap them to the posts tight. We all start reciting the price tag like we in assembly. "Handcrafted sailboat of fiberglass at one thousand one hundred ninety-five dollars."

"Unbelievable," I hear myself say and am really stunned. I read it again for myself just in case the group recitation put me in a trance. Same thing. For some reason this pisses me off. We look at Miss Moore and she lookin at us, waiting for I dunno what.

"Who'd pay all that when you can buy a sailboat set for a quarter at Pop's, a tube of glue for a dime, and a ball of string for eight cents? It must have a motor and a whole lot else besides," I say. "My sailboat cost me about fifty cents."

"But will it take water?" say Mercedes with her smart ass.

"Took mine to Alley Pond Park once," say Flyboy. "String broke, Lost it. Pity."

"Sailed mine in Central Park and it keeled over and sank. Had to ask my father for another dollar."

"And you got the strap," laugh Big Butt. "The jerk didn't even have a string on it. My old man wailed on his behind."

Little Q.T. was staring hard at the sailboat and you could see he wanted it bad. But he too little and somebody'd just take it from him. So what the hell. "This boat for kids, Miss Moore?"

"Parents silly to buy something like that just to get all broke up," say Rosie Giraffe.

"That much money it should last forever," I figure.

"My father'd buy it for me if I wanted it."

"Your father, my ass," say Rosie Giraffe getting a chance to finally push Mercedes.

"Must be rich people shop here," say Q.T.

"You are a very bright boy," say Flyboy. "What was your first clue?" And he rap him on the head with the back of his knuckles, since Q.T. the only one he could get away with. Though Q.T. liable to come up behind you years later and get his licks in when you half expect it.

"What I want to know is," I says to Miss Moore though I never talk to her, I wouldn't give the bitch that satisfaction, "is how much a real boat costs? I figure a thousand'd get you a yacht any day."

"Why don't you check that out," she says, "and report back to the group?" Which really pains my ass. If you gonna mess up a perfectly good swim day least you could do is have some answers. "Let's go in," she say like she got something up her sleeve. Only she don't lead the way. So me and Sugar turn the corner to where the entrance is, but when we get there I kinda hang back. Not that I'm scared, what's there to be afraid of, just a toy store. But I feel funny, shame. But what I got to be shamed about? Got as much right to go in as anybody. But somehow I can't seem to get hold of the door, so I step away for Sugar to lead. But she hangs back too. And I look at her and she looks at me and this is ridiculous. I mean, damn, I have never ever been shy about doing nothing or going nowhere. But then Mercedes steps up and then Rosie Giraffe and Big Butt crowd in behind and shove, and next thing we all stuffed into the doorway with only Mercedes squeezing past us, smoothing out her jumper and walking right down the aisle. Then the rest of us tumble in like a glued-together jigsaw done all wrong. And people lookin at us. And it's like the time me and Sugar crashed into the Catholic church on a dare. But once we got in there and everything so hushed and holy and the candles and the bowin and the handkerchiefs on all the drooping heads, I just couldn't go through with the plan. Which was for me to run up to the altar and do a tap dance while Sugar played the nose flute and messed around in the holy water. And Sugar kept givin me the elbow. Then later teased me so bad I tied her up in the shower and turned it on and locked her in. And she'd be there till this day if Aunt Gretchen hadn't finally figured I was lyin about the boarder takin a shower.

Same thing in the store. We all walkin on tiptoe and hardly touchin the games and puzzles and things. And I watched Miss Moore who is steady watchin us like she waitin for a sign. Like Mama Drewery watches the sky and sniffs the air and takes note of just how much slant is in the bird formation. Then me and Sugar bump smack into each other, so busy gazing at the toys, 'specially the sailboat. But we don't laugh and go into our fat-lady bump-stomach routine. We just stare at that price tag. Then Sugar run a finger over the whole boat. And I'm jealous and want to hit her. Maybe not her, but I sure want to punch somebody in the mouth.

"Watcha brings us here for, Miss Moore?"

"You sound angry, Sylvia. Are you mad about something?" Givin me one of them grins like she tellin a grown-up joke that never turns out to be funny. And she's lookin very closely at me like maybe she plannin to do my portrait from memory. I'm mad, but I won't give her that satisfaction. So I slouch around the store being very bored and say, "Let's go."

Me and Sugar at the back of the train watchin the tracks whizzin by large then small then gettin gobbled up in the dark. I'm thinkin about this tricky toy I saw in the store. A clown that somersaults on a bar then does chin-ups just cause you yank lightly at his leg. Cost $35. I could see me askin my mother for a $35 birthday clown. "You wanna who that costs what?" she'd say, cocking her head to the side to get a better view of the hole in my head. Thirty-five dollars could buy new bunk beds for Junior and Gretchen's boy. Thirty-five dollars and the whole household could go visit Granddaddy Nelson in the country. Thirty-five dollars would pay for the rent and the piano bill too. Who are these people that spend that much for performing clowns and $1,000 for toy sailboats? What kinda work they do and how they live and how come we ain't in on it? Where we are is who we are, Miss Moore always pointin out. But it don't necessarily have to be that way, she always adds then waits for somebody to say that poor people have to wake up and demand their share of the pie and don't none of us know what kind of pie she talkin about in the first damn place. But she ain't so smart cause I still got her four dollars from the taxi and she sure ain't gettin it. Messin up my day with this shit. Sugar nudges me in my pocket and winks.

Miss Moore lines us up in front of the mailbox where we started from, seem like years ago, and I got a headache for thinkin so hard. And we lean all over each other so we can hold up under the draggy-ass lecture she always finishes us off with at the end before we thank her for borin us to tears. But she just looks at us like she readin tea leaves. Finally she say, "Well, what did you think of F.A.O. Schwartz?"

Rosie Giraffe mumbles, "White folks crazy."

"I'd like to go there again when I get my birthday money," says Mercedes, and we shove her out the pack so she has to lean on the mailbox by herself.

"I'd like a shower. Tiring day," say Flyboy.

Then Sugar surprises me by sayin, "You know, Miss Moore, I don't think all of us here put together eat in a year what that sailboat costs." And Miss Moore lights up like somebody goosed her. "And?" she say, urging Sugar on. Only I'm standin on her foot so she don't continue.

"Imagine for a minute what kind of society it is in which some people can spend on a toy what it would cost to feed a family of six or seven. What do you think?"

"I think," say Sugar pushing me off her feet like she never done before, cause I whip her ass in a minute, "that this is not much of a democracy if you ask me. Equal chance to pursue happiness means an equal crack at the dough, don't it?" Miss Moore is besides herself and I am disgusted with Sugar's treachery. So I stand on her foot one more time to see if she'll shove me. She shuts up, and Miss Moore looks at me, sorrowfully I'm thinkin. And somethin weird is going on, I can feel it in my chest.

"Anybody else learn anything today?" lookin dead at me. I walk away and Sugar has to run to catch up and don't even seem to notice when I shrug her arm off my shoulder.

"Well, we got four dollars anyway," she says.

"Uh hunh."

"We could go to Hascombs and get half a chocolate layer and then go to the Sunset and still have plenty money for potato chips and ice-cream sodas."

"Uh hunh."

"Race you to Hascombs," she say.

We start down the block and she gets ahead which is O.K. by me cause I'm goin to the West End and then over the Drive to think this day through. She can run if she want to and even run faster. But ain't nobody gonna beat me at nuthin.

CRITICAL THINKING QUESTIONS

1. What is the lesson taught? Is it a cruel lesson which robs the children of their innocence?

2. Is the author also teaching the reader a lesson? If so, what is the larger *issue* here?

WRITING TOPIC

Think of a young person you would like to teach a lesson. Describe that person in a paragraph, and then create a "lesson plan" for instruction.
Objective: To teach _____ to

_____

_____

Instructional Plan _____

_____

_____

_____

_____

_____ (you may need more space)

Outcomes (what thinking or behavior do you want to see in this person as a result of your lesson?): _____

_____

_____

_____

Raymond Carver

Cathedral

This blind man, an old friend of my wife's, he was on his way to spend the night. His wife had died. So he was visiting the dead wife's relatives in Connecticut. He called my wife from his in-laws'. Arrangements were made. He would come by train, a five-hour trip, and my wife would meet him at the station. She hadn't seen him since she worked for him one summer in Seattle ten yeas ago. But she and the blind man had kept in touch. They made tapes and mailed them back and forth. I wasn't enthusiastic about his visit. He was no one I knew. And his being blind bothered me. My idea of blindness came from the movies. In the movies, the blind moved slowly and never laughed. Sometimes they were led by seeing-eye dogs. A blind man in my house was not something I looked forward to.

That summer in Seattle she had needed a job. She didn't have any money. The man she was going to marry at the end of the summer was in officers' training school. He didn't have any money, either. But she was in love with the guy, and he was in love with her, etc. She'd seen something in the paper: HELP WANTED— *Reading to Blind Man*, and a telephone number. She phoned and went over, was hired on the spot. She'd worked with this blind man all summer. She read stuff to him, case studies, reports, that sort of thing. She helped him organize his little office in the county social-service department. They'd become good friends, my wife and the blind man. How do I know these things? She told me. And she told me something else. On her last day in the office, the blind man asked if he could touch her face. She agreed to this. She told me he touched his fingers to every part of her face, her nose—even her neck! She never forgot it. She even tried to write a poem about it. She was always trying to write a poem. She wrote a poem or two every year, usually after something really important had happened to her.

When we first started going out together, she showed me the poem. In the poem, she recalled his fingers and the way they had moved around over her face. In the poem, she talked about what she had felt at the time, about what went through her mind when the blind man touched her nose and lips. I can remember I didn't think much of the poem. Of course, I didn't tell her that. Maybe I just don't understand poetry. I admit it's not the first thing I reach for when I pick up something to read.

Anyway, this man who'd first enjoyed her favors, the officer-to-be, he'd been her childhood sweetheart. So okay. I'm saying that at the end of the summer she let the blind man run his hands over her face, said goodbye to him, married her childhood etc., who was now a commissioned officer, and she moved away from Seattle. But they'd kept in touch, she and the blind man. She made the first contact after a year or so. She called him up one night from an Air Force base in Alabama. She wanted to talk. They talked. He asked her to send him a tape and tell him about her life. She did this. She sent the tape. On the tape, she told the blind man about her husband and about their life together in the military. She told the blind man she loved her husband but she didn't like it where they lived and she didn't like it that he was a part of the military-industrial thing. She told the blind man she'd written a poem and he was in it. She told him that she was writing a poem about what it was like to be an Air Force officer's wife. The poem wasn't finished yet. She was still writing it. The blind man made a tape. He sent her the tape. She made a tape. This went on for years. My wife's officer was posted to one base and then another. She sent tapes from Moody AFB, McGuire, McConnell, and finally Travis, near Sacramento, where one night she got to feeling lonely and cut off from people she kept losing in that moving-around life. She got to feeling she couldn't go it another step. She went in and swallowed all the pills and capsules in the medicine chest and washed them down with a bottle of gin. Then she got into a hot bath and passed out.

But instead of dying, she got sick. She threw up. Her officer—why should he have a name? he was the childhood sweetheart, and what more does he want?—came home from somewhere, found her, and called the ambulance. In time, she put it all on a tape and sent the tape to the blind man. Over the years, she put all kinds of stuff on tapes and sent the tapes off lickety-split. Next to writing a poem every year, I think it was her chief means of recreation. On one tape, she told the blind man she'd decided to live away from her officer for a time. On another tape, she told him about her divorce. She and I began going out, and of course she told her blind man about it. She told him everything, or so it seemed to me. Once she asked me if I'd like to hear the latest tape from the blind man. This was a year ago. I was on the tape, she said. So I said okay, I'd listen to it. I got us drinks and we settled down in the living room. We made ready to listen. First she inserted the tape into the player and adjusted a couple of dials. Then she pushed a lever. The tape squeaked and someone began to talk in this loud voice. She lowered the volume. After a few minutes of harmless chitchat, I heard my own name in the mouth of this stranger, this blind man I didn't even know! And then this: "From all you've said about him, I can only conclude—" But we were interrupted, a knock at the door, something, and we didn't ever get back to the tape. Maybe it was just as well. I'd heard all I wanted to.

Now this same blind man was coming to sleep in my house.

"Maybe I could take him bowling," I said to my wife. She was at the draining board doing scalloped potatoes. She put down the knife she was using and turned around.

"If you love me," she said, "you can do this for me. If you don't love me, okay. But if you had a friend, any friend, and the friend came to visit, I'd make him feel comfortable." She wiped her hands with the dish towel.

"I don't have any blind friends," I said.

"You don't have *any* friends," she said. "Period. Besides," she said, "goddamn it, his wife's just died! Don't you understand that? The man's lost his wife!"

I didn't answer. She'd told me a little about the blind man's wife. Her name was Beulah. Beulah! That's a name for a colored woman.

"Was his wife a Negro?" I asked.

"Are you crazy?" my wife said. "Have you just flipped or something?" She picked up a potato. I saw it hit the floor, then roll under the stove. "What's wrong with you?" she said. "Are you drunk?"

"I'm just asking," I said.

Right then my wife filled me in with more detail than I cared to know. I made a drink and sat at the kitchen table to listen. Pieces of the story began to fall into place.

Beulah had gone to work for the blind man the summer after my wife had stopped working for him. Pretty soon Beulah and the blind man had themselves a church wedding. It was a little wedding—who'd want to go to such a wedding in the first place?—just the two of them, plus the minister and the minister's wife. But it was a church wedding just the same. It was what Beulah had wanted, he'd said. But even then Beulah must have been carrying the cancer in her glands. After they had been inseparable for eight years—my wife's word, *inseparable*—Beulah's health went into a rapid decline. She died in a Seattle hospital room, the blind man sitting beside the bed and holding on to her hand. They'd married, lived and worked together, slept together—had sex, sure—and then the blind man had to bury her. All this without his having ever seen what the goddamned woman looked like. It was beyond my understanding. Hearing this, I felt sorry for the blind man for a little bit. And then I found myself thinking what a pitiful life this woman must have led. Imagine a woman who could never see herself as she was seen in the eyes of her loved one. A woman who could go on day after day and never receive the smallest compliment from her beloved. A woman whose husband could never read the expression on her face, be it misery or something better. Someone who could wear makeup or not—what difference to him? She could, if she wanted, wear green eyeshadow around one eye, a straight pin in her nostril, yellow slacks and purple shoes, no matter. And then to slip off into death, the blind man's hand on her hand, his blind eyes streaming tears—I'm imagining now—her last thought maybe this: that he never even knew what she looked like, and she on an express to the grave. Robert was left with a small insurance policy and half of a twenty-peso Mexican coin. The other half of the coin went into the box with her. Pathetic.

So when the time rolled around, my wife went to the depot to pick him up. With nothing to do but wait—sure, I blamed him for that—I was having a drink and watching the TV when I heard the car pull into the drive. I got up from the sofa with my drink and went to the window to have a look.

I saw my wife laughing as she parked the car. I saw her get out of the car and shut the door. She was still wearing a smile. Just amazing. She went around to the other side of the car to where the blind man was already starting to get out. This blind man, feature this, he was wearing a full beard! A beard on a blind man! Too much, I say. The blind man reached into the back seat and dragged out a suitcase. My wife took his arm, shut the car door, and, talking all the way, moved him down the drive and then up the steps to the front porch. I turned off the TV. I finished my drink, rinsed the glass, dried my hands. Then I went to the door.

My wife said, "I want you meet Robert. Robert, this is my husband. I've told you all about him." She was beaming. She had this blind man by his coat sleeve.

The blind man let go of his suitcase and up came his hand. I took it. He squeezed hard, held my hand, and then he let it go.

"I feel like we've already met," he boomed.

"Likewise," I said. I didn't know what else to say. Then I said. "Welcome. I've heard a lot about you." We began to move then, a little group, from the porch into the living room, my wife guiding him by the arm. The blind man was carrying his suitcase in his other hand. My wife said things like, "To your left here, Robert. That's right. Now watch it, there's a chair. That's it. Sit down right here. This is the sofa. We just bought this sofa two weeks ago."

I started to say something about the old sofa. I'd like that old sofa. But I didn't say anything. Then I wanted to say something else, small-talk, about the scenic ride along the Hudson. How going *to* New York, you should sit on the right-hand side of the train, and coming *from* New York, the left-hand side.

"Did you have a good train ride?" I said, "Which side of the train did you sit on, by the way?"

"What a question, which side!" my wife said. "What's it matter which side?" she said.

"I just asked," I said.

"Right side," the blind man said. "I hadn't been on a train in nearly forty years. Not since I was a kid. With my folks. That's been a long time. I'd nearly forgotten the sensation. I have winter in my beard now," he said. "So I've been told, anyway. Do I look distinguished, my dear?" the blind man said to my wife.

"You look distinguished, Robert," she said. "Robert," she said. "Robert, it's just so good to see you."

My wife finally took her eyes off the blind man and looked at me. I had the feeling she didn't like what she saw. I shrugged.

I've never met, or personally known, anyone who was blind. This blind man was late forties, a heavy-set, balding man with stooped shoulders, as if he carried a great weight there. He wore brown slacks, brown shoes, a light-brown shirt, a tie, a sports coat. Spiffy. He also had this full beard. But he didn't use a cane and he didn't wear dark glasses. I'd always thought dark glasses were a must for the blind. Fact was, I wished he had a pair. At first glance, his eyes looked like anyone else's eyes. But if you looked close, there was something different about them. Too much white in the iris, for one thing, and the pupils seemed to move round in the sockets without his knowing it or being able to stop it. Creepy. As I stared at his face, I saw the left pupil turn in toward his nose while the other made an effort to keep in one place. But it was only an effort, for that eye was on the roam without knowing it or wanting it to be.

I said, "Let me get you a drink. What's your pleasure? We have a little of everything. It's one of our pastimes."

"Bub, I'm a Scotch man myself," he said fast enough in this big voice.

"Right," I said. Bub! "Sure you are. I knew it."

He let his fingers touch his suitcase, which was sitting alongside the sofa. He was taking his bearings. I didn't blame him for that.

"I'll move that up to your room," my wife said.

"No, that's fine," the blind man said loudly. "It can go up when I go up."

"A little water with the Scotch?" I said.

"Very little," he said.

"I knew it," I said.

He said, "Just a tad. The Irish actor, Barry Fitzgerald? I'm like that fellow. When I drink water, Fitzgerald said, I drink water. When I drink whiskey, I drink whiskey." My wife laughed. The blind man brought his hand up under his beard. He lifted his beard slowly and let it drop.

I did the drinks, three big glasses of Scotch with a splash of water in each. Then we made ourselves comfortable and talked about Robert's travels. First the long flight from the West Coast to Connecticut, we covered that. Then from Connecticut up here by train. We had another drink concerning that leg of the trip.

I remembered having read somewhere that the blind didn't smoke because, as speculation had it, they couldn't see the smoke they exhaled. I thought I knew that much and that much only about blind people. But this blind man smoked his cigarette down to the nubbin and then lit another one. This blind man filled his ashtray and my wife emptied it.

When we sat down at the table for dinner, we had another drink. My wife heaped Robert's plate with cube steak, scalloped potatoes, green beans. I buttered him up two slices of bread. I said, "Here's bread and butter for you." I swallowed some of my drink. "Now let us pray," I said, and the blind man lowered his head. My wife looked at me, her mouth agape. "Pray the phone won't ring and the food doesn't get cold," I said.

We dug in. We ate everything there was to eat on the table. We ate like there was no tomorrow. We didn't talk. We ate. We scarfed. We grazed that table. We were into serious eating. The blind man had right away located his foods, he knew just where everything was on his plate. I watched with admiration as he used his knife and fork on the meat. He'd cut two pieces of meat, fork the meat into his mouth, and then go all out for the scalloped potatoes, the beans next, and then he'd tear off a hunk of buttered bread and eat that. He'd follow this up with a big drink of milk. It didn't seem to bother him to use his fingers once in a while, either.

We finished everything, including half a strawberry pie. For a few moments, we sat as if stunned. Sweat beaded on our faces. Finally, we got up from the table and left the dirty plates. We didn't look back. We took ourselves into the living room and sank into our places again. Robert and my wife sat on the sofa. I took the big chair. We had us two or three more drinks while they talked about the major things that had come to pass for them in the past ten yeas. For the most part, I just listened. Now and then I joined in. I didn't want him to think I'd left the room, and I didn't want her to think I was feeling left out. They talked of things that had happened to them—to them!—these past ten years. I waited in vain to hear my name on my wife's sweet lips: "And then my dear husband came into my life"—something like that. But I heard nothing of the sort. More talk of Robert. Robert had done a little of everything, it seemed, a regular blind jack-of-all trades. But most recently he and his wife had had an Amway distributorship, from which, I gathered, they'd earned their living, such as it was. The blind man was also a ham radio operator. He talked in his loud voice about conversations he'd had with fellow operators in Guam, in the Philippines, in Alaska, and even in Tahiti. He said he'd have a lot of friends there if he ever wanted to go visit those places. From time to time, he'd turn his blind face toward me, put his hand under his beard, ask me something. How long had I been in my present position? (Three years.) Did I like my work? (I didn't.) Was I going to stay with it? (What were the options?) Finally, when I thought he was beginning to run down, I got up and turned on the TV.

My wife looked at me with irritation. She was heading toward a boil. Then she looked at the blind man and sad, "Robert, do you have a TV?"

The blind man said, "My dear, I have two TVs. I have a color set and a black-and-white thing, an old relic. It's funny, but if I turn the TV on, and I'm always turning it on, I turn on the color set. It's funny, don't you think?"

I didn't know what to say to that. I had absolutely nothing to say to that. No opinion. So I watched the news program and tried to listen to what the announcer was saying.

"This is a color TV," the blind man said. "Don't ask me how, but I can tell."

"We traded up a while ago," I said.

The blind man had another taste of his drink. He lifted his beard, sniffed it, and let it fall. He leaned forward on the sofa. He positioned his ashtray on the coffee table, then put the lighter to his cigarette. He leaned back on the sofa and crossed his legs at the ankles.

My wife covered her mouth, and then she yawned. She stretched. She said, "I think I'll go upstairs and put on my robe. I think I'll change into something else. Robert, you make yourself comfortable," she said.

"I'm comfortable," the blind man said.

"I want you to feel comfortable in this house," she said.

"I am comfortable," the blind man said.

After she'd left the room, he and I listened to the weather report and then to the sports roundup. By that time, she'd been gone so long I didn't know if she was going to come back. I thought she might have gone to bed. I wished she'd come back downstairs. I didn't want to be left alone with a blind man. I asked him if he wanted another drink, and he said sure. Then I asked if he wanted to smoke some dope with me. I said I'd just rolled a number. I hadn't, but I planned to do so in about two shakes.

"I'll try some with you," he said.

"Damn right," I said. "That's the stuff."

I got our drinks and sat down on the sofa with him. Then I rolled us two fat numbers. I lit one and passed it. I brought it to his fingers. He took it and inhaled.

"Hold it as long as you can," I said. I could tell he didn't know the first thing.

My wife came back downstairs wearing her pink robe and her pink slippers.

"What do I smell?" she said.

"We thought we'd have us some cannabis," I said.

My wife gave me a savage look. Then she looked at the blind man and said, "Robert, I didn't know you smoked."

He said, "I do now, my dear. There's a first time for everything. But I don't feel anything yet."

"This stuff is pretty mellow," I said. "This stuff is mild. It's dope you can reason with," I said. "It doesn't mess you up."

"Not much it doesn't, bub," he said, and laughed.

My wife sat on the sofa between the blind man and me. I passed her the number. She took it and toked and then passed it back to me. "Which way is this going?" she said. Then she said, "I shouldn't be smoking this. I can hardly keep my eyes open as it is. That dinner did me in. I shouldn't have eaten so much."

"It was the strawberry pie," the blind man said. "That's what did it," he said, and he laughed his big laugh. Then he shook his head.

"There's more strawberry pie," I said.

"Do you want some more, Robert?" my wife said.

"Maybe in a little while," he said.

We gave out attention to the TV. My wife yawned again. She said, "Your bed is made up when you feel like going to bed, Robert. I know you must have had a long day. When you're ready to go to bed, say so." She pulled his arm. "Robert?"

He came to and said, "I've had a real nice time. This beats tapes, doesn't it?"

I said, "Coming at you," and I put the number between his fingers. He inhaled, held the smoke, and then let it go. It was like he'd been doing it since he was nine years old.

"Thanks, bub," he said. "But I think this is all for me. I think I'm beginning to feel it," he said. He held the burning roach out for my wife.

"Same here," she said. "Ditto. Me, too." She took the roach and passed it to me. "I may just sit here for a while between you two guys with my eyes closed. But don't let me bother you, okay? Either one of you. If it bothers you, say so. Otherwise, I may just sit here with my eyes closed until you're ready to go to bed," she said. "Your bed's made up, Robert, when you're ready. It's right next to our room at the top of the stairs. We'll show you up when you're ready. You wake me up now, you guys, if I fall asleep." She said that and then she closed her eyes and went to sleep.

The news program ended. I got up and changed the channel. I sat back down on the sofa. I wished my wife hadn't pooped out. Her head lay across the back of the sofa, her mouth open. She'd turned so that her robe had slipped away from her legs, exposing a juicy thigh. I reached to draw her robe back over her, and it was then that I glanced at the blind man. What the hell! I flipped the robe open again.

"You say when you want some strawberry pie," I said.

"I will," he said.

I said, "Are you tired? Do you want me to take you up to your bed? Are you ready to hit the hay?"

"Not yet," he said. "No, I'll stay up with you, bub. If that's all right. I'll stay up until you're ready to turn in. We haven't had a chance to talk. Know what I mean? I feel like me and her monopolized the evening." He lifted his beard and he let it fall. He picked up his cigarettes and his lighter.

"That's all right," I said. Then I said, "I'm glad for the company."

And I guess I was. Every night I smoked dope and stayed up as long as I could before I fell asleep. My wife and I hardly ever went to bed at the same time. When I did go to sleep, I had these dreams. Sometimes I'd wake up from one of them, my heart going crazy.

Something about the church and the Middle Ages was on the TV. Not your run-of-the-mill TV fare. I wanted to watch something else. I turned to the other channels. But there was nothing on them, either. So I turned back to the first channel and apologized.

"Bub, it's all right," the blind man said. "It's fine with me. Whatever you want to watch is okay. I'm always learning something. Learning never ends. It won't hurt me to learn something tonight. I got ears," he said.

We didn't say anything for a time. He was leaning forward with his head turned at me, his right ear aimed in the direction of the set. Very disconcerting. Now and then his eyelids drooped and then they snapped open again. Now and then he put his fingers into his beard and tugged, like he was thinking about something he was hearing on the television.

On the screen, a group of men wearing cowls was being set upon and tormented by men dressed in skeleton costumes and men dressed as devils. The men dressed as devils wore devil masks, horns, and long tails. This pageant was part of a procession. The Englishman who was narrating the thing said it took place in Spain once a year. I tried to explain to the blind man what was happening.

"Skeletons," he said. "I know about skeletons," he said, and he nodded.

The TV showed this one cathedral. Then there was a long, slow look at another one. Finally, the picture switched to the famous one in Paris, with its flying buttresses and its spires reaching up to the clouds. The camera pulled away to show the whole of the cathedral rising above the skyline.

There were times when the Englishman who was telling the thing would shut up, would simply let the camera move around over the cathedrals. Or else the camera would tour the countryside, men in fields walking behind oxen. I waited as long as I could. Then I felt I had to say something. I said, "They're showing the outside of this cathedral now. Gargoyles. Little statues carved to look like monsters. Now I guess they're in Italy. Yeah, they're in Italy. There's paintings on the walls of this one church."

"Are those fresco paintings, bub?" he asked, and he sipped from his drink.

I reached for my glass. But it was empty. I tried to remember what I could remember. "You're asking me are those frescoes?" I said. "That's a good question. I don't know."

The camera moved to a cathedral outside Lisbon. The differences in the Portuguese cathedral compared with the French and Italian were not that great. But they were there. Mostly the interior stuff. Then something occurred to me, and I said, "Something has occurred to me. Do you have any idea what a cathedral is? What they look like, that is? Do you follow me? If somebody says cathedral to you, do you have any notion what they're talking about? Do you know the difference between that and a Baptist church, say?"

He let the smoke dribble from his mouth. "I know they took hundreds of workers fifty or a hundred years to build," he said. "I just heard the man say that, of course. I know generations of the same families worked on a cathedral. I heard him say that, too. The men who began their life's work on them, they never lived to see the completion of their work. In that wise, bub, they're no different from the rest of us, right?" He laughed. Then his eyelids drooped again. His head nodded. He seemed to be snoozing. Maybe he was imagining himself in Portugal. The TV was showing another cathedral now. This one was in Germany. The Englishman's voice droned on. "Cathedrals," the blind man said. He sat up and rolled his head back and forth. "If you want the truth, bub, that's about all I know. What I just said. What I heard him say. But maybe you could describe one to me? I wish you'd do it. I'd like that. If you want to know, I really don't have a good idea."

I stared hard at the shot of the cathedral on the TV. How could I even begin to describe it? But say my life depended on it. Say my life was being threatened by an insane guy who said I had to do it or else.

I stared some more at the cathedral before the picture flipped off into the countryside. There was no use. I turned to the blind man and said, "To begin with, they're very tall." I was looking around the room for clues. "They reach way up. Up and up. Toward the sky. They're so big, some of them, they have to have these supports. To help hold them up, so to speak. These supports are called buttresses. They remind me of viaducts, for some reason. But maybe you don't know viaducts, either? Sometimes the cathedrals have devils and such carved into the front. Sometimes lords and ladies. Don't ask me why this is," I said.

He was nodding. The whole upper part of his body seemed to be moving back and forth.

"I'm not doing so good, am I?" I said.

He stopped nodding and leaned forward on the edge of the sofa. As he listened to me, he was running his fingers through his beard. I wasn't getting through to him, I could see that. But he waited for me to go on just the same. He nodded, like he was trying to encourage me. I tried to think what else to say. "They're really big," I said. "They're massive. They're built of stone. Marble, too, sometimes. In those olden days, when they built cathedrals, men wanted to be closed to God. In those olden days, God was an important part of everyone's life. You could tell this from their cathedral-building. I'm sorry," I said, "but it looks like that's the best I can do for you. I'm just no good at it."

"That's all right, bub," the blind man said. "Hey, listen. I hope you don't mind my asking you. Can I ask you something? Let me ask you a simple question, yes or no. I'm just curious and there's no offense. You're my host. But let me ask if you are in any way religious? You don't mind my asking?"

I shook my head. He couldn't see that, though. A wink is the same as a nod to a blind man. "I guess I don't believe in it. In anything. Sometimes it's hard. You know what I'm saying?"

"Sure, I do," he said.

"Right," I said.

The Englishman was still holding forth. My wife sighed in her sleep. She drew a long breath and went on with her sleeping.

"You'll have to forgive me," I said. "But I can't tell you what a cathedral looks like. It just isn't in me to do it. I can't do any more than I've done."

The blind man sat very still, his head down, as he listened to me.

I said, "The truth is, cathedrals don't mean anything special to me. Nothing. Cathedrals. They're something to look at on late-night TV. That's all they are."

It was then that the blind man cleared his throat. He brought something up. He took a handkerchief from his back pocket. Then he said. "I get it, bub. It's okay. It happens. Don't worry about it," he said. "Hey, listen to me. Will you do me a favor? I got an idea. Why don't you find us some heavy paper? And a pen. We'll do something. We'll draw one together. Get us a pen and some heavy paper. Go on, bub, get the stuff," he said.

So I went upstairs. My legs felt like they didn't have any strength in them. They felt like they did after I'd done some running. In my wife's room, I looked around. I found some ballpoints in a little basket on her table. And then I tried to think where to look for the kind of paper he was talking about.

Downstairs, in the kitchen, I found a shopping bag with onion skins in the bottom of the bag. I emptied the bag and shook it. I brought it into the living room and sat down with it near his legs. I moved some things, smoothed the wrinkles from the bag, spread it out on the coffee table.

The blind man got down from the sofa and sat next to me on the carpet.

He ran his fingers over the paper. He went up and down the sides of the paper. The edges, even the edges. He fingered the corners.

"All right," he said. "All right, let's do her."

He found my hand, the hand with the pen. He closed his hand over my hand. "Go ahead, bub, draw," he said. "Draw. You'll see. I'll follow along with you. It'll be okay. Just begin now like I'm telling you. You'll see. Draw," the blind man said.

So I began. First I drew a box that looked like a house. It could have been the house I lived in. Then I put a roof on it. At either end of the roof, I drew spires. Crazy.

"Swell," he said. "Terrific. You're doing fine," he said. "Never thought anything like this could happen in your lifetime, did you, bub? Well, it's a strange life, we all know that. Go on now. Keep it up."

I put in windows with arches. I drew flying buttresses. I hung great doors. I couldn't stop. The TV station went off the air. I put down the pen and closed and opened my fingers. The blind man felt around over the paper. He moved the tips of his fingers over the paper, all over what I had drawn, and he nodded.

"Doing fine," the blind man said.

I took up the pen again, and he found my hand. I kept at it. I'm no artist. But I kept drawing just the same.

My wife opened up her eyes and gazed at us. She sat up on the sofa, her robe hanging open. She said, "What are you doing? Tell me, I want to know."

I didn't answer her.

The blind man said, "We're drawing a cathedral. Me and him are working on it. Press hard," he said to me. "That's right. That's good," he said. "Sure. You got it, bub. I can tell. You didn't think you could. But you can, can't you? You're cooking with gas now. You know what I'm saying? We're going to really have us something here in a minute. How's the old arm?" he said. "Put some people in there now. What's a cathedral without people?"

My wife said, "What's going on? Robert, what are you doing? What's going on?"

"It's all right," he said to her. "Close your eyes now," the blind man said to me.

I did it. I closed them just like he said.

"Are they closed?" he said. "Don't fudge."

"They're closed," I said.

"Keep them that way," he said. He said, "Don't stop now. Draw."

So we kept on with it. His fingers rode my fingers as my hand went over the paper. It was like nothing else in my life up to now.

Then he said, "I think that's it. I think you got it," he said. "Take a look. What do you think?"

But I had my eyes closed. I thought I'd keep them that way for a little longer. I thought it was something I ought to do.

"Well?" he said. "Are you looking?"

My eyes were still closed. I was in my house. I knew that. But I didn't feel like I was inside anything.

"It's really something," I said.

CRITICAL THINKING QUESTIONS

1. The narrator undergoes a transformation at the end of the story as he sits drawing with the blind man on the carpet. Do people actually gain insight in an instant as happens here, or is such a change more likely to occur in fiction?

2. Although teachers like to think education helps make human beings more sensitive to the needs of others, is that always the case? From your *personal experience,* how do you think people learn compassion? Can it be taught?

WRITING TOPIC

Write a brief personal experience essay about a time in your life when you gained insight into something. What had your attitude been previously? What triggered the insight? How did your attitude change?

Edwidge Danticat

The Book of the Dead

My father is gone. I am slouched in a cast-aluminum chair across from two men, one the manager of the hotel where we're staying and the other a policeman. They are waiting for me to explain what has become of him, my father.

The manager—"Mr. Flavio Salinas," the plaque on his office door reads—has the most striking pair of chartreuse eyes I have ever seen on a man with an island-Spanish lilt to his voice.

The officer is a baby-faced, short white Floridian with a pot belly.

"Where are you and your daddy from, Ms. Bienaimé?" he asks.

I answer "Haiti," even though I was born and raised in East Flatbush, Brooklyn, and have never visited my parents' birthplace. I do this because it is one more thing I have longed to have in common with my parents.

The officer plows forward. "You down here in Lakeland from Haiti?"

"We live in New York. We were on our way to Tampa."

I find Manager Salinas's office gaudy. The walls are covered with orange-and-green wallpaper, briefly interrupted by a giant gold-leaf-bordered print of a Victorian cottage that somehow resembles the building we're in. Patting his light-green tie, he whispers reassuringly, "Officer Bo and I will do the best we can to help you find your father."

We start out with a brief description: "Sixty-four, five feet eight inches, two hundred and twenty pounds, moon-faced, with thinning salt-and-pepper hair. Velvet-brown eyes—"

"Velvet-brown?" says Officer Bo.

"Deep brown—same color as his complexion."

My father has had partial frontal dentures for ten years, since he fell off his and my mother's bed when his prison nightmares began. I mention that, too. Just the dentures, not the nightmares. I also bring up the claw-shaped marks that run from his left ear down along his cheek to the corner of his mouth—the only visible reminder of the year he spent at Fort Dimanche, the Port-au-Prince prison ironically named after the Lord's Day.

"Does your daddy have any kind of mental illness, senility?" asks Officer Bo.

"No."

"Do you have any pictures of your daddy?"

I feel like less of a daughter because I'm not carrying a photograph in my wallet. I had hoped to take some pictures of him on our trip. At one of the rest stops I bought a disposable camera and pointed it at my father. No, no, he had protested, covering his face with both hands like a little boy protecting his cheeks from a slap. He did not want any more pictures taken of him for the rest of his life. He was feeling too ugly.

"That's too bad," says Officer Bo. "Does he speak English, your daddy? He can ask for directions, et cetera?"

"Yes."

"Is there anything that might make your father run away from you—particularly here in Lakeland?" Manager Salinas interjects. "Did you two have a fight?"

I had never tried to tell my father's story in words before now, but my first sculpture of him was the reason for our trip: a two-foot-high mahogany figure of my father, naked, crouching on the floor, his back arched like the curve of a crescent moon, his downcast eyes fixed on his short stubby fingers and the wide palms of his hands. It was hardly revolutionary, minimalist at best, but it was my favorite of all my attempted representations of him. It was the way I had imagined him in prison.

The last time I had seen my father? The previous night, before falling asleep. When we pulled into the pebbled driveway, densely lined with palm and banana trees, it was almost midnight. All the restaurants in the area were closed. There was nothing to do but shower and go to bed.

"It is like a paradise here," my father said when he saw the room. It had the same orange-and-green wallpaper as Salinas's office, and the plush green carpet matched the walls. "Look, Annie," he said, "it is like grass under our feet." He was always searching for a glimpse of paradise, my father.

He picked the bed closest to the bathroom, removed the top of his gray jogging suit, and unpacked his toiletries. Soon after, I heard him humming, as he always did, in the shower.

After he got into bed, I took a bath, pulled my hair back in a ponytail, and checked on the sculpture—just felt it a little bit through the bubble padding and carton wrapping to make sure it wasn't broken. Then I slipped under the covers, closed my eyes, and tried to sleep.

I pictured the client to whom I was delivering the sculpture: Gabrielle Fonteneau, a young woman about my age, an actress on a nationally syndicated television series. My friend Jonas, the principal at the East Flatbush elementary school where I teach drawing to fifth graders, had shown her a picture of my "Father" sculpture, and, the way Jonas told it, Gabrielle Fonteneau had fallen in love with it and wished to offer it as a gift to her father on his birthday.

Since this was my first big sale, I wanted to make sure that the piece got there safely. Besides, I needed a weekend away, and both my mother and I figured that my father, who watched a lot of television, both in his barbershop and at home, would enjoy meeting Gabrielle, too. But when I woke up the next morning my father was gone.

I showered, put on my driving jeans and a T-shirt, and waited. I watched a half hour of midmorning local news, smoked three mentholated cigarettes even though we were in a nonsmoking room, and waited some more. By noon, four hours had gone by. And it was only then that I noticed that the car was still there but the sculpture was gone.

I decided to start looking for my father: in the east garden, the west garden, the dining room, the exercise room, and in the few guest rooms cracked open while the maid changed the sheets; in the little convenience store at the Amoco gas station nearby; even in the Salvation Army thrift shop that from a distance seemed to blend into the interstate. All that waiting and looking actually took six hours, and I felt guilty for having held back so long before going to the front desk to ask, "Have you seen my father?"

I feel Officer Bo's fingers gently stroking my wrist. Up close he smells like fried eggs and gasoline, like breakfast at the Amoco. "I'll put the word out with the other boys," he says. "Salinas here will be in his office. Why don't you go back to your room in case he shows up there?"

I return to the room and lie in the unmade bed, jumping up when I hear the click from the electronic key in the door. It's only the housekeeper. I turn down the late-afternoon cleaning and call my mother at the beauty salon where she perms, presses, and braids hair, next door to my father's barbershop. But she isn't there. So I call my parents' house and leave the hotel number on their machine. "Please call me as soon as you can, Manman. It's about Papi."

Once, when I was twelve, I overheard my mother telling a young woman who was about to get married how she and my father had first met on the sidewalk in front of Fort Dimanche the evening that my father was released from jail. (At a dance, my father had fought with a soldier out of uniform who had him arrested and thrown in prison for a year.) That night, my mother was returning home from a sewing class when he stumbled out of the prison gates and collapsed into her arms, his face still bleeding from his last beating. They married and left for New York a year later. "We were like two seeds planted in a rock," my mother had told the young woman, "but somehow when our daughter, Annie, came we took root."

My mother soon calls me back, her voice staccato with worry.
"Where is Papi?"
"I lost him."
"How you lost him?"
"He got up before I did and disappeared."
"How long he been gone?"
"Eight hours," I say, almost not believing myself that it's been that long.
My mother is clicking her tongue and humming. I can see her sitting at the kitchen table, her eyes closed, her fingers sliding up and down her flesh-colored stockinged legs.
"You call police?"
"Yes."
"What they say?"
"To wait, that he'll come back."

My mother is thumping her fingers against the phone's mouthpiece, which is giving me a slight ache in my right ear.

"Tell me where you are," she says. "Two more hours and he's not there, call me, I come."

I dial Gabrielle Fonteneau's cellular-phone number. When she answers, her voice sounds just as it does on television, but more silken and seductive without the sitcom laugh track.

"To think," my father once said while watching her show, "Haitan-born actresses on American television."

"And one of them wants to buy my stuff," I'd added.

When she speaks, Gabrielle Fonteneau sounds as if she's in a place with cicadas, waterfalls, palm trees, and citronella candles to keep the mosquitoes away. I realize that I, too, am in such a place, but I can't appreciate it.

"So nice of you to come all this way to deliver the sculpture," she says. "Jonas tell you why I like it so much? My papa was a journalist in Port-au-Prince. In 1975, he wrote a story criticizing the dictatorship, and he was arrested and put in jail."

"Fort Dimanche?"

"No, another one," she says. "Caserne. Papa kept track of days there by scraping lines with his fingernails on the walls of his cell. One of the guards didn't like this, so he pulled out all his fingernails with pliers."

I think of the photo spread I saw in the *Haitian Times* of Gabrielle Fonteneau and her parents in their living room in Tampa. Her father was described as a lawyer, his daughter's manager; her mother a court stenographer. There was no hint in that photograph of what had once happened to the father. Perhaps people don't see anything in my father's face, either, in spite of his scars.

"We celebrate his birthday on the day he was released from prison," she says. "It's the hands I love so much in your sculpture. They're so strong."

I am drifting away from Gabrielle Fonteneau when I hear her say, "So when will you get here? You have instructions from Jonas, right? Maybe we can make you lunch. My mother makes great *lanbi*."

"I'll be there at twelve tomorrow," I say. "My father is with me. We are making a little weekend vacation of this."

My father loves museums. When he isn't working in his barbershop, he's often at the Brooklyn Museum. The ancient Egyptian rooms are his favorites.

"The Egyptians, they was like us," he likes to say. The Egyptians worshipped their gods in many forms and were often ruled by foreigners. The pharaohs were like the dictators he had fled. But what he admires most about the Egyptians is the way they mourned.

"Yes, they grieve," he'll say. He marvels at the mummification that went on for weeks, resulting in bodies that survived thousands of years.

My whole adult life, I have struggled to find the proper manner of sculpting my father, a man who learned about art by standing with me most of the Saturday mornings of my childhood, mesmerized by the golden masks, the shawabtis, and Osiris, ruler of the underworld.

When my father finally appears in the hotel-room doorway, I am awed by him. Smiling, he looks like a much younger man, further bronzed after a long day at the beach.

"Annie, let your father talk to you." He walks over to my bed, bends down to unlace his sneakers. "*On ti koze*, a little chat."

"Where were you? Where is the sculpture, Papi?" I feel my eyes twitching, a nervous reaction I inherited from my mother.

"That's why we need to chat," he says. "I have objections with your statue."

He pulls off his sneakers and rubs his feet with both hands.

"I don't want you to sell that statue," he says. Then he picks up the phone and calls my mother.

"I know she called you," he says to her in Creole. "Her head is so hot. She panics so easily. I was just out walking, thinking."

I hear my mother lovingly scolding him and telling him not to leave me again. When he hangs up the phone, he picks up his sneakers and puts them back on.

"Where is the sculpture?" My eyes are twitching so hard now that I can barely see.

"Let us go," he says. "I will take you to it."

As my father maneuvers the car out of the parking lot, I tell myself he might be ill, mentally ill, even though I have never detected anything wrong beyond his prison nightmares. I am trying to piece it together, this sudden yet familiar picture of a parent's vulnerability. When I was ten yeas old and my father had the chicken pox, I overheard him say to a friend on the phone, "The doctor tells me that at my age chicken pox can kill a man." This was the first time I realized that my father could die. I looked up the word "kill" in every dictionary and encyclopedia at school, trying to comprehend what it meant, that my father could be eradicated from my life.

My father stops the car on the side of the highway near a manmade lake, one of those artificial creations of the modern tropical city, with curved stone benches surrounding stagnant water. There is little light to see by except a half-moon. He heads toward one of the benches, and I sit down next to him, letting my hands dangle between my legs.

"Is this where the sculpture is?" I ask.

"In the water," he says.

"O.K.," I say. "But please know this about yourself. You are an especially harsh critic."

My father tries to smother a smile.

"Why?" I ask.

He scratches his chin. Anger is a wasted emotion, I've always thought. My parents got angry at unfair politics in New York or Port-au-Prince, but they never got angry at my grades—at all the B's I got in everything but art classes—or at my not eating vegetables or occasionally vomiting my daily spoonful of cod-liver oil.

Ordinary anger, I thought, was a weakness. But now I am angry. I want to hit my father, beat the craziness out of his head.

"Annie," he says. "When I first saw your statue, I wanted to be buried with it, to take it with me into the other world."

"Like the ancient Egyptians," I say.

He smiles, grateful, I think, that I still recall his passions.

"Annie," he asks, "do you remember when I read to you from 'The Book of the Dead'?"

"Are you dying?" I say to my father. "Because I can only forgive you for this if you are. You can't take this back."

He is silent for a moment too long.

I think I hear crickets, though I cannot imagine where they might be. There is the highway, the cars racing by, the half-moon, the lake dug up from the depths of the ground, the allée of royal palms beyond. And there is me and my father.

"You remember the judgment of the dead," my father says, "when the heart of a person is put on a scale. If it is heavy, then this person cannot enter the other world."

It is a testament to my upbringing that I am not yelling at him.

"I don't deserve a statue," he says, even while looking like one: the Madonna of Humility, for example, contemplating her losses in the dust.

"Annie, your father was the hunter," he says. "He was not the prey."

"What are you saying?" I ask.

"We have a proverb," he says. "'One day for the hunter, one day for the prey.' Your father was the hunter. He was not the prey." Each word is hard won as it leaves my father's mouth, balanced like those hearts on the Egyptian scale.

"Annie, when I saw your mother the first time, I was not just out of prison. I was a guard in the prison. One of the prisoners I was questioning had scratched me with a piece of tin. I went out to the street in a rage, blood all over my face. I was about to go back and do something bad, very bad. But instead comes your mother. I smash into her, and she asks me what I am doing there. I told her I was just let go from prison and she held my face and cried in my hair."

"And the nightmares, what are they?"

"Of what I, your father, did to others."

"Does Manman know?"

"I told her, Annie, before we married."

I am the one who drives back to the hotel. In the car, he says, "Annie, I am still your father, still your mother's husband. I would not do these things now.

When we get back to the hotel room, I leave a message for Officer Bo, and another for Manager Salinas, telling them that I have found my father. He has slipped into the bathroom, and now he runs the shower at full force. When it seems that he is never coming out, I call my mother at home in Brooklyn.

"How do you love him?" I whisper into the phone.

My mother is tapping her fingers against the mouthpiece.

"I don't know, Annie," she whispers back, as though there is a chance that she might also be overheard by him. "I feel only that you and me, we saved him. When

I met him, it made him stop hurting the people. This is how I see it. He was a seed thrown into a rock, and you and me, Annie, we helped push a flower out of a rock."

When I get up the next morning, my father is already dressed. He is sitting on the edge of his bed with his back to me, his head bowed, his face buried in his hands. If I were sculpting him, I would make him a praying mantis, crouching motionless, seeming to pray while waiting to strike.

With his back still turned, my father says, "Will you call those people and tell them you have it no more, the statue?"

"We were invited to lunch there. I believe we should go."

He raises his shoulders and shrugs. It is up to me.

The drive to Gabrielle Fonteneau's house seems longer than the twenty-four hours it took to drive from New York: the ocean, the palms along the road, the highway so imposingly neat. My father fills in the silence in the car by saying, "So now you know, Annie, why your mother and me, we have never returned home."

The Fonteneaus' house is made of bricks of white coral, on a cul-de-sac with a row of banyans separating the two sides of the street.

Silently, we get out of the car and follow a concrete path to the front door. Before we can knock, an older woman walks out. Like Gabrielle, she has stunning midnight-black eyes and skin the color of sorrel, with spiralling curls brushing the sides of her face. When Gabrielle's father joins her, I realize where Gabrielle Fonteneau gets her height. He is more than six feet tall.

Mr. Fonteneau extends his hands, first to my father and then to me. They're large, twice the size of my father's. The fingernails have grown back, thick, densely dark, as though the past had nestled itself there in black ink.

We move slowly through the living room, which has a cathedral ceiling and walls covered with Haitan paintings—Obin, Hyppolite, Tiga, Duval-Carrié. Out on the back terrace, which towers over a nursery of orchids and red dracaenas, a table is set for lunch.

Mr. Fonteneau asks my father where his family is from in Haiti, and my father lies. In the past, I thought he always said a different province because he had lived in all those places, but I realize now that he says this to keep anyone from tracing him, even though twenty-six years and eighty more pounds shield him from the threat of immediate recognition.

When Gabrielle Fonteneau makes her entrance, in an off-the-shoulder ruby dress, my father and I stand up.

"Gabrielle," she says, when she shakes hands with my father, who blurts out spontaneously, "You are one of the flowers of Haiti."

Gabrielle Fonteneau tilts her head coyly.

"We eat now," Mrs. Fonteneau announces, leading me and my father to a bathroom to wash up before the meal. Standing before a pink seashell-shaped sink, my father and I dip our hands under the faucet flow.

"Annie," my father says, "we always thought, your mother and me, that children could raise their parents higher. Look at what this girl has done for her parents."

During the meal of conch, plantains, and mushroom rice, Mr. Fonteneau tries to draw my father into conversation. He asks when my father was last in Haiti.

"Twenty-six years," my father replies.

"No going back for you?" asks Mrs. Fonteneau.

"I have not had the opportunity," my father says.

"We go back every year to a beautiful place overlooking the ocean in the mountains in Jacmel," says Mrs. Fonteneau.

"Have you ever been to Jacmel?" Gabrielle Fonteneau asks me.

I shake my head no.

"We are fortunate," Mrs. Fonteneau says, "that we have another place to go where we can say our rain is sweeter, our dust is lighter, our beach is prettier."

"So now we are tasting rain and weighing dust," Mr. Fonteneau says, and laughs.

"There is nothing like drinking the sweet juice from a green coconut you fetched yourself from your own tree, or sinking your hand in sand from the beach in your own country," Mrs. Fonteneau says.

"When did you ever climb a coconut tree?" Mr. Fonteneau says, teasing his wife.

I am imagining what my father's nightmares might be. Maybe he dreams of dipping his hands in the sand on a beach in his own country and finds that what he comes up with is a fist full of blood.

After lunch, my father asks if he can have a closer look at the Fonteneaus' backyard garden. While he's taking the tour, I confess to Gabrielle Fonteneau that I don't have the sculpture.

"My father threw it away," I say.

Gabrielle Fonteneau frowns.

"I don't know," she says. "Was there even a sculpture at all? I trust Jonas, but maybe you fooled him, too. Is this some scam, to get into our home?"

"There was a sculpture," I say. "Jonas will tell you that. My father just didn't like it, so he threw it away."

She raises her perfectly arched eyebrows, perhaps out of concern for my father's sanity or my own.

"I'm really disappointed," she says. "I wanted it for a reason. My father goes home when he looks at a piece of art. He goes home deep inside himself. For a long time, he used to hide his fingers from people. It's like he was making a fist all the time. I wanted to give him this thing so that he knows we understand what happened to him."

"I am truly sorry," I say.

Over her shoulders, I see her parents guiding my father through rows of lemongrass. I want to promise her that I will make her another sculpture, one especially modelled on her father. But I don't know when I will be able to work on anything again. I have lost my subject, the father I loved as well as pitied.

In the garden, I watch my father snap a white orchid from its stem and hold it out toward Mrs. Fonteneau, who accepts it with a nod of thanks.

"I don't understand," Gabrielle Fonteneau says. "You did all this for nothing."

I wave to my father to signal that we should perhaps leave now, and he comes toward me, the Fonteneaus trailing slowly behind him.

With each step he rubs the scars on the side of his face.

Perhaps the last person my father harmed had dreamed this moment into my father's future—his daughter seeing those marks, like chunks of warm plaster still clinging to a cast, an questioning him about them, giving him a chance to either lie or tell the truth. After all, we have the proverb, as my father would say: "Those who give the blows may try to forget, but those who carry the scars must remember."

CRITICAL THINKING QUESTIONS

1. Certainly the parents lied to their daughter about the father's deeds. But what if they had told the truth to their daughter from the very beginning? Would the truth then have been any less devastating to the father–daughter relationship? Maybe the truth is not always what children need. We grow up learning to value telling the truth, but can you argue that there are times when lying is the better course within families, communities, and countries? Make a *syllogism* (see Chapter One) that expresses your reasoning for a particular situation (generalization, example, conclusion).

2. Can people change and deserve to be forgiven for their past deeds? Are some deeds beyond forgiveness?

Nadine Gordimer

Terminal

"Even the cat buries its dirt; I carry mine around with me." She thought of saying it aloud many times in the weeks after she came home from the hospital. She did not know if he would decide to laugh—whether they would go so far as to laugh. The only time the existence of such a contraption had ever been mentioned by them before the illness happened was a few years ago, when—exchanging sheets of newspaper as they usually did, lovely weekend mornings in bed—she had been reading some article about unemployment and teenage prostitutes, and had remarked to him, my God, the job the welfare people found for this girl was in a factory that makes those rubber bag things for people who have to have their stomachs cut out—no wonder she went on the streets, poor little wretch. . . .

She remembered that morning, that newspaper, clearly. More and more of their conversation kept coming back. They had drifted to talk about the dreariness of industrialization; how early Marxists had ascribed this to alienation, which would disappear when the means of production were owned by the workers, but the factories of the Soviet Union and China were surely just as dreary as those of the West? And she remembered she had reminded him (they had visited Peking together) that at least the Chinese factory workers had ten-minute breaks for compulsory calisthenics twice a day—and he had said, would you swap that for a tea break and a fag?

The rubber thing that went past on the assembly belt before the sixteen-year-old future prostitute was remote from the two of them, laughing in bed on a Sunday morning, as the life of any factory worker.

Now the contraption was attached to her own body. It issued from her, from the small wound hidden under her clothing. She had moved from their shared bed and he understood without a word. She had been taught at the hospital how to deal with the thing, it was horribly private in a way natural functions were not, since natural functions were—had been—experienced by them both. She was alone with her dirt.

The doctors said the thing would be taken away in time. Six weeks, the first one predicted, not more than three months was what the second one told her. They should have coordinated their fairy story. They said that (after six weeks or three months) everything would be reconnected inside her. The wound that was kept open would be sewn up. She would be whole again, repaired, everything would work. She would go back to her teaching at the music school. She could go back there now—why not?—if she wanted to, so long as she didn't tire herself. But she didn't want to, carrying that thing with her. She had to listen to more stories—from encouraging friends—about how wonderfully other people managed, lived perfectly

534

normal lives. Even a member of the British royal family, it was said. She shut them up with the fairy story, saying, but for me it's only for six weeks (or three months), I don't have to manage. He bought her two beautiful caftans, choosing them himself, and so perfectly right for her, just her colors, her style—in her pleasure she forgot (which she knew later was exactly what he hoped) she would be wearing them to cover that thing. She put on one or the other when the friends came to visit, and her outfit was admired, they said she must be malingering, she looked so marvelous. He confirmed to them that she was making good progress.

They had talked, once, early on. They had talked before that, in their lives, in the skein of their mingled lives—but how impersonal it was, really, then! A childish pact, blood-brotherhood; on a par with that endlessly rhetorical question, d'you love me, will you always love me: if either of us were to be incurably ill, neither would let the other suffer, would they? But when it happens—well, it never happens. Not in that silly, dramatic, clear-cut abstraction. Who can say what is "incurable"? Who can be sure what suffering is terminal, not worth prolonging in order to survive it? This one had a breast off twenty years ago, and is still going to the races every week. That one lost his prostate, can be seen knocking back gin-and-tonics at any cocktail party, with his third wife.

But just before she went into the hospital for the exploratory operation she found the time and place to reaffirm. "If it turns out to be bad, if it gets very bad . . . at any time, you promise you'll help me out of it. I would do it for you." He couldn't speak. She was lying with him in the dark; he nodded so hard the pact was driven into her shoulder by his chin. The bone hurt her. Then he made love to her, entering her body in covenant.

After the operation she found the tube leading out of her, the contraption. They did not talk again; only of cheerful things, only of getting better. The thing—the wound it issued from, that, unlike any other wound, couldn't be allowed to close, was like a contingent love affair concealed in his life or hers whose weight would tear their integument if admitted. They smiled at each other at once, every time their eyes met. It couldn't be borne, after all. There had to be a fairy story. It was told over and over, every day, in every plan they made for next week or next month or next year, never blinking an eyelid; in every assumption of continuing daily life neither believed. There were no words that were not lies. *Did the groceries come. There's been another hijacking. Are you all right in that chair. They say the election's set for Spring. We need new wine glasses. I should write letters. Order coffee and matches. Another crisis in the Middle East. Draw the curtains, the sun's in your eyes. I must have my hair done, Thursday.* If she took his hand now, it was only in the lie of immortality. The flesh, therefore, was not real for them anymore.

There was only one thing left that could not, by its very nature, have become a lie. There was only one place where love could survive: life was betrayed, but the covenant was not with life.

He drove her to the hairdresser that Thursday afternoon and when he came to fetch her he told her she looked pretty. She thanked him awkwardly as a girl with her first compliment. Beneath it she was overcome—the first strong emotion except fear and disgust, for many months—by an overwhelming trust in him. That night, alone in the room that was now her bedroom she counted out the hoarded pills and, before she washed them down with plain water, set under the paper-weight of her cigarette lighter her note for him. "Keep your promise. Don't have me revived."

Ever since she was a child she had understood it as a deep sleep, that's all. Ever since she saw the first bird, lying under a hedge, whose eyes hadn't opened when it was poked with a twig. But one can only be aware of a sleep as one awakens from it, and so one will never be aware of that deep sleep—she had no fear of death but now she had the terror of feeling herself waking from it, herself coming back from what was not death at all, then, could not be. Her eyelids were rosy blinds through which light glowed. She opened them on the glossy walls of a hospital room. There was a hand in hers; his.

CRITICAL THINKING QUESTIONS

1. The friend obviously does not fulfill his promise, his obligation. Is that a violation of the trust placed in him?

2. Occasionally one reads of an elderly person who kills his or her spouse to ease his or her suffering. Such an act conflicts with forces in our society that argue against it (the courts, religious teachings). Under what *premises* do individuals act who choose to ignore these forces?

WRITING TOPIC

Is "mercy killing" (or active euthanasia) justifiable? Do some research on the topic (you can use "physician-assisted suicide" as a search term as well). Based on your study of your research and some literature selections in this chapter, write your own argument that defends or refutes the ethical and moral justification of active euthanasia (also see Olds's poem, "The Promise").

Nathaniel Hawthorne

The Maypole of Merry Mount

There is an admirable foundation for a philosophic romance in the curious history of the early settlement of Mount Wollaston, or Merry Mount. In the slight sketch here attempted, the facts, recorded on the grave pages of our New England annalists, have wrought themselves, almost spontaneously, into a sort of allegory. The masques, mummeries, and festive customs, described in the text, are in accordance with the manners of the age. Authority on these points may be found in Strutt's Book of English Sports and Pastimes.

Bright were the days at Merry Mount, when the Maypole was the banner staff of that gay colony! They who reared it, should their banner be triumphant, were to pour sunshine over New England's rugged hills, and scatter flower seeds throughout the soil. Jollity and gloom were contending for an empire. Midsummer eve had come, bringing deep verdure to the forest, and roses in her lap, of a more vivid hue than the tender buds of Spring. But May, or her mirthful spirit, dwelt all the year round at Merry Mount, sporting with the Summer months, and revelling with Autumn, and basking in the glow of Winter's fireside. Through a world of toil and care she flitted with a dreamlike smile, and came hither to find a home among the lightsome hearts of Merry Mount.

Never had the Maypole been so gayly decked as at sunset on midsummer eve. This venerated emblem was a pine-tree, which had preserved the slender grace of youth, while it equalled the loftiest height of the old wood monarchs. From its top streamed a silken banner, colored like the rainbow. Down nearly to the ground the pole was dressed with birchen boughs, and others of the liveliest green, and some with silvery leaves, fastened by ribbons that fluttered in fantastic knots of twenty different colors, but no sad ones. Garden flowers, and blossoms of the wilderness, laughed gladly forth amid the verdure, so fresh and dewy that they must have grown by magic on that happy pine-tree. Where this green and flowery splendor terminated, the shaft of the Maypole was stained with the seven brilliant hues of the banner at its top. On the lowest green bough hung an abundant wreath of roses, some that had been gathered in the sunniest spots of the forest, and others, of still richer blush, which the colonists had reared from English seed. O, people of the Golden Age, the chief of your husbandry was to raise flowers!

But what was the wild throng that stood hand in hand about the Maypole? It could not be that the fauns and nymphs, when driven from their classic groves and homes of ancient fable, had sought refuge, as all the persecuted did, in the fresh woods of the West. These were Gothic monsters, though perhaps of Grecian ancestry. On the shoulders of a comely youth uprose the head and branching antlers of a stag; a second, human in all other points, had the grim visage of a wolf; a third, still with the trunk and limbs of a mortal man, showed the beard and horns of a venerable he-goat. There was the likeness of a bear erect, brute in all but his hind legs, which were adorned with pink silk stockings. And here again, almost as wondrous, stood a real bear of the dark forest, lending each of his fore paws to the grasp of a human hand, and as ready for the dance as any in that circle. His inferior nature rose half way, to meet his companions as they stooped. Other faces wore the similitude of man or woman, but distorted or extravagant, with red noses pendulous before their mouths, which seemed of awful depth, and stretched from ear to ear in an eternal fit of laughter. Here might be seen the Savage Man, well known in heraldry, hairy as a baboon, and girdled with green leaves. By his side, a noble figure, but still a counterfeit, appeared an Indian hunter, with feathery crest and wampum belt. Many of this strange company wore foolscaps, and had little bells appended to their garments, tinkling with a silvery sound, responsive to the inaudible music of their gleesome spirits. Some youths and maidens were of soberer garb, yet well maintained their places in the irregular throng by the expression of wild revelry upon their features. Such were the colonists of Merry Mount, as they stood in the broad smile of sunset round their venerated Maypole.

Had a wanderer, bewildered in the melancholy forest, heard their mirth, and stolen a half-affrighted glance, he might have fancied them the crew of Comus, some already transformed to brutes, some midway between man and beast, and the others rioting in the flow of tipsy jollity that foreran the change. But a band of Puritans, who watched the scene, invisible themselves, compared the masques to those devils and ruined souls with whom their superstition peopled the black wilderness.

Within the ring of monsters appeared the two airiest forms that had ever trodden on any more solid footing than a purple and golden cloud. One was a youth in glistening apparel, with a scarf of the rainbow pattern crosswise on his breast. His right hand held a gilded staff, the ensign of high dignity among the revellers, and his left grasped the slender fingers of a fair maiden, not less gayly decorated than himself. Bright roses glowed in contrast with the dark and glossy curls of each, and were scattered round their feet, or had sprung up spontaneously there. Behind this lightsome couple, so close to the Maypole that its boughs shaded his jovial face, stood the figure of an English priest, canonically dressed, yet decked with flowers, in heathen fashion, and wearing a chaplet of the native vine leaves. By the riot of his rolling eye, and the pagan decorations of his holy garb, he seemed the wildest monster there, and the very Comus of the crew.

"Votaries of the Maypole," cried the flower-decked priest, "merrily, all day long, have the woods echoed to your mirth. But be this your merriest hour, my hearts! Lo, here stand the Lord and Lady of the May, whom I, a clerk of Oxford, and high priest of Merry Mount, am presently to join in holy martrimony. Up with your nimble spirits, ye morris-dancers, green men, and glee maidens, bears and wolves, and horned gentlemen! Come; a chorus now, rich with the old mirth of Merry England, and the wilder glee of this fresh forest; and then a dance, to show the youthful pair what life is made of, and how airily they should go through it! All ye that love the Maypole, lend your voices to the nuptial song of the Lord and Lady of the May!"

This wedlock was more serious than most affairs of Merry Mount, where jest and delusion, trick and fantasy, kept up a continual carnival. The Lord and Lady of the May, though their titles must be laid down at sunset, were really and truly to be partners for the dance of life, beginning the measure that same bright eve. The wreath of roses, that hung from the lowest green bough of the Maypole, had been twined for them, and would be thrown over both their heads, in symbol of their flowery union. When the priest had spoken, therefore, a riotous uproar burst from the rout of monstrous figures.

"Begin you the stave, reverend Sir," cried they all; "and never did the woods ring to such a merry peal as we of the Maypole shall send up!"

Immediately a prelude of pipe, cithern, and viol, touched with practised minstrelsy, began to play from a neighboring thicket, in such a mirthful cadence that the boughs of the Maypole quivered to the sound. But the May Lord, he of the gilded staff, chancing to look into his Lady's eyes, was wonder struck at the almost pensive glance that met his own.

"Edith, sweet Lady of the May," whispered he reproachfully, "is yon wreath of roses a garland to hang above our graves, that you look so sad? O, Edith, this is our golden time! Tarnish it not by any pensive shadow of the mind; for it may be that nothing of futurity will be brighter than the mere remembrance of what is now passing."

"That was the very thought that saddened me! How came it in your mind too?" said Edith, in a still lower tone than he, for it was high treason to be sad at Merry Mount. "Therefore do I sigh amid this festive music. And besides, dear Edgar, I struggle as with a dream, and fancy that these shapes of our jovial friends are visionary, and their mirth unreal, and that we are no true Lord and Lady of the May. What is the mystery in my heart?"

Just then, as if a spell has loosened them, down came a little shower of withering rose leaves from the Maypole. Alas, for the young lovers! No sooner had their hearts glowed with real passion than they were sensible of something vague and unsubstantial in their former pleasures, and felt a dreary presentiment of inevitable change. From the moment that they truly loved, they had subjected themselves to earth's doom of care and sorrow, and troubled joy, and had no more a home at Merry Mount. That was Edith's mystery. Now leave we the priest to marry them, and the masquers to sport round the Maypole, till the last sunbeam be withdrawn from its summit, and the shadows of the forest mingle gloomily in the dance. Meanwhile, we may discover who these gay people were.

Two hundred years ago, and more, the old world and its inhabitants became mutually weary of each other. Men voyaged by thousands to the West: some to barter glass beads, and such like jewels, for the furs of the Indian hunter; some to conquer virgin empires; and one stern band to pray. But none of these motives had much weight with the colonists of Merry Mount. Their leaders were men who had sported so long with life, that when Thought and Wisdom came, even these unwelcome guests were led astray by the crowd of vanities which they should have put to flight. Erring Thought and perverted Wisdom were made to put on masques, and play the fool. The men of whom we speak, after losing the heart's fresh gayety, imagined a wild philosophy of pleasure, and came hither to act out their latest daydream. They gathered followers from all that giddy tribe whose whole life is like the festal days of soberer men. In their train were minstrels, not unknown in London streets; wandering players, whose theatres had been the halls of noblemen; mummers, rope-dancers, and mountebanks, who would long be missed at wakes, church ales, and fairs; in a word, mirth makers of every sort, such as abounded in that age, but now began to be discountenanced by the rapid growth of Puritanism. Light had their footsteps been on land, and as lightly they came across the sea. Many had been maddened by their previous troubles into a gay despair; others were as madly gay in the flush of youth, like the May Lord and his Lady; but whatever might be the quality of their mirth, old and young were gay at Merry Mount. The young deemed themselves happy. The elder spirits, if they knew that mirth was but the counterfeit of happiness, yet followed the false shadow wilfully, because at least her garments glittered brightest. Sworn triflers of a lifetime, they would not venture among the sober truths of life not even to be truly blest.

All the hereditary pastimes of Old England were transplanted hither. The King of Christmas was duly crowned, and the Lord of Misrule bore potent sway. On the Eve of St. John, they felled whole acres of the forest to make bonfires, and danced by the blaze all night, crowned with garlands, and throwing flowers into the flame. At harvest time, though their crop was of the smallest, they made an image with the sheaves of Indian corn, and wreathed it with autumnal garlands, and bore it home triumphantly. But what chiefly characterized the colonists of Merry Mount was their veneration for the Maypole. It has made their true history a poet's tale. Spring decked the hallowed emblem with young blossoms and fresh green boughs; Summer brought roses of the deepest blush, and the perfected foliage of the forest; Autumn enriched it with that red and yellow gorgeousness which converts each wildwood leaf into a painted flower; and Winter silvered it with sleet, and hung it around with icicles, till it flashed in the cold sunshine, itself a frozen sunbeam. Thus each alternate season did homage to the Maypole, and paid it a tribute of its own richest splendor. Its votaries danced round it, once, at least, in every month; sometimes they called it their religion, or their altar; but always, it was the banner staff of Merry Mount.

Unfortunately, there were men in the new world of a sterner faith then those Maypole worshippers. Not far from Merry Mount was a settlement of Puritans, most dismal wretches, who said their prayers before daylight, and then wrought in the forest or the cornfield till evening made it prayer time again. Their weapons were always at hand to shoot down the straggling savage. When they met in conclave, it was never to keep up the old English mirth, but to hear sermons three hours long, or to proclaim bounties on the heads of wolves and the scalps of Indians. Their festivals were fast days and their chief pastime the singing of psalms. Woe to the youth or maiden who did but dream of a dance! The selectman nodded to the constable; and there sat the light-heeled reprobate in the stocks; or if he danced, it was round the whipping-post, which might be termed the Puritan Maypole.

A party of these grim Puritans, toiling through the difficult woods, each with a horseload of iron armor to burden his footsteps, would sometimes draw near the sunny precincts of Merry Mount. There were the silken colonists, sporting round their Maypole; perhaps teaching a bear to dance, or striving to communicate their mirth to the grave Indian; or masquerading in the skins of deer and wolves, which they had hunted for that especial purpose. Often, the whole colony were playing at blindman's buff, magistrates and all, with their eyes bandaged, except a single scapegoat, whom the blinded sinners pursued by the tinkling of the bells at his garments. Once, it is said, they were seen following a flower-decked corpse, with merriment and festive music, to his grave. But did the dead man laugh? In their quietest times, they sang ballads and told tales, for the edification of their pious visitors; or perplexed them with juggling tricks; or grinned at them through horse collars; and when sport itself grew wearisome, they made game of their own stupidity, and began a yawning match. At the very least of these enormities, the men of iron shook their heads and frowned so darkly that the revellers looked up imagining that a momentary cloud had overcast the sunshine, which was to be perpetual there. On the other hand, the Puritans affirmed that, when a psalm was pealing from their place of worship, the echo which the forest sent them back seemed often like the chorus of a jolly catch, closing with a roar of laughter. Who but the fiend, and his bond slaves, the crew of Merry Mount, had thus disturbed them? In due time, a feud arose, stern and bitter on one side, and as serious on the other as anything could be among such light spirits as had sworn allegiance to the Maypole. The future complexion of New England was involved in this important quarrel. Should the grizzly saints establish their jurisdiction over the gay sinners, then would their spirits darken all the clime, and make it a land of clouded visages, of hard toil, of sermon and psalm forever. But should the benner staff of Merry Mount be fortunate, sunshine would break upon the hills, and flowers would beautify the forest, and late posterity do homage to the Maypole.

After these authentic passages from history, we return to the nuptials of the Lord and Lady of the May. Alas! we have delayed too long, and must darken our tale too suddenly. As we glance again at the Maypole, a solitary sunbeam is fading from the summit, and leaves only a faint, golden tinge blended with the hues of the rainbow banner. Even that dim light is now withdrawn, relinquishing the whole domain of Merry Mount to the evening gloom, which has rushed so instantaneously from the black surrounding woods. But some of these black shadows have rushed forth in human shape.

Yes, with the setting sun, the last day of mirth had passed from Merry Mount. The ring of gay masquers was disordered and broken; the stag lowered his antlers in dismay; the wolf grew weaker than a lamb; the bells of the morris-dancers tinkled with tremulous affright. The Puritans had played a characteristic part in the Maypole mummeries. Their darksome figures were intermixed with the wild shapes of their foes, and made the scene a picture of the moment, when waking thoughts start up amid the scattered fantasies of a dream. The leader of the hostile party stood in the centre of the circle, while the route of monsters covered around him, like evil spirits in the presence of a dread magician. No fantastic foolery could look him in the face. So stern was the energy of his aspect, that the whole man, visage, frame, and soul, seemed wrought of iron, gifted with life and thought, yet all of one substance with his head-piece and breastplate. It was the Puritan of Puritans; it was Endicott himself!

"Stand off, priest of Baal!" said he, with a grim frown, and laying no reverent hand upon the surplice. "I know thee, Blackstone!* Thou art the man who couldst not abide the rule even of thine own corrupted church, and hast come hither to preach iniquity, and to give example of it in thy life. But now shall it be seen that the Lord hath sanc-tified this wilderness for his peculiar people. Woe unto them that would defile it! And first, for this flower-decked abomination, the altar of thy worship!"

And with his keen sword Endicott assaulted the hallowed Maypole. Nor long did it resist his arm. It groaned with a dismal sound; it showered leaves and rose-buds upon the remorseless enthusiast; and finally, with all its green boughs and rib-bons and flowers, symbolic of departed pleasures, down fell the banner staff of Merry Mount. As it sank, tradition says, the evening sky grew darker, and the woods threw forth a more sombre shadow.

"There," cried Endicott, looking triumphantly on his work, "there lies the only Maypole in New England! The thought is strong within me that, by its fall, is shad-owed forth the fate of light and idle mirth makers, amongst us and our posterity. Amen, saith John Endicott."

"Amen!" echoed his followers.

But the votaries of the Maypole gave one groan for their idol. At the sound, the Puritan leader glanced at the crew of Comus, each a figure of broad mirth, yet, at this moment, strangely expressive of sorrow and dismay.

"Valiant captain," quoth Peter Palfrey, the Ancient of the band, "what order shall be taken with the prisoners?"

"I thought not to repent me of cutting down a Maypole," replied Endicott, "yet now I could find in my heart to plant it again, and give each of these bestial pa-gans one other dance round their idol. It would have served rarely for a whipping-post!"

"But there are pine-trees enow," suggested the lieutenant.

"True, good Ancient," said the leader. "Wherefore, bind the heathen crew, and bestow on them a small matter of stripes apiece, as earnest of our future justice. Set some of the rogues in the stocks to rest themselves, so soon as Providence shall bring us to one of our own well-ordered settlements where such accommodations

---

*Did Governor Endicott speak less positively, we should suspect a mistake here. The Rev. Mr. Blackstone, though an eccentric, is not known to have been an immoral man. We rather doubt his iden-tity with the priest of Merry Mount. [Hawthorne's note]

may be found. Further penalties, such as branding and cropping of ears, shall be thought of hereafter."

"How many stripes for the priest?" inquired Ancient Palfrey.

"None as yet," answered Endicott, bending his iron frown upon the culprit. "It must be for the Great and General Court to determine, whether stripes and long imprisonment, and other grievous penalty, may atone for his transgressions. Let him look to himself! For such as violate our civil order, it may be permitted us to show mercy. But woe to the wretch that troubleth our religion."

"And this dancing bear," resumed the officer. "Must he share the stripes of his fellows?"

"Shoot him through the head!" said the energetic Puritan. "I suspect witchcraft in the beast."

"Here be a couple of shining ones," continued Peter Palfrey, pointing his weapon at the Lord and Lady of the May. "They seem to be of high station among these misdoers. Methinks their dignity will not be fitted with less than a double share of stripes."

Endicott rested on this sword, and closely surveyed the dress and aspect of the hapless pair. There they stood, pale, downcast, and apprehensive. Yet there was an air of mutual support and of pure affection, seeking aid and giving it, that showed them to be man and wife, with the sanction of a priest upon their love. The youth, in the peril of the moment, had dropped his gilded staff, and thrown his arm about the Lady of the May, who leaned against his breast, too lightly to burden him, but with weight enough to express that their destinies were linked together, for good or evil. They looked first at each other, and then into the grim captain's face. There they stood, in the first hour of wedlock, while the idle pleasures, of which their companions were the emblems, had given place to the sternest cares of life, personi-fied by the dark Puritans. But never had their youthful beauty seemed so pure and high as when its glow was chastened by adversity.

"Youth," said Endicott, "ye stand in an evil case thou and thy maiden wife. Make ready presently, for I am minded that ye shall both have a token to remember your wedding day!"

"Stern man," cried the May Lord, "how can I move thee? Were the means at hand, I would resist to the death. Being powerless, I entreat! Do with me as thou wilt, but let Edith go untouched!"

"Not so," replied the immitigable zealot. "We are not wont to show an idle courtesy to that sex, which requireth the stricter discipline. What sayest thou, maid? Shall thy silken bridegroom suffer thy share of the penalty, besides his own?"

"Be it death," said Edith, "and lay it all on me!"

Truly, as Endicott had said, the poor lovers stood in a woeful case. Their foes were triumphant, their friends captive and abased, their home desolate, the be-nighted wilderness around them, and a rigorous destiny, in the shape of the Puritan leader, their only guide. Yet the deepening twilight could not altogether conceal that the iron man was softened; he smiled at the fair spectacle of early love; he al-most sighed for the inevitable blight of early hopes.

"The troubles of life have come hastily on this young couple," observed Endicott. "We will see how they comport themselves under their present trials ere we burden them with greater. If, among the spoil, there be any garments of a more decent fashion, let them be put upon this May Lord and his Lady, instead of their glistening vanities. Look to it, some of you."

"And shall not the youth's hair be cut?" asked Peter Palfrey, looking with abhorrence at the lovelock and long glossy curls of the young man.

"Crop it forthwith, and that in the true pumpkin-shell fashion," answered the captain. "Then bring them along with us, but more gently than their fellows. There be qualities in the youth, which may make him valiant to fight, and sober to toil, and pious to pray; and in the maiden, that may fit her to become a mother in our Israel, bringing up babes in better nurture than her own hath been. Nor think ye, young ones, that they are the happiest, even in our lifetime of a moment, who misspend it in dancing round a Maypole!"

And Endicott, the severest Puritan of all who laid the rock foundation of New England, lifted the wreath of roses from the ruin of the Maypole, and threw it, with his own gauntleted hand, over the heads of the Lord and Lady of the May. It was a deed of prophecy. As the moral gloom of the world overpowers all systematic gayety, even so was their home of wild mirth made desolate amid the sad forest. They returned to it no more. But as their flowery garland was wreathed of the brightest rose that had grown there, so, in the tie that united them, were intertwined all the purest and best of their early joys. They went heavenward, supporting each other along the difficult path which it was their lot to tread, and never wasted one regretful thought of the vanities of Merry Mount.

CRITICAL THINKING QUESTIONS

1. Immigrants to a new country usually are absorbed into that culture. If you moved to Holland, for example, your children would be Dutch and their children would look at you as the grandparent with the funny accent. How is it that Europeans were not absorbed into the Native American culture here? Did Europeans ever adopt the Native American lifestyle?

2. In what ways have whites attempted to force their culture on Native Americans? Is it merely a question of power? If the Native Americans had the rifles, what values might our communities exhibit (make an *inference* here based on what facts you know)?

WRITING TOPIC

What would you censor in contemporary culture? Select something, even if it might seem trivial. Describe at least two reasons that, in your eyes, justify such censorship.

Herman Melville

Bartleby the Scrivener

A Story of Wall Street

I am a rather elderly man. The nature of my avocations for the last thirty years has brought me into more than ordinary contact with what would seem an interesting and somewhat singular set of men, of whom as yet nothing that I know of has ever been written:—I mean the law-copyists or scriveners. I have known very many of them, professionally and privately, and if I pleased, could relate divers histories, at which good-natured gentlemen might smile, and sentimental souls might weep. But I waive the biographies of all other scriveners for a few passages in the life of Bartleby, who was a scrivener and the strangest I ever saw, or heard of. While of other law-copyists I might write the complete life, of Bartleby nothing of that sort can be done. I believe that no materials exist for a full and satisfactory biography of this man. It is an irreparable loss to literature. Bartleby was one of those beings of whom nothing is ascertainable, except from the original sources, and in his case those are very small. What my own astonished eyes saw of Bartleby, *that* is all I know of him, except, indeed, one vague report which will appear in the sequel.

Ere introducing the scrivener, as he first appeared to me, it is fit I make some mention of myself, my *employés*, my business, my chambers, and general surroundings; because some such description is indispensable to an adequate understanding of the chief character about to be presented.

Imprimis. I am a man who, from his youth upward, has been filled with a profound conviction that the easiest way of life is the best. Hence, though I belong to a profession proverbially energetic and nervous, even to turbulence, at times, yet nothing of that sort have I ever suffered to invade my peace. I am one of those unambitious lawyers who never addresses a jury, or in any way draws down public applause; but in the cool tranquility of a snug retreat, do a snug business among rich men's bonds and mortgages and title-deeds. All who know me, consider me an eminently *safe* man. The late John Jacob Astor, a personage little given to poetic enthusiasm, had no hesitation in pronouncing my first grand point to be prudence; my next, method. I do not speak it in vanity, but simply record the fact, that I was not unemployed in my profession by the late John Jacob Astor; a name which, I admit, I love to repeat, for it hath a rounded and orbicular sound to it, and rings like unto bullion. I will freely add, that I was not insensible to the late John Jacob Astor's good opinion.

Some time prior to the period at which this little history begins, my avocations had been largely increased. The good old office, now extinct in the State of New

York, of a Master in Chancery, had been conferred upon me. It was not a very arduous office, but every pleasantly remunerative. I seldom lose my temper; much more seldom indulge in dangerous indignation at wrongs and outrages; but I must be permitted to be rash here and declare, that I consider the sudden and violent abrogation of the office of Master in Chancery, by the new Constitution, as a——premature act; inasmuch as I had counted upon a life-lease of the profits, whereas I only received those of a few short years. But this is by the way.

My chambers were upstairs at No.——Wall street. At one end they looked upon the white wall of the interior of a spacious skylight shaft, penetrating the building from top to bottom. This view might have been considered rather tame than otherwise, deficient in what landscape painters call "life." But if so, the view from the other end of my chambers offered, at least, a contrast, if nothing more. In that direction my windows commanded an unobstructed view of a lofty brick wall, black by age and everlasting shade; which wall required no spy-glass to bring out its lurking beauties, but for the benefit of all near-sighted spectators, was pushed up to within ten feet of my window panes. Owing to the great height of the surrounding buildings, and my chambers being on the second floor, the interval between this wall and mine not a little resembled a huge square cistern.

At the period just preceding the advent of Bartleby, I had two persons as copyists in my employment, and a promising lad as an office-boy. First, Turkey; second, Nippers; third, Ginger Nut. These may seem names, the like of which are not usually found in the Directory. In truth they were nicknames, mutually conferred upon each other by my three clerks, and were deemed expressive of their respective persons or characters. Turkey was a short, pursy Englishman of about my own age, that is, somewhere not far from sixty. In the morning, one might say, his face was of a fine florid hue, but after twelve o'clock, meridian—his dinner hour—it blazed like a grate full of Christmas coals; and continued blazing—but, as it were, with a gradual wane—till 6 o'clock P.M. or thereabouts, after which I saw no more of the proprietor of the face, which, gaining its meridian with the sun, seemed to set with it, to rise, culminate, and decline the following day, with the like regularity and undiminished glory. There are many singular coincidences I have known in the course of my life, not the least among which was the fact, that exactly when Turkey displayed his fullest beams from his red and radiant countenance, just then, too, at that critical moment, began the daily period when I considered his business capacities as seriously disturbed for the remainder of the twenty-four hours. Not that he was absolutely idle, or averse to business then; far from it. The difficulty was, he was apt to be altogether too energetic. There was a strange, inflamed, flurried, flighty recklessness of activity about him. He would be incautious in dipping his pen into his inkstand. All his blots upon my documents, were dropped there after twelve o'clock, meridian. Indeed, not only would he be reckless and sadly given to making blots in the afternoon, but some days he went further, and was rather noisy. At such times, too, his face flamed with augmented blazonry, as if cannel coal had been heaped on anthracite. He made an unpleasant racket with his chair; spilled his sand-box; in mending his pens, impatiently split them all to pieces, and threw them on the floor in a sudden passion; stood up and leaned over his table, boxing his papers about in a most indecorous manner, very sad to behold in an elderly man like him. Nevertheless, as he was in many ways a most valuable person to me, and all the time before twelve o'clock, meridian, was the quickest, steadiest creature, too, accomplishing a great deal of work in a style not easy to be matched—for these reasons, I was willing to overlook his eccentricities, though indeed, occasionally, I remonstrated with him. I did this very gently, however, because, though the civilest, nay, the blandest and most reverential of men in the morning, yet in the afternoon he was disposed, upon provocation, to be slightly rash with his tongue, in fact, insolent. Now, valuing his morning services as I did, and resolving not to lose them—yet, at the same time, made uncomfortable by his inflamed ways after twelve o'clock; and being a man of peace, unwilling by my admonitions to call forth unseemly retorts from him—I took upon me, one Saturday noon (he was always worse on Saturdays), to hint to him, very kindly, that perhaps now that he was growing old, it might be well to abridge his labours; in short, he need not come to my chambers after twelve o'clock, but, dinner over, had best go home to his lodgings and rest himself till tea-time. But no; he insisted upon his afternoon devotions. His countenance became intolerably fervid, as he oratorically assured me—gesticulating, with a long ruler, at the other side of the room—that if his services in the morning were useful, how indispensable, then, in the afternoon?

"With submission, sir," said Turkey on this occasion, "I consider myself your right-hand man. In the morning I but marshal and deploy my columns; but in the afternoon I put myself at their head, and gallantly charge the foe, thus!"—and he made a violent thrust with the ruler.

"But the blots, Turkey," intimated I.

"True,—but, with submission, sir, behold these hairs! I am getting old. Surely, sir, a blot or two of a warm afternoon is not to be severely urged against grey hairs. Old age—even if it blot the page—is honourable. With submission, sir, we *both* are getting old."

This appeal to my fellow-feeling was hardly to be resisted. At all events, I saw that go he would not. So I made up my mind to let him stay, resolving, nevertheless, to see to it, that during the afternoon he had to do with my less important papers.

Nippers, the second on my list, was a whiskered, sallow, and, upon the whole, rather piratical-looking young man of about five and twenty. I always deemed him the victim of two evil powers—ambition and indigestion. The ambition was evinced by a certain impatience of the duties of a mere copyist—an unwarrantable usurpation of strictly professional affairs, such as the original drawing up of legal documents. The indigestion seemed betokened in an occasional nervous testiness and grinning irritability, causing the teeth to audibly grind together over mistakes committed in copying; unnecessary maledictions, hissed, rather than spoken, in the heat of business; and especially by a continual discontent with the height of the table where he worked. Though of a very ingenious mechanical turn, Nippers could never get this table to suit him. He put chips under it, blocks of various sorts, bits of pasteboard, and at last went so far as to attempt an exquisite adjustment by final pieces of folded blotting-paper. But no invention would answer. If, for the sake of easing his back, he brought the table lid at a sharp angle well up toward his chin, and wrote there like a man using the steep roof of a Dutch house for his desk—then he declared that it stopped the circulation in his arms. If now he lowered the table to his waistbands, and stooped over it in writing, then there was a sore aching in his back. In short, the truth of the matter was, Nippers knew not what he wanted. Or, if he wanted anything, it was to be rid of a scrivener's table altogether. Among the manifestations of his diseased ambition was a fondness he had for receiving visits from certain ambiguous-looking fellows in seedy coats, whom he called his clients. Indeed I was aware that not only was he, at times, considerable of a ward-politician, but he occasionally did a little business at the Justices' courts, and was not unknown on the steps of the Tombs. I have good reason to believe, however, that one individual who called upon him at my chambers, and who, with a grand air, he insisted was his client, was no other than a dun, and the alleged title-deed, a bill. But with all his failings, and the annoyances he caused me, Nippers, like his compatriot Turkey, was a very useful man to me; wrote a neat, swift hand; and, when he chose, was not deficient in a gentlemanly sort of deportment. Added to this, he always dressed in a gentlemanly sort of way; and so, incidentally, reflected credit upon my chambers. Whereas with respect to Turkey, I had much ado to keep him from being a reproach to me. His clothes were apt to look oily and smell of eating-houses. He wore his pantaloons very loose and baggy in summer. His coats were execrable; his hat not to be handled. But while the hat was a thing of indifference to me, inasmuch as his natural civility and deference, as a dependent Englishman, always led him to doff it the moment he entered the room, yet his coat was another matter. Concerning his coats, I reasoned with him; but with no effect. The truth was, I suppose, that a man with so small an income, could not afford to sport such a lustrous face and a lustrous coat at one and the same time. As Nippers once observed, Turkey's money went chiefly for red ink. One winter day I presented Turkey with a highly-respectable looking coat of my own, a padded grey coat, of a most comfortable warmth, and which buttoned straight up from the knee to the neck. I thought Turkey would appreciate the favour, and abate his rashness and obstreperousness of afternoons. But no. I verily believe that buttoning himself up in so downy and blanketlike a coat had a pernicious effect upon him; upon the same principle that too much oats are bad for horses. In fact, precisely as a rash, restive horse is said to feel his oats, so Turkey felt his coat. It made him insolent. He was a man whom prosperity harmed.

Though concerning the self-indulgent habits of Turkey I had my own private surmises, yet touching Nippers I was well persuaded that whatever might be his faults in other respects, he was, at least, a temperate young man. But, indeed, nature herself seemed to have been his vintner, and at his birth charged him so thoroughly with an irritable, brandy-like disposition, that all subsequent potations were needless. When I consider how, amid the stillness of my chambers, Nippers would sometimes impatiently rise from his seat, and stooping over his table, spread his arms wide apart, seize the whole desk, and move it, and jerk it, with a grim, grinding motion on the floor, as if the table were a perverse voluntary agent, intent on thwarting and vexing him; I plainly perceive that for Nippers, brandy and water were altogether superfluous.

It was fortunate for me that, owing to its peculiar cause—indigestion—the irritability and consequent nervousness of Nippers, were mainly observable in the morning, while in the afternoon he was comparatively mild. So that Turkey's paroxysms only coming on about twelve o'clock, I never had to do with their eccentricities at one time. Their fits relieved each other like guards. When Nippers's was on, Turkey's was off; and *vice versa*. This was a good natural arrangement under the circumstances.

Ginger Nut, the third on my list, was a lad some twelve years old. His father was a carmen, ambitious of seeing his son on the bench instead of a cart, before he died. So he sent him to my office as student at law, errand boy, and cleaner and sweeper, at the rate of one dollar a week. He had a little desk to himself, but he did not use it much. Upon inspection, the drawer exhibited a great array of the shells of various sorts of nuts. Indeed, to this quick-witted youth the whole noble science of the law was contained in a nut-shell. Not the least among the employments of Ginger Nut, as well as one which he discharged with the most alacrity, was his duty as cake and apple purveyor for Turkey and Nippers. Copying law papers being proverbially a dry, husky sort of business, my two scriveners were fain to moisten their mouths very often with Spitzenbergs to be had at the numerous stalls nigh the Custom House and Post Office. Also, they sent Ginger Nut very frequently for that peculiar cake—small, flat, round, and very spicy—which he had been named by them. Of a cold morning, when business was but dull, Turkey would gobble up scores of these cakes, as if they were mere wafers—indeed they sell them at the rate of six or eight for a penny—the scrape of his pen blending with the crunching of the crisp particles in his mouth. Of all the fiery afternoon blunders and flurried rashness of Turkey, was his once moistening a ginger-cake between his lips, and clapping it on to a mortgage for a seal. I came within an ace of dismissing him then. But he mollified me by making an oriental bow and saying—"With submission, sir, it was generous of me to find you in stationery on my own account."

Now my original business—that of a conveyancer and title hunter, and drawer-up of recondite documents of all sorts—was considerably increased by receiving the master's office. There was now great work for scriveners. Not only must I push the clerks already with me, but I must have additional help. In answer to my advertisement, a motionless young man one morning stood upon my office threshold, the door being open, for it was summer. I can see that figure now—pallidly neat, pitiably respectable, incurably forlorn! It was Bartleby.

After a few words touching his qualifications, I engaged him, glad to have among my corps of copyists a man of so singularly sedate an aspect, which I thought might operate beneficially upon the flighty temper of Turkey, and the fiery one of Nippers.

I should have stated before that ground glass folding-doors divided my premises into two parts, one of which was occupied by my scriveners, the other by myself. According to my humour I threw open these doors, or closed them. I resolved to assign Bartleby a corner by the folding-doors, but on my side of them, so as to have this quiet man within easy call, in case any trifling thing was to be done. I placed his desk close up to a small side-window in that part of the room, a window which originally had afforded a lateral view of certain grimy back-yards and bricks, but which, owing to subsequent erections, commanded at present no view at all, though it gave some light. Within three feet of the panes was a wall, and the light came down from far above, between two lofty buildings, as from a very small opening in a dome. Still further to a satisfactory arrangement, I procured a high green folding screen, which might entirely isolate Bartleby from my sight, though not remove him from my voice. And thus, in a manner, privacy and society were conjoined.

At first Bartleby did an extraordinary quantity of writing. As if long famishing for something to copy, he seemed to gorge himself on my documents. There was no pause for digestion. He ran a day and night line, copying by sun-light and by candle-light. I should have been quite delighted with his application, had he been cheerfully industrious. But he wrote on silently, palely, mechanically.

It is, of course, an indispensable part of a scrivener's business to verify the accuracy of his copy, word by word. Where there are two or more scriveners in an office, they assist each other in this examination, one reading from the copy, the other holding the original. It is a very dull, wearisome, and lethargic affair. I can readily imagine that to some sanguine temperaments it would be altogether intolerable. For example, I cannot credit that the mettlesome poet Byron would have contentedly sat down with Bartleby to examine a law document of, say, five hundred pages, closely written in a crimpy hand.

Now and then, in the haste of business, it had been my habit to assist in comparing some brief document myself, calling Turkey or Nippers for this purpose. One object I had in placing Bartleby so handy to me behind the screen, was to avail myself of his services on such trivial occasions. It was on the third day, I think, of his being with me, and before any necessity had arisen for having his own writing examined, that, being much hurried to complete a small affair I had in hand, I abruptly called to Bartleby. In my haste and natural expectancy of instant compliance, I sat with my head bent over the original on my desk, and my right hand sideways, and somewhat nervously extended with the copy, so that immediately upon emerging from his retreat, Bartleby might snatch it and proceed to business without the least delay.

In this very attitude did I sit when I called to him, rapidly stating what it was I wanted him to do—namely, to examine a small paper with me. Imagine my surprise, nay, my consternation, when without moving from his privacy, Bartleby in a singularly mild, firm voice, replied, "I would prefer not to."

I sat awhile in perfect silence, rallying my stunned faculties. Immediately it occurred to me that my ears had deceived me, or Bartleby had entirely misunderstood my meaning. I repeated my request in the clearest tone I could assume. But in quite as clear a one came the previous reply, "I would prefer not to."

"Prefer not to," echoed I, rising in high excitement, and crossing the room with a stride. "What do you mean? Are you moonstruck? I want you to help me compare this sheet here—take it," and I thrust it towards him.

"I would prefer not to," said he.

I looked at him steadfastly. His face was leanly composed; his grey eye dimly calm. Not a wrinkle of agitation rippled him. Had there been the least uneasiness, anger, impatience or impertinence in his manner; in other words, had there been anything ordinarily human about him, doubtless I should have violently dismissed him from the premises. But as it was, I should have as soon thought of turning my pale plaster-of-paris bust of Cicero out of doors. I stood gazing at him awhile, as he went on with his own writing, and then reseated myself at my desk. This is very strange, thought I. What had one best do? But my business hurried me. I concluded to forget the matter for the present, reserving it for my future leisure. So calling Nippers from the other room, the paper was speedily examined.

A few days after this, Bartleby concluded four lengthy documents, being quadruplicates of a week's testimony taken before me in my High Court of Chancery. It became necessary to examine them. It was an important suit, and great accuracy was imperative. Having all things arranged, I called Turkey, Nippers and Ginger Nut from the next room, meaning to place the four copies in the hands of my four clerks, while I should read from the original. Accordingly Turkey, Nippers and Ginger Nut had taken their seats in a row, each with his document in hand, when I called to Bartleby to join this interesting group.

"Bartleby! quick, I am waiting."

I heard a slow scrape of his chair legs on the uncarpeted floor, and soon he appeared standing at the entrance of his hermitage.

"What is wanted?" said he mildly.

"The copies, the copies," said I hurriedly. "We are going to examine them. There"—and I held toward him the fourth quadruplicate.

"I would prefer not to," he said, and gently disappeared behind the screen.

For a few moments I was turned into a pillar of salt, standing at the head of my seated column of clerks. Recovering myself, I advanced toward the screen, and demanded the reason for such extraordinary conduct.

"*Why* do you refuse?"

"I would prefer not to."

With any other man I should have flown outright into a dreadful passion, scorned all further words, and thrust him ignominiously from my presence. But there was something about Bartleby that not only strangely disarmed me, but in a wonderful manner touched and disconcerted me. I began to reason with him.

"These are your own copies we are about to examine. It is labour saving to you, because one examination will answer for your four papers. It is common usage. Every copyist is bound to help examine his copy. Is it not so? Will you not speak? Answer!"

"I prefer not to," he replied in a flute-like tone. It seemed to me that while I had been addressing him, he carefully revolved every statement that I made; fully comprehended the meaning; could not gainsay the irresistible conclusion; but, at the same time, some paramount consideration prevailed with him to reply as he did.

"You are decided, then, not to comply with my request—a request made according to common usage and common sense?"

He briefly gave me to understand that on that point my judgment was sound. Yes: his decision was irreversible.

It is not seldom the case that when a man is browbeaten in some unprecedented and violently unreasonable way, he begins to stagger in his own plainest faith. He begins, as it were, vaguely to surmise that, wonderful as it may be, all the justice and all the reason are on the other side. Accordingly, if any disinterested persons are present, he turns to them for some reinforcement for his own faltering mind.

"Turkey," said I, "what do you think of this? Am I not right?"

"With submission, sir," said Turkey, with his blandest tone, "I think that you are."

"Nippers," said I, "what do *you* think of it?"

"I think I should kick him out of the office."

(The reader of nice perceptions will here perceive that, it being morning, Turkey's answer is couched in polite and tranquil terms but Nippers's reply in ill-tempered ones. Or, to repeat a previous sentence, Nippers's ugly mood was on duty, and Turkey's off.)

"Ginger Nut," said I, willing to enlist the smallest suffrage in my behalf, "what do *you* think of it?"

"I think, sir, he's a little *luny*," replied Ginger Nut, with a grin.

"You hear what they say," said I, turning towards the screen, "come forth and do your duty."

But he vouchsafed no reply. I pondered a moment in sore perplexity. But once more business hurried me. I determined again to postpone the consideration of this dilemma to my future leisure. With a little trouble we made out to examine the papers without Bartleby, though at every page or two, Turkey deferentially dropped his opinion that this proceeding was quite out of the common; while Nippers, twitching in his chair with a dyspeptic nervousness, ground out between his set teeth occasional hissing maledictions against the stubborn oaf behind the screen. And for his (Nippers's) part, this was the first and the last time he would do another man's business without pay.

Meanwhile Bartleby sat in his hermitage, oblivious to everything but his own peculiar business there.

Some days passed, the scrivener being employed upon another lengthy work. His late remarkable conduct led me to regard his ways narrowly. I observed that he never went to dinner; indeed that he never went any where. As yet I had never of my personal knowledge known him to be outside of my office. He was a perpetual sentry in the corner. At about eleven o'clock though, in the morning, I noticed that Ginger Nut would advance towards the opening in Bartleby's screen, as if silently beckoned thither by a gesture invisible to me where I sat. The boy would then leave the office jingling a few pence, and reappear with a handful of gingernuts which he delivered in the hemitage, receiving two of the cakes for his trouble.

He lives, then, on ginger-nuts, thought I; never eats a dinner; properly speaking; he must be a vegetarian then; but no; he never eats even vegetables, he eats nothing but ginger-nuts. My mind then ran on in reveries concerning the probable effects upon the human constitution of living entirely on ginger-nuts. Ginger-nuts are so called because they contain ginger as one of their peculiar constituents, and the final flavouring one. Now what was ginger? A hot, spicy thing. Was Bartleby hot and spicy? Not at all. Ginger, then, had no effect upon Bartleby. Probably he preferred it should have none.

Nothing so aggravates an earnest person as a passive resistance. If the individual so resisted be of a not inhumane temper, and the resisting one perfectly harmless in his passivity; then, in the better moods of the former, he will endeavour charitably to construe to his imagination what proves impossible to be solved by his judgment. Even so, for the most part, I regarded Bartleby and his ways. Poor fellow! thought I, he means no mischief; it is plain he intends no insolence; his aspect sufficiently evinces that his eccentricities are involuntary. He is useful to me. I can get along with him. If I turn him away, the chances are he will fall in with some less indulgent employer, and then he will be rudely treated, and perhaps driven forth miserably to starve. Yes. Here I can cheaply purchase a delicious self-approval. To befriend Bartleby; to humour him in his strange wilfulness, will cost me little or nothing, while I lay up in my soul what will eventually prove a sweet morsel for my conscience. But this mood was not invariable with me. The passiveness of Bartleby sometimes irritated me. I felt strangely goaded on to encounter him in new opposition, to elicit some angry spark from him answerable to my own. But indeed I might as well have essayed to strike fire with my knuckles against a bit of Windsor soap. But one afternoon the evil impulse in me mastered me, and the following little scene ensued:

"Bartleby," said I, "when those papers are all copied, I will compare them with you."

"I would prefer not to."

"How? Surely you do not mean to persist in that mulish vagary?"

No answer.

I threw open the folding-doors near by, and turning upon Turkey and Nippers, exclaimed in an excited manner:

"He says, a second time, he won't examine his papers. What do you think of it, Turkey?"

It was afternoon, be it remembered. Turkey sat glowing like a brass boiler, his bald head steaming, his hands reeling among his blotted papers.

"Think of it?" roared Turkey; "I think I'll just step behind his screen, and black his eyes for him!"

So saying, Turkey rose to his feet and threw his arms into a pugilistic position. He was hurrying away to make good his promise, when I detained him, alarmed at the effect of incautiously rousing Turkey's combativeness after dinner.

"Sit down, Turkey," said I, "and hear what Nippers has to say. What do you think of it, Nippers? Would I not be justified in immediately dismissing Bartleby?"

"Excuse me, that is for you to decide, sir. I think his conduct quite unusual, and indeed unjust, as regards Turkey and myself. But it may only be a passing whim."

"Ah," exclaimed I, "You have strangely changed your mind then—you speak very gently of him now."

"All beer," cried Turkey; "gentleness is effects of beer—Nippers and I dined together to-day. You see how gentle *I* am, sir. Shall I go and black his eyes?"

"You refer to Bartleby, I suppose. No, not to-day, Turkey," I replied; "pray, put up your fists."

I closed the doors, and again advanced towards Bartleby. I felt additional incentives tempting me to my fate. I burned to be rebelled against again. I remembered that Bartleby never left the office.

"Bartleby," said I, "Ginger Nut is away; just step round to the Post Office, won't you? (it was but a three minutes' walk), and see if there is anything for me."

"I would prefer not to."

"You *will* not?"

"I *prefer* not."

I staggered to my desk, and sat there in a deep study. My blind inveteracy returned. Was there any other thing in which I could procure myself to be ignominiously repulsed by this lean, penniless wight?—my hired clerk? What added thing is there, perfectly reasonable, that he will be sure to refuse to do?

"Bartleby!"

No answer.

"Bartleby," in a louder tone.

No answer.

"Bartleby," I roared.

Like a very ghost, agreeably to the laws of magical invocation, at the third summons, he appeared at the entrance of his hermitage.

"Go to the next room, and tell Nippers to come to me."

"I prefer not to," he respectfully and slowly said, and mildly disappeared.

"Very good, Bartleby," said I, in a quiet sort of serenely severe self-possessed tone, intimating the unalterable purpose of some terrible retribution very close at hand. At the moment I half intended something of the kind. But upon the whole, as it was drawing towards my dinner-hour, I thought it best to put on my hat and walk home for the day, suffering much from perplexity and distress of mind.

Shall I acknowledge it? The conclusion of this whole business was, that it soon became a fixed fact of my chambers, that a pale young scrivener; by the name of Bartleby, had a desk there; that he copied for me at the usual rate of four cents a folio (one hundred words); but he was permanently exempt from examining the work done by him, that duty being transferred to Turkey and Nippers, out of compliment doubtless to their superior acuteness; moreover, said Bartleby was never on any account to be despatched on the most trivial errand of any sort; and that even if entreated to take upon him such a matter, it was generally understood that he would prefer not to—in other words, that he would refuse point-blank.

As days passed on, I became considerably reconciled to Bartleby. His steadiness, his freedom from all dissipation, his incessant industry (except when he chose to throw himself into a standing revery behind his screen), his great stillness, his unalterableness of demeanour under all circumstances, made him a valuable acquisition. One prime thing was this,—*he was always there;*—first in the morning, continually through the day, and the last at night. I had a singular confidence in his honesty. I felt my most precious papers perfectly safe in his hands. Sometimes to be sure I could not, for the very soul of me, avoid falling into sudden spasmodic passions with him. For it was exceeding difficult to bear in mind all the time those strange peculiarities, privileges, and unheard of exemptions, forming the tacit stipulations on Bartleby's part under which he remained in my office. Now and then, in the eagerness of despatching pressing business, I would inadvertently summon Bartleby, in a short, rapid tone, to put his finger, say, on the incipient tie of a bit of red tape with which I was about compressing some papers. Of course, from behind the screen the usual answer, "I prefer not to," was sure to come; and then, how could a human creature with the common infirmities of our nature, refrain from bitterly exclaiming upon such perverseness—such unreasonableness. However, every added repulse of this sort which I received only tended to lessen the probability of my repeating the inadvertence.

Here it must be said, that according to the custom of most legal gentlemen occupying chambers in densely-populated law buildings, there were several keys to my door. One was kept by a woman residing in the attic, which person weekly scrubbed and daily swept and dusted my apartments. Another was kept by Turkey for convenience sake. The third I sometimes carried in my own pocket. The fourth I knew not who had.

Now, one Sunday morning I happened to go to Trinity Church, to hear a celebrated preacher, and finding myself rather early on the ground, I thought I would walk round to my chambers for awhile. Luckily I had my key with me; but upon applying it to the lock, I found it resisted by something inserted from the inside. Quite surprised, I called out; when to my consternation a key was turned from within; and thrusting his lean visage at me, and holding the door ajar, the apparition of Bartleby appeared, in his shirt sleeves, and otherwise in a strangely tattered dishabille, saying quietly that he was sorry, but he was deeply engaged just then, and—preferred not admitting me at present. In a brief word or two, he moreover added, that perhaps I had better walk round the block two or three times, and by that time he would probably have concluded his affairs.

Now, the utterly unsurmised appearance of Bartleby, tenanting my law-chambers of a Sunday-morning, with his cadaverously gentlemanly *nonchalance*, yet withal firm and self-possessed, had such a strange effect upon me, that incontinently I slunk away from my own door, and did as desired. But not without sundry twinges of impotent rebellion against the mild effrontery of this unaccountable scrivener. Indeed, it was his wonderful mildness chiefly, which not only disarmed me, but unmanned me, as it were. For I consider that one, for the time, is in a way unmanned when he tranquilly permits his hired clerk to dictate to him, and order him away from his own premises. Furthermore, I was full of uneasiness as to what Bartleby could possibly be doing in my office in his shirt sleeves, and in an otherwise dismantled condition of a Sunday morning. Was anything amiss going on? Nay, that was out of the question. It was not to be thought of for a moment that Bartleby was an immoral person. But what could he be doing there—copying? Nay again, whatever might be his eccentricities, Bartleby was an eminently decorous person. He would be the last man to sit down to his desk in any state approaching to nudity. Besides, it was Sunday; and there was something about Bartleby that forbade the supposition that he would by any secular occupation violate the proprieties of the day.

Nevertheless, my mind was not pacified; and full of a restless curiosity, at last I returned to the door. Without hindrance I inserted my key, opened it, and entered. Bartleby was not to be seen. I looked around anxiously, peeped behind his screen; but it was very plain that he was gone. Upon more closely examining the place, I surmised that for an indefinite period Bartleby must have ate, dressed, and slept in my office, and that too without plate, mirror, or bed. The cushioned seat of a ricketty old sofa in one corner bore the faint impress of a lean, reclining form. Rolled away under his desk, I found a blanket; under the empty grate, a blacking box and brush; on a chair, a tin basin, with soap and a ragged towel; in a newspaper a few crumbs of ginger-nuts and a morsel of cheese. Yes, thought I, it is evident enough that Bartleby has been making his home here, keeping bachelor's hall all by himself. Immediately then the thought came sweeping across me, What miserable friendlessness and loneliness are here revealed! His poverty is great; but his solitude, how horrible! Think of it. Of a Sunday, Wall street is deserted as Petra; and every night of every day it is an emptiness. The building too, which of week-days hums with industry and life, at nightfall echoes with sheer vacancy, and all through Sunday is forlorn. And here Bartleby makes his home; sole spectator of a solitude which he has seen all populous—a sort of innocent and transformed Marius brooding among the ruins of Carthage!

For the first time in my life a feeling of overpowering stinging melancholy seized me. Before, I had never experienced aught but a not-unpleasing sadness. The bond of a common humanity now drew me irresistibly to gloom. A fraternal melancholy! For both I and Bartleby were sons of Adam. I remembered the bright silks and sparkling faces I had seen that day, in gala trim, swan-like sailing down the Mississippi of Broadway; and I contrasted them with the pallid copyist, and thought to myself, Ah, happiness courts the light, so we deem the world is gay; but misery hides aloof, so we deem that misery there is none. These sad fancyings—chimeras, doubtless, of a sick and silly brain—led on to other and more special thoughts, concerning the eccentricities of Bartleby. Presentiments of strange discoveries hovered round me. The scrivener's pale form appeared to me laid out, among uncaring strangers, in its shivering winding sheet.

Suddenly I was attracted by Bartleby's closed desk, the key in open sight left in the lock.

I mean no mischief, seek the gratificatioin of no heartless curiosity, thought I; besides, the desk is mine, and its contents, too, so I will make bold to look within. Everything was methodically arranged, the papers smoothly placed. The pigeon holes were deep, and, removing the files of documents, I groped into their recesses. Presently I felt something there, and dragged it out. It was an old bandana handkerchief, heavy and knotted. I opened it, and saw it was a savings' bank.

I now recalled all the quiet mysteries which I had noted in the man. I remembered that he never spoke but to answer; that though at intervals he had considerable time to himself, yet I had never seen him reading—no, not even a newspaper; that for long periods he would stand looking out, at his pale window behind the screen, upon the dead brick wall; I was quite sure he never visited any refectory or eating-house; while his pale face clearly indicated that he never drank beer like Turkey, or tea and coffee even, like other men; that he never went anywhere in particular that I could learn; never went out for a walk, unless indeed that was the case at present; that he had declined telling who he was, or whence he came, or whether he had any relatives in the world; that though so thin and pale, he never complained of ill health. And more than all, I remembered a certain unconscious air of pallid—how shall I call it?—of pallid haughtiness, say, or rather an austere reserve about him, which had positively awed me into my tame compliance with his eccentricities, when I had feared to ask him to do the slightest incidental thing for me, even though I might know, from his long-continued motionlessness, that behind his screen he must be standing in one of those dead-wall reveries of his.

Revolving all these things, and coupling them with the recently discovered fact that he made my office his constant abiding place and home, and not forgetful of his morbid moodiness; revolving all these things, a prudential feeling began to steal over me. My first emotions had been those of pure melancholy and sincerest pity; but just in proportion as the forlornness of Bartleby grew and grew to my imagination, did that same melancholy merge into fear, that pity into repulsion. So true it is, and so terrible, too, that up to a certain point the thought or sight of misery enlists our best affections; but, in certain special cases, beyond that point it does not. They err who would assert that invariably this is owing to the inherent selfishness of the human heart. It rather proceeds from a certain hopelessness of remedying excessive and organic ill. To a sensitive being, pity is not seldom pain. And when at last it is perceived that such pity cannot lead to effectual succour, common sense bids the soul be rid of it. What I saw that morning persuaded me that the scrivener was the victim of innate and incurable disorder. I might give alms to his body; but his body did not pain him; it was his soul that suffered, and his soul I could not reach.

I did not accomplish the purpose of going to Trinity Church that morning. Somehow, the things I had seen disqualified me for the time from church-going. I walked homeward, thinking what I would do with Bartleby. Finally, I resolved upon this:—I would put certain calm questions to him the next morning, touching his history, &c., and if he declined to answer them openly and unreservedly (and I supposed he would prefer not), then to give him a twenty dollar bill over and above whatever I might owe him, and tell him his services were no longer required; but that if in any other way I could assist him, I would be happy to do so, especially if he desired to return to his native place, wherever that might be, I would willingly help to defray the expenses. Moreover, if, after reaching home, he found himself at any time in want of aid, a letter from him would be sure of a reply.

The next morning came.

"Bartleby," said I, gently calling to him behind his screen.

No reply.

"Bartleby," said I, in a still gentler tone, "come here; I am not going to ask you to do anything you would prefer not to do—I simply wish to speak to you."

Upon this he noiselessly slid into view.

"Will you tell me, Bartleby, where you were born?"

"I would prefer not to."

"Will you tell me *anything* about yourself?"

"I would prefer not to."

"But what reasonable objection can you have to speak to me? I feel friendly towards you."

He did not look at me while I spoke, but kept his glance fixed upon my bust of Cicero, which, as I then sat, was directly behind me, some six inches above my head.

"What is your answer, Bartleby?" said I, after waiting a considerable time for a reply, during which his countenance remained immovable, only there was the faintest conceivable tremor of the white attenuated mouth.

"At present I prefer to give no answer," he said, and retired into his hermitage.

It was rather weak in me I confess, but his manner on this occasion nettled me. Not only did there seem to lurk in it a certain calm disdain, but his perverseness seemed ungrateful, considering the undeniable good usage and indulgence he had received from me.

Again I sat ruminating what I should do. Mortified as I was at his behaviour, and resolved as I had been to dismiss him when I entered my office, nevertheless I strangely felt something superstitious knocking at my heart, and forbidding me to carry out my purpose, and denouncing me for a villain if I dared to breathe one bitter word against this forlornest of mankind. At last, familiarly drawing my chair behind his screen, I sat down and said: "Bartleby, never mind then about revealing your history; but let me entreat you, as a friend, to comply as far as may be with the usages of this office. Say now you will help to examine papers to-morrow or next day: in short, say now that in a day or two you will begin to be a little reasonable:—say so, Bartleby."

"At present I would prefer not to be a little reasonable," was his mildly cadaverous reply.

Just then the folding-doors opened, and Nippers approached. He seemed suffering from an unusually bad night's rest, induced by severer indigestion than common. He overheard those final words of Bartleby.

"*Prefer not,* eh?" gritted Nippers—"I'd *prefer* him, if I were you, sir," addressing me—"I'd *prefer* him; I'd give him preferences, the stubborn mule! What is it, sir, pray, that he *prefers* not to do now?"

Bartleby moved not a limb.

"Mr. Nippers," said I, "I'd prefer that you would withdraw for the present."

Somehow, of late I had got into the way of involuntarily using this word "prefer" upon all sorts of not exactly suitable occasions. And I trembled to think that my contact with the scrivener had already and seriously affected me in a mental way. And what further and deeper aberration might it not yet produce? This apprehension had not been without efficacy in determining me to summary means.

As Nippers, looking very sour and sulky, was departing, Turkey blandly and deferentially approached.

"With submission, sir," said he, "yesterday I was thinking about Bartleby here, and I think that if he would but prefer to take a quart of good ale every day, it would do much towards mending him, and enabling him to assist in examining his papers."

"So you have got the word, too," said I, slightly excited.

"With submission, what word, sir," asked Turkey, respectful crowding himself into the contracted space behind the screen, and by so doing, making me jostle the scrivener. "What word, sir?"

"I would prefer to be left alone here," said Bartleby, as if offended at being mobbed in his privacy.

"*That's* the word, Turkey," said I— "*that's* it."

"Oh, *prefer?* oh, yes—queer word. I never used it myself. But, sir, as I was saying, if he would but prefer—"

"Turkey," interrupted I, "you will please withdraw."

"Oh certainly, sir, if you prefer that I should."

As he opened the folding-door to retire, Nippers at his desk caught a glimpse of me, and asked whether I would prefer to have a certain paper copied on blue paper or white. He did not in the least roguishly accent the word prefer. It was plain that it involuntarily rolled from his tongue. I thought to myself, surely I must get rid of a demented man, who already has in some degree turned the tongues, if not the heads, of myself and clerks. But I thought it prudent not to break the dismission at once.

The next day I noticed that Bartleby did nothing but stand at his window in his dead-wall revery. Upon asking him why he did not write, he said that he had decided upon doing no more writing.

"Why, how now? what next?" exclaimed I, "do no more writing?"

"No more."

"And what is the reason?"

"Do you not see the reason for yourself?" he indifferently replied.

I looked steadfastly at him, and perceived that his eyes looked dull and glazed. Instantly it occurred to me, that his unexampled diligence in copying by his dim window for the first few weeks of his stay with me might have temporarily impaired his vision.

I was touched. I said something in condolence with him. I hinted that, of course, he did wisely in abstaining from writing for a while, and urged him to embrace that opportunity of taking wholesome exercise in the open air. This, however, he did not do. A few days after this, my other clerks being absent, and being in a great hurry to dispatch certain letters by the mail, I thought that, having nothing else earthly to do, Bartleby would surely be less inflexible than usual, and carry these letters to the Post Office. But he blankly declined. So, much to my inconvenience, I went myself.

Still added days went by. Whether Bartleby's eyes improved or not, I could not say. To all appearance, I thought they did. But when I asked him if they did, he vouchsafed no answer. At all events, he would do no copying. At last, in reply to my urgings, he informed me that he had permanently given up copying.

"What!" exclaimed I; "suppose your eyes should get entirely well—better than ever before—would you not copy then?"

"I have given up copying," he answered and slid aside.

He remained, as ever, a fixture in my chamber. Nay—if that were possible—he became still more of a fixture than before. What was to be done? He would do nothing in the office: why should he stay there? In plain fact, he had now become a millstone to me, not only useless as a necklace, but afflictive to bear. Yet I was sorry for him. I speak less than truth when I say that, on his own account, he occasioned me uneasiness. If he would but have named a single relative or friend, I would instantly have written, and urged their taking the poor fellow away to some convenient retreat. But he seemed alone, absolutely alone in the universe. A bit of wreckage in the mid-Atlantic. At length, necessities connected with my business tyrannized over all other considerations. Decently as I could, I told Bartleby that in six days' time he must unconditionally leave the office. I warned him to take measures, in the interval, for procuring some other abode. I offered to assist him in this endeavour, if he himself would but take the first step towards a removal. "And when you finally quit me, Bartleby," added I, "I shall see that you go away not entirely unprovided. Six days from this hour, remember."

At the expiration of that period, I peeped behind the screen, and lo! Bartleby was there.

I buttoned up my coat, balanced myself; advanced slowly towards him, touched his shoulder, and said, "The time has come; you must quit this place; I am sorry for you; here is money; but you must go."

"I would prefer not," he replied, with his back still towards me.

"You *must*."

He remained silent.

Now I had an unbounded confidence in this man's common honesty. He had frequently restored to me sixpences and shillings carelessly dropped upon the floor, for I am apt to be very reckless in such shirt-button affairs. The proceeding then which followed will not be deemed extraordinary.

"Bartleby," said I, "I owe you twelve dollars on account; here are thirty-two; the odd twenty are yours.—Will you take it?" and I handed the bills towards him.

But he made no motion.

"I will leave them here then," putting them under a weight on the table. Then taking my hat and cane and going to the door, I tranquilly turned and added— "After you have removed your things from these offices, Bartleby, you will of course lock the door—since every one is now gone for the day but you—and if you please, slip your key underneath the mat, so that I may have it in the morning. I shall not see you again; so good-bye to you. If hereafter in your new place of abode I can be of any service to you, do not fail to advise me by letter. Good-bye, Bartleby, and fare you well."

But he answered not a word; like the last column of some ruined temple, he remained standing mute and solitary in the middle of the otherwise deserted room.

As I walked home in a pensive mood, my vanity got the better of my pity. I could not but highly plume myself on my masterly management in getting rid of Bartleby. Masterly I call it, and such it must appear to any dispassionate thinker. The beauty of my procedure seemed to consist in its perfect quietness. There was no vulgar bullying, no bravado of any sort, no choleric hectoring, no striding to and fro across the apartment, jerking out vehement commands for Bartleby to bundle himself off with his beggarly traps. Nothing of the kind. Without loudly bidding Bartleby depart—as an inferior genius might have done—I *assumed* the ground that depart he must; and upon that assumption built all I had to say. The more I thought over my procedure, the more I was charmed with it. Nevertheless, next morning, upon awakening, I had my doubts,—I had somehow slept off the fumes of vanity. One of the coolest and wisest hours a man has, is just after he awakes in the morning. My procedure seemed as sagacious as ever,—but only in theory. How it would prove in practice—there was the rub. It was truly a beautiful thought to have assumed Bartleby's departure; but, after all, that assumption was simply my own, and none of Bartleby's. The great point was, not whether I had assumed that he would quit me, but whether he would prefer so to do. He was more a man of preferences than assumptions.

After breakfast, I walked down town, arguing the probabilities *pro* and *con.* One moment I thought it would prove a miserable failure, and Bartleby would be found all alive at my office as usual; the next moment it seemed certain that I should see his chair empty. And so I kept veering about. At the corner of Broadway and Canal Street, I saw quite an excited group of people standing in earnest conversation.

"I'll take odds he doesn't," said a voice as I passed.

"Doesn't go?—done!" said I, "put up your money."

I was instinctively putting my hand in my pocket to produce my own, when I remembered that this was an election day. The words I had overheard bore no reference to Bartleby, but to the success or non-success of some candidate for the mayoralty. In my intent frame of mind, I had, as it were, imagined that all Broadway shared in my excitement, and were debating the same question with me. I passed on, very thankful that the uproar of the street screened my momentary absentmindedness.

As I had intended, I was earlier than usual at my office door. I stood listening for a moment. All was still. He must be gone. I tried the knob. The door was locked. Yes, my procedure had worked to a charm; he indeed must be vanished. Yet a certain melancholy mixed with this: I was almost sorry for my brilliant success. I was fumbling under the door mat for the key, which Bartleby was to have left there for me, when accidentally my knee knocked against a panel, producing a summoning sound, and in response a voice came to me from within— "Not yet; I am occupied."

It was Bartleby.

I was thunderstruck. For an instant I stood like the man who, pipe in mouth, was killed one cloudless afternoon long ago in Virginia, by summer lightning; at his own warm open window he was killed, and remained leaning out there upon the dreamy afternoon, till some one touched him, and he fell.

"Not gone!" I murmured at last. But again obeying that wondrous ascendency which the inscrutable scrivener had over me—and from which ascendency, for all my chafing, I could not completely escape—I slowly went down stairs and out into the street, and while walking round the block, considered what I should next do in this unheard-of perplexity. Turn the man out by an actual thrusting I could not; to drive him away by calling him hard names would not do; calling in the police was an unpleasant idea; and yet, permit him to enjoy his cadaverous triumph over me,— this too I could not think of. What was to be done? or, if nothing could be done, was there anything further that I could *assume* in the matter? Yes, as before I had prospectively assumed that Bartleby would depart, so now I might retrospectively assume that departed he was. In the legitimate carrying out of this assumption, I might enter my office in a great hurry, and pretending not to see Bartleby at all, walk straight against him as if he were air. Such a proceeding would in a singular degree have the appearance of a home-thrust. It was hardly possible that Bartleby could withstand such an application of the doctrine of assumptions. But, upon second thought, the success of the plan seemed rather dubious. I resolved to argue the matter over with him again.

"Bartleby," said I, entering the office, with a quietly severe expression, "I am seriously displeased. I am pained, Bartleby. I had thought better of you. I had imagined you of such a gentlemanly organization, that in any delicate dilemma a slight hint would suffice—in short, an assumption; but it appears I am deceived. Why," I added, unaffectedly starting, "you have not even touched that money yet," pointing to it, just where I had left it the evening previous.

He answered nothing.

"Will you, or will you not, quit me?" I now demanded in a sudden passion, advancing close to him.

"I would prefer *not* to quit you," he replied, gently emphasizing the *not*.

"What earthly right have you to stay here? Do you pay any rent? Do you pay my taxes? Or is this property yours?"

He answered nothing.

"Are you ready to go on and write now? Are your eyes recovered? Could you copy a small paper for me this morning? or help examine a few lines? or step round to the Post Office? In a word, will you do any thing at all, to give a colouring to your refusal to depart the premises?"

He silently retired into his hermitage.

I was now in such a state of nervous resentment that I thought it but prudent to check myself, at present, from further demonstrations. Bartleby and I were alone. I remembered the tragedy of the unfortunate Adams and the still more unfortunate Colt in the solitary office of the latter; and how poor Colt, being dreadfully incensed by Adams, and imprudently permitting himself to get wildly excited, was at unawares hurried into his fatal act—an act which certainly not man could possibly deplore more than the actor himself. Often it had occurred to me in my ponderings upon the subject, that had that altercation taken place in the public street, or at a private residence, it would not have terminated as it did. It was the circumstance of being alone in a solitary office, upstairs, of a building entirely unhallowed by humanizing domestic associations—an uncarpeted office, doubtless, of a dusty, haggard sort of appearance;—this it must have been, which greatly helped to enhance the irritable desperation of the hapless Colt.

But when this old Adam of resentment rose in me and tempted me concerning Bartleby, I grappled him and threw him. How? Why, simply by recalling the divine injunction: "A new commandment give I unto you that ye love one another." Yes, this it was that saved me. Aside from higher considerations, charity often operates as a vastly wise and prudent principle—a great safeguard to its possessor. Men have committed murder for jealousy's sake, and anger's sake, and hatred's sake, and selfishness' sake, and spiritual pride's sake; but no man that ever I heard of, ever committed a diabolical murder for sweet charity's sake. Mere self-interest, then, if no better motive can be enlisted, should, especially with high-tempered men, prompt all beings to charity and philanthropy. At any rate, upon the occasion in question, I strove to drown my exasperated feelings towards the scrivener by benevolently construing his conduct. Poor fellow, poor fellow! thought I, he doesn't mean any thing; and besides, he has seen hard times, and ought to be indulged.

I endeavoured also immediately to occupy myself, and at the same time to comfort my despondency. I tried to fancy that in the course of the morning, at such time as might prove agreeable to him, Bartleby, of his own free accord, would emerge from his hermitage, and take up some decided line of march in the direction of the door. But no. Half-past twelve o'clock came; Turkey began to glow in the face, overturn his inkstand, and become generally obstreperous; Nippers abated down into quietude and courtesy; Ginger Nut munched his noon apple; and Bartleby remained standing at his window in one of his profoundest dead-wall reveries. Will it be credited? Ought I to acknowledge it? That afternoon I left the office without saying one further word to him.

Some days now passed, during which at leisure intervals I looked a little into "Edwards on the Will," and "Priestly on Necessity." Under the circumstances, those books induced a salutary feeling. Gradually I slid into the persuasion that these troubles of mine, touching the scrivener, had been all predestinated from eternity, and Bartleby was billeted upon me for some mysterious purpose of an all-wise Providence, which it was not for a mere mortal like me to fathom. Yes, Bartleby, stay there behind your screen, thought I; I shall persecute you no more; you are harmless and noiseless as any of these old chairs; in short, I never feel so private as when I know you are here. At least I see it, I feel it; I penetrate to the predestinated purpose of my life. I am content. Others may have loftier parts to enact; but my mission in this world, Bartleby, is to furnish you with office room for such period as you may see fit to remain.

I believe that this wise and blessed frame of mind would have continued with me had it not been for the unsolicited and uncharitable remarks obtruded upon me by my professional friends who visited the rooms. But thus it often is, that the constant friction of illiberal minds wears out at last the best resolves of the more generous. Though to be sure, when I reflected upon it, it was not strange that people entering my office should be struck by the peculiar aspect of the unaccountable Bartleby, and so be tempted to throw out some sinister observations concerning him. Sometimes an attorney having business with me, and calling at my office and finding no one but the scrivener there, would undertake to obtain some sort of precise information from him touching my whereabouts; but without heeding his idle talk, Bartleby would remain standing immovable in the middle of the room. So, after contemplating him in that position for a time, the attorney would depart, no wiser than he came.

Also, when a Reference was going on, and the room full of lawyers and witnesses and business was driving fast, some deeply occupied legal gentle man present, seeing Bartleby wholly unemployed, would request him to run round to his (the legal gentleman's) office and fetch some papers for him. Thereupon, Bartleby would tranquilly decline, and yet remain idle as before. Then the lawyer would give a great stare, and turn to me. And what could I say? At last I was made aware that all through the circle of my professional acquaintance, a whisper of wonder was running round, having reference to the strange creature I kept at my office. This worried me very much. And as the idea came upon me of his possibly turning out a long-lived man, and keep occupying my chambers, and denying my authority; and perplexing my visitors; and scandalizing my professional reputation; and casting a general gloom over the premises; keeping soul and body together to the last upon his savings (for doubtless he spent but half a dime a day), and in the end perhaps outlive me, and claim possession of my office by right of his perpetual occupancy: as all these dark anticipations crowded upon me more and more, and my friends continually intruded their relentless remarks upon the apparition in my room, a great change was wrought in me. I resolved to gather all my faculties together, and for ever rid me of this intolerable incubus.

Ere resolving any complicated project, however, adapted to this end, I first simply suggested to Bartleby the propriety of his permanent departure. In a calm and serious tone, I commended the idea to his careful and mature consideration. But having taken three days to meditate upon it, he apprised me that his original determination remained the same; in short, that he still preferred to abide with me.

What shall I do? I now said to myself, buttoning up my coat to the last button. What shall I do? what ought I to do? what does conscience say I *should* do with this man, or rather ghost? Rid myself of him, I must; go, he shall. But how? You will not thrust him, the poor, pale, passive mortal,—you will not thrust such a helpless creature out of your door? you will not dishonour yourself by such cruelty? No, I will not, I cannot do that. Rather would I let him live and die here, and then mason up his remains in the wall. What then will you do? For all your coaxing, he will not budge. Bribes he leaves under your own paper-weight on your table; in short, it is quite plain that he prefers to cling to you.

Then something severe, something unusual must be done. What! surely you will not have him collared by a constable, and commit his innocent pallor to the common jail? And upon what ground could you procure such a thing to be done?— a vagrant, is he? What! he a vagrant, a wanderer, who refuses to budge? It is because he will *not* be a vagrant, then, that you seek to count him *as* a vagrant. That is too absurd. No visible means of support: there I have him. Wrong again: for indubitably he *does* support himself, and that is the only unanswerable proof that any man can show of his possessing the means so to do. No more then. Since he will not quit me, I must quit him. I will change my offices; I will move elsewhere; and give him fair notice, that if I find him on my new premises I will then proceed against him as a common trespasser.

Acting accordingly, next day I thus addressed him: "I find these chambers too far from the City Hall; the air is unwholesome. In a word, I propose to remove my offices next week, and shall no longer require your services. I tell you this now, in order that you may seek another place."

He made no reply, and nothing more was said.

On the appointed day I engaged carts and men, proceeded to my chambers, and having but little furniture, everything was removed in a few hours. Throughout all, the scrivener remained standing behind the screen, which I directed to be re-moved the last thing. It was withdrawn; and being folded up like a huge folio, left him the motionless occupant of a naked room. I stood in the entry watching him a moment, while something from within me upbraided me.

I re-entered, with my hand in my pocket—and—and my heart in my mouth.

"Good-bye, Bartleby; I am going—good-bye, and God some way bless you; and take that," slipping something in his hand. But it dropped upon the floor and then—strange to say—I tore myself from him whom I had so longed to be rid of.

Established in my new quarters, for a day or two I kept the door locked, and started at every footfall in the passages. When I returned to my rooms after any lit-tle absence, I would pause at the threshold for an instant, and attentively listen, ere applying my key. But these fears were needless. Bartleby never came nigh me.

I thought all was going well, when a perturbed looking stranger visited me, in-quiring whether I was the person who had recently occupied rooms at No.——Wall street.

Full of forebodings, I replied that I was.

"Then sir," said the stranger, who proved a lawyer, "you are responsible for the man you left there. He refuses to do any copying, he refuses to do anything; and he says he prefers not to; and he refuses to quit the premises."

"I am very sorry, sir," said I, with assumed tranquillity, but an inward tremor, "but, really, the man you allude to is nothing to me—he is no relation or apprentice of mine, that you should hold me responsible for him."

"In mercy's name, who is he?"

"I certainly cannot inform you. I know nothing about him. Formerly I employed him as a copyist; but he has done nothing for me now for some time past."

"I shall settle him then,—good morning, sir."

Several days passed, and I heard nothing more; and though I often felt a charitable prompting to call at the place and see poor Bartleby, yet a certain squeamishness of I know not what withheld me.

All is over with him, by this time, thought I at last, when through another week no further intelligence reached me. But coming to my room the day after, I found several persons waiting at my door in a high state of nervous excitement.

"That's the man—here he comes," cried the foremost one, whom I recognized as the lawyer who had previously called upon me alone.

"You must take him away, sir, at once," cried a portly person among them, advancing upon me, and whom I knew to be the landlord of No.——Wall street. "These gentlemen, my tenants, cannot stand it any longer; Mr. B——," pointing to the lawyer, "has turned him out of his room, and he now persists in haunting the building generally, sitting upon the banisters of the stairs by day, and sleeping in the entry by night. Everybody here is concerned; clients are leaving the offices; some fears are entertained of a mob; something you must do, and that without delay."

Aghast at this torrent, I fell back before it, and would fain have locked myself in my new quarters. In vain I persisted that Bartleby was nothing to me—no more than to any one else there. In vain:—I was the last person known to have anything to do with him, and they held me to the terrible account. Fearful then of being exposed in the papers (as one person present obscurely threatened) I considered the matter, and at length said, that if the lawyer would give me a confidential interview with the scrivener, in his (the lawyer's) own room, I would that afternoon strive my best to rid them of the nuisance they complained of.

Going up stairs to my old haunt, there was Bartleby silently sitting upon the banister at the landing.

"What are you doing here, Bartleby?" said I.

"Sitting upon the banisters," he mildly replied.

I motioned him into the lawyer's room, who then left us.

"Bartleby," said I, "are you aware that you are the cause of great tribulation to me, by persisting in occupying the entry after being dismissed from the office?"

No answer.

"Now one of two things must take place. Either you must do something, or something must be done to you. Now what sort of business would you like to engage in? Would you like to re-engage in copying for some one?"

"No; I would prefer not to make any change."

"Would you like a clerkship in a dry-goods store?"

"There is too much confinement about that. No, I would not like a clerkship; but I am not particular."

"Too much confinement," I cried, "why you keep yourself confined all the time!"

"I would prefer not to take a clerkship," he rejoined, as if to settle that little item at once.

"How would a bartender's business suit you? There is no trying of the eyesight in that."

"I would not like it at all; though, as I said before, I am not particular."

His unwonted wordiness inspirited me. I returned to the charge.

"Well then, would you like to travel through the country collecting bills for the merchants? That would improve your health."

"No, I would prefer to be doing something else."

"How then would going as a companion to Europe to entertain some young gentleman with your conversation,—how would that suit you?"

"Not at all. It does not strike me that there is anything definite about that. I like to be stationary. But I am not particular."

"Stationary you shall be then," I cried, now losing all patience, and for the first time in all my exasperating connection with him fairly flying into a passion. "If you do not go away from these premises before night, I shall feel bound—indeed I *am* bound—to—to—to quit the premises myself!" I rather absurdly concluded, knowing not with what possible threat to try to frighten his immobility into compliance. Despairing of all further efforts, I was precipitately leaving him, when a final thought occurred to me—one which had not been wholly unindulged before.

"Bartleby," said I, in the kindest tone I could assume under such exciting circumstances, "will you go home with me now—not to my office, but my dwelling—and remain there till we can conclude upon some convenient arrangement for you at our leisure? Come, let us start now, right away."

"No: at present I would prefer not to make any change at all."

I answered nothing; but effectually dodging every one by the suddenness and rapidity of my flight, rushed from the building, ran up Wall street toward Broadway, and then jumping into the first omnibus was soon removed from pursuit. As soon as tranquillity returned I distinctly perceived that I had now done all that I possibly could, both in respect to the demands of the landlord and his tenants, and with regard to my own desire and sense of duty, to benefit Bartleby, and shield him from rude persecution. I now strove to be entirely care-free and quiescent; and my conscience justified me in the attempt; though indeed it was not so successful as I could have wished. So fearful was I of being again hunted out by the incensed landlord and his exasperated tenants, that, surrendering my business to Nippers, for a few days I drove about the upper part of the town and through the suburbs, in my rockaway; crossed over to Jersey City and Hoboken, and paid fugitive visits to Manhattanville and Astoria. In fact I almost lived in my rockaway for the time.

When again I entered my office, lo, a note from the landlord lay upon the desk. I opened it with trembling hands. It informed me that the writer had sent to the police, and had Bartleby removed to the Tombs as a vagrant. Moreover, since I knew more about him than any one else, he wished me to appear at that place, and make a suitable statement of the facts. These tidings had a conflicting effect upon me. At first I was indignant; but at last almost approved. The landlord's energetic, summary disposition had led him to adopt a procedure which I do not think I would have decided upon myself; and yet as a last resort, under such peculiar circumstances, it seemed the only plan.

As I afterwards learned, the poor scrivener, when told that he must be conducted to the Tombs, offered not the slightest obstacle, but in his own pale, unmoving way silently acquiesced.

Some of the compassionate and curious bystanders joined the party; and headed by one of the constables, arm-in-arm with Bartleby, the silent procession filed its way through all the noise, and heat, and joy of the roaring thoroughfares at noon.

The same day I received the note I went to the Tombs, or, to speak more properly, the Halls of Justice. Seeking the right officer, I stated the purpose of my call, and was informed that the individual I described was indeed within. I then assured the functionary that Bartleby was a perfectly honest man, and greatly to be a compassionated (however unaccountable) eccentric. I narrated all I knew, and closed by suggesting the idea of letting him remain in as indulgent confinement as possible till something less harsh might be done—though indeed I hardly knew what. At all events if nothing else could be decided upon, the alms-house must receive him. I then begged to have an interview.

Being under no disgraceful charge, and quite serene and harmless in all his ways, they had permitted him freely to wander about the prison, and especially in the inclosed grass-platted yards thereof. And so I found him there, standing all alone in the quietest of the yards, his face toward a high wall—while all around, from the narrow slits of the jail windows, I thought I saw peering out upon him the eyes of murderers and thieves.

"Bartleby!"

"I know you," he said, without looking around,— "and I want nothing to say to you."

"It was not I that brought you here, Bartleby," said I, keenly pained at his implied suspicion. "And to you, this should not be so vile a place. Nothing reproachful attaches to you by being here. And see, it is not so sad a place as one might think. Look, there is the sky and here is the grass."

"I know where I am," he replied, but would say nothing more, and so I left him.

As I entered the corridor again a broad, meat-like man in an apron accosted me, and jerking his thumb over his shoulder said— "Is that your friend?"

"Yes."

"Does he want to starve? If he does, let him live on the prison fare, that's all."

"Who are you?" asked I, not knowing what to make of such an unofficially speaking person in such a place.

"I am the grub-man. Such gentlemen as have friends here, hire me to provide them with something good to eat."

"Is this so?" said I, turning to the turnkey.

He said it was.

"Well then," said I, slipping some silver into the grub-man's hands (for so they called him), "I want you to give particular attention to my friend there: let him have the best dinner you can get. And you must be as polite to him as possible."

"Introduce me, will you?" said the grub-man, looking at me with an expression which seemed to say he was all impatience for an opportunity to give a specimen of his breeding.

Thinking it would prove of benefit to the scrivener, I acquiesced; and asking the grub-man his name, went up with him to Bartleby.

"Bartleby, this is Mr. Cutlets; you will find him very useful to you."

"Your sarvant, sir, your sarvant," said the grub-man, making a low salutation behind his apron. "Hope you find it pleasant here, sir;—spacious grounds—apartments, sir—hope you'll stay with us some time—try to make it agreeable. May Mrs. Cutlets and I have the pleasure of your company to dinner, sir, in Mrs. Cutlets' private room?"

"I prefer not to dine to-day," said Bartleby, turning away. "It would disagree with me; I am unused to dinners." So saying, he slowly moved to the other side of the inclosure and took up a position fronting the dead-wall.

"How's this?" said the grub-man, addressing me with a stare of astonishment. "He's odd, ain't he?"

"I think he is a little deranged," said I, sadly.

"Deranged? deranged is it? Well now, upon my word, I thought that friend of yourn was a gentleman forger; they are always pale and genteel-like, them forgers. I can't help pity 'em—can't help it, sir. Did you know Monroe Edwards?" he added touchingly, and paused. Then, laying his hand pityingly on my shoulder, sighed, "he died of the consumption at Sing-Sing. So you weren't acquainted with Monroe?"

"No, I was never socially acquainted with any forgers. But I cannot stop longer. Look to my friend yonder. You will not lose by it. I will see you again."

Some few days after this, I again obtained admission to the Tombs, and went through the corridors in quest of Bartleby; but without finding him.

"I saw him coming from his cell not long ago," said a turnkey, "maybe he's gone to loiter in the yards."

So I went in that direction.

"Are you looking for the silent man?" said another turnkey passing me. "Yonder he lies—sleeping in the yard there. 'Tis not twenty minutes since I saw him lie down."

The yard was entirely quiet. It was not accessible to the common prisoners. The surrounding walls, of amazing thickness, kept off all sounds behind them. The Egyptian character of the masonry weighed upon me with its gloom. But a soft imprisoned turf grew under foot. The heart of the eternal pyramids, it seemed, wherein by some strange magic, through the clefts grass-seed, dropped by birds, had sprung.

Strangely huddled at the base of the wall—his knees drawn up, and lying on his side, his head touching the cold stones—I saw the wasted Bartleby. But nothing stirred. I paused; then went close up to him stooped over, and saw that his dim eyes were open; otherwise he seemed profoundly sleeping. Something prompted me to touch him. I felt his hand, when a tingling shiver ran up my arm and down my spine to my feet.

The round face of the grub-man peered upon me now. "His dinner is ready. Won't he dine to-day, either? Or does he live without dining?"

"Lives without dining," said I, and closed the eyes.

"Eh!—He's asleep, ain't he?"

"With kings and counsellors," murmured I.

There would seem little need for proceeding further in this history. Imagination will readily supply the meagre recital of poor Bartleby's interment. But ere parting with the reader, let me say, that if this little narrative has sufficiently interested him, to awaken curiosity as to who Bartleby was, and what manner of life he led prior to the present narrator's making his acquaintance, I can only reply, that in such curiosity I fully share—But am wholly unable to gratify it. Yet here I hardly know whether I should divulge one little item of rumour, which came to my ear a few months after the scrivener's decease. Upon what basis it rested, I could never ascertain; and hence, how true it is I cannot now tell. But inasmuch as this vague report has not been without a certain strange suggestive interest to me, however sad, it may prove the same with some others; and so I will briefly mention it. The report was this: that Bartleby had been a subordinate clerk in the Dead Letter Office at Washington, from which he had been suddenly removed by a change in the administration. When I think over this rumour I cannot adequately express the emotions which seize me. Dead letters! Does it not sound like dead men? Conceive a man by nature and misfortune prone to a pallid hopelessness: can any business seem more fitted to heighten it than that of continually handling these dead letters, and assorting them for the flames? For by the cartload they are annually burned. Sometimes from out the folded paper the pale clerk takes a ring—the finger it was meant for, perhaps, moulders in the grave; a bank-note sent in swiftest charity—he whom it would relieve, nor eats nor hungers any more; pardon for those who died despairing; hope for those who died unhoping; good tidings for those who died stifled by unrelieved calamities. On errands of life, these letters speed to death.

Ah, Bartleby! Ah, humanity!

CRITICAL THINKING QUESTIONS

1. Bartleby, who seems powerless, manipulates his boss and co-workers. How is he able to do this?

2. What responsibility do we have for people who make illogical choices? Can you think of examples? When you create a *moral argument* such as this, where do you look for supporting evidence?

WRITING TOPIC

Bartleby is a little bit like a stray dog or cat—once he moves into your house, you are faced with the obligation to care for him. Write an essay in which you defend or take issue with such an obligation.

Tim O'Brien

The Things They Carried

First Lieutenant Jimmy Cross carried letters from a girl named Martha, a junior at Mount Sebastian College in New Jersey. They were not love letters, but Lieutenant Cross was hoping, so he kept them folded in plastic at the bottom of his rucksack. In the late afternoon, after a day's march, he would dig his foxhole, wash his hands under a canteen, unwrap the letters, hold them with the tips of his fingers, and spend the last hour of light pretending. He would imagine romantic camping trips into the White Mountains in New Hampshire. He would sometimes taste the envelope flaps, knowing her tongue had been there. More than anything, he wanted Martha to love him as he loved her, but the letters were mostly chatty, elusive on the matter of love. She was a virgin, he was almost sure. She was an English major at Mount Sebastian, and she wrote beautifully about her professors and roommates and midterm exams, about her respect for Chaucer and her great affection for Virginia Woolf. She often quoted lines of poetry; she never mentioned the war, except to say, Jimmy, take care of yourself. The letters weighed 10 ounces. They were signed Love, Martha, but Lieutenant Cross understood that Love was only a way of signing and did not mean what he sometimes pretended it meant. At dusk, he would carefully return the letters to his rucksack. Slowly, a bit distracted, he would get up and move among his men, checking the perimeter, then at full dark he would return to his hole and watch the night and wonder if Martha was a virgin.

The things they carried were largely determined by necessity. Among the necessities or near-necessities were P-38 can openers, pocket knives, heat tabs, wristwatches, dog tags, mosquito repellent, chewing gum, candy, cigarettes, salt tablets, packets of Kool-Aid, lighters, matches, sewing kits, Military Payment Certificates, C rations, and two or three canteens of water. Together, these items weighed between 15 and 20 pounds, depending upon a man's habits or rate of metabolism. Henry Dobbins, who was a big man, carried extra rations; he was especially fond of canned peaches in heavy syrup over pound cake. Dave Jensen, who practiced field hygiene, carried a toothbrush, dental floss, and several hotel-sized bars of soap he'd stolen on R&R in Sydney, Australia. Ted Lavender, who was scared, carried tranquilizers until he was shot in the head outside the village of Than Khe in mid-April. By necessity, and because it was SOP, they all carried steel helmets that weighed 5 pounds including the liner and camouflage cover. They carried the standard fatigue jackets and trousers. Very few carried underwear. On their feet they carried jungle boots—2.1 pounds—and Dave Jensen carried three pairs of socks and a can of Dr. Scholl's foot powder as a precaution against trench foot. Until he was shot, Ted

Lavender carried six or seven ounces of premium dope, which for him was a necessity. Mitchell Sanders, the RTO, carried condoms. Norman Bowker carried a diary. Rat Kiley carried comic books. Kiowa, a devout Baptist, carried an illustrated New Testament that had been presented to him by his father, who taught Sunday school in Oklahoma City, Oklahoma. As a hedge against bad times, however, Kiowa also carried his grandmother's distrust of the white man, his grandfather's old hunting hatchet. Necessity dictated. Because the land was mined and booby-trapped, it was SOP for each man to carry a steel-centered, nylon-covered flak jacket, which weighed 6.7 pounds, but which on hot days seemed much heavier. Because you could die so quickly, each man carried at least one large compress bandage, usually in the helmet band for easy access. Because the nights were cold, and because the monsoons were wet, each carried a green plastic poncho that could be used as a raincoat or groundsheet or makeshift tent. With its quilted liner, the poncho weighed almost two pounds, but it was worth every ounce. In April, for instance, when Ted Lavender was shot, they used his poncho to wrap him up, then to carry him across the paddy, then to lift him into the chopper that took him away.

To carry something was to hump it, as when Lieutenant Jimmy Cross humped his love for Martha up the hills and through the swamps. In its intransitive form, to hump meant to walk, or to march, but it implied burdens far beyond the intransitive.

Almost everyone humped photographs. In his wallet, Lieutenant Cross carried two photographs of Martha. The first was a Kodacolor snapshot signed Love, though he knew better. She stood against a brick wall. Her eyes were gray and neutral, her lips slightly open as she stared straight-on at the camera. At night, sometimes, Lieutenant Cross wondered who had taken the picture, because he knew she had boyfriends, because he loved her so much, and because he could see the shadow of the picture-taker spreading out against the brick wall. The second photograph had been clipped from the 1968 Mount Sebastian yearbook. It was an action shot— women's volleyball—and Martha was bent horizontal to the floor, reaching, the palms of her hands in sharp focus, the tongue taut, the expression frank and competitive. There was no visible sweat. She wore white gym shorts. Her legs, he thought, were almost certainly the legs of a virgin, dry and without hair, the left knee cocked and carrying her entire weight, which was just over one hundred pounds. Lieutenant Cross remembered touching that left knee. A dark theater, he remembered, and the movie was *Bonnie and Clyde,* and Martha wore a tweed skirt, and during the final scene, when he touched her knee, she turned and looked at him in a sad, sober way that made him pull his hand back, but he would always remember the feel of the tweed skirt and the knee beneath it and the sound of the gunfire that killed Bonnie and Clyde, how embarrassing it was, how slow and oppressive. He remembered kissing her good night at the dorm door. Right then, he thought, he should've done something brave. He should've carried her up the stairs to her room and tied her to the bed and touched that left knee all night long. He should've risked it. Whenever he looked at the photographs, he thought of new things he should've done.

What they carried was partly a function of rank, partly of field specialty.

As a first lieutenant and platoon leader, Jimmy Cross carried a compass, maps, code books, binoculars, and a .45-caliber pistol that weighed 2.9 pounds fully loaded. He carried a strobe light and the responsibility for the lives of his men.

As an RTO, Mitchell Sanders carried the PRC-25 radio, a killer, 26 pounds with its battery.

As a medic, Rat Kiley carried a canvas satchel filled with morphine and plasma and malaria tablets and surgical tape and comic books and all the things a medic must carry, including M&M's for especially bad wounds, for a total weight of nearly 20 pounds.

As a big man, therefore a machine gunner, Henry Dobbins carried the M-60 which weighed 23 pounds unloaded, but which was almost always loaded. In addition, Dobbins carried between 10 and 15 pounds of ammunition draped in belts across his chest and shoulders.

As PFCs or Spec 4s, most of them were common grunts and carried the standard M-16 gas-operated assault rifle. The weapon weighed 7.5 pounds unloaded, 8.2 pounds with its full 20-round magazine. Depending on numerous factors, such as topography and psychology, the riflemen carried anywhere from 12 to 20 magazines, usually in cloth bandoliers, adding on another 8.4 pounds at minimum, 14 pounds at maximum. When it was available, they also carried M-16 maintenance gear—rods and steel brushes and swabs and tubes of LSA oil—all of which weighed about a pound. Among the grunts, some carried the M-79 grenade launcher, 5.9 pounds unloaded, a reasonably light weapon except for the ammunition, which was heavy. A single round weighed 10 ounces. The typical load was 25 rounds. But Ted Lavender, who was scared, carried 34 rounds when he was shot and killed outside Than Khe, and he went down under an exceptional burden, more than 20 pounds of ammunition, plus the flak jacket and helmet and rations and water and toilet paper and tranquilizers and all the rest, plus the unweighed fear. He was dead weight. There was no twitching or flopping. Kiowa, who saw it happen, said it was like watching a rock fall, or a big sandbag or something—just boom, then down—not like the movies where the dead guy rolls around and does fancy spins and goes ass over teakettle—not like that, Kiowa said, the poor bastard just flat-fuck fell. Boom. Down. Nothing else. It was a bright morning in mid-April. Lieutenant Cross felt the pain. He blamed himself. They stripped off Lavender's canteens and ammo, all the heavy things, and Rat Kiley said the obvious, the guy's dead, and Mitchell Sanders used his radio to report one U.S. KIA and to request a chopper. Then they wrapped Lavender in his poncho. They carried him out to a dry paddy, established security, and sat smoking the dead man's dope until the chopper came. Lieutenant Cross kept to himself. He pictured Martha's smooth young face, thinking he loved her more than anything, more than his men, and now Ted Lavender was dead because he loved her so much and could not stop thinking about her. When the dustoff arrived, they carried Lavender aboard. Afterward they burned Than Khe. They marched until dusk, then dug their holes, and that night Kiowa kept explaining how you had to be there, how fast it was, how the poor guy just dropped like so much concrete. Boom-down, he said. Like cement.

In addition to the three standard weapons—the M-60, M-16, and M-79— they carried whatever presented itself, or whatever seemed appropriate as a means of killing or staying alive. They carried catch-as-catch-can. At various times, in various situations, they carried M-14s and CAR-15s and Swedish Ks and grease guns and captured AK-47s and Chi-Coms and RPGs and Simonov carbines and black market Uzis and .38-caliber Smith & Wesson handguns and 66 mm LAWs and shot-guns and silencers and blackjacks and boyonets and C-4 plastic explosives. Lee Strunk carried a slingshot; a weapon of last resort, he called it. Mitchell Sanders carried brass knuckles. Kiowa carried his grandfather's feathered hatchet. Every third or fourth man carried a Claymore antipersonnel mine—3.5 pounds with its firing device. They all carried fragmentation grenades—14 ounces each. They all carried at least one M-18 colored smoke grenade—24 ounces. Some carried CS or tear gas grenades. Some carried white phosphorus grenades. They carried all they could bear, and then some, including a silent awe for the terrible power of the things they carried.

In the first week of April, before Lavender died, Lieutenant Jimmy Cross received a good-luck charm from Martha. It was a simple pebble, an ounce at most. Smooth to the touch, it was a milky white color with flecks of orange and violet, oval-shaped, like a miniature egg. In the accompanying letter, Martha wrote that she had found the pebble on the Jersey shoreline, precisely where the land touched water at high tide, where things came together but also separated. It was this separate-but-together quality, she wrote, that had inspired her to pick up the pebble and to carry it in her breast pocket for several days, where it seemed weightless, and then to send it through the mail, by air, as a token of her truest feelings for him. Lieutenant Cross found this romantic. But he wondered what her truest feelings were, exactly, and what she meant by separate-but-together. He wondered how the tides and waves had come into play on that afternoon along the Jersey shoreline when Martha saw the pebble and bent down to rescue it from geology. He imagined bare feet. Martha was a poet, with the poet's sensibilities, and her feet would be brown and bare, the toenails unpainted, the eyes chilly and somber like the ocean in March, and though it was painful, he wondered who had been with her that afternoon. He imagined a pair of shadows moving along the strip of sand where things came together but also separated. It was phantom jealousy, he knew, but he couldn't help himself. He loved her so much. On the march, through the hot days of early April, he carried the pebble in his mouth, turning it with his tongue, tasting sea salt and moisture. His mind wandered. He had difficulty keeping his attention on the war. On occasion he would yell at his men to spread out the column, to keep their eyes open, but then he would slip away into daydreams, just pretending, walking barefoot along the Jersey shore, with Martha, carrying nothing. He would feel himself rising. Sun and waves and gentle winds, all love and lightness.

What they carried varied by mission.

When a mission took them to the mountains, they carried mosquito netting, machetes, canvas tarps, and extra bug juice.

If a mission seemed especially hazardous, or if it involved a place they knew to be bad, they carried everything they could. In certain heavily mined AOs, where the land was dense with Toe Poppers and Bouncing Betties, they took turns humping a 28-pound mine detector. With its headphones and big sensing plate, the equipment was a stress on the lower back and shoulders, awkward to handle, often useless because of the shrapnel in the earth, but they carried it anyway, partly for safety, partly for the illusion of safety.

On ambush, or other night missions, they carried peculiar little odds and ends. Kiowa always took along his New Testament and a pair of moccasins for silence. Dave Jensen carried night-sight vitamins high in carotene. Lee Strunk carried his slingshot; ammo, he claimed, would never be a problem. Rat Kiley carried brandy and M&M's candy. Until he was shot, Tel Lavender carried the starlight scope, which weighed 6.3 pounds with its aluminum carrying case. Henry Dobbins carried his girlfriend's pantyhose wrapped around his neck as a comforter. They all carried ghosts. When dark came, they would move out single file across the meadows and paddies to their ambush coordinates, where they would quietly set up the Claymores and lie down and spend the night waiting.

Other missions were more complicated and required special equipment. In mid-April, it was their mission to search out and destroy the elaborate tunnel complexes in the Than Khe area south of Chu Lai. To blow the tunnels, they carried one-pound blocks of pentrite high explosives, four blocks to a man, 68 pounds in all. They carried wiring, detonators, and battery-powered clackers. Dave Jensen carried earplugs. Most often, before blowing the tunnels, they were ordered by higher command to search them, which was considered bad news, but by and large they just shrugged and carried out orders. Because he was a big man, Henry Dobbins was excused from tunnel duty. The others would draw numbers. Before Lavender died there were 17 men in the platoon, and whoever drew the number 17 would strip off his gear and crawl in headfirst with a flashlight and Lieutenant Cross's .45-caliber pistol. The rest of them would fan out as security. They would sit down or kneel, not facing the hole, listening to the ground beneath them, imagining cobwebs and ghosts, whatever was down there—the tunnel walls squeezing in—how the flashlight seemed impossibly heavy in the hand and how it was tunnel vision in the very strictest sense, compression in all ways, even time, and how you had to wiggle in—ass and elbows—a swallowed-up feeling—and how you found yourself worrying about odd things: Will your flashlight go dead? Do rats carry rabies? If you screamed, how far would the sound carry? Would your buddies hear it? Would they have the courage to drag you out? In some respects, though not many, the waiting was worse than the tunnel itself. Imagination was a killer.

On April 16, when Lee Strunk drew the number 17, he laughed and muttered something and went down quickly. The morning was hot and very still. Not good,

Kiowa said. He looked at the tunnel opening, then out across a dry paddy toward the village of Than Khe. Nothing moved. No clouds or birds or people. As they waited, the men smoked and drank Kool-Aid, not talking much, feeling sympathy for Lee Strunk but also feeling the luck of the draw. You win some, you lose some, said Mitchell Sanders, and sometimes you settle for a rain check. It was a tired line and no one laughed.

Henry Dobbins ate a tropical chocolate bar. Ted Lavender popped a tranquilizer and went off to pee.

After five minutes, Lieutenant Jimmy Cross moved to the tunnel, leaned down, and examined the darkness. Trouble, he thought—a cave-in maybe. And then suddenly, without willing it, he was thinking about Martha. The stresses and fractures, the quick collapse, the two of them buried alive under all that weight. Dense, crushing love. Kneeling, watching the hole, he tried to concentrate on Lee Strunk and the war, all the dangers, but his love was too much for him, he felt paralyzed, he wanted to sleep inside her lungs and breathe her blood and be smothered. He wanted her to be a virgin and not a virgin, all at once. He wanted to know her. Intimate secrets: Why poetry? Why so sad? Why that grayness in her eyes? Why so alone? Not lonely, just alone—riding her bike across campus or sitting off by herself in the cafeteria—even dancing, she danced alone—and it was the aloneness that filled him with love. He remembered telling her that one evening. How she nodded and looked away. And how, later, when he kissed her, she received the kiss without returning it, her eyes wide open, not afraid, not a virgin's eyes, just flat and uninvolved.

Lieutenant Cross gazed at the tunnel. But he was not there. He was buried with Martha under the white sand at the Jersey shore. They were pressed together, and the pebble in his mouth was her tongue. He was smiling. Vaguely, he was aware of how quiet the day was, the sullen paddies, yet he could not bring himself to worry about matters of security. He was beyond that. He was just a kid at war, in love. He was twenty-four years old. He couldn't help it.

A few moments later Lee Strunk crawled out of the tunnel. He came up grinning, filthy but alive. Lieutenant Cross nodded and closed his eyes while the others clapped Strunk on the back and made jokes about rising from the dead.

Worms, Rat Kiley said. Right out of the grave. Fuckin' zombie.

The men laughed. They all felt great relief.

Spook city, said Mitchell Sanders.

Lee Strunk made a funny ghost sound, a kind of moaning, yet very happy, and right then, when Strunk made that high happy moaning sound, when we went *Ahhooooo*, right then Ted Lavender was shot in the head on his way back from peeing. He lay with his mouth open. The teeth were broken. There was a swollen black bruise under his left eye. The cheekbone was gone. Oh shit, Rat Kiley said, the guy's dead. The guy's dead, he kept saying, which seemed profound—the guy's dead. I mean really.

The things they carried were determined to some extent by superstition. Lieutenant Cross carried his good-luck pebble. Dave Jensen carried a rabbit's foot. Norman Bowker, otherwise a very gentle person, carried a thumb that had been presented to him as a gift by Mitchell Sanders. The thumb was dark brown, rubbery to the touch, and weighed four ounces at most. It had been cut from a VC corpse, a boy of fifteen or sixteen. They'd found him at the bottom of an irrigation ditch, badly burned, flies in his mouth and eyes. The boy wore black shorts and sandals. At the time of his death he had been carrying a pouch of rice, a rifle and three magazines of ammunition.

You want my opinion, Mitchell Sanders said, there's a definite moral here.

He put his hand on the dead boy's wrist. He was quiet for a time, as if counting a pulse, then he patted the stomach, almost affectionately, and used Kiowa's hunting hatchet to remove the thumb.

Henry Dobbins asked what the moral was.

Moral?

You know. *Moral.*

Sanders wrapped the thumb in toilet paper and handed it across to Norman Bowker. Three was no blood. Smiling, he kicked the boy's head, watched the flies scatter, and said, It's like with that old TV show—Paladin. Have gun, will travel.

Henry Dobbins thought about it.

Yeah, well, he finally said. I don't see no moral.

There it *is*, man.

Fuck off.

They carried USO stationery and pencils and pens. They carried Sterno, safety pins, trip flares, signal flares, spools of wire, razor blades, chewing tobacco, liberated joss sticks and statuettes of the smiling Buddha, candles, grease pencils, *The Stars and Stripes,* fingernail clippers, Psy Ops leaflets, bush hats, bolos, and much more. Twice a week, when the resupply choppers came in, they carried hot chow in green mermite cans and large canvas bags filled with iced beer and soda pop. They carried plastic water containers, each with a two-gallon capacity. Mitchell Sanders carried a set of starched tiger fatigues for special occasions. Henry Dobbins carried Black Flag insecticide. Dave Jensen carried empty sandbags that could be filled at night for added protection. Lee Strunk carried tanning lotion. Some things they carried in common. Taking turns, they carried the big PRC-77 scrambler radio, which weighed 30 pounds with its battery. They shared the weight of memory. They took up what others could no longer bear. Often, they carried each other, the wounded or weak. They carried infections. They carried chess sets, basketballs, Vietnamese-English dictionaries, insignia of rank, Bronze Stars and Purple Hearts, plastic cards imprinted with the Code of Conduct. They carried diseases, among them malaria and dysentery. They carried lice and ringworm and leeches and paddy algae and various rots and molds. They carried the land itself—Vietnam, the place, the soil—a powdery orange-red dust that covered their boots and fatigues and faces. They carried the sky. The whole atmosphere, they carried it, the humidity, the monsoons, the stink of fungus and decay, all of it, they carried gravity. They moved like mules. By daylight they took sniper fire, at night they were mortared, but it was not battle, it was just the endless march, village to village, without purpose, nothing won or lost. They marched for the sake of the march. They plodded along slowly, dumbly, leaning forward against the heat, unthinking, all blood and bone, simple grunts, soldiering with their legs, toiling up the hills and down into the paddies and across the rivers and up again and down, just humping, one step and then the next and then another, but no volition, no will, because it was automatic, it was anatomy, and the war was entirely a matter of posture and carriage, the hump was everything, a kind of inertia, a kind of emptiness, a dullness of desire and intellect and conscience and hope and human sensibility. Their principles were in their feet. Their calculations were biological. They had no sense of strategy or mission. They searched the villages without knowing what to look for, not caring, kicking over jars of rice, frisking children and old men, blowing tunnels, sometimes setting fires and sometimes not, then forming up and moving on to the next village, then other villages, where it would always be the same. They carried their own lives. The pressures were enormous. In the heat of early afternoon, they would remove their helmets and flak jackets, walking bare, which was dangerous but which helped ease the strain. They would often discard things along the route of march. Purely for comfort, they would throw away rations, blow their Claymores and grenades, no matter, because by nightfall the resupply choppers would arrive with more of the same, then a day or two later still more, fresh watermelons and crates of ammunition and sunglasses and woolen sweaters—the resources were stunning—sparklers for the Fourth of July, colored eggs for Easter—it was the great American war chest—the fruits of science, the smokestacks, the canneries, the arsenals at Hartford, the Minnesota forests, the machine shops, the vast fields of corn and wheat—they carried like freight trains; they carried it on their backs and shoulders—and for all the ambiguities of Vietnam, all the mysteries and unknowns, there was at least the single abiding certainty that they would never be at a loss for things to carry.

After the chopper took Lavender away, Lieutenant Jimmy Cross led his men into the village of Than Khe. They burned everything. They shot chickens and dogs, they trashed the village well, they called in artillery and watched the wreckage, then they marched for several hours through the hot afternoon, and then at dusk, while Kiowa explained how Lavender died, Lieutenant Cross found himself trembling.

He tried not to cry. With his entrenching tool, which weighed five pounds, he began digging a hole in the earth.

He felt shame. He hated himself. He had loved Martha more than his men, and as a consequence Lavender was now dead, and this was something he would have to carry like a stone in his stomach for the rest of the war.

All he could do was dig. He used his entrenching tool like an ax, slashing, feeling both love and hate, and then later, when it was full dark, he sat at the bottom of his foxhole and wept. It went on for a long while. In part, he was grieving for Ted Lavender, but mostly it was for Martha, and for himself, because she belonged to another world, which was not quite real, and because she was a junior at Mount

Sebastian College in New Jersey, a poet and a virgin and uninvolved, and because he realized she did not love him and never would.

Like cement, Kiowa whispered in the dark. I swear to God—boom, down. Not a word.

I've heard this, said Norman Bowker.

A pisser, you know? Still zipping himself up. Zapped while zipping.

All right, fine. That's enough.

Yeah, but you had to see it, the guy just—

I *heard*, man. Cement. So why not shut the fuck *up?*

Kiowa shook his head sadly and glanced over at the whole where Lieutenant Jimmy Cross sat watching the night. The air was thick and wet. A warm dense fog had settled over the paddies and there was the stillness that precedes rain.

After a time Kiowa sighed.

One thing for sure, he said. The lieutenant's in some deep hurt. I mean that crying jag—the way he was carrying on—it wasn't fake or anything, it was real heavy-duty hurt. The man cares.

Sure, Norman Bowker said.

Say what you want, the man does care.

We all got problems.

Not Lavender.

No, I guess not, Bowker said. Do me a favor, though.

Shut up?

That's a smart Indian. Shut up.

Shrugging, Kiowa pulled off his boots. He wanted to say more, just to lighten up his sleep, but instead he opened his New Testament and arranged it beneath his head as a pillow. The fog made things seem hollow and unattached. He tried not to think about Ted Lavender, but then he was thinking how fast it was, no drama, down and dead, and how it was hard to feel anything except surprise. It seemed unchristian. He wished he could find some great sadness, or even anger, but the emotion wasn't there and he couldn't make it happen. Mostly he felt pleased to be alive. He liked the smell of the New Testament under his cheek, the leather and ink and paper and glue, whatever the chemicals were. He liked hearing the sounds of night. Even his fatigue, it felt fine, the stiff muscles and the prickly awareness of his own body, a floating feeling. He enjoyed not being dead. Lying there, Kiowa admired Lieutenant Jimmy Cross's capacity for grief. He wanted to share the man's pain, he wanted to care as Jimmy Cross cared. And yet when he closed his eyes, all he could think was Boom-down, and all he could feel was the pleasure of having his boots off and the fog curling in around him and the damp soil and the Bible smells and the plush comfort of night.

After a moment Norman Bowker sat up in the dark.

What the hell, he said. You want to talk, *talk*. Tell it to me.

Forget it.

No, man, go on. One thing I hate, it's a silent Indian.

For the most part they carried themselves with poise, a kind of dignity. Now and then, however, there were times of panic, when they squealed or wanted to squeal but couldn't, when they twitched and made moaning sounds and covered their heads and said Dear Jesus and flopped around on the earth and fired their weapons blindly and cringed and sobbed and begged for the noise to stop and went wild and made stupid promises to themselves and to God and to their mothers and fathers, hoping not to die. In different ways, it happened to all of them. Afterward, when the firing ended, they would blink and peek up. They would touch their bodies, feeling shame, then quickly hiding it. They would force themselves to stand. As if in slow motion, frame by frame, the world would take on the old logic—absolute silence, then the wind, then sunlight, then voices. It was the burden of being alive. Awkwardly, the men would reassemble themselves, first in private, then in groups, becoming soldiers again. They would repair the leaks in their eyes. They would check for casualties, call in dust-offs, light cigarettes, try to smile, clear their throats and spit and begin cleaning their weapons. After a time someone would shake his head and say. No lie, I almost shit my pants, and someone else would laugh, which meant it was bad, yes, but the guy had obviously not shit his pants, it wasn't that bad, and in any case nobody would ever do such a thing and then go ahead and talk about it. They would squint into the dense, oppressive sunlight. For a few moments, perhaps, they would fall silent, lighting a joint and tracking its passage from man to man, inhaling, holding in the humiliation. Scary stuff, one of them might say. But then someone else would grin or flick his eyebrows and say, Roger-dodger, almost cut me a new asshole, *almost.*

There were numerous such poses. Some carried themselves with a sort of wistful resignation, others with pride or stiff soldierly discipline or good humor or macho zeal. They were afraid of dying but they were even more afraid to show it.

They found jokes to tell.

They used a hard vocabulary to contain the terrible softness. *Greased* they'd say. *Offed, lit up, zapped while zipping.* It wasn't cruelty, just stage presence. They were actors. When someone died, it wasn't quite dying, because in a curious way it seemed scripted, and because they had their lines mostly memorized, irony mixed with tragedy, and because they called it by other names, as if to encyst and destroy the reality of death itself. They kicked corpses. They cut off thumbs. They talked grunt lingo. They told stories about Ted Lavender's supply of tranquilizers, how the poor guy didn't feel a thing, how incredibly tranquil he was.

There's a moral here, said Mitchell Sanders.

They were waiting for Lavender's chopper, smoking the dead man's dope.

The moral's pretty obvious, Sanders said, and winked. Stay away from drugs. No joke, they'll ruin your day every time.

Cute, said Henry Dobbins.

Mind blower, get it? Talk about wiggy. Nothing left, just blood and brains.

They made themselves laugh.

There it is, they'd say. Over and over—there it is, my friend, there it is—as if the repetition itself were an act of poise, a balance between crazy and almost crazy, knowing without going, there it is, which meant be cool, let it ride, because Oh yeah man, you can't change what can't be changed, there it is, there it absolutely and positively and fucking well *is.*

They were tough.

They carried all the emotional baggage of men who might die. Grief, terror, love, longing—these were intangibles, but the intangibles had their own mass and specific gravity, they had tangible weight. They carried shameful memories. They carried the common secret of cowardice barely restrained, the instinct to run or freeze or hide, and in many respects this was the heaviest burden of all, for it could never be put down, it required perfect balance and perfect posture. They carried their reputations. They carried the soldier's greatest fear, which was the fear of blushing. Men killed, and died, because they were embarrassed not to. It was what had brought them to the war in the first place, nothing positive, no dream of glory or honor, just to avoid the blush of dishonor. They died so as not to die of embarrassment. They crawled into tunnels and walked point and advanced under fire. Each morning, despite the unknowns, they made their legs move. They endured. They kept humping. They did not submit to the obvious alternative, which was simply to close the eyes and fall. So easy, really. Go limp and tumble to the ground and let the muscles unwind and not speak and not bulge until your buddies picked you up and lifted you into the chopper that would roar and dip its nose and carry you off to the world. A mere matter of falling, yet no one ever fell. It was not courage, exactly; the object was not valor. Rather, they were too frightened to be cowards.

By and large they carried these things inside, maintaining the masks of composure. They sneered at sick call. They spoke bitterly about guys who had found release by shooting off their own toes or fingers. Pussies, they'd say. Candy-asses. It was fierce, mocking talk, with only a trace of envy or awe, but even so the image played itself out behind their eyes.

They imagined the muzzle against flesh. So easy: squeeze the trigger and blow away a toe. They imagined it. They imagined the quick, sweet pain, then the evacuation to Japan, then a hospital with warm beds and cute geisha nurses.

And they dreamed of freedom birds.

At night, on guard, staring into the dark, they were carried away by jumbo jets. They felt the rush of takeoff. *Gone!* they yelled. And then velocity—wings and engines—a smiling stewardess—but it was more than a plane, it was a real bird, a big sleek silver bird with feathers and talons and high screeching. They were flying. The weights fell off; there was nothing to bear. They laughed and held on tight, feeling the cold slap of wind and altitude, soaring, thinking *It's over, I'm gone!*—they were naked, they were light and free—it was all lightness, bright and fast and buoyant, light as light, a helium buzz in the brain, a giddy bubbling in the lungs as they were taken up over the clouds and the war, beyond duty, beyond gravity and mortification and global entanglements—*Sin loi!* they yelled. *I'm sorry, motherfuckers, but I'm out of it, I'm goofed, I'm on a space cruise, I'm gone!*—and it was a restful, unencumbered sensation, just riding the light waves, sailing that big silver freedom bird over the mountains and oceans, over America, over the farms and great sleeping cities and cemeteries and highways and the golden arches of McDonald's, it was flight, a kind of fleeing, a kind of falling, falling higher and higher, spinning off the edge of the earth and beyond the sun and through the vast, silent vacuum where there were no burdens and where everything weighed exactly nothing—*Gone!* they screamed. *I'm sorry but I'm gone!*—and so at night, not quite dreaming, they gave themselves over to lightness, they were carried, they were purely borne.

On the morning after Ted Lavender died, First Lieutenant Jimmy Cross crouched at the bottom of his foxhole and burned Martha's letters. Then he burned the two photographs. There was a steady rain falling, which made it difficult, but he used heat tabs and Sterno to build a small fire, screening it with his body, holding the photographs over the tight blue flame with the tips of his fingers.

He realized it was only a gesture. Stupid, he thought. Sentimental, too, but mostly just stupid.

Lavender was dead. You couldn't burn the blame.

Besides, the letters were in his head. And even now, without photographs, Lieutenant Cross could see Martha playing volleyball in her white gym shorts and yellow T-shirt. He could see her moving in the rain.

When the fire died out, Lieutenant Cross pulled his poncho over his shoulders and ate breakfast from a can.

There was no great mystery, he decided.

In those burned letters Martha had never mentioned the war, except to say, Jimmy, take care of yourself. She wasn't involved. She signed the letters Love, but it wasn't love, and all the fine lines and technicalities did not matter. Virginity was no longer an issue. He hated her. Yes, he did. He hated her. Love, too, but it was a hard, hating kind of love.

The morning came up wet and blurry. Everything seemed part of everything else, the fog and Martha and the deepening rain.

He was a soldier, after all.

Half smiling, Lieutenant Jimmy Cross took out his maps. He shook his head hard, as if to clear it, then bent forward and began planning the day's march. In ten minutes, or maybe twenty, he would rouse the men and they would pack up and head west, where the maps showed the country to be green and inviting. They would do what they had always done. The rain might add some weight, but otherwise it would be one more day layered upon all the other days.

He was realistic about it. There was that new hardness in his stomach. He loved her but he hated her.

No more fantasies, he told himself.

Henceforth, when he thought about Martha, it would be only to think that she belonged elsewhere. He would shut down the daydreams. This was not Mount Sebastian, it was another world, where there were no pretty poems or midterm exams, a place where men died because of carelessness and gross stupidity. Kiowa was right. Boomdown, and you were dead, never partly dead.

Briefly, in the rain, Lieutenant Cross saw Martha's gray eyes gazing back at him.

He understood.

It was very sad, he thought. The things men carried inside. The things men did or felt they had to do.

He almost nodded at her, but didn't.

Instead he went back to his maps. He was now determined to perform his duties firmly and without negligence. It wouldn't help Lavender, he knew that, but from this point on he would comport himself as an officer. He would dispose of his good-luck pebble. Swallow it, maybe, or use Lee Strunk's slingshot, or just drop it along the trail. On the march he would impose strict field discipline. He would be careful to send out flank security, to prevent straggling or bunching up, to keep his troops moving at the proper pace and at the proper interval. He would insist on clean weapons. He would confiscate the remainder of Lavender's dope. Later in the day, perhaps, he would call the men together and speak to them plainly. He would accept the blame for what had happened to Ted Lavender. He would be a man about it. He would look them in the eyes, keeping his chin level, and he would issue the new SOPs in a calm, impersonal tone of voice, a lieutenant's voice, leaving no room for argument or discussion. Commencing immediately, he'd tell them, they would no longer abandon equipment along the route of march. They would police up their acts. They would get their shit together, and keep it together, and maintain it neatly and in good working order.

He would not tolerate laxity. He would show strength, distancing himself.

Among the men there would be grumbling, of course, and maybe worse, because their days would seem longer and their loads heavier, but Lieutenant Jimmy Cross reminded himself that his obligation was not to be loved but to lead. He would dispense with love; it was not now a factor. And if anyone quarreled or complained, he would simply tighten his lips and arrange his shoulders in the correct command posture. He might give a curt little nod. Or he might not. He might just shrug and say, Carry on, then they would saddle up and form into a column and move out toward the villages west of Than Khe.

CRITICAL THINKING QUESTIONS

1. Despite its terrible consequences, war is sometimes remembered as a time of bonding and friendship like no other. What is there in such a horrible situation that could make men later miss it?

2. Sometimes the Vietnam War is portrayed to young people as the only war which fostered demonstrations and civil disobedience. Were there protests against our involvement in World War I or II, or is the Hollywood image of happy, singing Army volunteers accurate?

Ed Vega

Spanish Roulette

Sixto Andrade snapped the gun open and shut several times and then spun the cylinder, intrigued by the kaleidoscopic pattern made by the empty chambers. He was fascinated by the blue-black color of the metal, but more so by the almost toy-like quality of the small weapon. As the last rays of sunlight began their retreat from the four-room tenement flat, Sixto once again snapped the cylinder open and began loading the gun. It pleased him that each brass and lead projectile fit easily into each one of the chambers and yet would not fall out. When he had finished inserting the last of the bullets, he again closed the cylinder and, enjoying the increased weight of the gun, pointed it at the ceiling and pulled back the hammer.

"What's the piece for, man?"

Sixto had become so absorbed in the gun that he did not hear Willie Collazo, with whom he shared the apartment, come in. His friend's question came at him suddenly, the words intruding into the world he had created since the previous weekend.

"Nothing," he said, lowering the weapon.

"What do you mean, 'nothing?'" said Willie. "You looked like you were ready to play Russian roulette when I came in, bro."

"No way, man," said Sixto, and as he had been shown by Tommy Ramos, he let the hammer fall back gently into place. "It's called Spanish roulette," he added, philosophically.

Willie's dark face broke into a wide grin and his eyes, just as if he were playing his congas, laughed before he did. "No kidding, man," he said. "You taking up a new line of work? I know things are rough but sticking up people and writing po-etry don't go together."

Sixto put the gun on the table, tried to smile but couldn't, and recalled the last time he had read at the cafe on Sixth Street. Willie had played behind him, his hands making the drums sing a background to his words. "I gotta take care of some business, Willie," he said, solemnly, and, turning back to his friend, walked across the worn linoleum to the open window of the front room.

"Not like that, *panita*," Willie said as he followed him.

"Family stuff, bro."

"Who?"

"My sister," Sixto said without turning.

"Mandy?"

Sixto nodded, his small body taut with the anger he had felt when Mandy had fin-ished telling him of the attack. He looked out over the street four flights below and

584

fought an urge to jump. It was one solution but not *the* solution. Despairingly, he shook his head at the misery below: burned out buildings, torched by landlords because it was cheaper than fixing them; empty lots, overgrown with weeds and showing the ravages of life in the neighborhood. On the sidewalk, the discarded refrigerator still remained as a faceless sentinel standing guard over the lot, its door removed too late to save the little boy from Avenue B. He had been locked in it half the day while his mother, going crazy with worry, searched the streets so that by the time she saw the blue-faced child, she was too far gone to understand what it all meant.

He tried to cheer himself up by focusing his attention on the children playing in front of the open fire hydrant, but could not. The twilight rainbow within the stream of water, which they intermittently shot up in the air to make it cascade in a bright arc of white against the asphalt, was an illusion, *un engaño,* a poetic image of his childhood created solely to contrast his despair. He thought again of the crushed innocence on his sister's face and his blood felt like sand as it ran in his veins.

"You want to talk about it?" asked Willie.

"No, man," Sixto replied. "I don't."

Up the street, in front of the *bodega,* the old men were already playing dominoes and drinking beer. Sixto imagined them joking about each other's weaknesses, always, he thought ironically, with respect. They had no worries. Having lived a life of service to that which now beckoned him, they could afford to be light-hearted. It was as if he had been programmed early on for the task now facing him. He turned slowly, wiped an imaginary tear from his eyes and recalled his father's admonition about crying: "*Usted es un machito y los machos no lloran,* machos don't cry." How old had he been? Five or six, no more. He had fallen in the playground and cut his lip. His father's friends had laughed at the remark, but he couldn't' stop crying and his father had shaken him. *"Le dije que usted no es una chancleta. ¡Apréndalo bien!"* "You are not a girl, understand that once and for all!"

Concerned with Sixto's mood, once again Willie tried drawing him out. "*Coño,* bro, she's only fifteen," he said. "*¿Qué pasó?*"

The gentleness and calm which Sixto so much admired had faded from Willie's face and now mirrored his own anguish. It was wrong to involve his friend but perhaps that was part of it. Willie was there to test his resolve. He had been placed there by fate to make sure the crime did not go unpunished. In the end, when it came to act, he'd have only his wits and manhood.

"It's nothing, bro," Sixto replied, walking back into the kitchen. "I told you, family business. Don't worry about it."

"Man, don't be like that."

There was no injury in Willie's voice and as if someone had suddenly punched him in the stomach to obtain a confession, the words burst out of Sixto.

"*Un tipo la mangó en el rufo,* man. Some dude grabbed her. You happy now?"

"Where?" Willie asked, knowing that uttering the words was meaningless. "In the projects?"

"Yeah, last week. She got let out of school early and he grabbed her in the elevator and brought her up to the roof."

"And you kept it all in since you came back from your Mom's Sunday night?"

"What was I supposed to do, man? Go around broadcasting that my sister got took off?"

"I'm sorry, Sixto. You know I don't mean it like that."

"I know, man. I know."

"Did she know the guy? *Un cocolo*, right? A black dude. They're the ones that go for that stuff."

"No, man. It wasn't no *cocolo*."

"But she knew him."

"Yeah, you know. From seeing him around the block. *Un bonitillo*, man. Pretty dude that deals coke and has a couple of women hustling for him. A dude named Lino."

"*¿Bien blanco?* Pale dude with Indian hair like yours?"

"Yeah, that's the guy."

"Drives around in a gold Camaro, right?"

"Yeah, I think so." Willie nodded several times and then shook his head.

"He's Shorty Pardo's cousin, right?" Sixto knew about the family connection but hadn't wanted to admit it until now.

"So?" he said, defiantly.

"Those people are crazy, bro," said Willie.

"I know."

"They've been dealing *tecata* up there in El Barrio since forever, man. Even the Italians stay clear of them, they're so crazy."

"That doesn't mean nothing to me," said Sixto, feeling his street manhood, the bravado which everyone develops growing up in the street, surfacing. Bad talk was the antidote to fear and he wasn't immune to it. "I know how crazy they are, but I'm gonna tell you something. I don't care who the dude is. I'm gonna burn him. Gonna set his heart on fire with that piece."

"Hey, go easy, *panita*," said Willie. "Be cool, bro. I know how you feel but that ain't gonna solve nothing. You're an artist, man. You know that? A poet. And a playwright. You're gonna light up Broadway one of these days." Willie was suddenly silent as he reflected on his words. He sat down on one of the kitchen chairs and lowered his head. After a few moments he looked up and said: "Forget what I said, man. I don't know what I'm talking about. I wouldn't know what to do if that happened to one of the women in my family. I probably would've done the dude in by now. I'm sorry I said anything. I just don't wanna see you messed up. And I'm not gonna tell you to go to the cops, either."

Sixto did not answer Willie. They both knew going to the police would serve no purpose. As soon as the old man found out, he'd beat her for not protecting herself. It would become a personal matter, as if it had been he who had submitted. He'd rant and rave about short skirts and lipstick and music and then compare everything to the way things were on the island and his precious hometown, his beloved Cacimar, like it was the center of the universe and the place where all the laws governing the human race had been created. But Sixto had nothing to worry

about. He was different from his father. He was getting an education, had been enlightened to truth and beauty and knew about equality and justice. Hell, he was a
new man, forged out of steel and concrete, not old banana leaves and coconuts. And
yet, he wanted to strike back and was sick to his stomach because he wanted Lino
Quintana in front of him, on his knees, begging for mercy. He'd smoke a couple of
joints and float back uptown to the Pardo's turf and then blast away at all of them
like he was the Lone Ranger.

He laughed sarcastically at himself and thought that in the end he'd probably
back down, allow the matter to work itself out and let Mandy live with the scar for
the rest of her life. And he'd tell himself that rape was a common thing, even in
families, and that people went on living and working and making babies like a
bunch of zombies, like somebody's puppets without ever realizing who was pulling
the strings. It was all crazy. You were born and tagged with a name: Rodríguez,
Mercado, Torres, Cartagena, Pantoja, Maldonado, Sandoval, Ballester, Nieves,
Carmona. All of them, funny-ass Spanish names. And then you were told to speak
English and be cool because it was important to try and get over by imitating the
Anglo-Saxon crap, since that's where all the money and success were to be found.
Nobody actually came out and said it, but it was written clearly in everything you
saw, printed boldly between the lines of books, television, movies, advertising. And
at the place where you got your love, your mother's milk, your rice and beans, you
were told to speak Spanish and be respectful and defend your honor and that of the
women around you.

"I'm gonna burn him, Willie," Sixto repeated. "Gonna burn him right in his
güevos. Burn him right there in his balls so he can feel the pain before I blow him
away and let God deal with him. He'll understand, man, because I don't." Sixto felt
the dizzying anger blind him for a moment. "*Coño,* man, she was just fifteen," he
pleaded, as if Willie could absolve him of his sin before it had been committed. "I
have to do it, man. She was just a kid. *Una nena,* man. A little innocent girl who
dug Latin music and danced only with her girlfriends at home and believed all the
nonsense about purity and virginity, man. And now this son of a bitch went and did
it to her. *Le hizo el daño.*"

That's what women called it. That damage. And it was true. Damaged goods.
He didn't want to believe it but that's how he felt. In all his educated, enlightened
splendor, that's how he felt. Like she had been rendered untouchable, her female-
ness soiled and smeared forever. Like no man would want to love her, knowing
what had happened. The whole thing was so devastating that he couldn't imagine
what it was like to be a woman. If they felt even a little of what he was experiencing,
it was too much. And he, her own brother, already talking as if she were dead.
That's how bad it was. Like she was a memory.

"I'm gonna kill him, Willie," said Sixto once more, pounding on the wall. "*¡Lo
mato, coño! Lo mato, lo mato,*" he repeated the death threat over and over in a frenzy.
Willie stood up and reached for his arm but Sixto pulled roughly away. "It's cool,
man," he said, and put his opened hands in front of him. "I'm all right. Everything's
cool."

"Slow down," Willie pleaded. "Slow down."

"You're right, man. I gotta slow down." Sixto sat down but before long was up again. "Man, I couldn't sleep the last couple of nights. I kept seeing myself wearing the shame the rest of my life. I gave myself every excuse in the book. I even prayed, Willie. Me, a spic from the streets of the Big Apple, hip and slick, writing my *jíbaro* poetry; *saliéndome las palabras de las entrañas; inventando foquin mundos* like a god; like *foquin* Juracán pitching lightning bolts at the people to wake them from their stupor, man. Wake them up from their lethargy and their four-hundred-year-old sleep of self-induced tyranny, you know?"

"I understand, man."

"Willie, man, I wanted my words to thunder, to shake the earth *pa' que la gente le pida a Yuquiyú que los salve.*"

"And it's gonna be that way, bro. You're the poet, man. The voice."

"And me praying. Praying, man. And not to Yuquiyú but to some distorted European idea. I'm messed up, bro. Really messed up. Writing all this jive poetry that's supposed to incite the people to take up arms against the oppressor and all the while my heart is dripping with feelings of love and brotherhood and peace like some programmed puppet, Willie."

"I hear you."

"I mean, I bought all that stuff, man. All that liberal American jive. I bought it. I marched against the war in Vietnam, against colonialism and capitalism, and for the Chicano brothers cracking their backs in the fields, marched till my feet were raw, and every time I saw lettuce or grapes, I saw poison. And man, it felt right, Willie."

"It was a righteous cause, man."

"And I marched for the independence of the island, of Puerto Rico, Willie: *de Portorro, de Borinquen, la buena, la sagrada, el terruño, madre de todos nosotros; bendita seas entre todas las mujeres y bendito sea el fruto de tu vientre pelú.* I marched for the land of our people and it felt right."

"It is right, man."

"You know, once and for all I had overcome all the anger of being a colonized person without a country and my culture being swallowed up, digested and thrown back up so you can't even recognize what it's all about. I had overcome all the craziness and could stand above it; I could look down on the brothers and sisters who took up arms in '50 and '54 when I wasn't even a fantasy in my pop's mind, man. I could stand above all of them, even the ones with their bombs now. I could pay tribute to them with words but still judge them crazy. And it was okay. It felt right to wear two faces, to go back and forth from poetic fury to social condescension or whatever you wanna call it. I thought I had it beat with the education and the poetry and opening up my heart like some long-haired, brown-skinned hippy. And now this. I'm a hypocrite, man."

Like the water from the open fire hydrant, the words had rushed out of him. And yet he couldn't say exactly what it was that troubled him about the attack on his sister, couldn't pinpoint what it was that made his face hot and his blood race angrily in his veins. Willie, silenced by his own impotence, sat looking at him. He knew he could neither urge him on nor discourage him and inevitably he would have to stand aside and let whatever was to happen run its course. His voice almost a whisper, he said, "It's okay, Sixto. I know how it feels. Just let the pain come out, man. Just let it out. Cry if you have to."

But the pain would never leave him. Spics weren't Greeks and the word katharsis had no meaning in private tragedy. Sixto's mind raced back into time, searching for an answer, knowing, even as it fled like a wounded animal seeking refuge from its tormentors, that it was an aimless search. It was like running a maze. Like the rats in the psychology films and the puzzles in the children's section of weekend newspapers. One followed a path with a pencil until he came to a dead end, then retraced his steps. Thousands of years passed before him in a matter of minutes.

The Tainos: a peaceful people, some history books said. No way, he thought. They fought the Spaniards, drowned them to test their immortality. And their *caciques* were as fierce and as brave as Crazy Horse or Geronimo. Proud chiefs they were. Jumacao, Daguao, Yaureibo, Caguax, Agueybaná, Mabodamaca, Aymamón, Urayoán, Orocobix, Guarionex all fought the Spaniards with all they had ... *guasábara ... guasábara ... guasábara ...* their battle cry echoing through the hills like an eerie phantom; they fought their horses and dogs; they fought their swords and guns and when there was no other recourse, rather than submitting, they climbed sheer cliffs and, holding their children to their breasts, leapt into the sea.

And the blacks: *los negros,* whose blood and heritage he carried. They didn't submit to slavery but escaped and returned to conduct raids against the oppressors, so that the whole *negrito lindo* business, so readily accepted as a term of endearment, was a joke, an appeasement on the part of the Spaniards. The *bombas* and *bembas* and *ginganbó* and their all night dances and *oraciones* to Changó: warrior men of the Jelofe, Mandingo, Mende, Yoruba, Dahomey, Ashanti, Ibo, Fante, Baule and Congro tribes, choosing battle over slavery.

And the Spaniards: certainly not a peaceful people. For centuries they fought each other and then branched out to cross the sea and slaughter hundreds of thousands of Indians, leaving an indelible mark on entire civilizations, raping and pillaging and gutting the earth of its riches, so that when it was all done and they laid in a drunken stupor four hundred years later, their pockets empty, they rose again to fight themselves in civil war.

And way back, way back before El Cid Campeador began to wage war: The Moors. *Los moros ... alhambra, alcázar, alcohol, almohada, alcade, alboroto ...* NOISE ... CRIES OF WAR ... A thousand years the maze traveled and it led to a dead end with dark men atop fleet Arabian stallions, dark men, both in visage and intent, raising their scimitars against those dishonoring their house ... they had invented algebra and Arabic numbers and it all added up to war ... there was no other way ...

"I gotta kill him, bro," Sixto heard himself say. "I gotta. Otherwise I'm as good as dead."

One had to live with himself and that was the worst part of it; he had to live with the knowledge and that particular brand of cowardice that eroded the mind and destroyed one's soul. And it wasn't so much that his sister had been wronged. He'd seen that. The injury came from not retaliating. He was back at the beginning. Banana leaves and coconuts and machete duels at sundown. Just like his father and his *jíbaro* values. For even if the aggressor never talked, even if he never mentioned his act to another soul for whatever reason, there was still another person, another member of the tribe, who could single him out in a crowd and say to himself: "That one belongs to me and so does his sister."

Sixto tried to recall other times when his manhood had been challenged, but it seemed as if everything had happened long ago and hadn't been important: kid fights over mention of his mother, rights of ownership of an object, a place in the hierarchy of the block, a word said of his person, a lie, a bump by a stranger on a crowded subway train—nothing ever going beyond words or at worst, a sudden shoving match quickly broken up by friends.

But this was different. His brain was not functioning properly, he thought. He tried watching himself, tried to become an observer, the impartial judge of his actions. Through a small opening in his consciousness, he watched the raging battle. His heart called for the blood of the enemy and his brain urged him to use caution. There was no thought of danger, for in that region of struggle, survival meant not so much escaping with his life, but conquering fear and regaining his honor.

Sixto picked up the gun and studied it once more. He pushed the safety to make sure it was locked and placed the gun between the waistband of his pants and the flesh of his stomach. The cold metal sent slivers of ice running down his legs. It was a pleasant sensation, much as if a woman he had desired for some time had suddenly let him know, in an unguarded moment, that intimacy was possible between them. Avoiding Willie's eyes, he walked around the kitchen, pulled out his shirt and let it hang out over his pants. It was important that he learn to walk naturally and reduce his self-consciousness about the weapon. But it was his mind working tricks again. Nobody would notice. The idea was to act calmly. That's what everyone said: the thieves, the cheap stickup men who mugged old people and taxi drivers; the burglars who, like vultures, watched the movement of a family until certain that they were gone, swooped down and cleaned out the apartment, even in the middle of the day; the check specialists, who studied mailboxes as if they were bank vaults so they could break them open and steal welfare checks or fat letters from the island on the chance they might contain money orders or cash. They all said it. Even the young gang kids said it. Don't act suspiciously. Act as if you were going about your business.

Going to shoot someone was like going to work. That was it. He'd carry his books and nobody would suspect that he was carrying death. He laughed inwardly at the immense joke. He'd once seen a film in which Robert Mitchum, posing as a preacher, had pulled a derringer out of a Bible in the final scene. Why not. He'd hollow out his Western Civilization text and place the gun in it. It was his duty. The act was a way of surviving, of earning what was truly his. Whether a pay check or an education, it meant nothing without self-respect.

But the pieces of the puzzle did not fit and Sixto sat down dejectedly. He let his head fall into his hands and for a moment thought he would cry. Willie said nothing and Sixto waited, listening, the void of silence becoming larger and larger, expanding so that the sounds of the street, a passing car, the excitement of a child, the rushing water from the open hydrant, a mother's window warning retreated, became fainter and seemed to trim the outer edges of the nothingness within the silence. He could hear his own breathing and the beating of his heart and still he waited.

And then slowly, as if waking from a refreshing sleep, Sixto felt himself grow calmer and a pleasant coldness entered his body as heart and mind finally merged and became tuned to his mission. He smiled at the feeling and knew he had gone through the barrier of doubt and fear which had been erected to protect him from himself, to make sure he did not panic at the last moment. War had to be similar. He had heard the older men, the ones who had survived Vietnam, talk about it. Sonny Maldonado with his plastic foot, limping everywhere he went, quiet and unassuming, talked about going through a doorway and into a quiet room where one died a little and then came out again, one's mind alive but the rest of the body already dead to the upcoming pain.

It had finally happened, he thought. There was no anger or regret, no rationalizations concerning future actions. No more justifications or talk about honor and dignity. Instead, Sixto perceived the single objective coldly. There was neither danger nor urgency in carrying out the sentence and avenging the wrong. It seemed almost too simple. If it took years he knew the task would be accomplished. He would study the habits of his quarry, chart his every movement, and one day he'd strike. He would wait in a deserted hallway some late night, calmly walk out of the shadows, only his right index finger and his brain connected and say: "How you doing, Lino?" and his voice alone would convey the terrible message. Sixto smiled to himself and saw, as in a slow motion cinematic shot, his mind's ghost delicately squeeze the trigger repeatedly, the small animal muzzle of the gun following Lino Quintana's body as it fell slowly and hit the floor, the muscles of his victim's face twitching and life ebbing away forever. It happened all the time and no one was ever discovered.

Sixto laughed, almost too loudly. He took the gun out from under his shirt and placed it resolutely on the table. "I gotta think some more, man," he said. "That's crazy rushing into the thing. You wanna a beer, Willie?"

Willie was not convinced of his friend's newly found calm. Reluctantly, he accepted the beer. He watched Sixto and tried to measure the depth of his eyes. They had become strangely flat, the glint of trust in them absent. It was as if a thin, opaque veil had been sewn over the eyes to mask Sixto's emotions. He felt helpless but said nothing. He opened the beer and began mourning the loss. Sixto was right, he thought. It was Spanish roulette. Spics were born and the cylinder spun. When it stopped one was handed the gun and, without looking, had to bring it to one's head, squeeze the trigger and take his chances.

The belief was pumped into the bloodstream, carved into the flesh through generations of strife, so that being was the enactment of a ritual rather than the beginning of a new life. One never knew his own reactions until faced with Sixto's dilemma. And yet the loss would be too great, the upcoming grief too profound and the ensuing suffering eternal. The violence would be passed on to another generation to be displayed as an invisible coat of arms, much as Sixto's answer had come to him as a relic. His friend would never again look at the world with wonder, and poetry would cease to spring from his heart. If he did write, the words would be guarded, careful, full of excuses and apologies for living. Willie started to raise the beer in a toast but thought better of it and set the can on the table.

"Whatever you do, bro," he said, "be careful."

"Don't worry, man," Sixto replied. "I got the thing under control." He laughed once again and suddenly his eyes were ablaze were hatred. He picked up the gun, stuck it back into his pants and stood up. "No good, man," he said, seemingly to himself, and rushed out, slamming the door of the apartment behind him.

Beyond the sound of the door, Willie could hear the whirring cylinder as it began to slow down, each minute click measuring the time before his friend had to raise the weapon to his head and kill part of himself.

CRITICAL THINKING QUESTIONS

1. There is a clear conflict in this story between the forces of learning and the forces of violence. Should Willie intervene? Which is the good side?

2. How do the main characters define the concept of justice?

WRITING TOPICS

1. Assuming Willie would argue for the poetic/learning side while Sixto would argue for the necessity for revenge, write a dialogue between the two men in which each states his side of the argument.

2. Acting as a third party mediator, construct a Rogerian-style conclusion to the argument.

Gwendolyn Brooks

The Boy Died in My Alley

Without my having known.
Policeman said, next morning,
"Apparently died Alone."
"You heard a shot?" Policeman said.
Shots I hear and Shots I hear.
I never see the dead.

The Shot that killed him yes I heard
as I heard the Thousand shots before;
careening tinnily down the nights
across my years and arteries.

Policeman pounded on my door.
"Who is it?" "POLICE!" Policeman yelled.
"A boy was dying in your alley.
A boy is dead, and in your alley.
And have you known this Boy before?"

I have known this Boy before.
I have known this Boy before, who
ornaments my alley.
I never saw his face at all.
I never saw his futurefall.
But I have known this Boy.

I have always heard him deal with death.
I have always heard the shout, the volley.
I have closed my heart-ears late and early.
And I have killed him ever.

I joined the Wild and killed him
with knowledgeable unknowing.
I saw where he was going.
I saw him Crossed. And seeing.
I did not take him down.

He cried not only "Father!"
but "Mother!
Sister!
Brother!"
The cry climbed up the alley.
It went up to the wind.
It hung upon the heaven
for a long
stretch-strain of Moment.

The red floor of my alley
is a special speech to me.

WRITING TOPIC

Write a paper analyzing the writer's concern for this dead boy. Why does she
feel this guilt?

Martín Espada

Bully

Boston, Massachusetts, 1987

In the school auditorium,
the Theodore Roosevelt statue
is nostalgic
for the Spanish-American War,
each fist lonely for a saber
or the reins of anguish-eyed horses,
or a podium to clatter with speeches
glorying in the malaria of conquest.

But now the Roosevelt school
is pronounced *Hernández*.
Puerto Rico has invaded Roosevelt
with its army of Spanish-singing children
in the hallways,
brown children devouring
the stockpiles of the cafeteria,
children painting *Taíno* ancestors
that leap naked across murals.

Roosevelt is surrounded
by all the faces
he ever shoved in eugenic spite
and cursed as mongrels, skin of one race,
hair and cheekbones of another.

Once Marines tramped
from the newsreel of his imagination;
now children plot to spray graffiti
in parrot-brilliant colors
across the Victorian mustache
and monocle.

CRITICAL THINKING QUESTIONS

1. What is the poet's *claim of value* about Theodore Roosevelt?
2. On which rhetorical appeal does he base his argument?

3. Find examples of *connotative language* (see Glossary). Do these word usages contribute to or detract from the poet's argument?

WRITING TOPIC

Assume a role as Theodore Roosevelt's defender. Do some research and write a rebuttal to Espada's poem's argument. Or, using your research and Espada's poem as evidence, write a Rogerian argument that evaluates Roosevelt's legacy.

Carolyn Forché

The Colonel

What you have heard is true. I was in his house. His wife carried a tray of coffee and sugar. His daughter filed her nails, his son went out for the night. There were daily papers, pet dogs, a pistol on the ion beside him. The moon swung bare on its black cord over the house. On the television was a cop show. It was in English. Broken bottles were embedded in the walls around the house to scoop the kneecaps from a man's legs or cut his hands to lace. On the windows there were gratings like those in liquor stores. We had dinner, rack of lamb, good wine, a gold bell was on the table for calling the maid. The maid brought green mangoes, salt, a type of bread. I was asked how I enjoyed the country. There was a brief commercial in Spanish. His wife took everything away. There was some talk then of how difficult it had become to govern. The parrot said hello on the terrace. The colonel told it to shut up, and pushed himself from the table. My friend said to me with his eyes: say nothing. The colonel returned with a sack used to bring groceries home. He spilled many human ears on the table. They were like dried peach halves. There is no other way to say this. He took one of them in his hands, shook it in our faces, dropped it into a water glass. It came alive there. I am tired of fooling around he said. As for the rights of anyone, tell your people they can go fuck themselves. He swept the ears to the floor with his arm and held the last of his wine in the air. Something for your poetry, no? he said. Some of the ears on the floor caught this scrap of his voice. Some of the ears on the floor were pressed to the ground.

CRITICAL THINKING QUESTIONS

1. In terms of persuasion, the colonel is not subtle. What is the by-product of his approach to persuasion? Think about what usually happens to dictators in the end.

2. Is there no way to argue with such a man as the Colonel except through violence?

WRITING TOPIC

The Colonel does not care about the rights of anyone, and in his situation he seems to be able to get away with this approach to governing and controlling people. Threatening people with physical violence creates an effective short-term argument; however, the byproduct is anger and hostility which, in the long run, often is counterproductive. Using examples, argue that the carrot is more powerful than the stick.

Robert Frost

Mending Wall

Something there is that doesn't love a wall,
That sends the frozen-ground-swell under it,
And spills the upper boulders in the sun;
And makes gaps even two can pass abreast.
The work of hunters is another thing:
I have come after them and made repair
Where they have left not one stone on a stone,
But they would have the rabbit out of hiding,
To please the yelping dogs. The gaps I mean,
No one has seen them made or heard them made,
But at spring mending-time we find them there.
I let my neighbor know beyond the hill;
And on a day we meet to walk the line
And set the wall between us once again.
We keep the wall between us as we go.
To each the boulders that have fallen to each.
And some are loaves and some so nearly balls
We have to use a spell to make them balance:
"Stay where you are until our backs are turned!"
We wear our fingers rough with handling them.
Oh, just another kind of outdoor game,
One on a side. It comes to little more:
There where it is we do not need the wall:
He is all pine and I am apple orchard.
My apple trees will never get across
And eat the cones under his pines, I tell him.
He only says, "Good fences make good neighbors."
Spring is the mischief in me, and I wonder
If I could put a notion in his head:
"*Why* do they make good neighbors? Isn't it
Where there are cows? But here there are no cows.
Before I built a wall I'd ask to know
What I was walling in or walling out,
And to whom I was like to give offense.
Something there is that doesn't love a wall,
That wants it down." I could say "Elves" to him,

But it's not elves exactly, and I'd rather
He said it for himself. I see him there
Bringing a stone grasped firmly by the top
In each hand, like an old-stone savage armed.
He moves in darkness as it seems to me,
Not of woods only and the shade of trees.
He will not go behind his father's saying,
And he likes having thought of it so well
He says again, "Good fences make good neighbors."

CRITICAL THINKING QUESTIONS

1. How does the speaker use *logos* appeal to argue against the fence between him and his neighbor?

2. In lines 32 and 33, the speaker says, "Before I built a wall I'd ask to know/ What I was walling in or walling out." When fences are not walling in, what might they be walling out?

3. Whose viewpoint do you support, the speaker's—"Something there is that doesn't love a wall"—or the neighbor's—"Good fences make good neighbors"?

WRITING TOPIC

Although in the United States, we often advocate the idea of individual independence and free expression, there are limits (*walls*) which most of us accept. Select a group of people who push against these limits, and defend or criticize its position.

A. E. Housman

The Laws of God, the Laws of Man

The laws of God, the laws of man,
He may keep that will and can;
Not I: let God and man decree
Laws for themselves and not for me;
And if my ways are not as theirs
Let them mind their own affairs.
Their deeds I judge and much condemn,
Yet when did I make laws for them?
Please yourselves, say I, and they
Need only look the other way.
But no, they will not; they must still
Wrest their neighbour to their will,
And make me dance as they desire
With jail and gallows and hell-fire.
And how am I to face the odds
Of man's bedevilment and God's?
I, a stranger and afraid
In a world I never made.
They will be master, right or wrong;
Though both are foolish, both are strong.
And since, my soul, we cannot fly
To Saturn nor to Mercury,
Keep we must, if keep we can,
These foreign laws of God and man.

CRITICAL THINKING QUESTIONS

1. What argument does the speaker make against laws? On which rhetorical appeal does it rely?
2. What argument does the speaker make for obeying laws? On which rhetorical appeal is it based?
3. Overall, what is the speaker's claim? Do you agree or disagree, and why?

Langston Hughes

Theme for English B

The instructor said,

> *Go home and write*
> *a page tonight.*
> *And let that page come out of you—*
> *Then, it will be true.*

I wonder if it's that simple?
I am twenty-two, colored, born in Winston-Salem.
I went to school there, then Durham, then here
to this college on the hill above Harlem.
I am the only colored student in my class.
The steps from the hill lead down into Harlem,
through a park, then I cross St. Nicholas,
Eighth Avenue, Seventh, and I come to the Y,
the Harlem Branch Y, where I take the elevator
up to my room, sit down, and write this page:

It's not easy to know what is true for you or me
at twenty-two, my age. But I guess I'm what
I feel and see and hear, Harlem, I hear you:
hear you, hear me—we two—you, me, talk on this page.
(I hear New York, too.) Me—who?

Well, I like to eat, sleep, drink, and be in love.
I like to work, read, learn, and understand life.
I like a pipe for a Christmas present,
or records—Bessie, bop, or Bach.
I guess being colored doesn't make me *not* like
the same things other folks like who are other races.
So will my page be colored that I write?
Being me, it will not be white.
But it will be
a part of you, instructor.
You are white—
yet a part of me, as I am a part of you.
That's American.

Sometimes perhaps you don't want to be a part of me.
Nor do I often want to be a part of you.
But we are, that's true!
As I learn from you,
I guess you learn from me—
although you're older—and white—
and somewhat more free.

This is my page for English B.

CRITICAL THINKING QUESTIONS

1. What power issues is the poem's speaker addressing?

2. In resolving his power issues, what Rogerian position does the speaker articulate? What is your opinion of this position?

WRITING TOPICS

1. Writing in the first person, create an argument for preserving a tradition found within your family or community. Use anecdotes and narrative to make this tradition clear for the reader.

2. Read several articles about *multiculturalism* so you understand the term and some of the controversy surrounding it. Many colleges and universities have multicultural requirements; argue for or against maintaining a multicultural requirement on your campus.

Denise Levertov

Everything That Acts Is Actual

From the tawny light
from the rainy nights
from the imagination finding
itself and more than itself
alone and more than alone
at the bottom of the well where the moon lives,
can you pull me

into December? a lowland
of space, perception of space
towering of shadows of clouds blown upon
clouds over
          new ground, new made
under heavy December footsteps? *the only
way to live?*

The flawed moon
acts on the truth, and makes
an autumn of tentative
silences.
You lived, but somewhere else,
your presence touched others, ring upon ring,
and changed. Did you think
I would not change?

CRITICAL THINKING QUESTIONS

1. How should individuals carry out the responsibility to see beauty and to know truth in their daily lives?

2. Has your "presence touched others"? In particular, have you touched someone in an especially positive way?

James Merrill

Casual Wear

Your average tourist: Fifty. 2.3
Times married. Dressed, this year, in Ferdi Plinthbower
Originals. Odds 1 to 9
Against her strolling past the Embassy

Today at noon. Your average terrorist:
Twenty-five. Celibate. No use for trends,
At least in clothing. Mark, though, where it ends.
People have come forth made of colored mist

Unsmiling on one hundred million screens
To tell of his prompt phone call to the station,
"Claiming responsibility"—devastation
Signed with a flourish, like the dead wife's jeans.

WRITING TOPIC

Read about a particular terrorist activity somewhere in the world. Then read further to gain some understanding of the group's motivation. Write a letter to the *New York Times* in which a leader of this group justifies its activities.

John Milton

When I Consider How My Light Is Spent

When I consider how my light is spent,
  Ere half my days in this dark world and wide,
  And that one talent which is death to hide
Lodged with me useless, though my soul more bent
To serve therewith my Maker, and present
  My true account, lest He returning chide;
  "Doth God exact day-labor, light denied?"
I fondly ask. But Patience, to prevent
That murmur, soon replies, "God doth not need
  Either man's work or His own gifts. Who best
  Bear His mild yoke, they serve Him best. His state
Is kingly: thousands at His bidding speed,
  And post o'er land and ocean without rest;
  They also serve who only stand and wait."

CRITICAL THINKING QUESTIONS

1. According to Milton, in deciding how to use one's individual talents, what value assumption or *warrant* about the purpose of one's life underlies that choice? Do you accept this warrant?

2. In your opinion, what values should inform one's choice of a career or profession?

Naomi Shihab Nye

Famous

The river is famous to the fish.

The loud voice is famous to silence,
which knew it would inherit the earth
before anybody said so.

The cat sleeping on the fence is famous to the birds
watching him from the birdhouse.

The tear is famous, briefly, to the cheek.
The idea you carry close to your bosom
is famous to your bosom.

The boot is famous to the earth,
more famous than the dress shoe,
which is famous only to floors.

The bent photograph is famous to the one who carries it
and not at all famous to the one who is pictured.

I want to be famous to shuffling men
who smile while crossing streets,
sticky children in grocery lines,
famous as the one who smiled back.

I want to be famous in the way a pulley is famous,
or a buttonhole, not because it did anything spectacular,
but because it never forgot what it could do.

CRITICAL THINKING QUESTIONS

1. What is Nye's *implied claim* for evaluating the concept of famous?
2. How does popular culture generally portray images of fame? What definition of "famous" do these images suggest?

WRITING TOPIC

Compare and contrast Nye's viewpoint on famous and the viewpoint projected by popular culture. What values do you think should be associated with famous? Based on your consideration of these perspectives, write your own argument for defining famous.

Sharon Olds

The Promise

With the second drink, at the restaurant,
holding hands on the bare table
we are at it again, renewing our promise
to kill each other. You are drinking gin,
night-blue juniper berry
dissolving in your body, I am drinking Fumé,
chewing its fragrant dirt and smoke, we are
taking on earth, we are part soil already,
and always, wherever we are, we are also in our
bed, fitted naked closely
along each other, half passed out
after love, drifting back and
forth across the border of consciousness, our
bodies buoyant, clasped. Your hand
tightens on the table. You're a little afraid
I'll chicken out. What you do not want
is to lie in a hospital bed for a year
after a stroke, without being able to
think or die, you do not want
to be tied to a chair like my prim grandmother,
cursing. The room is dim around us,
ivory globes, pink curtains
bound at the waist, and outside
a weightless bright lifted-up
summer twilight. I tell you you don't
know me if you think I will not
kill you. Think how we have floated together
eye to eye, nipple to nipple,
sex to sex, the halves of a single creature
drifting up to the lip of matter
and over it—you know me from the bright, blood-
flecked delivery room, if a beast
had you in its jaws I would attack it, if the ropes
binding your soul are your own wrists I will cut them.

CRITICAL THINKING QUESTIONS

1. What is this poem's *implied claim* on the issue of active euthanasia or "mercy killing"?

2. What *evidence* does the speaker provide in making her case for keeping "our promise/ to kill each other . . ."? On which *rhetorical appeal* does she rely?

3. How successful is the speaker in persuading you that she must keep the promise?

WRITING TOPIC

Read about Dr. Jack Kervorkian, the doctor who has carried out assisted suicides. In two columns, list the doctor's arguments for carrying out assisted suicides and across from those the court's arguments for ruling against him. Which side of the argument do you support?

Linda Pastan

Ethics

In ethics class so many years ago
our teacher asked this question every fall:
if there were a fire in a museum
which would you save, a Rembrandt painting
or an old woman who hadn't many
years left anyhow? Restless on hard chairs
caring little for pictures or old age
we'd opt one year for life, the next for art
and always half-heartedly. Sometimes
the woman borrowed my grandmother's face
leaving her usual kitchen to wander
some drafty, half-imagined museum.
One year, feeling clever, I replied
why not let the woman decide herself?
Linda, the teacher would report, eschews
the burdens of responsibility.
This fall in a real museum I stand
before a real Rembrandt, old woman,
or nearly so, myself. The colors
within this frame are darker than autumn,
darker even than winter—the browns of earth,
though earth's most radiant elements burn
through the canvas. I know now that woman
and painting and season are almost one
and all beyond saving by children.

WRITING TOPIC

Pastan argues that we cannot expect children to make the kind of ethical decision her teacher posed. In contrast, however, many people argue that today education does not teach values. Write a description of several times during your
childhood, in school or out of school, when you received values instruction.

John F. Kennedy

Inaugural Address

My Fellow Citizens:

We observe today not a victory of party but a celebration of freedom—symbolizing an end as well as a beginning—signifying renewal as well as change. For I have sworn before you and Almighty God the same solemn oath our forebears prescribed nearly a century and three quarters ago.

The world is very different now. For man holds in his mortal hands the power to abolish all form of human poverty and to abolish all form of human life. And yet the same revolutionary beliefs for which our forebears fought are still at issue around the globe—the belief that the rights of man come not from the generosity of the state but from the hand of God.

We dare not forget today that we are the heirs of that first revolution. Let the word go forth from this time and place, to friend and foe alike, that the torch has been passed to a new generation of Americans—born in this century, tempered by war, disciplined by a cold and bitter peace, proud of our ancient heritage—and unwilling to witness or permit the slow undoing of those human rights to which this nation has always been committed, and to which we are committed today.

Let every nation know, whether it wish us well or ill, that we shall pay any price, bear any burden, meet any hardship, support any friend or oppose any foe in order to assure the survival and success of liberty.

This much we pledge—and more.

To those old allies whose cultural and spiritual origins we share, we pledge the loyalty of faithful friends. United, there is little we cannot do in a host of new cooperative ventures. Divided, there is little we can do—for we dare not meet a powerful challenge at odds and split asunder.

To those new states whom we now welcome to the ranks of the free, we pledge our word that one form of colonial control shall not have passed merely to be replaced by a far more iron tyranny. We shall not always expect to find them supporting our every view. But we shall always hope to find them strongly supporting their own freedom—and to remember that, in the past, those who foolishly sought to find power by riding on the tiger's back inevitably ended up inside.

To those people in the huts and villages of half the globe struggling to break the bonds of mass misery, we pledge our best efforts to help them help themselves, for whatever period is required—not because the communists are doing it, not because we seek their votes, but because it is right. If the free society cannot help the many who are poor, it can never save the few who are rich.

To our sister republics south of our border, we offer a special pledge—to convert our good words into good deeds—in a new alliance for progress—to assist free men and free governments in casting off the chains of poverty. But this peaceful revolution of hope cannot become the prey of hostile powers. Let all our neighbors know that we shall join with them to oppose aggression or subversion anywhere in the Americas. And let every other power know that this Hemisphere intends to remain the master of its own house.

To that world assembly of sovereign states, the United Nations, our last best hope in an age where the instruments of war have far outpaced the instruments of peace, we renew our pledge of support—to prevent its becoming merely a forum for invective—to strengthen its shield of the new and the weak—and to enlarge the area to which its writ may run.

Finally, to those nations who would make themselves our adversary, we offer not a pledge but a request: that both sides begin anew the quest for peace, before the dark powers of destruction unleashed by science engulf all humanity in planned or accidental self-destruction.

We dare not tempt them with weakness. For only when our arms are sufficient beyond doubt can we be certain beyond doubt that they will never be employed.

But neither can two great and powerful groups of nations take comfort from their present course—both sides overburdened by the cost of modern weapons, both rightly alarmed by the steady spread of the deadly atom, yet both racing to alter that uncertain balance of terror that stays the hand of mankind's final war.

So let us begin anew—remembering on both sides that civility is not a sign of weakness, and sincerity is always subject to proof. Let us never negotiate out of fear. But let us never fear to negotiate.

Let both sides explore what problems unite us instead of belaboring the problems that divide us.

Let both sides, for the first time, formulate serious and precise proposals for the inspection and control of arms—and bring the absolute power to destroy other nations under the absolute control of all nations.

Let both sides join to invoke the wonders of science instead of its terrors. Together let us explore the stars, conquer the deserts, eradicate disease, tap the ocean depths and encourage the arts and commerce.

Let both sides unite to heed in all corners of the earth the command of Isaiah—to "undo the heavy burdens . . . (and) let the oppressed go free."

And if a beach-head of cooperation can be made in the jungles of suspicion, let both sides join in the next task: creating, not a new balance of power, but a new world of law, where the strong are just and the weak secure and the peace preserved forever.

All this will not be finished in the first one hundred days. Nor will it be finished in the first one thousand days, nor in the life of this Administration, nor even perhaps in our lifetime on this planet. But let us begin.

In your hands, my fellow citizens, more than in mine, will rest the final success or failure of our course. Since this country was founded, each generation has been summoned to give testimony to its national loyalty. The graves of young Americans who answered that call encircle the globe.

Now the trumpet summons us again—not as a call to bear arms, though arms we need—not as a call to battle, though embattled we are—but a call to bear the burden of a long twilight struggle, year in and year out, "rejoicing in hope, patient in tribulation"—a struggle against the common enemies of man: tyranny, poverty, disease and war itself.

Can we forge against these enemies a grand and global alliance, North and South, East and West, that can assure a more fruitful life for all mankind? Will you join in that historic effort?

In the long history of the world, only a few generations have been granted the role of defending freedom in its hour of maximum danger. I do not shrink from this responsibility—I welcome it. I do not believe that any of us would exchange places with any other people or any other generation. The energy, the faith and the devotion which we bring to this endeavor will light our country and all who serve it— and the glow from that fire can truly light the world.

And so, my fellow Americans: ask not what your country will do for you—ask what you can do for your country.

My fellow citizens of the world: ask not what America will do for you, but what together we can do for the freedom of man.

Finally, whether you are citizens of America or of the world, ask of us the same high standards of strength and sacrifice that we shall ask of you. With a good conscience our only sure reward, with history the final judge of our deeds, let us go forth to lead the land we love, asking His blessing and His help, but knowing that here on earth God's work must truly be our own.

CRITICAL THINKING QUESTIONS

1. Notice how short the paragraphs are in this address. What effect does this structure have on the listener or reader?

2. What *rhetorical devices* do you see Kennedy using in this address? Make a list of pairs of words Kennedy uses, such as *united/divided* or *not because/but because*.

3. In what sense does this address argue for power, and in what sense does it argue for responsibility?

WRITING TOPIC

Read one other inaugural address by a U.S. president. Summarize and compare the arguments offered by Kennedy and the president you selected.

George Orwell

A Hanging

It was in Burma, a sodden morning of the rains. A sickly light, like yellow tinfoil, was slanting over the high walls into the jail yard. We were waiting outside the condemned cells, a row of sheds fronted with double bars, like small animal cages. Each cell measured about ten feet by ten and was quite bare within except for a plank bed and a pot for drinking water. In some of them brown, silent men were squatting at the inner bars, with their blankets draped round them. These were the condemned men, due to be hanged within the next week or two.

One prisoner had been brought out of his cell. He was a Hindu, a puny wisp of a man, with a shaven head and vague liquid eyes. He had a thick, sprouting mustache, absurdly too big for his body, rather like the mustache of a comic man on the films. Six tall Indian warders were guarding him and getting him ready for the gallows. Two of them stood by with rifles and fixed bayonets, while the others handcuffed him, passed a chain through his handcuffs and fixed it to their belts, and lashed his arms tight to his sides. They crowded very close about him, with their hands always on him in a careful, caressing grip, as though all the while feeling him to make sure he was there. It was like men handling a fish which is still alive and may jump back into the water. But he stood quite unresisting, yielding his arms limply to the ropes, as though he hardly noticed what was happening.

Eight o'clock struck and a bugle call, desolately thin in the wet air, floated from the distant barracks. The superintendent of the jail, who was standing apart from the rest of us, moodily prodding the gravel with his stick, raised his head at the sound. He was an army doctor, with a gray toothbrush mustache and a gruff voice. "For God's sake, hurry up, Francis," he said irritably. "The man ought to have been dead by this time. Aren't you ready yet?"

Francis, the head jailer, a fat Dravidian in a white drill suit and gold spectacles, waved his black hand. "Yes sir, yes sir," he bubbled. "All iss satisfactorily prepared. The hangman iss waiting. We shall proceed."

"Well, quick march, then. The prisoners can't get their breakfast till this job's over."

We set out for the gallows. Two warders marched on either side of the prisoner, with their rifles at the slope; two others marched close against him, gripping him by arm and shoulder, at though at once pushing and supporting him. The rest of us, magistrates and the like, followed behind. Suddenly, when we had gone ten yards, the procession stopped short without any order or warning. A dreadful thing had happened—a dog, come goodness knows whence, had appeared in the yard. It came bounding among us with a loud volley of barks and leapt round up wagging its whole body, wild with glee at finding so many human beings together. It was a large woolly dog, half Airedale, half pariah. For a moment it pranced around us, and then, before anyone could stop it, it had made a dash for the prisoner, and jumping up tried to lick his face. Everybody stood aghast, too taken aback even to grab the dog.

"Who let that bloody brute in here?" said the superintendent angrily. "Catch it, someone!"

A warder detached from the escort charged clumsily after the dog, but it danced and gamboled just out of his reach, taking everything as part of the game. A young Eurasian jailer picked up a handful of gravel and tried to stone the dog away, but it dodged the stones and came after us again. Its yaps echoed from the jail walls. The prisoner, in the grasp of the two warders, looked on incuriously, as though this was another formality of the hanging. It was several minutes before someone managed to catch the dog. Then we put my handkerchief through its collar and moved off once more, with the dog still straining and whimpering.

It was about forty yards to the gallows. I watched the bare brown back of the prisoner marching in front of me. He walked clumsily with his bound arms, but quite steadily, with that bobbing gait of the Indian who never straightens his knees. At each step his muscles slid neatly into place, the lock of hair on his scalp danced up and down, his feet printed themselves on the wet gravel. And once, in spite of the men who gripped him by each shoulder, he stepped lightly aside to avoid a puddle on the path.

It is curious; but till that moment I had never realized what it means to destroy a healthy, conscious man. When I saw the prisoner step aside to avoid the puddle, I saw the mystery, the unspeakable wrongness, of cutting a life short when it is in full tide. This man was not dying, he was alive just as we are alive. All the organs of his body were working—bowels digesting food, skin renewing itself, nails growing, tissues forming—all toiling away in solemn foolery. His nails would still be growing when he stood on the drop, when he was falling through the air with a tenth-of-a-second to live. His eyes saw the yellow gravel and the gray walls, and his brain still remembered, foresaw, reasoned—even about puddles. He and we were a party of men walking together, seeing, hearing, feeling, understanding the same world; and in two minutes, with a sudden snap, one of us would be gone—one mind less, one world less.

The gallows stood in a small yard, separate from the main grounds of the prison, and overgrown with tall prickly weeds. It was a brick erection like three sides of a shed, with planking on top, and above that two beams and a crossbar with the rope dangling. The hangman, a gray-haired convict in the white uniform of the prison, was waiting beside his machine. He greeted us with a servile crouch as we entered. At a word from Francis the two warders, gripping the prisoner more closely than ever, half led, half pushed him to the gallows and helped him clumsily up the ladder. Then the hangman climbed up and fixed the rope round the prisoner's neck.

We stood waiting, five yards away. The warders had formed in a rough circle round the gallows. And then, when the noose was fixed, the prisoner began crying out to his god. It was a high, reiterated cry of "Ram! Ram! Ram! Ram!" not urgent and fearful like a prayer or cry for help, but steady, rhythmical, almost like the tolling of a bell. The dog answered the sound with a whine. The hangman, still standing on the gallows, produced a small cotton bag like a flour bag and drew it down over the prisoner's face. But the sound, muffled by the cloth, still persisted, over and over again: "Ram! Ram! Ram! Ram! Ram!"

The hangman climbed down and stood ready, holding the lever. Minutes seemed to pass. The steady, muffled crying from the prisoner went on and on, "Ram! Ram! Ram!" never faltering for an instant. The superintendent, his head on his chest, was slowly poking the ground with his stick; perhaps he was counting the cries, allowing the prisoner a fixed number—fifty, perhaps, or a hundred. Everyone had changed color. The Indians had gone gray like bad coffee, and one or two of the bayonets were wavering. We looked at the lashed, hooded man on the drop, and listened to his cries—each cry another second of life; the same thought was in all our minds; oh, kill him quickly, get it over, stop that abominable noise!

Suddenly the superintendent made up his mind. Throwing up his head he made a swift motion with his stick. "Chalo!" he shouted almost fiercely.

There was a clanking noise, and then dead silence. The prisoner had vanished, and the rope was twisting on itself. I let go of the dog, and it galloped immediately to the back of the gallows; but when it got there it stopped short, barked, and then retreated into a corner of the yard, where it stood among the weeds, looking timorously out at us. We went round the gallows to inspect the prisoner's body. He was dangling with his toes pointed straight downwards, very slowly revolving, as dead as a stone.

The superintendent reached out with his stick and poked the bare brown body; it oscillated slightly. "*He's* all right," said the superintendent. He backed out from under the gallows, and blew out a deep breath. The moody look had gone out of his face quite suddenly. He glanced at his wristwatch. "Eight minutes past eight. Well, that's all for this morning, thank God."

The warders unfixed bayonets and marched away. The dog, sobered and conscious of having misbehaved itself, slipped after them. We walked out of the gallows yard, past the condemned cells with their waiting prisoners, into the big central yard of the prison. The convicts, under the command of warders armed with lathis, were already receiving their breakfast. They squatted in long rows, each man holding a tin pannikin, while two warders with buckets marched around ladling out rice; it seemed quite a homely, jolly scene, after the hanging. An enormous relief had come upon us now that the job was done. One felt an impulse to sing, to break into a run, to snigger. All at once everyone began chattering gaily.

The Eurasian boy walking beside me nodded towards the way we had come, with a knowing smile: "Do you know sir, our friend (he meant the dead man) when he heard his appeal had been dismissed, he pissed on the floor of his cell. From fright. Kindly take one of my cigarettes, sir. Do you not admire my new silver case, sir? From the boxwallah, two rupees eight annas. Classy European style."

Several people laughed—at what, nobody seemed certain.

Francis was walking by the superintendent, talking garrulously: "Well, sir, all has passed off with the utmost satisfactoriness. It was all finished—flick! Like that. It iss not always so—oah, no! I have known cases where the doctor wass obliged to go beneath the gallows and pull the prisoner's legs to ensure decease. Most disagreeable!"

"Wriggling about, eh? That's bad," said the superintendent.

"Ach, sir, it iss worse when they become refractory! One man, I recall, clung to the bars of hiss cage when we went to take him out. You will scarcely credit, sir, that it took six warders to dislodge him, three pulling at each leg. We reasoned with him, 'My dear fellow,' we said, 'think of all the pain and trouble you are causing to us!' But no, he would not listen! Ach, he wass very troublesome!"

I found that I was laughing quite loudly. Everyone was laughing. Even the superintendent grinned in a tolerant way. "You'd better all come out and have a drink," he said quite genially. "I've got a bottle of whiskey in the car. We could do with it."

We went through the big double gates of the prison into the road. "Pulling at his legs!" exclaimed a Burmese magistrate suddenly, and burst into a loud chuckling. We all began laughing again. At that moment Francis' anecdote seemed extraordinarily funny. We all had a drink together, native and European alike, quite amicably. The dead man was a hundred yards away.

CRITICAL THINKING QUESTIONS

1. The powers of peace and order have structured this execution perfectly, and all the details seem so right, so correct. What small event allows Orwell to see past all the trappings of justice being carried out?

2. Why does everyone laugh at the end? Surely an execution cannot be humorous.

Katherine Anne Porter

To Dr. William Ross

March 4, 1951

Dear Dr. Ross,

I cannot possibly sign the oath of allegiance you sent me, and I'm sorry I was not told in your first letter that this would be required of me, for a good deal of time and trouble would have been spared both of us.

This is the first time I've encountered this dangerous nonsense, but I have known from the beginning what my answer must be. My memory goes back easily thirty years to the time this law was passed in Colorado, in a time of war, fright and public hysteria being whipped up by the same kind of people who are doing this work now. Only now we're worse for thirty years of world disaster.

I believed then, and still do believe, that this requirement of an oath of allegiance was more of a device for embarrassing and humiliating honest persons than an effective trap for traitors and subversive people. We, all of us, do quite a lot of ceremonial oath-taking on many important occasions of life as an act of faith, a public testimony of honorable intention, and it is the mere truth that an oath binds only those persons who meant to keep their promises anyway, with or without an oath. The others cannot be touched or controlled in any such way. We all know this so why assist at such a cynical fraud.

I'm entirely hostile to the principle of Communism and to every form of totalitarian society, whether it calls itself Communism, Fascism, or whatever. I feel indeed that Communism and Fascism are two names for the same thing, that the present struggle is really a civil war between two factions of totalitarianism. But Fascism is older, more insidious, harder to identify, easier to disguise. No one can be a Communist without knowing what he is doing. A man may be a most poisonous Fascist without even in the least recognizing his malady.

It is not the oath itself that troubles me. There is nothing in it I do not naturally and instinctively observe as I have and will. My people are the old stock. They helped to found colonies, to break new trails, and to survey wildernesses. They set up little log cabin academies, all the way from Virginia and Pennsylvania to Kentucky and clear into Texas. They have fought in all the wars, they have been governors of states, and military attachés, and at least one ambassador among us. We're not suspect, nor liable to the questionings of the kind of people we would never have invited to our tables.

You can see what the root of my resentment is. My many family branches helped to make this country. My feeling about my country and its history is as tender and intimate as about my own parents, and I really suffer to have them violated by the irresponsible acts of cheap politicians who prey on public fears in times of trouble and force their betters into undignified positions.

Our duty, Dr. Ross, is to circumvent them. To see through them and stop them in their tracks in time and not to be hoodwinked or terrorized by them, not to rationalize and excuse that weakness in us which leads us to criminal collusion with them for the sake of our jobs or the hope of being left in peace. That is not the road to any kind of safety. Nothing really effective is being done here against either Communism or Fascism, at least not by the politicians because they do not want anything settled. Their occupation and careers would be gone. We're going to be made sorry very soon for our refusal to reject unconditionally the kind of evil that disguises itself as patriotism, as love of virtue, as religious faith, as the crusador against the internal enemy. These people are themselves the enemy.

I do not propose to sit down quietly and be told by them what my duty is to my country and my government. My feelings and beliefs are nothing they could understand. I do not like being told that I must take an oath of allegiance to my government and flag under the threat of losing my employment if I do not. This is blackmail, and I have never been blackmailed successfully yet and do not intend to begin now.

So please destroy the contract we have made, as it is no longer valid. I know I run some little risk of nasty publicity in this matter. I hope not. I am not in the least a martyr. I have no time for heroics and indeed distrust them deeply. I am an artist who wishes to be left in peace to do my work. I hope that work will speak in the long run very clearly for me and all my kind, will be in some sort my testimony and my share of the battle against the elements of corruption and dissolution that come upon us so insidiously from all sides we hardly know where to begin to oppose them.

You may say this is a great how-do-you-do about a small matter. I can only say it is not a small matter when added to all other small matters of the kind that finally make an army of locusts.

Dr. Ross, I thank you for your courteous letter and hope you will take my word that this letter has nothing personal in it. That towards you I intend nothing but human respect in the assurance that I believe I understand your situation which must be extremely difficult.

What has this kind of meanness and cheapness to do with education? What is wrong that undesirable applicants for the faculty are not quietly discovered and refused before they are appointed? Why must a person like me be asked to do a stupid, meaningless thing because one person with a bad political record got into your college once? No, I can't have it, and neither can you. The amusing side of all this brou-ha-ha is I really did not expect to have any occasion to mention the flag or the laws of Colorado or the Communist Alger Hiss or even the Fascist Senator McCarthy. I meant to talk about literature, life understood and loved in terms of the human heart in the personal experience. The life of the imagination and the search for the true meaning of our fate in this world, of the soul as a pilgrim on a stony path and of faithfulness to an ideal good and tenacity in the love of truth. Whether or not we ever find it, we still must look for it to the very end.

Any real study of great literature must take in human life at every possible level and search out every dark corner. And its natural territory is the whole human experience, no less. It does not astonish me that young people love to hear about these things, love to talk about them, and think about them. It is sometimes surprising to me how gay my classes can be, as if we had found some spring of joy in the tragic state to which all of us are born. This is the service the arts do, and the totalitarian's first idea is to destroy exactly this. They can do great harm but not for long. I am not in the least afraid of them.

With my sincere good wishes, and apologies for this overlong letter,

Yours,
Katherine Anne Porter

CRITICAL THINKING QUESTIONS

1. Why does the writer make the loose distinction between Communism and Fascism? Does she imply by this definition that Dr. Ross may be a Fascist?

2. When she describes her role as a teacher, how does that affect her appeal to *ethos?*

Tom Regan

Religion and Animal Rights

In its simplest terms the animal rights position I uphold maintains that such diverse practices as the use of animals in science, sport and recreational hunting, the trapping of furbearing animals for vanity products, and commercial animal agriculture are categorically wrong—wrong because these practices systematically violate the rights of the animals involved. Morally, these practices ought to be abolished. That is the goal of the *social* struggle for animal rights. The goal of our *individual* struggle is to divest ourselves of our moral and economic ties to these injustices—for example, by not wearing the skins of dead animals and by not eating their decaying corpses.

Not a few people regard the animal rights position as extreme, calling, as it does, for the abolition of certain well-entrenched social practices rather than for their "humane" reform. And many seem to imagine that once this label ("extreme") is applied, the need for further refutation evaporates. After all, how can such an "extreme" moral position be correct?

I addressed this question in a recent speech, reminding my audience of a few "extreme" moral positions we all accept:

Rape is *always* wrong.

Child pornography is *always* wrong.

Racial and sexual discrimination are *always* wrong.

I went on to note that when an injustice is absolute, as is true of each of the examples just cited, then one must oppose it absolutely. It is not reformed, more humane child pornography that an enlightened ethic calls for; it is its abolition that is required—it is this *extreme* position we must uphold. And analogous remarks apply in the case of the other examples.

Once this much is acknowledged, it is evident (or at least it should be) that those who oppose or resist the animal rights position will have to do better than merely attach the label "extreme" to it. Sometimes "extreme" positions about what is wrong are right.

Of course, there are two obvious differences between the animal rights position and the other examples of extreme views I have given. The latter views are very generally accepted, whereas the former position is not. And unlike these very generally accepted views, which concern wrongful acts done to human beings, the animal rights position concerns the (alleged) wrongfulness of treating animals (nonhuman animals, that is) in certain ways. Those who oppose or resist the animal rights position might seize upon these two differences in an effort to justify themselves in accepting extreme positions regarding rape and child abuse, for example, while rejecting the "extremism" of animal rights.

But neither of these differences will bear the weight of justification. That a view (whether moral or otherwise) is very generally accepted is not a sufficient reason for accepting it as true. There was a time when the shape of the earth was very generally believed to be flat, and when the presence of physical and mental handicaps was very generally thought to make the people who bore them morally inferior. That very many people believed these falsehoods obviously did not make them true. We won't discover or confirm what's true by taking a vote.

The reverse of the preceding also can be demonstrated. That a view (moral or otherwise) is not generally accepted is not a sufficient reason for judging it to be false. When those lonely few first conjectured that the earth is round and that women are the moral equals of men, they conjectured truly, notwithstanding how grandly they were outnumbered. The solitary person who, in Thoreau's enduring image, marches to a different drummer, may be the only person to apprehend the truth.

The second difference noted above is more problematic. That difference cites the fact that child abuse and rape, for example, involve evils done to human beings, while the animal rights position claims that certain (alleged) evils are done to non-human animals. Now, there is no question that this does constitute a difference. The question is, is this a *morally relevant difference*—a difference, that is, that would justify us in accepting the extreme opposition we judge to be appropriate in the case of child abuse and rape, for example, but, which most people resist or abjure in the case of, say, vivisection. For a variety of reasons I do not myself think that this difference is a morally relevant one. Permit me to explain why.

Viewed scientifically, this second difference succeeds only in citing a biological difference: The victims of rape and child abuse belong to one species (the species *Homo sapiens*) whereas the (alleged) victims of vivisection and trapping belong to other species (the species *Canis lupus,* for example). But biological differences *inside* the species *Homo sapiens* do not justify radically different treatment among those individual humans who differ biologically (for example, in terms of sex, or skin color, or chromosome count). Why, then, should biological differences *outside* our species count morally? If having one eye or deformed limbs does not disqualify a human being from moral consideration equal to that given to those humans who are more fortunate, how can it be rational to disqualify a rat or a wolf from equal moral consideration because, unlike us, they have paws and a tail?

Some of those who resist or oppose the animal rights position might have recourse to "intuition" at this point. They might claim that one either "sees" that the principal biological difference at issue (namely, species membership) *is* a morally relevant one, or does *not* see this. No *reason* can be given as to why belonging to the species *Homo sapiens* gives one a superior moral status, just as no *reason* can be given as to why belonging to the species *Canis lupus* gives wolves an inferior moral status (if wolves have a moral status at all). This difference in moral status can only be grasped immediately, without making an inference, by an exercise of intuitive reason. This moral difference is "self-evident"—or so it will be claimed by those who claim to "intuit" it.

However attractive this appeal to intuition may seem to some, it woefully fails to bear the weight of justification. The plain fact is, people have claimed to "intuit" differences in the comparative moral standing of individuals and groups *inside* the human species, and these alleged "intuitions," we all would agree, are painful symptoms of unquestioned and unjustifiable prejudice. Over the course of history, for example, many men have "intuited" the moral superiority of men when compared with that of women, and many white-skinned humans have "intuited" the moral superiority of white-skinned humans when compared with humans having different skin colors. If this is a matter of intuition, then no reason can be given for this superiority. No inference is (or can be) required, no evidence adduced. One either "sees" it, or one doesn't. It's just that those who do "see" it (or so they will insist) apprehend the truth, while those whose deficient intuitive faculties prevent them from "seeing" it fail to do so.

I cannot believe that any thoughtful person will be taken in by this ruse. Appeals to "intuition" in these contexts are symptomatic of unquestioned and unjustifiable moral prejudices. What prompts or encourages men to "see" their moral superiority over women are the sexual prejudices men bring with them, not what is to be found in the existence of sexual differences themselves. And the same is true, *mutatis mutandis,* of "seeing" moral superiority in racial or other biological differences between humans.

That much established, the weakness of appeals to intuition in the case at hand should be apparent. Since intuition is not to be trusted when questions of the comparative moral standing of biologically different individuals *inside* the species *Homo sapiens* are at issue, it cannot be rational to assume or insist that such appeals can or should be trusted when questions of the comparative moral standing of individuals *outside* the species are at issue. Moreover, since appeals to intuition in the former case turn out to be symptomatic of unquestioned and unjustifiable moral prejudices, rather than being revelatory of some important moral truth, it is not unreasonable to suspect that the same diagnosis applies to appeals to intuition in the latter case. If true, then those who "intuit" the moral superiority of all members of the species *Homo sapiens* over all members of every other species, also emerge as the unwitting victims or the willful perpetrators of an unquestioned and unjustifiable moral prejudice.

"Speciesism" is the name given to this (alleged) prejudice. This idea has been characterized in a variety of ways. For present purposes let us begin with the following twofold characterization of what I shall call "categorical speciesism."

Categorical speciesism is the belief that (1) the inherent value of an individual can be judged solely on the basis of the biological species to which that individual belongs, and that (2) all the members of the species *Homo sapiens* have equal inherent value, while all the members of every other species lack this kind of value, simply because all and only humans are members of the species *Homo sapiens.*

In speaking of inherent value, both here and throughout what follows, I mean something that coincides with Kant's famous idea of "end-in-itself." Individuals who have inherent value, in other words, have value in their own right, apart from their possible utility for others; as such, these individuals are never to be treated in ways that reduce their value to their possible usefulness for others; they are always to be treated as "ends-in-themselves," not as "means merely." Categorical speciesism, then, holds that all and only humans have this kind of value precisely because all and only humans belong to the species *Homo sapiens*.

I have already indicated why I believe that appeals to intuition cannot succeed in establishing the truth of categorical speciesism as so characterized. How, then, might the prejudicial character of speciesism be established?

Part of that answer is to be found when we pause to consider the nature of the animals we humans hunt, trap, eat and use for scientific purposes. Any person of common sense will agree that these animals bring the mystery of consciousness to the world. These animals, that is, not only are *in* the world, they are aware *of it*—and also of their "inner" world. They see, hear, touch and feel; but they also desire, believe, remember and anticipate.

If anyone questions my assessment of the common sense view about these animals, then I would invite them to speak with people who share their lives with dogs or cats or horses, or others who know the ways or wolves or coyotes, or still others who have had contact with any bird one might wish to name. Common sense clearly is on the side of viewing these animals as unified psychological beings, individuals who have a biography (a psychological life-story), not merely a biology. And common sense is not in conflict with our best science here. Indeed, our best science offers a scientific corroboration of the common sense view.

That corroboration is to be found in a set of diverse but related considerations. One is evolutionary theory, which implies that (1) the more complex has evolved from the less complex, that (2) members of the species *Homo sapiens* are the most complex life form of which we are aware, that (3) members of our species bring a psychological presence to the world, that (4) the psychological capacities we find in humans have evolved over time, and that (5) these capacities would not have evolved at all and would not have been passed on from one generation to the next if they (that is, these capacities) failed to have adaptive value—that is, if they failed to offer advantages to our species in its ongoing struggle to survive in an ever-changing environment.

Given these five points, it is entirely consistent with the main thrust of evolutionary theory, and is, indeed, required by it, to maintain that the members of some species of nonhuman animals are like us in having the capacity to see and hear and feel, for example, as well as to believe and desire, to remember and anticipate.

Certainly this is what Darwin thinks, as is evident when he writes of the animals we humans eat and trap, to use just two instances, that they differ psychologically (or mentally) from us in degree, not in kind.

A second, related consideration involves comparative anatomy and physiology. Everything we know about nature must incline us to believe that a complex structure has a complex reason for being. It would therefore be an extraordinary lapse of form if we humans had evolved into complicated psychological creatures, with an underlying anatomical and physiological complexity, while other species of animals had evolved to have a more or less complex anatomy and physiology, very much like our own in many respects, and yet lacked—*totally* lacked—any and every psychological capacity. If nature could respond to this bizarre suggestion, the verdict we would hear would be, "Nonsense!"

Thus it is, then, that both common sense and our best science speak with one voice regarding the psychological nature we share with the nonhuman animals I have mentioned—those, for example, many people stew, roast, fry, broil and grill for the sake of their gustatory desires and delights. When the dead and putrefying bodies of these animals are eaten, our psychological kin are consumed.

Recall the occasion for this review of relevant scientific considerations. Categorical speciesism, which I characterized earlier, is not shown to be a moral prejudice merely because those who accept it are unable to prove its truth. This much has been conceded and, indeed, insisted upon. What more, then, would have to be established before the charge of moral prejudice could be made to stick? Part of that answer is to be found in the recent discussion of what common sense and our best science contribute to our understanding of the nonhuman animals we have been discussing. Both agree that these animals are fundamentally like ordinary human beings—like you and me. For, like us, these animals have a unified psychological presence in the world, a life-story that is uniquely their own, a separate biography. In the simplest terms *they are somebody, not something*. Precisely because this similarity is so well established, grounded in the opinions, as Aristotle would express this, of both "the many and the wise," any substantive moral position at odds with it seems dubious to say the least.

And categorical speciesism, as I have characterized it, *is* at odds with the joint verdict of common sense and our best science. For once the appeal to intuition is denied (and denied for good reasons), the onus of justification must be borne by the speciesist to cite some unique feature of being human that would ground the attribution of inherent value exclusively to human beings, a task that we now see is all but certain to end in failure, given the biographical status humans share with those nonhuman animals to whom I have been referring. Rationally considered, we must judge similar cases similarly. This is what the principle of formal justice requires, what respect for logical consistency demands. Thus, since we share a biographical presence in the world with these animals, it seems arbitrary and prejudicial in the extreme to insist that all humans have a kind of value that every other animal lacks.

In response to this line of argument people who wish to retain the spirit of speciesism might be prompted to alter its letter. This position I shall call modified speciesism. According to this form of speciesism those nonhuman animals who, like us, have a biographical presence in the world have *some* inherent value, it's just that the degree of inherent value they have *always is less* than that possessed by human beings. And if we ask why this is thought to be so, the answer modified speciesism offers is the same as categorical speciesism: The degree of value differs because humans belong to a particular species to which no other animal belongs—the species *Homo sapiens*.

I think it should be obvious that modified speciesism is open to many of the same kinds of damaging criticisms as categorical speciesism. What, we may ask, is supposed to be the basis of the alleged superior value of human beings? Will it be said that one simply "intuits" this? Then all the same difficulties this appeal faced in the case of categorical speciesism will resurface and ultimately swamp modified speciesism. To avoid this, will it be suggested that the degree of inherent value an individual possesses depends on the relative complexity of that individual's psychological repertoire—the greater the complexity, the greater the value? Then modified speciesism simply will not be able to justify the ascription of superior inherent value to all human beings when compared with every nonhuman animal. And the reason it will not be able to do this is simple: Some nonhuman animals bring to their biography a degree of psychological complexity that far exceeds what is brought by some human beings. One need only to compare, say, the psychological repertoire of a healthy two year old chimp, or dog, or hog, or robin to that of a profoundly handicapped human of any age, to recognize the incontrovertible truth of what I have just said. Not all human beings have richer, more complex biographies than every nonhuman animal.

How are speciesists to get around this fact—for get around it they must, because fact it is. There is a familiar theological answer to this question; at least it is familiar to those who know something of the Judeo-Christian religious traditions, as these traditions sometimes have been interpreted. That answer states that human beings—all of us—are inherently more valuable than any other existing individual because we are spiritually different and, indeed, unique. This uniqueness stems from our having been created in the image of God, a status we share with no other creature. If, then, it is true that all humans uniquely image God, then we are able to cite a real (spiritual) difference between every member of our species and the countless numbers of the millions of other species of creaturely life. And, if, moreover, this difference is a morally relevant one, then speciesists might seem to be in a position to defend their speciesism (and this is true whether they are categorical or moderate speciesists) in the face of the demands of formal justice. After all, that principle requires that we judge similar cases similarly, whereas any two individuals—the one human, the other of some other species—will not be relevantly similar, given the hypothesis of the unique spiritual worth of all human beings.

Now I myself am not ill-disposed to the idea of there being something about us humans that gives us a unique spiritual worth, nor am I ill-disposed to the idea that the ground of this worth is to be found or explicated in the idea that we humans uniquely "image" God. Not surprisingly, therefore, the interpretation of these ideas I favor, while it concedes this (possible) difference between humans and the rest of creation, does not yield anything like the results favored by speciesism, whether categorical or moderate. Let me explain.

The position I favor is the one that interprets our divine "imaging" in terms of our moral responsibility: By this I mean that we are expressly chosen by God to be God's vice-regent in the day-to-day affairs of the world; we are chosen by God, that is, to be as loving in our day-to-day dealings with the created order, as God was in creating that order in the first place. In *this* sense, therefore, there *is* a morally relevant difference between human beings and every other creaturely expression of God. For it is only members of the human species who are given the awesome freedom and responsibility to be God's representative within creation. And it is, therefore, only we humans who can be held morally blameworthy when we fail to do this, and morally praiseworthy when we succeed.

Within the general context of this interpretation of our unique "imaging" of God, then, we find a morally relevant difference between God's creative expression in the human and God's creative expression in every other aspect of creation. But— as should be evident—this difference *by itself* offers neither aid nor comfort to speciesism, of whatever variety. For to agree that only humans image God, in the sense that only humans have the moral responsibility to be loving toward God's creation, in no way entails either that all and only humans have inherent value (so-called categorical speciesism) or that all and only humans have a superior inherent value (modified speciesism, as I called it). It is perfectly consistent with our unique status as God's chosen representative within creation that *other* creatures have inherent value and possess it to a degree equal to that possessed by human beings. Granted, our uniqueness lies in our moral responsibility to God and to God's creation, including, of course, all members of the human family. But this fact, assuming it to be a fact, only answers the question, "Which among God's creatures are capable of acting rightly or wrongly (or, as philosophers might say, 'are moral agents')?" What this fact, assuming it to be one, does not answer are the questions, "To which creatures can we act rightly or wrongly?" and "What kind of value do other creatures have?"

Every prejudice dies hard. Speciesism is no exception. That it is a prejudice and that, by acting on it, we humans have been, and continue to be, responsible for an incalculable amount of evil, an amount of truly monumental proportions, is, I believe, as true as it is regrettable. In my philosophical writings over the past fifteen years I have endeavored to show how this tragic truth can be argued for on wholly secular grounds. On this occasion I have looked elsewhere for support—have in fact looked to the original saga of creation we find in *Genesis*—in the hope that we might there find a religious or theological account that resonates with the secular case for animal rights. Neither case—not the secular and not the religious—has, or can have, the conclusiveness of a proof in, say, geometry. I say "can have" because I am reminded of Aristotle's astute observation, that it is the mark of an educated person not to demand "proof" that is inappropriate for a given subject matter. And whatever else we might think of moral thought, I believe we at least can agree that it is importantly unlike geometry.

It remains true, nonetheless, that my attempt to explain and defend as egalitarian this view of the inherent value of humans and other animals must face a number of important challenges. For reasons of length, if for no other, I cannot on this occasion characterize or respond to all these challenges, no even all the most fundamental ones. The best I can do, before concluding, is describe and defuse two of them.

The first begins by observing that, within the traditions of Judaism and Christianity, *every form of life,* not simply humans and other animals, is to be viewed as expressive of God's love. Thus, to attempt to "elevate" the value of nonhuman animals, as I might be accused of having done, could be viewed as having the unacceptable consequence of negating or reducing the value of everything else.

I think this objection misses the mark. There is nothing in the animal rights philosophy (nothing, that is, in the kind of egalitarianism I have endeavored to defend) that either denies or diminishes the value of fruits, nuts, grains and other forms of vegetative life, or that refuses to accept the possibility that these and the rest of creation are so many ways in which God's loving presence is manifested. Nor is there anything in this philosophy that disparages the wise counsel to treat all of creation gently and appreciatively. It is an arrogant, unbridled anthropocentrism, often aided and abetted in our history by an arrogant, unbridled Christian theology, not the philosophy of animal rights, that has brought the earth to the brink of ecological disaster.

Still, this philosophy does find in humans and other animals, because of our shared biographical status in creation, a kind of value—inherent value—which other creatures fail to possess, either not at all or at least not to the degree in which humans and other animals possess it. Is it possible to defend this view? I believe it is, both on the grounds of a purely secular moral philosophy and by appeal to Biblical authority. The secular defense I have attempted to offer elsewhere and will not repeat here. As for the Christian defense, I shall merely reaffirm the vital importance (in my view) of *Genesis 1,* as well as (to my mind) the more than symbolic significance of the covenant, and note that in both we find Biblical sanction for viewing the value of animals to be superior to that of vegetables. After all, we do not find carrots and almonds included in the covenant, and we do find God expressly giving these and other forms of vegetative life to us, as our food, in *Genesis'* first creation saga. In a word, then, vegetative life was meant to be used by us, thus giving it utility value for us (which does not mean or entail that we may use these life forms thoughtlessly or even irreverently).

So much for the first challenge. The second one emanates from quite a different source and mounts a quite different objection. It begins by noting the large disparities that exist in the quality of life available to those who are affluent (the "haves") and those who are poor (the "have-nots"), especially those who live in the so-called "Third World." "It is all fine and good to preach the gospel of animal rights to those people who have the financial and other means to practice it, if they choose to do so," this objection states, "but please do spare us your self-righteous denunciation of the struggling (and often starving) masses of people in the rest of the world, who really have no choice but to eat animals, wear their skins, and use them in other ways. To condemn these people is to value animal life above human life. And this is misanthropy at its worst."

Now, this particular variation on the familiar theme of misanthropy (at least this is familiar to advocates of animal rights) has a point, up to a point. The point it has, is that it would be self-righteous to condemn the people in question for acting as they do, especially if we are acting worse than they are (as well we may be). But, of course, nothing in what I have argued supports such a condemnation, and this for the simple reason that I have nowhere argued that people who eat animals, or who hunt and trap them, or who cut their heads off or burst their intestines in pursuit of "scientific knowledge," either are or must be *evil* people. The position I have set forth concerns the moral wrongness of what people do, not the *vileness of their character*. In my view, it is entirely possible that good people sometimes do what is wrong, and evil people sometimes do what is right.

Indeed, not only is this possible, it frequently happens, and among those circumstances in which it does, some concern the actions performed by people in the Third World. At least this is the conclusion we reach if we take the philosophy of animal rights seriously. To make my meaning clearer, consider the following example. Suppose we chance upon a tribe of hunter-gatherers who annually, on a date sacred to their tradition, sacrifice the most beautiful female child to the gods, in the hope that the tribe will prosper in the coming year. In my view this act of human sacrifice is morally wrong and ought to be stopped (which does *not* mean that we should invade with tanks and flame-throwers to stop it!). From this moral assessment of what these human beings do, however, it does not follow that we should judge them to be evil, vicious people. It could well be that they act from only the best intentions and with nothing but the best motives. Nevertheless, what they do, in my judgment, is morally wrong.

What is true of the imaginary case of this tribe, is no less true of real-life cases where people in the Third World raise and kill animals for food, cruelly subject other animals to forced labor, and so on. Anytime anyone reduces the inherent value of a nonhuman animal to that animal's utility value for human beings, what is done, in my view, is morally wrong. But it does not follow from this that we should make a negative moral judgment about the character of the human moral agents involved, especially if, as is true in the Third World, there are mitigating circumstances. For it often happens that people who do what is morally wrong should be *excused* from moral blame and censure. A person who shoots a family member, for example, in the mistaken belief that there is a burglar in the house, does what is wrong and yet may well *not* be morally blameworthy. Similarly, those people in the Third World who act in ways that are prohibited by respect for the rights of animals, do what is wrong. But because of the harsh, uncompromising exigencies of their life, where they are daily faced with the demand to make truly heroic sacrifices, where indeed it often is a matter of their life or their death that hangs in the balance, the people of the Third World in my view should be excused from our harsh, uncompromising judgments of moral blame. The circumstances of their life, one might say, are as mitigating as any circumstances can be.

In light of the preceding remarks, I hope it is clear why it would be a bad reading of the philosophy of animal rights, to charge its proponents with a hearty appetite, if not for animal flesh then at least for self-righteousness. When we understand the difference between morally assessing a person's act and that person's character, and when we take cognizance of the appropriateness of reducing or erasing moral blame in the face of mitigating circumstances, then the proponents of animal rights should be seen to be no more censorious or "self-righteous" than the proponents of any other moral philosophy.

The challenge to lead a good, respectful, loving life just in our dealings within the human family is onerous and demanding. How much more onerous and demanding must it be, therefore, if we widen the circle of the moral community to include the whole of creation. How might we begin to meet this enlarged challenge? Doubtless there are many possible places to begin, some of which will be more accessible to some than to others. For my part, however, I cannot help believing that an appropriate place to begin is with the food on our plates. For here we are faced with a direct personal choice, over which we exercise absolute sovereign authority. Such power is not always within our grasp. How little influence we really have, you and I, on the practices of the World Bank, the agrarian land-reform movement, the call to reduce armed conflicts, the cessation of famine and the evil of abject poverty! These large-scale evils stand beyond the reach of our small wills.

But not the food on our plates. Here we are at liberty to exercise absolute control. And here, then, we ought to be asking ourselves, "Which of those choices I can make are most in accord with the idea of the integrity of creation?"

When we consider the biographical and, I dare say, the spiritual kinship we share with those billions of animals raised and slaughtered for food; when, further, we inform ourselves of the truly wretched conditions in which most of these animals are raised, not to mention the deplorable methods by which they are transported and the gruesome, blood-soaked reality of the slaughterhouse; and when, finally, we take honest stock of our privileged position in the world, a position that will not afford us the excuse from moral blame shared by the desperately poor who, as we say, "really have no choice"—when we consider all these factors, then the case for abstaining from animal flesh has the overwhelming weight of both impartial reason and a spiritually-infused compassion on its side.

True, to make this change will involve some sacrifices—in taste perhaps, in convenience certainly. And yet the whole fabric of Christian *agape* is woven from the threads of sacrificial acts. To abstain, on principle, from eating animals, therefore, although it is not the end-all, can be the begin-all of our conscientious effort to journey back to (or toward) Eden, can be one way (among others) to re-establish or create that relationship to the earth which, if *Genesis 1* is to be trusted, was part of God's original hopes for and plans in creation. It is the integrity of this creation we seek to understand and aspire to honor. In the choice of our food, I believe, we see, not in a glass darkly, but face to face, a small but not unimportant part of both the challenge and the promise of Christianity and animal rights.

CRITICAL THINKING QUESTIONS

1. The author systematically destroys all the arguments we commonly hear for eating meat. Does he convince you to become a vegetarian? If so, why? If not, why not?

2. Whether or not you are convinced by Regan's argument, what do you consider to be his most effective *evidence?*

WRITING TOPIC

Regan says, "The challenge to lead a good, respectful, loving life just in our dealings within the human family is onerous and demanding. How much more onerous and demanding must it be, therefore, if we widen the circle of the moral community to include the whole of creation." While you may not be ready to include the "whole of creation," create a moral argument advocating a change in our behavior toward some particular creature in this world.

Richard Wright

from Black Boy

One morning I arrived early at work and went into the bank lobby where the Negro porter was mopping. I stood at a counter and picked up the Memphis *Commercial Appeal* and began my free reading of the press. I came finally to the editorial page and saw an article dealing with one H. L. Mencken. I knew by hearsay that he was the editor of the *American Mercury*, but aside from that I knew nothing about him. The article was a furious denunciation of Mencken, concluding with one, hot, short sentence: Mencken is a fool.

I wondered what on earth this Mencken had done to call down upon him the scorn of the South. The only people I had ever heard denounced in the South were Negroes, and this man was not a Negro. Then what ideas did Mencken hold that made a newspaper like the *Commercial Appeal* castigate him publicly? Undoubtedly he must be advocating ideas that the South did not like. Were there, then, people other than Negroes who criticized the South? I knew that during the Civil War the South had hated northern whites, but I had not encountered such hate during my life. Knowing no more of Mencken than I did at that moment, I felt a vague sympathy for him. Had not the South, which had assigned me the role of a non-man, cast at him its hardest words?

Now, how could I find out about this Mencken? There was a huge library near the riverfront, but I knew that Negroes were not allowed to patronize its shelves any more than they were the parks and playgrounds of the city. I had gone into the library several times to get books for the white men on the job. Which of them would now help me to get books? And how could I read them without causing concern to the white men with whom I worked? I had so far been successful in hiding my thoughts and feelings from them, but I knew that I would create hostility if I went about this business of reading in a clumsy way.

I weighed the personalities of the men on the job. There was Don, a Jew; but I distrusted him. His position was not much better than mine and I knew that he was uneasy and insecure; he had always treated me in an offhand, bantering way that barely concealed his contempt. I was afraid to ask him to help me to get books; his frantic desire to demonstrate a racial solidarity with the whites against Negroes might make him betray me.

Then how about the boss? No, he was a Baptist and I had the suspicion that he would not be quite able to comprehend why a black boy would want to read Mencken. There were other white men on the job whose attitudes showed clearly that they were Kluxers or sympathizers, and they were out of the question.

There remained only one man whose attitude did not fit into an anti-Negro category, for I had heard the white men refer to him as a "Pope lover." He was an Irish Catholic and was hated by the white Southerners. I knew that he read books, because I had got him volumes from the library several times. Since he, too, was an object of hatred, I felt that he might refuse me but would hardly betray me. I hesitated, weighing and balancing the imponderable realities.

One morning I paused before the Catholic fellow's desk.

"I want to ask you a favor," I whispered to him.

"What is it?"

"I want to read. I can't get books from the library. I wonder if you'd let me use your card?"

He looked at me suspiciously.

"My card is full most of the time," he said.

"I see," I said and waited, posing my question silently.

"You're not trying to get me into trouble, are you, boy?" he asked, staring at me.

"Oh, no, sir."

"What book do you want?"

"A book by H. L. Mencken."

"Which one?"

"I don't know. Has he written more than one?"

"He has written several."

"I didn't know that."

"What makes you want to read Mencken?"

"Oh, I just saw his name in the newspaper," I said.

"It's good of you to want to read," he said. "But you ought to read the right things."

I said nothing. Would he want to supervise my reading?

"Let me think," he said. "I'll figure out something."

I turned from him and he called me back. He stared at me quizzically.

"Richard, don't mention this to the other white men," he said.

"I understand," I said. "I won't say a word."

A few days later he called me to him.

"I've got a card in my wife's name," he said. "Here's mine."

"Thank you, sir."

"Do you think you can manage it?"

"I'll manage fine," I said.

"If they suspect you, you'll get in trouble," he said.

"I'll write the same kind of notes to the library that you wrote when you sent me for books," I told him. "I'll sign your name."

He laughed.

"Go ahead. Let me see what you get," he said.

That afternoon I addressed myself to forging a note. Now, what were the names of books written by H. L. Mencken? I did not know any of them. I finally wrote what I thought would be a foolproof note: *Dear Madam: Will you please let this nigger boy*—I used the word "nigger" to make the librarian feel that I could not possibly be the author of the note—*have some books by H. L. Mencken?* I forged the white man's name.

I entered the library as I had always done when on errands for whites, but I felt that I would somehow slip up and betray myself. I doffed my hat, stood a respectful distance from the desk, looked as unbookish as possible, and waited for the white patrons to be taken care of. When the desk was clear of people, I still waited. The white librarian looked at me.

"What do you want, boy?"

As though I did not possess the power of speech, I stepped forward and simply handed her the forged note, not parting my lips.

"What books by Mencken does he want?" she asked.

"I don't know, ma'am," I said, avoiding her eyes.

"Who gave you this card?"

"Mr. Falk," I said.

"Where is he?"

"He's at work, at the M—— Optical Company," I said. "I've been in here for him before."

"I remember," the woman said. "But he never wrote notes like this."

Oh, God, she's suspicious. Perhaps she would not let me have the books? If she had turned her back at that moment, I would have ducked out the door and never gone back. Then I thought of a bold idea.

"You can call him up, ma'am," I said, my heart pounding.

"You're not using these books, are you?" she asked pointedly.

"Oh, no, ma'am. I can't read."

"I don't know what he wants by Mencken," she said under her breath.

I knew now that I had won; she was thinking of other things and the race question had gone out of her mind. She went to the shelves. Once or twice she looked over her shoulder at me, as though she was still doubtful. Finally she came forward with two books in her hand.

"I'm sending him two books," she said. "But tell Mr. Falk to come in next time, or send me the names of the books he wants. I don't know what he wants to read."

I said nothing. She stamped the card and handed me the books. Not daring to glance at them, I went out of the library, fearing that the woman would call me back for further questioning. A block away from the library I opened one of the books and read a title: *A Book of Prefaces.* I was nearing my nineteenth birthday and I did not know how to pronounce the word "preface." I thumbed the pages and saw strange words and strange names. I shook my head, disappointed. I look at the other book; it was called *Prejudices.* I knew what that word meant; I had heard it all my life. And right off I was on guard against Mencken's books. Why would a man want to call a book *Prejudices?* The word was so stained with all my memories of racial hate that I could not conceive of anybody using it for a title. Perhaps I had made a mistake about Mencken? A man who had prejudices must be wrong.

When I showed the books to Mr. Falk, he looked at me and frowned.

"That librarian might telephone you," I warned him.

"That's all right," he said. "But when you're through reading those books, I want you to tell me what you get out of them."

That night in my rented room, while letting the hot water run over my can of pork and beans in the sink, I opened *A Book of Prefaces* and began to read. I was jarred and shocked by the style, the clear, clean, sweeping sentences. Why did he write like that? And how did one write like that? I pictured the man as a raging demon, slashing with his pen, consumed with hate, denouncing everything American, extolling everything European or German, laughing at the weaknesses of people, mocking God, authority. What was this? I stood up, trying to realize what reality lay behind the meaning of the words . . . Yes, this man was fighting, fighting with words. He was using words as a weapon, using them as one would use a club. Could words be weapons? Well, yes, for here they were. Then, maybe, perhaps, I could use them as a weapon? No. It frightened me. I read on and what amazed me was not what he said, but how on earth anybody had the courage to say it.

Occasionally I glanced up to reassure myself that I was alone in the room. Who were these men about whom Mencken was talking so passionately? Who was Anatole France? Joseph Conrad? Sinclair Lewis, Sherwood Anderson, Dostoevski, George Moore, Gustave Flaubert, Maupassant, Tolstoy, Frank Harris, Mark Twain, Thomas Hardy, Arnold Bennett, Stephen Crane, Zola, Norris, Gorky, Bergson, Ibsen, Balzac, Bernard Shaw, Dumas, Poe, Thomas Mann, O. Henry, Dreiser, H. G. Wells, Gogol, T. S. Eliot, Gide, Baudelaire, Edgar Lee Masters, Stendhal, Turgenev, Huneker, Nietzsche, and scores of others? Were these men real? Did they exist or had they existed? And how did one pronounce their names?

I ran across many words whose meanings I did not know, and I either looked them up in a dictionary or, before I had a chance to do that, encountered the word in a context that made its meaning clear. But what strange world was this? I concluded the book with the conviction that I had somehow overlooked something terribly important in life. I had once tried to write, had once reveled in feeling, had let my crude imagination roam, but the impulse to dream had been slowly beaten out of me by experience. Now it surged up again and I hungered for books, new ways of looking and seeing. It was not a matter of believing or disbelieving what I read, but of feeling something new, of being affected by something that made the look of the world different.

As dawn broke I ate my pork and beans, feeling dopey, sleepy. I went to work, but the mood of the book would not die; it lingered, coloring everything I saw, heard, did. I now felt that I knew what the white man were feeling. Merely because I had read a book that had spoken of how they lived and thought, I identified myself with that book. I felt vaguely guilty. Would I, filled with bookish notions, act in a manner that would make the whites dislike me?

I forged more notes and my trips to the library became frequent. Reading grew into a passion. My first serious novel was Sinclair Lewis's *Main Street*. It made me see my boss, Mr. Gerlad, and identify him as an American type. I would smile when I saw him lugging his golf bags into the office. I had always felt a vast distance separating me from the boss, and now I felt closer to him, though still distant. I felt now that I knew him, that I could feel the very limits of his narrow life. And this had happened because I had read a novel about a mythical man called George F. Babbitt.

The plots and stories in the novels did not interest me so much as the point of view revealed. I gave myself over to each novel without reserve, without trying to criticize it; it was enough for me to see and feel something different. And for me, everything was something different. Reading was like a drug, a dope. The novels created moods in which I lived for days. But I could not conquer my sense of guilt, my feeling that the white men around me knew that I was changing, that I had begun to regard them differently.

Whenever I brought a book to the job, I wrapped it in newspaper—a habit that was to persist for years in other cities and under other circumstances. But some of the white men pried into my packages when I was absent and they questioned me.

"Boy, what are you reading those books for?"

"Oh, I don't know, sir."

"That's deep stuff you're reading, boy."

"I'm just killing time, sir."

"You'll addle your brains if you don't watch out."

I read Dreiser's *Jennie Gerhardt* and *Sister Carrie* and they revived in me a vivid sense of my mother's suffering; I was overwhelmed. I grew silent, wondering about the life around me. It would have been impossible for me to have told anyone what I derived from these novels, for it was nothing less than a sense of life itself. All my life had shaped me for the realism, the naturalism of the modern novel, and I could not read enough of them.

Steeped in new moods and ideas, I bought a ream of paper and tried to write; but nothing would come, or what did come was flat beyond telling. I discovered that more than desire and feeling were necessary to write and I dropped the idea. Yet I still wondered how it was possible to know people sufficiently to write about them? Could I ever learn about life and people? To me, with my vast ignorance, my Jim Crow station in life, it seemed a task impossible of achievement. I now knew what being a Negro meant. I could endure the hunger. I had learned to live with hate. But to feel that there were feelings denied me, that the very breath of life itself was beyond my reach, that more than anything else hurt, wounded me. I had a new hunger.

CRITICAL THINKING QUESTIONS

1. Wright wants a library card in order to read and grow intellectually. Perhaps today he would have been looking for access to a computer. Read about the computer divide. Fifty years later are we still dividing access to knowledge according to wealth if not race?

2. Have you ever wanted or needed something that someone else in power has denied you? If so, did the situation make you angry? Like James Baldwin and other African-American artists, especially jazz musicians, Richard Wright spent years living in France. Look up the meaning of the word *expatriate*. Can you imagine situations that would lead you to leave your country?

CHAPTER ACTIVITIES

1. Advertising has created a popular image of the young computer genius who has become a millionaire by age 30, and while their numbers may not be large, in fact, there are such people driving their Ferraris through Silicon Valley as you read this question. Suppose for a moment you created and sold your own dot-com company, leaving you with a net worth of fifty million dollars. Assuming money is power, you certainly will have the power to do many things, but once you have bought mom and dad a nice retirement home and satisfied your own desire to trek through the Himalayas, what next? To what degree do you have responsibilities to your fellow human beings? Create a specific plan for using your assets, and argue that it is the best choice (literature suggestions: Brooks's "The Boy Died in My Alley" and Kennedy's "Inaugural Address").

2. Here is a hypothetical situation: The United States is at war in the Middle East, and China has stepped into the conflict. Our government has stated one objective in this war is to restore human rights to the besieged countries. However, everyone understands that this war is also over oil: we win and life goes on normally; we lose and gas goes up to six dollars a gallon while our economy unravels and depression looms. And in this ground war, fought by high-tech infantry, Americans are dying in large numbers. The draft has been reinstated, and your number is called. It's the front lines for you. But there is an alternative. The Scandinavian countries as well as Canada have denounced this war and openly accept conscientious objectors. What are your responsibilities? What do you do? Make a decision and support it (literature suggestions: Owen's "*Dulce et Decorum Est*" and O'Briens "On the Rainy River").

3. In her book, *The Perfect Vehicle: What It Is About Motorcycles*, Melissa Holbrook Pierson says,

   > Our aim . . . it seems [is] to accumulate goods. At the end of this metaphoric road stands the non-metaphoric Kmart, glistening like Oz and filled to the rafters with a hundred cheap mementos of wildflowers, in forms of candle, air freshener, sachet, cologne, bath bead, potpourri, and incense stick. In its prior life, of course, the ground under the big store bloomed with wildflowers.[1]

   What is our personal responsibility toward the natural world, toward what we term our *natural resources?* What power do we have to influence events? Of course, the word *resources* implies something to be used, yet how far do we go? Read about the conflicts between jobs and the environment that have been prominent in this country. Does the need to preserve age-old redwood forests outweigh loggers' need for paychecks in California? Are fish in the Gulf of

---

[1]Melissa Holbrook Pierson, *The Perfect Vehicle: What It Is About Motorcycles* (New York: W. W. Norton, 1997), p. 153.

Mexico more important than jobs for the commercial fishermen living along that coast? Conflicts such as these are usually settled in the courts. Read about one of these or a similar conflict, and, as you read, create a list of emotionally charged *diction* used by both sides. Then moving past the emotional appeals (*pathos*), write your own decision to resolve the conflict (literature suggestions: Kumin's "Woodchucks" and Regan's "Religion and Animal Rights").

4. As a manager of a department, you have the power and responsibility to hire and fire a group of twelve accountants. One employee in particular causes you concern. She contributes to the overall positive atmosphere of the department because of her caring approach to her fellow workers; however, although she seems to be trying, she is not productive. The result is that others must carry her share of the work, which, in turn, reduces their productivity. She is a single mother trying to raise two sons and needs this job, but even though you have discussed the situation with her, there has been no improvement over the past year. Do you exercise your power and terminate her, or do you let the situation continue? No matter what you decide, write Ms. Jones a letter explaining and justifying your decision (literature suggestion: Melville's "Bartleby the Scrivener").

5. Since we seem to share the desire to vanquish our enemies, revenge is sometimes called *sweet*. But is revenge sweet? We often applaud the person who has suffered unfair treatment when he or she finally triumphs. And we, ourselves, cannot but feel a twinge of joy when the court finally forces that unscrupulous car dealer to pay us back the money he unjustly took from us and offer an apology. But is revenge always sweet? Situations often are not as simple and clearcut as they appear on the surface. Read the story, "Spanish Roulette," and the poem, "Bully," in this chapter, and then write an extended definition of the word *revenge*. In your extended definition, you might include examples from history, literature, and personal experience, but be sure to focus on the conflicts this impulse for revenge creates in people.

Appendix A

Notes on the Writing Process

CLARIFYING A SUBJECT, PURPOSE, AND AUDIENCE

In Chapter One, we introduced a specific rhetorical triangle from Aristotle's *Rhetoric* which denotes three types of appeals to audience—*ethos, logos, pathos.* Another rhetorical triangle, commonly associated with the writing process, denotes the relationship among the subject, the purpose, and the audience. For example, in the sample essay in Chapter Two (page 33), "Yes, the Future Looks Bright, but the Moment is Hell," student writer Shawn Mullin addresses the subject of college students' working. His audience is his peers, college students, and his purpose is to convince fellow students that if they do choose to work, they should not work more than 20 hours a week. However, in the longer, research-based essay (page 47), "Who Are the Real Victims of Alcoholism?", student writer Meredith Newmon Blanco envisions a broader and more general audience—not only her college peers but also adults, younger and older, in the community. Her subject is victims of alcoholism, and her purpose is to inform her readers about certain victims and to *move* them to feel concern for these victims. For both Shawn and Meredith, finding their *subject (what do I want to write about?)*, designating their *audience (whom do I want to target?)*, and clarifying their *purpose (what effect do I want to have on readers?)* were critical, early stage steps in their writing process.

For many writers, finding a subject seems to present the biggest challenge. Here is where journal/freewriting, reading, and talking with others/class discussions can provide the requisite spark. For example, in a National Public Radio interview, poet Stephen Dunn said that if he waited for his "muse" or inspiration before beginning to write, he would not get any poems written. Dunn said he must sit down and begin to write, and in the process of writing, he finds a subject for his poem. Like the poet Dunn, student writers Shawn and Meredith began their search for a subject by writing *freely* and *for themselves*. In considering his essay assignment criteria (a short, first-person argument based on personal experience), Shawn began freewriting about an immediate personal predicament—how to celebrate his six-month anniversary with his girlfriend—which led him to his subject, working and the college student. Similarly, Meredith, in writing a journal response to Molly Peacock's poem, "Say You Love Me," found her subject for a longer, research-based, argument paper on alcoholism. With a palpable connection to their subjects, Shawn and Meredith were motivated to move forward from the private to the public realm of communication—to the process of producing writing about a specific *subject*, with a specific *purpose*, and for a specific *audience*.

ORGANIZING A LONGER, RESEARCH-BASED ARGUMENT PAPER

The Heart of an Argument Is Its *Claim*: Claims of Fact, Value, and Policy

The *subject* of an argument is, by definition, an *issue*, a debatable topic. One way for a writer to ascertain that his or her subject is debatable is to frame the topic as an *issue question*. Prompted by her response to Peacock's poem, Meredith narrowed her research focus from the general topic of alcoholism to children of alcoholic parents. Meredith articulated her issue as the question, "Who Are the Real Victims of Alcoholism?", which she later decided to use as her essay title, thus, setting a tone of inquiry and also suggesting an argumentative stance toward her subject.

The *purpose* of an argument is wedded to the writer's *claim*. In articulating the claim, the writer asserts his or her response to the issue question or subject of the argument. Because the claim of an argument is the thesis or main point of the essay, its clarity and scope are crucial in producing a successful argument. Chapter One discusses three central types of claim: *claim of fact, claim of value, claim of policy*. Determining which type of claim best suits one's purpose provides a key organizing tool for creating an effective argument.

For example, let's consider the subject of global warming. Alarmed by record heat and droughts, one may be motivated to find out what action could be taken to slow down or reverse this recent warming trend. By framing the issue question—how can we alleviate the detrimental effects of global warming?—one has set the stage for writing a *claim of policy* argument. Preliminary research, however, would reveal that the scientific community itself is debating the "fact or myth" of global warming. In constructing his argument, the writer could not *assume* the "fact" of global warming without also ignoring compelling counterarguments. Thus, if he persists with a claim of policy argument on global warming, he first would need to address the issue question—what is global warming?—and then proceed to propose his specific action for alleviating the harm caused by global warming. All in all, quite a task! Returning to the initial question of choosing a type of claim, the writer may well decide to limit himself to a *claim of fact* argument: "Key factors contributing to the harmful effects of global warming are. . . ." Similarly, in her argument paper on victims of alcoholism, Meredith settled on a claim of fact argument. By concluding her argument with a "call to action," Meredith seeks to motivate her audience to act on this information; however, the thrust of her argument has been to establish a factual basis for her claim that children are the real victims of alcoholism.

Some issues readily lend themselves to a *claim of policy* argument. For example, the link between tobacco smoke and lung cancer has long been documented; recent debate has centered on *what to do* about the public health problems caused by tobacco smoke (claim of policy issue). Similarly, let's consider the policy debate over mandatory uniforms in public schools. Most reasonable persons fully endorse the value of orderly conduct and respect for others in the public school classroom; however, many reasonable persons dispute the policy of mandating school uniforms as a means of creating a constructive climate in the classroom.

A *claim of value* is intrinsic to many claim of policy arguments. A *claim of policy* argument, for example, would advocate the legalization of physician-assisted suicide for terminally ill persons. In supporting this policy proposal, the writer would need to address the ethical issue of the quality of life/dignity of dying. She would attempt to convince her readers that the individual's right to choose when and how one dies is preferable to the experience of unremitting pain and suffering. On the other hand, to argue against physician-assisted suicide, a writer would *evaluate* the procedure, hoping to convince readers that it would be a detrimental policy for society to sanction. In this case, the writer would assert a *claim of value* as his main argument. When a writer's central purpose is to critique or evaluate his subject, he formulates a *claim of value* for his argument.

The Body of an Argument Is Its *Support*: Appeals to *Ethos*, *Logos*, and *Pathos*

The primary responsibility for a writer of an argument is not simply to state an opinion, conclusion, or judgment (to make a claim), but to demonstrate to an audience why the claim holds merit and is worthy of thoughtful consideration, adoption, and action. To support the claim, the writer draws on sources—*primary* (firsthand experience, observations, interviews, and personal accounts) and *secondary* (reported facts and information). Because one of the writer's principal concerns is to build respect and trust *(ethos)* with her target audience, the writer evaluates and selects evidence with her audience's needs in mind. The writer must envision her audience as "real" persons with their own emotions and biases, beliefs and values, and intellectual and social backgrounds. As with all levels of communication, the key to success is to establish a bond of respect: to demonstrate respect for and to earn respect from one's audience.

In selecting evidence to build support and establish credibility, a writer draws on material that will appeal to an audience's "heart"—emotions and beliefs—or *pathos*, and to an audience's "head"—logic and reasoning—or *logos*. Or course, just as the heart and head are part of the same human being, so is there often an overlap between material that appeals to the audience's emotions and reasoning. But for the purpose of *organizing* support for an argument, a writer may decide which of his evidence primarily appeals to *logos* and which primarily appeals to *pathos*, and thus, group or "chunk" his supporting materials. For example, in her argument paper on victims of alcoholism, Meredith's main body of evidence—statistical data and factual information from researchers—appeals to *logos*. However, to appeal to *pathos*, she breaks up the factual evidence with vivid quotes from Peacock's poem that evoke her audience's emotions. Moreover, Meredith frames her essay with appeals to *pathos:* by leading in with a personal anecdote and by concluding with the articulation of a common ground belief (*warrant*) in the value of children.

Counterarguments, Concessions, and Refutations

Depending on the rhetorical context or the current climate of controversy surrounding an issue, some arguments are more sharply divisive than others. The climate of controversy surrounding Meredith's argument, for example, might be described as seasonably comfortable. Her purpose was not to argue for or against her subject (of course, no one "supports" victims of alcoholism—be they children or adults) but to heighten her audience's awareness and concern about the victims of alcoholism. On the other hand, the current issue of physician-assisted suicide draws clear dissension; likewise, the enduring issue surrounding the value of civil disobedience for protesting an injustice can evoke clashing opinions. Thus, the writer should assess the climate of controversy surrounding an issue and its effect on his or her audience's prior knowledge, beliefs, and opinions. The writer also should be willing to reconsider and evaluate his own opinions as he confronts new information about his issue. Throughout the research process, the writer should be formulating his claim based on a thorough and critical investigation of information involving multiple and diverse perspectives on the issue.

To compose her argument, the writer determines which opposing views or *counterarguments* are significant in arguing her claim. Based on her investigation and evaluation of the evidence, the writer may choose to make some *concessions*, that is, to acknowledge the validity of aspects of the opposing viewpoints. For example, in the case of global warming, the writer may acknowledge that factual records of climate factors are relatively recent and, therefore, offer some credence to the challenge that global warming is not a direct result of modern industrial and technological factors but, instead, a normal and natural climatic phenomenon. Admitting this possibility, the writer would offer a *limited concession;* however, the writer could immediately follow her concession with a *refutation* which would provide compelling factual evidence that weighs in more heavily on the side of industrial and technological factors as primary causes of global warming.

By addressing opposing viewpoints, the writer strengthens her position with a broader audience—those who are undecided or skeptical about global warming, as well as with those who are predisposed to see technological advancement as a threat to the purity of the environment. Through the dialectical process of counterargument, concession, and refutation, the writer demonstrates fair-mindedness and reasonableness (appeal to *ethos*), and thus, reinforces the bond of respect and trust between writer and audience.

The Rogerian Argument

The Rogerian approach to argument takes fair-mindedness and reasonableness a step further. Carl Rogers, a well-known psychologist, suggested that more is to be gained through compromise than through confrontation. Thus, the Rogerian argument seeks out an area in which both sides' positions overlap and uses that overlap as a basis for compromise. Of course, compromise means each side must relinquish something; however, in the end, the positive result also means no one goes away defeated and angry. Student Russell Schneider demonstrates the Rogerian approach in his paper as he finds common ground between two sides of an issue and reaches a compromise at the end.

To Obey or Not to Obey

Once again it is election time in America—another chance for the average American to voice his or her opinion on what direction the country should take in the next four years. Casting a vote, John Q. Taxpayer gets a voice in determining how some of his money will be spent, which issues will take priority and which will get pushed aside until the next election year. But what if choosing another president is not enough? What if John Q. Taxpayer believes his government is corrupt and defies his moral principles, for example, because it condones abortion or capital punishment? What actions can he take? He could write a letter to his senator or even to the president himself. Or he could organize a protest outside of the White House with speeches condemning the government, marches disrupting traffic on Pennsylvania Avenue, and a mock ceremony shredding the American flag. Would this street protest constitute civil disobedience? And if so, is it justifiable? When, if ever, is it morally defensible to break a law?

To answer these questions about civil disobedience, one must first answer another question. What role should government play in limiting or controlling personal choice? How far any particular individual is willing to push the limits of the law depends largely upon his or her feelings of loyalty and patriotism to the nation. One who holds the ideas of loyalty and patriotism in the highest regard is less willing to upset the order of his government. In an excerpt from Plato's *Crito*, written over two thousand years ago,

Socrates, a citizen of Athens, explains his view that citizens are forever indebted to their nation. Speaking on behalf of the Athenian government, Socrates asks Crito, "Well, then, since you were brought into the world and nurtured and educated by us, can you deny in the first place that you are our child and slave, as your fathers were before you?" (Plato 664). This question clearly indicates Socrates's firm belief that the individual is beholden to the state as the child is to the parent; he owes nothing less than his life to the state. Therefore, one has no alternative but to obey the laws of his nation. Socrates continues,

> Has a philosopher like you failed to discover that our country is more to be valued and higher and holier far than mother or father or any ancestor. . . . And when we are punished by her, whether with imprisonment or stripes, the punishment is to be endured in silence, and if she leads us to wounds or death in battle, thither we follow as is right; . . . (Plato 664)

In Socrates's opinion, obedience to the state should dictate one's behavior and actions.

If a citizen considers a law to unjust or the government corrupt, according to Socrates, one should attempt to convince the leaders to change the law and, thus, to remedy the flaw. If, however, the individual is unsuccessful in having the laws changed, then one can choose to relocate to another country. But if one rejects this option and chooses to remain in the country, he must submit to the laws as they stand, even when he considers them unjust. Socrates proclaims, "He who has experience in the manner in which we order justice and administer the state, and still remains, has entered into an implied contract that he will do as we command him" (Plato 664–5). Socrates, in choosing to remain in Athens, accepts the rule of law which has declared him guilty of corrupting the youth and sentenced him to death.

On the other hand, the nineteenth-century American, Henry David Thoreau, places the authority of the individual above that of the government. In his argument "Civil Disobedience," Thoreau contends that the government exists solely to serve the people. Instead of the citizens' being loyal to the government, the government should be loyal to its citizens. Thoreau suggests that the government's role in the everyday lives of citizens should be limited to an absolute minimum: "'That government is best which governs not at all';. . . . Government is at best but an expedient; . . . " (Thoreau 676). Thoreau makes it clear that he is not a supporter of strong national government; in fact, he rebukes it as a not so necessary evil. Moreover, he specifically addresses the ideas of persons (such as Socrates) who believe in obeying laws deemed unjust until such time as the laws can be amended:

> Unjust laws exist: Shall we be content to obey them, [and] endeavor to amend them, . . . or shall we disobey them at once? Men generally . . . think that they ought to wait until they have persuaded the majority to alter them. They think that, if they should resist, the remedy would be worse than the evil. But it is the fault of the government itself that the remedy *is* worse than the evil. *It* makes it worse. (682)

Here Thoreau suggests that the government is to blame for any violence that might occur in revolution. He shows signs of a strong will and limited patience. Later, Thoreau states, "As for adopting the ways which the State has provided for remedying the evil, I know not of such ways. They take too much time, and a man's life will be gone" (683). The individual, according to Thoreau, is more effective and efficient than the State in addressing problems of evil and corruption.

However, Thoreau does not appear to advocate violence in any form. Instead he suggests a more passive approach to resistance: "What I have to do is to see that I do not lend myself to the wrong which I condemn" (683). Thoreau himself refused to pay a poll tax that would fund the United States's war on Mexico in 1848, which in his opinion, constituted an unjust act of aggression. For his refusal to pay the tax, Thoreau spent one night in jail—not a news-breaking incident, but his example gives credence to his willingness to break the law and to accept his punishment in order to make his disapproval known.

Both Socrates and Thoreau offer persuasive arguments for their opposing positions on the value of civil disobedience—the authority of the government and its laws versus the authority of the individual and his or her moral conscience. Socrates believes that citizens owe their government unequivocal loyalty and must obey its laws, even those they deem unfair or immoral. Thoreau, on the contrary, believes that citizens should not tolerate injustice or moral failings in their government and should act to rectify the situation, even if it means breaking the law. Given the merit of both arguments, how should Jane Q. Citizen respond to a law she considers to be unjust or immoral?

Although Socrates and Thoreau advocate opposing positions, they share essential common ground: Both men believe that the individual is directly responsible for addressing and responding to the laws of one's country. Above all, they both believe that the individual must acknowledge and accept the consequences of his or her response to the laws—whether that action is one of obedience or disobedience. And finally, each individual must determine what he or she is willing to do to bring about a fair and just government. Whether a person chooses to lobby his or her congressional representative or to chain him or herself to the White House fence is an individual decision.

Works Cited

Plato. From *Crito*. Trans. Benjamin Jowett, 3rd ed. New York: Dial Press, 1982. Rpt. In *Elements of Argument: A Text and Reader*. Annette T. Rottenberg. 6th ed. Boston: Bedford/St. Martin's, 2000. 663–667.

Thoreau, Henry David. "Civil Disobedience." In *Elements of Argument: A Text and Reader*. Annette T. Rottenberg. 6th ed. Boston: Bedford/St. Martin's, 2000. 676–693.

Appendix B

Notes on Using Sources and Creating a Draft

You can certainly write a college level paper expressing your opinions and insights on a given topic by using personal experience to support your claims. However, because such a paper is characterized by a subjective approach to your topic, professors most often expect you to move beyond the use of personal experience as evidence. In these cases, you will need to make use of evidence from outside sources. Once you choose to utilize support found in your reading of books and periodicals or in interviews of people with expertise in your subject, you face several tasks.

First, you must make accurate and fair use of the material in your paper. This task involves taking good notes and then deciding whether to *quote* directly or *paraphrase* that information as you integrate it into your composition. Secondly, you must follow a *documentation* system which will allow your reader to see the sources of this information. Although using only personal experience as evidence in support of your claims is much easier than utilizing outside sources, all academic disciplines require a systematic approach to research and documentation. Whether your paper is in anthropology or chemistry, economics or English, geology or art history, you will need to learn to use outside sources accurately and correctly.

Academic disciplines make use of several documentation systems. For example, the social sciences often use a system devised by the American Psychological Association (APA), while the humanities typically use one created by the Modern Language Association (MLA). Other academic documentation systems include the Chicago Manual of Style and Turabian. However, since your papers written for this course will fall under the category *humanities,* the following explanation will center on the Modern Language Association (MLA) style.

THE PRELIMINARY BIBLIOGRAPHY

Typically, you will begin to think about a topic by examining your own ideas and experiences associated with it before moving beyond that subjective analysis to discuss your ideas with friends and classmates. Inevitably, however, you will need to read about your topic in books, periodicals, and on Web sites to gain a broader understanding. As you undertake this research, you will want to maintain a list of the sources you examine; this list is called a *preliminary bibliography*. In making this list, get into the habit of recording initially as much bibliographic information as is available—author, title, date of publication, Web address, page or paragraph numbers, etc.—because you will need this information when you compose the actual bibliography for your finished paper. Nothing is more frustrating than finishing a paper only to discover you must try to locate the source of a quote you found three weeks earlier when you first began the project. Make your preliminary bibliography a working list, crossing out sources that prove unusable and making quick notes below sources to help you identify their potential use in your paper.

AVOIDING PLAGIARISM WITH NOTE-TAKING

Plagiarism means making use of someone's ideas or facts without giving him or her credit. In other words, plagiarism is equivalent to theft, and thieves, when caught, are punished. Most first-year college students hear several lectures on the sins of plagiarism. Unfortunately, while a few students knowingly take others' ideas and pass them off as their own, many more students commit the sin of plagiarism unintentionally because they do not understand how to make use of ideas and facts from outside sources.

To avoid charges of plagiarism, begin by taking *accurate notes*. As you examine materials from your preliminary bibliography, you will need to record the facts and ideas you think you might find useful for your paper. [*Hint:* Many handbooks advocate the use of note cards; you might want to read through a handbook's chapter on the use of note cards.] Whether you take your notes on 3 × 5 index cards, on a legal pad, or on the back of your electric bill, one concept is particularly important—*make a clear distinction between your words and the words of the author.* Unless you put quotes around the author's words, in a few days you will be unable to distinguish yours from the author's. In fact, when you have the opportunity, photocopy or print the page containing the information you think you might use in your paper. In addition, record the source, as well as the page number where you find your information. In the case of Web pages without page numbers, you will have to record the paragraph number. [*Hint:* Write this bibliographic information on any photocopies or printouts you make.] For example, here is a periodical source and a Web site:

> Binder, Leonard. "U.S. Policy in the Middle East." *Current History*
>   Jan. 1997: 4.

> *Thomas: Legislative Information on the Internet.* 26 May 1999. Lib.
>   of Congress, Washington. Par. 6. 03 January 2001.
>   <http://thomas.loc.gov>.

You may read information in your sources which you do not have to document; this information is called *common knowledge*. For instance, you may read that the United States military suffered many casualties during the worst battles of World

War II; however, that information is common knowledge, and even though you also make that statement in your paper, there is no need to document the source. On the other hand, if you read that 3,200 Americans were wounded or killed at the Battle of the Bulge—information that is not common knowledge—you would have to document the source of that statistic in your paper. [*Hint:* Because deciding what is common knowledge can be a bit confusing, when in doubt, cite the source.]

As you take notes, you may encounter long passages which you want to record. In those cases, students traditionally *paraphrase* the material; that is, they read the passage and then, using their own words, express the ideas briefly but accurately. In your notes, *always put quotes around any words that are the author's*—later, as you write your paper, you do not want to wonder if your notes reflect a direct quote or a paraphrase. Again, if you have the opportunity to photocopy or print out the page of your source, you can easily resolve that ambiguity.

Paraphrased material is run into the text of your paper and is never enclosed in quotation marks. Paraphrasing means completely rephrasing a quotation so that only the core or central idea of the original is retained; it is not enough just to change a few of the words, here and there. Also, even when paraphrasing, an in-text note is required.

A *direct quotation* is an exact restatement of a writer's or a speaker's words. It is always documented with its source, usually through the use of an in-text note. Short direct quotations are always enclosed in quotation marks. Longer direct quotations, more than four typed lines, are indented ten spaces from the left margin and double-spaced, using no quotation marks unless they were in the original. Here is an example:

> If one is going to help a child of an alcoholic, one must know what alcoholism is. Alcoholism is defined as,
>
> > primary chronic disease with genetic, psychosocial and environmental factors influencing its development and manifestations. The disease is often progressive and fatal. Continuous or periodic characterizes it: impaired control over drinking, preoccupation with the drug alcohol, use of alcohol despite adverse consequences, and distortions in thinking most notably denial. ("Definition," par. 4)

Paraphrasing a passage can be quite difficult, especially for inexperienced writers, because the task involves making judgments and interpretations. Unintentional plagiarism can be the result. For this reason, some professors ask students to avoid the use of paraphrasing altogether. If you feel uncomfortable paraphrasing, you might rely on direct quotes until you have the opportunity to gain some experience. [*Hint:* If your school has a writing center, that setting would afford you a good place to practice this skill. You might try paraphrasing a passage and then taking it to a tutor along with the original in order to get some criticism of your efforts.] Paraphrasing is a challenging skill, one you will need to practice and master.

USING YOUR SOURCES AND CREATING A DRAFT

You have thought about your topic, discussed it with friends and classmates, and read about it in various periodicals, books, and electronic sources. You have an angle you want to explore and a tentative claim you wish to make. You have a collection of notes, photocopies of sources, a preliminary bibliography, and a general·idea of where you want this paper to go. Now comes the time to sit down and create a draft.

Write out your claim in a single, concise sentence at the top of your paper. Draw a box around it if you are writing in longhand; bold it if you are using a word processor. If you are starting early and can afford the time, plant that claim in your mind and then give your subconscious a day or two to work on it. If you are writing a paper that is due in a day or two, you will just have to begin.

CITATIONS

Once you begin to write and make use of your research, you will encounter several challenges. First, you will need to integrate your facts, quotes, and paraphrased material into your paper. To achieve coherence and clarity, always introduce each piece of outside evidence, making clear to the reader the purpose of placing this quote or paraphrase in this particular spot in your paper. Some students' first research papers neglect this important element, and, as a consequence, their papers read as if they merely dropped their quotes randomly onto the pages. Secondly, you will need to document your statements with in-text parenthetical notes showing the sources of your information; this is called *parenthetical documentation.*

In MLA style, the in-text parenthetical notes usually include the author's last name or, if an author's name is not given with the source, the title as well as the page number or paragraph number, all enclosed in parentheses. Remember this key principle: *You must use in-text parenthetical notes for direct quotations; for paraphrases or summaries of another person's words; and for facts, figures, or concepts that originated in someone else's work.* For example, if you are citing a fact you found in an article by Sharon Johnson, called "Cosmetic Surgery" and published on page 114 of the magazine *Science* on October 14, 1992, the parenthetical note would look like this: (Johnson 114). It would be placed at the end of the sentence containing that fact. In cases where your source does not include an author, you use the title to identify the source. If there is no page number, as is often the case with Web sites, you must count the paragraphs on the site and include the source's paragraph number in your parenthetical note: ("Postmodern Culture," par. 6). [*Hint:* The *MLA Handbook for Writers of Research Papers,* 5th ed. (1999) is an excellent source for bibliographic information. Also you can look at the organization's Web site (http://www.mla.org) for updates and further explanations.]

The purpose of documentation is to give credit to the originators of any material that is not your own. However, documentation also serves another purpose: to allow your readers to locate the information you used and evaluate it for themselves. In effect, you are sharing the information you have found, a consideration which becomes increasingly important as you continue in higher education.

In order to fulfill these two purposes, your readers must be able to find the complete bibliographic information for each of your sources. You have provided the key name or title in your parenthetical citation, immediately after your use of the information in your paper. Now the reader can turn to the last page of your paper to see the bibliographic entry for each of these sources; that means you must create a *Works Cited* page.

THE WORKS CITED PAGE

The final page of your paper is the Works Cited page, which is a list of the sources you directly cited in your paper. These citations are arranged alphabetically by the author's last name or by the first word in the title (excluding *the, a,* or *an*). The specific details to be included in each entry vary, according to the nature of the source—book, article, Web site, interview, etc. For the specific details required, you will need to consult a handbook or go to one of the many Web sites devoted to documentation. Here is an example from a student paper:

Works Cited

"Alcoholism and Alcohol-Related Problems: A Sobering Look." *Infinet Internet Service. National Council on Alcohol and Drug Dependency.* 13 Nov. 1999. <http://www.ncadd.org>.

"Answers to Frequently Asked Questions about Being a Child of an Alcoholic." *Infinet Internet Service. National Council of Alcohol and Drug Dependency.* 11 Nov. 1999. <http://www.alcoholism help.com>.

"Chemical Dependency: Myths and Facts about Alcoholism." *Infinet Internet Service. Baptist Hospital East.* 13 Nov. 1999. <http://www.baptisteast.com>.

"Children of Alcoholics: Important Facts." *Infinet Internet Service.* August, 1998. *National Association of Children of Alcoholics.* 13 Nov. 1999. <http://www.healthorg/nacoa/impfacts.htm>.

"Definition of Alcoholism." *Infinet Internet Service.* 25 Feb 1990. *National Council on Alcoholism and Drug Dependency.* 11 Nov. 1999. <http://www.ncadd.org>.

FYI: Drinking in America." *Infinet Internet Service. National Council of Alcohol and Drug Dependency.* 12 Nov. 1999. <http://www.ncadd.org/fyidina.html>.

Peacock, Molly. "Say You Love Me." *Literature: Reading and Writing the Human Experience.* 7th ed. Richard Abcarian and Marvin Klotz, eds. New York: St. Martin's Press, 1998. 1056–1057.

Weddle, Charles D. and Phillip Wishon. "Children of Alcoholics." *Children Today* Jan–Feb. 1986: 8–12.

STRATEGY QUESTIONS FOR ORGANIZING
YOUR ARGUMENT PAPER

1. How will you *introduce* your issue? What will be your *lead-in "hook"* (an example, anecdote, scenario, startling statistic, provocative questions or statements, vivid description)? Is there an interesting fact or quotation you have come across which might make a catchy beginning for your introduction?

2. How much *background* (rhetorical context) will your readers need to understand this issue?

3. Where will you present the strongest statement of your *claim:* early on/at the end of your introduction (the conventional location), midway through the essay, or delayed/in your conclusion?

4. What are your three (or so) main supporting arguments (*subclaims*)? How should they be ordered? These subclaims should probably serve as body *paragraph topic sentences.*

5. What *authoritative evidence* do you have to support the subclaims you identified above? What evidence will you use to support your claim? Do you have the option to use personal experience? Have you found any authorities whom you can quote? Are there statistics or facts you need to present?

   a. What evidence do you have that will appeal to your readers' *logos?*

   b. What evidence do you have that will appeal to your readers' *pathos?* Will any of the creative literature you have read provide direct support for your claim? Will including it add an emotional impact to your essay, and, if so, where do you want that impact to appear in your paper?

   c. How can you best use these appeals? Where in the argument will they work the best to build your *ethos* with your readers?

6. Where will you address *opposing* viewpoints—in the first, middle, or last section of your body? Identify the main points of the opposing arguments, which also should be *paragraph topic sentences.*

7. How will you address the opposing arguments? What might readers say in opposition? "Yeah, but. . . . " objections will have some validity, and you need to address these concerns. Will you make some *concessions?* Finally, how will you *refute* the opposing arguments?

8. What questions of *style* and *tone* do you need to keep in mind as you write to ensure that you keep as many readers open to and interested in your argument? How do you want your *voice* to sound?

9. How will you *conclude* your paper? Will you use a value-based appeal (assert a *warrant*) in an attempt to strike common ground? Will you issue a specific "call to action"—suggest steps "we" can take . . . ?

[*Hint:* Think *chunks* . . . coherent "chunks" of evidence have a logical order and lead your readers to believe that your claim is the thinking person's response to the issue question.]

Glossary

Active voice   the construction of a sentence in which the subject of the sentence is the doer of the action, as opposed to *passive voice,* in which the object of the action is in the subject place. "John hit Joe" is active voice, while "Joe was hit by John" is passive voice.

Ad hominem   the fallacy of personal attack. Instead of arguing with someone's position, one attacks the person. "Mrs. X has had two affairs and does not deserve our vote."

Ad populum   the fallacy of substituting content with a "just plain folks" appeal.

Allegory   a work which may be seen totally or in part to represent a similar political or moral situation. *Aesop's Fables* or the *Stories of Brer Rabbit* are famous allegories.

Alliteration   the repetition of similar consonant sounds, e.g., *a fearsome food fight* or *an amorous aardvark.*

Ambiguity   intentionally vague meaning, sometimes leading the reader astray in argument or adding multiple levels of interpretation to literature.

Analogy   in argument, creating an explanation through point-by-point comparison, for example, comparing the perceived moral deterioration of the modern world with that of ancient Rome.

Anecdote   a brief story used within a larger work in order to illustrate an idea.

Annotation   a critical or explanatory note.

Appeal to authority   in argument, an appeal for support based on the widely accepted credibility of the witness; for example, suggesting that Dr. Spock, the noted baby doctor, held a similar position to your own on the subject of toilet training.

Archetype   a recurring image that evokes very basic associations seen in universal patterns of human experience.

Assertion   sometimes called the *claim* or the *thesis,* it is the speaker's or writer's statement of his or her position in an argument.

Assumption   in argument, an idea which the writer or speaker feels no need to support, prove or justify since he or she believes his or her audience will certainly hold it to be true. See also *Warrant.*

Audience   the readers or listeners for whom the writer composes, thus shaping or influencing the final product.

Begging the question   to use an argument that assumes exactly what the argument attempts to prove; for example, gun control goes against our freedom because it takes away our individual rights.

Caricature   a comic portrait of a person based on the exaggeration of several traits.

Character   the representation of a person in literature. A one-dimensional character is called a *flat* character, while one who is realistically complex is called a *round* character.

Claim   in argument, the main point, thesis, or assertion of the argument—what the speaker or writer wants his or her audience to think or do about an issue.

Cliché   a word or phrase overused and outworn to the point of losing its impact; for example, *the bottom line* or *put the pedal to the metal.* In literature, plot situations can be termed *cliché* or hackneyed.

Climax   the high point of interest and intensity after which the plot moves toward its conclusion. See also *Denouement.*

Conceit   in writing or speaking, the use of an elaborate or striking metaphor.

Concession   in argument, recognizing and acknowledging the validity of a portion of the opposition's point of view. In making a concession, the arguer can strengthen his or her *ethos* by demonstrating the character trait of fair-mindedness.

Conflict   the opposition which creates tension in literature. The opposing forces may be *external* when a character conflicts with other people, or they may be *internal* when a character faces conflicts within him or herself.

Connotation   the emotional or social meaning attached to a word beyond its literal, objective meaning. For example, in James Fenimore Cooper's story, "The Slaughter of the Pigeons," the word "slaughter" suggests a wanton and brutal assault. See also *Denotation.*

Crisis   the point of uncertainty and tension, leading to the plot's *climax.*

Deduction   the reasoning process which begins with a generalization, applies that generalization to a particular instance, and then draws a conclusion based on that application. See also *Induction*.

Denotation   the dictionary definition of a word—its literal and explicit meaning. See also *Connotation*.

Denouement   the climax or final coming together of all plot elements in a drama or narrative once the conflicts are resolved. See also *Climax*.

Diction   the writer's choice of words.

Didactic   when an author wishes to teach a lesson or instruct his or her audience through his or her writing.

Documentation   a way of attributing sources of words and concepts, usually following MLA or APA parenthetical style.

Dramatic irony   a situational irony in which an audience's wider understanding highlights a character's limited vision.

Either-or reasoning   sometimes called the *black and white* or *false dillemma fallacy;* in argument, such reasoning is characterized by over-simplification that presents an issue only in two ways, either X or Y.

Ellipses   the three periods used to indicate words left out of a direct quote; e.g., "I shall never . . . return to this area of the country."

Emphasis   in writing, the use of repetition, syntax, and word placement to draw the reader's attention to a word or idea.

Equivocation   in argument, the intentional use of a word which has more than one interpretation and thus misleads the reader or listener.

Ethos   the appeal first mentioned by Aristotle through which the writer or speaker evokes his or her credibility and trustworthiness; e.g., a teenager wishing to stay out past curfew might ask his or her parents, "Have I ever done anything to lead you to mistrust me?"

Euphemism   a word used in place of a harsher word, e.g., "passed away" used instead of "died." Such words sometimes can mask the truth of an issue.

Evidence   in argument, there are many types of evidence, but the most common are personal experience or first-person accounts, *logos* or the use of facts and objective reports, *ethos* or the use of character and credibility, and *pathos* or the use of value-based and emotional appeals.

Exposition   that portion of a drama or narrative which introduces the facts of setting, plot, and character to the audience.

Fact   verifiable information; a statement that can be proven true or false. "Texas is located near New Jersey," is stated as a fact although, of course, it is false.

Fallacy   illogical reasoning; often an intentional flaw created to manipulate the evidence and mislead one's audience, but sometimes an unknowing flaw in reasoning due to one's carelessness or ignorance.

False analogy   a false comparison, sometimes expressed as "comparing apples and oranges." People might say that like Rome, America is destined for destruction; however, modern America is quite unlike ancient Rome.

Figurative language   language using imaginative comparison, such as *metaphor* and *simile.*

Flashback   a return, out of chronological order, to an earlier point in the plot, often used in fiction and film.

Foil character   a minor character designed to reflect the qualities of a major character through contrast.

Foreshadowing   a hint or suggestion of what is to come.

Image   a reference in literature which calls to mind vivid details of sight, sound, smell, taste, and touch.

Induction   a process of reasoning that begins by one's examining details in order to arrive at a generalization. In moving from specific evidence to articulating a probable conclusion, one makes an *inductive leap.* When one moves hastily from inadequate evidence to a generalization, this leap in reasoning represents flawed reasoning, commonly called, *jumping to a conclusion.*

Inference   S. I. Hayakawa defines it as "a statement about the unknown based on the known." Unlike a fact, an inference cannot be proven true or false since it is a probable explanation or interpretation of evidence.

Interpretation   moving beyond line-by-line explication of a work to an examination of themes, implications, and broader meanings.

Irony   a humorous or sarcastic statement whose words mean the opposite of their usual use, or in literature, the contrast between a character's perception and the truth known to the reader or audience.

Issue   a topic of argument which generates tension because both sides have some reasonable aspects to their arguments.

Logos   in argument, the rhetorical appeal which Aristotle identified as the arguer's use of reasoning and logic to persuade his or her audience to accept the claim.

Metaphor without using "like" or "as," this device describes something as if it were something quite different. "That man is an angel."

Mood the emotional quality of a work created through the writer's choice of imagery and setting. One might say Shakespeare's *Romeo and Juliet* is a "tragic and somber" play, while Harvey Fierstein's *On Tidy Endings* is "both funny and sad, and yet, uplifting."

Narration the recounting of a series of plot events in order to tell a story. A *narrator* relates these events to the reader.

Non-sequitur in argument, a common fallacy, meaning "it does not follow"; the reasoning does not follow logically between clauses within a sentence or between consecutive sentences.

Pathos the quality in literature which arouses pity; in argument, an emotional or value-based appeal. When an emotional appeal replaces content, it is called the fallacy of *ad misercordium* or appeal to pity and fear.

Persona literally translated as a "mask"; the identity or image the writer presents in poetry, fiction, or argument.

Plagiarism a writer's failure to give credit for words or concepts from another source.

Plot the chain of events in literature, what happens next.

Point-of-view the speaker or narrator of a work through which the audience or readers perceive the details of plot and character. The point-of-view may be omniscient, limited, or objective, as well as first-, second-, or third-person.

Post hoc **fallacy** Incorrectly attributing a cause and effect relationship; often called the false cause fallacy.

Premise the main idea, hypothesis, or underlying principle in an argument.

Protagonist the central character or actor in literature.

Red herring the fallacy of leading the reader astray by bringing up a different issue as bait to capture the reader's interest, thus distracting him or her from the real issue.

Refutation attempting to prove an argument wrong.

Rhetorical question asking a question as a way to involve the reader in the issue at hand. In this way, the writer sets him or herself up to answer the question that has been planted in the reader's mind.

Stacking the evidence the writer or speaker purposefully ignores opposing evidence to create a one-sided argument.

Stream-of-consciousness a narrative technique in which the author may reveal the emotions, perceptions, and thoughts of a character on a conscious or unconscious level.

Subplot a story that runs parallel to the main plot of a narrative, sometimes reinforcing the central theme.

Syllogism in argument, Aristotle's three-part method of deductive reasoning, beginning with a major premise, followed by a minor premise, and ending with a conclusion.

Syntax the arrangement of words, phrases, and clauses forming sentences.

Theme a recurring, unifying idea running through a piece of literature. To discover *plot*, readers may ask the question, "what happens next?"; whereas, to discover *theme*, readers may answer the question, "why?"

Tone a speaker's or writer's attitude toward his or her subject and audience, often conveyed through diction.

Tragedy traditionally the fall of a great person through his or her own errors in judgment, as in the case of Creon in *Antigone*. In modern literature, the term is often applied to the downfall of less highly placed characters.

Tragic flaw a character's shortcoming which leads to disaster, for example, greed, lust, pride, or merely poor judgment.

Voice the writer's personality or image constructed by the reader, often conveyed to the reader by the writer's sentence style and diction. See also *Persona* and *Tone*.

Warrant a general principle or premise, stated or unstated, which the arguer assumes his or her audience accepts as valid or true, often a value-based principle. For example, in opposing abortion, pro-life advocates assume that life has human value from the moment of conception.

Authors' Biographical Notes

Abbey, Edward (1927–1989) Although born and raised on a farm in Pennsylvania, Abbey lived in the Southwest from 1947 until his death. A passionate defender of wilderness, his book, *Desert Solitaire* (1968), helped to launch the environmental movement. His novel, *The Monkey Wrench Gang* (1975), about a group of environmental guerilla's plot to blow up Glen Canyon Dam of the Colorado River, is credited with influencing radical environmental groups such as Earth First!.

Bambara, Toni Cade (b. 1939) Bambara grew up in New York City and became a welfare investigator and a community activist. In 1970, she adopted the name "Bambara" from a signature she found in her great-grandmother's trunk. She has edited anthologies of black literature and published two collections of short stories, *Gorilla, My Love* (1972) and *The Sea Birds are Still Alive* (1977).

Bass, Rick (b. 1959) Bass, who lives in northwest Montana, is the author of fourteen books of fiction and nonfiction, including *The Watch* (1994), *The Sky, the Stars, the Wilderness* (1977), *Wild to the Heart*, and *Colter: The True Story of the Best Dog I Ever Had* (2000).

Brooks, Gwendolyn (1917–2000) Brooks won the Pulitzer Prize in 1950 for her collection of poetry, *Annie Allen*. Since then she has continued to write and was named the poet laureate of Illinois in 1969. Her poems reflect the diction and syntax of black street life. *The Bean-Eaters* was published in 1960, followed by *Beckonings* in 1975 and *To Disembark* in 1981.

Carson, Rachel (1907–1964) A scientist and writer, Carson's *The Sea Around Us* won the 1952 National Book Award. Her book, *Silent Spring* (1962), alerted the nation about the dangers of widespread and indiscriminate use of pesticides and chemical fertilizers. In 1963, the National Wildlife Federation recognized Carson as Conservationist of the Year.

Carver, Raymond (1938–1988) Raised in a working-class environment in the Pacific Northwest, Carver worked at many jobs while writing stories about the lives of everyday working people who feel trapped by their surroundings. His writing has been collected in *Fires: Essays, Poems, and Stories* (1989).

660

Chopin, Kate (1851–1904) In defiance of contemporary restraints, Chopin often wrote about strong, independent, female characters. She also wrote frankly about her characters' sexual feelings and, for that reason, caused a literary scandal. Her novels have recently found a sympathetic audience.

Cleary, Michael (b. 1945) Cleary grew up in upstate New York and now teaches college English in Fort Lauderdale, Florida, where he writes poetry. His first book of poems is *Hometown,* published in 1992.

Clifton, Lucille (b. 1936) A graduate of Howard University, Clifton has published seven books of poetry and fifteen children's books. She now teaches creative writing at the University of California, Santa Cruz.

Cooper, James Fenimore (1789–1851) Considered by critics to be the first successful American novelist, Cooper created the character Natty Bumppo in his famous *Leather-Stocking Tales,* depicting life on the frontier. The collection includes the well-known novels, *The Last of the Mohicans* (1826) and *The Deerslayer* (1841).

Crane, Stephen (1871–1900) Crane spent his brief life involved with writing, working with newspapers, serving as a war correspondent, and composing fiction. "A Bride Comes to Yellow Sky" was produced as a result of the year he spent traveling in the West. His best-known novel, *The Red Badge of Courage,* was published in 1895.

Danticat, Edwidge (b. 1969) Born in Haiti, Danticat came to the United States when she was twelve years old. She received her M.A. from Barnard College and M.F.A. from Brown University. Danticat won a 1995 Pushcart Short Story Prize, and her first novel, *Breath, Eyes, Memory,* was highly praised. *Krik? Krak!* was a National Book Award Finalist in 1995.

Dickey, James (1923–1997) Born in Buckhead, Georgia, Dickey flew combat missions in World War II and also served in the U.S. Air Force during the Korean War. A poet, novelist, and essayist, Dickey received a number of awards, including the 1966 National Book Award for Poetry; also, Dickey was invited to read at the inauguration of President Jimmy Carter (1977). Among his collections of poetry are *Buckdancer's Choice* (1965), *The Strength of Fields* (1979), and *The Whole Motion: Collected Poems, 1945–1992* (1992). Dickey's novel, *Deliverance* (1970), an international bestseller, was made into a popular movie.

Dillard, Annie (b. 1945) Dillard, born in Pittsburgh, Pennsylvania, won the 1975 Pulitzer Prize for general nonfiction for *Pilgrim at Tinker Creek.* Author of essays, a memoir, poetry, and literary criticism, her many published works include *An American Childhood* (1987), *The Writing Life* (1989), *Mornings like This: Found Poems* (1995), and *For the Time Being* (1999).

Eliot, T. S. [Thomas Stearns] (1888–1965) Although born in St. Louis and educated at Harvard, Eliot emigrated to England and became a British citizen in 1927. *Prufrock and Other Observations* was published in 1917 during World War I. He won the Nobel Prize for Literature in 1948.

Emerson, Ralph Waldo (1803–1882) The son of a prominent Unitarian minister in Boston, Emerson graduated from Harvard University in 1821, and briefly attended Harvard's Unitarian Divinity School. Emerson was ordained to be a preacher at a Boston Unitarian church in 1829, but increasingly skeptical about Christianity, he resigned in 1832. His first book, *Nature* (1836), reveals Emerson's passion for idealistic philosophies, ancient and modern, particularly, Transcendentalism. Besides his writings, Emerson was a frequent lecturer and a prominent figure on the social and intellectual landscape of the nineteenth century. His many published books include essays, journal writings, and the texts of his sermons, lecturers, and letters.

Erdrich, Louise (b. 1954)   Edrich is the author of three novels, *Love Medicine, The Beet Queen,* and *Tracks.* She has also written two volumes of poetry and is the co-author with her late husband, Michael Dorris, of *The Crown of Columbus.* Erdrich was born in Minnesota to Chippewa and German parents.

Espada, Martín (b. 1957)   An attorney who was born in the housing projects of Brooklyn, Espada's poems often highlight the social inequities of urban America. His book, *Rebellion Is the Circle of a Lover's Hands,* won the Peterson Poetry Prize in 1991.

Fierstein, Harvey (b. 1954)   Fierstein wrote a series of one-act plays, *Torch Song Trilogy,* between 1976 and 1979. An acclaimed actor on and off Broadway, he also wrote the book for the musical version of *La Cage aux Folles.*

Forché, Carolyn (b. 1950)   After attending schools in Michigan and Ohio, Forche moved to the Southwest where she lived among Pueblo Indians. Later, she documented civil rights violations in El Salvador for Amnesty International. Her published books of poetry include *Gathering the Tribes* in 1975, *The Country Between Us* in 1981, and *The Angel of History* in 1994.

Franklin, John Hope (b. 1915)   A history professor and author, Franklin has served as the chair of the President's Initiative on Race. His books include *Racial Equality in America* (1976) and *The Color Line: Legacy for the Twenty-first Century* (1993). Currently, Franklin is associated with Duke University.

Frost, Robert (1874–1963)   Frost was born in San Francisco but is best known for his relationship with New England, where he lived most of his life. *A Boy's Will,* his first collection of poems, was published by 1913 and Frost continued to write and publish poetry through 1962. He won four Pulitzer Prizes for his work and will always be remembered for reading his poems, "Dedication" and "The Gift Outright," at the inauguration of President John F. Kennedy in 1961.

Giovanni, Nikki (b. 1943)   Born in Knoxville, Tennessee, Giovanni is a poet, writer, lecturer, and professor of creative writing. She has published many books of poetry as well as an autobiography, *Gemini: An Extended Autobiographical Statement on My First Twenty-Five Years of Being a Black Poet* (1971).

González, Genaro (b. 1949)   A psychology professor at the University of Texas at Pan American, González received the National Endowment for the Arts Creative Writing Award in 1990. His book, *Only Sons* (1991), is a collection of interconnected stories about characters who live along the Mexican-American border.

Gordimer, Nadine (b. 1923)   Gordimer, born an English-speaking Jew in South Africa, resented the white supremacist attitudes embodied in the system of Apartheid.

The topic of her fiction has most often been the relations between blacks and whites in South Africa. She received the Nobel Prize in Literature in 1994.

Grahn, Judy (b. 1940)   After growing up in New Mexico where she worked at several blue-collar jobs, Grahn moved to California and founded the Diana Press. Her work includes volumes of poetry and the nonfiction work, *Another Mother Tongue: Gay Words, Gay Worlds* (1984).

Hardy, Thomas (1840–1928)   A major British novelist, Hardy also wrote poems throughout his career. *Tess of the D'Urbervilles* and *The Mayor of Casterbridge* are two of his many novels. At age 60 he turned entirely to poetry, publishing *Late Lyrics and Earlier* in 1922. *Winter Words in Various Moods and Metres* was published posthumously in 1928.

Hawthorne, Nathaniel (1804–1864)   A Massachusetts author whose fiction draws on romance and psychological realism, Hawthorne found much of his material in New England's Puritan history. Besides his many short stories, he is best known for his novels, *The Scarlet Letter* (1850) and *The House of Seven Gables* (1851).

Hayden, Robert (1913–1980)   Hayden was a professor of English at several universities, primarily at Fisk University. During his teaching years, he published multiple volumes of poetry, including *The Night-Blooming Cereus* in 1972.

Heaney, Seamus (b. 1939)   An Irish poet, Heaney won the Noble Prize for Literature in 1995. *Government of the Tongue* was published in 1988, and *The Redress of Poetry* in 1995. In 1998, he published *Opened Ground: Selected Poems 1966–1996*.

Hogan, Linda (b. 1947)   Hogan, a member of the Chickasaw tribe, grew up in Oklahoma and Colorado in a military family. Her writings center on the traditional, indigenous relationship of humans to the land, animals, and plants. *Seeing Through the Sun* won the American Book Award in 1986.

Housman, A. E. (1859–1936)   Housman was a classics professor at Cambridge University in England. He published a collection of poems, *A Shropshire Lad*, in 1896, and his *Complete Poems* was published in 1956.

Houston, Pam (b. 1962)   Houston has published several books of fiction, including *Cowboys Are My Weakness* (1992) and *Waltzing the Cat* (1999). She has worked as a wilderness guide, teacher, and writer.

Hughes, Langston (1902–1967)   Born in Joplin, Missouri, Hughes became a major force in the Harlem Renaissance. He was among the first successful African American writers in the United States and published poetry, novels, plays as well as children's books and song lyrics.

Huxley, Aldous (1894–1963)   The grandson of the famous English biologist T. H. Huxley, Huxley pursued a wide range of intellectual interests throughout his life. He was a prolific writer, best known for *Brave New World*, written in 1932.

Jewett, Sarah Orne (1849–1909)   Born in South Berwick, Maine, Jewett began publishing stories and sketches in her twenties, when she developed a correspondence with the prominent author Harriet Beecher Stowe. Among Jewett's books are *A White Heron and Other Stories* (1886) and *The Country of the Pointed Firs* (1896).

King, Martin Luther, Jr. (1929–1968)   One of the most prominent civil rights leaders of the twentieth century, King was born in Atlanta and was the grandson and son of ministers. After receiving degrees from Morehouse College and Crozier Theological Seminary, he attended Boston University, earning his Ph.D. (1955) and D.D. (1959). In his decade of leadership of the civil rights movement, King was influenced by the example of Mahatma Gandhi who led a bloodless rebellion against British colonial rule in India. King instituted training for his nonviolent campaign of protest. In 1963, King delivered his famous speech, "I Have a Dream," and in 1964, *Letter from Birmingham City Jail* was published. King received the Nobel Prize for Peace in 1964, but in 1968, at the height of his work for civil rights, King was assassinated in Memphis, Tennessee. Among his published works are *The Measure of a Man* (1968), *I've Been to the Mountaintop* (1994), and *A Knock at Midnight: Inspiration from the Great Sermons of Reverend Martin Luther King, Jr.* (1998).

Kinnell, Galway (b. 1927)   Kinnell grew up in Providence, Rhode Island, and attended Princeton University where he and poet W. S. Merwin were classmates. Besides writing poetry and teaching at colleges and universities, Kinnell has been director of an adult education program in Chicago, a journalist in Iran, and a fieldworker for voter registration in the South in the 1960s. Among his poetry collections are *What a Kingdom It Was* (1960), *Body Rags* (1969), *The Past* (1985), and *Imperfect Thirst* (1994).

Knight, Etheridge (1933–1991)   Knight, who grew up in the South, was sentenced to twenty years in Indiana State Prison for a robbery in 1960. *Poems from Prison* was published in 1968, and he won the American Book Award in 1987 for *The Essential Etheridge Knight* (1986).

Kramer, Peter D. (b. 1948)   A professor of clinical psychiatry at Brown University, Kramer's book, *Listening to Prozac: A Psychiatrist Explores Mood-Altering Drugs and the Meaning of Self* (1993), was a national bestseller. He is a contributor of numerous articles to journals and the author of a monthly column in *Psychiatric Times.*

Kumin, Maxine (b. 1925)   Winner of the Pulitzer Prize and the Ruth Lily Poetry Prize, Kumin lives in New Hampshire. She has written novels, collections of short stories, and children's and nonfiction books. Recent books include *Connecting the Dots: Poetry* (1996), *Women, Animals, and Vegetables: Essays and Stories* (1996), and *Inside the Halo and Beyond: The Anatomy of a Recovery* (2000).

Lee, Cherylene (n.d.)   Born and raised in Los Angeles, Lee is a prize-winning writer whose fiction and poetry have appeared in many anthologies. Her plays have been produced in a variety of venues, including the Mark Taper Forum in Los Angeles and the Pan Asian Repertory in New York.

Le Guin, Ursula K. (b. 1929)   A highly versatile writer, Le Guin is perhaps best known for her science fiction and fantasy works, notably, *The Left Hand of Darkness* (1969), *The Lathe of Heaven* (1971), and *The Dispossessed* (1974). Less overtly political, her more recent book, *Buffalo Gals and Other Animal Presences* (1987), examines fundamental relationships between human and nonhuman animals. In addition to science fiction awards, Le Guin has received a National Book Award and a Newberry Honor Medal for children's literature.

Leopold, Aldo (1876–1944)   A conservationist, forester, professor, and writer, Leopold was a founding member of the Wilderness Society in 1934, and an influential advocate of an ecological perspective on wildlife and land management issues. In his book which addresses this concept, *The Sand County Almanac* (1949), Leopold uses a reflective, meditative prose style, which contributes to the book's universal appeal.

Levertov, Denise (1923–1997)   Levertov was a nurse in London during World War II and later moved to New York where William Carlos Williams guided her career as a poet. She has published widely, her recent books being *Evening Train* and *New and Selected Essays*, both published in 1992.

London, Jack (1876–1916)   Born in San Francisco, London began earning his own living at age fifteen, by working in a canning factory, a laundry, and as a sailor. Fully aligned with working-class persons, he joined the Socialist Labor Party. London produced a number of works of fiction, among them, *The Call of the Wild* (1903), *Son of the Wolf* and *South Sea Tales* (1912).

McKay, Claude (1890–1948)   Originally from Jamaica, McKay was an important figure during the Harlem Renaissance when black writers found their voice in America. He wrote novels and plays but is best remembered for his poems. *Home to Harlem* was published in 1928.

Meinke, Peter (b. 1932)   Meinke was born in Brooklyn, New York, and attended Hamilton College. He received his doctorate in literature from the University of Minnesota. His poetry has appeared in many magazines and journals since the 1970s. *Liquid Paper: New and Selected Poems* was published in 1991. He now teaches at Eckerd College in St. Petersburg, Florida.

Melville, Herman (1819–1891)   Melville wrote two novels, *Typee* (1846) and *Omoo* (1847), based on his experiences at sea on a whaling vessel and on a navy frigate. His most important novel was *Moby Dick* (1851). Although his early novels were popular, he soon fell into obscurity, not to be rediscovered until after World War I. *Moby Dick* is now considered an American classic.

Merrill, James (1926–1995)   Independently wealthy, Merrill published poetry throughout his life, beginning with *First Poems* in 1951 and ending with *Selected Poems* in 1992. During that time, he won two Pulitzer Prizes and two National Book Awards.

Miller, Arthur (b. 1915)   Although *Death of a Salesman* (1945) continues to be his most successful play, Miller has had a long career a playwright, winning both the Pulitzer Prize and the New York Drama Critics Circle Award. His play, *The Crucible* (1953), grew out of his disdain for the anti-communist fervor of the McCarthy-era House Un-American Activities Committee.

Milton, John (1608–1674)   Milton worked for Oliver Cromwell during the civil war between the king and Parliament but was arrested when the monarchy was restored. During the last fourteen years of his life, he retired from public life and wrote his epic poems, *Paradise Lost* (1667) and *Paradise Regained* (1671).

Momaday, N. Scott (b. 1934)   A Kiowa who often explores Native American history and culture in his writing, Momaday received his doctoral degree from

Stanford University. His novel, *House Made of Dawn,* won a Pulitzer Prize in 1969 and helped to spark the Native American renaissance.

Mukherjee, Bharati (b. 1940)   Mukherjee was born in Calcutta, India to a wealthy family and learned to write at age three. She received her doctorate in English from the University of Iowa and now teaches at the University of California at Berkeley. She has written many short stories and recently published a novel, *Leave It to Me* (1997), in which a young woman seeks revenge on parents who abandoned her.

Murray, Pauli (1910–1985)   Murray, who grew up in Durham, North Carolina, worked to dismantle the barriers of race and gender and founded the National Organization of Women (NOW) in the early 1970s. She published *Proud Shoes: The Story of an American Family* in 1956, *Dark Testament and Other Poems* in 1970, and her autobiographical *Song in a Watery Throat: An American Pilgrimage* in 1987.

Ng, Fae Myenne (b. 1957)   Born in San Francisco and raised in Chinatown, Ng's first novel, *Bone* (1993), received widespread recognition. Her award-winning stories have been published in many periodicals, including *Harpr's* magazine. She has won the Pushcart Prize for short fiction and a McDowell Fellowship.

Nye, Naomi Shihab (b. 1952)   An American singer and writer with Palestinian roots, Nye has published children's books as well as poetry. Her poetry collections include *Hugging the Jukebox* (1982), *Words Under the Words: Selected Poems* (1995), and *Fuel* (1998).

Oates, Joyce Carol (b. 1938)   Oates, a prolific writer who has published over one hundred stories and forty books, is a professor at Princeton University. Her novels, *Because It Is Bitter, and Because It Is My Heart* (1990) and *What I Lived For* (1994), received widespread critical attention.

O'Brien, Tim (b. 1946)   After graduation from college, O'Brien served as an infantry man in Vietnam, where he won the Purple Heart. Upon returning home, he began to write about his war experiences. His novel, *Going After Cacciato* (1978), won the National Book Award.

Okita, Dwight (b. 1958)   An American of Japanese descent, Okita was born and raised in Chicago. His collection of poems is *Crossing with the Light* (1992).

Olds, Sharon (b. 1942)   A professor and writer, Olds is a much-published contemporary American poet. Her poetry collections include *The Father* (1992), *The Wellspring* (1995), *The Gold Cell* (1997), and *Blood, Tin, Straw* (1999). Olds lives and teaches in New York City.

Oliver, Mary (b. 1935)   Oliver was born in Cleveland and attended Ohio State and Vassar. She first published a collection of poetry in 1963, *No Voyage and Other Poems.* Her book, *New and Selected Poems,* won the National Book Award for poetry in 1992.

Orwell, George (1903–1950)   A writer and socialist, Orwell lived in poverty and associated with laborers early in his writing career. He later fought in the Spanish civil war and went on to write *Animal Farm* (1945) and *1984* (1949), both illustrating his distaste for totalitarian governments.

Owen, Wilfred (1893–1918)   Owen was an English poet who died in France during World War I at the young age of twenty-five before his career ever began. Twenty-four of his poems were published after his death.

Paley, Grace (b. 1922)   A fiction writer and teacher of creative writing, Paley was born and raised in New York City. Perhaps reflecting her native New York City, her stories often bristle with humor and toughness in their tone and theme. Paley has two published volumes of stories, *The Little Disturbances of Man* (1959) and *Enormous Changes at the Last Minute* (1975).

Pastan, Linda (b. 1932)   Pastan lives in Potomac, Maryland, and was the Poet Laureate of Maryland from 1990 to 1995. Her book, *PM/AM: New and Selected Poems* was nominated for the National Book Award.

Plato (427–347 B.C.)   A Greek philosopher born in Athens, Plato was an *idealist*. He wrote thirty dialogues in which Socrates, an Athenian philosopher twenty-five years older than Plato, is the principal speaker.

Piercy, Marge (b. 1936)   Piercy is a poet and novelist who presently lives on Cape Cod. Her recent collection of poems include *Mars and Her Children* (1992) and *What Are Big Girls Made Of?* (1996).

Porter, Katherine Anne (1890–1980)   A fiction writer who also played small parts in films and worked in journalism, Porter is considered a Southern writer. Her book, *Collected Stories,* won both the National Book Award and the Pulitzer Prize in 1967.

Power, Susan (b. 1961)   Power, a member of the Standing Rock Sioux tribe, was educated at Radcliffe/Harvard and Harvard Law School. Her novel, *Grass Dancer,* was published in 1994.

Quiñonez, Ernesto (b. 1966)   *Bodega Dreams* is the first novel by Quiñonez. He currently teaches fourth grade in the New York public schools and is writing his second novel.

Randall, Dudley (b. 1914)   Randall founded Broadside Press in 1965, where he published African American writers. His collected poetry is found in *More to Remember: Poems of Four Decades* (1971) and *A Litany of Friends: New and Selected Poems* (1981).

Regan, Tom (b. 1938)   A leading philosopher in the animal protection movement, Regan's book, *The Case for Animal Rights* (1984), brought the subject of animal rights to new levels of serious discussion within scholarly circles. He is a professor of philosophy at North Carolina State University.

Rich, Adrienne (b. 1929)   Rich was a Phi Beta Kappa graduate of Radcliffe in 1951, the year she published her first collection of poetry, *A Change of World.* Since then she has won many awards, including the National Book Award for poetry in 1974. *An Atlas of the Difficult World* was published in 1992.

Rilke, Rainer Maria (1875–1926)   One of the most famous German poets, Rilke served as secretary to the French sculptor Rodin. He published *New Poems* in 1907. Later, living in Switzerland, he wrote *Sonnets to Orpheus* (1923) and *The Duino Elegies* (1923).

Robinson, Edwin Arlington (1869–1935)   Robinson created psychological portraits of small-town citizens in his poems and received three Pulitzer Prizes for his work.

Rodriguez, Richard (b. 1944)   His book, *Hunger of Memory: The Education of Richard Rodriguez* (1982), focuses on the issues of education and ethnic identity.

Days of Obligation (1992) was nominated for the Pulitzer Prize. Rodriguez appears on the "The News Hour with Jim Lehrer" on PBS.

Roethke, Theodore (1908–1963)   Roethke grew up in Michigan and attended the University of Michigan and Harvard University. He won the Pulitzer Prize for poetry in 1954 for *The Waking: Poems 1933–1953*. He also won two National Book Awards for poetry.

Rogers, Pattiann (b. 1940)   Rogers has won grants from the National Endowment for the Arts and the Guggenheim Foundation. She has published several books of poetry, including *Splitting and Binding* (1989) and *Firekeeper: New and Selected Poems* (1994). In *The Dream of the Marsh Hen: Writing as Reciprocal Creation* (1999), Rogers explores her writing process.

Rukeyser, Muriel (1913–1980)   Born in New York City, Rukeyser was a poet and social activist who published many books of poetry, including *Body of Waking* (1958) and *Collected Poems* (1978).

Sandburg, Carl (1878–1967)   Sandburg grew up in Illinois and often wrote about Chicago, for example, in *Chicago Poems* (1916) and *Smoke and Steel* (1920). In 1939, he received the Pulitzer Prize in history for his biography of Lincoln, and in 1951, won again in poetry for his *Complete Poems of 1950*.

Sanders, Scott Russell (b. 1945)   Born in Memphis, Sanders has published many essays, novels, and children's books. His latest books are *Hunting for Hope* (1998) and *The Country of Language* (1999). He is a professor of English at Indiana University.

Sexton, Anne (1928–1974)   Sexton was born in Newton, Massachusetts. She attended poetry workshops in the late 1950s in the Boston area and began writing poetry at age twenty-eight. She received the Pulitzer Prize for *Live or Die* (1967) and taught creative writing and continued writing poetry until her death by suicide.

Silko, Leslie Marmon (b. 1948)   Silko grew up on the Laguna Pueblo Reservation and has taught college English at Navajo Community College, the University of Arizona, and the University of New Mexico. She has published poetry and fiction since 1974.

Snyder, Gary (b. 1930)   Born in San Francisco, Snyder studied Asian languages at University of California, Berkeley, worked as a logger, studied Buddhism in Japan, and shipped as a crew member on oil tankers. His poems draw on images from nature, Native American culture, and Buddhism. Of his many books of poetry, *Regarding Wave* was published in 1970.

Song, Cathy (b. 1955)   Song, who lives in Hawaii, first published *Picture Bride* in 1983, for which she won the National Book Critics Circle Award. Her collection of poems, *School Figures,* was published in 1994.

Sophocles (c. 496–c. 405)   Sophocles was a tragic poet and playwright in ancient Greece. Previously a priest and a general, Sophocles is best known for his *Oedipus* trilogy, which includes the play *Antigone.*

Stafford, William (1914–1992)   Stafford earned his doctorate from Iowa State University. He was a conscientious objector during World War I and later taught at Lewis and Clark College in Oregon. His 1963 collection of poetry, *Traveling through the Dark,* won the National Book Award for poetry.

Strand, Mark (b. 1934) Although born in Canada, Strand was named U.S. Poet Laureate in 1990. *Selected Poems* was published in 1980 and *The Continuous Life* in 1990. In 1993, he received the Bollingen Prize. Strand is presently a professor at the University of Utah.

Stevens, Harper (b. 1971) Born on Floriada's Gulf Coast panhandle, Stevens did doctoral work in historical linguistics and worked in the publishing field before turning to writing. She is currently working on a collection of fiction set on the Gulf Coast.

Terkel, Studs (b. 1912) Terkel is associated with Chicago, where he lives and works. He most often focuses his attention on working-class, everyday people. His book, *Race: How Blacks and Whites Think and Feel about the American Obsession*, was published in 1992.

Thoreau, Henry David (1817–1862) Thoreau wrote the classic, *Walden, or Life in the Woods* (1854), based on his experience of living a simple life in a cabin by Walden Pond near Boston. An outspoken social critic, he opposed slavery and the Mexican War of 1846 to 1848. His published lecture on civil disobedience influenced Martin Luther King, Jr.

Updike, John (b. 1932) A writer and lecturer, Updike has published many novels and collections of short stories, including *Pigeon Feathers and Other Stories* in 1962. Contemporary urban and suburban people are the focus of Updike's stories. In a series of four novels—*Rabbit Run, Rabbit Redux, Rabbit is Rich,* and *Rabbit at Rest*—Updike dramatizes the life of Harry "Rabbit" Angstrom who confronts the realities of his present life while longing for his idealized vision of a past life. Updike's recent novels include *Brazil* (1994) and *In the Beauty of the Lilies* (1996).

Vega, Ed (b. 1936) Vega is a Puerto Rican fiction writer who has lived in New York since 1949. In 1985, he published *The Comeback*, a novel satirizing ethnic autobiography and the identity crisis. *Casualty Report*, his third book, was published in 1991.

Villanueva, Alma Luz (b. 1944) Villanueva's fiction often appears in anthologies. Her novel *Desire* was published in 1998. *Weeping Woman: La Ilorna and Other Stories* came out in 1994.

Vonnegut, Kurt (b. 1922) Vonnegut is the author of short stories, essays, novels, and plays. He is best known for his novels, *Slaughterhouse Five* (1969) and *Breakfast of Champions* (1973).

Walker, Alice (b. 1944) Born in Eatonton, Georgia, Walker attended Spelman College and received her B.A. from Sarah Lawrence College. A poet, writer, lecturer, and professor, Walker also co-produced the film documentary, *Warrior Marks* (1993). Walker has won numerous awards for her poems and novels, including the 1983 Pulitzer Prize for fiction and American Book Award for *The Color Purple*. Other publications include *Revolutionary Petunias and Other Poems* (1973) and the novel, *Possessing the Secret of Joy* (1992).

Walker, Margaret (b. 1915) Born in Birmingham, Alabama, the daughter of college professors, Walker published *Jubilee* in 1966, a novel which imagines the Civil War and emancipation from the slave's point of view. Her collection of poetry, *For My People,* was published in 1942.

Warren, Robert Penn (1905–1989)   Warren won the Pulitzer Prize in 1947, 1957, and 1978. Additionally, he was named the first American Poet Laureate in 1985. His most acclaimed novel is *All the King's Men,* published in 1946. His poetry collections include *Promises* (1957) and *New and Selected Poems* (1985).

Welty, Eudora (b. 1909)   Welty is the author of numerous works of fiction, including *The Optimist's Daughter,* which won the Pulitzer Prize in 1972. Born in Jackson, Mississippi, Welty roots the actual settings of her stories in the Southern region she knows firsthand; meanwhile, the thematic implications far extend those geographical borders.

Whitman, Walt (1819–1892)   Whitman worked as a journalist in the New York area most of his life, but with the publication of *Leaves of Grass* in 1855, he assured himself of an important place in world literature. His poetry focuses on the American landscape and its people.

Wilbur, Richard (b. 1921)   Wilbur is a prolific poet who has taught at Harvard University. Wellesley College, and Wesleyan University. His many books include *The Poems of Richard Wilbur* (1963), *Waking to Sleep* (1969), and *The Mind-Reader* (1976).

Woolfe, Virginia (1882–1941)   Woolfe was a major English novelist who quickly became the center of the Bloomsbury Group before World War I. Her novels *Mrs. Dalloway* and *To the Lighthouse,* published in 1925 and 1927, are always counted as major examples of the modern novel. Her bouts of depression led to her suicide in 1941.

Wordsworth, William (1770–1850)   Wordsworth was the English poet who introduced Romanticism with its interest in nature. The natural world, Wordsworth believed, held the power to heal some of the abuses inflicted upon society by urbanization. He is most famous for *The Lyrical Ballads* (1798) and *The Excursion* (1814).

Wright, James (1927–1980)   Wright was born in Martins Ferry, Ohio. After serving in World War II, he attended college, receiving a Fulbright Scholarship to the University of Vienna and his Ph.D. from Washington University. He taught at Hunter College in New York from 1966 to 1980. His many volumes of poetry include *The Branch Will Not Break* (1963), *Collected Poems* (1971), and *This Journey* (1982). Wright won the 1972 Pulitzer Prize for *Collected Poems.*

Wright, Richard (1908–1960)   Born in Roxie, Mississippi, Wright graduated as valedictorian of his high school class in 1925, although during his youth he was often close to starvation. Fifteen years later, he published his novel, *Native Son,* and in 1945, his autobiography, *Black Boy,* brought him much critical acclaim.

Author and Title Index

Subject Index

Credits